HEALTH CARE

IN CANADA

HEALTH CARE *Ethics* IN CANADA

Françoise **BAYLIS**
Department of Philosophy
University of Tennessee

Jocelyn **DOWNIE**
Doctoral Candidate
University of Michigan

Benjamin **FREEDMAN**
Professor, McGill Centre for Medicine, Ethics and Law
Clinical Ethicist, Mortimer B. Davis – Jewish General Hospital of Montreal

Barry **HOFFMASTER**
Director, Westminster Institute for Ethics and Human Values
Professor, Departments of Philosophy and Family Medicine
University of Western Ontario

Susan **SHERWIN**
Professor, Departments of Philosophy and Women's Studies
Dalhousie University

HARCOURT
BRACE
CANADA

Harcourt Brace & Company, Canada

Toronto Montreal Fort Worth New York Orlando
Philadelphia San Diego London Sydney Tokyo

Canadian Cataloguing in Publication Data

Main entry under title:

Health care ethics in Canada

Includes bibliographical references.
ISBN 0–7747–3288–1
1. Medical ethics – Canada.   I. Baylis, Françoise,1961–

R724.H43 1995   174′.2′0971   C94–931796–9

Publisher: Heather McWhinney
Editor and Marketing Manager: Christopher Carson
Projects Manager: Marguerite Martindale
Projects Co-ordinator: Laura Paterson Pratt
Director of Publishing Services: Jean Davies
Editorial Manager: Marcel Chiera
Supervising Editor: Semareh Al-Hillal
Production Editor: Laurel Parsons
Production Manager: Sue-Ann Becker
Production Supervisor: Carol Tong
Copy Editor: Ingrid Berzins
Cover Design: Opus House
Cover Photo: W. Westheimer/Masterfile
Interior Design: boyes and connolly
Typesetting and Assembly: True to Type Inc.
Printing and Binding: Best Book Manufacturers, Inc.

♾ This book was printed in Canada on acid-free paper.

1 2 3 4 5   99 98 97 96 95

Preface

The field of health care ethics has grown and changed substantially over the past three decades; this book uniquely reflects both the history of contemporary health care ethics and new developments and directions in the field. Initially, health care ethics seemed to involve applying general moral theories or moral principles to cases to arrive at decisions. As the limitations of this method were recognized, alternative approaches emerged, for example, attempts to reprise the notion of casuistry and to use narratives to gain moral insight. More recently, the limitations of a case-oriented approach to health care ethics have been emphasized by feminist writers and others who are concerned with the impact of social and institutional settings in which health care is delivered. Similarly, the narrow focus on physician–patient decision making that has been characteristic of much work in health care ethics is now widely criticized. This focus assumes that health care involves only two people, whereas in reality patients are members of intricate social networks and health care is largely practiced in teams. Health care ethics is now starting to expand its vision to take account of these realities. Another important development has been a recognition of the cultural context of health care. For a long time the role of culture in health care was invisible. Now, the profound ways in which culture affects the delivery of health care and thus the nature of health care ethics are being appreciated. All of these changes are represented in this book.

Another noteworthy feature of the book is its Canadian focus. Many of the selections are written by Canadians who work in health care ethics. The Canadian focus is broader than that, however. Although some moral issues are borderless, the contexts in which ethical issues arise always are important in shaping how those issues are perceived and resolved. Questions about the allocation and rationing of health care resources, for example, assume a distinctive cast in Canada's government-funded health care system. As well, the approaches taken to some moral issues have been significantly affected by legal rulings from the Supreme Court of Canada, with respect to abortion and assisted suicide, for example. Canadian public policy also has had a substantial impact on health care ethics. Government departments have issued influential reports on the concepts of health and health care, for instance, and recently the Royal Commission on New Reproductive Technologies investigated the issue of assisted reproduction throughout the country and made policy recommendations. The study of health care ethics in Canada needs to appreciate the distinctive history and nature of the questions in this country, along with the distinctive contributions Canadians have made to them.

The book is divided into three sections: The Nature and Context of Health Care Ethics; Decision Making in Health Care; and Decisions Near the Beginning and End of Life. The chapters in each section include a brief introduction and summary of the selections; several articles that explore relevant issues and, whenever possible, present opposing views; suggested further readings; and questions to consider.

This book will be a useful resource for health care ethics courses in university departments, for example, in philosophy, the social sciences, and the humanities, as well as in professional schools, for example, law, medicine, and nursing. The book also should be a useful resource for health care practitioners and others interested in the field who may not have the benefit of a formal course.

Acknowledgements

The Westminster Institute for Ethics and Human Values in London, Ontario provided financial and administrative support for the preparation of this book. We are grateful to the Board of Governors of the Westminster Institute for making this project possible. The staff of the Institute worked diligently in assembling the manuscript. Judy Noordermeer and Seanna-Lin Brodie-Keys flawlessly supervised the details of putting the chapters together and securing the necessary permissions. They gracefully coped with myriad changes and ensured that everything went smoothly. Janet Baldock processed the introductory materials for the chapters with her usual impressive speed and accuracy. Edith Richardson ensured that all our bibliographic needs and problems were handled promptly and with care. We thank them all for their essential contributions to this book.

We also thank our editors, Chris Carson and Laura Paterson Pratt, for their unfailing support and help. They forced us to make some difficult decisions that, in the end, have made this a better book than it otherwise would have been. And they kept us close to the deadlines we were supposed to meet.

A Note from the Publisher
Thank you for selecting *Health Care Ethics in Canada*, by Françoise Baylis, Jocelyn Downie, Benjamin Freedman, Barry Hoffmaster, and Susan Sherwin. The authors and publisher have devoted considerable time to the careful development of this book. We appreciate your recognition of this effort and accomplishment.

We want to hear what you think about *Health Care Ethics in Canada*. Please take a few minutes to fill in the stamped student reply card at the back of the book. Your comments and suggestions will be valuable to us as we prepare new editions and other books.

Contents

Part One

The Nature and Context of Health Care Ethics

Chapter 1

Theory and Method in Health Care Ethics

Introduction

The field of health care ethics is concerned with the identification and investigation of ethical problems that arise in the realm of health and health services. Despite the common agenda of people working in this broad area, however, there is much dispute about the best approach to take in addressing issues. In this chapter, we explore some of the many proposals that theorists have offered on the question of strategy.

Although in many cases we may arrive at the same resolution of a problem through different routes, in other cases, the choice of theory and strategy may determine the direction and outcome of our inquiry. Different strategies are likely to direct our attention to different features of a problem and, hence, may result in different analyses and conclusions. The theoretic orientation we adopt for exploring topics in health care ethics can have a significant influence on the selection of problems that we recognize as important and on the solutions we take to be morally acceptable.

Some Familiar Distinctions

One way of distinguishing among approaches in health care ethics is to focus on the central distinctions that exist among basic ethical theories. Many theorists identify the distinction between consequentialist and deontological theories as the most important difference in orientation among ethical theories.

Consequentialist (or teleological) theories are characterized as theories that evaluate the moral rightness or wrongness of actions in terms of the moral desirability of their consequences. The best-known forms of consequentialism are the many variations of utilitarianism: these are theories in which actions are right if they produce the greatest balance of happiness over unhappiness (or pleasure over pain, or satisfaction of preferences) for everyone concerned. Thus, people who adopt a consequentialist moral theory try to evaluate the moral acceptability of an action or practice by trying to predict its likely consequences; they then consider whether these consequences are better (in terms of happiness produced or suffering avoided) than those produced by any alternative action or practice that might be pursued. The most famous classical statement of utilitarianism is offered by John Stuart Mill (1971). Some contemporary examples of the use of utilitarian theory in health care ethics are offered by Peter Singer (1979) and L.W. Sumner (1981).

Deontological theories can be readily distinguished from consequentialist theories by the fact that they treat moral worth as separate from the production of happiness or the satisfaction of preferences. Deontological theorists believe that moral duties arise from adherence to fundamental moral rules and that at least some of these rules are justified independently of the consequences that follow from our actions. The most important deontologist is the eighteenth-century theorist Immanuel Kant, who argued that morality requires a certain form of universality and so it must exist apart from the accidental history of any individual's personal preferences or pleasures (1964). Kant's theory is complex and not easily summarized, but much of its practical import is captured by appeal to the first two formulations of what he considered to be the fundamental moral rule, termed "the categorical imperative." In the first version, Kant claimed that morality dictates that we act only on maxims (or rules) that we can, without contradiction, will to be universal laws. Kant argues, for example, that it is possible to will that telling the truth be a universal law, but that lying cannot be willed to be a universal law without running into contradictions. The second formulation of the categorical imperative directs us to treat human persons always as ends in themselves and never merely as means to someone else's ends. Contemporary versions of deontological approaches to health care ethics are provided by H. Tristram Engelhardt, Jr. (1986) and Eike-Henner W. Kluge (1992).

When consequentialists are confronted by moral dilemmas, they seek to determine what options are available and which of these options will result in the most desirable or least undesirable consequences. Deontologists seek the most fundamental moral rule that applies. Much work in health care ethics, however, does not manifest a rigid commitment to either a consequentialist or a deontological model. Instead, a pluralistic or mixed conception approach is adopted, one that appeals sometimes to consequences and sometimes to basic moral rules. The obvious difficulty for this alternative is determining which approach is appropriate for a given problem.

Another issue in ethical theory that is significant for health care ethics concerns the proper focus for ethics. While much work in contemporary ethics and applied ethics accepts the assumption that ethics is primarily concerned with the moral evaluation and justification of actions or practices, there are other long-standing traditions in ethics.

For example, some ethicists focus on justice rather than on matters of individual action (e.g., Rawls 1971). Others believe that virtue or the evaluation of an individual's character takes priority; rather than examining actions in abstraction from those who perform them, as action-based theories tend to do, virtue-based theories focus more heavily on the person whose behaviour is explored (e.g., Foot 1978). Still other theorists focus on questions of moral or individual rights as the basis of ethical evaluation as, for instance, in Judith Jarvis Thomson (1990). And some place priority on relationships between people, rather than looking only at the behaviour of individuals in isolation from their social circumstances (e.g., Gilligan 1982).

Moreover, these theories are just some of the most prominent among current Western thinkers; other cultural traditions involve quite different understandings of the world and the moral values that should inform human behaviour. Hence, we can widen the field of available moral perspectives and strategies even further by taking account of different cultural perspectives. But within this cursory review, it is impossible to list all the variations in ethical perspective that influence thought in health care ethics.

The scope, terms, agenda, methodology, and application of ethics are matters of continuing controversy. Although these debates have been going on for centuries, there is still widespread disagreement about many of the fundamental issues. Theories in this area are subject to intense scrutiny, but the fact that the main theories retain committed proponents in the face of such critical review is evidence of their plausibility. Hence, it can be anticipated that different readers will be attracted to different types of ethical theory.

Some readers may find that they do not need to resolve the eternal questions of moral theory to proceed to address the complex practical issues of health care ethics. Many health care ethicists choose to sidestep the difficult and seemingly irresolvable conflicts of traditional ethics and seek alternative moral approaches that will inform the specific tasks confronting them. Some theorists have gone so far as to explicitly advocate disregard for the broader ethical theories; they urge us to address problems in the contexts in which they arise through the ancient practice of casuistry or systematic case analysis (Jonsen and Toulmin 1988).

The Selections

The selections included in this chapter constitute a range of methodological proposals for health care ethics. They represent some of the current trends that influence discussion of specific issues in this field, but they are by no means exhaustive.

The excerpt from Paul Ramsey's influential book, *The Patient as Person* (1970), is an example of an explicitly religious perspective in health care ethics (in this case,

Christianity). Many people consider their religious beliefs to be the foundation of their ethical views, and theological writers have always been prominent in the debates of ethics and health care ethics. Nonetheless, much of the current writing in health care ethics (and most of the articles included in this collection) are written from a secular perspective; that is, the arguments presented are not dependent on or unique to any specific religious perspective.

In the second selection, Peter Singer provides a very clear statement of his preference for a utilitarian approach to moral reasoning. He begins by exploring the nature of ethics and concludes that moral reasoning involves the adoption of a universal point of view. He then argues that utilitarian reasoning can be deduced from the universal aspect of ethics and is, in fact, common to all universal approaches — that is, that all moral reasoning involves at least a core of utilitarian reasoning. Since he considers utilitarianism to be adequate to resolve all moral questions, he argues that there is no need to complicate our moral theory by adding further controversial premises.

H. Tristram Engelhardt, Jr., in contrast, supports a deontological approach to bioethics. In his pursuit of a foundational basis for a secular bioethics, he settles on two principles as central: autonomy and beneficence. He observes that neither of these principles is justified by its consequences, but rather by the fact that it is an expression of mutual respect, which is at the heart of any ethical system. Although he recognizes that in practice the principle of beneficence is likely to lead us to attend to the consequences of proposed actions, he argues that the principle of autonomy is to be followed no matter what the consequences.

The excerpt from the introductory chapter in the widely cited textbook, *Principles of Biomedical Ethics*, by Tom L. Beauchamp and James F. Childress (1994), recommends a strategy for addressing issues in health care ethics that is characterized as the "four-principles approach." Like Engelhardt, Beauchamp and Childress turn to a set of principles to resolve moral problems but, unlike him, they sidestep the controversies associated with choosing between deontological and consequential theories. They propose that we concentrate on a few moral principles that are compatible with many variations of both kinds of theory (as well as with the moral views of people who approach ethics from a particular set of religious beliefs or a commitment to virtue or rights theory). These principles can serve as the foundation for more specific moral rules which we can apply to particular cases. The four moral principles that Beauchamp and Childress identify as central to deliberations about health care ethics are the principles of respect for autonomy, nonmaleficence, beneficence, and justice.

In the final selection, Rosemarie Tong explains how feminist approaches to health care ethics differ from traditional approaches. Feminists appreciate the complexity of the moral issues that arise in health care, and that complexity is reflected in the diversity of their work. Different ontological assumptions about the nature of the self and connections among selves, as well as different epistemological assumptions about the nature of knowledge in general and medical knowledge in particular, lead to different versions of feminist health care ethics. What feminist approaches share, however, are a concern with questions of power, specifically questions about male domination and female subordination, and three methodological strategies: asking the woman question, employing consciousness-raising, and engaging in feminist practical reasoning. By regarding these matters as morally relevant, proponents of feminist ethics are able to identify problematic aspects of situations and practices that remain invisible in traditional health care ethics writings.

Conclusion

The various proposals surveyed and sampled in this chapter differ dramatically in their understandings of what topics ought to be explored and how investigations should proceed in health care ethics. The particular theoretical orientation one adopts significantly influences the selection of problems to be studied and the framing of those problems. These choices, in turn, affect the solutions that are considered and chosen. These methodological questions are still being contested; there is no unanimity among health care ethicists about the best strategy or approach to take to the ethical problems that arise in health care. Differences in ethical approach account for much of the complexity and richness of the debates that occur within the field. The very definition of the subject matter is constantly evolving and expanding as new perspectives engage with older, more established proposals. Moreover, the practical work of trying out different approaches to resolving specific ethical issues in the concrete realities of health care can help to inform and transform the largely abstract moral theories of philosophical ethics.

References

Engelhardt, H. Tristram, Jr. 1986. *The foundations of bioethics*. New York: Oxford University Press.

Foot, Philippa. 1978. *Virtues and vices and other essays in moral philosophy*. Berkeley: University of California Press.

Gilligan, Carol. 1982. *In a different voice: Psychology theory and women's development*. Cambridge, MA: Harvard University Press.

Jonsen, Albert R., and Stephen Toulmin, 1988. *The Abuse of casuistry*. Berkeley: University of California Press.

Kant, Immanuel. 1964. *Groundwork of the metaphysic of morals*, H.J. Paton, trans. New York: Harper & Row (originally published in 1785).

Kluge, Eike-Henner W. 1992. *Biomedical ethics in a Canadian context*. Scarborough, Ont.: Prentice-Hall Canada.

Mill, John Stuart. 1971. *Utilitarianism*. Indianapolis: Bobbs-Merrill (originally published in 1861).

Rawls, John. 1971. *A theory of justice.* Cambridge: Harvard University Press.

Singer, Peter. 1979. *Practical ethics.* Cambridge, MA: Cambridge University Press.

Sumner, L.W. 1981. *Abortion and moral theory.* Princeton: Princeton University Press.

Thomson, Judith Jarvis. 1990. *The realm of rights.* Cambridge: Harvard University Press.

1   The Patient as Person

Paul Ramsey

This volume undertakes to examine some of the problems of medical ethics that are especially urgent in the present day. These are by no means technical problems on which only the experts (in this case, the physician) can have an opinion. They are rather the problems of human beings in situations in which medical care is needed. Birth and death, illness and injury are not simply events the doctor attends. They are moments in every human life. The doctor makes decisions as an expert but also as a man among men; and his patient is a human being coming to his birth or to his death, or being rescued from illness or injury in between.

Therefore, the doctor who attends *the case* has reason to be attentive to the patient as person. Resonating throughout his professional actions, and crucial in some of them, will be a view of man, an understanding of the meaning of the life at whose first or second exodus he is present, a care for the life he attends in its afflictions. In this respect the doctor is quite like the rest of us, who must yet depend wholly on him to diagnose the options, perhaps the narrow range of options, and to conduct us through the one that is taken.

To take up for scrutiny some of the problems of medical ethics is, therefore, to bring under examination at once a number of crucial human moral problems. These are not narrowly defined issues of medical ethics alone. Thus this volume has — if I may say so — the widest possible audience. It is addressed to patients as persons, to physicians of patients who are persons — in short, to everyone who has had or will have to do with disease or death. The question, What ought the doctor do? is only a particular form of the question, What should be done?

This, then, is a book *about ethics*, written by a Christian ethicist. I hold that medical ethics is consonant with the ethics of a wider human community. The former is (however special) only a particular case of the latter. The moral requirements governing the relations of physician to patients and researcher to subjects are only a special case of the moral requirements governing any relations between man and man. Canons of loyalty to patients or to joint adventurers in medical research are simply particular manifestations of canons of loyalty of person to person generally. Therefore, in the following chapters I undertake to explore a number of medical covenants among men. These are the covenant between physician and patient, the covenant between researcher and "subject" in experiments with human beings, the covenant between men and a child in need of care, the covenant between the living and the dying, the covenant between the well and the ill or with those in need of some extraordinary therapy.

We are born within covenants of life with life. By nature, choice, or need we live with our fellowmen in roles or relations. Therefore we must ask, What is the meaning of the faithfulness of one human being to another in every one of these relations? This is the ethical question.

At crucial points in the analysis of medical ethics, I shall not be embarrassed to use as an interpretative principle the Biblical norm of *fidelity to covenant*, with the meaning it gives to *righteousness* between man and man. This is not a very prominent feature in the pages that follow, since it is also necessary for an ethicist to go as far as possible into the technical and other particular aspects of the problems he ventures to take up. Also, in the midst of any of these urgent human problems, an ethicist finds that he has been joined — whether in agreement or with some disagreement — by men of various persuasions, often quite different ones. There is in actuality a community of moral discourse concerning the claims of persons. This is the main appeal in the pages that follow.

Still we should be clear about the moral and religious premises here at the outset. I hold with Karl Barth that covenant-fidelity is the inner meaning and purpose of our creation as human beings, while the whole of creation is the external basis and condition of the possibility of covenant. This means that the conscious acceptance of covenant responsibilities is the inner meaning of even the "natural" or systemic relations into which we are born and of the institutional relations or roles we enter by choice, while this fabric provides the external framework for human fulfillment in explicit covenants among men. The practice of medicine is one such covenant. *Justice, fairness, righteousness, faithfulness, canons of loyalty, sanctity of life, hesed, agape* or *charity* are some of the names given to the moral quality of attitude and of action owed to all men by any man who steps into a covenant with another man — by any man who, so far as he is a religious man, explicitly acknowledges that we are a covenant people on a common pilgrimage.

The chief aim of the chapters to follow is, then, simply to explore the meaning of *care*, to find the actions and abstentions that come from adherence to *covenant*, to ask the meaning of the sanctity of life, to articulate the requirements of steadfast *faithfulness* to a fellow man. We shall ask, What are the moral claims upon us in crucial medical situations and human relations in which some decision must be made about how to show respect for, protect, preserve, and honor the life of fellow man?

Just as man is a *sacredness in the social and political order*, so he is a *sacredness in the natural, biological order*. He is a sacredness in bodily life. He is a person who within the ambience of the flesh claims our care. He is an embodied soul or ensouled body. He is therefore a sacredness in illness and in his dying. He is a sacredness in the fruits of the generative processes. (From some point he is this if he has any sanctity, since it is undeniably the case that men are never more than, from generation to generation, the products of human generation.) The sanctity of human life prevents ultimate trespass upon him even for the sake of treating his bodily life, or for the sake of others who are also only a sacredness in their bodily lives. Only a being who is a sacredness in the social order can withstand complete dominion by "society" for the sake of engineering civilizational goals — withstand, in the sense that the engineering of civilizational goals cannot be accomplished without denying the sacredness of the human being. So also in the use of medical or scientific technics. . . .

---

2   Practical Ethics

Peter Singer

. . . What is it to make a moral judgment, or to argue about an ethical issue, or to live according to ethical standards? How do moral judgments differ from other practical judgments? Why do we regard a woman's decision to have an abortion as raising an ethical issue, but not her decision to change her job? What is the difference between a person who lives by ethical standards and one who doesn't?

All these questions are related, so we only need to consider one of them; but to do this we need to say something about the nature of ethics. Suppose that we have studied the lives of a number of different people, and we know a lot about what they do, what they believe, and so on. Can we then decide which of them are living by ethical standards and which are not?

We might think that the way to proceed here is to find out who believes it wrong to lie, cheat, steal, and so on and does not do any of these things, and who has no such beliefs, and shows no such restraint in their actions. Then those in the first group would be living according to ethical standards and those in the second group would not be. But this procedure mistakenly assimilates two distinctions: the first is the distinction between living according to (what we judge to be) the right ethical standards and living according to (what we judge to be) mistaken ethical standards; the second is the distinction between living according to some ethical standards, and living according to no ethical standards at all. Those who lie and cheat, but do not believe what they are doing to be wrong, may be living according to ethical standards. They may believe, for any of a number of possible reasons, that it is right to lie, cheat, steal, and so on. They are not living according to conventional ethical standards, but they may be living according to some other ethical standards.

This first attempt to distinguish the ethical from the nonethical was mistaken, but we can learn from our mistakes. We found that we must concede that those who hold unconventional ethical beliefs are still living according to ethical standards, *if they believe, for any reason, that it is right to do as they are doing.* The italicised condition gives us a clue to the answer we are seeking. The notion of living according to ethical standards is tied up with the notion of defending the way one is living, of giving a reason for it, of justifying it. Thus people may do all kinds of things we regard as wrong, yet still be living according to ethical standards, if they are prepared to defend and justify what they do. We may find the justification inadequate, and may hold that the actions are wrong, but the attempt at justification, whether successful or not, is sufficient to bring the person's conduct within the domain of the ethical as opposed to the non-ethical. When, on the other hand, people cannot put forward any justification for what they do, we may reject their claim to be living according to ethical standards, even if what they do is in accordance with conventional moral principles.

We can go further. If we are to accept that a person is living according to ethical standards, the justification must be of a certain kind. For instance, a justification in terms of self-interest alone will not do. When Macbeth, contemplating the murder of Duncan, admits that only 'vaulting ambition' drives him to do it, he is admitting that the act cannot be justified ethically. 'So that I can be king in his place' is not a weak attempt at an ethical justification for assassination; it is not the sort of reason that counts as an ethical justification at all. Self-interested acts must be shown to be compatible with more broadly based ethical principles if they are to be ethically defensible, for the notion of ethics carries with it the idea of something bigger than the individual. If I am to defend my conduct on ethical grounds, I cannot point only to the benefits it brings me. I must address myself to a larger audience.

From ancient times, philosophers and moralists have expressed the idea that ethical conduct is acceptable from a point of view that is somehow universal. The 'Golden Rule' attributed to Moses, to be found in the book of Leviticus and subsequently repeated by Jesus, tells us to go beyond our own personal interest and 'love they neighbour as thyself' — in other words, give the same weight to the interests of others as one gives to one's own interests. The same idea of putting oneself in the position of another is involved in the other Christian formulation of the commandment, that we do to others as we would have them do to us. The Stoics held that ethics derives from a universal natural law. Kant developed this idea into his famous formula: 'Act only on that maxim through which you can at the same time will that it should become a universal law.' Kant's theory has itself been modified and developed by R.M. Hare, who sees universalisability as a logical feature of moral judgments. The eighteenth-century British philosophers Hutcheson, Hume, and Adam Smith appealed to an imaginary 'impartial spectator' as the test of a moral judgment, and this theory has its modern version in the Ideal Observer theory. Utilitarians, from Jeremy Bentham to J.J.C. Smart, take it as axiomatic that in deciding moral issues 'each counts for one and none for more than one'; while John Rawls, a leading contemporary critic of utilitarianism, incorporates essentially the same axiom into his own theory by deriving basic ethical principles from any imaginary choice in which those choosing do not know whether they will be the ones who gain or lose by the principles they select. Even Continental European philosophers like the existentialist Jean-Paul Sartre and the critical theorist Jürgen Habermas, who differ in many ways from their English-speaking colleagues — and from each other — agree that ethics is in some sense universal.

One could argue endlessly about the merits of each of these characterisations of the ethical; but what they have in common is more important than their differences. They agree that an ethical principle cannot be justified in relation to any partial or sectional group. Ethics takes a universal point of view. This does not mean that a particular ethical judgment must be universally applicable. Circumstances alter causes, as we have seen. What it does mean is that in making ethical judgments we go beyond our own likes and dislikes. From an ethical point of view, the fact that it is I who benefit from, say, a more equal distribution of income and you who lose by it, is irrelevant. Ethics requires us to go beyond 'I' and 'you' to the universal law, the universalisable judgment, the standpoint of the impartial spectator or ideal observer, or whatever we choose to call it.

Can we use this universal aspect of ethics to derive an ethical theory that will give us guidance about right and wrong? Philosophers from the Stoics to Hare and Rawls have attempted this. No attempt has met with general acceptance. The problem is that if we describe the universal aspect of ethics in bare, formal terms, a wide range of ethical theories, including quite irreconcilable ones, are compatible with this notion of universality; if, on the other hand, we build up our description of the universal aspect of ethics so that it leads us ineluctably to one particular ethical theory, we shall be accused of smuggling our own ethical beliefs into our definition of the ethical — and this definition was supposed to be broad enough, and neutral enough, to encompass all serious candidates for the status of 'ethical theory'. Since so many others have failed to overcome this obstacle to deducing an ethical theory from the universal aspect of ethics, it would be foolhardy to attempt to do so in a brief introduction to a work with a quite different aim. Nevertheless I shall propose something only a little less ambitious. The universal aspect of ethics, I suggest, does provide a persuasive, although not conclusive, reason for taking a broadly utilitarian position.

My reason for suggesting this is as follows. In accepting that ethical judgments must be made from a universal point of view, I am accepting that my own interests cannot, simply because they are my interests, count more than the interests of anyone else. Thus my very natural concern that my own interests be looked after must, when I think ethically, be extended to the interests of others. Now, imagine that I am trying to decide between two possible courses of action — perhaps whether to eat all the fruits I have collected myself, or to share them with others. Imagine, too, that I am deciding in a complete ethical vacuum, that I know nothing of any ethical considerations — I am, we might say, in a pre-ethical stage of thinking. How would I make up my mind? One thing that would be still relevant would be how the possible courses of action will affect my interests. Indeed, if we define 'interests' broadly enough, so that we count anything people desire as in their interests (unless it is incompatible with another desire or desires), then it would seem that at this pre-ethical stage, only one's own interests can be relevant to the decision.

Suppose I then begin to think ethically, to the extent of recognising that my own interests cannot count for more, simply because they are my own, than the interests of others. In place of my own interests, I now have to take into account the interests of all those affected by my decision. This requires me to weigh up all these interests and adopt the course of action most likely to maximize the interests of those affected. Thus at least at some level in my moral reasoning I must choose the course of action that has the best consequences, on balance, for all affected. (I say 'at some level in my moral reasoning' because, as we shall see later, there are utilitarian reasons for believing that we ought not to try to calculate these consequences for every ethical decision we make in our daily lives, but only in very unusual circumstances, or perhaps when we are reflecting on our choice of general principles to guide us in future. In other words, in the specific example given, at first glance one might think it obvious that sharing the fruit that I have gathered has better consequences for all affected than not sharing them. This may in the end also be the best general principle for us all to adopt, but before we can have grounds for believing this to be the case, we must also consider whether the effect of a general practice of sharing gathered fruits will benefit all those affected, by bringing about a more equal distribution, or whether it will reduce the amount of food gathered, because some will cease to gather anything if they know that they will get sufficient from their share of what others gather.)

The way of thinking I have outlined is a form of utilitarianism. It differs from classical utilitarianism in that 'best consequences' is understood as meaning what, on balance, furthers the interests of those affected, rather than merely what increases pleasure and reduces pain. (It has, however, been suggested that classical utilitarians like Bentham and John Stuart Mill used 'pleasure' and 'pain' in a broad sense that allowed them to include achieving what one desired as a 'pleasure' and the reverse as a 'pain'. If this interpretation is correct, the difference between classical utilitarianism and utilitarianism based on interests disappears.)

What does this show? It does not show that utilitarianism can be deduced from the universal aspect of ethics. There are other ethical ideals — like individual rights, the sanctity of life, justice, purity, and so on — that are universal in the required sense, and are, at least in some versions, incompatible with utilitarianism. It does show that we very swiftly arrive at an initially utilitarian position once we apply the universal aspect of ethics to simple, pre-ethical decision making. This, I believe, places the onus of proof on those who seek to go beyond utilitarianism. The utilitarian position is a minimal one, a first base that we reach by universalising self-interested decision making. We cannot, if we are to think ethically, refuse to take this step. If we are to be persuaded that we should go beyond utilitarianism and accept non-utilitarian moral rules or ideals, we need to be provided with good reasons for taking this further step. Until such reasons are produced, we have some grounds for remaining utilitarians. . . .

3   The Foundations of Bioethics

H. Tristram Engelhardt, Jr.

. . . The principles of autonomy and beneficence ground and summarize two central moral points of view: (1) that in terms of which one considers what it means to act with authority, within one's rights, and (2) that in terms of which one considers what it means to do good and avoid evil. Each is justified through being tied to an inescapable element of meaning. The principle of autonomy is inescapable, insofar as one asks the question whether one (or another) has acted rightly in the sense of with moral authority. The principle of beneficence is inescapable insofar as one asks a question regarding the good one ought to achieve or evil one ought to avoid for others. The principles express the fact that the moral point of view is one of beneficence within constraints of respect for persons.

The Tension between the Principles

Neither the principle of autonomy nor that of beneficence is justified in terms of its consequences. They are rather summaries of unavoidable areas of personal conduct. They are in this sense deontological principles, in that their rightness is not defined in terms of their consequences. However, concrete rules of beneficence are likely to be teleological in being justified in terms of their consequences. Concrete applications of the principle of autonomy, in contrast, bind, even if they have negative consequence for liberty. The principle of autonomy, which is justified in terms of the morality of mutual respect, does not focus on freedom as a value, but on respect for freedom as the possibility for general moral authority and justified worthiness of blame and praise. It is not goal or consequence oriented (i.e., teleological). Physician–patient agreements (e.g., a physician's agreement to keep a patient's disclosures confidential) bind in terms of the principle of autonomy, independently of their consequences. Rules for free and informed consent that are based on mutual respect also bind independently of their consequences. The sphere of the principle of autonomy, in its application, remains in its core deontological. It grounds rights and obligations independently of concerns for achieving what is good and avoiding what is evil. The sphere of the principle of beneficence, in its application, becomes teleological. It grounds particular rights and obligations in terms of their achieving what is good and avoiding what is harmful (though the general principle is not so justified). A particular rule of beneficence that caused more harm than good would lose its justification. Thus, a rule for distributing health care resources on grounds of beneficence would be defeated if it failed to provide more benefits than alternative rules. The two principles thus lead to contrasting spheres of moral discourse: one deontologically oriented, the other teleologically oriented.[1]

These dimensions of morality appear to be sufficiently distinct so as to allow for an important form of tension. An act can be justified within one dimension of morality but not within the other. Thus, one has conflicts of the general sort, "X has a right (obligation) to do A but it is wrong." One might advance as an example of this general formula, "Physicians have a right to do what they want to with their spare time, even when they could easily contribute a small portion of that spare time to aiding indigent patients, but it is wrong not to use some of that time to aid those patients." One has a conflict between the morality of mutual respect and the morality of welfare. Still, one cannot specify the morality of welfare without appealing to mutual agreement and therefore to the morality of mutual respect.

The principles of autonomy and beneficence are thus both mutually supporting, as well as the root of ineradicable conflicts in the moral life. Goods and harms become moral goods and harms in the embrace of a community with a moral vision. However, such a community can have moral authority only through respecting the principle of moral autonomy. Yet the principle of autonomy requires acquiescing in the choice by others of harms they hold to be goods, which may be at odds with the views of the moral community, for example, a young man deciding to commit suicide after sustaining nonfatal but disfiguring burns or individuals choosing within the rules of a medical insurance system in ways that will in the end subvert that very system through escalating costs. Respect for freedom and interest in the good will conflict.

Since views of the good are divergent, there will be no moral authority to stop persons from peaceably pursuing their view of the good life alone or with consenting others. One might think of a community attempting to bring its members to realize a higher level of health and to lower certain health care costs by stopping smoking and engaging in exercise programs. What of the sedentary smokers who do not judge that such is worth the effort? The achievement of the communal view of the good will often fall prey to the free choice of individuals not to aid its prospering. Such dissenters from an orthodox vision of the good can be characterized as having valued personal freedoms higher than other goods or as having embraced a different view of the good life with a different schedule of the relative significance of costs and benefits. As such, they remind us of the community's lack of authority to constrain individuals from such deviance. Such dissenters also underscore the tension between respecting freedom and acting benevolently, especially on a social level.

Dissenters not only underscore the tension between the principles of autonomy and beneficence, but in so doing they also indicate how a community can fragment into numerous communities, each with its own view of the good life. The arrangements can be complicated. Communities can in various areas overlap and separate. Consider how reform and orthodox Jewish physicians and patients may commonly presuppose certain views about the goods proper to the practice of medicine and still disagree regarding others. This fragmentation of the view of the good life leads, as has already been noted, to the tensions expressed in the application of the principle of nonmaleficence. Unlike other analyses, this volume supports the reduction of the principle of nonmaleficence to the conflict between the general and particular perspectives within the principle of beneficence.[2] This tension is exemplified when a physician is asked by a patient to achieve for the patient what the patient holds to be a good but what the physician holds to be a harm. . . .

The Principles of Bioethics

In approaching the problems of moral judgment in bioethics, we have then two major moral principles. Their character reflects the fact that they are principles for resolving moral disputes among individuals who do not share a common moral vision. They have their place through sustaining the ethical fabric of a secular pluralism. They sustain the possibility of moral discourse in secular pluralist societies where no one moral sense can be established. They function also as guides for tracing the lineage of supposed authority for public policy. Public policy that lacks a morally justified authority is without moral force. One might think here of laws of forbidding aiding and abetting the suicide of competent individuals.[3] Such laws are without moral authority at least as long as the individuals have not explicitly ceded their right to suicide (e.g., one might imagine that officers in the armed forces might be required to relinquish that right under specified conditions as a condition for their commission). On the other hand, laws protecting human research subjects against being used in experimentation without their consent carry moral authority in that they are grounded in the very notion of protecting the peaceable community. They spring from the notion of the morality of mutual respect.

Other areas of public policy have less certain moral authority. It will be clear how to use commonly owned resources in ways that support the common good. The provision of a mix of preventive and primary health care out of common funds would appear reasonable. However, arguments can reasonably be advanced for various mixtures, including a major preponderance of either preventive or primary health care. The actual character of public health policy will thus have to be created by common agreement and will not be discoverable by an inspection of the principle of beneficence in isolation. One will need to appeal to the principle of autonomy as the basis for the common fashioning of particular programs of beneficence. In most cases, one finds both principles intertwined. These two principles are principles in the sense of being *principia*. They indicate foundations for major elements of the moral life. . . .

Notes

1. I distinguish here between deontological principles as those that cannot be reduced to interests in the achievement of particular goods or values, and teleological principles that can be so reduced. As John Rawls indicates, "A deontological theory [is] one that either does not specify the good independently from the right, or does not interpret the right as maximizing the good." *Theory of Justice* (Cambridge, Mass.: Harvard University Press, 1971), p. 30. In contrast, within teleological theories, "the good is de-

fined independently from the right, and then the right is defined as that which maximizes the good." Ibid., p. 24.

2. For a treatment of nonmaleficence as an independent principle, see Tom L. Beauchamp and James F. Childress, *Principles of Biomedical Ethics*, 2d ed. (New York: Oxford University Press, 1983). pp. 106–47.

3. H. Tristram Engelhardt, Jr., and Michele Malloy, "Suicide and Assisting Suicide: A Critique of Legal Sanctions." *Southwestern Law Review* 36 (November 1982): 1003–37.

4   Morality and Moral Justification

Tom L. Beauchamp & James F. Childress

. . . The upshot of our analysis of coherence and specification is the following: One goal of a moral theory, and central to its account of justification, is to move from general levels of theory to particular rules, judgments, and policies that are in close proximity to everyday decisions in the moral life. Like a tributary with many forks into different territories, the principles and rules in a theory can be made to fork outward through specification and feed different parts of the moral life. Appropriate specification conserves or elevates the coherence already present in the theory. When moral conflicts occur, specification supplies an *ideal* of repeated coherence testing and modification of a principle or rule until the conflict is specified away, *but* specification is also a useful tool for the development of *policies* in biomedical ethics.

To accept this ideal is not to assume that conflicts can always be specified away by developing rules or policies. The moral life will be plagued by contingent conflicts that cannot be eliminated. Our pragmatic goal should be a method of resolution that often helps, not a method that will invariably resolve our problems.

Balancing and Overriding

Principles, rules, and rights require *balancing* no less than *specification*. Principles (and the like) direct us to certain forms of conduct, but principles by themselves do not settle conflicts of principle. Whereas specification entails a substantive development of the meaning and scope of norms, balancing consists of deliberation and judgment about the relative weights of norms. Balancing sometimes occurs in specification, and specification also sometimes occurs in balancing. Specification and balancing can best be conceived as mutually facilitative approaches, methods, or strategies that fit coherently within the larger method of coherence outlined above. Balancing is especially useful for individual cases, whereas specification is especially useful for policy development.

Avoiding Balancing through "Absolute" Norms   Throughout this book we view the norms to be balanced — principles, rules, rights, and the like — as *prima facie* and not as absolute, as rules of thumb, or as hierarchically (lexically or serially) ordered. However, some specified norms are virtually absolute, and therefore usually escape the need to balance. Examples include prohibition of cruelty and torture, where these actions are defined as gratuitous infliction of pain and suffering. (Other prohibitions, such as rules against murder, are absolute only because of the meaning of their terms. For example, to say "murder is categorically wrong" is to say "unjustified killing is unjustified.")

Defensible substantive absolutes are thorough and decisive specifications of principles. They are rare and rarely play a role in moral controversy. More interesting are norms that are formulated with the goal of including all legitimate exceptions, but whose formulation remains controversial. An example is "Always obtain oral or written informed consent for medical interventions with competent patients, *except* in emergencies, in low-risk situations, or when patients have waived their rights to adequate information." The norm clearly needs interpretation and a specification of what constitutes an informed consent, an emergency, a waiver, and a low risk, but this rule would be absolute if all legitimate exceptions were included in its formulation and specification. Depending on how far specification goes and whether all exceptions are built in and defended, a rule could turn out to be legitimately absolute and thereby escape balancing because its potential for conflict with other principles and rules would have been eliminated. However, if such rules exist, they are rare. Moreover, in light of the enormous range of possibilities for contingent conflicts among rules, absolute rules are best construed as ideals rather than finished products. . . .

The Place of Principles

We defend what has sometimes been called the *four-principles approach* to biomedical ethics,[1] and also called, somewhat disparagingly, *principlism*.[2] These principles initially derive from considered judgments in the common morality and medical tradition that form our starting point in this volume. For example, the principle of beneficence derives, in part, from long-standing, professional role obligations in medicine to provide medical benefits to patients. Our goal is to specify and balance these principles by the methods of ethical theory previously discussed. Both the set of principles and the content ascribed to the principles are based on our attempts to put the common morality as a whole into a coherent package.

In this section we sketch our ethical framework by providing an analytical breakdown of its elements. We distinguish several types of normative action guides as components in our framework, including principles, rules, rights, and virtues. Although rules, rights, and virtues are of the highest importance for health care ethics, principles provide the most abstract and comprehensive norms in the framework. These principles will be individually analyzed in later chapters. This chapter presents only the structural shell.

Four Clusters of Basic Principles

We begin with our assumptions. That four clusters of moral "principles" (in another framework they might be developed as "rights," "virtues," or "values") are central to biomedical ethics is a conclusion we have reached by the search for considered judgments and coherence, not a position that receives an argued defense. However, we will in later chapters defend the choice of each principle as well as the independent significance of each. We also operate with only a loose distinction between rules and principles. Both are normative generalizations that guide actions, but, as we analyze them, *rules* are more specific in content and more restricted in scope than principles. Principles do not function as precise action guides that inform us in each circumstance how to act in the way more detailed rules do. *Principles* are general guides that leave considerable room for judgment in specific cases and that provide substantive guidance for the development of more detailed rules and policies. This limitation is no defect in principles; rather, it is a part of the moral life in which we are expected to take responsibility for the way we bring principles to bear in our judgments about particular cases. We also need to distinguish both rules and principles from the coherent, systematic body of norms that comprise *theories*. Our discussion of the coherence theory has already given some insight into our views about the nature of theory and its construction.

The four clusters of principles are (1) respect for autonomy (a norm of respecting the decisionmaking capacities of autonomous persons), (2) nonmaleficence (a norm of avoiding the causation of harm), (3) beneficence (a group of norms for providing benefits and balancing benefits against risks and costs), and (4) justice (a group of norms for distributing benefits, risks, and costs fairly). Nonmaleficence and beneficence have played a central historical role in medical ethics, whereas respect for autonomy and justice were neglected in traditional medical ethics but have came into prominence because of recent developments. . . .

Notes

1. See, for example, Raanam Gillon and Ann Lloyd, eds. *Principles of Health Care Ethics* (London: John Wiley & Sons, 1993).

2. K. Danner Clouser and Bernard Gert, "A Critique of Principlism," *The Journal of Medicine and Philosophy* 15 (April 1990): 232.

---

5   What's Distinctive about Feminist Bioethics?

Rosemarie Tong

Many critics wonder what distinctive insights feminism has to offer the field of bioethics. Some traditional bioethicists might ask whether feminists' reliance on concepts such as choice, control, caring, and relationships really represents a significant departure from Tom Beauchamp and James Childress's reliance on the principles of autonomy, beneficence, non-maleficence, and justice.[1] Aren't the former simply the latter restated? After all, isn't autonomy about choice and justice about relationships? Moreover, isn't beneficence about caring and non-maleficence about not controlling others? Other critics could argue that feminists, with their search for paradigmatic cases to guide the resolution of particular medical dilemmas, are simply echoing casuists such as Albert Jonsen and Stephen Toulmin,[2] or imitating communitarians' emphasis on virtues, role responsibilities, and cultural practices.[3] Yet others might point to the similarities between feminist theorists and ideal discourse or conversationalist attempts to create moral consensus through discussion and sharing ideas,[4] stressing the perspectival nature of moral knowledge. Finally, traditional bioethicists could claim that feminist bioethics is merely a species of the genus "contextual ethics," the latest attempt to steer a mid-course between what Robert

L. Holmes has termed "moral legalism" (the view that the rightness or wrongness of an act is determined by its adherence to certain rules, principles, or commandments) on the one hand,[5] and what he has termed "moral particularism" (the view that moral rightness or wrongness of an act depends solely on the situation in which it is performed) on the other.[6]

The claim that feminist bioethics borrows ideas from non-feminist moral perspectives should not distress feminist bioethicists. We are, after all, not blank slates, nor do we frame new philosophical notions within a vacuum. During training at an institution of higher learning, feminist bioethicists learn much about deontology[7] and utilitarianism,[8] nearly as much about virtue ethics[9] and moral-sentiment ethics,[10] and at least something about one or more less emphasized ethical perspectives: for example, Sartre's existentialism,[11] Habermas's discourse ethics,[12] Rorty's pragmatic ethics,[13] or MacIntyre's communitarian ethics.[14] Therefore, we as feminist bioethicists should not be faulted for building upon what we have been taught and have come to value. Rather, we should be credited for how we have transformed and improved our initial knowledge base. Feminist bioethics work within the parameters of a recognizable ethical framework — in most cases a contextual one, but in some cases one that favors principles over situations as the ultimate moral determinant,[15] or vice versa.[16] The choice of an ethical framework is not therefore the distinguishing mark of a feminist approach to bioethics. Rather, feminist approaches to bioethics are distinctive because of the complex combinations of politics, ontology, and epistemology that make their common methodology an effective means for discerning instances of gender oppression or neglect.

Feminists do not pride themselves on the simplicity of their approaches to bioethics — they do not shave with Ockham's razor — but on their complexity. Typically, feminist bioethics do not draw sharp lines between ethics and politics. On the contrary, for feminist bioethicists the crucial ethical questions to ask are questions about power, specifically questions about male domination and female subordination. Thus, guiding every feminist approach to bioethics is at least one feminist political perspective; that is, a coherent undergirding notion of the causes underlying women's subordination to men, coupled with a refined program of action aimed at eliminating the systems and attitudes that oppress women.

Feminist political perspectives are numerous: liberal, Marxist, radical, psychoanalytic, socialist, cultural, multicultural, global, ecological, existentialist, and postmodern.[17] Each of these feminist analyses of the distribution of power identifies a particular factor as the *primary* cause of women's subordinate status: for example, biology, economics, law, education, national boundaries, language, and so on. Admitting, however, that *all* of these factors have contributed more or less strongly to "women's estate," an increasing number of feminist bioethicists are describing themselves as "eclectic feminists."[18] Eclectic feminist bioethicists use two or more feminist political perspectives to guide their analytical forays into the realm of medicine. For example, they might use liberal, Marxist, radical, and cultural feminist perspectives to consider the positive and negative dimensions of surrogate motherhood. The contracted mother can be viewed as a woman exercising her enhanced procreative options, a baby machine or fetal container, a reproductive prostitute, or a woman helping another woman.[19] Which of these descriptions best fits the contracted mother is, of course, a matter of considerable debate among all feminist bioethicists, be they "eclectic" or firmly committed to one and only one feminist political perspective.

Not only do a wide variety of feminist political perspectives orient the thinking of feminist bioethicists, so too do a wide variety of ontological assumptions. Feminist ontologies are as numerous as feminist political perspectives, though they tend to cluster into two groups: those that view the self as definitively separate from others and those that describe the self as essentially connected to others. This significant contrast is typified in the differences between liberal feminists on the one hand and radical and cultural feminists on the other.

Like traditional liberals, liberal feminists endorse the so-called male ontology, in which the self is not only essentially separate from other selves, but also depends upon this separation for her freedom. Autonomy is the human value *par excellence* through which a woman achieves her full human potential. To be sure, autonomy is not an unalloyed blessing. In her struggle to maximize her self-interest, the autonomous self leads a particularly difficult existence. According to legal theorist Robin West, this separation leads to a fear of annihilation by others. The interests of separate individuals collide, and conflict arises. When the self is not warring with others, the autonomous self's separateness produces a feeling of alienation from others.[20] Nonetheless, liberal feminists urge women to pay this high price so that they can have the same opportunities, occupations, rights, and privileges men have had. Indeed, in their drive for women's sameness with men, liberal feminists have sometimes denied women's unique qualities.[21] They have cautioned women against emphasizing their differences from men, viewing these biologically-produced and/or culturally shaped "othernesses" as traps that limit women to the role of maintaining the human species, while men strive to elevate it to greater heights.

In contrast, most radical and cultural feminists have rejected "male" ontology and the separation thesis that guides it. In its place they endorse a "female" ontology, guided by a connection thesis. Indeed, as Robin West notes, it is the central insight of radical and cultural feminists "that women are 'essentially connected,' not 'essentially separate,' from the rest of human life, both materially, through pregnancy, intercourse, and breast-feeding, and existentially, through the moral and practical life."[22] Yet, as West also observes, cultural feminists — thinkers like Carol Gilligan[23] and Nel Noddings[24] — and radical feminists — thinkers like Andrea Dworkin,[25] Gena Corea,[26] and Catherine MacKinnon[27] — have reacted very differently to women's connectedness.

Radical feminists have emphasized the negative side of the connection thesis. Connections set women up for exploitation and misery: "Invasion and intrusion, rather than intimacy, nurturance, and care, is the 'unofficial story' of women's subjective experience of connections.[28] Women are connected to others, most especially through the experiences of heterosexual intercourse and child-bearing. Beneath the sugar coating, however, these experiences leave an aftertaste of violation. This type of harm, because of its link to these specific experiences, is unique to women in a way that men can never fully understand. Women do not fear either annihilation by the other or alienation from the other as much as they dread occupation by the other: the uninvited penis, the unwanted fetus.[29]

Agreeing with radical feminists that connection is women's fundamental reality, cultural feminists have stressed the positive side of this state of affairs, praising women's capacities for sharing, giving, nurturing, sympathizing, empathizing, and above all, connecting. Women's bodies link one generation to another, a unique ability conferring strength. The fact that they menstruate, gestate, and lactate gives women a unique perspective on the meaning of human connection. For women, connection is not about signing contracts, but about people using their blood, sweat, and tears to bind each other together in close familial and friendship relationships.[30]

Since most people, including most feminists, find themselves torn between the positive and negative dimensions of separation and connection, respectively, feminist bioethicists are increasingly driven toward what I term "ontological vacillation." We are never quite sure whether our self is whole or fragmented, or whether we are most ourselves when we are alone or when we are with others. Feminist bioethicists are particularly aware of the self-other dynamic because disease, decay, and death threaten even the strongest sense of self, and also because in our moments of suffering and pain we tend to experience ourselves as both radically alone and fundamentally united with all of human creation.

In the act of disclosing the ethical, political, and onological perspectives that motivate their distinct approach to biomedical problems, feminist bioethicists simultaneously reveal the feminist epistemologies that orient their observations about how women fare in the medical establishment. Like other feminist perspectives, feminist approaches to knowledge are multiple. According to Katharine T. Bartlett, rational-empirical epistemology, standpoint epistemology, postmodern anti-epistemology, and, most recently, positionalist epistemology are some of the leading feminist means of knowing.[31] Using their epistemological approach of choice, feminist bioethicists attempt to ascertain, for example, the actual health status of both sexes and to determine how far that condition deviates from what justice prescribes.

Feminist bioethicists who adopt a rational-empirical epistemology believe, for instance, that current medical practice is not objective, but hope to make it more objective by providing more facts (as opposed to myths or stereotypes) about women. The knowledge needed to create good, just, and rational medical practice is out there — it is just a matter of discovering and acknowledging all of the true facts. The physical and emotional pain experienced by women during their menopause has always been a fact — (male) physicians simply had to learn to take their female patients seriously before they could recognize that this pain was all over women's bodies and not simply "in their heads."[32]

Like feminist bioethicists who adopt a rational-empirical epistemology, feminist bioethicists who adopt a standpoint epistemology believe that there is objective knowledge, but they doubt that all rational agents necessarily see the same thing when the facts stare them in the face.[33] Standpoint epistemologists credit women, for example, with being able to see things about reality that men do not typically see. Because the "master's position" in any set of dominating social relations — the general position of men vis-à-vis women — "tends to produce distorted visions of the real regularities and underlying causal tendencies in social relations,"[34] men experience their power over women as normal, even beneficial. According to feminist standpoint theorists, this is not women's experience. Women see systems of male domination and female subordination for what they really are: abnormal and harmful ways for men and women to relate. Social position, rather than being irrelevant, determines the way in which we see the facts, including fundamental facts about the human body and mind.

Significantly, there do not seem to be any feminist *bioethicists* — at least I cannot think of one — who adopt postmodern anti-epistemology. That this should be the case should not surprise us. Feminist postmodernists chastise feminists who *theorize* about women's status in society; they accuse them of simply imitating the kind of universalist, absolutistic, deductivist "male thinking" that insists on telling as absolute truth one and only one story. For the postmodern anti-epistemologist, there is no truth; instead there are only shifting, ephemeral, changing realities that evolve within different social contexts.[35] Given that such a viewpoint provides no solid ground for advocating or criticizing medical reform, feminist bioethicists tend to steer clear of it. Since life and death decisions must be made in medicine, we need to hold some position from which to reason concerning the best choice.

Finally, there are an increasing number of feminist bioethicists, including myself, who work out of a positional epistemological framework. We believe in truth, a self, and reality, but insist that they are all partial, provisional, and changing in nature. Knowledge comes from experience, and since our experiences are necessarily limited, our truths are never total. We are never quite objective enough because we can never step out of ourselves completely. If I wish to secure a broader truth than my own — which is white, heterosexual, Eastern-European, well-educated, socially-advantaged, fertile, able-bodied, Catholic, female, etc. — then I must talk to as many "others" as possible. The truth emerges through "solidarity in politics" and "shared conversations in epistemology."[36] Everyone's knowledge about medicine and health care, including women's knowledge, is limited.

Not surprisingly, positionality in epistemology is highly compatible with contextualism in ethics, eclecticism in feminist politics, and vacillation in feminist ontology. I suspect that it is this compatibility which helps me and others to make good use of what Bartlett and others have identified as the three standard elements of feminist methodology: asking the woman question, employing consciousness-raising, and engaging in feminist practical reasoning.[37]

The *woman question* challenges the supposed objectivity of medicine, as well as claiming that many of the "facts" about female "nature" actually result from values founded on biased social construction. Gender bias can and does misshape the precepts and practices of medicine. It creeps in when physicians treat all human bodies as if they were all male bodies — viewing them as dysfunctional if they fail to function like male bodies or showing no curiosity or interest in their unique problems.

Consciousness-raising invites women to weave their personal experiences into a tapestry that has a wider meaning for all women. Women who share "ob-gyn" stories, for example, often come to realize that their feelings of having been treated as a girl rather than a woman are not unique to them but common to most women in this society. Increasingly convinced that not they but the "system" is crazy, such women routinely gain the courage and confidence to challenge those who presume to know what is best for them.

Feminist practical reasoning helps feminist bioethicists achieve a reflective equilibrium between principles, rules, ideals, values, and virtues on the one hand and actual cases in which moral decisions must be made on the other. Feminism enhances classical Aristotelian practical reasoning by stressing the importance of *listening* as well as speaking in the course of a moral dialogue, for moral choices are made in most cases between several moral agents rather than isolated within one individual. Ethics requires communication, corroboration, and collaboration; thankfully, it also means we are not alone as we grapple with applying ethics to particular situations. As I conceive feminist practical reasoning, it accepts our limited ability to explain and justify our decisions and actions to each other even as it insists that we try harder to find the words that will make us not only "partners in virtue" but "friends in action."[38]

To be sure, *non-feminist* contextualists in ethics, vacillators in ontology, and positionalists in epistemology will raise many of the same questions about cases and come to many of the same conclusions I do. But there are still some questions they will not ask and some conclusions they will not draw, because they lack what I and other feminist bioethicists have: namely, a feminist political perspective and methodology. Think of it this way. Most of the ingredients a Chinese chef uses can be found in any chef's kitchen: meat, fish, rice, eggs, etc. However, a few of them are unlikely to be found in the kitchen of any chef who does not do Chinese cooking, like certain Chinese vegetables and spices. Moreover, a Chinese chef will combine the more common ingredients in uncommon ways — pineapple with chicken, for instance. It is the combination of these culinary innovations with the staples found in any chef's kitchen that accounts for why the food I eat at the Lotus tastes differently from the food I eat at El Cancun. Feminist bioethicists offer non-feminist bioethicists the equivalent of a distinct eating experience; the fact that some of the philosophical "ingredients" may also be found elsewhere does not detract from the ability of feminist bioethicists to offer an innovative and significant new "recipe." This analogy is not meant to suggest that feminist bioethics is a matter of mere taste. Rather, it means that feminist bioethicists, because of their political, ontological, and epistemological assumptions are more likely to raise important questions about women and to offer answers unlikely to occur to anyone but someone with a women's eyes. Of course, questions about women are not the only important questions to be asked. Feminist bioethicists trust others to use the eyes of their own gender, race, class, culture, and so on, to search the field of bioethics, and to raise other important questions accordingly, so that we can find mutually-agreeable ways to weaken patterns of human domination and subordination in the realm of medicine, including patterns of male domination and female subordination.

Endnotes

1. Tom L. Beauchamp and James F. Childress, *Principles of Biomedical Ethics*, 4th ed. (New York: Oxford University Press, 1994).
2. Albert R. Jonsen and Stephen Toulmin, *The Abuse of Casuistry: A History of Moral Reasoning* (Berkeley, CA: University of California Press, 1988).
3. Alasdair MacIntyre, *After Virtue* (Notre Dame, IN: University of Notre Dame Press, 1981).
4. Jurgen Habermas, *The Philosophical Discourse of Modernity*, trans. Frederick Lawrence (Cambridge, MA: MIT Press, 1987), and Richard Rorty, *Contingency, Irony, and Solidarity* (New York: Cambridge University Press, 1989).
5. Holmes claims that the following standard ethical theories express the view he terms "moral legalism:" ethical egoism, divine command theory, Kantianism, utilitarianism, principle of justice, ethics of love, and

ethics of nonviolence. As he sees it, each of these theories is guided by a principle that is viewed as the ultimate norm to which all moral judgments must be referred. See Robert L. Holmes, *Basic Moral Philosophy* (Belmont, CA: Wadsworth, 1993), p.44.

6. Holmes claims that Aristotle is probably a "moral particularist." He also classifies H.A. Prichard, W.D. Ross, the existentialists, and John Dewey as "moral particularists." See Holmes, *Basic Moral Philosophy*, p.46.

7. Immanuel Kant, *Critique of Practical Reason and Other Writings in Moral Philosophy*, ed. and trans. Lewis White Beck (Chicago: University of Chicago Press, 1949).

8. John Stuart Mill, *Utilitarianism* (New York: Liberal Arts Press, 1953).

9. Aristotle, "Nichomachean Ethics," in *The Basic Works of Aristotle*, ed. Richard McKeon (New York: Random House, 1941).

10. David Hume, *An Inquiry Concerning the Principles of Morals*, ed. Charles W. Hendel (Indianapolis, IN: Bobbs-Merrill Co., 1957).

11. Jean-Paul Sartre, *Existentialism and Human Emotions* (New York: Philosophical Library, 1957).

12. Jurgen Habermas, *The Philosophical Discourse of Modernity*.

13. Richard Rorty, *Contingency, Irony, and Solidarity*.

14. MacIntyre, *After Virtue*.

15. Laura Purdy has defended utilitarian ethics on several occasions. See Laura M. Purdy, *In Their Best Interest* (Ithaca, NY: Cornell University Press, 1992), pp.234–246.

16. Linda Bell has developed a feminist version of existentialist ethics that fits Holmes's description of "moral particularism." Linda Bell, *Rethinking Ethics in the Midst of Violence: A Feminist Approach to Freedom* (Lanaham, MD: Rowman and Littlefield, 1993).

17. See, for example, Alison M. Jaggar, *Feminist Politics and Human Nature* (Totowa, NJ; Rowman and Allenheld, 1983), and Rosemarie Tong, *Feminist Thought: A Comprehensive Introduction* (Boulder, CO: Westview, 1989).

18. Susan Sherwin, *No Longer Patient: Feminist Ethics and Health Care* (Philadelphia: Temple University, 1992), pp.32–34.

19. See, for example, Christine Overall, *Ethics and Human Reproduction* (Boston, MA: Unwin Hyman, 1987).

20. Robin C. West, "Jurisprudence and Gender," *The University of Chicago Law Review* 55 (Winter 1988): 5–12.

21. It is important to note that not all liberal feminists stress women's sameness with men. See Mary Joe Frug, *Postmodern Legal Feminism* (New York: Routledge, 1991), pp.ix–xxxv; 3–52.

22. West, "Jurisprudence and Gender," p.3.

23. Carol Gilligan, *In a Different Voice* (Cambridge, MA: Harvard University Press, 1982).

24. Nel Noddings, *Caring: A Feminine Approach to Ethics and Moral Education* (Berkeley, CA: University of California Press, 1984).

25. Andrea Dworkin, *Woman Hating: A Radical Look at Sexuality* (New York: E.P. Dutton, 1974).

26. Genea Corea, *The Mother Machine: Reproductive Technologies from Artificial Insemination to Artificial Wombs* (New York: Harper & Row, 1985).

27. Catharine A. MacKinnon, *Feminism Unmodified: Discourses on Life and the Law* (Cambridge, MA: Harvard University Press, 1977).

28. West, "Jurisprudence and Gender," p.29.

29. Ibid., pp.29–36.

30. See, for example, Caroline Whitbeck, "A Different Reality: Feminist Ontology," in Ann Garry and Marilyn Pearsall, eds. *Women, Knowledge, and Reality: Explorations in Feminist Philosophy* (Boston: Unwin Hyman, 1989), pp.51–76.

31. Katharine T. Bartlett, "Feminist Legal Methods (1990)," in *Feminist Legal Theory: Foundations*, ed. D. Kelly Weisberg (Philadelphia: Temple University Press, 1993), pp.558–566.

32. Joan C. Callahan, ed. *Menopause: A Midlife Passage* (Bloomington: Indiana University Press, 1993).

33. Sherwin, *No Longer Patient*, pp.13–57.

34. Sandra Harding, *The Science Question in Feminism* (Ithaca, NY: Cornell University Press, 1986), p.191.

35. Toril Moi, *Sexual/Textual Politics: Feminist Literary Theory* (New York: Methuen, 1985), pp.130–131.

36. Donna Haraway, "Situated Knowledges: The Science Question in Feminism and the Privilege of Partial Perspective," in *Simians,*

Cyborgs and Women (New York: Routledge, 1991), p.191.

37. Bartlett, "Feminist Legal Methods," pp.551–557.

38. Aristotle, "Nicomachean Ethics," Book VIII.

Chapter 1

Questions to Consider

1. Consider a moral dilemma that might arise in a health care context; for example, whether or not to lie to a patient if it is feared that the truth will be devastating and the lie unlikely to be discovered. Compare and contrast the different ways this problem might be approached by the different authors represented in this chapter (i.e., what questions would each begin with in investigating such an issue?).

2. What does Paul Ramsey mean by "covenant"? How might this concept inform our investigations in the area of health care ethics?

3. What specific considerations does Peter Singer propose we attend to in reflecting on ethical problems? How would he account for the moral values expressed by the principles of justice and respect for autonomy?

4. Explain the tension that H. Tristram Engelhardt, Jr., speaks of between the principles of autonomy and beneficence. Give an example of a case where this tension is apparent and explain the role of each principle in this conflict.

5. What role do Beauchamp and Childress assign to moral principles in their view of moral deliberation and justification? How does their proposal differ from those of other authors in this chapter?

6. What are some examples of questions that would not be asked and conclusions that would not be drawn in health care ethics by those who do not adopt a feminist political perspective and methodology?

Further Readings

Callahan, Daniel. 1973. Bioethics as a discipline. *Hastings Center Studies* 1(1): 66–73.

Caplan, Arthur L. (1980). Ethical engineers need not apply: The state of applied ethics today. *Science, Technology, and Human Values* 6:24–32.

Clouser, K. Danner. 1978. Bioethics. *Encyclopedia of Bioethics*, vol. 1, (115–27). New York: Free Press.

Downie, R. S., and K. C. Calman. 1987. *Healthy respect: Ethics in health care*. Boston: Faber and Faber.

Hoffmaster, Barry. 1991. The theory and practice of applied ethics. *Dialogue* 3:213–34.

Holmes, Helen B., and Laura M. Purdy, eds. 1992. *Feminist perspectives in medical ethics*. Bloomington: Indiana University Press.

Kymlicka, Will. 1993. Approaches to the ethical issues raised by the Royal Commission's mandate. In Royal Commission on New Reproductive Technologies, *New Reproductive Technologies: Ethical Aspects* (Vol. 1 of the Research Studies, 1–46). Ottawa: Minister of Supply and Services Canada.

Pellegrino, Edmund D., and David C. Thomasma. 1981. *A philosophical basis of medical practice*. New York: Oxford University Press.

Rachels, James. 1980. Can ethics provide answers? *Hastings Center Report* 10(3): 32–40.

Sherwin, Susan. 1992. *No longer patient: Feminist ethics and health care*. Philadelphia: Temple University Press.

Chapter 2

Pluralism and Multiculturalism

Chapter 2

Introduction

The profound ways in which cultural beliefs and values affect our understanding of disease and illness and our reactions to them, and the ways in which those beliefs affect how health care is delivered, are becoming more widely appreciated. Cultural differences are apparent in basic styles of medical practice. Whereas doctors in the United States rely extensively on tests to arrive at a diagnosis, for example, physicians in Europe make more use of their clinical skills in examining patients and of the histories they obtain by talking with patients. This difference has been noted since the early 1900s. A Parisian physician who toured American hospitals in 1912 was surprised at the number of laboratory tests routinely ordered for patients. He observed that the tests seemed "like the Lord's rain, to descend from Heaven on the just and on the unjust in the most impartial fashion," and he surmised that "the diagnosis and treatment of a given patient depended more on the result of these various tests than on the symptoms present in the case" (Payer 1988, 140).

Differences in treatment also have been traced to culture. American physicians, for example, begin treating human immunodeficiency virus (HIV) infection with the drug zidovudine (AZT) earlier than French physicians do (Feldman 1992). American physicians start treatment for patients with CD4$^+$ lymphocyte counts (the cells initially targeted by HIV) below 500×10^6 per litre, while French physicians wait for counts below 200×10^6 per litre. One theory attributes this difference to the different models for AIDS found in the two countries: in the United States the primary model is cancer, whereas in France it is tuberculosis. As well, the approach to tuberculosis differs in the two countries. In the United States skin tests are used to screen the population for tuberculosis and prophylaxis with isoniazid is given to those with known exposure. In France, where the prevalence of tuberculosis has been higher, most of the population is now vaccinated. Moreover, in France, resistance to isoniazid is not uncommon. Their experience with tuberculosis, it is hypothesized, disposes French physicians to conceptualize acquired immunodeficiency syndrome (AIDS) largely as an infectious disease and thus to be sensitive to the problems of toxicity and resistance to drugs associated with infectious diseases:

> . . . the French experience with tuberculosis seems to inform their approach to AIDS, itself a chronic, difficult-to-treat infection. Concerned over the development of resistant strains of HIV in the population, the French intervene later in the course of the illness (Feldman 1992, 348).

These examples suggest that culture is implicated, in fundamental ways, in how health care is understood and delivered.

Cultural differences can be even more dramatic. Although criteria for brain death have been adopted in North America and have made more hearts available for transplantation, brain death has not been accepted in Japan. An explanation of the Japanese resistance is complicated, but in part it involves some pervasive cultural beliefs and values, such as the respect accorded ancestors and the obligations owed to them, the anthropomorphization of the spirit of a deceased person, and the lack of a tradition of altruistic giving to unknown others (Lock and Honde 1990).

The approach to abortion also is different in Japan (Nesbitt 1994). The Japanese word for abortion, "ryuzan," does not distinguish between a spontaneous abortion or miscarriage and an induced abortion. Abortion is not encouraged in Japan, but neither are women blamed for terminating pregnancies. The Japanese response to abortion is influenced by the Buddhist notion of karma, which determines the destiny of persons in their present and future lives. Rituals are performed to dispel the bad karma resulting from an abortion. Parents memorialize and apologize to the spirit of an aborted fetus, called a "mizuko," by setting up altars in their homes and making daily offerings of rice, water, and money. As well, there are temples that serve as memorials for aborted and miscarried fetuses. Toys are left at these temples for "mizuko" to play with, along with piles of flat stones so that the "mizuko" can climb to heaven. A Canadian who lived in Japan for two years regards these cultural practices as "a solution to the problem of abortion that addresses both the spiritual and practical needs of women who want abortions" (Nesbitt 1994).

It is easier to identify cultural differences in health care than it is to know what to make of them, however. The initial difficulty is to establish what kind of challenge cultural differences raise for health care ethics. Some cultural differences can be readily accommodated within health care systems, given an understanding of and sensitivity to those differences. When life support is stopped for a Muslim patient, for example, certain customs are supposed to be observed (Klessig 1992, 318). When a Muslim dies, a non-Muslim is not supposed to touch the body; health care providers could respect this custom simply by wearing gloves. As well, family members should be permitted to turn the bed so that the patient is facing Mecca at the time of death, and they should be allowed to recite the Koran. Respecting these customs would not be too onerous.

Sometimes an appropriate response involves a departure from the customs of both intersecting cultures. A hospital in Toronto, for example, is now offering childbirth classes to pregnant Somali women, from which men are excluded (Morrissey 1993). Fathers have become routinely involved in childbirth preparation in Canada, but the presence of men in the Somali class would, it is felt, inhibit the women. Here deviation from the established practice of childbirth preparation in Canada is necessary to counter the male domination inherent in Somali culture.

Other responses are more controversial. In New Jersey, for example, the law that applies to the determination of death contains a conscience clause that respects the religious beliefs of those who do not accept brain death (Olick 1991). The exemption is intended primarily for some members of the Orthodox Jewish community, but also for some Native Americans and some Japanese, whose religious and cultural under-standings might be violated by declarations of brain death. Implicit in this legal policy is the view that the determination of death is not exclusively a medical judgement but also involves value judgements. Most jurisdictions regard the need for a uniform standard of death to be so strong that a statutory conscience clause is precluded. The approach in New Jersey has been hailed, however, as "a new direction for the de-velopment of public policy governing the declaration of death in pluralistic communities" (Olick 1991, 285).

Some commentators see the challenges that cultural differences pose for both health care and health care ethics as deep and threatening:

> Much of modern medical practice is laced with land mines because it is predicated on the assumption that the person experiencing illness is the one to make health care decisions and who has a right, indeed almost a duty, to be told the diagnosis and prognosis. Ideas like autonomy, independence, and competence undergird communication processes and the physician–patient relationship. Serious questions can be raised about the appropriateness of these assumptions, especially when dealing with immigrant or other groups with cultural values vastly different from those underpinning biomedicine . . . (Barker 1992, 251).

The suggestion here is that fundamental concepts of health care ethics in North America, such as autonomy and competence, as well as the practices that instantiate these concepts, such as obtaining informed consent and truth telling, are inappropriate in certain cultures.

Other cultures might, for example, have an understanding of what it means to be a person that does not emphasize individualism or prize self-determination and control. Or a culture might value a family more than the individuals who comprise that family. Is the individualistic, autonomy-based conception of health care ethics that prevails in North America appropriate for cultures that do not share the assumptions upon which it is grounded? And if not, what is the proper response? Tolerance or conformity? That is the more difficult and penetrating challenge that cultural diversity presents.

Such questions challenge not only health care ethics but morality in general because they raise the issue of whether moral standards are universal or culturally relative. Cultural differences can be taken to show that morality is somehow dependent upon or relative to culture. This claim, in turn, can be understood to entail that what is morally right or wrong is what people in a given culture believe is right or wrong; in other words, there are no universal notions of right and wrong, only notions of right-for-this-culture and wrong-for-this-culture. Advocates of this position seem forced to accept the moral permissibility of some abhorrent practices, however. If a culture believes, for example, that it is right to excise the genitals of girls, then why is that practice not right-for-that-culture? On what moral basis could anybody outside the culture criticize or try to stop the practice?

Defenders of the universality of morality hold that moral standards can be justified on grounds that transcend idiosyncratic cultural differences. Morality concerns what is common to human beings as human beings, not as members of a particular culture. The daunting problems for this position are to identify the universal features of human beings that are morally relevant and to justify the moral requirements that are taken to follow from them.

The Selections

The selections in this chapter show how cultural differences arise with respect to the withdrawal of life support, truth telling, and research involving human subjects. The first selection by Jill Klessig uses case examples to illustrate how the customs and practices that surround death and the withdrawal of life support vary across cultures. Klessig discusses the beliefs and values behind these differences as well as appropriate responses to them.

The next two selections deal with telling the truth about terminal illnesses. Antonella Surbone, an Italian physician who has practised in the United States, questions how appropriate the North American policy of informing patients that they are terminally ill would be in Italy. Italian medical ethics holds that physicians have a duty to provide "the most serene information about the diagnosis," and that physicians could be justified in not revealing a serious prognosis to a patient and instead informing the family. Surbone believes that "ethics is inevitably connected to cultural values," and that "both the Italian and the American ways are ethical in their context." Edmund Pellegrino replies that truth telling is not a "cultural artifact." Truth telling is founded on the principle of autonomy, which is "a valid and universal principle because it is based on what it is to be human." This exchange raises the theoretical question of whether morality is universal or culturally relative in the context of an important practical issue in health care ethics.

The last three selections by Michele Barry, Marcia Angell, and Lisa Newton also raise the issue of the universality of moral standards. Should North American standards for the ethical conduct of research involving human subjects be applied in other countries? Do these standards represent universally binding moral requirements, or would their imposition manifest "ethical imperialism" and lack of respect for the different moral customs and traditions of the countries in which the research is to be conducted?

Conclusion

Deciding how to respond to cultural differences in health care clearly is not easy. There are important distinctions among the cultural differences. Similarly, there is enormous variability among the individual members of a cultural group. Care must be taken not to label or stereotype persons on the basis of their culture(s). Sometimes cultural differences will need to be respected, and sometimes uniform policies will need to be formulated. One difficulty is figuring out when and where there should be a uniform public culture of health care ethics. Another is determining whether morality has the resources to provide that uniformity.

References

Barker, Judith C. 1992. Cultural diversity: Changing the context of medical practice. *Western Journal of Medicine* 157:248–54.

Feldman, Jamie. 1992. The French are different: French and American medicine in the context of AIDS. *Western Journal of Medicine* 157:345–49.

Klessig, Jill. 1992. The effect of values and culture on life-support decisions. *Western Journal of Medicine* 157:316–22.

Lock, Margaret, and Christina Honde. 1990. Reaching consensus about death: Heart transplants and cultural identity in Japan. In *Social science perspectives on medical ethics*, G. Weisz, ed., 99–119. Boston: Kluwer Academic Press.

Morrissey, Deborah. 1993. Childbirth Course Aimed at Somali Women. *Hospital News* April 3.

Nesbitt, Kiri. 1994. Abortion and Karma: A Japanese Perspective. *The Globe and Mail* Jan. 25, A22.

Olick, Robert S. 1991. Brain death, religious freedom, and public policy: New Jersey's landmark legislative initiative. *Kennedy Institute of Ethics Journal* 1:275–88.

Payer, Lynn. 1988. *Medicine & culture.* New York: Henry Holt.

6   The Effect of Values and Culture on Life-Support Decisions

Jill Klessig

Many challenges to the physician–patient relationship occur in the period around a patient's death. Even in the best of circumstances, discussing starting and stopping life support is emotionally demanding. Poor communication between the physician and the patient or the patient's family can turn this situation into a nightmare. The psychological damage cannot be undone and may cloud the last memories the family has of the patient. Similarly, the physician will always carry the knowledge that the situation might have been handled better.

Instances of poor communication can occur if the cultural values of the health care professional and the patient are different, and each is unaware of the reasons underlying the other's behavior or viewpoint. This frequently leads to frustration, anger, and stereotyping. The problem is especially important when life-support measures are being discussed, as cultural patterns have great strength and influence in the period around a death.[1] It is unacceptable for a health professional to be ignorant or insensitive to the cultural beliefs of a dying patient. . . .

It is not ethnicity per se but the social experiences of different groups that help shape particular cultural organization and value systems. These systems undergo constant, although sometimes slow, change as the social experiences of groups vary. Furthermore, all cultures are composed of individuals and, thus, intracultural variation can be as great as, or sometimes even greater than, intercultural variation.

I present this discussion to help physicians understand why patients might react in the way described, especially when such behavior is different from the physicians' expectations. I do not imply that any single member of an ethnic group will respond in the specific way or for the particular reasons mentioned here. To assume that a patient will react in a particular way can be as detrimental to the physician–patient relationship as ignoring the fact that differences exist among patients. Patients should always be treated as individuals first and members of a cultural group or groups second.

Religion is referred to here for several reasons. Religion is often important in shaping values and the moral fiber of societies and thus can help explain differing views toward death. In addition, often even persons who are not active in any religion revert to their religious roots when faced with death.[2]

. . . The behaviors surrounding death are among the most resistant to change of any cultural or subcultural pattern.[3] Thus, in times of crisis, patients may return to cultural and religious traditions regardless of their socioeconomic status.

Iranians

Case Example

The patient, a 17-year-old Iranian girl, had a long history of diabetes mellitus with numerous episodes of ketoacidosis. On the day of admission, she was found unconscious. When the paramedics arrived she was asystolic, but a cardiac rhythm was restored en route to the emergency department. She was admitted to the intensive care unit (ICU) on full ventilatory support. On evaluation she was found to be brain dead. The family was informed of the diagnosis and the fact that legally she was dead. They objected to removing the ventilator and insisted on many unnecessary medical procedures. They remained in the ICU most of the time, interfering with the care of other patients. The physicians felt that the family was being unreasonable and inappropriate. On the second day of admission when the family was not present, life support was stopped. When the patient's parents found out what had happened, they became irate and refused to leave the ICU. The attending physician talked to them for a few minutes, became irritated, and left. The resident left in tears when the family told her that she had "murdered" the patient.

Discussion

Iranian patients are usually opposed to stopping life support in any situation. There appears to be little difference in the responses of the Muslims and the Christians in the study group, thus indicating that the trend was based in culture, not religion. Because, however, religious values have tremendous influence on societal norms, and the predominant moral code of Iran is based on Islamic traditions, those will be discussed.

Life and death are viewed as controlled by God.[4,5] All persons are entrusted with their body, and it is their moral duty to seek medical help when needed. The right to die is not recognized.[6] Because only God can decide when someone will die and all are mandated to seek medical attention, life support is viewed as an obligation, not an option. Although stopping supportive measures is thought to be "playing God," starting these measures is not: instituting life support is an appropriate use of the "gift" of medical technology that has been given to humanity. Thus, to argue with Iranian patients or their families that to start therapy is also interfering with the will of God carries little moral validity.

The opposition to stopping life support holds true even if a patient is in considerable pain. Long-term suffering presents an opportunity to show courage and faith in God,[7] and taking a life to relieve suffering is forbidden.[5] Individual duress is acceptable if it obviates the societal duress of going against moral standards.[4]

Of note, these rules do not necessarily hold in the case of a defective newborn. Some people believe that evil spirits entered the child, and it is no longer human.[8] In these cases it might be permissible to withhold support, including nutrition.

Initiating a discussion of the issues of life support might anger a patient or family. This is based on the conviction that to tell a patient that there is no hope may hasten the dying process and is thus considered inappropriate and insensitive.[9] Given the necessity of obtaining informed consent in the United States, however, some form of dialogue about the terminal nature of a patient's disease is usually necessary. The manner in which such discussion is initiated is important. In Iranian culture it is rude to go directly to the point.[9] The physician should approach the subject slowly, first engaging in small talk. The family dynamics should also be investigated. If a patient is female, she may be under the guardianship of a male family member.[10] The patient's autonomy may not be honored if her decision is not in agreement with her husband's or father's.

In general, the concept of options and patient autonomy is foreign to traditional Iranian culture.[9] Patients are not used to being asked to make choices and may delay doing so. The health care team may become impatient with the patient or family because they "cannot make up their minds" when, in fact, the patient is expecting the physician to make the decisions regarding care.

Other factors can affect decisions about supportive measures in Iranian patients:

- The family's definition of death needs to be considered. In the case discussed here, the family felt that their daughter was still alive because she had a heartbeat and her skin was warm. Thus, to them, removing the ventilator was tantamount to murder.
- In Iran and in many other Middle Eastern countries, the family is expected to be demanding.[9] This shows concern for their family member. This is why the patient's family in this case stayed in the ICU and was so insistent on a wide range of medical care. Not to have done so would have indicated that they did not care about their daughter. Although physicians often become frustrated with this demanding behavior, to understand the reasons behind it may help alleviate some of the friction it causes.
- If a decision is made to stop life support in a Muslim patient, certain customs should be observed. The family should be allowed to stay in the room and recite the Koran (*Qur'an*) so that these are the last words the patient hears.[2,10] In addition,

family members should be allowed to move the bed so that the patient is facing Mecca when he or she dies. Finally, when a Muslim dies, a non-Muslim is not supposed to touch the body, so gloves should be worn.[11,12]

Korean Americans

Case Example

The patient, a 54-year-old Korean man, was admitted to the hospital with idiopathic pulmonary fibrosis. His condition deteriorated rapidly, and it was clear that death would occur within the next week. His physicians wanted to issue a do-not-resuscitate order, but his family disagreed, insisting that everything be done to keep him alive until arrangements could be made to fly him to Korea. The house staff thought that the family was unreasonable about the patient's prognosis and was causing him undue suffering. The family did not understand why the physicians were being so insensitive.

Discussion

There is little in the medical literature about Koreans and their views towards ethical issues in medicine, especially life support. The following factors are important, however: First, most Koreans are religious, with Buddhism and Protestantism exerting the greatest influence.[13–15] Many Koreans interpret stopping life support as interfering with God's will, although starting such measures is not. There is also still a strong Taoist influence in Korea, which places a great value on longevity.[13]

Another, perhaps more important, issue is that of filial piety, or loyalty to one's parents. In Korea as in many Asian countries, elders are to be respected and cared for.[13,14,16,17] Children, especially the oldest son, owe their life to their parents. They are responsible for the parents and must preserve their lives at all cost. To agree to stopping life support, even if this is a parent's desire, may dishonor the family member in the eyes of relatives or the community. How people's actions are viewed by others is important.[18]

In addition to respect for elders, there is also a traditional concept of obedience to the male head of the family. This tradition has been shown to be still present in Korean-American families,[19(p115)] and physicians may find that the father or husband makes life-support decisions about all family members.

Traditional values dictate that a patient die at home.[18] Thus, in this case example, the patient's family was aware of the terminal nature of his illness but wanted to keep him alive long enough to get him back to Korea. The fact that he would die en route was not important to them: the action was more important and preserved their honor.

Chinese Americans

Case Example

The patient, a 69-year-old Chinese-American woman, was admitted with complete right hemiparesis and aphasia due to a stroke. She had a history of several previous infarcts, with a resulting dementia. A feeding tube was placed, but the patient repeatedly pulled it out. The family was asked to consent to a gastrostomy tube for feeding. They refused and, in addition, asked that all intravenous hydration be discontinued. Because of a question the patient's son had asked about the cost of nursing homes, the intern was certain that the family wanted the patient to die so they would not have to spend their potential inheritance on her care. The intern wanted to get a court order for the gastrostomy tube.

Discussion

Literature about traditional Chinese culture provides some explanations for the bipolar trend — both to stop life support and to believe strongly that all measures should be continued. For centuries the moral outlook of China has been shaped by Confucianism, Taoism, Buddhism, and, more recently, Marxism. This has led to an ethical perspective that is strongly virtue oriented.[20,21] What is valued is not life itself but living in an ideal way. Taoism advocates nonaction and allowing things to be, and Buddhism emphasizes the transitoriness of life.[22] ("Death is only the vanishing of the human body, the true body exists forever."[23(p13)]) These viewpoints, combined with the concept of *Ren* (benevolence, kindheartedness, humaneness),[24] lead many patients or their families to the belief that nature should be allowed to take its course, especially when a patient is suffering. Chinese philosophy has long included the right to choose death,[25] and there is evidence that most Chinese approve of passive euthanasia.[26]

In addition, each person is seen as part of the whole community, and individual actions must always take into consideration the effects on society.[21,27] Thus, economic factors become an issue.[28] If life support is a financial burden on the family, the patient or family is likely to request that it be stopped.[29] An explanation for this view can be found in the teachings of Buddha: The principles of justice and compassion are central.[30] Justice requires an appropriate distribution of health care resources. Compassion encompasses justice. Thus, a patient who decides to forgo life-support measures so the family does not suffer, either emotionally or financially, is performing an act of compassion, which is highly valued.

Opposed to this is a traditional Chinese view that life should be valued and preserved at all costs and that physicians should do their best to save lives.[26,29] This is partially based on the first Buddhist precept that prohibits killing, even when a person is suffering from a painful and incurable disease.[29] There is also the concern that to stop life support is to interfere with a person's *karma* — the idea that suffering is the result of some past deed and if the karma is not "worked out" in this life, the patient will be forced to suffer again in the next life.[30] Yet another factor involved is the concept of filial piety,[24,26,29,31] discussed earlier.

Orthodox and Non-Orthodox Jews

Case Example
The patient, a 34-year-old man with alcoholic liver disease, was admitted with his tenth episode of massive hematemesis over the past six months. During his previous admission 14 days before, the patient received 110 units of fresh frozen plasma and 68 units of red cells. On admission the patient had alcohol on his breath. After 24 hours he was still requiring constant transfusions. The attending physician decided to stop all blood products. On hearing this, the Jewish intern caring for the patient vehemently argued that such action was wrong and then left the ICU extremely upset.

Discussion
When raising the issue of life support with Jewish patients, identifying which sect they are associated with is essential. There is a great dichotomy between the views of Orthodox and non-Orthodox Jews. Both views are discussed here.

Traditional Orthodox teachings are firmly in favor of continuing life support. An Orthodox patient may become upset at a health care team for even bringing up the subject of stopping life-support measures. Reasons for this can be found in Orthodox teaching that takes a strong prolife stance. Life is sacred and is to be preserved whenever possible.[32-34] Thus, it is mandatory to maintain one's health[34] and to seek health care when needed.[33] In addition, the traditional interpretation of the Bible says that physicians are mandated to save life when able[33,34] and definitely should not assist a patient's death. (Someone who even closes the eyes of a dying person while the soul is departing is classified as a murderer.[35]) So strong is the requirement to preserve life that the risk of loss of life supercedes most laws of the Sabbath.[33] Every life is of infinite worth, and even one moment of life is to be valued as if it were a month or a year. The sanctity of life is more important than its quality. Furthermore, physicians cannot make a judgment about another person's quality of life because life may have meaning under all conditions, even when the suffering is immense.[36] Thus, conservative interpretations of Jewish moral standards command that patients seek life-support measures and compel physicians to provide them. Although autonomy is valued, wishes that do not comply with these moral standards are not be honored.[32]

On discussing his feelings, the intern in this case indicated that he was Orthodox and that he believed that not giving blood to this patient was wrong. This is an important case example because it shows how conflicts due to differences in values do not always come from patients. Physicians, too, carry value systems that relate to their past experiences, upbringing, and ethnic identity. Health care professionals need to be aware of their own biases when dealing with these potentially difficult situations.

The views explored here are not necessarily held by non-Orthodox Jews. Possible reasons for this include that Judaism does not glorify suffering by assigning it the redeeming features that other faiths do. No one is required to withstand intractable pain to preserve life.[37] Judaism is committed to use all available resources to alleviate suffering to every extent possible.[38] Thus, pain should be treated. Prolonging the dying process is also prohibited.[33] Exactly what constitutes this dying process is unclear, but traditionally a person who is dying (*a goses*) is one who will not live more than 72 hours.[34] In this situation, it is permissible to stop life support because it is only prolonging the dying process. Another reason for being against life-prolonging measures is that Jews do not have the same belief in an afterlife or reincarnation that other faiths do. There is the feeling that "when it's over, it's over," and there is no point in prolonging futile care.

African Americans

Case Example

The patient, a 32-year-old African-American man, was admitted after receiving a stab wound to the heart. He had a cardiac arrest in the emergency department, suffering severe brain damage. A month later the patient had no notable return of cognitive function, although he was responsive to pain. He had continuous fevers, though no source of infection was found. The ICU team wished to issue a do-not-resuscitate order, stop antibiotic therapy, and transfer him to the general medical ward. The patient's wife disagreed and threatened to sue the hospital if these plans were carried out.

Discussion

An exploration of the views that African Americans hold toward do-not-resuscitate orders and life support is especially important because of the higher prevalence in the African-American community (than in the general population) of conditions likely to result in the need for a discussion of such issues. Overall, African Americans have higher incidences of cancer, accidents, the acquired immunodeficiency syndrome, hypertension, diabetes mellitus, and low-birth-weight babies[39-46]; they also have less access to needed primary health care.[47]

As is the case with all groups, African Americans cannot be lumped together, as past experiences, religion, and politics are extremely varied. Because of centuries of slavery and racism, their experiences in the United States are dissimilar from all other groups. Patients who recently arrived in the United States from Africa cannot be included in this group, as they have different experiences and medical belief systems.

Although the literature is sparse, there is some support for the finding that African-American patients are more likely to want life-support measures to be continued. Port and co-workers found fewer deaths due to the termination of dialysis in African-American patients than in whites.[48]

Several factors may influence decisions about life-support options. First, African Americans tend to be more religious and more devout than whites.[49] Many patients said that they would continue all measures until the end because it "is wrong" to stop and miracles are always possible. Patients said that they would feel enormous guilt about stopping support. This relates to both strong religious convictions and the observation that, in general, African Americans highly value their elders, long life (regardless of suffering), and the will to survive.[50-53] A physician's statement that the situation is hopeless may not be adequate: only God knows for sure. This may represent a distrust of the medical community rather than strictly religious conviction.

In addition there are still problems with racism in the medical establishment. It has been shown that African-American patients receive less intense care[54] and are more likely to be negatively stereotyped than other patients.[55] These issues, combined with the perception of some African-American patients that their hospital stay was too short and the care less than satisfactory,[56] may lead to concerns that life support was stopped prematurely because of the patient's race.

Filipino Americans

Case Example

The patient, a 44-year-old Filipino woman with metastatic breast cancer, was admitted with shortness of breath. On admission the house staff discussed the possibility of a do-not-resuscitate order with her. She agreed. Later, while the attending physician was examining the patient with her family in the room, he again brought up the subject of a do-not-resuscitate order. This time she denied that it was what she wanted. On leaving the room, the attending physician expressed displeasure with the resident who had initiated the order "without the patient's consent."

Discussion

The Republic of the Philippines is a diverse nation comprising more than 7,000 islands and with a culture that has been influenced by many countries and religions.[57] Compounding this diversity is the fact that there have been several different waves of immigration to the United States from the Philippines, with each group having unique experiences and backgrounds that would influence their belief systems. Despite this variety, most Filipino patients are apparently opposed to stopping life support.

Many of the Filipinos who have immigrated to the United States are Catholic[58] and believe that patients or physicians should not interfere with God's plan. The Catholic Church abhors "suicide" for any reason,[59] and it is morally wrong to encourage death with any action or omission. Thus, religious conviction is a major reason for continuing life support. Respect for elders is also important, as with Korean and Chinese patients.

The Filipino family greatly influences patients' decisions about health care.[57] Harmony is valued, and personal needs are subjugated to keeping group harmony. Thus, in this case, the patient actually did want the do-not-resuscitate order to be written and did not want life-support measures started. Her family objected, however, and because outright disagreement was to be avoided, she changed her mind.

The perceived cause of a patient's illness can also be a factor in decisions about supportive care. For example, for some Filipinos, illness may be attributed to a punishment from God,[56] and thus it would not be appropriate to interfere. Others believe that people die because they have offended or are possessed by a spirit, a belief that is common throughout Southeast Asia.[60,61] Patients or families may be reluctant to stop life support before the causative agent has been addressed. For example, the brother of a patient thought that she became ill because she swept dirt on a spirit who was walking by, thus offending the spirit. He believed that if the patient apologized enough she would get better, so stopping the ventilator was not appropriate.

Mexican Americans

Case Example

The patient, a 43-year-old Mexican-American woman, was admitted with known metastatic breast cancer. On admission she said she wanted no heroic measures done. Over the next 24 hours her condition rapidly deteriorated, and she became comatose with imminent respiratory arrest. The issue of a do-not-resuscitate order was discussed with the patient's children. They were aware of her wishes but insisted that she be incubated, at least until their father was able to come from Mexico.

Discussion

Mexicans have a rich heritage, with their present culture influenced by indigenous native traditions as well as customs and beliefs imported from Spain and Africa. Mexican Americans have had these traditions modified further by the dominant American culture. This has led to a unique and diversified culture that only partially resembles those of other Spanish-speaking countries. Although Mexican Americans are the largest group of Latino patients,[6] a substantial number of persons come from other Hispanic countries. The following comments should not be assumed to relate to these other groups.

Mexican Americans' beliefs about illness causation are important in determining their views about life support. Health is a gift from God, and ill health, including accidents, may be due to a punishment from God or the saints. The suffering incurred is part of God's plan and should not be interfered with. Conversely, a patient may believe that the illness is caused by evil spirits or the Devil[62-65] and that a *curandero* (healer) may be able to cure the patient, even when Western medical practices have failed.

Other issues are equally important when discussing life support with Mexican-American patients. First, there is always hope the patient may get better, so to stop life support may cause the Mexican-American family great feelings of guilt. In addition, Mexican Americans believe that enduring sickness is a sign of strength.[65] Some studies suggest that Mexican Americans may have more fear of dying than other ethnic groups.[49] Last, more than 85% of Mexican Americans are Catholic[49] and against anything that hastens death.[66(p282)]

When a patient is terminally ill, the family is involved in all aspects of decision making. The well-being of the family is valued over that of individual members. Traditionally the father or husband is the head of the household,[67,68] and he should make or agree with all decisions. The wife's input is usually influential, however, even when it is not highly visible.

When discussing life support, physicians need to be aware of the concept of courtesy as it pertains to Mexican-American patients. Directly contradicting a physician is considered rude or disrespectful.[62,67] Thus, a physician may think that a patient and the patient's family are in agreement with the plan of action when in fact they are strongly opposed to it. There is also still a strong tendency toward paternalism,[69] and physicians may be expected to make life-support decisions for their patients.

Summary

The frustration that health care professionals experience when treating patients from different ethnic backgrounds can be mitigated by exploring the cultural foundation of the behaviour in question. Variants of the factors discussed in this article occur in diverse cultures, although their degree of influence may vary. In addition, people who have identical reactions when confronted with the subject of stopping life support may have entirely different reasons for their behavior. Thus, when discussing do-not-resuscitate orders with patients from any culture, it is best to explore the following issues:

- What do they think about the sanctity of life?
- What is their definition of death?
- What is their religious background, and how active are they currently?
- What do they believe are the causal agents in illness, and how do these relate to the dying process?
- What is the patient's social support system?
- Who makes decisions about matters of importance in the family?

Health care professionals should remember that many patients have immigrated from countries where as much as three fourths of the population does not have access to basic health needs, such as clean drinking water. They have never before faced "high-tech" health care and do not have a clear concept of the implications or consequences of initiating life support. Finally, the concept of patient autonomy that is so highly valued in Western culture, and is the basis of many life-support decisions, is not as important in other cultures.

When faced with life-and-death decisions, all patients draw on a lifetime of experiences for strength and guidance in making decisions. Patients' societal traditions affect their interpretation of past experiences but are not the only factors involved. Each patient must be seen as a person who has a unique belief system, with ethnic background only a part, albeit an important part, of the equation. By discussing life-support issues in a culturally sensitive way, a physician can turn a potentially exasperating experience into an enriching one, with understanding and respect, if not agreement.

References

1. Counts D: The good death and Kaliai: Preparation for death in West New Britain, In Kalish R(Ed): Death and Dying: Views From Many Cultures. Farmingdale, NY, Baywood, 1980, pp 39–46

2. Walker C: Attitudes to death and bereavement among cultural minority groups. Nurs Times 1982; 78:2106–2109

3. Moore J: The death culture of Mexico and Mexican-Americans. Omega 1970; 1: 271–291

4. Sachedina AA: Islamic views on organ transplantation. Transplant Proc 1988; 20(suppl I):1084–1088

5. Hathout H: Islamic basis for biomedical ethics, In Transcultural Dimensions of Medical Ethics, Symposium Proceedings. Washington, DC, Fidia Research Foundation, 1990, pp 25–26

6. Andrews M, Hanson P: Religious beliefs: Implications for nursing practice, In Boyle JS, Andrews M (Eds): Transcultural Concepts in Nursing Care. Glenview, Ill, Scott, Foresman, 1989, pp 357–417

7. Al-Mutawa M: Health care ethics in Kuwait. Hastings Cent Rep 1989; 19:S11–12

8. Shiloh A: The interaction between the Middle Eastern and Western systems of medicine. Soc Sci Med 1968; 2:235–248

9. Meleis I, Jonsen R: Ethical crises and cultural differences. West J Med 1983; 138:889–893

10. Henley A: Asian Patients in Hospital and at Home. London, Great Britain, King Edward's Hospital Fund, 1979 [distributor Pitman Medical]

11. Black J: Broaden your mind about death and bereavement in certain ethnic groups in Britain. Br Med J 1987; 295:536–539

12. McAvoy B, Donaldson L: Health Care for Asians. Cambridge, Great Britain, Oxford University Press, 1990

13. Korean Overseas Information Service: A Handbook of Korea. Seoul, Korea, Samkhwai Printing, 1990

14. Pang KY: The practice of traditional Korean medicine in Washington, DC. Soc Sci Med 1989; 28:875–884

15. Religions. Seoul, Korea, Korean Overseas Information Service, 1983

16. Pang KY: *Hwabyung*: The construction of a Korean popular illness among Korean elderly immigrant women in the United States. Cult Med Psychiatry 1990; 14:495–512

17. Customs and Traditions. Seoul, Korea, Overseas Information Service. 1982

18. Chung HJ: Understanding the Oriental maternity patient. Nurs Clin North Am 1977; 12:67–75

19. Yu EY, Phillips E, Yan ES: Koreans in Los Angeles: Prospects and Promises. Los Angeles, Calif, Koryo Research Institute, 1982

20. Qiu RZ; Medical Ethics and Chinese Culture. Transcultural Dimensions of Medical Ethics, Symposium Proceedings. Washington, DC, Fidia Research Foundation, 1990

21. Fox RC, Swazey JP: Medical morality is not bioethics — Medical ethics in China and the United States. Perspect Biol Med 1984; 27:336–360

22. Chen-Louie T: Nursing care of Chinese American patients, *In* Orque M, Blocks B, Monrroy LSA (Eds): Ethnic Nursing Care: A Multicultural Approach. St. Louis, Mo, CV Mosby, 1983

23. The Teachings of Buddha. Tokyo, Japan, Dosaido Printing, 1966

24. Ren-Zong Q [Qiu RZ]: Medicine — The art of humaneness; On the ethics of traditional Chinese medicine. J Med Philos 1988; 13:277–300

25. Xu TM: China: Moral puzzles. Hastings Cent Rep 1990; 20:24–25

26. Pu SD: Euthanasia in China: A report. J Med Philos 1988; 16:131–138

27. Qiu RZ: Economics and medical decision-making: A Chinese perspective. Sem Perinatol 1987; 11:262–263

28. Fox S: China: Diary of a barefoot bioethicist. Hastings Cent Rep 1984; 14:18–20

29. Qiu RZ: Morality in flux: Medical ethics dilemmas in the People's Republic of China. Kennedy Inst Ethics J 1991; 1:16–27

30. Ratanakui P: Bioethics in Thailand: The struggle for Buddhist solutions. J Med Philos 1988; 13:301–312

31. Qiu RZ: 'No feeding tubes for me!' (Commentary). Hastings Cent Rep 1987; 17:S23–26

32. Steinberg A: Bioethics: Secular philosophy, Jewish law and modern medicine. Isr J Med Sci 1989; 25:404–409

33. Rosner F: The physician–patient relationship: Responsibilities and limitations, *In* Meier L (Ed): Jewish Values in Health and Medicine. Lanham, Md, University Press of America. 1991, pp 95–110

34. Perlin E: Jewish medical ethics and the care of the elderly. Pharos 1990; 53:2–5

35. The Talmud. Shabbat 151b

36. Frankl VE: The meaning of suffering, *In* Meier L (Ed): Jewish Values in Bioethics. New York, NY, Human Sciences Press, 1986, pp 117–123

37. Bleich D: Care of the terminally ill. *In* Meier L (Ed): Jewish Values in Health and

Medicine. Lanham, Md, University Press of America, 1991, pp 141–161

38. Glick SM: A view from Sinai — A Jewish Perspective on Biomedical Ethics. Symposium Proceedings: Transcultural Dimensions of Medical Ethics. Washington, DC, Fidia Research Foundation, 1990, pp 19–21

39. AMA Council on Ethical and Judicial Affairs: Black-white disparities in health care. Conn Med, 1990; 54:625–628

40. Joseph S: AIDS in the black community: Public health implications. J Natl Med Assoc 1988; 80:1173–1178

41. Johnson C: Meeting the health care needs of our nation's black elderly. J Natl Med Assoc 1990; 82:823–827

42. Evans T. Being black in America is hazardous to your health. J Natl Med Assoc 1988; 80:253–255

43. Barber J: Black Americans in crisis. J Natl Med Assoc 1990: 82:664–665

44. Dowling P, Fisher M: Maternal factors and low birthweight infants: A comparison of blacks with Mexican-Americans. J Fam Pract 1987; 25:153–158

45. Miller W, Cooper R: Rising lung cancer death rates among black men: The importance of occupation and social class. J Natl Med Assoc 1982; 74:253–258

46. Raju T, Hager S: The dilemma of less than 500 grams birth: Epidemiologic considerations. Am J Perinatol 1986; 3:327–331

47. Hayward RA, Shapiro MF, Freeman HE, Corey CR: Inequities in health services among insured Americans — Do working-age adults have less access to medical care than the elderly? N Engl J Med 1988; 318:1507–1512

48. Port FK, Wolfe RA, Hawthorne VM, Ferguson CW: Discontinuation of dialysis therapy as a cause of death. AM J Nephrol 1989; 9:145–149

49. Kalish R, Reynolds DK: Death and Ethnicity: A Psychocultural Study. Los Angeles, Calif, University of Southern California Press, 1976, pp 200–221

50. Lundgren L: Hospice: Concept and implementation in the black community. J Commun Health Nurs 1986; 3:137–144

51. Spector R: Cultural Diversity in Health and Illness. New York, NY, Appleton Century-Crofts, 1979

52. Swanson WC, Harter CL: How do elderly blacks cope in New Orleans? Aging Human Dev 1971; 2:210–216

53. Koenig R, Goldner N, Kresojevich R, Lockwood G: Ideas about illness of elderly black and white in an urban hospital. Aging Hum Dev 1971; (2):217–225

54. Yergan J, Flood AB, LoGerfo JP, Diehr P: Relationship between patient race and the intensity of hospital services. Med Care 1987; 25:592–603

55. Johnson SM, Kurtz ME, Tomlinson T, Howe KR: Students' stereotypes of patients as barriers to clinical decision-making. J Med Educ 1986; 61(pt 1):727–735

56. Blendon RJ, Aiken LH, Freeman HE, Corey CR: Access to medical care for black and white Americans — A matter of continuing concern. JAMA 1989; 261:278–281

57. Orque M: Nursing care of Filipino American Patients. In Orque M, Block B, Monrroy LSA (Eds): Ethnic Nursing Care: A Multicultural Approach. St Louis, Mo, CV Mosby, 1983, pp 149–182

58. Anderson JN: Health and illness in Philipino immigrants. West J Med 1983; 139:811–819 [7–15]

59. Veith I: Changing concepts of health care: An historian's view. West J Med 1980; 133:532–538

60. Sharp PT: Ghosts, witches, sickness and death: The traditional interpretation of injury and disease in a rural area of Papua New Guinea. Papua New Guinea Med J 1982; 25:108–115

61. Orque M: Nursing care of South Vietnamese patients. In Orque M, Block B, Monrroy LSA (Eds): Ethnic Nursing Care: A Multicultural Approach. St Louis, Mo, CV Mosby, 1983, pp 245–269

62. Kuipers J: Mexican Americans. In Giger J, Davidhizar R (Eds): Transcultural Nursing: Assessment and Intervention. St. Louis, Mo, Mosby Year Book, 1991, pp 185–202

63. Gonzales HH: Health care needs of the Mexican American. In Ethnicity and Health Care. New York, NY, National League Nursing, 1976, pp 21–28

64. Dorsey PR, Jackson HQ: Cultural health traditions: The Latino/Chicano perspective. In Branch M, Paxton P (Eds): Providing Safe Nursing Care for Ethnic People of

Color. New York, NY, Appleton-Century-Crofts, 1976, pp 41–80

65. Schur C, Bernstein A, Berk M: The importance of distinguishing Hispanic subpopulations in the use of medical care. Med Care 1987; 25:627–641

66. Dubois MJ: The dying human in Christian philosophy, *In* de Vries A, Carmi A (Eds): The Dying Human. Ramat Gan, Tel Aviv, Israel, Turtledove Publishing, 1979, pp 275–285

67. Murillo N: The Mexican American family. *In* Martinez RA (Ed): Hispanic Culture and Health Care. St Louis, Mo, CV Mosby, 1978, pp 3–18

68. Monrroy LSA: Nursing care of Raza/Latina patients. *In* Orque M. Block B. Monrroy LSA (Eds): Ethnic Nursing Care: A Multicultural Approach. St Louis, Mo, CV Mosby, 1983, pp 115–148

69. Escobar A: Human dying has changed. Bull Pan Am Health Organ 1990; 24:446–453

7   Truth Telling to the Patient

Antonella Surbone

And you shall know the truth, and the truth shall make you free. (John 8:32)

When I started writing this letter last year, I was practicing medical oncology in the United States. My work, based on providing thorough information to every patient, was that of an expert in a particular field as well as an educator. By explaining diagnosis, prognosis, and treatment options to the patient, I was creating the basis for freedom: freedom not only from symptoms and disease, but also freedom to make informed choices. At the same time, I grew to believe that truth telling goes far beyond providing mere information. Truth is not just the opposite of a lie, not just the sum of correct statements, but a reciprocal state in the patient–physician relationship. This relationship is established on the basis of mutual responsibilities. In such a context, information should never become a way of delegating the entire burden of medical decisions to the patient, thus limiting medical responsibilities. Truth should expand rather than limit professional responsibilities.

The Italian Deontology Code and Withholding Truth

While reflecting on my responsibility to provide patients with information, which is an ethical duty of American physicians,[1] I often thought of the different approaches used in my country of origin, Italy, where patients are not always informed of their diagnosis and prognosis. In medical school at the University of Turin in the late 1970s, I learned the Italian Deontology Code, written by the Italian Medical Association, which included the following statement: "A serious or lethal prognosis can be hidden from the patient, but not from the family."[2]

During my first year of oncology fellowship in Italy in 1983, a middle-aged businessman was told he had gastritis, when dying of chachexia from end-stage carcinoma; a young, divorced housewife was told she had arthritis while receiving palliative radiation therapy for chemotherapy-resistant metastatic breast cancer; and a college student was told he had drug-induced hepatitis, but he was indeed progressing toward liver failure from widespread hepatic involvement with lymphoma. In each case the patient's family or only one family member was informed of the true diagnosis and prognosis. A ritual started, composed of sotto voce conversations between the physician and family members outside the patient's room: "Doctor, don't speak too loud" or "Doctor, tell me how much time is left for my husband because I have to prepare." In each case, the patients knew or at least strongly suspected the truth, but they were part of a generally accepted farce of deception that prevented open discussion about the truth and how to act on it. Consequences of such deception varied from the unresolved financial problems left at the businessman's death, to the stressful, secret, and unsuccessful attempt of the dying single mother to find a way to provide for the future of her four children.

In 1986, an Italian public television survey of a sample population representative of the entire nation showed that Italians were more or less equally divided in their preferences for truth telling in medicine. A 1991 study of 1171 breast cancer patients and their physicians and surgeons in general hospitals in Italy evaluated the frequency of disclosure of the diagnosis of operable breast cancer.[3] Only 47% of these patients reported having been told that they had cancer, and 25% of their physicians stated they had not given accurate information. After reading the results of this study, I asked myself, from an assimilated American perspective, how could such women not participate in the decision to undergo mastectomy or breast-conserving surgery, especially in those cases where we predict the outcomes to be equivalent?[4]

Later in 1991, I accepted my present position as vice-chairman in the oncology department of Santa Chiara Hospital in Pisa, Italy. The situation in the Italian medical world is rapidly evolving, with malpractice lawsuits increasing and the public skepticism of physicians on the rise.[5,6] It is in this reality that bioethical issues, including patients' rights to information, are the subject of frequent discussions among physicians.

The Deontology Code was revised in 1989 and it now reads as follows:

> The physician has the duty to provide the patient — according to his cultural level and abilities to understand — the most serene information about the diagnosis, the prognosis and the therapeutic perspectives and their consequences; in the awareness of the limits of medical knowledge, in the respect of the person's rights, to foster the best compliance to the therapeutic proposals. Each question asked

by the patient has to be accepted and answered clearly. The physician might evaluate, specifically in relationship with the patient's reactions, the opportunity not to reveal to the patient or to mitigate as serious or lethal prognosis. In this case it will have to be communicated to the family. In any event, the patient's will, freely expressed, should represent for the physician [an] element to which he will inspire his behavior.[7]

With regard to informed consent and participation in clinical studies, the Code states "experimentation is subordinated to the consent of the subject which has to be — if possible — freely expressed in writing."[8] In each of these statements the possibility of truth withholding still exists, and I think this can only be understood by considering the Italian cultural background.

I must first stress that I believe that ethics is inevitably connected to cultural values and, therefore, varies in different societies. This requires an implicit understanding of the dichotomy between believing in absolute values and respecting the pluralism of different cultures. This is to say, as difficult as it may sound for someone only used to one culture, that both the Italian and the American ways are ethical in their context.

Autonomia e Isolamento

First, the Italian culture is strongly bound to the Greek and Latin approaches to medicine. "To benefit, at least not to harm," wrote Hippocrates. Benefit is the priority in the patient–physician relationship. In a recent public debate in Rome among physicians and journalists on truth telling, even those stating that information is the basis for the contract between patient and physician stressed that the first aim of such a contract is not information, but what is good for the patient.[9] In bioethics, practical directions derive from a balance between the two principles of beneficence and autonomy. While the concept of beneficence is quite similarly perceived in Italy and in the United States, autonomy is certainly viewed in different ways.

In the Italian culture, autonomy (*autonomia*) is often synonymous for isolation (*isolamento*). The Italian patient is frequently viewed as being unable to learn enough to make appropriate autonomous health care decisions. Autonomy thus would easily become isolation for a person overwhelmed by complicated and frightening information that does not develop into knowledge. If information does not create knowledge, it does not create a positive autonomy. Protecting the ill family member from painful information is seen as essential for keeping the family together and not allowing the ill member to suffer alone. In addition, many Italians find it difficult to openly confront sickness and death.

Today, many Americans usually demand and are given information that enables them to make decisions either autonomously or with a physician's advice about their health care. Ancient Greek philosophers disputed the possibility of effectively communicating knowledge. Contemporary Italian attitudes perpetuate the belief that patients will never acquire enough knowledge to enable them to fully and appropriately participate in their care. As a result, the Italian physician remains a powerful, distant figure exercising unilateral decisions on the basis of knowledge that is assumed incommunicable.[10] "It is difficult to remain Imperator in the presence of a physician," said the Roman Emperor Hadrian in the second century,[11] and this seems to hold true even today.

Truth and the Therapeutic Relationship

We should never forget that the ill person, because of the nature of disease itself, is in a "uniquely dependent state."[12] The Italian Deontology Code thus allows physicians to use their experience and expertise to understand each patient and to establish how much information the patient can accept and process and in what manner the information is best conveyed. Any connection between patient and physician should be therapeutic. I firmly believe that truth is essential for a therapeutic relationship,[13] but I have to acknowledge that the Italian society is not prepared for the American way.

On the other hand, the Italian medical scene is rapidly changing, and physicians are now confronted with medicolegal issues that did not exist a few years ago. Although strongly believing in the truth, I am concerned that Italian physicians may communicate vast amounts of complicated information to unprepared patients only out of fear of litigation. Should this happen, it probably will not give rise to real truth telling and may result in exhaustive lists of information that will not improve the patient-physician relationship.

The Italian bioethical situation regarding truth telling to patients is often compared with the US situation a few decades ago.[14] I believe Italians should not borrow the American way, but they should learn from Americans and try to find a better Italian way. I already see signs of this happening. There are now courses in bioethics at the universities in Florence and Rome, updates on bioethics in some regions of Italy,[15] medical meetings on truth telling[16] and communicating with patients,[17] and a project to establish a database for national and international bioethical issues.[18] From the patients' side, a spontaneous organization called "Tribunale per i Diritti del Malato" (Court for the Patient's Rights) now exists.[19]

For now, when dealing with my patients, I try to tell them the complete truth. But there are times when this is not so easy. For example, when faced with a family repeatedly asking me not to use the word "cancer," I rely on nonverbal communication to establish a truthful and therapeutic relationship with the patient. In all instances, I make an effort to listen to the patients and to respect their need for information. Since I believe the suffering person knows the truth, I think the only way to respect both Italian ethical principles and the patient's autonomy and dignity is to let the patient know that there are no barriers to communication and to the truth.

I hope all my Italian patients will soon ask me for the truth, and I hope I will never give information just for medicolegal reasons. Moreover, I hope I will contribute — together with my colleagues — to a positive change in our society.

Notes

1. Ad Hoc Committee on Medical Ethics. American College of Physicians Ethics Manual, I: history of medical ethics, the physician and the patient, the physician's relationship to other physicians, the physician and society. *Ann Intern Med.* 1984; 101: 129–137.

2. Federazione Nazionale degli Ordini dei Medici Chirurghi e degli Odontoiatri. *Guida all'Esercizio Professionale per i Medici-Chirurghi e degli Odontoiatri.* Turin, Italy: Edizioni Medico Scientifiche; 1987:66–67.

3. Mosconi P, Meyerowitz BE, Liberati MC, et al. Disclosure of breast cancer diagnosis: patient and physician reports. *Ann Oncol.* 1991;2:273–280.

4. Treatment of early-stage breast cancer. *JAMA.* 1991;265:391–395. NIH Consensus Conference.

5. Sabbioni MEE. Speech is silver, silence is gold? *Ann Oncol.* 1991;2:234.

6. Boeri S. Medici e no. *Panorama.* 1992; 1349: 38–42.

7. Codice Deontologico 1989: informazione e consenso del paziente, art 39. In: Ordine dei Medici. ed. *Annuario dell'Ordine dei Medici della Provincia di Torino.* Turin, Italy: Ordine dei Medici; 1990:27.

8. Codice Deontologico 1989: sperimentazione, art 49. In: Ordine dei Medici. ed. *Annuario dell'Ordine dei Medici della Provincia di Torino.* Turin, Italy: Ordine dei Medici; 1990:28.

9. Il Medico d'Italia. Informazione al malato: come, quando e perché. *Organo Ufficiale della Federazione Nazionale degli Ordini dei Medici Chirurghi e degli Odontoiatri.* 1991;4:1–2

10. Zittoun R. Patient information and participation. In: Holland JC, Zittoun R. eds. *Psychosocial Aspects of Oncology.* Berlin, Germany: Springer-Verlag; 1990:27–44.

11. Yourcenar M. *Memoires d'Hadrien suivi de Carnets de notes de memoires d'Hadrien.* Paris, France: Gallimard; 1974.

12. Pellegrino ED. Altruism, self-interest, and medical ethics. *JAMA.* 1987;258:1939–1940.

13. Suchman AL, Matthews DA. What makes the patient-doctor relationship therapeutic? exploring the connexional dimension of medical care. *Ann Intern Med.* 1988; 108: 125–130.

14. Novack DH, Plumer R, Smith RL, et al. Changes in physicians' attitudes toward telling the cancer patient. *JAMA.* 1979; 241: 897–900.

15. Corso di formazione sulle tematiche bioetiche connesse al trattamento sanitario. Unità Sanitaria Locale 12, Pisa, Italy. January–February 1992.

16. Il Medico d'Italia. Come informare il paziente grave. *Organo Ufficiale della Federazione Nazionale degli Ordini dei Medici Chirurghi e degli Odontoiatri.* 1992;30:17.

17. Il Medico d'Italia. Come costruire e migliorare il rapporto medico–paziente. *Organo Ufficiale della Federazione Nazionale degli Ordini dei Medici Chirurghi e degli Odontoiatri.* 1992;26:16.

18. Il Medico d'Italia. Al via una banca dati sulla bioetica. *Organo Ufficiale della Federazione Nazionale degli Ordini dei Medici Chirurghi e degli Odontoiatri.* 1992;40:4.

19. Tribunale per i Diritti del Malato. Sezione di Pisa, Ospedale Santa Chiara. Carta dei diritti del cittadino malato. Pisa, Italy. 1984.

8   Is Truth Telling to the Patient a Cultural Artifact?

Edmund D. Pellegrino

In this issue of *JAMA*, Antonella Surbone, MD, describes her dilemma in trying to transfer the ideals of medical ethics she learned in the United States to her native Italy.[1] From her experience in the United States, she found that truth telling and respect for autonomy have become virtual moral absolutes. On the other hand, in Italy, families and physicians often shield patients from painful truths and difficult decisions. As Dr Surbone points out, what is beneficent in one country may seem maleficent in another country.

This contrast in moral perspectives, of course, is not unique to the difference between Italy and North America. It has become a worldwide problem as newer models of medical ethics nurtured in the individualistic soil of North America are introduced to other countries with different moral traditions.[2] But similar contrasts may exist within a country, for example, between northern and southern Italy, or between the multiple ethnic groups in the United States.[3] Everywhere, as cultural groups attain freedom of expression, physicians and patients must relate with each other across ethical barriers especially with respect to the importance of autonomy.

These contrasts raise some provocative questions. Is medical ethics a cultural artifact such that a universal medical ethic is not viable? How should physicians who are dedicated to the best interests of their patients conduct therapeutic relationships with patients whose cultural values differ materially from their own?

These questions invite a critical reexamination of the foundation and meaning of autonomy and its relationship with truth telling. Such reflection suggests that autonomy is not and cannot be unequivocally interpreted. Some of the dilemma is more superficial than real and derives from a narrow interpretation of the concept of autonomy.

Autonomy entered medical ethics as part of a system of prima facie principles devised to deal with moral pluralism. Prima facie principles, such as autonomy, nonmaleficence, beneficence, and justice, are those that ought to be respected unless powerful reasons for overriding them can be adduced.[4,5] In this system, each principle is given equal weight. Priorities among principles can be established only when the detailed circumstances of a particular decision are known. No principle, including autonomy, is granted a priori moral hegemony over the others.

The principle of autonomy is grounded in respect for persons and the acknowledgement that as rational beings we have the unique capability to make reasoned choices. Through these choices we plan and live lives for which we are morally accountable. Inhibiting an individual's capability to make these personal choices is a violation of his or her integrity as a person and thus a maleficent act.

Autonomy, therefore, is not in fundamental opposition with beneficence as is too often supposed, but in congruence with it. Problems arise when the content of what is beneficent is defined by others such as family members or physicians. This may be warranted when we are mentally incompetent, when our choices harm others, or when we make choices that contravene good medical practice or harm us seriously. In the absence of these limitations, competent humans are owed the freedom to define beneficence in terms of their own values. This does not mean that all values are morally equivalent or defensible, but only that as humans we are owed respect for the choices we voluntarily make.

In North America, in the United States in particular, autonomy has tended to become a moral absolute. The reasons for this are multiple. They include improved education of the public, a strong tradition of privacy rights and personal liberty, a distrust of authority and the possibilities of medical technology, and the loosening of family and community identification. In this context, truth telling is a necessary corollary, since human capability for autonomous choices cannot function if truth is withheld, falsified, or otherwise manipulated. Truth telling is essential to informed consent, the instrument whereby personal autonomy is expressed in concrete decisions.

Respect for autonomy and truth telling are intrinsic to beneficent medical care for many people in the North American context. It does not follow, however, that this concept of autonomy is always beneficent or that it must be accepted by, or imposed on, everyone living in the United States or elsewhere.

For one thing, autonomous patients are free to use their autonomy as they see fit — even to delegate it when this fits their own concept of beneficence. Some patients need a more authoritative approach than others. This approach is legitimate when, for example, despite efforts to inform and empower patients to make their own decisions, patients find themselves unable or unwilling to cope with choices. Such patients may feel sincerely that a close friend or family member would be able to make decisions that better protect their values than they could make themselves. Such a delegation of decision-making authority may be explicit or implicit depending on the dominant ethos.

In some parts of Italy, among many ethnic groups in the United States, and in large parts of the world, this delegation of authority is culturally implicit. In such contexts, the uniformity of the practice suggests that delegation of decision making is an expectation of the sick person that need not be explicit. To thrust the truth or the decision on a patient who expects to be buffeted against news of impending death is a gratuitous and harmful misinterpretation of the moral foundation for respect for autonomy. In many cultures clinicians encounter patients who are fully aware of the gravity of their condition but choose to play out the drama in their own way. This may include not discussing the full or obvious truth. This is a form of autonomy, if it is implicitly and mutually agreed on, between physician and patient. However, autonomy should not be violated by a misconceived attempt to be morally rigorous. Withholding the truth from a patient demands, of course, the utmost care in responding to any occasion when the patient wishes to exert more control.

Among most North American physicians, the withholding of truth, in whole or in part, is a therapeutic privilege accepted as morally licit when we have substantial evidence that offering the patient the truth has a significant probability of causing harm, for example, emotional damage or suicide. This "privilege" must be used rarely and with utmost care since it is so easily abused.

Treating patients within the conception of beneficence defined by their own cultural ideas is a form of therapeutic privilege. However, a palpable risk of harm in knowing the truth must exist that must not be outweighed by the risk of withholding the truth. The amount, manner, and timing of truth telling or truth withholding are crucial factors for which there is no ready formula.

Thus, autonomy cannot be an absolute principle with a priori precedence over other prima facie principles. Rather, the judicious exercise of respect for autonomy means that health professionals must act in a manner that enables and empowers patients to make decisions and act in a way that is most in accord with their values.

That the patient may draw these values from the circumambient culture does not make autonomy or medical ethics a cultural artifact. Autonomy is still a valid and universal principle because it is based on what it is to be human. The patient must decide how much autonomy he or she wishes to exercise, and this amount can vary from culture to culture.

It seems probable that the democratic ideals that lie behind the contemporary North American concept of autonomy will spread and that something close to it will be the choice of many individuals in other countries. What then does the physician do when a society is in transition as Dr Surbone suggests is the case in Italy today, or when many different cultures make up one society as is the case in the United States? To preserve both autonomy and beneficence, physicians must get to know their patients well enough to discern when, and if, those patients wish to contravene the mores of prevailing medical culture. This requires a degree of familiarity and sensitivity increasingly difficult to come by, but morally inescapable for every physician who practices in today's morally and culturally diverse world society.

Notes

1. Surbone A. Truth telling to the patient. *JAMA*. 1992;268:1661–1662.
2. Pellegrino ED, Mazzarella P, Corsi P. eds. *Transcultural Dimensions in Medical Ethics*. Frederick, Md: University Publishing Group. In press.
3. Flack HE, Pellegrino ED, eds. *African American Perspectives on Biomedical Ethics*. Washington, DC: Georgetown University Press; 1992.
4. Beauchamp TL, Childress JF. *Principles of Bioethics*, 3rd ed. New York, NY: Oxford University Press; 1989.
5. Ross WD. *The Right and the Good*. Indianapolis, Ind: Hackett Publishing Company; 1988:33–34.

9 Ethical Considerations of Human Investigation in Developing Countries: The AIDS Dilemma

Michele Barry

As pressure mounts within the scientific community to find a vaccine and develop strategies for the treatment of human immunodeficiency virus (HIV) infection, researchers are turning to developing countries, especially in sub-Saharan Africa, where large patient population at risk for HIV infection can be identified and studied. Research funding is being offered by the National Institutes of Health and other agencies to establish collaborative study units, and American and European investigators, often unfamiliar with the culture, customs, and economic pressures within these developing countries, are designing large-scale studies. Although there is an urgent need to control the acquired immunodeficiency syndrome (AIDS), consideration must be given to the ethical implications and cultural obstacles involved in conducting research in developing nations.

The basic ethical principles that guide human investigation, as defined by the Helsinki Declaration and the Nuremberg Code,[1] need to be interpreted and applied within different cultural settings, many of which were unfamiliar to the international bodies that originally formulated these principles. The basic bioethical principles may have very different meanings in such settings; foreign investigators need to be sensitive to these different perspective before conducting studies. Given the urgency of research on AIDS and the difficulties that are being encountered and will undoubtedly persist, I believe that a careful examination of cross-cultural bioethics is critical at this time. In this paper, the immediate problem associated with AIDS research in developing countries are reviewed in the context of four principles — autonomy, beneficence, nonmaleficence, and justice.

Autonomy and Informed Consent

"Autonomy" is a term derived from the Greek *autos* ("self") and *nomos* ("rule"). In present-day American society, personhood is conceived in terms emphasizing autonomy — i.e., individual rights, self-determination, and privacy.[2] The Nuremberg Code requires that participation in biomedical research be based on freedom of individual choice, with no element of coercion or constraint. It dictates further that a person should understand the subject matter of the research sufficiently to make an enlightened decision.[1] Thus, the nature, duration, and purpose of an experiment, the methods of experimentation, the possible effects on health, and all the inconveniences entailed by the experiment need to be made known to a participant.

Applying the concept of autonomy and the requirement of informed consent may present difficulties in cultures where personal choice is extremely limited. For example, in some central African cultures the concept of personhood differs so fundamentally from that in Western cultures that many Bantu languages lack terms corresponding to the English word "person."[2] Personhood is defined by one's tribe, village, or social group. Whereas in Western terms selfhood emphasizes the individual, in certain African societies it cannot be extricated from a dynamic system of social relationships, both of kinship and of community as defined by the village.[2] Thus, an investigator seeking informed consent from persons in such a setting may need to approach community elders for their consent before attempting to obtain informed consent from individual persons. Clearly, the question of who gives informed consent — heads of households, elders, individual persons, the tribe, the ministry of health, or the government — needs to be asked with cultural sensitivity.

Ideally, each potential research subject should comprehend the nature of the investigation before providing valid informed consent.[1] The information should be communicated and interpreted culturally so that it does not become overwhelming and senseless. Unfortunately, when language barriers exist and such concepts as germ theory or viral agents are alien, a description of an AIDS-related investigation, even a simple seroprevalence study, becomes difficult to relay to participants. Illiteracy may be a problem as well, but it must never be confused with lack of intelligence.[3] Often investigators write detailed descriptions of studies to demonstrate to American human-investigation committees that informed consent is being pursued, yet they bypass the important step of making the information culturally comprehensible. I favor local community involvement, and when appropriate the oral and pictorial depiction of concepts. When possible, cultural and societal precepts should be incorporated into the information supplied to participants and into public education about high-risk behavior and AIDS.

Nonmaleficence and Beneficence

The principle of nonmaleficence is associated with the maxim of *primum non nocere* — "first, do no harm." The principle of beneficence requires not only that we refrain from harming the patients but also that we contribute to their general welfare and health. Risk-benefit assessment for collaborative research in AIDS may be different when it is interpreted in the context of different cultures and political settings. As the Helsinki Declaration emphasizes, during human investigations the interests of science and society should never take precedence over considerations of a subject's well-being.[1] Yet in non-autonomous populations, health policy decisions and risk–benefit analyses often place state interests above concern for the individual. For example, during a recent study in Tanzania with which I was associated, on HIV seroprevalence in pregnant women and infant cord blood, health officials insisted that the women not be told what they were being tested for, or given the results. The host country's decision was based on the judgment that the results could provoke hysteria within the population about the disease with no cure and for which limited resources were available, even for palliative treatment. The American collaborator was placed in an ethical quandary about whether to continue the field study, because the American protocol, approved by a human-investigation committee, called for informed consent and the dissemination of test results. At the host country's request, serum samples were collected anonymously, but because of ethical concerns analysis of the samples in the United States has not been completed. Certainly, large studies of seroprevalence have been conducted in the United States without disclosure, but typically they have had the informed consent of the participating study group. Although no one is overtly harmed by closed studies, the beneficent treatment of research subjects should include, at a minimum, educational programs and access to the results of anonymous testing.

Limited resources may compound the risk–benefit dilemma for a developing nation. Since many countries cannot afford costly confirmation by Western blotting during large studies of seroprevalence, should asymptomatic subjects be informed of a single positive enzyme-linked immunosorbent assay? On the other hand, large seroprevalence studies with no disclosure withhold information that might lead to a change in high-risk behavior and thus save lives. Funding agencies should try to make confirmation by Western blotting possible during collaborative studies in Africa. Full disclosure — ideally with Western blot confirmation — permits self-protection, the protection of others, and the possibility of treatment should future therapeutic breakthrough occur.[4]

The risk–benefit assessment of AIDS-related research in the developing world may involve political as well as cultural and ethical concerns. American investigators must be aware of the political and economic ramifications of their research. For countries in which the chief industry is tourism, adverse or false publicity about AIDS can disrupt fragile economies.[5] For example, the 1987 *Fodor's Kenya*[6] speculates that in some African countries the HIV infection rate may be 30 percent of the total population. This statement has no scientific support, least of all in Kenya, where well-conducted studies of seroprevalence have shown much lower rates in the general population.[7] Similarly, the efforts of American researchers to locate the origins of the AIDS virus in western or central Africa have created political controversy and discrimination against African students travelling abroad.[7] The legacy of exploitation by colonialists in many developing countries engenders suspicion even when well-intentioned research on AIDS-vaccine trials is proposed. As a result, certain ministries of health in sub-Saharan Africa have banned the exportation of any body fluid or tissue culture, even if it is ostensibly unrelated to HIV study. Many developing nations rightly take pride in new scientific and laboratory achievements and find it offensive when, for expedience, American investigators take African serum samples to the United States to be examined and processed. In the past, results have often been published even before data were shared with the host country. For all the urgency of AIDS research, human research performed in a developing country without joint collaboration, training, or education can become exploitative or at least be so perceived. Too often, external interests are served with little immediate benefit to the host country or individual subject. As a result, social and racial divisions between nations can become aggravated.

Justice

The principle of justice is concerned with fairness. Neither the benefits nor the burdens of research should be unjustly distributed.[8] Under the principle of justice, research subjects should be chosen for reasons directly related to the scientific question under study and not because of their easy availability, their compromised position, or their ability to be manipulated.[9,10] For example, the mere presence of a highly accessible high-risk population in Africa, for which a low-cost vaccine trial would be feasible, does not constitute sufficient justification for using Africans as subjects.[10] Although there may be scientific interest in studying groups of Africans with different transmission risks in order to evaluate the efficacy of a vaccine, it would be unethical to subject Africans to a disproportionate share of the research risks without an equal share of the benefits.[10] A financial commitment by the developed world will therefore be required to provide an affordable or subsidized vaccine to the developing world.

The principle of justice also implies that resources be allocated in the way that best benefits the society being studied. For many developing countries, AIDS morbidity and even AIDS mortality are seen to be problems less urgent than malnutrition, malaria, tuberculosis, or even the diseases preventable by available immunizations. The World Health Organization report of December 1987 describes 73,747 cases of AIDS from 129 countries. Of these, 48,138 were from the United States and 8652 were from 37 African countries.[11] Although the latter figure clearly represents underreporting, the number of deaths from nutritional diseases alone in Africa almost certainly far exceeds AIDS mortality. Preventing the deaths of skilled, productive adults from heterosexually transmitted HIV infection must become a health priority in the developing world, but should money and manpower be diverted from reducing infant mortality due to diarrhea, malaria, or diseases preventable by immunization? For the proper allocation of resources, AIDS research and educational programs must be put into perspective alongside primary health care programs. Outside investigators need to consider the health care priorities of the collaborating nation and must try to satisfy both internal and external interests. Long-term support in the form of the commitment of labratories, the training of local staff, or the development of educational exchange programs can mitigate feelings of exploitation and benefit both nations mutually

Human-Investigation Committees and Developing Nations

The provisions for the review of research involving human subjects may be influenced by politics, the existing organization of medical practice and research, and the degree of autonomy accorded to medical researchers in the field.[12] Whatever the circumstances, there is a responsibility to defend the principles of autonomy, nonmaleficence, beneficence, and justice while conducting human investigation, as emphasized in the Helsinki Declaration and the Nuremberg Code. Research protocols should be subjected to independent ethical review by the initiating country or agency, using ethical standards as stringent as those applied to research carried out within the developed country.[12] Difficulty may arise in collaborative ventures when a host country is forced to maintain foreign standards; these demands may rekindle past resentments of colonialist policy. Sensitivity to the charge of "ethical imperialism" and to health policy decisions made by the host country is important. Mutually acceptable ethical standards can be agreed on easily if a prospective review is approached jointly.

Such deliberations should include attending to the issue of patient confidentiality. Can investigators ensure confidentiality in a foreign society? Is it possible to ensure anonymity in small village settings? Will government have access to the names of persons who are HIV positive? To ensure patient rights, outside investigators should be asking such questions. Local religious, university, or community leaders can often help with the answers.

I suggest working with a local review board composed of both medical professionals and laymen qualified to represent local community, cultural, and moral values. This board should consist of people uninfluenced by the prospect of money, prestige, or personal gain from the project. If no such board exists in the developing nation, the public health ministry or host institution can help in composing one that will maintain ongoing independent review of a project. Such ongoing evaluation is important, because protocols are often revised for expedience in the field.

Conclusion

Clearly, AIDS is a devastating health problem for the entire world. The most recent estimate by the World Health Organization is that between 5 and 10 million people are currently infected.[11] The reality is that for all countries, AIDS research is crucial. Despite the potential problems we have described, collaborative work should be encouraged and funded. Yet investigations need to be culturally sensitive, and research ethics need to be made culturally relevant. The formulation of codified principles to guide human investigation permits just and beneficial collaborative research across cultural barriers.

References
1. Beauchamp TL, Childress JF, eds. Principles of biomedical ethics. 2nd ed. Oxford: Oxford University Press, 1983:339–43.
2. De Craemer W. A cross-cultural perspective on personhood. Milbank Mem Fund Q 1983; 61:19–34.
3. Setiloane GM. African traditional views. In: Benatar SR, ed. Ethical and moral issues in contemporary medical practice. Capetown, South Africa: UCT Printing Department, 1986:32–5.
4. Curran WJ. AIDS research and "the window of opportunity." N Engl J Med 1985; 312:903–4.
5. Norman C. Politics and science clash on African AIDS. Science 1985; 230:1140–2.
6. Fodor's Kenya. Rev. ed. New York: David McKay, 1987.
7. Sabatier RC. Social, cultural and demogra-

phic aspects of AIDS. West J Med 1988;
147:713–5.

8. Beauchamp TL, Childress JF. eds. Principles
of biomedical ethics. 2nd ed. Oxford: Oxford University Press, 1983:183–220.

9. National Commission for the Protection of
Human Subjects of Biomedical and Behavioral Research. The Belmont report: ethical
principles and guidelines for the protection
of human subjects of research. Washington,
D.C.: Department of Health, Education,

and Welfare, 1979:5. (DHEW publication
no. (05) 9–12065.)

10. Christakis NA. The ethical design of an
AIDS vaccine trial in Africa. Hastings Cent
Rep 1988; 18(3):31–7.

11. AIDS worldwide. Lancet 1988; 1:252–3.

12. Proposed international guidelines for biomedical research involving human subjects.
Geneva: World Health Organization
1981:1–49.

10   Ethical Imperialism? Ethics in International Collaborative Clinical Research

Marcia Angell

. . . It is often argued that . . . insisting on certain ethical standards when doing research in another country is a form of imperialism and therefore inappropriate. Why should we believe that ethical principles that make sense in one culture are necessarily right in another? More specifically, why should researchers be expected to obtain informed consent in a society that places little value on individual autonomy? This argument has appeal to those who are concerned with tolerance and cooperation among different societies. Any notion of equality among societies, after all, demands that we recognize one another's traditions and not try to impose foreign ones. Many see this position as a step toward countering the long history of exploitation of the Third World by the developed countries. According to this view, if informed consent is not an accepted concept in a society or if a community leader customarily speaks for the members of the community, we should not insist that subjects give informed consent. To do so, it is said, would constitute ethical imperialism.

The problem with this argument is the implication that ethical standards are matters of custom, like table manners, and that their content is irrelevant as long as they are indigenous. It further presupposes that all members of a community share its dominant values. This ethical relativism gives the same weight to practices that would sharply curtail individual freedom (whether by tradition or by a community leader) as to those that would protect it. Does this make sense? Consider an analogy. Does apartheid offend universal standards of justice, or does it instead simply represent a South African custom that should be seen as morally neutral? If the latter view is accepted, then ethical principles are not much more than a description of the mores of a society. I believe they must have more meaning than that. There must be a core of human rights that we would wish to see honored universally, despite local variations in their superficial aspects. Ethical standards in medicine similarly cannot be relative; they must be judged by their substance. The force of local custom or law cannot justify abuses of certain fundamental rights, and the right of self-determination, on which the doctrine of informed consent is based, is one of them.

Furthermore, if we accept the view that ethical standards in clinical research are relative, we may create a situation in which Western researchers use Third World populations to do studies they could not do at home because they would be considered unethical. Researchers would be tempted to short-circuit the sometimes onerous requirements for protecting human subjects by appealing to this ethical relativism. What would follow, then, would be true imperialism in the sense of exploitation — the very opposite of what the proponents of honoring local traditions would wish.

This is not to say that Western researchers should not make appropriate accommodations to local custom, as Dr. Barry points out.[1] Local sensitivities should be respected. It may be necessary, for example, to obtain permission from community leaders to enroll members of the community in a clinical study or from a husband to enroll his wife. Such permission should not, however, be a substitute for informed consent from the subjects themselves or be allowed to override a refusal. Similarly, conveying the information necessary to give informed consent may be very difficult and require a good deal of ingenuity, but it must be done. In such ways, the ethical requirements of performing clinical research in Third World societies may be more, rather than less, exacting.

Fundamental principles of humane research, however, should not be compromised. Human subjects in any part of the world should be protected by an irreducible set of ethical standards, including the requirements that they not be subjected to unreasonable risks and that they be asked for informed consent to participate. When Western researchers collaborate on studies performed in the Third World, it is particularly important that they adhere to these standards. . . .

References

1. Barry M. Ethical considerations of human investigation in developing countries: the AIDS dilemma. N Engl J Med 1988; 319: 1083–6.

11   Ethical Imperialism and Informed Consent

Lisa H. Newton

AIDS has presented the field of bioethics with a series of fascinating problems, sharpening concerns for privacy and autonomy (involuntary testing and divulgence of results), maximization of patient well-being (determining the extent of treatment for terminally ill AIDS patients), and justice (allocations of scarce resources in terminal illnesses).

Among the more interesting is the dilemma presented and discussed by Michele Barry of Yale in the *New England Journal of Medicine*,[1] commented upon editorially by Marcia Angell in the same issue.[2] When doing AIDS research among the tribes of sub-Saharan Africa, where "self" is often undeveloped as a concept and it is not traditional to ask individuals to make decisions for "themselves," should the same standards of "informed consent" be applied in the course of the trials, as would be required if the study were conducted in (say) New Haven? Or, instead, should cultural tradition be honored, when it requires only the permission of the leader of the community to commit its citizens to the research, or the consent of the head of the household to enroll members of the family? To accept the community standard of "consent" (i.e., that permission of the community leader suffices) might seem to be exploitative of the subjects, who get no real chance to understand the research on their own and make their own choices; on the other hand, insisting on Yale University-level standards of individual consent seems to be "ethical imperialism," the coercive and inappropriate imposition of Western morality.

For the sake of discussion, we will have to make certain assumptions about the studies in question. First of all, the research must pass scientific muster: no one doubts the importance of AIDS research, but each proposal must have a reasonable chance of advancing our knowledge of the disease, or it cannot be carried out on human subjects. Second, it must not impose excessive risk on the subjects, as would, say, a study that called for the introduction of live AIDS virus into an uninfected subject. (For purposes of this discussion, we will assume that the study calls for drawing blood to determine HIV seroprevalence, like the study with which Michele Barry was associated.[3]) Third, the case cannot be one where securing informed consent is possible, but just not required by the local authorities. If the trusting community is perfectly willing to let you go ahead and draw their blood on the say-so of the head man alone, while you feel yourself obliged to check this permission with each person whose blood shall be drawn, and it is perfectly feasible (and harmless) to run that check, then there is no reason not to do it, and the standard obligation to secure individual consent should prevail. Fourth, the problem cannot be one of communication only; there are ways to communicate all that a reasonable person might want to know about a study, with pictures if necessary, to any competent person.

For the dilemma to make sense, there must be very good reasons not to communicate the normally required information to the subject, good reasons not to obtain informed consent as we understand it. In general, these reasons will derive from our general duty of nonmaleficence: where it appears that disclosure of information about the study will do the subject more harm than good, we have a good reason not to disclose, and we shall have to see if our duty to protect and enhance autonomy should prevail against it. Such harm might include undue (groundless) fear of damage from the procedures in the study, futile (irremediable) fear of the disease itself, and the possibility of creating a community climate of fear in the process of raising the profile of the investigators and of the research itself. There is the more subtle harm of undermining the social trust of the community: when the head man consented, and that is all the consent that is required in this community, why are the investigators apparently seeking further individual commitments from the community members? Isn't the head man to be trusted? Are the normal procedures of the community unworthy of credence, contemptible in the eyes of more advanced societies, that such elaborate procedures are introduced to replace them?

Are Ethical Standards Universal?

Marcia Angell asks what she takes to be the key question: "Should ethical standards be substantially the same everywhere, or is it inevitable that they differ from region to region, reflecting local beliefs and custom?"[4] Her answer to that question is that ethical standards are, inevitably, the same everywhere — to call a standard moral, or ethical, as opposed to legal or conventional, is by definition to call it universal, and independent of local custom. Further, ethical standards do not change with time, for they derive from human nature itself, which does not change (or at least has not changed in historical time). The standards, or fundamental moral principles, that she seeks are always and everywhere the same. But that's not the real question.

For starters, we noted above that objections to seeking informed consent are often based on the principle of nonmaleficence. That principle is at least as important as the principle of respect for persons, on which autonomy, and the demand that individual choice be taken into account, and hence the requirement for informed consent in human subjects research, are based. When we discuss the necessity of informed consent in this research, we must balance the importance of honoring choice with the importance of doing no harm. Second, the principles do not usually have only one application in any complex case. The informed consent requirement, as above, is derived from the principle of respect for individual autonomy, protected by a strict requirement of informed consent, it can still be argued that it has another equally valid application in respect for the integrity of the community, requiring that local custom and beliefs be honored, not because they are the highest morality there is, but because respect for those who have forged a common life around those beliefs demands that the beliefs be acknowledged by any who come to do business there and that people be allowed to operate in accordance with them.

Third, only part of the question has to do with dealing with people who have customs at odds with our own. Striking a balance between respecting choice and doing no harm can be just as great a problem in our own country and culture, under suitable circumstances, and the answer will be just as unclear as in sub-Saharan Africa; the perceptions of harm will differ, but that makes no difference to the fundamental argument. Only one aspect of the dilemma is really culturally significant: seeking informed consent to research from individuals may tend to weaken the social fabric of a non-individualist society, forcing it to deal with values it does not hold and possibly sowing disorder that the community will have to reap long after the investigators have gone home. Is this infusion of alien practices really respectful to the participants in the study, all of whom will suffer if community order breaks down? Are we compelled by a moral necessity — a necessity known best, perhaps, to Yale's earliest students, the evangelical missionaries who brought the "truth" of Christianity to backward countries — to preach individualism to communities that reject it?

Two observations come to mind; I will make one and conclude with the other. First, the question comes at an awkward time for Western social philosophy. As readers of Robert Bellah's *Habits of the Heart* will be aware, our vaunted individualism is coming under severe scrutiny;[5] it is questionable that it has been an unmitigated good for our own civilization, and very questionable that it is up to standard for export. We ought, in truth, to be suitably humble about the worth of procedures developed only to cater to a very Western weakness.

Second, and more important, the whole controversy illustrates an aspect of bioethics in general, and human subjects research literature in particular, that needs to be pointed out and studied for its own sake, for it manifests the very disease it takes as its subject. It is certain that universal ethical standards should be applied without discrimination throughout the world, but it is "ethical imperialism" at its worst to assume that the informed consent requirement, which does indeed serve one (only one) moral principle in the Western setting, is in itself such a universal ethical standard. It compounds that error with worse, when a decision is taken, or suggested, that research be brought to a halt[6] or denied publication[7] for failure to carry out the informed consent requirement to the letter, no matter how inappropriate the requirement may be to the setting of the research. The point of the enterprise seems to have been lost.

The point of the enterprise, after all, was to acquire generalizable knowledge about medical matters, in this case about HIV seroprevalence in a high risk population. The disease is unquestionably dreadful, and the people serving as subjects for this research will probably benefit from any knowledge gained, perhaps more than the people of Western countries with lower incidence of disease. How can it be a sign of our respect for the people, or of our concern for their welfare, that we are willing to suppress research that is conducted according to the laws and customs of the countries in which it is being carried on?

Or is such disrespect part of the intention of the requirement and its enforcement? After all, the insistence on making our cooperation contingent upon their adherence to our rules may make a good deal of sense if such adherence is part of the program we bring with us. When the Yale-educated medical missionaries went to those same countries, they often insisted on Holy Baptism as a condition for medical care; our investigators may be insisting on jot and tittle of informed consent as a condition for carrying on essential research, as part of a conscious program of instilling a respect for individual rights among people perceived as oppressively backward on such matters. But are our clinical investigators really qualified for such liberal missionary work — better, is this really part of the investigator's job? Especially given the doubt surrounding the value of individualism and individual rights at present, the investigator might better stick to the research, and accept the local assessment as to adequate protection of individual rights.

References

1. Barry, M.: Ethical considerations of human investigation in developing countries. *New England Journal of Medicine* 1988; 319:1083–86.
2. Angell, M.: Ethical imperialism? Ethics in international collaborative clinical research. *New England Journal of Medicine* 1988; 319:1081–83.
3. Barry, op.cit., p. 1084.
4. Angell, op.cit., p. 1081.
5. Bellah, R.N., et al: *Habits of the Heart*, New York, Harper & Row, 1988.
6. Barry, op.cit., p. 1984.
7. Angell, op.cit., p. 1083.

Chapter 2

Questions to Consider

1. According to Pellegrino, the principle of autonomy is universal because it is grounded in what it means to be human. How does one determine what the distinctive features of being human are? Does this kind of view assume there is a unique human nature? And how does an understanding of what it means to be human entail any moral conclusions?
2. What does the concept of autonomy mean, and how can it be applied in a culture in which the concept of personhood is so different that the language contains no word equivalent to the English word "person"?
3. Angell contends that there are certain fundamental human rights that are universal. What would make something a "fundamental human right"? How would one determine what fundamental human rights there are? Would respect for autonomy be one of these rights?
4. Defenders of the universality of morality often concede that appropriate accommodation to local customs must be made when applying universal moral standards in diverse cultures. What does "appropriate accommodation" mean, and why does this concession not amount to admitting the truth of cultural relativism?
5. What does the charge of ethical imperialism mean? Is it "ethical imperialism" if a doctor in Canada refuses to perform female circumcision when asked to do so by a family from a culture in which this is a custom? Is it ethical imperialism if Canadians campaign to have female circumcision banned in a country in which it has been customarily practised? If ethical standards are universal, what is the difference?

Further Readings

Christakis, Nicholas A. 1992. Ethics are local: Engaging cross-cultural variation in the ethics for clinical research. *Social Science and Medicine* 35:1079–91.

Feldman, Eric. 1985. Medical ethics the Japanese way. *Hastings Center Report* 15(5):21–24.

Galanti, Geri-Ann. 1991. *Caring for patients from different cultures*. Philadelphia: University of Pennsylvania Press.

Gordon, Deborah R. 1990. Embodying illness, embodying cancer. *Culture, Medicine and Psychiatry* 14:275–97.

Gutmann, Amy. 1993. The challenge of multiculturalism in political ethics. *Philosophy and Public Affairs* 22:171–206.

Halevy, Amir, and Baruch, Brody. 1993. Brain death: Reconciling definitions, criteria, and tests. *Annals of Internal Medicine* 119:519–25.

IJsselmuiden, Carel B., and Ruth R. Faden. 1992. Research and informed consent in africa — another look. *New England Journal of Medicine* 326:830–34.

Kimura, Rihito. 1991. Japan's dilemma with the

definition of death. *Kennedy Institute of Ethics Journal* 1:123–31.

Levine, Robert J. 1993. New international ethical guidelines for research involving human subjects. *Annals of Internal Medicine* 119:339–41.

Meleis, Afaf Ibrahim, and Albert R. Jonsen. 1983. Ethical crises and cultural differences. *Western Journal of Medicine* 138:889–93.

Pellegrino, Edmund D., Patricia Mazzarella, and Pietro Corsi. 1992. *Transcultural dimensions in medical ethics*. Frederick, Md.: University Publishing Group.

van der Kwaak, Anke. 1992. Female circumcision and gender identity: A questionable alliance. *Social Science and Medicine* 35:777–87.

Chapter 3

Health Care in Canada

Chapter 3

Introduction

Ethical questions about health care cannot be meaningfully addressed outside the context in which those questions arise. That context includes the political, economic, and legal forces that impinge upon the delivery of health care; it also includes the values that are immanent in a health care system. The Canadian health care system is currently in flux, and as the system changes, so do its underlying values. To make informed judgements about what is happening, the values that shape and direct the provision of health care in Canada, and the goals of the health care system, need to be understood and assessed.

The design, structure, and operation of different health care systems manifest different values. The core values of the Canadian health care system are contained in the guiding principles of the Canada Health Act. To obtain the full federal contribution to health care funding, provincial health care plans must provide coverage that is universal, comprehensive, accessible, portable, and publicly administered. Determining what those five general values require in practice is not easy, however.

What, for example, does "comprehensive" coverage mean? If a province were to identify a limited set of services deemed "medically necessary" and to insure only those services, would that count as comprehensive coverage? Would allowing individuals to purchase services that were no longer insured violate the values of universality and accessibility? Those who object to allowing health care services to be purchased privately (so-called "privatization") worry about the introduction of a "two-tier" system in Canada. But a two-tier system already exists in a number of respects. Canadians pay privately for prescription drugs, dental services, prostheses and devices, cosmetic surgery, and *in vitro* fertilization, for example. As well, those who can afford it can have "preferred accommodation" — private or semi-private rooms — in hospitals and can travel to the United States to obtain services that either are not available in Canada or have lengthy waiting lists here.

Would the introduction of so-called "user fees" (currently prohibited by s. 19 of the Canada Health Act) violate the values of accessibility and universality? Opponents of user fees worry that requiring patients to pay even a nominal amount every time they visit a doctor or an emergency department would be a substantial deterrent to seeking care, especially for the poor. If user fees were introduced and functioned as a deterrent, those who are already disadvantaged would delay obtaining treatment and thus would enter the health care system when their illnesses are more serious and more expensive to treat. On the other hand, it can be argued that user fees would decrease frequent, excessive patient demands on the system and would impose discipline on physicians by making them more circumspect about the tests and treatments they recommend. The additional revenue from user fees then could be used to relieve the mounting pressure for cutbacks and change.

The core values embedded in the Canada Health Act comprise a moral vision of health and health care. In Canada, health care is regarded as a common good to which all of us, as moral equals, are entitled. Our public system of health care displays our shared concern and responsibility for one another and differentiates Canada from the United States, where health care is regarded more as a commodity. It is often pointed out that our willingness to help and protect others is "an essential part of what makes us Canadians" (Dossetor 1994, 10).

We can turn to the Canada Health Act for an explicit statement of the values behind our health care system, but no comparable articulation of the goals of the system exists. Even to question the goals of a health care system might seem gratuitous because the answer appears so obvious, but what exactly is a health care system supposed to do? Just provide health care? That would restrict the goal to treating diseases and illnesses after they occur. Would it not make more sense to try to prevent disease, illness, and accidents, that is, to keep people healthy in the first place? The Preamble to the Canada Health Act explicitly endorses prevention and health promotion. In the Preamble, Parliament recognizes

> that Canadians can achieve further improvements in their well-being through combining individual lifestyles that emphasize fitness, prevention of disease and health promotion with collective action against the social, environmental and occupational causes of disease, and that they desire a system of health services that will promote physical and mental health and protection against disease.

Canada has been an international leader in developing a broad conception of health. The report, "A New Perspective on the Health of Canadians," issued in 1974 by Marc Lalonde, minister of National Health and Welfare at the time, introduced the notion of a "health field" intended to encompass all matters affecting health. The four main elements that comprise the health field in the Lalonde report are human biology, environment, lifestyle, and health care organizations. The Lalonde report has been widely acclaimed for its persuasive and perceptive identification of a broad range of "determinants" of health, and that enlarged understanding of health is evident in the Preamble to the Canada Health Act. But how can a health care system attempt to deal with all the factors that influence health? Is such an ambitious undertaking at all feasible? How much would it cost? And would it be morally desirable if it substantially infringed on the freedom of individuals to decide how they want to live?

Alternatively, we might try to identify the goals of our health care system by analyzing the notion of health. But health has proved difficult to define. The World Health Organization's definition takes health to be "a state of complete physical, mental, and social well-being and not merely the absence of disease or infirmity." Including "social well-being" in a definition of health, it has been pointed out, "turns the enduring problem of human happiness into one more medical problem, to be dealt with by scientific means" (Callahan 1973). Given that health care still has a long way to go in dealing with a host of physical diseases, optimism about its ability to foster "complete mental and social well-being" seems misplaced. And even if it did have this ability, whether so many human problems should be "medicalized" is highly questionable. Moreover, broad definitions of health raise the same questions about feasibility, cost, and moral permissibility as long lists of the determinants of health. Ascertaining the proper goals and scope of a health care system is not nearly as easy as it seems.

One change that is substantially altering the Canadian health care system is the shift to providing more care in the home and community instead of in institutions. Psychiatric patients and persons who are developmentally delayed or mentally handicapped already have been "deinstitutionalized." Now the same policy is being implemented with respect to long-term and chronic care. The goal is to keep patients, most of whom are elderly, out of chronic care hospitals, nursing homes, and homes for the aged and provide the care they need in their homes and communities. As with the first two movements, the current shift to home and community care is motivated by humanitarian as well as economic concerns. Providing care in the home or community is intended to promote both the well-being and autonomy of patients, two values central to the delivery of health care. But as happened with the first two movements, the danger is that the resources necessary to provide adequate home and community care will not be forthcoming. Upon whom, then, will the responsibility for providing this care fall? Upon the same people who have traditionally assumed that responsibility:

... we have a social history of placing the responsibility of family care almost entirely upon the shoulders of women. This model for caring finds the personal health needs of women caregivers at the bottom of the healthcare agenda. What is troubling about the current move to shift more health care into the home is the expectation that unpaid, non-professional women will be providing the care (i.e., mothers, sisters, daughters, wives, etc.) (Kieser 1994, 1).

The resources necessary for workable home care do not appear to be forthcoming, yet the transition proceeds. That reality raises serious questions of social justice as the burden of providing care falls disproportionately upon women. This issue highlights how moral concerns are vitally implicated in the operation of a health care system, even if they do not receive the attention they deserve.

The Selections

The first selection, from the document, "Achieving Health for All: A Framework for Health Promotion," by Jake Epp, former minister of National Health and Welfare, briefly reviews changes in the definition of health and outlines three principal challenges for Canada's health care system. As long as infectious disease remained the primary cause of illness and death, health was defined as the absence of disease. When infectious diseases were largely brought under control around the middle of this century, health came to be understood as a state of complete physical, mental, and social well-being. Now health is seen as a resource for living, "an essential dimension of the quality of our lives." Changes in how health is perceived are accompanied by changes in how the goals of a health care system are formulated. According to the minister, the main challenges for health care as Canada enters the twenty-first century are reducing inequities in health between low-income and high-income groups; finding better ways to prevent injuries, illnesses, disabilities, and chronic diseases; and enhancing people's ability to contend with disabilities, chronic conditions, and mental health problems.

The second selection, from "Nurturing Health," a report of the Ontario Premier's Council on Health Strategy, builds on the pioneering work of the Lalonde report by carefully examining the factors in the social environment that affect health status. These factors include early childhood experience, hierarchical positions at work, workplace hazards, employment status, family and friendship supports, and environmental factors. The report stresses the difference, as does the Lalonde report, between health and health care. While universal access to health care helps those who become ill, it does little to reduce overall disparities in health status. The report also emphasizes that a healthy lifestyle is not solely a matter of individual choice.

In the final selection Raisa Deber provides a concise survey of the political, legal, and economic dimensions of the Canadian health care system. She corrects a number of misconceptions about the operation of the system and examines the economic pressures impinging on it, along with various alternatives being adopted to deal with those pressures. Deber is optimistic that Canada will be able to preserve a health care system that is "both popular and, in general, highly successful."

Conclusion

What does the future hold for our understanding of health and health care in Canada? Perhaps the next transformation of the concept of health will be caused by genetics. Patricia Baird, a medical geneticist and chairperson of Canada's Royal Commission on New Reproductive Technologies, is convinced that "as a society we need to change our view of disease as an outside enemy — and find a new way of thinking about illness" (Baird 1990, 203). She argues that it is "too simplistic" to regard the determinants of health as external because there is a major internal determinant of disease: "Far from being a rare cause of disease, genetic factors are a very important determinant of health or illness in developed countries" (Baird 1990, 203–204). Abby Lippman, on the other hand, deplores what she calls the "geneticization" that such a view promotes (Lippman 1993). Lippman argues that there is no objective and value-free conception of health and illness, and she is concerned about the consequences of emphasizing the genetic contribution to disease:

> I worry about giving genes prominence in contemporary constructions of health and disorder because social, political and ethical claims will be quite different when a condition is seen as a failure of our genes rather than a failure, for example, in providing essential resources for health (Lippman 1993, 53).

Given all the genetic research that is under way, how we construe the notions of genetic health and genetic disease will be a major influence on our health care system (see Chapter 10 for more on this matter).

Perhaps the most that can be said about the Canadian health care system is that it will be substantially different in the twenty-first century. The shape it assumes will depend crucially on whether our commitment to the egalitarian values in the Canada Health Act, values that symbolize both our mutual dependency and our solidarity, remains steadfast, or whether our altruism succumbs to the combined forces of economics and individualism.

References

Baird, P.A. 1990. Genetics and health care: A paradigm shift. *Perspectives in Biology and Medicine*, 33:203–13.

Callahan, Daniel. 1973. The WHO definition of "health." *Hastings Center Studies*, 1(3): 77–87.

Canada Health Act, R.S.C., 1985, c. C-6.

Dossetor, John B. 1994. Can a charitable foundation give good health care? *Bioethics Bulletin*, 6(2): 9–10.

Kieser, Doris M. 1994. The squeeze of health care from hospital to home: The impact on Women. *Bioethics Bulletin*, 6(2): 1–3.

Lalonde, Marc. 1974. *A New Perspective on the Health of Canadians*. Ottawa: Government of Canada.

Lippman, Abby. 1993. Worrying — and worrying about — the geneticization of reproduction and health. In *Misconceptions: The Social Construction of Choice and the New Reproductive and Genetic Technologies*, Gwynne Basen, Margrit Eichler, and Abby Lippman, eds., 39–65. Hull, Que.: Voyageur Publishing.

---

12   Achieving Health for All

Jake Epp

Canada has built a strong health care system and has achieved for its people a level of health of which we are all proud. We want to continue in this tradition. While it is true that the prospects for health of the average Canadian have improved over recent decades, there nevertheless remain three major challenges which are not being adequately addressed by current health policies and practices:

- disadvantaged groups have significantly lower life expectancy, poorer health and a higher prevalence of disability than the average Canadian;
- various forms of preventable diseases and injuries continue to undermine the health and quality of life of many Canadians;
- many thousands of Canadians suffer from chronic disease, disability, or various forms of emotional stress, and lack adequate community support to help them cope and live meaningful, productive and dignified lives.

The times in which we live are characterized by rapid and irreversible social change. Shifting family structures, an aging population and wider participation by women in the paid work force are all exacerbating certain health problems and creating pressure for new kinds of social support. They are forcing us also to seek new approaches for dealing effectively with the health concerns of the future. . . .

. . . In the past, when infectious disease was the predominant cause of illness and death, health was defined in terms of the absence of disease. By the mid 1900s, however, we had reduced the incidence of many of these infections, and health had come to mean more than simply not being ill. It was now defined as a state of complete physical, mental and social well-being. In 1974, a federal publication entitled *A New Perspective on the Health of Canadians* put forward the view that people's health was influenced by a broad range of factors: human biology, lifestyles, the organization of health care, and the social and physical environment in which people live. This representation of the factors contributing to health legitimized the idea of developing health policies and practices within a broader context.

Today, we are working with a concept which portrays health as a part of everyday living, an essential dimension of the quality of our lives. "Quality of life" in this context implies the opportunity to make choices and to gain satisfaction from living. Health is thus envisaged as a resource which gives people the ability to manage and even to change their surroundings. This view of health recognizes freedom of choice and emphasizes the role of individuals and communities in defining what health means to them.

Viewed from this perspective, health ceases to be measurable strictly in terms of illness and death. It becomes a state which individuals and communities alike strive to achieve, maintain or regain, and not something that comes about merely as a result of treating and curing illnesses and injuries. It is a basic and dynamic force in our daily lives, influenced by our circumstances, our beliefs, our culture and our social, economic and physical environments. . . .

. . . As we broaden and deepen our understanding of health, we begin to perceive with greater clarity the importance and magnitude of the challenges now looming in the field of health. . . .

Challenge I: Reducing Inequities

The first challenge we face is to find ways of reducing inequities in the health of low- versus high-income groups in Canada.

There is disturbing evidence which shows that despite Canada's superior health services system, people's health remains directly related to their economic status. For example, it has been reported that men in the upper income group live six years longer than men with a low income. The difference is a few years less for women. With respect to disabilities, the evidence is even more startling. Men in upper income groups can expect 14 more disability-free years than men with a low income; in the case of women, the difference is eight years.

Among low-income groups, people are more likely to die as a result of accidental falls, chronic respiratory disease, pneumonia, tuberculosis and cirrhosis of the liver. Also, certain conditions are more prevalent among Canadians in low-income groups; they include mental health disorders, high blood pressure and disorders of the joints and limbs.

Within the low-income bracket, certain groups have a higher chance of experiencing poor health than others. Older people, the unemployed, welfare recipients, single women supporting children and minorities such as natives and immigrants all fall into this category. More than one million children in Canada are poor. Poverty affects over half of single-parent families, the overwhelming majority of them headed by women. These are the groups for whom "longer life but worsening health" is a stark reality.

So far, we have not done enough to deal with these disparities. As we search for health policies which can take this country confidently into the future, it is obvious that the reduction of health inequities between high- and low-income groups is one of our leading challenges.

Challenge II: Increasing the Prevention Effort

Our second challenge is to find new and more effective ways of preventing the occurrence of injuries, illnesses, chronic conditions and their resulting disabilities.

Prevention involves identifying the factors which cause a condition and then reducing or eliminating them. Immunization and the chlorination of drinking water are prime examples of measures introduced to prevent and reduce the incidence of infectious disease. In the last century, through the efforts of public health, the practice of prevention gained wide acceptance. In fact, many prevention measures we take for granted today were initiated during the 19th century.

In recent years, the preventive effort has been extended into the area of individual lifestyle and behaviour. The realization that smoking, alcohol consumption and high-fat diets were contributing variously to lung cancer, cirrhosis of the liver, cardiovascular disease and motor vehicle accidents, led us to turn our attention to reducing risk behaviour and trying to change people's lifestyles.

Unfortunately, the causal relationships between behaviour and health are not nearly as clear-cut as they are between "germs" and disease. Today's illnesses and injuries and the disabilities to which they give rise are the result of numerous interacting factors.

This means that prevention is a far more complex undertaking than we may at one time have imagined.

In spite of this, there is considerable scope for prevention. Already, children have been among the main beneficiaries. In prenatal and neo-natal care, preventive measures have brought about a marked reduction in infant mortality. Notable progress has also been achieved in preventing learning disabilities, and preventive measures are helping, for example, to overcome the difficulties associated with dyslexia, hyperactivity and speech and hearing impairments. With regard to adults, it is estimated that the use of preventive measures can lead to a future 50 per cent reduction in the incidence of lung cancer and heart disease.

Challenge III: Enhancing People's Capacity to Cope

In this century, chronic conditions and mental health problems have replaced communicable diseases as the predominant health problems among Canadians in all age groups. Our third challenge is to enhance people's ability to manage and cope with chronic conditions, disabilities and mental health problems.

Conditions such as arthritis, hypertension, respiratory ailments, dependence on drugs and chronic depression can all limit people's capacity to work, to take care of themselves, to perform the activities of daily living and to enjoy life.

Canada is experiencing an "age boom", and the number of older people in this country will more than double within the next thirty-five years. Thus, for Canada's older population, coping with chronic conditions and the disabilities to which they give rise, is a particular concern. It is often hard for those seniors who are incapacitated by disabilities to function independently. Everyday tasks, such as taking a shower or opening a jar, become difficult or even unmanageable.

It is particularly important to ensure that people are supported in the area of mental health. Obviously, we cannot afford to diminish our efforts to assist those who are suffering from serious mental illness; however, it is essential that we assign equal priority to helping people remain mentally healthy.

Surveys indicate that many Canadians find their lives stressful. Women are more vulnerable in this regard. The fact that women are prescribed tranquillizers and anti-depressants more than twice as often as men is a telling sign of the emotional strain women are experiencing. For some, it may be the changing and uncertain nature of their role that is unduly stressful. Others may be overwhelmed by the burden of caring for family members, particularly those who are chronically ill or disabled. For both men and women, job burnout is taking an increasing toll. The changing nature of social roles and factors such as unemployment have also had a bearing on the emotional well-being of men, who may encounter health problems including ulcers, dependence on alcohol and depression.

We know that anxiety, tension, sadness, loneliness, insomnia and fatigue are often symptoms of mental stress which find expression in many forms, including child abuse, family violence, drug and alcohol misuse and suicide. Problems associated with mental stress may occur in times of crisis, or be the result of accumulated life circumstances.

Our challenge is to provide the skills and the community support needed by people with disabilities and mental health problems if they are to manage effectively, lead stable lives and improve the quality of their lives. We must also recognize the importance of ensuring that informal care-givers have access to the support they need. Many people, especially women, care for others on a regular basis. The health and capacity of these individuals to manage is no less important than the health of those for whom they care. Homemakers, home care nursing, respite care and postal alert are services which enhance the coping capacity of both those with disabilities and their care-givers.

Reducing inequities, widening the prevention effort and enhancing people's ability to cope are the principal challenges confronting us as Canada enters the 21st century. It is toward these challenges that we must dedicate our efforts and resources.

---

13   Nurturing Health

Ontario Premier's Council on Health Strategy

At the turn of the 20th century, public health measures were widely recognized as important health safeguards. But in the following decades — indeed for most of this century — health became almost entirely equated with curative medicine.

More recently, an increasing number of Canadians are beginning to realize the fundamental importance of social and physical environments to individual health. . . .

The 1974 publication of the internationally-acclaimed federal report *A New Perspective on the Health of Canadians*[1] represented an important milestone in the evolving concept of health.

The federal report identified the central importance of health care organization, social and physical environments, lifestyle and behaviour. But the Lalonde report, as it is known, did not speak to the differences in social environment between the various subgroups in society. The social environment of the poor, for instance, is clearly different from that of the middle class which is different from that of the wealthy.

Universal access to quality medical care is an important principle in Canadian society. Canada spends more on health care (on a per person basis) than any other industrialized country with national health insurance.[2] But the availability of high quality medical care does not mean there is equal access to health, which remains an unevenly distributed resource. And some countries have better overall health, as measured by length of life, than we do.[3]

To understand disparities in health status and to formulate policies to improve health, Canadians must also recognize that a healthful lifestyle is not just a matter of individual choice.

In Ontario, as in Canada, the health of the population as measured by mortality (death) and morbidity (disease) is expressed as health status within each income group. People in lower socio-economic groups experience worse health and die sooner than people in middle income groups, who in turn experience worse health and die sooner than individuals in higher income groups. While universal access to medical care can help people who become ill, it has little effect on differences in health status between income groups.[4]

- A baby born to parents living in a poor neighbourhood in an Ontario city in 1986 was twice as likely to die in infancy as a baby born to parents living in a wealthy neighbourhood.[5]
- In 1986, a poor man in urban Ontario would live, on average, 5.3 years less than a rich man, while a poor woman would live 1.8 fewer years than a rich woman.

These gradients in health status are rooted in the social environment. Children born to parents in lower socio-economic groups, for instance, are more likely than those in higher socio-economic groups to have low birth weights, to have difficulty in school, to eat less wholesomely, and to drop out of school.

Although the biggest difference in health status is found between the top group and the bottom group, the largest group affected is the middle classes.

A growing body of national and international research has identified a long list of important factors in the social environment that influence the health status of in-dividuals. As this report will show, these factors include: early childhood experience; hierarchical positions at work; workplace hazards; family and friendship support; em-ployment status; and environmental factors.

This report focuses on a review of the research on the health effects of these factors which, while sometimes admittedly broad and general-sounding, are measured by the specific and unequivocal yardsticks of mortality.

It is clear to this committee that public policy has a vital, active role to play in providing, and equalizing, the opportunities for optimal health. . . .

A Framework on the Determinants of Health

I. Introduction to the Concept

Attitudes to health have been dominated by a viewpoint that equates health status with the availability of physicians and hospitals. This belief is reflected in the size of the current health care industry which represents the largest cluster of economic activity in all modern states.[6]

This popular myth, which could be described as a "thermostat" model of illness, has hampered wider consideration of the meaning of health. As a framework for understanding the determinants of health, it is limited to a focus on departures from health (illness) and the corresponding health care system.

In this perspective, the causes of ill health to a person are like cold and wind to a house: they are external factors that public policy cannot control. The only possible response, then, is to attempt to diminish illness by "turning up the furnace" — by putting more money into the health care system, and specifically into treatment.

The problem is, there does not appear to be an optimum temperature. Rather, the furnace is fueled by "unmet needs" and the belief that "more is always better" as well as many other factors.[7] Health is also influenced by many other elements. In fact, we know that there is no simple, positive relationship between spending on formal health care and the population's health status. There is growing concern in all developed countries regarding the cost of health care.

This "thermostat" idea has led to the current situation where medical care, hospital care, laboratory tests and prescription drugs absorb most of our attention and money when it comes to addressing poor health. In Canada, this stems in part from the national origins of medicare which began as insurance to cover the costs of doctors and hospitals.

We know now that increased spending on formal health care in developed economies is not having a corresponding positive impact on health status. At the same time, there is growing evidence that population health status may be significantly influenced by measures taken outside the formal health care system.

Clearly, a broader framework than the "thermostat" model is needed — one that reflects a wider range of relationships among the determinants of health.

Recently, health has come to be closely associated with individual lifestyle.[8] Unhealthy activities, such as smoking, are often referred to as self-imposed risks resulting from individual choice. This attitude, when not accompanied by a recognition that much behaviour is socially-derived, sets the scene for blaming the victim.

It is important to consider the nature of "choice" in these "personal decisions." As American public health expert Nancy Milio notes:

> . . . people with lesser incomes are forced to choose among fewer alternatives for coping. Thus a greater share of them turn to what is at hand — alcohol, cigarettes, food — all economically accessible in an affluent society if substituted for other things. And they turn most to the least costly (cigarettes) or most available (excess calories).[9]

When health is not viewed strictly as an individual matter, and the links between health and social environment are openly acknowledged, it becomes possible to think about the problem of poor health in a different light. As a result, different policy issues can emerge.

Our society has also become accustomed to unnecessarily high levels of measurable hazard in the human-built physical environment. Much can be done, for instance, to reduce air pollution, traffic fatalities and occupational illnesses. To fuel reform, we must demonstrate that many of the accidents that people have come to accept as inevitable are in fact preventable and that system-wide changes can improve the physical environment and our health. . . .

II. Social Environment and Health: The Research

Wide disparities in health status are not unique to Canada and the relationship between characteristics of the social environment, socio-economic status and health is not a new discovery. Canadian and international research is underscoring the role that various social and economic factors play in determining people's health. The research has been broken down into five categories: health services; work hierarchy; unemployment; social networks; and prenatal/early childhood.

1) Health Care   Because of its vital role in improving ill health, effective medical treatment is an important determinant of health. Its very success, however, has resulted in a tendency for the public to overestimate medicine's contribution to health. Practising doctors frequently express frustration about how they are usually able to treat only the symptoms, not the causes, of ill health. They are acutely aware of the impact of the social environment on health and yet cannot tackle the problem directly.

Today, there is limited scope for effective medical intervention with many of the leading causes of death. While there are a few new effective treatments for particular types of cancer, primarily in children, for instance, there has been little overall improvement in the last 20 years in the outlook for people suffering from the most common forms of cancer.[10]

The mortality rate for cardiovascular disease, the largest cause of premature death in Canada, has fallen steadily in the past 25 years.[11] But researchers have concluded that medical intervention is responsible for only a small portion of this improvement. They suspect that factors such as changes in social environment and in individual behaviour (such as smoking and eating habits) explain much of the remaining decline in death rates.

2) Work Hierarchy and the Organization of Work   A study of the British civil service[12] reveals noteworthy mortality differences for most causes of death between four classes of male civil servants. Over the period studied, those in the lowest grade died at three times the rate of those in the highest grade.

The study findings are all the more noteworthy because none of the employees was living in poverty, and all had good job security. They all worked in the same location (London) and were not exposed to industrial hazards.

The biggest gap was for lung cancer, chronic bronchitis and other respiratory disease, which are all strongly smoking-related. The extent of smoking differed markedly between the civil service grades. The study showed that 29 per cent of the top grade civil servants smoked, compared to 68 per cent of the bottom grade.

This gradient in smoking behaviour raises the question of how this behaviour is a product of the social environment. The study also found, however, that non-smoking lower grade civil servants had higher death rates due to chronic heart disease and other causes (not including cancer) than their higher grade counterparts.

Another British study concluded that the organization of work, and in particular the freedom to make decisions, are the basis for the strong link between social class and heart disease.[13] Reviewing international research, the authors found that the lower the "decision latitude" at work, the higher the proportion of smokers. Examining the links between social class and chronic heart disease on an international level, and considering the evidence from the civil service study, the researchers suggest that:

above a threshold of poverty, position on the social hierarchy per se may be a more important determinant of health and disease than material conditions.

This study also noted that while blood pressure rates were similar between high grade and low grade male civil servants in Britain while at work, the rates fell much more for upper grade men than for lower grade men when they were at home.

Latitude in decision-making is only one of the important factors in the organization of work that impacts on health. Workplace social support, as measured by the number and quality of interaction with co-workers, also has an effect on health. Health is also affected by the stress related demands of a job such as the pace of work, the frequency of deadlines and reporting requirements.[14]

A recent study of Swedish workers examined the health effects of work control and social support on work stress and cardiovascular disease. Cardiovascular disease occurred most often among those in high demand jobs, with a low level of both work control and social supports.[15]

3) Unemployment   Research on the health effects of unemployment has been conducted at both a population level (where variations in the rates of unemployment are linked to variations in official mortality and morbidity figures) and on a smaller scale and case study basis.

A Danish study on unemployment and mortality found a significantly higher death rate — between 40 and 50 per cent higher — among the unemployed than the employed. The study, which covered the decade from 1970 to 1980, found increased mortality from all the five major causes of death, especially from suicide or accidents. In areas of the country with higher overall unemployment rates, the relative death rate among the unemployed was lower.

Increased mortality among the unemployed was interpreted to be a consequence of two factors: health-related selection (those who were unemployed because they were sick) and increased susceptibility associated with the psychosocial stress of unemployment.[16]

A review of the research on unemployment and health completed for the World Health Organization (WHO) found that:

> high levels of unemployment and economic instability cause a significant increase in the levels of mental ill health and also have adverse effects on the physical health not only of the unemployed but also of their families and the community in general.[17]

The WHO review stated that research into the experience of unemployed people has "consistently shown that unemployment of more than a few weeks' duration causes physiological stress. This may in turn lead to an increase in blood pressure and heart disease."

Using data from the 1978 Canada Health Survey, one Canadian study found that:

The unemployed reported significantly more psychological distress, anxiety, and depressive symptoms, disability days, activity limitation, health problems, hospitalization and visits and telephone calls to physicians than did the employed.[18]

Lower-income unemployed people reported more anxiety and depressive symptoms than higher-income unemployed.

More recently, a preliminary analysis of Statistics Canada's 1989 General Social Survey found that the unemployed and those in insecure full-time employment reported lower health and life satisfaction than the employed in secure jobs. . . .

Other studies have supported the view that unemployment or the threat of unemployment is a major stress factor. And the "stress response as such (i.e. elevated blood pressure, elevated blood lipid levels etc.) plus stress-related behaviour (i.e. weight gain, smoking etc.) are both risk factors in the pathogenesis of cardiovascular disease."[19]

The majority of doctors in a Swedish study felt that unemployment led to certain disease symptoms and an increase in the demand for medical care. When the doctors were asked what measures should be taken to improve health, they gave highest priority to measures to defeat unemployment.[20]

4) Social Networks   Researchers in the United States have found a clear link between social support networks and death rates, suggesting that social relationships (or the lack thereof) constitute a major risk factor for health.

A study done in California found that, for both men and women, the more social contacts people had, the lower their mortality rate.[21] The study established four categories from least to most social connections. It found that for men 60 to 69 years old the death rate among those with the least connections was four out of 10 compared to two out of 10 for those with the most connections. Comparable figures among women were three out of 10 and one out of ten.

Overall, men with the least number of social contacts are more than twice as likely to die as their same-age counterparts having many contacts. For women, those with the least contacts are almost three times as likely to die at a given age.

It has long been known that married people live longer than unmarried people. A link between widowhood and higher rates of illness and death is similarly well established. The California study also found, however, that a variety of social and community ties influence death rates.

Subsequent research in the United States and elsewhere has confirmed the California results,[22] leading to the observation that social relationships may rival the effects of well-established health risk factors such as smoking, blood pressure, obesity and physical activity.

5) Prenatal/Early Childhood Conditions   Research also shows that prenatal and early childhood conditions have a clear impact on health.

The way in which children are cared for at an early age can influence their coping skills — and, by association, their health — not only for the rest of their childhoods but also for their entire lives.

A recent review of the research on early childhood interventions by the Ontario Ministry of Community and Social Services concludes that primary prevention projects for children can be successful.[23] The review recommends integrated programs of services to families and children because:

> . . . the close association between poverty and risk holds for every component of risk — from premature birth to poor health and nutrition, from failure to develop warm, secure, trusting relationships early in life to child abuse, from family stress to failure to master social skills. Programs aimed at any one risk will be helpful, but since the risk factors interact, programs aimed at multiple risk factors should produce greater, more stable and longer term effects.

The report warns that it is an illusion to believe that "single, simple, relatively inexpensive, one-shot programs can produce long-term positive advantages for economically disadvantaged children."[24]

However, prenatal programs to prevent low birth weight babies (LBW, 2500 grams or less) can produce unambiguous, long-term positive advantages.[25] LBW is a known risk factor for mortality and disease and Canada has a higher rate of LBW babies than countries such as Norway, France, Japan and Sweden.[26]

LBW babies have a 40-times-greater chance of dying during the first four weeks of life than do newborns whose birth weight is higher.[27] As well, among LBW babies there is a greater prevalence of neurological deficits, congenital abnormalities, and retarded development.[28]

Research shows a strong relationship between lower socio-economic status and the risk of having a LBW baby. A Montreal study[29] found that a high incidence of LBW babies is also associated with a mother's age (under 20 or 35 or older), level of education (less than 11 years), and marital status (unmarried). There is evidence that intervention can reduce the incidence of infant mortality and LBW babies.

A key intervention to prevent LBW babies is improved nutrition for the mother. In the United States, the Special Supplemental Food Program for Women, Infants and

Children (WIC) found that food supplements were instrumental in reducing the incidence of LBW and premature babies.[30]

Some studies point to interventions, and to family and individual characteristics, which may at least partially offset the harmful effects of poverty on the physical and mental health of the children.

The American Perry Preschool Program[31] is one of the most important in a series of preschool projects that provided the empirical basis for "Head Start" and other early childhood programs.

The Perry Preschool Program involved five groups of children who were followed until age 19. Poor youngsters were randomly assigned to either an enriched preschool program or to a control group. In early childhood, those in the enriched program demonstrated higher intellectual performance than the control group. In elementary school, the same group showed better scholastic placement and achievement.

By adolescence, those from the enriched pre-school program had a lower rate of delinquency, a higher rate of high school graduations and a higher rate of employment. As well, those from the enriched program had comparatively less drug abuse and a lower teenage pregnancy rate.

It should be noted, however, that these programs, as part of an American policy, provide early childhood programs to a very limited number of eligible disadvantaged children. With improved accessibility, early childhood programs may go a long way to offset the harmful effects of poverty on the physical and mental health of children.

III. Physical Environment and Health: The Research

Any planning for health must address the importance of both the human-made and the natural environment.

We recognize that the boundary between the physical environment can become blurred because of the complex interaction of the two. For the purposes of this report, however, physical environment is defined as structures or conditions that can be physically altered.

In some cases, policy options with respect to the physical environment are more obvious than those pertaining to the social environment. On the other hand, the "blind spots" that prevent policy makers from recognizing the need for reform can be formidable obstacles.

A myriad of environmental factors influence health. For the sake of brevity we have chosen to highlight three that we believe have significant, and readily understandable, health effects.

1) Occupational Health   Adults who work outside the home spend about one-quarter of their life in the workplace, yet many have little choice about, or control over, their work setting.

Workplace injuries and occupational illness exact a large toll in terms of diminishing the health of workers, yet many workplace injuries and illnesses are preventable. A recent study from the Organization for Economic Co-operation and Development (OECD), however, notes that occupational injury rates in Canada rose by about one-third from 1955 to 1987.[32] During the same period, rates declined by half in France, Germany and the United Kingdom and by one-third in Sweden, Austria and Belgium.

In Ontario in 1988 alone, 293 people lost their lives due to occupational illness or injury and more than 215,000 lost-time claims were made to the Workers' Compensation Board (WCB).[33] The latter figure understates injury and illness since some workplace accidents go unreported to the WCB.

2) Motor Vehicle Injuries   Motor vehicle accidents are the third leading cause (after cancer and heart disease) of potential years of life lost in Canada.[34] (This measurement looks at years of life lost before age 75, which is not the average life expectancy, so that deaths at earlier ages are seen to result in a greater loss of life.) Yet for years, officials concerned with health paid scant attention to the thousands of lives lost, and injuries caused, by motor vehicle accidents.

In Ontario, motor vehicle accidents are the leading cause of death for people aged 15 to 24 years old, and the second major cause of death (after suicide) for people 25 to 34 years old.[35]

In 1987, 1,229 people died in Ontario motor vehicle accidents and 121,089 were injured.[36]

People concerned about road safety are particularly frustrated by the fact that governments do not promote or adopt measures known to be effective in preventing injury. Leon Robertson of the epidemiology department at Yale University notes:

> One can ask in almost any community and find where the local 'dead man's' curve is located. What is not so easily found are public officials who understand that there are remedies, such as enhanced perception of curvature, energy absorbing guardrails, and removal of rigid objects . . . The attitude too often seems to be that human beings who are not perfect deserve the death penalty.[37]

Robertson notes that the maximum speed capacity of most vehicles is twice the maximum legal speed limit and that "such capability is contrary both to goals of safety and fuel economy."[38]

Transport Canada estimates that about 70 per cent of Canadian drivers and passengers use seat belts[39] and that if this level were pushed to 95 per cent by 1995, some 13,000 fatalities and 340,000 injuries could be avoided over a 20 year period.[40]

Federal officials note that West Germany, the United Kingdom and parts of Australia have already achieved 95 per cent compliance with seat belt laws.[41] They add, however, that for Canada to reach that level requires enforcement and persuasion on a scale not yet seen in this country.

3) Air Pollution   The devastating effects of air pollution have been underscored recently by revelations from Eastern Europe, where enforcement of standards has been extremely lax.

In Upper Silesia, a highly industrialized region of Poland, residents suffer from 15 per cent more cases of circulatory disease, 30 per cent more cancer, 47 per cent more respiratory problems, 100 per cent more diabetes and 100 per cent more liver disease deaths than the national average, according to a World Bank study and to reports from local health officials.[42]

In the West, where air pollution has been more vigorously controlled, the health effects are nonetheless discernible. A study of southern Ontario, for example, found a consistent link during the summer between hospital admissions for respiratory illness, the temperature, and the levels of sulphate and ozone in the air.[43]

While standards for outdoor air pollution have existed for many years, attention has shifted recently to the importance of indoor air pollution, since most individuals spend 75 to 90 per cent of their time indoors, in residence or public buildings.[44]

Research has shown, for instance, that one-third of non-smokers' lung cancer deaths are caused by exposure to the smoking of other people (so-called passive smoking). This public health risk is "larger than the hazardous air pollutants from all regulated industrial emissions combined."[45]

IV. Individual Responses (Psychoneuroimmunology)

There is growing evidence that mental health influences physical well-being although the exact pathways and the biological mechanisms are not yet clear. Animal experiments show a direct linkage between the central nervous system and the immune system. It appears that soluble factors, often referred to as cytokines, enable the central nervous system to communicate with the immune system.[46]

Psychological factors, which work through the central nervous system, may well influence the body's host defence system, perhaps through making peoples' vulnerability to disease depend on the state of the body's immune system.

There is clear evidence, for instance, of immune suppression in recent widowers and clinically depressed people. Recently widowed people also have a higher death rate than married people of the same age[47] (see Social Networks).

A Stanford University study of cancer deaths shows the importance of psychological factors in human disease.[48] Among women with serious breast cancer, those who engaged in supportive group psychotherapy lived, on average, one and a half years longer than those in a control group who did not have the psychotherapy. Both groups underwent standard medical therapy.

The psychiatrist who conducted this research, Dr. Spiegel, cautions that therapy may have led to better compliance with doctor orders; but clearly, something about being in these groups helped these women live longer.

This relationship between psychological factors and the immune system may be a key to explaining health outcomes related to income, unemployment, work hierarchy, span of control and social support.

V. Productivity, Wealth and Health: The Research

In his pioneering work *The Modern Rise of Population*,[49] Thomas McKeown showed that the dramatic decline in mortality from infectious diseases from the early 1800s to the middle 1970s could not be wholly, or even primarily, explained by medical interventions or public health measures.

Instead, he attributed 70 to 75 per cent of the gain in life expectancy to factors associated with the increased prosperity that resulted from the industrial revolution. It is thought that improved nutrition was the major influence.

Today, the firmest data on health determinants link health status to income. There is a strong correlation, for instance, between income and life expectancy in Canadian males.[50]

But income data are really a proxy of socio-economic status. It is not money itself, but the conditions, opportunities and amenities provided by money that are important to health.

1) Social Rank and Health   Canadian data indicate a clear link between socio-economic status and health status.

In the Canada Health Promotion Survey of 1985, people surveyed were asked to rate their own health, activity limitations and happiness. A recently published special review of the survey data found that:

> For persons aged 25 to 64, health status and quality of life are clearly lowest among the poor, those with little education, the unemployed and persons whose main activity is keeping house, while they

are highest among the rich, the university educated, and those employed in professional/managerial occupations. This confirms other studies (which show) . . . the poorer you are, the less healthy you are likely to be, over a shorter lifetime.[51]

Researchers Russell Wilkins and Owen Adams created a measurement of health called "health expectancy" based on 1978 data on mortality, long-term institutionalization and disability.[52] Their work showed that men in the top 20 per cent income bracket live on average six years longer than those in the bottom 20 per cent income bracket, and can expect 14 more years of life free of activity restriction.

For women, the comparable figures are three years, and an additional eight years of life free of activity restriction. The data also show that while women have longer life expectancies than men, that longer life is also subject to greater health limitations.

More recent research using Canada Pension Plan data found that the more a man earns in the 10 to 20 years before retirement, the longer he is likely to live. The study found a remarkable association between men's life expectancy at age 65 and their average annual income when they were age 42 to 64.

The disparity in life expectancy is striking: men in the bottom five per cent in earning in the two decades before retirement were twice as likely to die by the age of 70 than men in the top five per cent.[53]

British research indicates that the relative health inequalities between occupational classes persist over many decades, even though the causes of death have changed significantly.[54]

A recent Canadian study points to similar conclusions.[55] An update of research based on 1971 data of mortality rates in Canadian urban areas found that relative mortality (lowest compared to highest) between income groups narrowed only slightly in the 15 years between 1971 and 1986.

This study also showed that, over the 15-year time span, certain causes of death became more prevalent, some remained the same, and others declined as causes of death. (Deaths from lung cancer increased, for example, there was no change in deaths from breast cancer or alcoholism, and deaths due to infectious diseases declined.)

Together, the British and Canadian research seems to indicate that if certain diseases known to be associated with lower income groups were eliminated, the socio-economic differential would express itself through some other diseases.

This observation should not serve as an argument against tackling particular diseases that afflict those groups. It does suggest, however, that a disease-specific approach to health inequalities is not, in itself, adequate. More generally, it suggests some overall greater vulnerability to a variety of specific ailments among poorer as opposed to wealthier people.

2) Social Policy and Health   While disease-specific responses to health inequalities are not likely to be sufficient in reducing these disparities, social policy can make an important difference. Some of the poorer, Less-Developed Countries (LDCs) have succeeded in keeping their population much healthier than other LDCs with much higher per capita incomes through conscious policies to reduce health inequalities.[56]

Among developed countries, the importance of political will is underscored by the fact that some studies show that citizens of countries with a narrow range between the top and the bottom income groups have longer life expectancy.

In particular, the life expectancy in Scandinavian countries, where governments have consciously used social policy to equalize opportunities, is higher than in countries with higher per capita incomes, such as the United States.

Evidence of an important link between life expectancy and the distribution of income among a country's citizens was apparent in research which used 1970 life expectancy figures. This research shows an overall higher life expectancy in developed countries with a narrow range between lowest and highest income groups than in countries with a wider gap. The Netherlands, Sweden and Norway ranked at the top of the heap for life expectancy and a narrow range between top and bottom income groups. The United States, Spain, West Germany and France were clustered together at the lower end of the spectrum. Canada, Australia, and the United Kingdom were all in the middle.[57]

3) The Economy and Health   In the above sections we examined the relationship between socio-economic status (income) and health, and the relationship between income distribution and health. Clearly the socio-economic well-being of a population is related to national prosperity, as well as public policy.

Equally, how much a nation can afford to spend on the quality of the social environment (and hence nurturing opportunities for health, as well as access to health care) is directly related to its ability to generate income.

Japan presents an interesting example of how income, income distribution, and national prosperity are linked to health status. In this case, however, superior population health status does not appear to correspond with the high levels of expenditure on health care we have come to expect.[58]

Japan appears to bear out the importance of prosperity to longevity. From a middle-of-the-road position in life expectancy in 1965, the Japanese soared to top place in 1987. During the same period, the Japanese economy also accelerated. By 1987, Japan ranked 4th in GNP per capita of OECD countries after Switzerland, the United States and Norway.[59]

Researchers who have considered the impact of health care, diet, organization of work and other factors on longevity, speculate that the large and rapid improvement in life expectancy is due to the marked success of the Japanese economy.

Japanese gains in life expectancy have been dramatic. In 1955, the life expectancy at birth for Japanese males was 63.6 years; by 1986 the comparable figure was 75.2. For Japanese women, the comparable figures over that period were 67.8 to 80.9 years.[60]

Data from Eastern Europe lend credibility to the hypothesis linking life expectancy to economic prosperity. During the 1970s, life expectancy actually *declined* in Hungary and Poland during a period of economic deterioration.[61]

Another important factor in the Japanese life expectancy story is the distribution of income. In a review of the data, British researcher Michael Marmot notes that Japan, "with the fastest rate of growth of any OECD country, has the smallest relative differences in income between the top and the bottom 20 per cent of groups,"[62] and goes on to consider how this fact might relate to Japan's life expectancy gains.

The foregoing gains were made while Japan remained a relatively low-cost nation in terms of medical spending. In 1987, Japan spent an estimated 6.8 percent of its GDP on health care as compared to 11.2 percent in the United States and 8.6 in Canada.[63]

It will be interesting to see whether Japan's success can be sustained over time. Nonetheless, there are practical, economic considerations for those prosperous developed economies with high levels of expenditure on health care and low to middle-of-the road population health status. . . .

Health care, as the largest single industry in modern societies, represents a major commitment of resources. While our health care system must be subject to continuous quality improvement, increased spending on formal health care is not having a corresponding positive impact on health status. Furthermore, overexpansion of the formal health care system could potentially have negative effects as it competes for resources with other health enhancing activities, and as it eats up a greater and greater share of the nation's wealth.[64]

In terms of our basic thermostat, how much heat is enough? How can resources be directed towards intentional public policies that influence the other determinants of health as described above? . . .

This concludes the discussion of selected research on the determinants of health.

The determinants have been presented within an overall framework that extends well beyond a traditional understanding of health as dependent on our health care system. The new framework allows us to consider the dynamic interplay of many other factors that common sense alone tells us are important. Based on accumulating research evidence, it is clear that it is essential to adopt a new framework for understanding health. The challenge of the future lies in using this knowledge to develop effective public policies that will ensure a healthy and prosperous Ontario.

Endnotes

1. Lalonde, Marc. *A New Perspective on the Health of Canadians*. (Ottawa: Government of Canada, 1974).

2. U.S. Department of Health and Human Services. *Health Care Financing Review: International Comparison of Health Care Financing and Delivery: Data and Perspectives*. (Baltimore: Health Care Financing Administration, Dec. 1989) p. 4.

3. D'Arcy, Carl. "Levelling the Playing Field", a paper presented to the National Symposium about Families July, 1989 in Regina. See figure 5: Average Life Expectancy by Gender for Selected Countries.

4. A new federal study show that, despite the increasing amounts of money spent on the formal health care system in the past 15 years, there has not been a significant change in the relative health status of different socio-economic groups in the country and in the province. See endnote 3 for reference.

5. This, and the example immediately following, are drawn from: Wilkins, Russell, Adams and Branckner. "Changes in Mortality by Income in Urban Canada from 1971 to 1986: Diminishing Absolute Differences, Persistence of Relative Inequality." Joint study by the Health Policy Division, Communications and Information Branch, Health and Welfare Canada and Health Division, Statistics Canada. In press.

6. Evans, Robert G. and Stoddart, Greg L. "Producing Health, Consuming Health Care", Population Health Working Paper, No. 6. Canadian Institute for Advanced Research. May 1990.

7. ibid

8. For instance, a recent survey by the Ontario Hospital Association found that most respondents ranked personal behaviour very highly as a determinant of health, while income was seen to be only a minor contributor. Also, see Lalonde, Marc *A New Perspective on the Health of Canadians*, cited in endnote no. 1.

9. Milio, Nancy. *Promoting Health Through Public Policy*. (Ottawa: Canadian Public Health Association, 1986) p. 75.

10. Bailer, J. and Smith, E. (1986) "Progress Against Cancer?" *New England Journal of Medicine*, 314 (1986): 1227.

11. Rachlis, Michael and Kushner, Carol. *Second Opinion, What's Wrong with Canada's Health-Care System and How to Fix it* (Toronto: Collins, 1989) p. 169–170.

12. Wilkinson, Richard ed. *Class and Health* (London: Tavistock, 1986).

13. Marmot, Michael and Tores Theorell. "Social Class and Cardiovascular Disease: The Contribution of Work." *International Journal of Health Sciences* vol. 18. no. 4, 1988.

14. Ham, J. *Work and Health*, presentation to the Annual Convention, Association of Workers' Compensation Boards of Canada, St. John's, Newfoundland, August 1, 1990.

15. Johnson J.V., Hall, E.M. Job Strain, Work Place Social Support and Cardiovascular Disease: A Cross-sectional Study of a Random Sample of the Swedish Working Population. *American Journal of Public Health*, vol. 78, no. 10, October 1988, p. 1336–1342.

16. Iverson, Lars, Otto Anderson, Per Kragh Andersen et al. "Unemployment and mortality in Denmark, 1970–80." *British Medical Journal*, Vol. 295 (Oct. 10, 1987), p. 879–884.

17. Wescott, G. et al. (eds). *Health Policy Implications of Unemployment*. (Copenhagen: World Health Organization, 1985) p. 3.

18. D'Arcy, Carl. "Unemployment and Health: Data and Implications" *Canadian Journal of Public Health*, vol. 77, supplement 1, May/June 1986.

19. Swedish Government (HS 90 The Swedish Health Services in the 1990s) "Unemployment and Health," p. 17.

20. ibid

21. Berkman, Lisa and Leonard Syme. "Social Network, Host Resistance, and Mortality: A Nine-Year Follow-up Study of Alameda County Residents." *American Journal of Epidemiology*, vol. 109, no. 2, 1979.

22. House, James et al. "Social Relationships and Health" Science, vol. 241, p. 540–545, July 29, 1988.

23. "Better Beginnings, Better Futures: An Integrated Model of Primary Prevention of Emotional and Behavioral Problems." Ontario Ministry of Community and Social Services, Queen's Printer for Ontario, 1989.

24. ibid, p. 107.

25. Milio, Nancy. *Promoting Health Through Public Policy*. (Ottawa: Canadian Public Health Association, 1986) p. 21.

26. *The Health of Canada's Children: A Canadian Institute for Child Health Profile*. (Ottawa: The Canadian Institute of Child Health) 1990, p. 95 and p. 102.

27. Pelchat, Yolande and Wilkins, Russell. "Report on Births: Certain Sociodemographic and Health Aspects of Mothers and Newborns in Region 6A (Metropolitan Montreal) 1979–1983". (Montreal Association of Community Health Departments of Metropolitan Montreal (RDSCMM), April, 1987).

28. ibid

29. ibid

30. Lisbeth B. Schorr with Daniel Schorr. *Within Our Reach, Breaking the Cycle of Disadvantage*. (New York: Doubleday, 1988) p. 128, 129.

31. Berrueta-Clement, John et al. *Changed Lives, The Effects of the Perry Preschool Program on Youths Through Age 19*. (Ypsilanti, Michigan: High/Scope Press, 1989).

32. *The OECD Employment Outlook*. (Paris: The Organisation for Economic Co-operation and Development, 1989) p. 146.

33. Workers' Compensation Board. *Statistical Supplement to the 1988 Annual Report*, (Toronto: Worker's Compensation Board, 1989) p. 4–5.

34. Statistics Canada. *Causes of Death*, no. 84203, 1986.

35. From 1986 figures compiled for the Ministry of Transportation. For those 15 to 19 years old, motor vehicle accidents accounted for 41.1 per cent of deaths, followed by suicides, which accounted for 15.4 per cent. For ages 20 to 24 the comparable figures are 37.9 (MVA) and 18.3 (suicide), while for 25 to 34 years olds the figures are 21.6 (suicide) and 18.7 (MVA). For all age groups, MVA account for 1.6 of deaths, taking seventh place after leading causes such as cardiovascular disease, cancer and respiratory ailments.

36. According to the Ministry of Transportation reporting is behind schedule in Ontario due to changes in the way police reporting is recorded, which took effect Jan. 1, 1988.

37. Robertson, Leon S. "Behavioral and Environmental Interventions for Reducing Motor Vehicle Trauma," *Annual Review of Public Health*, p. 13–34, 1986.

38. ibid

39. *Transport Canada Road Safety*, no CL9001, February 1990.

40. Personal communication with John Lawson, Chief of Evaluation and Data Systems, Road Safety Branch, Transport Canada, 1990.

41. United States Department of Transport. National Highway Traffic Safety Administration. *Effectiveness of Safety Belt Use Laws: A Multinational Examination*. DOT document no. HS807018, October 1986.

42. Figures cited in article "Poland's Deadly Air," by Larry Tye, in The Toronto Star, Jan. 14, 1990. The article is a reprint from the Boston Globe.

43. Bates, David V. and Sizto, Ronnie. "Air Pollution and Hospital Admission in Southern Ontario: The Acid Summer Haze Effect," *Environment Research*, vol. 43, p. 317–331, 1987.

44. Leibowitz, M.D. "Health Effects of Indoor Pollutants". *Annual Review of Public Health*, vol. 4, p. 203–221, 1983.

45. Repace, J.F. "A Quantitative Estimate of Nonsmokers' Lung Cancer Risk from Passive Smoking," *Environment International*. vol. 11. p. 3–22, 1985.

46. Dantzer, Robert and Kelley, Keith W. "Stress and Immunity: An integrated view of relationships between the brain and the immune system." *Life Sciences*, vol. 44. p. 1995–2008, 1989.

47. Rees, W.P., Lutkins, S.G. "Mortality of Bereavement", *British Medical Journal*. 4:13–16, 1967.

48. Barinage, Marcia. "Can Psychotherapy Delay Cancer Deaths?" *Science*. vol. 246. October 1989.

49. McKeown, Thomas. *The Modern Rise of Population* (New York: Academic Press, 1976).

50. Wolfson, Michael et al. "Earnings and

Death — Effects Over a Quarter Century." Canadian Institute of Advanced Research, internal document #60, May 1990. (Toronto: CIAR, 1990).

51. Wilkins, Russell. "Special Study on the Socially and Economically Disadvantaged." Ottawa: Health and Welfare Canada. 1988.

52. Wilkins, Russell, and Adams. *Healthfulness of Life.* (Montreal: Institute for Research on Public Policy, 1978) p. 96.

53. Wolfson, Michael, et al. "Earnings and Death — Effects Over a Quarter Century" cited in endnote no. 48.

54. Black, D., Morris, J., Smith, C. and Townsend, P. *Inequalities in Health: The Black Report.* (New York: Penguin Books, 1982).

55. Wilkins, Russell, Adams, and Branckner. "Changes in Mortality by Income in Urban Canada from 1971 to 1986" cited in endnote no. 5.

56. For example, Sri Lanka, with a per capita income of $320 (U.S. 1982) has an infant mortality rate of 32 per 1,000 live births. Oman, on the other hand, had a per capita income of $6,090 but an infant mortality rate of 123. See Caldwell, John C., "Routes to Low Mortality in Poor Countries." *Population and Development Review*, vol. 12, no. 2. June 1986.

57. Wilkinson, Richard G. ed. *Class and Health.*, cited in endnote no. 12.

58. In 1987, in U.S. dollars, Japan spent $915 per person on health care. The same year, the United States ranked at the top in terms of per person spending on health care ($2,051) with Canada, at $1,483 ranking second. Cited in U.S. Department of Health and Human Services. *Health Care Financing Review: International Comparison of Health Care Financing and Delivery: Data and Perspectives*, cited in endnote no. 2.

59. Marmot, Michael and Smith, George Davey. "Why are the Japanese Living Longer?", *British Medical Journal*, vol. 299, p. 1547–1551, December 23–30, 1989.

60. ibid

61. Hertzman, Clyde. "Poland: Health and Environment in the Context of Socioeconomic Decline", HPRU 90:2D. Health Policy Research Unit, University of British Columbia, Vancouver, 1990.

62. Marmot, Michael and Smith, George Davey, "Why are the Japanese Living Longer?", cited in endnote no. 59.

63. U.S. Department of Health and Human Services. *Health Care Financing Review: International Comparison of Health Care Financing and Delivery: Data and Perspectives*, cited in endnote no. 2.

64. See Evans, Robert G. and Stoddard, Greg L., "Producing Health, Consuming Health Care". Cited in endnote 6.

14 Canadian Medicare: Can It Work in the United States? Will It Survive in Canada?

Raisa B. Deber

I. Introduction

Canada's system of universal health insurance, which, in a probable effort to confuse Americans, we call Medicare, is both popular and, in general, highly successful.[1] It combines relatively stable costs (admittedly at the high end for industrialized nations, but considerably less than the cost in the United States) with favorable health status measurements, universal coverage, and a high degree of public popularity. The Canadian model is a major point of pride for Canadians, and a model that is receiving increasing attention in the United States.[2] The system, however, is under increasing strain within Canada.[3] That fact must not rule out consideration of the Canadian model since many of the pressures are not unique to Canada. Rather, they are problems shared — to a greater or lesser degree — by most Western health systems, and include:

- increasing costs and an economy that may no longer be able to bear them;[4]
- the uncertain relationship between increased spending for medical services and improvements in health status;[5]
- the efficiency and effectiveness of existing delivery systems;[6] and
- responsiveness to consumer needs and demands.[7]

Therefore, a proper evaluation of the merits of the Canadian system focuses on its comparative ability to respond to seemingly universal problems. Of course, other issues are more idiosyncratic to Canada, particularly the impact of its constitutional crisis. . . .[8]

II. What Is the Canadian Health Care System?

Canada's health care system has been widely reported, and misreported, in the current U.S. debate about health care policy. Consider these excerpts from a speech given by former President George Bush:

The Canadian health care system, typical of a government-run national health care system, suffers from basic structural flaws that are bound to lead to long term problems with cost, access, and quality. . . .

Patients must endure long lines and wait for surgery and access to advanced technology. High quality care is rationed by limiting physician access to new, life-saving technologies. In British Columbia, for example, it takes an average of 6 months to get a coronary bypass, 3.5 months to get a tonsillectomy, 4 months to get a hysterectomy. For speedy and quality care, many Canadians simply go to the United States.

Neither providers nor consumers have incentives for efficiency or to control costs. Under Canada's National Health Care System, costs are growing faster than in the United States.

Instead of making their own choices, consumers under the Canadian model are forced to rely on government bureaucrats to make their health care choices.

A Canadian-style plan would require from $250 billion to $500 billion a year in new taxes.[9]

If this and similar alarms were accurate, few would advocate imposing such a flawed system on anyone. Fortunately, they are not. Canada's system indeed has its flaws, but they are not precisely those indicated by Mr. Bush's speechwriters.

First, it must be noted that Canada does not have a "government-run national health care system," but rather a series of provincial health insurance plans that work within a set of broad national standards. This is a direct consequence of the 1867 British North America Act, Canada's Constitution. This Act placed most of health care under provincial jurisdiction.[10] As a result, the Canadian health care system is essentially a series of provincially managed insurance plans that must comply with federal guidelines in order to obtain federal resources. Therefore, a Canadian-style plan in the United States would entail a series of state-run plans, rather than a single plan directed from Washington.

However, Canadian provinces vary greatly in size and fiscal capacity, as do American states. Accordingly, Canada's federal government became involved in providing revenues to the provinces through a variety of programs. "Fiscal federalism" has become an important component of most policy fields in Canada. In health care, its role has been crucial.[11]

The federal role in health care started with a series of special purpose grants for public health programs and hospital construction. Canadian Medicare began in the late 1950s with the Hospital Insurance and Diagnostic Services Act ("HIDS"),[12] which cost-shared provincial insurance for hospital-based services on the condition that the provinces comply with a series of national conditions. By 1961, all provinces and territories had set up participating plans. In 1966, the Medical Care Act[13] cost-shared physician services, and all provinces enacted participating plans by 1971. Although the 1977 Federal-

Provincial Fiscal Arrangements and Established Programs Financing Act ("EPF")[14] altered the funding formula away from cost sharing to a mixture of tax points and block funding,[15] the requirement to comply with the national conditions remained and was reinforced in the 1984 Canada Health Act.[16]

To receive federal cost sharing, these Acts specify that provincial plans must comply with a set of "national standards," often referred to as the "pillars of Medicare." They require that all provincial plans contain the following five elements:

1. *universal coverage* for all eligible residents. Narrow exclusions are provided for individuals otherwise covered, such as members of the military.
2. *comprehensive coverage* for all medically required hospital and physician services. This includes office visits and preventive care as well as drugs and diagnostic testing provided to inpatients. Most provinces also provide coverage for other sectors and services (particularly outpatient and home-based services, mental health and public health), although such services are not required under the federal legislation and, hence, are not considered "insured services" under Medicare.
3. *accessibility*. The definition of "reasonable access" in the Canada Health Act includes a prohibition of any direct charges for insured services, and, therefore, does not allow co-payments or deductibles for physician or hospital care.[17] In contrast, many of the provincial plans still use means tests and co-payments for services they choose to provide that are not required under Medicare (for example, drugs, ambulance services, and long-term care).
4. *portable coverage* for insured services anywhere in Canada. This requirement is essential to coordinating a series of provincially-run plans.
5. *public administration*, which means that there is, at best, a minimal role for private insurance in covering services not included in Medicare, such as semi-private rooms, drugs, or dental care. . . .

Federal revenue sharing plays a critical role in the Canadian model. Because significant fiscal disparities often exist across regions, federal cost sharing is essential to ensuring the provision of a uniform level of services nationwide. In fact, much of the current ferment over Canadian Medicare is traceable to the federal government's efforts to curb its budget deficit by reducing its commitment to revenue sharing. This has been accomplished by shifting the financial burden to the provinces through a series of unilateral alterations to the cost sharing formula. . . .[18]

. . . Canada's system is not a national health care system in two senses of the word "national." First, the system is not run by the national government, but by the provinces.[19]

Second, unlike the situation that prevailed in the United Kingdom until its recent reforms, service delivery remains private and patients have a free choice of providers. Government bureaucrats do not make health care choices in Canada. To the contrary, Canadian consumers arguably have more freedom of choice than their counterparts in the United States.[20]

Indeed, it is precisely this free choice that has led to the waiting list problem on which American critics of Canada's system like to focus. Because Canadian Medicare is not national, it is difficult to evaluate the truth about waiting lists, but the consensus is that the problem is severely overstated by American commentators.[21] In general, investigations demonstrate that much of the problem is attributable to a lack of coordination among providers, rather than a lack of resources.[22] In a private delivery system, each provider keeps its own waiting lists. Patients are likely to be on many lists, with popular providers oversubscribed at the same time that colleagues have openings. Without considerable excess capacity at every institution or a good system of coordination, bottlenecks are certain to arise.

The waiting list problem is also due in part to the fact that Canadian institutions are sometimes slow to respond to changes in practice patterns. In both British Columbia and Ontario, for example, the highly publicized problem of waiting lists for cardiac procedures appears to have arisen in part because of a shift in practice patterns — in particular, an increased rate of procedures performed in the over sixty-five population — that was not factored into demand estimates by the institutions providing those services. A combination of efficiency-enhancing maneuvers and modestly increased capacity essentially resolved the problem. In Ontario, physicians agreed on explicit case-selection criteria and a centralized registry was formed. Patients still had the option of waiting for the clinician of their choice, but physician-set triaging criteria ensured that urgent cases did not wait, while those anxious for surgery were made aware of available resources.[23]

Critics who allege that Canada has insufficient technology also fail to recognize inherent differences in the Canadian and American approaches to health care. A widely cited study by Dale Rublee has been used by some to argue that there is insufficient technology in Canada when compared with the United States by contrasting the number of units available for certain procedures, rather than the number of actual procedures performed.[24] In most provinces, however, deliberate government policies have restricted the number of available units. Consequently, Canadian units operate at far higher volumes than is the case in the United States, but procedure rates do not vary greatly between the two countries.[25] Many believe that restricting certain procedures to "centers of excellence" not only secures better outcomes,[26] but also may help avoid the overutilization of services that is frequently criticized in the United States.[27] Although precise evaluation is again hampered because the decentralized systems of private delivery in Canada do not, for the most part, keep centralized records, those studies that have examined numbers of procedures have concluded that Canadian patients are generally not denied access to possibly beneficial procedures.[28]

III. Consequences of the Canadian Model

Like all advanced, industrialized countries, Canada is experiencing cost pressure in its health care system. However, while Canada's system is expensive, it is far less so than the United States's.[29] A 1991 General Accounting Office ("GAO") Report suggests that the administrative savings from a single-payer model would probably generate enough resources to enable the extension of coverage to all Americans.[30] There is also substantial unmeasured savings in the Canadian system. Canadian have full coverage, with no co-payments or deductibles for insured services. In general, they do not have to receive a bill unless they desire semi-private hospital accommodations or a television set in their room. Accordingly, patients need not deal with the paperwork burden of dealing with the claims process.

Administrative simplicity also benefits providers and payment agencies. Most provinces have chosen to pay their hospitals on the basis of prospective global budgets. This reimbursement mechanism provides an excellent lever for macro-cost control. Moreover, Canadian hospitals typically require only very small accounting departments, which devote much of their time to dealing with American patients.

Most physicians are paid fee-for-service on the basis of a fee schedule that is negotiated between the provincial medical association and the provincial government. As the disadvantages of such a volume-driven practice have become more evident, however, efforts to cap total physician payments are underway in many provinces.[31] Still, Canadian doctors face far lower administrative costs than their American counterparts.[32] They need only deal with one payer and one set of forms, which the provinces are moving rapidly to computerize.

Another advantage for physicians and their patients is a higher degree of clinical autonomy than currently exists in much of the United States. Unlike American insurance companies, the provincial health insurance plans have made little effort to micro-manage clinical decisions.[33] In general, Canadian doctors do not have to cope with outside utilization review. Those processes that are in place are typically established within institutions by medical staff simply to help them manage their caseloads.

Since most providers "accept assignment" (or, in Canadian terms, are "opted in"), payment agencies have the much simpler task of sending monthly checks to providers, rather than reimbursing individual patient claims. Accordingly, their administrative costs are extremely low in international terms.[34] However, administrative simplicity also has disadvantages. Most obviously, there is a major impact on insurance companies and people seeking white-collar jobs; if no one has to fill out a form, no one need be hired to process it. More problematic is a comparative absence of management information, which, in turn, may hamper efforts to measure and improve the managerial efficiency of providers. Global budgets are relatively insensitive to cross-institutional differences in efficiency. At present, however, considerable efforts are being made to improve information systems, albeit on a voluntary basis, through such efforts as the Management Information System Project. . . .[35]

A global budget provides only a "macro" control mechanism. The major cost containment tool available to payment agencies is curbing that global budget, typically by giving increases below the rate of inflation. The task of deciding *how* to curb expenditures is left to providers. Thus, the Canadian government has operated in the pious hope that providers will curb unnecessary care and ensure that resources available to them are used cost-effectively. To some extent, Canadian providers have responded with voluntary efforts, such as rationing services within a region.

Nevertheless, there are few incentives for system-wide efficiency in the Canadian model. Taking an extreme example, it is unlikely that an institution will voluntarily choose to close its doors and transfer its programs elsewhere. Given a guaranteed global budget, there are no fiscal pressures that force it to do so. Accordingly, hospital closures are extremely rare in Canada, in marked contrast to recent experience in the United States.[36] This does have advantages, since it not only keeps facilities running at high occupancy rates, but also maintains access to care in rural and inner-city areas. Undeniably, inefficiencies remain in Canadian health care delivery that are not easily addressed within the current system. That has led some provincial governments to look more intensely at regional solutions and other mechanisms for altering service delivery patterns.[37]

Another disadvantage of existing Canadian funding mechanisms is that, by avoiding micro-management, the government might also find it difficult to distinguish between efficient and inefficient organizations. Continued fiscal restraint may lead to "death by a thousand cuts," with negative effects on both innovation and quality of care. A countervailing force is the continued popularity of Canadian Medicare. Any threats (real or imagined) to quality or accessibility evoke strong public opposition. The media have worked as a strong "watchdog" in this respect. However, if the current recession continues, there is a danger that locally instituted cuts may lead to gaps in service availability. Public fear of poorer quality may eventually lead to support for a "supplementary" private sector for those willing to pay more. In general, Canadian health policy experts are firmly opposed to any such developments. . . .[38]

V. The Current Health Care Debate within Canada

One never truly solves a problem, but merely replaces one set of problems with another.[39] The policy issue, then, is which set of problems one prefers. Having solved the access dilemma, Canada now faces another challenge: the problem that medical care has limits to its ability to improve health. What is termed the "determinants of health" perspective makes evident that additional investments in medical care do not necessarily lead to commensurate increases in health status. Indeed, the opportunity costs of foregone investments in education or regional development may, by increasing poverty, actually diminish health status.[40]

Consequently, all Canadian provincial governments are currently trying to curb health care costs without sacrificing what most agree is an excellent system. A number of alternatives are being tested. One is an effort by some provinces to exploit government's monopsony power through increasingly tough fee and budget negotiations, which, in turn, has led to confrontations with physicians.[41] Another is an increased emphasis on quality assurance and appropriateness.[42] In an effort to get "more bang for the buck," some provinces are trying to restructure institutions and encourage a more extensive rationalization of services. Others contemplate regionalization as a mechanism for shifting responsibility for maintaining a budget to another level of government. A major constraint on all of these activities is the popularity of Canada's health care system and public uneasiness with what is termed "two-tier" medicine. Here, the United States stands as a constant "evil example" of what can happen if Canadian Medicare is allowed to erode.

The real risk, though, is that it is always easier to shift costs than to cut them. The simplest mechanism, from the viewpoint of government, is to shift costs to the public. The Canada Health Act prohibits user fees for insured services,[43] so musing by provincial health ministers and premiers about the merits of a "modest" user fee has come to nothing. Nevertheless, there have been some minor efforts to de-insure services that appear not to be medically necessary (e.g., sterilization), or do not qualify as insured services in the first place (e.g., drug benefits and vision care). There is also musing about (if not much action on) shifting financing by making heavier use of "hidden" taxes, such as premiums or payroll taxes. In sum, although overall costs are up, it appears that proportionately less of them are now being borne by government.[44]

It must be recognized that Canada has not responded to higher costs by shedding people from coverage. This is in marked contrast to the United States, where current estimates place the number of uninsured at nearly fourteen percent.[45] Comparative cost figures must be weighed in that light.

Ironically, Canada's success in Medicare has highlighted the issue of how much good medicine can do. The simplest answer, of course, lies in the appropriateness movement, for it is difficult to quarrel with a desire to eliminate care that will not lead to improved health outcomes. At present, for example, Canadian governments and providers are paying at least rhetorical tribute to the concepts of "Continuous Quality Improvement," although it remains to be seen whether its potential can in fact be realized.[46] There is also a great need to shift to more effective delivery systems that de-emphasize institutions and physicians in favor of community-based care, produce curative care in favor of prevention, and use a narrow definition of health in favor of a recognition that health has many determinants, few of which are under the control of the health care system.[47]

In the final analysis, it is not clear how much these trends can do, or how much they will save, although there is clearly considerable scope for improving both quality and cost-effectiveness. Prevention has limits.[48] A person who did not die at age sixty from lung cancer may become an elderly person who needs expensive, long-term care. A patient treated at home might never have been admitted to an institution in the first place.[49] At some point, Canada, like all other nations, will have to make tough choices regarding how much care it wishes to deliver.

As a result, the future is likely to include major conflicts between nondiscrimination and sensitivity to the individual, on the one hand, and cost-effectiveness, on the other. As one example, in 1992, the Toronto newspapers reported a controversy arising from the birth of an infant with Down's syndrome and multiple medical problems, and the parents' fury that their child was not given a heart transplant. The hospital claimed that, in its view, the child was too ill to benefit. To the parents, this amounted to discrimination on the basis of handicap. A similar dilemma has confronted Oregon's attempt to ration care on the basis of purported impact on quality of life, which the Bush Administration said violated the Americans with Disabilities Act of 1990.[50]

This issue of limits will arise in many arenas. One clear example is human resources planning. Does Canada have too many doctors? If so, how can numbers be controlled without wasting highly skilled labor or discriminating against immigrants who wish to practice their profession? What are appropriate pay levels for unionized employees, including nurses? If pay is lower in the community than in hospitals, can wages be cut as care is shifted out of institutions?

Most analysts hope that Canadian governments can resist the politically tempting route of avoiding reform and just shifting costs to the private sector. That strategy is likely to raise the amount spent on medical care without improving the health of the population. If the Canadian economy recovers, it is likely that a combination of luck, political will, and the outcomes-appropriateness movement will help Canada preserve what most agree is an excellent system.

Notes

1. See Sharmila L. Mhatre & Raisa B. Deber, *From Equal Access to Health Care to Equitable Access to Health: a Review of Canadian Provincial Health Commissions and Reports*, 22 Int'l J. Health Serv. 645, 645 (1992). For further discussion of citizen satisfaction, see Robert J. Blendon et al., *Satisfaction With Health Systems In Ten Nations*, Health Aff., Spring 1992, at 185; Robert J. Blendon & Humphrey Taylor, *Views On Health Care: Public Opinion In Three Nations*, Health Aff., Spring 1989, at 149.

2. *See, e.g.*, General Accounting Office, Report to the Chairman, House Comm. on Gov't Operations, Canadian Health Insurance: Lessons for the United States (1991) [hereinafter GAO Report]; Robert G. Evans. *We'll Take Care of It For You: Health Care In the Canadian Community*. Daedalus, Fall 1988, at 157; Robert G. Evans, *Split Vision: Interpreting Cross-border Differences In Health Spending*, Health Aff., Winter 1988, at 17; Morris L. Barer & Robert G. Evans, *Interpreting Canada: Models, Mindsets and Myths*, Health Aff., Spring 1992, at 44, 45–46; Robert G. Evans, *U.S. Influence On Canada: Can We Prevent The Spread Of Kuru?*, in Restructuring Canada's Health Services System: How Do We Get There From Here? 143, 145 (Raisa B. Deber & Gail G. Thompson eds., 1992) [hereinafter *U.S. Influences On Canada*]: David U. Himmelstein & Steffie Woolhandler, *Cost Without Benefit: Administrative Waste In U.S. Health Care*, 314 New Eng. J. Med. 441, 445 (1986); Steffie Woolhandler & David U. Himmelstein, *The Deteriorating Administrative Efficiency Of The U.S. Health Care System*, 324 New Eng. J. Med. 1253 (1991) [hereinafter *Deteriorating Administrative Efficiency*].

3. See George K. Bryce, *Medicare On The Ropes*, 82 Can. J. Pub. Health 75 (1991). For suggested reforms, see Raisa B. Deber, Regulatory and Administrative Options for Canada's Health Care System, (Aug. 27, 1991) (unpublished manuscript prepared for The Health Action Lobby ("HEAL"), on file with the *American Journal of Law and Medicine*).

4. *See* Canada Department of Finance, Cost Of Government and Expenditure Management Study: Review of Federal and Provincial Cost-Containment Initiatives (1992) [hereinafter Ottawa Report]. *See also* British Columbia Royal Commission on Health Care and Costs, Closer to Home: Summary Of the Report of the British Columbia Royal Commission on Health Care and Costs 10–11 (1991) [hereinafter Closer to Home].

5. This argument was popularized by Victor R. Fuchs. *See* Victor R. Fuchs, Who Shall Live? Health, Economics, and Social Choice 6 (1974). *See also* Robert G. Evans & Greg L. Stoddart, Producing Health, Consuming Health Care 23–28 (May 1990) (Centre for Health Economics and Policy Analysis Working Paper No. 90–6, on file with the *American Journal of Law & Medicine*); Michael Rachlis & Carol Kushner, Second Opinion: What's Wrong with Canada's Health Care System and How to Fix It 4, 17–18 (1989).

6. *See, e.g.*, Closer to Home, *supra* note 4, at 15, 19–20; Rachlis & Kushner, *supra* note 5, at 4–5.

7. Richard B. Saltman & Casten von Otter, Planned Markets and Public Competition: Strategic Reform in Northern European Health Systems 81–82 (1992).

8. As described below in Part II, Canada's health care system is heavily intertwined with federal–provincial relations and, as such, is vulnerable to any constitutional

changes in the distribution of power among levels of government. Deber, supra note 3, at i.

9.   Press Release, President Bush's Plan for Comprehensive Health Care Reform (Aug. 2, 1992) (on file with the *American Journal of Law and Medicine*).

10. Can. Const. (Constitution Act, 1867) pt. VI (Distribution of Legislative Powers), § 92(7). Canada was established as a loose confederation of 4 provinces. The British North America ("BNA") Act of 1867, now known as the Constitution Act, 1867, set up an organizational structure for the new nation and divided powers between the provincial governments and the new national (federal) government in Ottawa. *See generally id*. The BNA Act assigned all matters of national concern, plus those endeavors likely to be costly, to the federal government, which had the broadest tax base. *Id*. § 91. Ottawa was given jurisdiction over such items as railways, canals, coinage, and, in the health area, quarantine, marine hospital, and health services for native peoples and the armed forces. *Id*. The provinces were given authority for those local concerns thought to be relatively inexpensive — including roads, education and "[t]he Establishment, Maintenance and Management of Hospitals, Asylums, Charities, and Eleemosynary Institutions in and for the Province, other than Marine Hospitals." *Id*. § 92(7). Municipal governments were given only such powers as the provinces would delegate to them. The federal role in health policy was, thus, formally limited to: (1) those few activities specified in the BNA Act (for example, health services for the armed forces, residents of the territories, and the native population, and powers over quarantine); and (2) the "health protection" concerns of food and drug safety, deemed to be under federal jurisdiction through its criminal law, trade and commerce, and "peace, order and good government" powers. *See* Peter W. Hogg, Constitutional Law of Canada 476–77 (3d ed. 1992).

11. *See, e.g.*, Malcolm G. Taylor, Health Insurance and Canadian Public Policy 381, 415 (1987); Eugene Vayda & Raisa B. Deber.

The Canadian Health-Care System: A Development Overview, in Canadian Health Care and the State: A Century of Evolution 125, 127 (C. David Naylor ed., 1992).

12. Hospital Insurance and Diagnostic Services Act, ch. 28. § §4, 5(2), 1956–1957 S.C. 155 (Can.).

13. Medical Care Act, R.S.C., ch. M–8, § §2, 5 (1970) (Can.).

14. Federal–Provincial Fiscal Arrangements and Established Programs Financing Act, ch. 10, 1976–1977 S.C. 301 (Can.), renamed by the Federal–Provincial Fiscal Arrangements and Federal Post-Secondary Education and Health Contributions Act, R.S.C., ch. F–8, §4 (1985) (Can.).

15. See Alistair Thompson, Financing Health Care 17 (Aug. 30. 1991) (unpublished manuscript, on file with the *American Journal of Law and Medicine*). Under the formula used for HIDS and the Medical Care Act, provincial governments received matching funds from the federal government for "shareable" expenditures, although the formula included provisions (e.g., using national cost data), which meant that federal payments amounted to slightly more than 50 percent of the costs of the poorer provinces. EPF altered the formula so that provinces would no longer have to compute eligible expenditures. Instead, the federal government divided its contribution into two pieces: (1) a direct grant, which became part of provincial general revenues; and (2) the federal lowering of federal tax rates for personal and corporate tax, which allowed provincial governments to increase their tax rates without increasing the total tax burden. The payments would increase, indexed to population growth in GNP. Subsequent unilateral decisions by the federal government to reduce the growth rate have meant that an increasing proportion of the transfer arises from the imputed value of the tax points. It is estimated that, if current trends continue, the cash portion of federal revenue-sharing will completely disappear within two decades. Michael Rachlis, The Impact of the 1991 Federal Budget on Health Care, Public Health Programs and the Health Status of Ontario Citizens 3 (May

8, 1991) (unpublished manuscript, on file with the *American Journal of Law and Medicine*): Bryce, *supra* note 3. at 75–76: Mhatre & Deber. *supra* note 1. at 646–47, 652–53.

16. Canada Health Act. R.S.C., ch. C-6. § §7–13(1985) (Can.). The Canada Health Act replaced HIDS and the Medical Care Act and reaffirmed the terms and conditions that provincial plans must meet to receive federal funding under EPF. *Id.* § 32.

17. *See* S. Heiber & R. Deber. *Banning Extra Billing in Canada: Just What the Doctor Didn't Order*, 13 Can. Pub. Pol'y 62, 66–67 (1987).

18. Rachlis, *supra* note 15, at 3.

19. See *supra* note 10 and accompanying text.

20. For example, the prohibition of direct charges to patients for insured services means that managed care programs in Canada cannot "lock in" their patients. *See* Marianne Lamb et al., Managed Care in Canada: The Toronto Hospital's Proposed Comprehensive Health Organization 67–69 (1991). Indigent care is also not an issue in a system with universal coverage. Patients have free choice of providers, without any limitations based on income or insurance coverage.

21. A primary cause for Canadians' going to the United States arises from Canada's universal system. In general, providers attempt to give priority to those with the highest medical needs. This may, on occasion, disgruntle wealthier individuals whose health would not be impaired by waiting, but who find it more convenient to "jump the queue." If such individuals choose to go to the United States at their own expense to make use of their neighbor's underutilized facilities, most Canadians have not regarded this as a policy disaster. Other pressure points can arise in border communities with insufficient population to warrant specialized facilities. Since individuals in those communities must travel for care, they may often prefer to go the shorter distance. Windsor, Ontario is a classic example, since the Detroit hospitals just across the river have considerable excess capacity and have actually tried to attract Canadian patients. In our view, neither explanation constitutes a structural weakness of the Canadian model.

22. C. David Naylor, *A Different View of Queues in Ontario*, Health Aff., Fall 1991, at 110, 114 [hereinafter A Different View]; Rachlis & Kushner, *supra* note 5, at 60–61.

23. *A Different View*, *supra* note 23, at 110, 115–16.

24. See Dale A. Rublee, *Medical Technology in Canada, Germany, and the United States*, Health Aff., Fall 1989, at 178.

25. Geoffrey Anderson et al., *Hospital Care for Elderly Patients with Diseases of the Circulatory System: A Comparison of Hospital Use in the United States and Canada*, 321 New Eng. J. Med. 1443 (1989). For a comparison of admissions, length of stay, and costs between United States and Canadian hospitals, see Donald A. Redelmeier & Victor R. Fuchs, *Hospital Expenditures in the United States and Canada*, 328 New Eng. J. Med. 772 (1993).

26. *See, e.g.*, Robert G. Hughes et al., *Hospital Volume and Patient Outcomes*, 26 Med. Care 1057, 1067 (1988).

27. Theodore R. Marmor, *Commentary on Canadian Health Insurance: Lessons for the United States*, 23 Int'l J. Health Services 45, 57 (1993).

28. *See* Anderson et al., *supra* note 25, at 1448.

29. Robert G. Evans et al., *Controlling Health Expenditures: The Canadian Reality*, 320 New Eng. J. Med. 571, 571, 572 (1989) [hereinafter *Controlling Health Expenditures*] George J. Scheiber & Jean Pierre Poullier, *International Health Care Expenditure Trends*, Health Aff., Fall 1989, at 169, 172. *See generally* Health Care Systems. [For information on the higher economic efficiency of single-payer systems, see generally *Organization for Economic Co-operation and Development, Health Care Systems in Transition. The Search for Efficiency* (1990).]

30. GAO Report, *supra* note 2, at 6–7, 63.

31. See Charles J. Wright, *Physician Remuneration: Fee-for-Service Must Go, But Then What?*, in Restructuring Canada's Health Services System: How Do We Get There From Here?, *supra* note 2, at 35, 37–38; Morris L. Barer et al., *Fee Controls as Cost Control: Tales from the Frozen North*, 66 Millbank Q. 1, 25, 32 (1988).

32. *See Deteriorating Administrative Efficiency*, *supra* note 2, at 1253; GAO Report, *supra* note

2, at 39–41. The extent of administrative savings is a contentious issue; for obvious reasons, the private insurance industry has challenged these estimates, but the direction is clear.

33. *See, e.g.*, Carolyn Tuohy, *Conflict and Accommodation in the Canadian Health System*, in Medicare at Maturity 393, 406–07, 422–23 (Robert G. Evans & G. Evans & Greg L. Stoddart eds., 1986); Carolyn J. Tuohy, *Medicine and the State in Canada: The Extrabilling Issue in Perspective*, 21 Can. J. Pol. Sci. 268, 294 (1988).

34. *See Controlling Health Expenditures, supra* note 29, at 472–73.

35. The Management Information System Project is a cooperative effort to determine standards for hospital information systems.

36. *See, e.g.*, Ross M. Mullner et al., *Rural Community Hospitals and Factors Correlated with Their Risk of Closing*, 104 Pub. Health Rep. 315, 315 (1989) (noting that as many as 600 of the remaining 2700 rural hospitals in the U.S. appear likely to close).

37. *See* Mhatre & Debre, *supra* note 1, at 662–64.

38. *See U.S. Influences on Canada, supra* note 2, at 144.

39. Aaron Wildavsky, Speaking Truth to Power: The Art and Craft of Policy Analysis 58 (1989).

40. *See* Evans & Stoddart, *supra* note 5, at 54–56. *See generally* Ontario Premier's Council on Health Strategy, Nurturing Health: A Framework on the Determinants of Health (1991) (summarizing how social, economic, and environmental factors outside the health care system play key roles in our individual and collective well-being).

41. *See* Jonathan Lomas et al., The Price of Peace: The Structure and Process of Physician Negotiations in Canada 3 (Aug. 1992) (Centre for Health Economics and Policy

Analysis Working Paper No. 92–17, on file with the *American Journal of Law and Medicine*).

42. *See, e.g.*, Donald M. Berwick, *Continuous Improvement as an Ideal in Health Care*, 320 New Eng. J. Med. 53–56 (1989) [hereinafter *Continuous Improvement*]: see also Donald M. Berwick, Curing Health Care (1990).

43. Heiber & Deber, *supra* note 17, at 66–67.

44. Data provided by the Policy, Planning and Information Branch of National Health and Welfare, Canada, indicates that the proportion of national health expenditures borne privately had increased from 23.6% in 1975 to an estimated 27.8% in 1990. Health and Welfare Canada Policy, Planning and Information Branch, Health Expenditures in Canada Fact Sheets (1993) (Table I). National health expenditures as a proportion of GDP had increased from 7.2% to 9.4% in that same period. *Id.*

45. Felicity Barringer, *Florida Enacts Law Seeking Insurance for All Employees*, N.Y. Times, Mar. 26, 1992, at B12.

46. *See Continuous Improvement, supra* note 42, at 54.

47. Mhatre & Deber, *supra* note 1, at 662–63.

48. See Louise B. Russell, Is Prevention Better Than Cure? (1986) (discussing the limitations of prevention).

49. William G. Weissert, *Cost-effectiveness of Home Care*, in Restructuring Canada's Health Services System: How Dow We Get There From Here?, *supra* note 2, at 89, 91.

50. The Clinton Administration reversed this ruling, granting Oregon a Medicaid waiver that cleared the way for its rationing experiment, but with major revisions of the plan's details. Robert Pear, *U.S. Backs Oregon's Health Plan for Covering All Poor People*, N.Y. Times, Mar. 19, 1993, at A8.

Chapter 3
Questions to Consider

1. Is health care special? Should it be regarded as a right to which everyone is equally entitled? Or should it be a commodity subject to the pressures of supply and demand?
2. How much emphasis should a health care system give to prevention and health promotion? Is there solid evidence that prevention and health promotion efforts are effective?
3. How is the notion of quality of life related to the definition of health? In what ways, if at all, are value judgements involved in the definition of health?
4. Would "privatization" of health care in Canada be a desirable way of responding to economic pressures on the system? Or would it simply shift costs from the public sector to the private sector without bringing about necessary reforms? What moral arguments are there in favour of and against privatization?

Further Readings

Caplan, Arthur L., H. Tristram Engelhardt, Jr., and James J. McCartney, eds. 1981. *Concepts of health and disease.* Don Mills, Ont.: Addison-Wesley Publishing Company.

Decter, Michael B. 1994. *Healing Medicare.* Dartmouth, N.S.: McGilligan Books.

Downie, R.S., Carol Fyfe, and Andrew Tannahill. 1990. *Health promotion: Models and values.* New York: Oxford University Press.

Evans, R.G. 1992. The Canadian health-care financing and delivery system: Its experience and lessons for other nations. *Yale Law & Policy Review*, 10:362–96.

Fried, Charles. 1975. Rights and health care: Beyond equity and efficiency. *New England Journal of Medicine* 293:241–45.

Fulton, M. Jane. 1993. *Canada's health care system: Bordering on the possible.* New York: Fulkner & Gray.

Hoffmaster, Barry. 1992. Values in preventive medicine. *Canadian Family Physician* 38:321–27.

Iglehart, John K. 1986. Canada's health care system. *New England Journal of Medicine* 315:202–208, 778–84, 1623–28.

Leichter, Howard M. 1991. *Free to be foolish: Politics and health promotion in the United States and Great Britain.* Princeton: Princeton University Press.

Manga, Pran. 1993. Health economics and the current health care cost crisis: Contributions and controversies. *Health and Canadian Society/Santé et société canadienne*, 1:177–203.

Rachlis, M., and Carol Kushner. 1989. *Second opinion: What's wrong with canada's health care system and how to fix it.* Toronto: Collins.

Sutherland, Ralph W., and M. Jane Fulton. 1988. *Health care in Canada: A description and analysis of Canadian health services.* Ottawa: The Health Group.

Chapter 4

Resource Allocation and Rationing

Chapter 4

Introduction

Health care systems in countries around the world are under increasing financial pressure. In Canada, the effects of economic constraints are becoming progressively more apparent. Hospitals are closing or amalgamating and laying off staff. Some hospital services are now being provided on an out-patient basis, and the length of time patients stay in the hospital is being shortened, leading to the criticism that patients are discharged "quicker and sicker." Provincial ministries of health are removing items from their lists of insured services. Waiting lists for health care services are springing up or lengthening. Talk about the need to ration health care, to institute "user fees," or to make people pay for some services that are currently free is becoming more common.

The financial pressures come from several sources. One is the success of medicine over the last half-century. Medicine can now diagnose and treat a panoply of diseases, with the result that people live longer than they used to. In those extended life spans, however, other problems arise, often of a serious and chronic nature. Rather than reducing the demand for resources, the achievements of medicine have increased that demand.

Medicine's success is in large part a result of new technologies, many of which are expensive. Dr. Maurice McGregor, former dean of medicine at McGill University and current chair of a Quebec commission on technology and medicine, has emphasized the extent to which "modern medicine is composed of modern technology":

> . . . [U]ntil about 40 years ago, our health professions had virtually no cures to offer at all. The principal cost involved in health services was for the comfort and support of the sick, and this cost was relatively low because patients either recovered or succumbed fairly rapidly. The interventions that medicine could make in the course of disease were so slight that a doctor could carry almost all equipment of importance around in a little black bag (McGregor 1989, 119).

Dr. McGregor provides examples of the impact of technology on medicine. Forty years ago, for instance, all a doctor treating kidney failure could do was relieve discomfort until death occurred. Now there are dialysis and transplantation programs at a cost of about $20 000 per year. And forty years ago, doctors could only wait for death when signs of heart block developed in elderly patients. Now cardiac pacemakers, at a cost of about $5 000, can be installed. That these technological advances are beneficial and worth their cost is not being disputed. The point is simply that they have a cost, and as more technologies are introduced and more patients use them, the overall cost of health care escalates.

Another financial factor is demographic — the aging of the population. The proportion of older persons in Canada has been increasing and will continue to increase for several decades. So not only must more problems be treated as people grow older, but there are more older people to treat.

Finally, in times of economic recession, less revenue is available for all purposes, including health care.

If these trends continue, hard choices about what health care services society can provide will be required. But an initial difficulty that we encounter in trying to comprehend the debate about the allocation and rationing of health care resources is fundamental disagreement about the nature of the problem, or indeed whether there really is a problem. The suggestion that health care resources will have to be "rationed" is provocative and controversial. There are those who argue that health care resources have always been rationed in a multitude of ways. For example, anyone who has sat in a crowded waiting room or emergency department knows that a doctor's time is a scarce resource. In this view, recent trends merely extend and exacerbate problems that are as old as health care.

Nevertheless, there are those who regard talk about rationing as misguided and even dangerous. They believe that the total resources society provides for health care are adequate. The problem, as they see it, is that those resources are maldistributed and are used inefficiently and ineffectively. They point out that many of the health care services currently provided have never been proved to be effective. Removing inefficiencies, restricting funding to services that have been demonstrated to be effective, and reallocating resources would, in this view, alleviate the financial pressures. What the health care system needs, in other words, is rationalization not rationing.

Yet another view is that a reform of society's priorities would solve the problem. Redirecting the billions of dollars spent annually on researching and marketing new cosmetic products, for example, would in itself be enough to fund health care now and for years to come.

Difficulty in coming to terms with the dispute about allocation and rationing is compounded by the complexity of the health care system. Indeed, the mechanisms and procedures for the delivery of health care services are so complex and varied, and sometimes so disjointed, that they appear to lack the coherence, consistency, and co-ordination necessary to constitute a "system" at all. Decisions about the use of health care resources are made at a variety of levels. At the top of the hierarchy, the "macro" level, the federal and provincial governments have to decide how much money to allocate to health care as opposed to, say, education, defence, the environment, and social services. Provincial ministries of health then have to decide how to apportion the money assigned to health care. How much should go to acute care, long-term care, and prevention? How much to community-based and home care? How much to the salaries of physicians? How much to drug plans?

As well, decisions have to be made about which services will be covered by provincial health insurance plans. It is now possible, for example, to cure snoring with laser surgery. For some families snoring is so disruptive that they are willing to pay about $1 200 to have the operation performed in a private clinic. One woman reports that her husband snored so loudly that he would wake up their teenage daughter sleeping in the next room; in fact, his snoring was so bad that even the cat wouldn't sleep with him (Taylor 1994). The operation is not covered by provincial health insurance, however. Why not? Is it because snoring is not a "medical" or "health" problem? Sometimes snoring is a sign of sleep apnea, a condition in which a person awakens briefly during the night, many times an hour, to gulp for air. The cause of sleep apnea is excess tissue in the back of the throat that prevents breathing. People who suffer from sleep apnea do not remember awakening, but they suffer from fatigue; moreover, the effort to breathe at night can impose a strain on their hearts, leading to cardiovascular disease. Perhaps snoring, or at least a certain kind of snoring, is a "medical" problem then. So is it not a sufficiently important problem for its treatment to be covered by provincial health insurance? How should decisions about which services to include in provincial insurance plans be made?

Even if a service is covered by a provincial insurance plan, that is not the end of the matter because questions about access to that service remain. The government also has to provide the capital and personnel funding necessary to offer that service. As well, accessibility can depend upon an evaluation of benefits. The Royal Commission on New Reproductive Technologies, for example, recommended that *in vitro* fertilization be an insured service, but the commission insisted that it not be provided to women with "unexplained infertility" because there is no evidence that it is beneficial in such circumstances (Royal Commission on New Reproductive Technologies 1993). In other countries, different limitations on access to *in vitro* fertilization have been proposed. Legislation under consideration in France, for example, would restrict access to in vitro fertilization to a woman and a man who had lived together for at least two years (Dorozynski 1994).

After "macro" allocation decisions have been made, institutions such as hospitals have to decide how to allot the global budgets they receive. How should funds be distributed across the many services and programs that a hospital provides? In a long-term care hospital, for example, how much money should go to chronic care, to rehabilitation services, and to palliative care? How much to social work, to physiotherapy, to occupational therapy, and to leisure and recreational programs? Directors or managers of programs and services then have to allocate their budgets. How many nurses does the unit need, for instance, and how should they be scheduled?

Finally, at the level of patient care, the "micro" level, a health care provider must decide how comprehensively to investigate a patient's problems and how aggressively to manage those problems. That decision has to be made in the context of the total group of patients for whom the health care provider is responsible. And how big is that group? Should health care providers think only about the welfare of their own patients or also about how resources could best be used for all patients in society? If the latter, they would be acting as "gatekeepers" to the health care system. Should they perform that function, particularly if it means not doing everything they might for their own patients?

The Selections

The first selection, by John Williams and Eric Beresford, reports the results of a survey of Canadian physicians who were asked to identify the health care resources that are in short supply and to describe how they deal with those shortages. The most critical problem in health care, according to these physicians, is the shortage of personnel, particularly nurses. Coping with scarce resources, the physicians recognize, forces them to address a conflict between their traditional loyalty to and advocacy for their own patients and their responsibility to be a "gatekeeper" of society's limited resources. Williams and Beresford emphasize the importance of considerations of justice in resolving questions about the distribution of scarce health care resources.

The two other selections discuss issues at the ends of the resource allocation hierarchy. Benjamin Freedman and Françoise Baylis discuss the "macro" allocation of health care resources. They recognize the need for a "demarcation principle," that is, a principle that would determine what services should be covered by provincial health insurance programs. They criticize what they call a "purposive" approach, one that attempts to use a definition of "health" or "health care" to decide what services are "medically necessary." A crucial problem for the purposive approach is that all attempts to define health are open to telling objections. As an alternative, they recommend a "functional" approach, one that asks instead whether a particular service would meet a demand that the health care system could satisfy efficiently. The advantages they see are that a functional approach is concerned with whether a service or procedure is good, worthwhile, and desired; it allows questions outside the realm of health care to be considered; and it requires that patients' perceptions of health care be understood and respected. Freedman and Baylis would not tackle the issue of paying for surgery for snoring, for example, by questioning whether it is medically necessary; instead, they would investigate the nature and seriousness of the problem and ask whether that problem is best dealt with by the health care system.

A continuing issue in the "micro" allocation of scarce resources concerns who should receive transplantable organs, particularly when they are lifesaving hearts or livers. George Annas distinguishes four major ways of making such tragic decisions: the market approach, the committee selection process, the lottery approach, and the customary approach. He outlines the strengths and weaknesses of each and argues for a combination of them that also incorporates significant public representation into the process.

Little has been written so far about allocation decisions at the intermediate, institutional level of the health care system. Recently there has been a call for developing a distinctive "hospital ethics" (Thompson 1992), but much work remains to be done in this area.

Conclusion

The issues that arise with respect to the allocation and rationing of health care resources involve fundamental theoretical questions about the nature of health and health care and fundamental ethical questions about the responsibilities of health care providers and the requirements of justice. The danger here is that, rather than guiding policies and decisions about allocation and rationing, ethical concerns will be swept aside in the economic rush to reduce deficits and promote efficiency.

References

Dorozynski, Alexander. 1994. France battles out bioethics bill. *BMJ* 308:290.

McGregor, Maurice. 1989. Technology and the allocation of resources. *New England Journal of Medicine* 320:118–20.

Royal Commission on New Reproductive Tech-nologies. 1993. *Proceed with Care*, vol. 1. Ottawa: Minister of Government Services Canada.

Taylor, Paul. 1994. Cutting Edge of Technology Used to Silence Snorers. *The Globe and Mail* Feb. 14, A1.

Thompson, Dennis F. 1992. Hospital ethics. *Cambridge Quarterly of Healthcare Ethics* 1:203–15.

15   Physicians, Ethics and the Allocation of Health Care Resources

John R. Williams & Eric B. Beresford

Introduction

As the gap between the demand for and the availability of health care resources grows wider, can physicians continue to abide by the injunctions of their codes of ethics "Do no harm" and "Consider first the well-being of the patient"? The physicians' role as advocate of the best interests of their patients, regardless of cost, conflicts with another role that they are often expected to fulfil, that of gatekeeper of society's scarce health care resources. The conflict between these roles can present ethical dilemmas for physicians as they try to balance their responsibilities to their patients, other patients in need of the same scarce resources, health care institutions, insurers, and society in general.

The conflict between the roles of the physician as patient advocate and as gatekeeper has become a topic of discussion for health care economists, sociologists, policy analysts, lawyers, ethicists and physicians.[1-9] However, relatively little attention has been given to the views of individual physicians. Since physicians control access to an estimated 80 per cent of health care expenditures,[1] their perceptions of the problems of allocation are an essential ingredient in any attempt to develop effective policies. We analyze the views of 25 Canadian physicians on this conflict of roles. We contend that the choice among these roles is a matter of ethics, and we present the main ethical considerations that should govern decisions. . . .

Current Shortages

According to the interview subjects, the most critical problem in health care, at least in hospitals, is the shortage of staff, especially nurses. This has adverse effects on the care given to patients: those needing emergency services and elective surgery are among the most disadvantaged. The main causes of the nursing shortage were identified as budget cutbacks, which have eliminated many nursing positions in the hospitals, and inadequate pay and status, which have driven many qualified nurses from their profession.

The nursing shortage leads to closure of hospital beds. A pediatrician reported that "we are funded for 212 beds but, because of the number of staff, we only operate at about 180. Presently, our staff shortage is such that we are really only at 140 to 150 beds. . . . Our burn unit tonight is closed: no staff."

A gynecologist commented "Because of the shortage at the present time, nurses are being pulled out of retirement without having appropriate upgrading, and nurses are being pulled in from other countries with rather uncertain standards. I can see the changes in our ward every day because the quality of care has changed for the worse. . . . Our laboratory staff including IV (intravenous) nurses and technicians are so rushed that mistakes happen more often, and as well they are unable to relate to the patients they are servicing. They treat their patients very much like objects."

Another example is the greater recourse to restraints for hallucinatory patients, especially during night shift: "Day shift can sometimes handle these patients without the application of restraints by manoeuvring and steering them in certain directions. When you have less staff on at night, they really do not have the option of managing things optimally and they resort more frequently to restraints" (psychiatrist).

The interview subjects complained that chronic patients occupy a large number of acute care beds — 10 to 20 per cent in one city — because there are so few chronic care facilities to which they can be discharged. Emergency departments are overcrowded because the wards are blocked, and since emergency cases generally have priority for acute care beds, elective admissions are postponed and waiting lists become longer. Even serious emergency cases cannot be guaranteed beds. According to a neurosurgeon, "Sometimes the restriction has been so great that the residents may spend nearly half their time in the emergency department trying to find other beds for patients in the town and trying to phone other residents on other services."

Residents, allied health practitioners, and some medical specialists were also mentioned as being in short supply. The strongest case for more personnel was made by those in charge of complex equipment. A radiation oncologist said, "I have a brand new machine sitting out there which one man gave $250,000 for last December 31. That machine is still in the box. I cannot take it out of there because I do not have the personnel to be able to use it." A diagnostic radiologist had a similar complaint: "I have not got the paid hours to operate my CT (computed tomography) scanner enough hours of the day. Here I have a $2,000,000 piece of equipment, and it should be operating at least 16 to 20 hours a day and I have difficulty operating it more than one shift because of the paid hours."

After personnel, the most often cited shortages are of equipment and tests. Physicians generally mentioned the same items of equipment in inadequate supply. These ranged from multi-million dollar radiological devices such as magnetic resonance imaging (MRI) scanners to dialysis machines to best quality plates, screws and prostheses for orthopedic surgery to more prosaic items: "Sure it would be nice to have our own scanner, but we cannot even get a photocopy machine to copy our medical reports" (psychiatrist). Some respondents had no problems with equipment; their requests for new pediatric monitors or dialysis machines had recently been answered. But others were discouraged by the fact that the annual hospital budget provided no more than 10 per cent of the amount that the medical staff had requested for new equipment.

The shortage of equipment and personnel results in limited access to tests. Waiting lists for CT scans were reported to be from five to eight weeks, and for MRI scans, up to one year. Some simple laboratory tests — screening for chlamydia was mentioned by a general practitioner — are not widely available because of government funding policies. Some tests are not done because of hospital budgetary restrictions: "For example, serum creatinine; we still do the creatinine but before it was a personalized check for patients with kidney transplants, so if there was an increase of 10 per cent you can pick it up and detect rejection. Now we cannot do that, even though the machines can do the job" (nephrologist).

Another restriction in hospitals, according to the interview subjects, is access to drugs. Many institutions have limited formularies, and physicians often have relatively little discretion in prescribing certain drugs, such as erythropoietin for dialysis patients and expensive antibiotics. One psychiatrist said that "in terms of drugs, we are very restricted. . . . Invariably the drugs we have are generics, but secondly they are limited . . . in their side effect profile. When you are dealing particularly with older people, who already have a number of other pharmaceutical agents, you have many fewer options and consequently you may have to run the risk of some kind of clash of medications with the effect upon the patient being potentially lethal." Two other psychiatrists said that a medication may be stocked by the hospital pharmacy only in tablet form, whereas the liquid form would be easier to administer.

Dealing with the Shortages

Some physicians reported that dealing with shortages presented no ethical dilemmas because they have no choice. They are gatekeepers in a very limited sense, since they have little discretion in the allocation of resources. Even though they believe that their patients are receiving inferior treatment, there is nothing they can do about it, because of the system's constraints. Such constraints operate with respect to all the shortages mentioned: access to hospital beds, tests and drugs.

When all beds in a hospital are full, patients are refused admission. A critical care physician said, "As a tertiary care hospital we often get referrals from primary and secondary care hospitals because of resource limitations on their side, so that they want to transfer the patient here. That is an easy situation to resolve: we tell them that we are sorry but we cannot accommodate their patient right now, and we have no idea what happens to them."

A diagnostic radiologist is in a similar position with regard to requests for tests: "I cannot accept, purely by resources alone and the waiting lists I have alluded to, I cannot accept to do patients who are not of this hospital unless they happen to be from another hospital or admitted to another hospital."

Some physicians reported that they have limited discretion in their choice of drugs. A neurologist said, "In this hospital the pharmacist will send over the generic drug no matter what is ordered." A nephrologist reported a similar policy, "There is a pharmacy committee, they decide, with aminoglycocide, for example, they decide which aminoglycocide we will use in the hospital. If I want another aminoglycocide, I can not get it. . . . Also a big expense is the new antibiotic. . . . I may have to ask the infectious disease consultant to authorize a new antibiotic, but if he disagrees, he will not authorize it."

Physicians in private practice feel less constrained by the system. They see themselves having options from which to choose. This makes their decision-making more complex than it is for those physicians who feel that they have no choices. A cardiologist exemplifies this view: "It is easy for me to take care of someone, for example, someone with chronic stable angina, and say, "I am going to see you four times a year," and schedule those according to my schedule. That is easy for me to do, and if I need money, I can see the same people six times a year instead of four. The patients are probably happy to do that and no one polices that."

Some physicians know how to circumvent the system's limitations by obtaining services for their patients or equipment for their wards from unconventional sources, such as private donors or voluntary organizations. Those in charge of admissions or access to tests also have discretion in their choice of patients, and they often have to choose which of two or more equally needy individuals should have first call on a limited resource.

For the physicians who think that they have discretion in allocating health care resources, there is a choice to be made between the two conflicting roles of being the advocate of their patient's best interests and the gatekeepers of society's scarce resources. As an obstetrician-gynecologist said, "I do not see how I could be the patient's physician and the gatekeeper at the same time. I really do not know how I could do that." He chooses not to act as a gatekeeper. Other physicians also see themselves mainly, if not exclusively, as their patient's advocate. A cardiologist works to "get my patients to jump the line," for example, in hospital admissions. He does this by establishing a reputation for efficient use of beds with the hospital responsible for admission, and by exerting pressure on these officials to give his patients preference.

To get his psychiatric patients admitted to acute care hospitals, a geriatrician undertakes "a lot of negotiations, shopping around, sometimes a degree of threatening, a lot of pleading. I just went through one of those. Finally it was resolved, probably because I had a personal connection with one of the psychiatrists on call and I think I traded on that." A critical care specialist explains his concept of patient advocacy: "I never have any difficulty, even for an outpatient, getting a test done on an urgent basis if necessary. What you have to do, though, is to take a little personal trouble. I phone the radiologist. I do not phone the booking clerk. That works fine. I suppose that may simply mean that my patients get preferential treatment because I am more aggressive. I see that as my job. You come to me, I am going to look after you. You go to somebody else, that is your tough luck."

None of the physicians interviewed, even those holding administrative positions, see themselves mainly as gatekeepers. However, many are concerned with the just distribution of resources among needy patients, so they fulfill the role of advocate or agent of society in addition to that of patient advocate. They implement the social advocate role in four ways: by voluntarily restraining their use of health care resources, by working with their colleagues to distribute the available resources fairly, by educating their patients not to make excessive demands, and by refusing unreasonable patient or family requests.

Many of the interview subjects claimed to practise restraint in their use of resources, especially tests. A general practitioner said, "I think we are all trained not to do tests needlessly. . . . I know with each test that I order I am thinking of the cost and balancing that out with the fear that I am going to miss certain diseases the tests are needed for." A pediatrician stated, "I guess I am always aware of those costs and I think it comes with experience, to a certain extent, so I would try to order a minimum number of tests and depend more on my clinical skills in making a diagnosis and treating a patient for any particular conditions."

In many institutions, physicians work together to establish procedures for dealing with resource shortages. At a community clinic, "the doctors at our regular meetings pull out charts at random and the chart is reviewed. If the test is not felt to be necessary, the other doctors will certainly comment on that." A obstetrician said that at his hospital, a second opinion is required before a cesarian section is performed. A neurologist said that "if the radiologists notice a doctor ordering a lot of scans that are negative and for questionable reasons, they will then start scrutinizing every request coming from that individual and they will turn them down."

Most physicians expressed reluctance about educating patients not to make unnecessary demands on the health care system. Their reasons were lack of time, since patient education is unremunerated, and a fear that the patient's confidence in them as their advocate would be weakened if they were told to take more responsibility for their, or their children's, health. The exceptions to this rule were physicians who staff emergency wards. They think that these wards are overused, but they are unsure about what to do to solve the problem. As one pediatrician said, "I do not think we should be giving . . . the message out to the public that they can come any time at any hour of the day or night and get any kind of service they feel they need. . . . [But] I cannot say to a mother at three in the morning — I cannot get upset with her because she came in. . . . It is not appropriate at that time to decide that you have to educate her that she should never come to the emergency room. . . . That has to be done one step before."

On the other hand, an obstetrician-gynecologist is more direct with his patients: "I get very annoyed at some of my patients and I tell them that they do not have to be here. 'It is not appropriate for you to be here,' and I look at them and say, 'You are just wasting your money. Yes, your money.' The patient will say, 'But it is the government;' and I say, 'But who is the government? It is you, you pay the bills. . . .' Once you explain that to them, you do not see them as often. Maybe they go to someone else, but I do not see them any more."

Physicians also ration health care resources by refusing unreasonable patient and family requests. Some physicians find this even more difficult than patient education, because of their reluctance to weaken their patient's confidence in them and because of the fear of litigation if something goes wrong. A frequent unreasonable demand is for sophisticated radiological testing. An orthopedic surgeon said that "people will regularly ask for scans, maybe CT scans. People refer now to these newer magnetic resonance tests and will ask for them, although, in many cases, a simple X-ray or a clinical examination will give us just as much information." How does he deal with such requests? "I simply say, it is not necessary. Or I tend to tell them that the cheaper test is just as good, if it is. . . . Most people are very reasonable, although they have the option, of course, of going to somebody else who might agree with them. Which happens."

A general practitioner also admitted difficulty in dealing with persistent patients: "If I know someone is a 'demanding' patient, I will try to meet their needs because I know if I do not, they will just go to someone else who may well give into their need right away." On the other hand, a critical care specialist claimed "to have my secretary very well trained to prioritize the patients with regard to medical emergency based on their condition, not their importance in society, nor what tends to be more relevant nowadays, how persistent they are in bothering her."

A frequent unreasonable request from families is for aggressive treatment of a terminally ill or even brain-dead patient. There is often reluctance to override the wishes of families in such cases, no matter how futile their requests. A hospital administrator said that in such cases, the family's wishes always prevail, "although I think the medical staff increasingly are trying to explain to families just what the prognosis is and what the likelihood is for any meaningful recovery." A geriatrician deals with these situations by "a lot of negotiation" and by offering the family a second opinion or even the transfer of the patient to another physician or another ward. A critical care specialist takes a different approach: "Sometimes I do not always give the family all the options at that point in time. If somebody who I think does not have a chance of recovering is in renal failure, then sometimes I will not talk to the family about dialysis or other life-sustaining therapies, even if they are saying, please do everything you can." A nephrologist is even more direct: "I had to fight with the children of a patient who was totally demented. They wanted me to continue dialysis. . . . I said I would stop it even if you take me to court because I could not stand the suffering of the patient."

Discussion

Eisenberg[1] lists several variables in physicians' practice patterns that lead to greater (or less) use of health care resources: the physician's perception of his or her self-interest, including economic factors, personal style, and practice environment; his or her role as patient advocate, acting on behalf of the patient's physical and economic health and personal preferences; his or her desire to provide the most good to the most people in need of medical care. All these factors enter into the physician's decision whether to undertake a medical intervention, as he or she seeks to maximize their combined value.

Although there are potential conflicts between the physician's welfare and that of his or her patients, Eisenberg contends that this is not a serious problem compared with the conflict between the needs of patients and the resources of society. He states: "Physicians seem to be most comfortable when they can consider only the welfare of their patients and themselves as the principal issues in medical care decisions (although they may claim to consider only the patient's benefit). While physicians may also be willing to weigh the effect of their decisions on the patient's family, they are generally less comfortable contemplating the impact of their decisions on the rest of society. They are generally unwilling to consider the effect of their individual decisions on the overall cost of medical care or the consumption of limited resources (be they beds, scarce drugs, or dollars). In fact, many doctors believe that these broader considerations have no place in an ethical physician's decision-making."

However accurate these observations might be with regard to the U.S.A., it is clear from our interview that some Canadian physicians take seriously their role as gatekeepers. This role is being forced on them by budgetary cutbacks, which lead to greater competition among patients for the same limited resources. Some physicians think that they have little if any discretion in helping their patients gain access to these resources. Others, however, see themselves as still possessing a high degree of authority in this regard, and they have to decide if they are going to act mainly or exclusively on behalf of their patients, or whether they will try to ensure a fair allocation of the available resources among all those in need.

Although it is seldom articulated as such, the choice is ethical, since it involves the rights and responsibilities of physicians and the exercise of justice in the distribution of social resources.[7] Furthermore, both roles of patient advocate and gatekeeper can be justified ethically. The arguments in favor of physicians doing everything possible for their patients, no matter what the cost, include the following:[5,6,8]

- Patients and society expect this of their physicians, and to do otherwise would be a breach of trust.
- The principle of patient autonomy, as reflected in the ethical and legal doctrine of informed consent, implies that physicians should respond to the needs of their patients rather than those of the institution or of society.
- Since each patient is unique, outside attempts to regulate medical decision-making result in inappropriate care for some patients.

A strong ethical case can also be made for the physician as gatekeeper of society's medical resources. The Royal College/Canadian Medical Association code of ethics states that ethical physicians "will accept their share of the profession's responsibility to society in matters relating to the health and safety of the public. . . ." The responsibility of physicians to their patients is not absolute: both as medical practitioners and as citizens, they have duties to other patients and to society. Physicians must be sensitive to the requirement of justice that their patients should not benefit unduly at the expense of others.[3]

Can these two roles be reconciled? Pellegrino, a physician–ethicist, believes so.[2] While upholding the primacy of the physician–patient relationship, he sees no contradiction between that and the physician–society relationship: "The physician . . . has a legitimate, indeed, a morally binding responsibility to function as a 'gatekeeper.' He must use his knowledge to practise competent, scientifically rational medicine. His guidelines should be a diagnostic elegance — just the right degree of economy of means in diagnosis — and therapeutic parsimony — just those treatments that are demonstrably beneficial and effective. . . ."

While some studies have shown that there is wasteful overtreatment in the health care system,[10,11] others argue that the elimination of this waste would not solve the problem of limited resources.[12,13] More rationing of these resources seems inevitable, and physicians are likely to be put under increasing pressure by hospitals, insurers and governments to serve as the agents of rationing. Such pressure should not be allowed to obscure the ethical character of allocation decisions. If questions of justice are avoided in the distribution of scarce health resources, it is likely that injustice will prevail. . . .

References

1. Eisenberg JM. Doctors' decisions and the cost of medical care. Ann Arbor: Health Administration Press, 1986.
2. Pellegrino EE. Rationing health care: The ethics of medical gatekeeping. J Contemporary Health Law Policy 1986;2:23–45.
3. Daniels N. Just health care. Cambridge: Cambridge University Press, 1985.
4. Reagan MD. Physicians as gatekeepers: A complex challenge. N Engl J Med 1987; 317: 1731–4
5. Manga P. The allocation of health care resources: Ethical and economic choices, conflicts and compromise. Numéro 33. Synthèse critique, Commission d'enquête sur les services de santé et les services sociaux. Québec: Les Publications du Québec, 1987.
6. Churchill LR. Rationing health care in America: Perceptions and principles of justice. Notre Dame: University of Notre Dame Press, 1987.
7. Grunberg F, Williams JR. Ethical responsibilities of physicians in the allocation of health care resources. Ann R Coll Physicians Surg Can 1988;21:311–5.
8. Cassell EJ. Do justice, love mercy: The inappropriateness of the concept of justice applied to bedside decisions. In: Shelp EE, ed. Justice and health care. Dordrecht, Reidel. 1981:75–82.
9. Linton AL. Would Hippocrates accept cost containment? Ann R Coll Physicians Surg Can 1988;21:21–4.
10. A similar study in the U.S.A. was reported by Elkowitz A. Physicians at the bedside: Practitioners' thoughts regarding bedside allocation of resources. J Med Humanities and Bioethics 1986;7:122–32.
11. Singer DE, Carr PL, Mulley AG, et al. Rationing intensive care: Physician responses to the resource shortage. N Engl J Med 1983;309:1155–60.
12. Strauss MJ, LoGerfo JP, Yeltatzie JA, et al. Rationing of intensive care unit services: An everyday occurrence. JAMA 1986; 255: 1143–6.
13. Callahan D. What kind of life: The limits of medical progress. New York: Simon and Schuster, 1990.

16   Purpose and Function in Government-Funded Health Coverage

Benjamin Freedman & Françoise Baylis

Government-funded health insurance schemes are under increasing pressure to reconcile finite medical resources with seemingly infinite demands for medical services. Consequently, problems regarding the macroallocation of available resources must constantly be readdressed. The substantive macroallocational questions are familiar: What portions of health care funding should be directed toward acute, chronic, or preventive care, or toward research in these respective areas? What, if any, provision should be made for the funding of novel therapies? When more than one approach to a disorder is available (e.g., medical or surgical treatment of angina pectoris), should the insurance program reward the use of the cheapest option (one assumption underlying the DRG system; see Wasserman 1983), the option which the physician believes is clinically preferable, or that which the patient prefers, perhaps on grounds of compatibility with lifestyle?

Questions such as these underline the need for a demarcation principle which government-funded health insurance programs could use to determine what should not be funded. The usefulness of such a principle is obvious, particularly from the government's perspective, when one considers how quickly new approaches to health care are adopted by health care providers (creating a demand for insurance reimbursement on their behalf). Current examples would include transportation, advanced diagnostic and imaging equipment, and expensive techniques for the treatment of infertility (most notoriously, *in vitro* fertilization). A demarcation principle would serve to limit the constantly expanding claims for health insurance coverage which feed upon (and, when successful, fuel) the unrealistic expectation that the government-funded health care system can guarantee everyone a long, happy, and productive life.

At present, the approach to funding adopted by government health care programs is eclectic. Aside from strictly medical concerns, attention is given to factors deriving from economics, politics, and public policy. Even within the mélange of compromise that constitutes health insurance, however, we may discern a basic theme of demarcation: absent special considerations, a purposive (deductive) approach is commonly used in deciding whether a specific service should be a covered benefit. The results of this theme may be reconstructed in almost syllogistic terms: the insurance scheme should fund that which yields, or leads to, health (major premise); the proposed service does (or does not) yield or lead to health (minor premise); therefore the proposed service should (should not) be reimbursed. Presented in this way, the deductive approach is, of course, an artificial reconstruction of a more complicated reality. In the cases that we will be presenting, however, it plausibly captures an important theme in insurance decision making as that is publicly presented.

The Preamble to the Ontario Health Insurance Plan's *Schedule of Benefits* (1983), for example, states at the outset that "Insured medical services are limited to the services which are medically necessary . . ." (p. 1). This we understand to mean that only those services designed to restore health ("medically necessary") are to be funded. The purposive concept of medical necessity is therefore ostensibly an *exclusive* criterion of demarcation — that is, a necessary but not sufficient condition for coverage. However, medical necessity also serves as an *inclusive* criterion of demarcation. The fitting of contact lenses, for example, is not a covered benefit unless it is being done to correct aphakia, myopia greater than nine diopters, irregular astigmatism, or keratoconus (p. 20). Similarly, other services commonly sought for reasons of vanity or convenience are not covered benefits unless they are called for by some substantial degree of medical necessity. A case in point is cosmetic surgery, which is not an insured benefit "except where medically required" (p. 19).

The deductive model, idealized as it is, is a plausible — sometimes, the *only* plausible — reconstruction of a number of specific decisions on insurance coverage. Although it is initially appealing, we shall argue that this form of reasoning results in some obvious inequalities and distortions in government coverage practice. An alternative approach, which may be termed functional or inductive, will be suggested. The functional approach would have us resolve the problem of demarcation by asking whether the specific service in question represents a demand which the health care system may efficiently satisfy. The question of whether the funded service supplies "health" or "health care" is thereby intentionally finessed.

The examples we shall be using are drawn largely from Canadian (and predominantly Ontarian) experiences. They are intended to serve for purposes of illustration alone. If successful, they point to problems and approaches generally prevalent among any government-funded insurance scheme which claims to comprehensively fund the health demands of the serviced population.

The Purposive Approach

In ordinary language, "purpose" broadly refers to the end one has in view in acting in a certain way (i.e., "purposively"). The use of the term implies the conscious choice of both a goal and an action designed to achieve the stated goal. By extension, we may think of objects as purposively designed. For example, a television receiver is built with the end of it serving as a decoder of electronic impulses. In designing it, a certain size and shape are chosen on the grounds of fitness toward that end (Turkel 1984); any components which prove unreliable in achieving that end are either discarded or redesigned. Social institutions, such as traffic regulation, can also be construed as purposive. A panoply of elements (road markings, rules, etc.) are chosen subordinate to the primary goal of the swift and accident-free motion of traffic.

Similarly, some view medical practice as a purposive enterprise. It is usual to distinguish medical from nonmedical interventions — to demarcate medical practice — by referring to current beliefs concerning what promotes or conserves health; in theory new forms of medical treatment are accepted into practice and old ones discarded on the basis of their fitness to serve the purpose of health. It is on this basis alone that physicians, in the course of their daily practice, "may, unquestioned and with impunity, slice, puncture, bind, grind, inject, and extract various organic and inorganic substances into and from" their patients (Freedman 1984, 5).

As health is the organizing principle and rule of demarcation for medical practice, it is natural to assume that this concept should apply as well to that system which funds medical practice. That is, it seems natural to assume that problems of demarcation in health care funding cannot be decided unless prior agreement has been arrived at concerning the definition of health, so that the nature of "medically necessary" services may be ascertained. By extension, a government-funded health insurance program may be purposively understood as an institution designed to secure health, although it is constrained by economic and political factors.

If the purpose of the government-funded insurance system is to promote health, and if that purpose is to serve as its rule of demarcation, a definition of health must be presented. However, the definition of health and related concepts (such as illness and disease) has resisted numerous scholarly efforts. Those definitions which have gained favorable attention have succeeded by stipulating a definition which could then be explicated or operationalized (Boorse 1975). But this approach will not serve the purposes of a government-funded health insurance scheme, since these purposes require a definition or an understanding of health with a basis in social consensus and usage.

The most widely known and most frequently criticized definition of health is found in the Preamble to the Constitution of the World Health Organization: "Health is a state of complete physical, mental and social well-being and not merely the absence of disease or infirmity" (WHO 1976). Daniel Callahan, a relatively sympathetic commentator on the WHO definition, notes nonetheless that this definition fosters "the cultural tendency to define all social problems, from war to crime on the streets, as 'health' problems" (Callahan 1973, 78). It "makes the medical profession the gate-keeper for happiness and social well-being . . . the final magic-healer of human misery" (p. 81).

These eloquent criticisms relate to the one point that makes the WHO definition of health inadequate for the purposes of our discussion: it provides a government-funded health insurance scheme with no rule of demarcation whatsoever. . . .

Mindful of the need for demarcation, Callahan offered the following definition of health as a counterproposal: "Health is a state of physical well-being," a state which need not be "complete" but must be "at least adequate, i.e., without significant impairment of function" (Callahan 1973, 87). With this narrow definition of health, mental illness would qualify as "ill health," if at all, only if it substantially interfered with functioning.

Would Callahan's definition, or one equally narrow, represent a satisfactory rule of demarcation for government-funded health insurance schemes? It is important to examine this question at some length, because the narrowness of the definition as well as its common-sense roots make it attractive to economically pressed governments. Therefore, even if Callahan would not use his definition of health as a rule of demarcation, governments faced with competing priorities might be tempted to do so.

In judging the adequacy of any proposed rule of demarcation, two different kinds of questions may be asked. First, *could* the rule serve (i.e., would it clearly distinguish between those services to be included and those to be excluded from the funding system)? Second, *should* the rule serve (i.e., if applied, would it yield satisfactory results)? The first question concerns the formal adequacy of the rule; the second, its substantive adequacy.

The notion of "well-being" and of "impairment of function" are two crucial elements of Callahan's definition which are unavoidably ambiguous; these ambiguities speak to the issue of formal adequacy. To revert to the example introduced earlier, consider a patient suffering from exercise-onset angina pectoris. Two types of treatment are available. One option is medical management, which requires of the patient a commitment to control of diet, a modification of activity, and the tolerance of some degree of continued pain. The alternative is surgical intervention, which avoids the above problems at the expense of discrete surgical risk and substantial surgical and hospitalization costs. An appeal to "well-being" and "functioning" fails to indicate which of these forms of treatment should appropriately be funded. The problem is further complicated when one considers that the judgments of the patient and of the physician may differ; and, whereas people tend to think of "health" or "therapy" as technical concepts whose application is in the hands of professionals, they tend to define other concepts like "well-being" and "functioning" for themselves. The formal adequacy of Callahan's definition is therefore in question.

What about the substantive adequacy of the definition as a demarcation rule? This may seem to beg the question. We need a demarcation rule because we don't know what should and what should not be funded; therefore, how can we question such a rule by saying that it includes the wrong items? But this point presumes a false dichotomy, as often occurs when applying deductive approaches to social questions. We may (we almost certainly do) have some idea of the results desired from a rule of demarcation. We likely wish to develop a demarcation rule to sharpen an initially hazy understanding, rather than to fill a total vacuum.

Substantively, a rule may be faulty because it is either overinclusive, underinclusive, or both. It would be overinconclusive because it fails to account for the quantity of resources expended in marginal improvements in well-being or functioning. It does not tell us when the game is no longer worth the candle; and, as was noted at the outset, it is because medicine continues to yield improvements in these parameters, albeit at ever-increasing expense, that the problem we are discussing arises.

Callahan's definition would be underinclusive as well, because if it were applied rigorously benign and worthwhile services would be excluded from coverage. In his concern to combat the view that medicine should be held responsible to deliver perfect happiness, Callahan eliminates any role medicine might legitimately satisfy in this direction. Sometimes medical expertise is necessary to provide a modicum of happiness; if the costs thereby incurred are trivial enough, and the benefits (even in mere happiness) great enough, why should the required service not be funded?

Consider the following. The removal of tattoos is not usually necessary to restore function; nor, strictly speaking, is it a necessary component of well-being. Yet, the safe eradication of tattoos may require medical expertise. In Ontario, in most cases the provincial health insurance scheme does not cover the cost of tattoo removal. However, an exception is made for the eradication of prisoner-of-war or concentration camp tattoos. In some isolated instances well-being or functioning might require the removal of such tattoos, and to these cases Callahan's principle would extend. But in the usual case physical well-being and functioning are not impaired by these offensive tattoos. Is it wrong to fund this service simply out of consideration for the victims' feelings, in a situation where practical concern for these feelings requires medical expertise?

Evidently a definition of health from either end of the continuum — the relatively inclusive WHO definition, and the rather exclusive definition proposed by Callahan

— will not serve as a satisfactory demarcation principle. However, quite apart from the specific problems arising from any particular definition of health, a further obstacle confronts the definitional approach to health care funding in that no definition of health has garnered general agreement. This lack of consensus is no mere accident. While on the surface the debate concerning the definition of health is technical in nature, it is clear in the writings of Szasz (1961), Kass (1975), and others that this debate serves an ideological role as well. Often the definitions advocated reflect broad views concerning such disparate issues as technocracy, nature versus nurture, and the allowable limits of eccentricity in liberal societies. Unhappily, therefore, it may be the case that consensus regarding the definition of health will have to wait for prior consensus on political and social ideology.

Also, the economic facts of health care may be another source of dissent regarding the definition of health and disease. Consider a study by Campbell, Scadding, and Roberts (1979), in which subjects were presented with a number of conditions and asked whether these represented "disease." The conditions ranged from malaria and tuberculosis to drowning and starvation. Physicians, and especially general practitioners, were more likely to characterize a condition as "disease" than were lay respondents. The authors suggest that the operational equivalents of "disease" are different in the two groups. For the layman, "disease" means "Do I need a doctor?" For the physician, it means "Is it useful for me to use this label?" An alternative suggestion compatible with the observed differences is that physicians, especially family practitioners, have a vested economic interest in broadening the scope of the term "disease."

We have been arguing that reliance upon the definition of health for the purposive elucidation of a government-funded insurance program is unlikely to result in a consensual, usable, and fair system. To this one might object that the preceding argument has erred in identifying the purpose of a government-funded health insurance system as the provision of "health." A health insurance system cannot provide *health*, but at best can only provide *health care*.

This amended purposive description is not, however, immune from the criticism noted above. The objection purports to take a realistic look at what the government-funded insurance system actually does: it funds "health care." This is presumed to be a less ambiguous concept than "health." However, the definition of health care itself is crucially dependent upon prior agreement on the definition of health, so the objection only succeeds in pushing the problems we have noted one step back.

Others will object that the health care system provides neither "health" nor "health care" but "medical care" *tout court*. This, however, is no more serious an objection, for although the term "medical care" is perhaps even less ambiguous than the term "health care," the problem remains in that "medical care" is commonly understood to require that a physician's expertise be applied on behalf of restoring or preserving the health of patients. Furthermore, if we were to be fully realistic, we would have to admit that government-funded health insurance systems do not fund medical care or health care any more than they fund health. Rather, they fund health care providers, as public monies are made available precisely to pay for medical services rendered.

Structural Deficiencies of the Purposive Approach

As noted above, the two definitions of health drawn from either end of the continuum fail to adequately demarcate insurable services. It does not necessarily follow from this, however, that a definition in between these extremes would not serve.

Allowing for the remote possibility that a consensual definition of health were to be adopted, some important structural problems would remain to confront any purposive system of government-funded health insurance. These problems derive from the approach's top-down, deductive fashion of reasoning, and therefore would not be solved by any improvement in the formulation of the premises. In particular, they would persist despite changes in the definition of health or health care.

An inherent problem with the purposive-deductive approach is its rationalization of the issue of demarcation. In principle, once the premises have been adopted, all of the solutions are present; as logicians say, deductive reasoning produces no new knowledge not already embedded in the premises. Two difficulties follow from this. The purposive approach does not in principle allow for an incremental solution to the issues, within which some procedures might be funded on a trial basis while other relevantly similar procedures await the lessons of experience. Furthermore, this rationalized approach does not permit any wisdom of quantification, a problem noted earlier in reference to Callahan. It does not allow us by its premises to say that some procedure does not fall on the "fundable" side of the demarcation line, but that it is still worthy of funding (e.g., tattoo removal), or alternatively that some procedure might fall on the "fundable" side of the demarcation line, but that it is nonetheless too expensive a proposition to fund (e.g., heart transplants).

A further problem is who decides whether some service is fundable under the definition consensually adopted. He almost certainly will be some professional: possibly the individual health care provider, but more likely some government official. Thus, control of the health insurance system passes into the hands of the technocracy, and the patient is lost in the shuffle, as is indeed lay input in general (which currently may be provided through political representation and control). How is the technocracy to resolve these problems? In the deductive mode of reasoning, issues of application are reduced to a search for semantic clarity and consensus. Practical issues of whether it is useful, fair, or right to cover a given treatment for a given condition are converted into an obsessive contemplation of the definition of health.

Problems of the Purposive Approach in Practice

The purposive-deductive approach is neccesarily obsessed with determining whether a condition is "really" an illness. Two representative cases illustrate this point, though many other examples could be cited if space permitted. Jane Smith (a real case, though not her real name) approached an endocrinologist with a presenting complaint of excessive growth of facial and body hair. After an extensive workup (covered, incidentally, by the provincial health plan) in which no endocrinological disorder was established, she was diagnosed as suffering from "essential hirsutism." Mrs. Smith then requested of the physician a referral to an electrolysist, in the belief that the health care plan would then cover the cost of treatment. This request was refused. She was told that if the condition was causing her acute discomfort or embarrassment, she could be referred to a psychiatrist, who could then make the referral for hair removal. The kinds of questions the psychiatrist would be likely to ask could equally well have been asked by the endocrinologist. However, he felt constrained by the purposive nature of the system to validate the electrolytic referral by means of special expertise (into mental illness) which he did not feel he possessed. Thus, inappropriate gatekeeping mechanisms which are both costly and inefficient were introduced. This case illustrates one way in which the technocratic and logomachistic tendencies of the purposive approach re-inforce one another.

To further illustrate this point, consider the treatment of infertility, which might include hormonal therapy or surgery as well as counselling. These therapies ordinarily are thought to fall within the boundaries of medical care. But the purposive approach must question whether infertility itself is really a "disease." If we look to an American example, Great Southern Life of Houston, a private insurance company, is reported as having denied coverage for *in vitro* fertilization on the grounds that it is "not a treatment of an illness" (*Surrogate Parenting News 1983*). Presumably a government-funded health care system similarly concerned with purposive considerations might apply the same reasoning.

Another distinction covertly used is that of the internal versus the external. There is a vague feeling that health care is a concept that relates to the individual rather than to the environment, and that fundable, fee-for-service health care interventions may be demarcated in part as those which represent internal adjustments to the human organism rather than modifications of the organism's environment. When a malnourished patient is nursed back to health through intravenous infusions, that is health care; when he or she is given money or remunerative employment supplying the wherewithal for self-nourishment, that is not health care.

The distinction makes less sense in other contexts. What of a patient suffering from a definable illness whose comprehensive treatment would include environmental modification? A major and growing current example are those patients suffering from pan-allergic syndromes. It is sometimes claimed that the alleviation of the symptoms from this disorder requires a total readjustment of the patient's living arrangements, such as moving into a cabin tiled with ceramics and discarding a wardrobe laced with allergens. Although this is asserted to be the treatment of choice, it is "external" and therefore not a covered benefit under the government health insurance scheme. Similarly, prosthetics that are implanted, like heart pacemakers, are covered benefits under Ontario's health insurance scheme, whereas externally attached prosthetics, like limbs, generally are not paid for by the Ontario Health Insurance Plan (OHIP).

The Functional Approach: An Alternative

Most social institutions are established with a purpose in view. When a government-funded health insurance program is initiated, the purpose is vaguely understood to contribute to the provision of health or health care. This original purpose is in fact critical to the establishment of a government health insurance program, which is often given higher priority than comparable welfare schemes dealing in less critical services and commodities. But once an insurance scheme is in place, it would be foolish to freeze the system in its embryonic state. With the continuing development of a health insurance plan, as it confronts issues of macroallocation and demarcation, there is no need to restrict it to the a priori wisdom that went into its establishment. On these grounds we advocate a functional approach to government health care funding.

In accordance with common usage, we define a "function" as any output of a system which is positively evaluated, whether that output was intentional or not.[1] Purposes are therefore a subset of functions, the latter including happy surprises in addition to anticipated outcomes. To revert to our earlier example, the purpose of a television set is to decode electronic signals. In most homes, however, it will also service a variety of additional functions: conversation piece, plant stand, and so on.

What would be distinctive about a functional approach to a government-funded health insurance plan? Three main differences stand between a purposive and a functional approach. These differences have to do with the characterization of those conditions which the government health insurance program should ameliorate, the demarcation of reimbursable from nonreimbursable services, and the relationship between the health plan and other government services.

With the purposive approach to the question of health care funding, funding decisions turn on whether a condition represents ill health, a disease, an illness. With a functional approach, in contrast, questions outside the realm of health are also considered. For example, has the condition resulted in impaired occupational performance? (In the infamous words of an anonymous Polish public health official, "Tuberculosis slows production.") Does the person afflicted with the condition experience disturbed functioning in other areas as a result? Is he severely distressed or depressed as a result of the condition? Is he experiencing pain? These types of considerations do sometimes appear in the purposive conception, but in a distorted, Procrustean way, as questions concerning "mental health" or "adjustment."

To illustrate this point, consider how the different approaches would deal with a difficult case of demarcation like sex-reassignment surgery. The purposive approach would need to discover whether the surgery represented the treatment of a genuine disease. In this context, the neologism "gender dysphoria" has been introduced, and psychiatrists continue to battle over its propriety and etiology. With a functional approach the questions considered in reaching a funding decision on a macro level (by bureaucrats) and in implementing the decision at the micro level (by physicians) are more straightforward. How seriously has the applicant's life been affected? How likely is it that he/she will improve with the treatment? Is the cost justified by these benefits? Admittedly, similar questions might be asked by psychiatrists in the gender dysphoria debate. We suggest, however, that such questions are both clearer and more realistic when not filtered through the prism of a definition of disease.

The second contrast between the purposive and the functional approach is evident when deciding about the funding of discrete services. Whereas with the purposive approach one asks whether some service represents health care, with the functional approach one would ask if the service or procedure is good, worthwhile, and desired.

Consider fertility interventions. For the vast majority of women, tubal ligation per se has almost no discrete medical justification (although it certainly will "cure" the "disorder" of fecundity). On these grounds, Kass (1975) has suggested that tubal ligation or vasectomy not be included within the medical orbit. But clearly, tubal ligation is a much-desired intervention; it has recently become the most popular form of female contraception in Canada. And clearly, medical expertise is necessary to provide ligations. Also, from the economic point of view of the insurance plan, sterilization is one of the most efficient interventions available, obviating both medical costs of parturition and costs of care of the (forever-to-remain) unborn. Whereas the purposive conception forces government health care officials to conceptualize health matters in futile and disingenuous ways, the functional conception allows one to examine the real underlying concerns. Does a requested procedure — for example, tubal ligation — represent a treatment whose cost is rationally proportionate to the need it serves?

When the issue is phrased in this way, we are required to confront questions which are never raised by the purposive approach. For example: Does the procedure in question address a human want or need, or perhaps something people ought to want or need? As difficult as these questions are, they seem to us to be the right ones to address. Among their advantages is the fact that their solution demands of us that we understand and respect the patient's perceptions of health care.

A recent study (Freedman 1983) yielded some suggestive data on this very point. The study included interviews of Canadian women applying for microsurgical attempts at reversing a prior ligation (tubal reanatomosis). During the interview, the women were asked "Do you see the reversal of the sterilization as a health procedure (like an appendectomy) or as a social procedure requiring medical assistance (like cosmetic surgery)? Most of these women, both in questionnaires and during the subsequent interviews, classified the procedure they requested as medical, but the interview responses of some of the women revealed ambivalence stemming from a variety of considerations. The following representative statements are worthy of careful consideration as they encapsulate a lay response to the issue of demarcation: "I think for my mental and emotional well-being it is necessary. It is not like cosmetic surgery, like something I could do. It is something that is inside of me. I never thought I'd feel as strongly about [it]." "No [it's not a social procedure] . . . I don't feel that having a tubal done is the same thing as having a reversal done. I'm having it [the reversal] done so that we can have children . . . So I really don't see it as being something that you do just to fit in. It's hard to explain but that's the way I feel about it."

How did these laypeople go about resolving this critical question of demarcation? What themes emerge from their responses? Hints are found of a variety of approaches, including the "internal/external" approach. However, their major point of consensus was the belief that because the procedure was so important to them personally, and because a doctor was needed to perform it, the procedure *must* be medical.

The population from which these responses were drawn would be expected to provide tendentious replies. It is in these women's interest to argue that the procedure they are requesting is medical in nature, and hence reimbursable. However, this fact only sharpens the point, because we would expect that they would be choosing the most persuasive demarcation principle available to support their claim.

The third divergence between the two approaches concerns the relationship between the health care system (and its public funding agent) and other elements of society. The purposive approach makes of the health care system a hermetically sealed enterprise, self-directed in terms of its original purpose and resistant to other legitimate social concerns and institutionalized values. On the other hand, with the functional approach, other social interests and resources are taken into account in deciding whether to supply a particular benefit when its request is justified in terms of health.

A functionalist perspective also allows one to consider whether the health care system is the best institution to respond to demands for particular needs. Needs (or wants) and the associated goods and services that have traditionally been seen as medical in nature may be better served by some other social institution. Alcoholism, obesity, and other diseases of lifestyle are notoriously resistant to treatment by the medical model. For the purposive approach, however, provided that these conditions are diseases and that a physician is prepared to "treat" them, such treatment would be insured. The fact that other social institutions could better deal with these conditions is irrelevant from a purposive perspective. With a functional approach one questions whether we might not be better served by "divestiture" of these conditions from medicine, at least at this point in time. Conversely, the health care system may be better suited to providing some needs which traditionally have been served outside the medical model. One such possibility might be the care of the families of dying patients by physicians, nurses, or medical social workers, a role traditionally relegated to pastors and family support systems. The funding of such a service should not wait upon the discovery of a new "disease" ("impending grief syndrome"), but should proceed immediately upon the recognition that these forms of care are valid, useful, and best accomplished within the institutions of the health care system.

Questions for the Functional Approach

It might seem that the functional approach is necessarily heir to all of the criticisms presented above concerning the WHO definition of health. Under a functional approach, as under the WHO definition, the full range of human suffering and discontent become potential targets of a government-supported health care system. In fact, some might even argue that the functional approach is even more latitudinous than WHO, although it is hard to imagine what has been left out once "a complete state of physical, mental and social well-being" has been included.

This criticism, however, dissolves in the face of a critical distinction. The problem with the WHO definition, which is that it fails to exclude anything from coverage, arises in the context of a purposive system. In contrast, with a functional approach to health care funding, demarcation does not end with the recognition of a need or demand for services, but rather only begins at this point. It must then be determined whether the health care system, with its particular expertise and modalities of intervention, may redress that need efficiently; whether another social program or practice would better serve; or whether the need is so difficult to satisfy or so at odds with other values that it should not be served at all.

The whole point of the functional approach is the recognition that decisions regarding coverage involve more than semantics. In a purposive approach, once we know that a procedure serves health, we have an argument (which, to be sure, might need to be tempered by political or economic realities) that it should be funded. In a functional approach, when we know that a procedure satisfies a demand, we simply know that it is *potentially* fundable — not that it should be funded, let alone that it should be funded by the health care system.

A further point worth noting is that since functionalism contains no single decision rule for demarcation, it must address new problems which do not trouble a purposive system. However, the fact that a theory raises new questions does not necessarily count as a strike against it, provided that the questions are ones which are worth confronting. In fact, a theory might be deficient precisely because it fails to raise questions which should be answered, as at times the purposive approach slurs over the complications faced by the functional approach. In general the new problems which the functional approach must address are actually complications which arise due to the fact that patient choice is allowed, and that services traditionally considered nonmedical may be included within the boundaries of health care; therefore, a greater range of alternatives must be considered. For example, a possible negative consequence of allowing patient choice is that the costs involved might be greater. This criticism, however, also applies to the purposive approach, as the following examples will serve to illustrate

Under the Ontario Health Insurance Plan postmastectomy breast reconstruction surgery is a covered service. This type of procedure fits comfortably within the naive notion of health services, since it involves a direct "internal" procedure on a patient's behalf. On the other hand, prosthetic devices, being "external," have not been a covered benefit for adults and have represented a repeated source of political contention. A system which proceeds under the strong purposive principle of demarcation does not recognize the need to fund environmental adjustments, since these would fall under the rubric of social welfare rather than health care. Ontario, therefore, has long refused to cover the costs of breast prostheses and surgical brassieres for victims of breast cancer, while still funding surgical breast reconstruction for those interested in pursuing that course.

A complicated situation arose in Ontario when a woman eligible for a breast reconstruction procedure offered to exchange this service for a Tucker valve set (a prosthetic device needed for "normal" speech after she had undergone a tracheotomy). The trade would have been cost-effective for the Ministry of Health, and might have saved $1000 or more. The insurance plan declined the offer as there was no apt bureaucratic means of accepting it, given that the health insurance plan funds "services" and not "goods" (*London Free Press* 1982).

Another Ontario woman suffering from a lung condition lived at home, using a mobile oxygen cart. Eventually her monthly oxygen bills — which the public health insurance program would not cover — rose to over $700. At this point, entering the hospital became, for her, the only practical economic move, because then the insurance plan would supply her with oxygen gratis. The average cost of inpatient hospital care was estimated at approximately ten times the cost of the oxygen alone (*London Free Press* 1984). This situation similarly indicates the unreasoning prejudice a purposive system may have against environmental adjustment.

A functional approach would deal with such situations differently since patient choice would be independently relevant (if not necessarily decisive) in determining fundability. The implications of this are obviously quite serious, particularly as patients persist in expressing individual preferences on this issue, a fact which must be taken seriously by a system concerned with lay input. Honoring the choice of patients will at times be far more expensive than acceding to the choice dictated by a purposive demarcation rule. Patient autonomy in relation to funding decisions has not been an issue; but, without presuming any particular resolution, we suggest that it should be.

A functional conception would need to reexamine funding of the diverse forms of health care practice. In Ontario's quasi-purposive system, all reimbursements flow directly to, or indirectly from, physicians. Doctors may perform a service directly, or engage another professional (e.g., psychologist, physiotherapist) on a salaried basis to work under their direction, with the physician billing the government insurance program. Since physicians are certified specialists in "health," this arrangement is acceptable (although certainly not inevitable) under a purposive system. Similarly, although a physician may bill for consultation with a patient, parent, or other physician, he or she may not bill for consultation with nonphysician providers of health care. If a child is experiencing behavioral problems in school which have concerned the school psychologist, the physician may charge the government insurance plan for consultation with the parents, who may serve as middlemen between the school psychologist and the physician; but if the physician wishes to discuss the matter with the psychologist directly, he must do so on his own account. A functional system would necessarily call such arrangements into question.

As a result, in implementing a functional approach, a comprehensive government health plan would face bureaucratic dislocation. How serious would this be? To this, three points can be made: some dislocation has already occurred; some dislocation is good; and remaining dislocations need not all be faced at once.

Some Dislocation Has Already Occurred

In Ontario, a system of psychiatric hospitals is run by the Ministry of Health. A system of facilities for the developmentally disabled is run by the Ministry of Community and Social Services (COMSOC). This kind of division would be preserved if a consistently functional approach were adopted. The facilities for the developmentally handicapped require a high level of expertise in development and programming, but the specific forms required — training of various sorts, behavioral techniques, and custodial care — are not specifically medical or nursing in nature (although both of these disciplines perform an important ancillary function). Indeed, because developmental handicap constitutes an "illness" under almost any definition, the division that currently exists between psychiatric and COMSOC facilities is inexplicable under a purposive conception.

Some Dislocation Is Good

Many of the decisions noted above (e.g., concerning prostheses and oxygen) would be inappropriate given a functionalist perspective. Their reversal involves dislocation in itself; but in the cases noted, that seems to be all to the good. Also, some bureaucratic awkwardness, intrinsic to a purposive system, would be resolved under a functional approach. While a physician may recover from the Ontario Health Insurance Plan on behalf of the examination of a patient carried out for investigation, confirmation, or documentation of an alleged sexual assault, a portion of its outlays on this behalf are then recovered from the Ministries of the Attorney General and the Solicitor General. Similar cumbersome paper shuffling may be involved in other instances which require medical expertise, albeit outside of medical treatment (e.g., in assessments of insurance or for the purpose of establishing workmen's compensation). It would seem that the only reason the money needs to be shuffled at present is to keep the accounts clear on behalf of a system that is purposively designed to fund health care.

Not All Dislocations Need Be Funded at Once

The saving grace of the functional approach is that it may, consistent with its own logic, be activated in an incrementalist fashion. The facts of bureaucratic life are, as are the facts of economic, political and medical life, all to be included within the calculation that should precede a decision on inclusion of a service within coverage.

In general, then, new questions of the division between medical and social services and of the cost-effectiveness of different modes of health care would directly arise under a functional system. Quantitative concerns would also need to be directly confronted: How serious is the need or desire? What value should be assigned to the honoring of the preferences of the patient? These questions need not be raised at all in a purposive system, which deals instead with questions concerning the nuances of the definitions of "health" and "health care." We will leave to others the task of parsing the seriousness of these questions. In choosing between these two approaches, however, we ought to consider which kinds of questions we want to contemplate, as well as which results we wish to achieve.

Notes
1. "... functional analysis seeks to understand a behavior pattern or a sociocultural institution by determining the role it plays in keeping the given system in proper working order or maintaining it as a going concern" (Hempel 1985). For a general discussion of the functional approach see the chapter "The Logic of Functional Analysis," pp. 297–330, in Hempel (1985).

References

Boorse, C. 1975. On The Distinction Between Disease and Illness. *Philosophy and Public Affairs* 5 (Fall): 49–68.

Callahan, D. 1973. The WHO Definition of "Health." *The Hastings Center Studies* 1: 77–87.

Campbell, E.J.M., J.G. Scadding, and R. S. Roberts. 1979. The Concept of Disease. *British Medical Journal* 2 (September): 757–62.

Freedman, B. 1983–85. Study of Ethical Issues In Infertility (unpublished material).

_____ 1985. Ethical Issues in Clinical Obstetrics and Gynecology. *Current Problems in Obstetrics, Gynecology and Fertility* 7 (March): 1–47.

Hempel, C.G. 1985. *Aspects of Scientific Explanation.* New York: The Free Press.

Kass, L.R. 1975. Regarding the End of Medicine and the Pursuit of Health. *The Public Interest* 40 (Summer): 11–42.

London Free Press. 1982. OHIP won't pay for vocal device it calls luxury. 5 June: 2.

London Free Press. 1984. Woman needing pure oxygen may be forced into hospital. 3 August: 12.

Ontario Health Insurance Plan. 1983. Ministry of Health of the Province of Ontario. *Schedule of Benefits: Physician Services.* 1 January.

Surrogate Parenting News. 1983. Insurance Coverage of In Vitro. 1 (October/November): 71–72.

Szasz, T. 1961. *The Myth of Mental Illness.* New York: Dell Publishing Co.

Taylor, F.K. 1971. A Logical Analysis of the Medico-Psychological Concepts of Disease. *Psychological Medicine* 1:356–64.

Turkel, Sherry. 1984. *The Second Self.* New York: Simon and Schuster.

Wasserman, J. 1983. How DRGs Work. *The Hastings Center Report* 13 (October): 24.

World Health Organization. 1976. Constitution of the World Health Organization. In *World Health Organization: Basic Documents,* ed. 26. Geneva: WHO.

17   The Prostitute, the Playboy, and the Poet: Rationing Schemes for Organ Transplantation

George J. Annas

In the public debate about the availability of heart and liver transplants, the issue of rationing on a massive scale has been credibly raised for the first time in United States medical care. In an era of scarce resources, the eventual arrival of such a discussion was, of course, inevitable.[1] Unless we decide to ban heart and liver transplantation, or make them available to everyone, some rationing scheme must be used to choose among potential transplant candidates. The debate has existed throughout the history of medical ethics. Traditionally it has been stated as a choice between saving one of two patients, both of whom require the immediate assistance of the only available physician to survive.

National attention was focused on decisions regarding the rationing of kidney dialysis machines when they were first used on a limited basis in the late 1960s. As one commentator described the debate within the medical profession:

> Shall machines or organs go to the sickest, or to the ones with most promise of recovery; on a first-come, first-served basis; to the most "valuable" patient (based on wealth, education, position, what?); to the one with the most dependents; to women and children first; to those who can pay; to whom? Or should lots be cast, impersonally and uncritically?[2]

In Seattle, Washington, an anonymous screening committee was set up to pick who among competing candidates would receive the life-saving technology. One lay member of the screening committee is quoted as saying:

> The choices were hard . . . I remember voting against a young woman who was a known prostitute. I found I couldn't vote for her, rather than another candidate, a young wife and mother. I also voted against a young man who, until he learned he had renal failure, had been a ne'er do-well, a real playboy. He promised he would reform his character, go back to school and so on, if only he were selected for treatment. But I felt I'd lived long enough to know that a person like that won't do what he was promising at the time.[3]

When the biases and selection criteria of the committee were made public, there was a general negative reaction against this type of arbitrary device. Two experts reacted to the "numbing accounts of how close to the surface lie the prejudices and mindless clichés that pollute the committee's deliberations," by concluding that the committee was "measuring persons in accordance with its own middle-class values." The committee process, they noted, ruled out "creative nonconformists" and made the Pacific Northwest "no place for a Henry David Thoreau with bad kidneys."[4] . . .

There are four major approaches to rationing scarce medical resources: the market approach; the selection committee approach; the lottery approach; and the "customary" approach.[1]

The Market Approach

The market approach would provide an organ to everyone who could pay for it with their own funds or private insurance. It puts a very high value on individual rights, and a very low value on equality and fairness. It has properly been criticized on a number of bases, including that the transplant technologies have been developed and are supported with public funds, that medical resources used for transplantation will not be available for higher priority care, and that financial success alone is an insufficient justification for demanding a medical procedure. Most telling is its complete lack of concern for fairness and equity.[5]

A "bake sale" or charity approach that requires the less financially fortunate to make public appeals for funding is demeaning to the individuals involved, and to society as a whole. Rationing by financial ability says we do not believe in equality, but believe that a price can and should be placed on human life and that it should be paid by the individual whose life is at stake. Neither belief is tolerable in a society in which income is inequitably distributed.

The Committee Selection Process

The Seattle Selection Committee is a model of the committee process. Ethic Committees set up in some hospitals to decide whether or not certain handicapped newborn infants should be given medical care may represent another.[6] These committees have developed because it was seen as unworkable or unwise to explicitly set forth the criteria on which selection decisions would be made. But only two results are possible, as Professor Guido Calabrezi has pointed out: either a pattern of decision-making will develop or it will not. If a pattern does develop (e.g., in Seattle, the imposition of middle-class values), then it can be articulated and those decision "rules" codified and used directly, without resort to the committee. If a pattern does not develop, the committee is vulnerable to the charge that it is acting arbitrarily, or dishonestly, and therefore cannot be permitted to continue to make such important decisions.[1]

In the end, public designation of a committee to make selection decisions on vague criteria will fail because it too closely involves the state and all members of society in explicitly preferring specific individuals over others, and in devaluing the interests those others have in living. It thus directly undermines, as surely as the market system does, society's view of equality and the value of human life.

The Lottery Approach

The lottery approach is the ultimate equalizer which puts equality ahead of every other value. This makes it extremely attractive, since all comers have an equal chance at selection regardless of race, color, creed, or financial status. On the other hand, it offends our notions of efficiency and fairness since it makes no distinctions among such things as the strength of the desires of the candidates, their potential survival, and their quality of life. In this sense it is a mindless method of trying to solve society's dilemma which is caused by its unwillingness or inability to spend enough resources to make a lottery unnecessary. By making this macro spending decision evident to all, it also undermines society's view of the pricelessness of human life. A first-come, first-served system is a type of natural lottery since referral to a transplant program is generally random in time. Nonetheless, higher income groups have quicker access to referral networks and thus have an inherent advantage over the poor in a strict first-come, first-served system.[7,8]

The Customary Approach

Society has traditionally attempted to avoid explicitly recognizing that we are making a choice not to save individual lives because it is too expensive to do so. As long as such decisions are not explicitly acknowledged, they can be tolerated by society. For example, until recently there was said to be a general understanding among general practitioners in Britain that individuals over age 55 suffering from end-stage kidney disease not be referred for dialysis or transplant. In 1984, however, this unwritten practice became highly publicized, with figures that showed a rate of new cases of end-stage kidney disease treated in Britain at 40 per million (versus the US figure of 80 per million) resulting in 1500–3000 "unnecessary deaths" annually.[9] This has, predictably, led to movements to enlarge the National Health Service budget to expand dialysis to meet this need, a more socially acceptable solution than permitting the now publicly recognized situation to continue.

In the US, the customary approach permits individual physicians to select their patients on the basis of medical criteria or clinical suitability. This, however, contains much hidden social worth criteria. For example, one criterion, common in the transplant literature, requires an individual to have sufficient family support for successful aftercare. This discriminates against individuals without families and those who have become alienated from their families. The criterion may be relevant, but it is hardly medical.

Similar observations can be made about medical criteria that include IQ, mental illness, criminal records, employment, indigency, alcoholism, drug addiction, or geographical location. Age is perhaps more difficult, since it may be impressionistically related to outcome. But it is not medically logical to assume that an individual who is 49 years old is necessarily a better medical candidate for a transplant than one who is 50 years old. Unless specific examination of the characteristics of older persons that make them less desirable candidates is undertaken, such a cut off is arbitrary, and thus devalues the lives of older citizens. The same can be said of blanket exclusions of alcoholics and drug addicts.

In short, the customary approach has one great advantage for society and one great disadvantage: it gives us the illusion that we do not have to make choices; but the cost is mass deception, and when this deception is uncovered, we must deal with it either by universal entitlement or by choosing another method of patient selection.

A Combination of Approaches

A socially acceptable approach must be fair, efficient, and reflective of important social values. The most important values at stake in organ transplantation are fairness itself, equity in the sense of equality, and the value of life. To promote efficiency, it is important that no one receive a transplant unless they want one and are likely to obtain significant benefit from it in the sense of years of life at a reasonable level of functioning.

Accordingly, it is appropriate for there to be an initial screening process that is based *exclusively* on medical criteria designed to measure the probability of a successful transplant, i.e., one in which the patient survives for at least a number of years and is rehabilitated. There is room in medical criteria for social worth judgments, but there is probably no way to avoid this completely. For example, it has been noted that "in many respects social and medical criteria are inextricably intertwined" and that therefore medical criteria might "exclude the poor and disadvantaged because health and socioeconomic status are highly interdependent."[10] Roger Evans gives an example. In the End Stage Renal Disease Program, "those of lower socioeconomic status are likely to have multiple comorbid health conditions such as diabetes, hepatitis, and hypertension" making them both less desirable candidates and more expensive to treat.[10]

To prevent the gulf between the haves and have nots from widening, we must make every reasonable attempt to develop medical criteria that are objective and independent of social worth categories. One minimal way to approach this is to require that medical screening be reviewed and approved by an ethics committee with significant public representation, filed with a public agency, and made readily available to the public for comment. In the event that more than one hospital in a state is offering a particular transplant service, it would be most fair and efficient for the individual hospitals to perform the initial medical screening themselves (based on the uniform, objective criteria), but to have all subsequent non-medical selection done by a method approved by a single selection committee composed of representatives of all hospitals engaged in the particular transplant procedure, as well as significant representation of the public at large.

As this implies, after the medical screening is performed, there may be more acceptable candidates in the "pool" than there are organs or surgical teams to go around. Selection among waiting candidates will then be necessary. This situation occurs now in kidney transplantation, but since the organ matching is much more sophisticated than in hearts and livers (permitting much more precise matching of organ and recipient), and since dialysis permits individuals to wait almost indefinitely for an organ without risking death, the situations are not close enough to permit use of the same matching criteria. On the other hand, to the extent that organs are specifically tissue- and size-matched and fairly distributed to the best matched candidate, the organ distribution system itself will resemble a natural lottery.

When a pool of acceptable candidates is developed, a decision about who gets the next available, suitable organ must be made. We must choose between using a conscious, value-laden, social worth selection criterion (including a committee to make the actual choice), or some type of random device. In view of the unacceptability and arbitrariness of social worth criteria being applied, implicitly or explicitly, by committee, this method is neither viable nor proper. On the other hand, strict adherence to a lottery might create a situation where an individual who has only a one-in-four chance of living five years with a transplant (but who could survive another six months without one) would get an organ before an individual who could survive as long or longer, but who will die within days or hours if he or she is not immediately transplanted. Accordingly, the most reasonable approach seems to be to allocate organs on a first-come, first-served basis to members of the pool but permit individuals to "jump" the queue if the second level selection committee believes they are in immediate danger of death (but still have a reasonable prospect for long-term survival with a transplant) and the person who would otherwise get the organ can survive long enough to be reasonably assured that he or she will be able to get another organ.

The first-come, first-served method of basic selection (after a medical screen) seems the preferred method because it most closely approximates the randomness of a straight lottery without the obviousness of making equity the only promoted value. Some unfairness is introduced by the fact that the more wealthy and medically astute will likely get into the pool first, and thus be ahead in line, but this advantage should decrease sharply as public awareness of the system grows. The possibility of unfairness is also inherent in permitting individuals to jump the queue, but some flexibility needs to be retained in the system to permit it to respond to reasonable contingencies.

We will have to face the fact that should the resources devoted to organ transplantation be limited (as they are now and are likely to be in the future), at some point it is likely that significant numbers of individuals will die in the pool waiting for a transplant. Three things can be done to avoid this: 1) medical criteria can be made stricter, perhaps by adding a more rigorous notion of "quality" of life to longevity and prospects for rehabilitation; 2) resources devoted to transplantation and organ procurement can be increased; or 3) individuals can be persuaded not to attempt to join the pool.

Of these three options, only the third has the promise of both conserving resources and promoting autonomy. While most persons medically eligible for a transplant would probably want one, some would not — at least if they understood all that was involved, including the need for a lifetime commitment to daily immunosuppression medications, and periodic medical monitoring for rejection symptoms. Accordingly, it makes public policy sense to publicize the risks and side effects of transplantation, and to require careful explanations of the procedure be given to prospective patients before they undergo medical screening. It is likely that by the time patients come to the transplant center they have made up their minds and would do almost anything to get the transplant. Nonetheless, if there are patients who, when confronted with all the facts, would voluntarily elect not to proceed, we enhance both their own freedom and the efficiency and cost-effectiveness of the transplantation system by screening them out as early as possible.

Conclusion

Choices among patients that seem to condemn some to death and give others an opportunity to survive will always be tragic. Society has developed a number of mechanisms to make such decisions more acceptable by camouflaging them. In an era of scarce resources and conscious cost containment, such mechanism will become public, and they will be usable only if they are fair and efficient. If they are not so perceived, we will shift from one mechanisms to another in an effort to continue the illusion that tragic choices really don't have to be made, and that we can simultaneously move toward equity of access, quality of services, and cost containment without any challenges to our values. Along with the prostitute, the playboy, and the poet, we all need to be involved in the development of an access model to extreme and expensive medical technologies with which we can live.

References

1. Calabresi G, Bobbit P: *Tragic Choices*. New York: Norton, 1978.
2. Fletcher J: Our shameful waste of human tissue. *In*: Cutler DR (ed): The Religious Situation. Boston: Beacon Press, 1969; 223–252.
3. Quoted in Fox R, Swazey J: The Courage to Fail. Chicago: Univ of Chicago Press, 1974; 232.
4. Sanders & Dukeminier: Medical advance and legal lag: hemodialysis and kidney transplantation. UCLA L Rev 1968: 15:357.
5. President's Commission for the Study of Ethical Problems in Medicine: *Securing Access to Health Care*. US Govt Printing Office, 1983; 25.
6. Annas GJ: Ethics committees on neonatal care: substantive protection or procedural diversion? Am J Public Health 1984; 74: 843–845.
7. Bayer R: Justice and health care in an era of cost containment: allocating scarce medical resources. Soc Responsibility 1984; 9:37–52.
8. Annas GJ: Allocation of artificial hearts in the year 2002: *Minerva v National Health Agency*. Am J Law Med 1977; 3:59–76.
9. Commentary: UK's poor record in treatment of renal failure. Lancet July 7, 1984; 53.
10. Evans R: Health care technology and the inevitability of resource allocation and rationing decisions, Part II. JAMA 1983; 249:2208, 2217.

Chapter 4

Questions to Consider

1. To what extent, if at all, should health care providers be "gatekeepers" for society? If they should function as gatekeepers, how are they to resolve the conflict between their traditional fiduciary duty to act only in the interests of their patients and their responsibility for ensuring that health care resources are distributed fairly?
2. Should "quality of life" be considered in deciding who should receive scarce health care resources? If so, how is quality of life to be understood and measured?
3. If patients are to be denied potentially beneficial treatment because of economic constraints, should they be informed of this denial and the reason for it, as well as the possible increased side effects and reduced effectiveness of the treatment that they can receive?
4. When confronted by financial restrictions that prevent their patients from receiving potentially beneficial treatment, should health care providers try to "game the system," that is, make special efforts to circumvent the rules on behalf of their own patients? If they do not do this, are they failing to be advocates for their patients? On the other hand, what would happen if every health care provider did this?
5. Should patients ever be denied health care on the grounds that their lifestyle is a cause of their disease or illness?

Further Readings

Angell, Marcia. 1993. The doctor as double agent. *Kennedy Institute of Ethics Journal*, 3:279–86.

Buchanan, Allen. 1981. Justice: A Philosophical Review. In *Justice and Health Care*, Earl E. Shelp, ed. 3–21. Boston: D. Reidel Publishing Co.

Callahan, Daniel. 1987. *Setting limits*. New York: Simon and Schuster.

Haas, Janet F. 1988. Admission to rehabilitation centers: Selection of patients. *Archives of Physical Medicine and Rehabilitation* 69:329–332.

Langford, Michael J. 1992. Who should get the kidney machine? *Journal of Medical Ethics* 18:12–17.

Morreim, E. Haavi. 1991. Gaming the system. *Archives of Internal Medicine* 151: 443–47.

Purtilo, Ruth B. 1992. Whom to treat first, and how much is enough? Ethical dilemmas that physical therapists confront as they compare individual patient's needs for treatment. *International Journal of Technology Assessment in Health Care*, 8:26–34.

Schwartz, Robert L. 1992. Making patients pay for their life-style choices. *Cambridge Quarterly of Healthcare Ethics*, 4:393–400.

Strosberg, Martin A., et al., eds. 1989. *Rationing of medical care for the critically ill*. Washington, D.C.: The Brookings Institution.

———, eds. 1992. *Rationing America's medical care: The Oregon plan and beyond*. Washington, D.C.: The Brookings Institution.

Veatch, Robert M. 1980. Voluntary risks to health. *JAMA* 243:50–55.

Williams, Alan. 1992. Cost-effectiveness analysis: Is it ethical? *Journal of Medical Ethics* 18:7–11.

Part Two

Decision Making in Health Care

Chapter 5

Patients and Providers

Chapter 5

Introduction

A principal concern of health care ethics has been recognizing patients' authority to make meaningful choices about their care. Traditionally, physicians have had the responsibility of deciding what is best for patients on the grounds that their medical training and expertise qualify them to make such judgements. That position, known as medical paternalism, has been widely criticized, however. There are three main criticisms. The first follows from the recognition that health care decisions, decisions about what investigative tests to undergo and what treatments to have, for instance, involve both facts and values. Doctors are likely to be in the best position to understand and appreciate the relevant facts. Patients, however, are likely to be in the best position to understand and appreciate the relevant values. Only patients can ultimately decide whether the risks of harm associated with an intervention are worth the benefits likely to be obtained. Because health care decisions crucially involve value judgements, those who are most qualified to assess and compare the values — patients themselves — should, in this view, be entitled to make the decisions.

Second, once the factual and evaluative components of health care decisions have been distinguished, arguing that physicians possess expertise in evaluative or moral matters because they possess expertise in clinical or scientific matters can be seen to be mistaken. This mistake has been called "the fallacy of generalization of expertise" (Veatch 1973). Having been disabused of the notion that doctors are moral experts, we can, in this view, come to realize that the responsibility for health care decisions should be vested in the patients who know their own values best.

Third, and perhaps most important, it is the patient's life that will be most significantly affected by any procedure. That fact alone, it is argued, gives patients the right to decide.

The critique of medical paternalism becomes particularly compelling to many people when the values in question are moral, as in an anecdote related by a journalist:

There is a family doctor in Fort Garry, Man., who still fumes with outrage when telling how a middle-aged couple asked him to prescribe contraceptive pills, for their 15-year-old daughter, "so we won't have to worry." What upset him most was they weren't angry with a teen-age girl behaving in a fashion that made unwanted pregnancy a possibility. "They blindly accepted that's the way things are, that 'it's all part of the new morality.' Their real concern was to avoid the consequences." He refused the prescription. In justification, he still argues provision of the Pill would be seen by the schoolgirl — and her friends — as tacit approval by both parents and society of that mystical teen-age activity, "going all the way." However, he still worries about the decision because he had, in effect, been forced to act on the basis of a moral judgment, and that was a burden he could have done without (Edmonds 1981).

This journalist strongly disapproves of such behaviour and suggests a model to govern interactions between physicians and patients:

I resent being the victim of idiosyncratic moral convictions of my doctors. The human consequences of being treated by a doctor who let his conscience be his guide are potentially appalling. In other fields — politics for instance, and the law — you're required to declare any conflict of interest. For patients, the most significant conflict of interest can often be between their needs and their doctor's morality, so there should be a similar, and mandatory, requirement for medical professionals. I don't want my doctor to have placed upon him the uncomfortable mantle of custodian of modern morality, as in the case of the schoolgirl and the Pill. On the other hand, I don't want the burden of his morals, either. I want a professional to tell me my options (Edmonds 1981).

In this view, the job of a doctor (and other professionals) is to explain the nature of the problem and the alternative ways of dealing with it to the patient (or client) and then allow the patient to choose. This recommendation has been called the "engineering model" of the physician–patient relationship because it regards a doctor as a technician or "an engineer, a plumber making repairs, connecting tubes and flushing out clogged systems, with no questions asked" (Veatch 1972).

Should doctors be regarded simply as engineers? The engineering model has been criticized on a number of grounds. For one thing, it assumes that a sharp distinction between facts and values is possible, and that physicians can and should be confined to dealing with just the facts. That view is unrealistic, however. Doctors make value judgements all the time, when, for example, they assess the risks of a procedure or decide that a change in a patient's condition is significant. The practice of medicine is not value free; to the contrary, it is value laden, so "the question is not whether the physician will make value judgments, but which value judgments he or she will make . . ." (Paris 1993, 356). Moreover, whether patients, who are vulnerable and whose decision-making capacities may be compromised by their illnesses, can actually engage in the kind of objective, rational decision making that this model assigns to them has been questioned. One physician, reacting to the difficulty of making decisions about the treatment of his own cancer, found that his experience as a patient substantiated his belief that physicians "must be authoritarian and paternalistic to some degree" (Ingelfinger 1980, 1509). Because he is convinced that a certain amount of authoritarianism, paternalism, and domination are essential to good medical care, this doctor emphatically rejects the engineering model: "A physician who merely spreads an array of vendibles in front of the patient and then says, 'Go ahead and choose, it's your life,' is guilty of shirking his duty, if not of malpractice" (Ingelfinger 1980, 1509).

An appreciation of both sides of this issue has led to calls for physicians and patients to share decision making (Veatch 1972; Brock 1991). That sounds like an appealing compromise, but it is not easy to see how the responsibility for a decision can, in the end, be shared. At some point doesn't one person have to say yes or no, and isn't that person then fully responsible for the decision?

A general problem with the attempt to devise models of the physician–patient relationship is the restricted focus of this approach. Concentrating on the physician–patient relationship assumes that decision making in health care involves only two people and that these two people are removed from their personal, institutional, cultural, and social contexts. Health care is largely a team effort, however, so the moral relationships between patients and all members of the team and among members of the team themselves also need to be addressed. When health care is provided by a team, clear and consistent communication with patients and their families or guardians becomes more challenging; preservation of confidentiality and protection of privacy also become more difficult when multiple parties are involved. The moral problems associated with a team approach to health care need to be pursued.

Another problem with normative models of the physician–patient relationship (models of how decisions *ought* to be made) is that they ignore the vital issue of power. Not all analysts of decision making in health care have been blind to power, however. One suggests that "the real issue underlying paternalism, especially of the medical variety, is the question of power":

> The physician's power is awesome, and power carries responsibility. When a doctor says, "the ultimate responsibility is mine," what he really means is that the power to decide and control the situation, for better or worse, resides in him and that fact burdens him with a great responsibility (Ladd 1980, 1129).

But the need to recognize power and assess its moral implications is not restricted to the physician–patient relationship. All health care providers should be sensitive to the dynamics of power in their interactions with patients. Although discussions of the physician's power are now emerging (Brody 1992), much more scrutiny needs to be given to power relationships throughout the health care system.

As well, the changing nature of relationships between health care providers and patients has to be understood in context. Recognition of patient sovereignty or autonomy is not a phenomenon unique to health care. It has occurred throughout society and derives in large part from an underlying social and political philosophy, namely, the liberalism that is so influential in North America. A classic defence of individual autonomy, provided by John Stuart Mill in his essay, *On Liberty*, published in 1859, is frequently cited in defence of patient autonomy. Mill says his aim in *On Liberty* is "to assert one very simple principle, as entitled to govern absolutely the dealings of society with the individual in the way of compulsion and control"; this principle is that

> the sole end for which mankind are warranted, individually or collectively, in interfering with the liberty of action of any of their number is self-protection. That the only purpose for which power can be rightfully exercised over any member of a civilized community, against his will, is to prevent harm to others. His own good, either physical or moral, is not a sufficient warrant. . . . The only part of the conduct of anyone for which he is amenable to society is that which concerns others. In the part which merely concerns himself, his independence is, of right, absolute. Over himself, over his own body and mind, the individual is sovereign (Mill 1956, 13).

That eloquently stated principle (which actually is not as simple as Mill supposed) and Mill's argument in *On Liberty* that individuals are the best judges of what is in their own best interest are used to reject medical paternalism. One important worry about Mill's position, however, is whether there is, in the health care realm or elsewhere in society, any conduct that is purely self-regarding, that is, whether there is any conduct whatsoever that *merely concerns* oneself and does not affect others. The strong individualism that such a liberal position promotes is now being criticized, by feminist writers who give more priority to relationships, and by social and political philosophers who give more priority to the community.

The Selections

The selections in this chapter present both the standard concern of health care ethics with analyzing the physician–patient relationship and the notions of autonomy and paternalism and moral issues pertinent to other health care providers. In the first selection, Ezekiel Emanuel and Linda Emanuel describe four models of the physician–patient relationship — the paternalistic model, the informative model, the interpretive model, and the deliberative model — and the different conception of patient autonomy embodied in each. They use a case to illustrate, under each model, how a physician would speak to a patient with breast cancer. Emanuel and Emanuel recognize that different models will be appropriate in different clinical circumstances, but argue that, for both descriptive and prescriptive reasons, the ideal physician–patient relationship should be understood in terms of the deliberative model.

In the second selection, Ellen Bernal questions whether nurses should try to construct a professional identity for themselves in terms of the role of patient advocate. She worries about the assumptions regarding the nature of nursing that are implicit in an advocacy model, and she is sceptical of the alliance of moral and political considerations that this movement produces. She prefers the development of a more co-operative model of the nursing profession.

Ruth Purtilo, in the final selection, analyzes the debate about autonomy and paternalism in the context of rehabilitation. She suggests that autonomy should not be the only, or even the most important, value in a moral assessment of the practices of rehabilitation teams. She also makes recommendations about how the model of team rehabilitation can be improved.

References

Brock, Dan W. 1991. The ideal of shared decision making between physicians and patients. *Kennedy Institute of Ethics Journal* 1:28–47.

Brody, Howard. 1992. *The healer's power*. New Haven: Yale University Press.

Edmonds, Alan. 1981. Dramatic Collisions Between Morality, Medicine. *Medical* Post, Feb. 24, 12.

Ingelfinger, Franz J. 1980. Arrogance. *New England Journal of Medicine* 303:1507–11.

Ladd, John. 1980. Medical Ethics: Who Knows Best? *Lancet* Nov. 22, 1127–29.

Mill, John Stuart. 1956. *On Liberty*. Indianapolis: Bobbs-Merrill (originally published in 1859).

Paris, John J., et al. 1993. Beyond autonomy: Physicians' refusal to use life-prolonging extracorporeal membrane oxygenation. *New England Journal of Medicine* 329:354–57.

Veatch, Robert M. 1972. Models for ethical medicine in a revolutionary age. *Hastings Center Report*, 2(3):5–7.

———. (1973). Generalization of expertise. *Hastings Center Studies* 1(2):29–40.

18   Four Models of the Physician–Patient Relationship

Ezekiel J. Emanuel & Linda L. Emanuel

During the last two decades or so, there has been a struggle over the patient's role in medical decision making that is often characterized as a conflict between autonomy and health, between the values of the patient and the values of the physician. Seeking to curtail physician dominance, many have advocated an ideal of greater patient control.[1,2] Others question this ideal because it fails to acknowledge the potentially imbalanced nature of this interaction when one party is sick and searching for security, and when judgments entail the interpretation of technical information.[3,4] Still others are trying to delineate a more mutual relationship.[5,6] This struggle shapes the expectations of physicians and patients as well as the ethical and legal standards for the physician's duties, informed consent, and medical malpractice. This struggle forces us to ask, What should be the ideal physician–patient relationship?

We shall outline four models of physician–patient interaction, emphasizing the different understanding of (1) the goals of the physician–patient interaction, (2) the physician's obligations, (3) the role of patient values, and (4) the conception of patient autonomy. To elaborate the abstract description of these four models, we shall indicate the types of response the models might suggest in a clinical situation. Third, we shall also indicate how these models inform the current debate about the ideal physician–patient relationship. Finally, we shall evaluate these models and recommend one as the preferred model.

As outlined, the models are Weberian ideal types. They may not describe any particular physician–patient interaction but highlight, free from complicating details, different visions of the essential characteristics of the physician–patient interaction.[7] Consequently, they do not embody minimum ethical or legal standards, but rather constitute relative ideals that are "higher than the law" but not "above the law."[8]

The Paternalistic Model

First is the *paternalistic* model, sometimes called the parental[9] or priestly[10] model. In this model, the physician–patient interaction ensures that patients receive the interventions that best promote their health and well-being. To this end, physicians use their skills to determine the patient's medical condition and his or her stage in the disease process and to identify the medical tests and treatments most likely to restore the patient's health or ameliorate pain. Then the physician presents the patient with selected information that will encourage the patient to consent to the intervention the physician considers best. At the extreme, the physician authoritatively informs the patient when the intervention will be initiated.

The paternalistic model assumes that there are shared objective criteria for determining what is best. Hence the physician can discern what is in the patient's best interest with limited patient participation. Ultimately, it is assumed that the patient will be thankful for decisions made by the physician even if he or she would not agree to them at the time.[11] In the tension between the patient's autonomy and well-being, between choice and health, the paternalistic physician's main emphasis is toward the latter.

In the paternalistic model, the physician acts as the patient's guardian articulating and implementing what is best for the patient. As such, the physician has obligations, including that of placing the patient's interest above his or her own and soliciting the views of others when lacking adequate knowledge. The conception of patient autonomy is patient assent, either at the time or later, to the physician's determinations of what is best.

The Informative Model

Second is the *informative* model, sometimes called the scientific,[9] engineering,[10] or consumer model. In this model, the objective of the physician–patient interaction is for the physician to provide the patient with all relevant information, for the patient to select the medical interventions he or she wants, and for the physician to execute the selected interventions. To this end, the physician informs the patient of his or her disease state, the nature of possible diagnostic and therapeutic interventions, the nature and probability of risks and benefits associated with the intervention, and any uncertainties of knowledge. At the extreme, patients could come to know all medical information relevant to their disease and available interventions and select the interventions that best realize their values.

The informative model assumes a fairly clear distinction between facts and values. The patient's values are well defined and known; what the patient lacks is facts. It is the physician's obligation to provide all the available facts, and the patient's values then determine what treatments are to be given. There is no role for the physician's values, the physician's understanding of the patient's values, or his or her judgment of the worth of the patient's values. In the informative mode, the physician is a purveyor of technical expertise, providing the patient with the means to exercise control. As technical experts, physicians have important obligations to provide truthful information, to maintain competence in their area of expertise, and to consult others when their knowledge or skills are lacking. The conception of patient autonomy is patient control over medical decision making.

The Interpretive Model

The third model is the *interpretive* model. The aim of the physician–patient interaction is to elucidate the patient's values and what he or she actually wants, and to help the patient select the available medical interventions that realize these values. Like the informative physician, the interpretive physician provides the patient with information on the nature of the condition and the risks and benefits of possible interventions.

Beyond this, however, the interpretive physician assists the patient in elucidating and articulating his or her values and in determining what medical interventions best realize the specified values, thus helping to interpret the patient's values for the patient.

According to the interpretive model, the patient's values are not necessarily fixed and known to the patient. They are often inchoate, and the patient may only partially understand them; they may conflict when applied to specific situations. Consequently, the physician working with the patient must elucidate and make coherent these values. To do this, the physician works with the patient to reconstruct the patient's goals and aspirations, commitments and character. At the extreme, the physician must conceive the patient's life as a narrative whole, and from this specify the patient's values and their priority.[12,13] Then the physician determines which tests and treatments best realize these values. Importantly, the physician does not dictate to the patient; it is the patient who ultimately decides which values and course of action best fit who he or she is. Neither is the physician judging the patient's values; he or she helps the patient to understand and use them in the medical situation.

In the interpretive model, the physician is a counselor, analogous to a cabinet minister's advisory role to a head of state, supplying relevant information, helping to elucidate values and suggesting what medical interventions realize these values. Thus the physician's obligations include those enumerated in the informative model but also require engaging the patient in a joint process of understanding. Accordingly, the conception of patient autonomy is self-understanding; the patient comes to know more clearly who he or she is and how the various medical options bear on his or her identity.

Table 5.1   Comparing the Four Models

	Informative	Interpretive	Deliberative	Paternalistic
Patient values	Defined, fixed, and known to the patient	Inchoate and conflicting, requiring elucidation	Open to development and revision through moral discussion	Objective and shared by physician and patient
Physician's obligation	Providing relevant factual information and implementing patient's selected intervention	Elucidating and interpreting relevant patient values as well as informing the patient and implementing the patient's selected intervention	Articulating and persuading the patient of the most admirable values as well as informing the patient and implementing the patient's selected intervention	Promoting the patient's well-being independent of the patient's current preferences
Conception of patient's autonomy	Choice of, and control over, medical care	Self-understanding relevant to medical care	Moral self-development relevant to medical care	Assenting to objective values
Conception of physician's role	Competent technical expert	Counselor or advisor	Friend or teacher	Guardian

The Deliberative Model

Fourth is the *deliberative model*. The aim of the physician–patient interaction is to help the patient determine and choose the best health-related values that can be realized in the clinical situation. To this end, the physician must delineate information on the patient's clinical situation and then help elucidate the types of values embodied in the available options. The physician's objectives include suggesting why certain health-related values are more worthy and should be aspired to. At the extreme, the physician and patient engage in deliberation about what kind of health-related values the patient could and ultimately should pursue. The physician discusses only health-related values, that is, values that affect or are affected by the patient's disease and treatments; he or she recognizes that many elements of morality are unrelated to the patient's disease or treatment and beyond the scope of their professional relationship. Further, the physician aims at no more than moral persuasion; ultimately, coercion is avoided, and the patient must define his or her life and select the ordering of values to be espoused. By engaging in moral deliberation, the physician and patient judge the worthiness and importance of the health-related values.

In the deliberative model, the physician acts as a teacher or friend,[14] engaging the patient in dialogue on what course of action would be best. Not only does the physician indicate what the patient could do, but, knowing the patient and wishing what is best, the physician indicates what the patient should do, what decision regarding medical therapy would be admirable. The conception of patient autonomy is moral self-development; the patient is empowered not simply to follow unexamined preferences or examined values, but to consider, through dialogue, alternative health-related values, their worthiness, and their implications for treatment.

Comparing the Four Models

The Table compares the four models on essential points. Importantly, all models have a role for patient autonomy; a main factor that differentiates the models is their particular conception of patient autonomy. Therefore, no single model can be endorsed because it alone promotes patient autonomy. Instead the models must be compared and evaluated, at least in part, by evaluating the adequacy of their particular conceptions of patient autonomy.

The four models are not exhaustive. At a minimum there might be added a fifth: the *instrumental* model. In this model, the patient's values are irrelevant; the physician aims for some goal independent of the patient, such as the good of society or furtherance of scientific knowledge. The Tuskegee syphilis experiment[15–17] and the Willowbrook hepatitis study[18,19] are examples of this model. As the moral condemnation of these cases reveals, this model is not an ideal but an aberration. Thus we have not elaborated it herein.

A Clinical Case

To make tangible these abstract descriptions and to crystallize essential differences among the models, we will illustrate the responses they suggest in a clinical situation, that of a 43-year-old premenopausal women who has recently discovered a breast mass. Surgery reveals a 3.5-cm ductal carcinoma with no lymph node involvement that is estrogen receptor positive. Chest roentgenogram, bone scan, and liver function tests reveal no evidence of metastatic disease. The patient was recently divorced and has gone back to work as a legal aide to support herself. What should the physician say to this patient?

In the paternalistic model a physician might say, "There are two alternative therapies to protect against recurrence of cancer in your breast: mastectomy or radiation. We now know that the survival with lumpectomy combined with radiation therapy is equal to that with mastectomy. Because lumpectomy and radiation offers the best survival and the best cosmetic result, it is to be preferred. I have asked the radiation therapist to come and discuss radiation treatment with you. We also need to protect you against the spread of cancer to other parts of your body. Even though the chance of recurrence is low, you are young, and we should not leave any therapeutic possibilities untried. Recent studies involving chemotherapy suggest improvements in survival without recurrence of breast cancer. Indeed, the National Cancer Institute recommends chemotherapy for women with your type of breast cancer. Chemotherapy has side effects. Nevertheless, a few months of hardship now are worth the potential added years of life without cancer."

In the informative model a physician might say, "With node-negative breast cancer there are two issues before you: local control and systemic control. For local control, the options are mastectomy or lumpectomy with or without radiation. From many studies we know that mastectomy and lumpectomy with radiation result in identical overall survival, about 80% 10-year survival. Lumpectomy without radiation results in a 30% to 40% chance of tumor recurrence in the breast. The second issue relates to systemic control. We know that chemotherapy prolongs survival for premenopausal women who have axillary nodes involved with tumor. The role for women with node-negative breast cancer is less clear. Individual studies suggest that chemotherapy is of no benefit in terms of improving overall survival, but a comprehensive review of all studies suggests that there is a survival benefit. Several years ago, the NCI suggested that for women like yourself, chemotherapy can have a positive therapeutic impact. Finally, let me inform you that there are clinical trials, for which you are eligible, to evaluate the benefits of chemotherapy for patients with node-negative breast cancer. I can enroll you in a study if you want. I will be happy to give you any further information you feel you need."

The interpretive physician might outline much of the same information as the informative physician, then engage in discussion to elucidate the patient's wishes, and conclude, "It sounds to me as if you have conflicting wishes. Understandably, you seem uncertain how to balance the demands required for receiving additional treatment, rejuvenating your personal affairs, and maintaining your psychological equilibrium. Let me try to express a perspective that fits your position. Fighting your cancer is important, but it must leave you with a healthy self-image and quality time outside the hospital. This view seems compatible with undergoing radiation therapy but not chemotherapy. A lumpectomy with radiation maximizes your chance of surviving while preserving your breast. Radiotherapy fights your breast cancer without disfigurement. Conversely, chemotherapy would prolong the duration of therapy by many months. Further, the benefits of chemotherapy in terms of survival are smaller and more controversial. Given the recent changes in your life, you have too many preoccupations to undergo months of chemotherapy for a questionable benefit. Do I understand you? We can talk again in a few days."

The deliberative physician might begin by outlining the same factual information, engage in a conversation to elucidate the patient's values, but continue, "It seems clear that you should undergo radiation therapy. It offers maximal survival with minimal risk, disfigurement, and disruption of your life. The issue of chemotherapy is different, fraught with conflicting data. Balancing all the options, I think the best one for you is to enter a trial that is investigating the potential benefit of chemotherapy for women with node-negative breast cancer. First, it ensures that you receive excellent medical care. At this point, we do not know which therapy maximizes survival. In a clinical study the schedule of follow-up visits, tests, and decisions is specified by leading breast cancer experts to ensure that all the women receive care that is the best available anywhere. A second reason to participate in a trial is altruistic: it allows you to contribute something to women with breast cancer in the future who will face difficult choices. Over decades, thousands of women have participated in studies that inform our current treatment practices. Without those women, and the knowledge they made possible, we would probably still be giving you and all other women with breast cancer mastectomies. By enrolling in a trial you participate in a tradition in which women of one generation receive the highest standard of care available but also enhance the care of women in future generations because medicine has learned something about which interventions are better. I must tell you that I am not involved in the study; if you elect to enroll in this trial, you will initially see another breast cancer expert to plan your therapy. I have sought to explain our current knowledge and offer my recommendation so you can make the best possible decision."

Lacking the normal interchange with patients, these statements may seem contrived, even caricatures. Nevertheless, they highlight the essence of each model and suggest how the objectives and assumptions of each inform a physician's approach to his or her patients. Similar statements can be imagined for other clinical situations such as an obstetrician discussing prenatal testing or a cardiologist discussing cholesterol-reducing interventions.

The Current Debate and the Four Models

In recent decades there has been a call for greater patient autonomy or, as some have called it, "patient sovereignty,"[20] conceived as patient *choice* and *control* over medical decisions. This shift toward the informative model is embodied in the adoption of business terms for medicine, as when physicians are described as health care providers and patients as consumers. It can also be found in the propagation of patient rights statements,[21] in the promotion of living will laws, and in rules regarding human experimentation. For instance, the opening sentences of one law state: "The Rights of the Terminally Ill Act authorizes an adult person to *control* decisions regarding administration of life-sustaining treatment. . . . The Act merely provides one way by which a terminally-ill patient's *desires* regarding the use of life-sustaining procedures can be legally implemented" (emphasis added).[22] Indeed, living will laws do not require or encourage patients to discuss the issue of terminating care with their physicians before signing such documents. Similarly, decisions in "right-to-die" cases emphasize patient control over medical decisions. As one court put it[23]:

> The right to refuse medical treatment is basic and fundamental. . . . Its exercise requires no one's approval. . . . *[T]he controlling decision belongs to a competent informed patient.* . . . It is not a medical decision for her physicians to make. . . . *It is a moral and philosophical decision that, being a competent adult, is [the patient's] alone.* (emphasis added)

Probably the most forceful endorsement of the informative model as the ideal inheres in informed consent standards. Prior to the 1970s, the standard for informed consent was "physician based."[24-26] Since 1972 and the *Canterbury* case, however, the emphasis has been on a "patient-oriented" standard of informed consent in which the physician has a "duty" to provide appropriate medical facts to empower the patient to use his or her values to determine what interventions should be implemented.[25-27]

> True consent to what happens to one's self is the informed exercise of a choice, and that entails an opportunity to evaluate knowledgeably the options available and the risks attendant upon each. . . . *[I]t is the prerogative of the patient, not the physician, to determine for himself the direction in which his interests seem to lie.* To enable the patient to chart his course understandably, some familiarity with the therapeutic alternatives and their hazards become essential.[27] (emphasis added)

Shared Decision Making

Despite its dominance, many have found the informative mode "arid."[20] The President's Commission and others contend that the ideal relationship does not vest moral authority and medical decision-making power exclusively in the patient but must be a process of shared decision making constructed around "mutual participation and respect."[20,28] The President's Commission argues that the physician's role is "to help the patient understand the medical situation and available courses of action, and the patient conveys his or her concerns and wishes."[20] Brock and Wartman[29] stress this fact-value "division of labor" — having the physician provide information while the patient makes value decisions — by describing "shared decision making" as a collaborative process

> in which both physicians and patients make active and essential contributions. Physicians bring their medical training, knowledge, and expertise — including an understanding of the available treatment alternatives — to the diagnosis and management of patients' condition. Patients bring knowledge of their own subjective aims and values, through which risks and benefits of various treatment options can be evaluated. With this approach, selecting the best treatment for a particular patient requires the contribution of both parties.

Similarly, in discussing ideal medical decision making, Eddy[30] argues for this fact-value division of labor between the physician and patient as the ideal:

> It is important to separate the decision process into these two steps. . . . The first step is a question of facts. The anchor is empirical evidence. . . . [T]he second step is a question not of facts but of personal values or preferences. The thought process is not analytic but personal and subjective. . . . [I]t is the patient's preferences that should determine the decision. . . . Ideally, you and I [the physicians] are not in the picture. What matters is what Mrs. Smith thinks.

This view of shared decision making seems to vest the medical decision-making authority with the patient while relegating physicians to technicians "transmitting medical information and using their technical skills as the patient directs."[20] Thus, while the advocates of "shared decision making" may aspire toward a mutual dialogue between physician and patient, the substantive view informing their ideal reembodies the informative model under a different label.

Other commentators have articulated more mutual models of the physician–patient interaction.[5,6,25] Prominent among these efforts is Katz'[31] *The Silent World of the Doctor and Patient*. Relying on a Freudian view in which self-knowledge and self-determination are inherently limited because of unconscious influences, Katz views dialogue as a mechanism for greater self-understanding of one's values and objectives. According to Katz, this view places a duty on physicians and patients to reflect and communicate so that patients can gain a greater self-understanding and self-determination. Katz' insight is also available on grounds other than Freudian psychological theory and is consistent with the interpretive model.[13]

Objections to the Paternalistic Model

It is widely recognized that the paternalistic model is justified during emergencies when the time taken to obtain informed consent might irreversibly harm the patient.[1,2,20] Beyond such limited circumstances, however, it is no longer tenable to assume that the physician and patient espouse similar values and views of what constitutes a benefit. Consequently, even physicians rarely advocate the paternalistic model as an ideal for routine physician–patient interactions.[32]

Objections to the Informative Model

The informative model seems both descriptively and prescriptively inaccurate. First, this model seems to have no place for essential qualities of the ideal physician–patient relationship. The informative physician cares for the patient in the sense of competently implementing the patient's selected interventions. However, the informative physician lacks a caring approach that requires understanding what the patient values or should value and how his or her illness impinges on these values. Patients seem to expect their physician to have a caring approach; they deem a technically proficient but detached physician as deficient, and properly condemned. Further, the informative physician is proscribed from giving a recommendation for fear of imposing his or her will on the patient and thereby competing for the decision making control that has been given to the patient.[25] Yet, if one of the essential qualities of the ideal physician is the ability to assimilate medical facts, prior experience of similar situations, and intimate knowledge of the patient's view into a recommendation designed for the patient's specific medical and personal condition,[3-5,25] then the informative physician cannot be ideal.

Second, in the informative model the ideal physician is a highly trained subspecialist who provides detailed factual information and competently implements the patient's preferred medical intervention. Hence, the informative model perpetuates and accentuates the trend toward specialization and impersonalization within the medical profession.

Most importantly, the informative model's conception of patient autonomy seems philosophically untenable. The informative model presupposes that persons possess known and fixed values, but this is inaccurate. People are often uncertain about what they actually want. Further, unlike animals, people have what philosophers call "second order desires," that is, the capacity to reflect on their wishes and to revise their own desires and preferences. In fact, freedom of the will and autonomy inhere in having "second order desires"[33–35] and being able to change our preferences and modify our identity. Self-reflection and the capacity to change what we want often require a "process" of moral deliberation in which we assess the value of what we want. And this is a process that occurs with other people who know us well and can articulate a vision of who we ought to be that we can assent to.[13] Even though changes in health or implementation of alternative interventions can have profound effects on what we desire and how we realize our desires, self-reflection and deliberation play no essential role in the informative physician–patient interaction. The informative model's conception of autonomy is incompatible with a vision of autonomy that incorporates second-order desires.

Objections to the Interpretive Model

The interpretive model rectifies this deficiency by recognizing that persons have second-order desires and dynamic value structures and placing the elucidation of values in the context of the patient's medical condition at the center of the physician–patient interaction. Nevertheless, there are objections to the interpretive model.

Technical specialization militates against physicians cultivating the skills necessary to the interpretive model. With limited interpretive talents and limited time, physicians may unwittingly impose their own values under the guise of articulating the patient's values. And patients, overwhelmed by their medical condition and uncertain of their own views, may too easily accept this imposition. Such circumstances may push the interpretive model towards the paternalistic model in actual practice.

Further, autonomy viewed as self-understanding excludes evaluative judgment of the patient's values or attempts to persuade the patient to adopt other values. This constrains the guidance and recommendations the physician can offer. Yet in practice, especially in preventive medicine and risk-reduction interventions, physicians often attempt to persuade patients to adopt particularly health-related values. Physicians frequently urge patients with high cholesterol levels who smoke to change their dietary habits, quit smoking, and begin exercise programs before initiating drug therapy. The justification given for these changes is that patients should value their health more than they do. Similarly, physicians are encouraged to persuade their human immunodeficiency virus (HIV)-infected patients who might be engaging in unsafe sexual practices either to abstain or, realistically, to adopt "safer sex" practices. Such appeals are not made to promote the HIV-infected patient's own health, but are grounded on an appeal for the patient to assume responsibility for the good of others. Consequently, by excluding evaluative judgments, the interpretive model seems to characterize inaccurately ideal physician–patient interactions.

Objections to the Deliberative Model

The fundamental objections to the deliberative model focus on whether it is proper for physicians to judge patients' values and promote particular health-related values. First, physicians do not possess privileged knowledge of the priority of health-related values relative to other values. Indeed, since ours is a pluralistic society in which people espouse incommensurable values, it is likely that a physician's values and view of which values are higher will conflict with those of other physicians and those of his or her patients.

Second, the nature of the moral deliberation between physician and patient, the physician's recommended interventions, and the actual treatments used will depend on the values of the particular physician treating the patient. However, recommendations and care provided to patients should not depend on the physician's judgment of the worthiness of the patient's values or on the physician's particular values. As one bioethicist put it:[36]

> The hand is broken; the physician can repair the hand; therefore the physician must repair the hand — as well as possible — without regard to personal values that might lead the physician to think ill of the patient or of the patient's values. . . . [A]t the level of clinical practice, medicine should be value-free in the sense that the personal values of the physician should not distort the making of medical decisions.

Third, it may be argued that the deliberative model misconstrues the purpose of the physician–patient interaction. Patients see their physicians to receive health care, not to engage in moral deliberation or to revise their values. Finally, like the interpretive model, the deliberative model may easily metamorphose into unintended paternalism, the very practice that generated the public debate over the proper physician–patient interaction.

The Preferred Model and the Practical Implications

Clearly, under different clinical circumstances different models may be appropriate. Indeed, at different times all four models may justifiably guide physicians and patients. Nevertheless, it is important to specify one model as the shared, paradigmatic reference; exceptions to use other models would not be automatically condemned, but would require justification based on the circumstances of a particular situation. Thus, it is widely agreed that in an emergency where delays in treatment to obtain informed consent might irreversibly harm the patient, the paternalistic model correctly guides physician–patient interactions. Conversely, for patients who have clear but conflicting values, the interpretive model is probably justified. For instance, a 65-year-old woman who has been treated for acute leukemia may have clearly decided against reinduction chemotherapy if she relapses. Several months before the anticipated birth of her first grandchild, the patient relapses. The patient becomes torn about whether to endure the risks of reinduction chemotherapy in order to live to see her first grandchild or whether to refuse therapy, resigning herself to not seeing her grandchild. In such cases, the physician may justifiably adopt the interpretive approach. In other circumstances, where there is only a one-time physician–patient interaction without an ongoing relationship in which the patient's values can be elucidated and compared with ideals, such as in a walk-in center, the informative model may be justified.

Descriptively and prescriptively, we claim that the ideal physician–patient relationship is the deliberative model. We will adduce six points to justify this claim. First, the deliberative model more nearly embodies our ideal of autonomy. It is an oversimplification and distortion of the Western tradition to view respecting autonomy as simply permitting a person to select, unrestricted by coercion, ignorance, physical interference, and the like, his or her preferred course of action from a comprehensive list of available options.[34,35] Freedom and control over medical decisions alone do not constitute patient autonomy. Autonomy requires that individuals critically assess their own values and preferences; determine whether they are desirable; affirm, upon reflection, these values as ones that should justify their actions; and then be free to initiate action to realize the values. The process of deliberation integral to the deliberative model is essential for realizing patient autonomy understood in this way.

Second, our society's image of an ideal physician is not limited to one who knows and communicates to the patient relevant factual information and competently implements medical interventions. The ideal physician — often embodied in literature, art, and popular culture — is a caring physician who integrates the information and relevant values to make a recommendation and, through discussion, attempts to persuade the patient to accept this recommendation as the intervention that best promotes his or her overall well-being. Thus, we expect the best physicians to engage their patients in evaluating discussions of health issues and related values. The physician's discussion does not invoke values that are unrelated or tangentially related to the patient's illness and potential therapies. Importantly, these efforts are not restricted to situations in which patients might make "irrational and harmful" choices[29] but extend to all health care decisions.

Third, the deliberative model is not a disguised form of paternalism. Previously there may have been category mistakes in which instances of the deliberative model have been erroneously identified as physician paternalism. And no doubt, in practice, the deliberative physician may occasionally lapse into paternalism. However, like the ideal teacher, the deliberative physician attempts to persuade the patient of the worthiness of certain values, not to impose those values paternalistically; the physician's aim is not to subject the patient to his or her will, but to persuade the patient of a course of action as desirable. In the Laws, Plato[37] characterizes this fundamental distinction between persuasion and imposition for medical practice that distinguishes the deliberative from the paternalistic model:

> A physician to slaves never gives his patients any account of his illness . . . the physician offers some order gleaned from experience with an air of infallible knowledge, in the brusque fashion of a dictator. . . . The free physician, who usually cares for free men, treats their disease first by thoroughly discussing with the patient and his friends his ailment. This way he learns something from the sufferer and si-multaneously instructs him. Then the physician does not give his medications until he has persuaded the patient; the physician aims at complete restoration of health by persuading the patient to comply with his therapy.

Fourth, physician values are relevant to patients and do inform their choice of a physician. When a pregnant woman chooses an obstetrician who does not routinely perform a battery of prenatal tests or, alternatively, one who strongly favors them; when a patient seeks an aggressive cardiologist who favors procedural interventions or one who concentrates therapy on dietary changes, stress reduction, and life-style mod-ifications, they are, consciously or not, selecting a physician based on the values that guide his or her medical decisions. And, when disagreements between physicians and patients arise, there are discussions over which values are more important and should be realized in medical care. Occasionally, when such disagreements undermine the phy-sician–patient relationship and a caring attitude, a patient's care is transferred to another physician. Indeed, in the informative model the grounds for transferring care to a new physician is either the physician's ignorance or incompetence. But patients seem to switch physicians because they do not "like" a particular physician or that physician's attitude or approach.

Fifth, we seem to believe that physicians should not only help fit therapies to the patients' elucidated values, but should also promote health-related values. As noted, we expect physicians to promote certain values, such as "safer sex" for patients with HIV or abstaining from or limiting alcohol use. Similarly, patients are willing to adjust their values and actions to be more compatible with health-promoting values.[38] This is in the nature of seeking a caring medical recommendation.

Finally, it may well be that many physicians currently lack the training and capacity to articulate the values underlying their recommendations and persuade patients that these values are worthy. But, in part, this deficiency is a consequence of the tendencies toward specialization and the avoidance of discussion of values by physicians that are perpetuated and justified by the dominant informative model. Therefore, if the deliberative model seems most appropriate, then we need to implement changes in medical care and education to encourage a more caring approach. We must stress understanding rather than mere provisions of factual information in keeping with the legal standards of informed consent and medical malpractice; we must educate physicians not just to spend more time in physician–patient communication but to elucidate and articulate the values underlying their medical care decisions, including routine ones; we must shift the publicly assumed conception of patient autonomy that shapes both the physician's and the patient's expectations from patient control to moral development. Most important, we must recognize that developing a deliberative physician–patient relationship requires a considerable amount of time. We must develop a health care financing system that properly reimburses — rather than penalizes — physicians for taking the time to discuss values with their patients.

Conclusion

Over the last few decades, the discourse regarding the physician–patient relationship has focused on two extremes: autonomy and paternalism. Many have attacked physicians as paternalistic, urging the empowerment of patients to control their own care. This view, the informative model, has become dominant in bioethics and legal standards. This model embodies a defective conception of patient autonomy, and it reduces the physician's role to that of a technologist. The essence of doctoring is a fabric of knowledge, understanding, teaching, and action, in which the caring physician integrates the patient's medical condition and health-related values, makes a recommendation on the appropriate course of action, and tries to persuade the patient of the worthiness of this approach and the values it realizes. The physician with a caring attitude is the ideal embodied in the deliberative model, the ideal that should inform laws and policies that regulate the physician–patient interaction.

Finally, it may be worth noting that the four models outlined herein are not limited to the medical realm: they may inform the public conception of other professional interactions as well. We suggest that the ideal relationships between lawyer and client,[14] religious mentor and laity, and educator and student are well described by the deliberative model, at least in some of their essential aspects.

Acknowledgements: We would like to thank Robert Mayer, MD, Craig Henderson, MD, Lynn Peterson, MD, and John Stoeckle, MD, as well as Dennis Thompson, PhD, Arthur Applbaum, PhD, and Dan Brock, PhD, for their critical reviews of the manuscript. We would also like to thank the "ethics and the professions" seminar participants, especially Robert Rosen, JD, Francis Kamm, PhD, David Wilkins, JD, and Oliver Avens, who enlightened us in discussions.

References

1. Veatch RM. *A Theory of Medical Ethics*. New York, NY: Basic Books Inc Publishers; 1981.

2. Macklin R. *Mortal Choices*. New York, NY: Pantheon Books Inc; 1987.

3. Ingelfinger FJ. Arrogance. *N Engl J Med*. 1980;304:1507.

4. Marzuk PM. The right kind of paternalism. *N Engl J Med*. 1985;313:1474–1476.

5. Siegler M. The progression of medicine: from physician paternalism to patient autonomy to bureaucratic parsimony. *Arch Intern Med*. 1985;145:713–715.

6. Szasz TS, Hollender MH. The basic models of the doctor-patient relationship. *Arch Intern Med*. 1956;97:585–592.

7. Weber M; Parsons T. ed. *The Theory of Social and Economic Organization*. New York, NY: The Free Press; 1974.

8. Ballantine HT. Annual discourse — the crisis in ethics, anno domini 1979. *N Engl J Med*. 1979;301:634–638.

9. Burke G. Ethics and medical decision-making *Prim Care*. 1980;7:615–624.

10. Veatch RM. Models for ethical medicine in a revolutionary age. *Hastings Cent Rep*. 1975;2:3–5.

11. Stone AA. *Mental Health and Law: A System in Transition*. New York, NY: Jason Aronson Inc; 1976.

12. MacIntyre A. *After Virtue*. South Bend, Ind: University of Notre Dame Press; 1981.

13. Sandel MJ. *Liberalism and the Limits of Justice*. New York, NY: Cambridge University Press; 1982.

14. Fried C. The lawyer as friend: the moral foundations of the lawyer client relationship. *Yale Law J*. 1976;85:1060–1089.

15. Jones JH. *Bad Blood*. New York, NY: Free Press; 1981.

16. *Final Report of the Tuskegee Syphilis Study Ad Hoc Advisory Panel*. Washington, DC: Public Health Service; 1973.

17. Brandt AM. Racism and research: the case of the Tuskegee Syphilis Study, *Hastings Cent Rep*. 1978;8:21–29.

18. Krugman S, Giles JP. Viral hepatitis: new light on an old disease. *JAMA*. 1970;212:1019–1029.

19. Ingelfinger FJ. Ethics of experiments on children. *N Engl J Med*. 1973;288:791–792.

20. President's Commission for the Study of Ethical Problems in Medicine and Biomedical and Behavioral Research. *Making Health Care Decisions*. Washington, DC: US Government Printing Office; 1982.

21. *Statement of a Patient's Bill of Rights*. Chicago, Ill: American Hospital Association; November 17, 1972.

22. Uniform Rights of the Terminally Ill Act. In: *Handbook of Living Will Laws*. New York, NY: Society for the Right to Die; 1987: 135–147.

23. *Bouvia v Superior Court*. 225 Cal Rptr 297 (1986).

24. *Natanson v Kline*, 350 P2d 1093 (Kan 1960).

25. Applebaum PS, Lidz CW, Meisel A. *Informed Consent: Legal Theory and Clinical Practice*. New York, NY: Oxford University Press Inc; 1987:chap 3.

26. Faden RR, Beauchamp TL. *A History and Theory of Informed Consent*, New York, NY: Oxford University Press Inc; 1986.

27. *Canterbury v Spence*, 464 F2d 772 (DC Cir 1972).

28. Brock D. The ideal of shared decision-making between physicians and patients. *Kennedy Institute J Ethics*. 1991;1:28–47.

29. Brock DW, Wartman SA. When competent patients make irrational choices. *N Engl J Med*. 1990;322:1595–1599.

30. Eddy DM. Anatomy of a decision. *JAMA*. 1990;263:441–443.

31. Katz J. *The Silent World of Doctor and Patient*. New York, NY: Free Press; 1984.

32. Tannock IF, Boyer M. When is a cancer treatment worthwhile? *N Engl J Med*. 1990; 322:989–990.

33. Frankfurt H. Freedom of the will and the concept of a person. *J Philosophy*. 1971; 68:5–20.

34. Taylor C. *Human Agency and Language*. New York, NY: Cambridge University Press; 1985:15–44.

35. Dworkin G. *The Theory and Practice of Autonomy*. New York, NY: Cambridge University Press; 1988:chap 1.

36. Gorovitz S. *Doctors' Dilemmas: Moral Conflict and Medical Care*. New York, NY: Oxford University Press Inc; 1982:chap 6.

37. Plato; Hamilton E, Cairns H, eds; Emanuel EJ, trans. *Plato: The Collected Dialogues*. Princeton, NJ: Princeton University Press; 1961: 720 c–e.

38. Walsh DC, Hingson RW, Merrigan DM, et al. The impact of a physician's warning on recovery after alchoholism treatment. *JAMA*. 1992:267;663–667.

19   The Nurse as Patient Advocate

Ellen W. Bernal

Since the 1970s an extensive discussion in nursing literature had been devoted to the suggestion that nurses be "patient advocates" whose primary responsibility is to protect patient rights and interests in the health care setting.[1] The obligation to patients represents an ideal; in actual practice, institutional and hierarchical constraints often prevent nurses from acting as advocates. Consequently, those espousing patient advocacy argue that unless nurses achieve greater professional autonomy, patients' rights will not be fully protected in hospital settings.[2]

The intertwining of professional and ethical concerns, whereby principles such as patient rights and autonomy are considered in the same context as the professional issue of freedom to practice, is worthy of note. Indeed, such intertwining is a distinguishing feature of nursing ethics in general. While medical ethics rarely needs to address the physician's freedom to establish a professional relationship with patients, nursing ethics had to deal with ongoing challenges to the freedom to practice, especially in hospital settings.

But even within the context of nursing ethics and its characteristic focus on professional issues, the advocacy literature is distinguished by the frequently explicit claim that patients' rights and interests can only be fully protected in hospital settings if nurses achieve greater professional autonomy. The claim may be misguided. Potential confusion may arise when a call for protection of patient rights is combined with a call for increased political power for nurses.[3]

While the specific features of patient advocacy continue to be debated, it is clear that the central idea — that the primary obligation of nurses is to patients, rather than to physicians or hierarchies within hospitals — has gained wide acceptance within the profession.

Revisions in the American Nurses' Association's Code for Nurses reflect this shift in professional viewpoint. The 1976 code not only omits statements, present in earlier versions, that obliged nurses to maintain confidence in physicians and obey their orders, but also explicitly uses the language of advocacy in its interpretive statements: "In the role of client advocate, the nurse must be alert to and take appropriate action regarding any instances of incompetent, unethical, or illegal practice(s) by any member of the health care team or the health care system itself, or any action on the part of others that is prejudicial to the client's best interests."[4]

The debate over nurses' role as patient advocate affords an opportunity to consider several key issues. First, over the past two decades, nurses' perception of their primary allegiance has shifted from physicians and hospitals to patients. Second, some of the advocacy literature explicitly combines professional aspirations with the expression of obligations to patients. To what extent is the combination of moral and political claims legitimate? Third, patient advocacy assumes that nurses bring a special moral perspective to hospital settings. What is the nature of this moral contribution, and do nurses in fact wish to accept this as a feature of their professional role?

The advocacy literature asserts the moral primacy of autonomy, currently accepted in Western culture, and as a result may risk an impoverished view of illness, suffering, and the obligations of the professional to the patient. Alternative models of the nurse–patient relationship such as the covenantal models already described in nursing literature, may offer a better construction of the relationship between nursing and the public.

The Advocacy Model

Before the advocacy model gained wide acceptance, nurses believed that their primary obligation was to obey physicians and maintain order within hospitals. This military sense of nursing identity originated in the context of the Crimean war, when Florence Nightingale brought order and greatly improved conditions to military hospitals. Upon her return to England in 1856, Nightingale worked to establish a training school for nurses that would eventually impart the same military discipline to civilian hospitals, through an emphasis on improved education and obedience to institutional hierarchies. Elements of the military ideal included unquestioning loyalty and obedience to the nurse's training school, hospital, and physician's orders; protection of the patient's faith in the physician, even in cases of physician error or incompetence; self-sacrifice under difficult working conditions; and the routine indications of discipline such as uniforms and deference to physicians. Despite evidence that some nursing leaders called attention to the conflicts in loyalty that could come about under this model, the military ideal provided an early sense of professional nursing identity.

The military language prevalent during the Nightingale era was gradually replaced by the language of advocacy. The primary role of advocacy is defined as the protection of patients' rights and interests. In one of the earliest pieces on the topic, Mary F. Kohnke suggests that advocacy means informing patients about their rights, providing facts about their health care situation, and supporting them in the decisions they make.[5] A more extensive development of this idea is found in a series of articles by George J. Annas, who claims that patients' rights need protection in hospital settings, and that nurses may be able to fill the role of "patient rights advocate."[6]

From the outset, the advocacy literature has frequently associated protection of patient rights with professional development. For example, Annas notes that advocacy will require a level of assertiveness that many nurses may not currently possess. If nurses provided organized support for the idea of patient rights, and taught students the art of advocacy in nursing schools, the position of the patient in the hospital and the public image of the nurse would both be enhanced. "Nurses so trained can act not only as independent practioners, but can also move into the direct care of patients as partners of doctors rather than servants to them." Similarly, Nancy Quinn and Anne Somers Walsh predict that if nurses support the consumers' movement in health care and become patient advocates, health care and nurses' professional status will improve, while Elsie and Bertram Bandman claim that "patient advocacy is integral with the expanding relationships nurses have in the care of their patients. Models of nurse–patient–physician relationships show that patient advocacy by nurses is essential to patients' health care rights."[7]

The next move in the debate was the claim that hospital power structures prevent nurses from identifying unsafe or unethical practices by instilling a fear of reprisal. That is to say, hospital nurses are limited in their ability to serve as patient advocates because they are *unable* to protect patients' rights. Unless hospital power structures are changed to permit greater autonomy for nurses, patient rights within hospitals will be compromised. In this view, set forth in an influential article by Roland R. Yarling and Beverly J. McElmurry, optimal protection of patient rights can only be achieved through the development of nurses' professional power:

> unless nursing, through the reform of the institution in which the majority of its members practice, acquires a balance of controlling power in the institution or creates new structures for the organization of practice, it cannot effectively implement standards of care for its own practice. If it cannot realize reform it will compromise the integrity of the nurse-patient relationship, which is the moral foundation of nursing, and it will have lost its status as a profession. Furthermore, the public will have lost its most valuable ally within the health care system. The one action that would most improve the quality of health care in this society is simple and direct: set the nurses free, set the nurses free.[8]

An Ethical Analysis of the Advocacy Argument

The advocacy literature expresses professional identity and aspirations in the context of present nursing practice, displaying a concern for public and interprofessional recognition of nursing's professional status along with the concern to promote patients' rights and best interests. The literature often describes nurses as symbols of moral order within hospitals, and may have captured the imagination of nurses because it seems to offer a constructive way out of current difficult practice conditions, while simultaneously enhancing patients' rights.

The use of autonomy in the arguments for patient advocacy is also worth noting. The image of the autonomous person is invoked for both the patient whose rights are threatened in the hospital and for the nurse whose moral agency is compromised by institutional power structures. In the most extreme formulation of patient advocacy, the autonomy of the patient is held to be contingent upon the autonomy of the nurse.

The combination of references to actual circumstances, professional frustration and aspiration, and powerful moral ideals tends to promote uncritical assent to the claims for patient advocacy.[9] Criticism of any one of these elements may lead to a defense of advocacy through an appeal to another component. For example, any empirical question raised about nurses' working conditions within hospital settings might be answered by an appeal to nurses' professional aspirations. In a similar fashion, criticism of the search for professional power can be turned aside through a reference to the ideal of autonomy. The complex relationships among the components of the argument may have contributed to the persistence of the advocacy model.

But it is important to distinguish between the interest generated by a model and its adequacy in describing professional realities, values, and ideals. Professional nursing needs to determine whether the current description of patient advocacy actually enhances, or is in fact a detriment to professional development. Toward this end, the elements of the model should be considered separately. For example, the empirical claims and assumptions present in the advocacy literature should be examined. Is the typical nurse more likely to identify ethical issues than members of other professions, or than the general public? Do nurses currently have adequate freedom to practice? What courses of action are available to nurses when they observe less than optimal care in hospitals or other settings? Do nurses exercise these options, if they are in fact currently available? When nurses hesitate to act because of fear of reprisal, how realistic is this fear? What is the relevance of the advocacy role to situations involving deficiencies in the practice of other nurses? Research in nursing ethics is currently examining related issues that could be extended and brought to bear on the concept of advocacy if the empirical claims used to argue for it could be separated from the accompanying moral principles and professional aspirations.

Professional identity also requires clear conceptual distinctions between intrinsic professional values, the instrumental need for adequate freedom to practice, and the more self-serving goal of increased professional status. Without this differentiation, a key feature of professional identity may be lost: the promise to provide services to the public as an intrinsic value, rather than as a means to achieve professional power. Professional autonomy is not an intrinsic value of nursing and does not constitute part of the services offered to the public.[10] Instead, the ability to take action is a condition for the exercise of other values that are intrinsic to the profession. While freedom to practice is certainly necessary, the advocacy literature repeatedly confuses the distinction between freedom to practice and the less disinterested goal of professional nursing development.

On the Moral Contribution of Nurses to Hospitals

The patient advocacy literature presents symbolic images of the nurse as an individual who identifies ethical concerns, yet because of institutional constraints must either set these concerns aside, or take unusually forceful action. If she sets the concerns aside, the nurse compromises personal integrity and the adequacy of patient care: if she takes action, she risks personal and professional harm.

Christine Mitchell's argument for nursing integrity signals the end of the notion that the military model of obedience can provide effective patient care in hospitals, and the beginning of the advocacy literature's claim that the nurse's freedom to act with integrity is essential to the support of patient rights and best interests. In a fictional account, Mitchell describes the moral discord faced by Nurse Andrews, who is caring for two neurologically injured patients, one an alert quadriplegic and the other a comatose individual with a poor prognosis. The two patients are attended by different physicians whose perspectives on cardiopulmonary resuscitation are different. The military model of obedience at the heart of Nurse Andrew's practice leads to inconsistency: she resuscitates the comatose patient several times, but allows the alert quadriplegic to die, despite his interest in recovering. Mitchell comments that "the individual nurse is severely handicapped in acting with integrity. Nurses' inter-professional relationships with physicians come into direct conflict with their relationships with patients. Consequently, the integrity of the whole health care system is threatened."[11] In this story, the nurse is portrayed as central to the protection of moral standards and consistent care within the hospital. When her integrity is compromised, the integrity of the institution is compromised as well.

In other advocacy stories the nurse attempts to champion patient rights and in the process either experiences or narrowly avoids personal harm. Leah Curtin provides a description of an actual situation. Jean S. is a staff nurse who is assigned to care for William R., a recently widowed man in his late sixties who was admitted to the hospital through the emergency room, where he presented with probable bowel obstruction. When the house surgeon operated, he found that Mr. R. had cancer; however, the physician believed that this diagnosis should not be shared with the patient. Jean S. attempted to convince the physician that this lack of disclosure was contrary to the rights of the patient and counterproductive to his well-being, but without success. When the patient continued to ask pointed questions regarding his health, the nurse did inform the patient about his condition. The grateful patient was then able to obtain assistance with home care through a local hospice association and later died peacefully at home. The attending physician was angry with the nurse and lodged a complaint of insubordination against her, but the director of nursing, social work services, and the chaplain's office supported her decision to share information. In Curtin's commentary upon this case, she observes that "although nurses have a moral duty to be honest in answering patients' questions, . . . it is unlikely that nurses will do so (at least in any great numbers) as long as physicians have the professional and institutional power to coerce and punish them."[12]

Whether the nurse in the advocacy stories chooses to act or to remain passive, she brings a moral point of view to patient care. The expectation that nurses are to display a special moral sensitivity, while a key feature of the notion of advocacy, is by no means new. In the culture of ancient Greece and Rome, the perception that women have a natural altruism and an ability to care for others gave a sense of moral obligation to their traditional domestic occupations, such as caring for the sick. But because these occupations were regarded as chores somehow natural to women, and because of women's comparative social invisibility, their work did not appear to merit special notice. Although some of the services performed by women were highly respected, such as preparing the dead for burial and assisting at childbirth, the surrounding culture did not confer professional status on women who performed these activities.[13]

Modern culture persists in the belief that women are naturally altruistic, and altruism is a foundational assumption in the professional development of nursing. The establishment of modern hospitals "played upon the contemporary assumption that there was a necessary and laudable conjunction between nursing and femininity; the trained sensibility of a middle-class woman could alone bring order and morality to the hospital's grim wards."[14] But the view that women are naturally altruistic has restricted the ability of nurses to achieve professional status. Demands for professional autonomy when made by women are taken to be self-interested rather than oriented toward the needs of others, and so are seen as unfeminine.[15]

Patient advocacy appears to offer a way out of this difficulty, as it draws upon the traditional belief that nurses bring civilizing, altruistic influence to hospitals, but is based on a changed notion of civic virtue. Instead of military obedience, the surrounding culture values individual rights. Proponents of patient advocacy imply that nurses are the professionals who — given adequate professional freedom — can best ensure the protecting of patient rights within hospitals. Through this maneuver nurses can make a claim for professional power without jeopardizing their traditional image of altruism, self-sacrifice, and high moral ideals.

The advocacy stories, however, contain questionable implications that should be considered carefully by anyone tempted to define nurses as patient advocates. First of all, they suggest that the core values of nursing are ephemeral, and that the profession will take up whatever values are current in the surrounding culture. The stories also contribute to the likelihood that the public will continue to perceive the nursing profession sentimentally, perpetuating longstanding stereotypes of nurses as martyrs or heroes. The martyr, a victim of circumstance, is sacrificed to save others who will not at first honor the sacrifice or recognize its importance. This is the nurse under the military model, who works long hours and sacrifices her own interests to care for the suffering and to save lives. In contrast, the hero, possessing unusual strength and courage, is engaged in a socially visible struggle. This is the nurse under the advocacy model, who both defends patients' rights and seeks to elevate nurses' professional status, in an adversarial struggle against the forces of institutional oppression. Both images are highly unrealistic. Professional authority has legitimate origins in nursing expertise and history, not in romantic images of nurses as guardians of morality. When nurses are portrayed in this fashion, nursing practice is burdened with unrealistic demands and barriers are erected between nurses and the other professionals with whom they cooperate.

The Ideal of Autonomy

Those who promote patient advocacy often confuse the need for an adequate level of professional freedom to practice with an idealized image of autonomy that has attained a privileged moral status in Western culture. In this idealized image, persons select actions from a wide array of choices and are unlimited by situational constraints. Such a vision of autonomy impoverishes our view of social relationships, illness, suffering, and the obligations of the professional to the patient.

On the patient advocate model, social relationships within the hospital are essentially adversarial and manipulative. The rights of the patient are threatened by caregivers and by the institution itself. Nurses' rights too are abridged by physicians, other professionals, and bureaucratic structures. The model assumes that most relationships within hospitals are based on self-preservation and self-interest, rather than on mutual cooperation toward a common end. Within this context, nurses become professionals who assert their own rights and the rights of patients when they are threatened by others. There is a tendency to protest and unmask others' motivations rather than to explore the purposes and ends of social relationships and one's own responsibilities in promoting them.

A misplaced emphasis on autonomy obscures the frequently positive aspects of social relationships within hospitals: the mutually affirmed goals of promoting the patient's best interest in accordance with patient choice and the responsible use of resources in the service of those ends. Although hospitals may sometimes fail in their efforts to achieve their goals, it is not clear that failures are due to a deficit in nursing autonomy. The call for an abstract and unadulterated ideal of autonomy disregards the freedom of action that nurses already have.[16]

It is also not clear that the vision of autonomy invoked by proponents of patient advocacy sufficiently honors the experience of illness for the patient in the hospital. When the patient is suffering and vulnerable, an emphasis on individual rights cannot fully characterize the nurse–client relationship, as Sally Gadow observes when she urges nurses to assist the patient to find meaning in the experience of illness.[17] The interests of third parties and communities are also not encompassed by notions of patient autonomy.

The ascendancy of autonomy in modern culture contributes to the likelihood that the role of nurse as patient advocate will be accepted uncritically, especially by those nurses who actually experience repressive working conditions in hospital settings. Nurses should consider whether a more effective contribution to the growth of professional identity might not be achieved by defining patient advocacy more precisely.

As it now stands, advocacy refers to situations in which the nurse protects the patient from the incompetent or unethical practice of another professional. But other professionals, such as patient representatives, also describe themselves as patient advocates. Are nurses to practice a distinctive, nurse-specific form of advocacy or is their advocacy to overlap that of other professionals?

Professional nursing might also wish to examine the public's perception of nursing's contribution to health care, and in particular whether the public wishes nurses to assume the role of patient advocate. While public expectations should not define professional identity, extreme disparities between them are an indication that professionals need to examine their assumptions regarding their role.

Nurses should also consider setting aside the idea that they are powerless within hospitals. It would seem to be far more productive to identify and extend currently available resources for action, rather than seeking an idealized version of autonomy that no one working in hospitals actually possesses. If nurses do have restricted autonomy, they are not alone. Increasingly, physicians have their autonomy limited by third-party payers, utilization review, and hospital administration. In any case, what is needed is not greater individuation for nurses but greater cooperation among all professionals who provide health care in a hospital setting.

Professional Virtue and the Model of a Covenant

With its perplexing claim that patient autonomy is contingent upon nursing autonomy, proponents of patient advocacy tend to disregard crucial empirical questions relating to nursing practice, and to offer an overly romanticized image of the nurse as a moral guardian within the hospital. It would seem important to investigate other descriptions of nursing authority to assess their contribution to the further development of professional identity.

A covenantal model of the professional–public relationship is one alternative that has been suggested. On William May's account, covenantal agreements described in the Bible are based on three elements that provide clues to authentic professional–public relationships: (1) an exchange of gifts, symbolizing mutual indebtedness; (2) an exchange of the promises, establishing a set of mutually affirmed intrinsic values; and (3) an ontological change in the persons who create the covenantal agreement. The individual becomes a professional when he or she is given freedom to practice by the public, on the basis of the professional's promise to remain faithful to the ideal of service.[18] These elements, which have their origins in ancient Hebrew thought, afford a different interpretation of issues raised by the proponents of patient advocacy: the relationship between professions and the public, the meaning of personal autonomy and illness, and intrinsic professional values.

A covenantal model calls attention to the reciprocal indebtedness of the public and the profession, suggesting that professional power is a gift from the public to the profession given in exchange for its expertise and orientation toward the service of others. Those who have adopted the notion that nurses should be patient advocates should consider whether the current model of advocacy can fully encompass the extent of services nursing traditionally offers. While protecting patient self-determination is certainly essential, nursing is also, in the language of the American Nurses' Association,

> the protection, promotion and restoration of health: the prevention of illness, and the alleviation of suffering in the care of clients, including individuals, family groups, and communities. In the context of these functions, nursing is defined as the diagnosis and treatment of human responses to actual or potential health problems.[19]

Patient advocacy represents only one feature of the range of professional services nursing provides.

Under a covenantal model, gifts are to some degree responsive to the needs and expectations of the recipients. Although the full extent of nursing's gift to the public may not be completely defined by the needs that the public perceives, if patients do not in fact expect or want nurses to be their advocates, the nurse's gift of advocacy may well go unappreciated. Patients presumably regard themselves and their families or other surrogates, rather than nurses, as the primary sources of self-determination, and expect nurses to respond to the wider variety of needs occasioned by illness and health care.

A related concern involves the connection between patient advocacy and professional autonomy. A gift given by the profession to the public should strengthen the covenantal relationship between the nurse and the patient rather than strengthen the profession's independent claim to professional status. A gift with this secondary motivation risks becoming illegitimately self-interested. The risk seems greater when the nurse is presented as the key to moral practice within hospital settings. Surely other professionals within hospitals also provide support for patient self-determination, rights, and interests. Nurses must carefully consider whether they wish to retain this image of moral centrality or whether it is in fact counter-productive to professional development.

A covenantal model describes persons as free to enter into agreements, establish moral principles, and keep promises. This account of practical autonomy, or autonomy within a situation, is an alternative to the more sweeping description of professional autonomy underlying the argument for patient advocacy, which tends to view persons as though they were abstracted from the social obligations, relationships, and contingencies that characterize actual social settings. A covenantal model more clearly engages actual experience, including the need to change institutions that are repressive and inimical to the covenantal relationship.

At present, patient advocacy does not provide a comprehensive description of the role and contributions of nursing. But the question of whether nurses currently possess adequate professional freedom to establish covenantal relationships with patients still remains. It seems clear that professional nursing has an extensive and historically based covenant with the general public. However, especially for nurses who practice in hospitals, the possibility of professional covenants with clients faces several challenges, not only because of the bureaucratic structures of hospitals and the history of the nurse–physician relationship, but also because of the way that nursing services within hospitals are al-located. When patients are admitted to hospitals by physicians, they have little choice regarding which nurses will take care of them. Changes in nursing personnel due to staffing patterns and the frequent lack of primary care nursing also contribute to dis-continuity in nurse–patient relationships. These structures place real limitations on hospital nurses' ability to enter into caregiving agreements with individual patients. At the same time, institutions do provide opportunities for cooperative change, which is especially likely to occur if nurses continue to demonstrate the essential contribution that the profession makes to overall patient well-being. The adversarial stance of the advocacy model may not be the best way to achieve needed change.

Professions modify their intrinsic values over time, in response to historical and social conditions. The conditions that prompted the call for patient advocacy should also prompt a consideration of alternative models, given advocacy's theoretical and prac-tical shortcomings. Such consideration will contribute to an expression of professional identity that reflects both the history and tradition of nursing and the challenges of modern practice.

Acknowledgements: This article benefitted greatly from comments received after presentation at the 1991 meeting of the Society for Health and Human Values.

References

1. Barbara K. Miller, Thomas J. Mansen, and Helen Lee, "Patient Advocacy: Do Nurses Have the Power and Authority to Act as Patient Advocate?" *Nursing Leadership* 6 (June 1983): 56–60; Gerald R. Winslow, "From Loyalty to Advocacy: A New Metaphor for Nursing," *Hastings Center Report* 14, no. 3 (1984): 32–40; and Terry Pence and Janice Cantrall, eds., *Ethics in Nursing: An Anthology* (New York: National League for Nursing, 1990).

2. George J. Annas, "The Patient Rights Advocate: Can Nurses Fill the Role?" *Supervisor Nurse* 5 (July 1974): 20–23, 25; Mary F. Kohnke, "The Nurse as Advocate," *American Journal of Nursing* 80 (November 1980): 2038–40; Christine Mitchell, "Integrity in Interprofessional Relationships," in *Responsibility in Health Care*, ed. George J. Agich (Dordrecht: D. Reidel, 1982); Darlene Trandel-Korenchuk and Keith Trandel-Korenchuk, "Nursing Advocacy of Patients' Rights: Myth or Reality?" *Nurse Practitioner* 8 (April 1983): 40–42.

3. See George J. Agich, "Professionalism and Ethics in Health Care," *Journal of Medicine and Philosophy* 5, no. 3 (1980): 186–99.

4. American Nurses' Association, *Code for Nurses with Interpretive Statements* (Kansas City: American Nurses' Association, 1976; 1985).

5. Kohnke, "The Nurse as Advocate."

6. George J. Annas, "Patient Rights: An Agenda for the '80s." *Nursing Law and Ethics* 3 (April 1981), reprinted in *Ethics in Nursing*, ed. Pence and Cantrall, pp. 75–82.

7. Annas, "The Patient Rights Advocate," p. 25; Nancy Quinn and Anne Somers, "The Patient's Bill of Rights: A Significant Aspect of the Consumer Revolution." *Nursing Outlook* 22 (April 1974):240–44; Elsie L. Bandman and Bertram Bandman. *Nursing Ethics Across the Life Span*, 2d ed. (Norwalk: Appleton and Lange, 1990), p. 21.

8. Roland R. Yarling and Beverly J. McElmurry, "The Moral Foundation of Nursing," *Advances in Nursing Science* 8, no. 2 (1986): 63–73.

9. Michael Polanyi, *Personal Knowledge: Towards a Post-Critical Philosophy* (New York: Harper Torchbooks, 1964).

10. John S. Packard and Mary Ferrara, "In Search of the Moral Foundation of Nursing," *Advances in Nursing Science* 10, no. 4 (1988): 60–71.

11. Mitchell, "Integrity in Interprofessional Relationships," pp. 163–84.

12. Leah Curtin and Josephine Flaherty, *Nursing Ethics: Theories and Pragmatics* (Bowie, Md.: Robert J. Brady Co., 1982), p. 333.

13. Natalie B. Kampen, "Before Florence Nightingale: A Prehistory of Nursing in Painting and Sculpture," in *Images of Nurses: Perspective from History, Art, and Literature*, ed. Anne Hudson Jones (Philadelphia: University of Pennsylvania Press, 1988), pp. 6–39.

14. Charles E. Rosenberg, *The Care of Strangers: The Rise of America's Hospital System* (New York: Basic Books, 1987), p. 212.

15. Susan Reverby, "A Caring Dilemma: Womanhood and Nursing in Historical Perspective," *Nursing Research* 36, no. 1 (1987): 5–11.

16. Anne H. Bishop and John R. Scudder, Jr., *The Practical, Moral and Personal Sense of Nursing: Phenomenological Philosophy of Practice* (Albany: State University of New York Press, 1990).

17. Sally Gadow, "Existential Advocacy: Philosophical Foundation of Nursing," in *Nursing Images and Ideals: Opening Dialogue with the Humanities*, ed. Stuart F. Spicker and Sally Gadow (New York: Springer, 1980), pp. 79–101.

18. William F. May, "Code and Covenant or Philanthropy and Contract?" in *Ethics in Medicine: Historical Perspectives and Contemporary Concerns*, ed. Stanley Joel Reiser, Arthur J. Dyck, and William J. Curran (Cambridge, Mass.: M.I.T. Press, 1977), pp. 65–76; see also Mary Carolyn Cooper, "Convenantal Relationships: Grounding for the Nursing Ethic," *Advances in Nursing Science* 10, no. 4 (1988): 48–59.

19. American Nurses' Association, *Code for Nurses*. Preamble.

20   Ethical Issues in Teamwork: The Context of Rehabilitation

Ruth B. Purtilo

"Teamwork" as an approach to the provision of health care services is a relatively modern phenomenon. Only during and after World War II has the notion gained wide acceptance. Today almost no health professional can imagine what it would be like to work outside of some type of team structure.[2]

The purpose of this paper is to evaluate the extent to which one type of health care team, the medical rehabilitation team, has succeeded in promoting the well-being of patients. It is impossible to evaluate fully the success of rehabilitation teams in helping rehabilitation patients receive better care than they would have received without the team approach. Nonetheless, one can subject the team approach to two basic criteria of good patient care: (1) technically competent care, and (2) personalized care, that is, care tailored to the individual patient.[14] We will examine how well rehabilitation teams fare in meeting these challenges.

Rehabilitation Teams and the Provision of Technically Competent Care

Licensure, standardized examination, and other mechanisms have been implemented to define standards of technical competence among health professionals and enforce sanctions against persons who fail to uphold them.

Competent care requires that each component team member skillfully applies his or her professional skills. At first blush, the plurality of the team suggests that checks and balances will be assured simply by virtue of the fact that each team member feels responsible for patient outcome, and will attempt to weed out weak, incompetent colleagues whose contribution may compromise an optimum outcome.

However, history is laced with accounts of health care providers who have protected incompetent colleagues well beyond any defensible moral limits of loyalty to fellow professionals. Part of the psychology of teams is that members experience their membership on a team as entailing "team loyalty" — a moral obligation of loyalty to other team members and to the team itself.[14] They may believe that they have voluntarily committed themselves to a type of "social contract," one that requires a good team member to protect team secrets, thereby promoting a tendency for cover-ups or protection of weaker members.[8] A troubling moral conflict arises when one's moral obligation of faithfulness to one's colleague does battle with one's moral obligations to patients. Therefore, holding peers accountable for incompetence may be made more difficult by the team ideal and team rhetoric. It cannot be assumed that competent interventions are fostered by the team approach.

Rehabilitation Teams and the Candidates' Welfare

Despite the importance of technical competence, neither the writings about health care providers in general, nor those about rehabilitation groups in particular, judge it as the sole criterion of good health care. Health professionals must also fulfill the stringent requirement of tailoring care to suit the individual who receives it. This requirement is adduced from the pervasive moral ideal of "respect for persons" in principle I of the 1981 American Medical Association *Principles of Medical Ethics*. A good intervention must fit within the context of the patient's needs, hopes, and fears. For example, following a shoulder disarticulation for cancer, a person who is well qualified medically to be fitted with an upper extremity prosthesis may be opposed to it on esthetic, financial, or religious grounds. Assuming that the individual understands the ramifications of each option, withholding the prosthesis would be judged the morally good course of action, despite the technical advantages of the prosthesis. Thus, the patient's or candidate's well-being becomes the reference point for judging whether the person is being treated with respect, and for ultimately determining the moral worth of the treatment program.

No other group of health professionals takes this highly personalized approach to treatment more seriously than rehabilitation specialists. Rehabilitation is explicitly designed to enable each individual to attain his or her highest possible level of functional independence given the constraints imposed by illness or injury. Goals rest on the ideal that maximal functioning will enable the person to engage in appropriate forms of interdependence with peers, employers, family members, and other social groups.[17] Rehabilitation teams may be distinguished in part from other health care teams by their explicit commitments to psychologic, social, and vocational outcomes, as well as medical outcomes. Rehabilitation team members are prized according to their willingness and capability to foster these more broadly defined outcomes in whatever form deemed fitting for an individual patient.

There is widespread agreement today that a necessary (although not always sufficient) requirement for assuring a good patient care outcome is to honor the patient's wishes or autonomy. The President's Commission for the Study of Ethical Problems in Medicine and Biomedical and Behavioral Research concluded that, even in decisions with consequences so serious that death will ensue, the competent patient's wishes should guide health care decisions.[15] The doctrine of informed consent, a governing concept in health care, is designed to enhance patient autonomy. How does patient autonomy fare within the rehabilitation team context? A vague idea of autonomy combined with team pressures may (although not inevitably will) compromise autonomy.

Autonomy and the Rehabilitation Process

While the notion of "autonomy" is often invoked in discussions about good patient care, only a loose (if any) definition of the concept is usually offered. As Beauchamp and Childress observe, such diverse philosophers as Kant, Mill, Sartre, Nietzche, and Hare have developed dissimilar views of autonomy and its role in morality. One emphasizes freedom of choice, while another focuses on the creation of one's own moral position, acceptance of responsibility for one's view, or the task of reconciling the tension between individual freedom and social and political constraints on one's own actions.[1] Beauchamp and Childress point out the important contributions of Kant and Mill to the development of the concept of autonomy as it is applied in the health professions today. Kant emphasizes the role of self-determination, being-in-control, making one's own choices in accord with principles that could be willed to be valid for everyone. His main contribution to a theory of autonomy probably is his emphasis on the importance of giving the right reasons for choice of a course of action. Conversely, Mill focuses on freedom of action, arguing that an individual's actions are legitimately constricted only when necessary to prevent harm to other individuals. Otherwise, each person should be permitted to act according to his or her own desires. Mill highlights the social-political context of action.

Rehabilitation team members have several means of expressing their commitment to the general ideal of patient autonomy, but none is more formal and explicit than the process of setting rehabilitation goals. Kant's interpretation of autonomy, entailing the ideal that we ought to respect an individual "as . . . rightfully a rational determiner of his or her own destiny,"[1] is precisely the message conveyed to a candidate as he or she begins discussion with the rehabilitation team when the goal setting process is initiated. The patient-candidate (a role transition not always made easily) is encouraged to take a more active, participatory role in developing himself or herself and is told outright that rehabilitation goals ultimately must be guided by the personal goals of the candidate (and, when present, the candidate's family). Most candidates initially are eager to take advantage of the "new lease on life." An individual who may have been a passive observer during the acute treatment phase of an injury or debilitating illness now is charged with "taking control."

The stage is set. While the intentions of all are to work together, disenchantment sometimes ensues because of a misunderstanding of how much self-determination the candidate really will have in the process of rehabilitation. The candidate may believe that his/her choices (hopes, desires, fears, and dreams) will dominate the direction of the rehabilitation program. At the same time, team members leave the initial goal-setting session eager to establish treatment priorities that will enable the candidate to make an appropriate adjustment to the disability. Writers in the independent living movement have observed that rehabilitation professionals focus their efforts on molding the individual candidate to cope with constraints engendered by disability in an able-bodied society.[7] Professionals define autonomy as limited by structural and environmental barriers. This interpretation of autonomy is akin to Mill's conception, in which freedom of action is the key to autonomy. Although respect for the person's choices governs the goalsetting process, an actual rehabilitation plan is fashioned with an emphasis on the constrictions that will have to be accommodated by the candidate. Rehabilitation professionals, who themselves may wish that the candidate could live life more fully in harmony with his or her desires, usually rationalize their emphasis on adjustment by drawing on the experience of other candidates: It is almost always inevitable that the affected person will have to make many accommodations. Therefore, in many cases, the two conceptions of autonomy lead to differing expectations and the envisioning of different treatment programs by candidate and rehabilitation team.

After the initial weeks or months of rehabilitation, the situation sometimes becomes yet more stultifying for all involved. The table summarizes six structural factors that act as barriers to candidates' attempts to stay involved in setting the direction of their rehabilitation. All but the first directly relate to team-organized approaches to treatment.

This summary highlights explanations for how the locus of authority progressively shifts from the individual candidate to the team. To be sure, team members may act as important checks and balances on each other by using their ongoing perceptions of the candidate's desires or needs as guides (e.g., "He told me . . ."; Well, yesterday he said . . ."), but these attempts by individual members to honor a candidate's self-determination may be insufficient to offset the shift in the direction of the team's collective judgments. Furthermore, it is possible that the candidate may tell members what he thinks each of them wants to hear; in such circumstances, self-determination has given way to the crying need for acceptance by team members. At this point even a Millsian ideal of autonomy — action carried out within constraints viewed by the larger society as necessary — is compromised. Desiring the security which requires that he depend

Table 5.2   Barriers to Rehabilitation Candidates' Autonomy

Factors	Candidate is:
1. "Can't turn back now"	Too invested to back out or change course of action.
2. Fatigue	Too engaged with multiple activities and team members to envision, or seek, alternatives.
3. Anxiety	Too anxious to risk new approaches, especially since so many team members appear largely in agreement about the course of action.
4. Gratitude	Too grateful for this opportunity or "gift" from the team to reject it, even though it may not seem completely suitable.
5. "Reasonable expectation"	Too convinced that the team demands the candidate's cooperation to risk engendering their hostility.
6. Team numbers	Too outnumbered to experience having any power to change the course of events.

on the team's judgment, and believing himself largely unknowing and impotent, the candidate is in danger of losing sight of what he or she wants.

Consider again the phenomenon of "adjustment to disability." We have implied that rehabilitation teamwork may lead to a compromise, even at times an opprobrious compromise, of the candidate's desires, hopes, and dreams. But we have also hinted that the team's emphasis on the necessity of helping the candidate "adjust" is a perspicacious approach to the candidate's actual dilemma. As Haas indicates, "judgment calls" by the team usually are based on their experience with many like-situated candidates.[10] For instance, rehabilitation team members observe time and time again that just as all persons alter their goals as time and events intervene, so much more must persons who have faced the exigencies of serious illness or injury do so. Candidates are faced with profound changes in the way their bodies look, work, and feel; they may encounter intense, negative responses of friends and loved ones as they lose the ability to carry out previously cherished mental or physical activities.[16] These factors may require that the rehabilitation team adopt an approach not guided entirely by the candidate's opinions; his or her cataclysm may bar a clear vision of who he or she will become in the future. Religious conceptions of death and resurrection may be apt in trying to assess what happens to a candidate during the rehabilitation process. Sometimes a "new" person seems to emerge from the old. To the extent that this occurs, the initial act of setting rehabilitation goals is but an exercise in the blind hope that the shadow which falls between the dream and the reality will not destroy the dream. More important, to the extent that the truly desired ends are not initially knowable by either the rehabilitation candidate or team members, the candidate's autonomy does fail to be reliable as the governing moral guide.

In summary, the ideal of autonomy as a guide for setting the course of action by the rehabilitation team is challenged throughout the treatment process. One might conclude that the rehabilitation team approach is able to uphold the highest moral values of health care only in the rare situations in which team and candidate are in complete agreement from the start. Another way to view the issue, however, is to propose that autonomy may be appropriate, but not the supreme or sole standard by which to judge the moral value of rehabilitation team practices.

Beneficence and Paternalism in the Rehabilitation Process

A richer portrayal includes the principles of "beneficence" as an appropriate moral standard to judge the extent to which a rehabilitation team's practices contribute to and support a morally good form of health care. Beneficence long has been held to include acts which contribute positively to the welfare of others, as well as acts intended to prevent or remove harm. While not always ascribed the moral stringency of a "duty" within philosophical thought, beneficence has been treated as a duty by others, including many writing in medical ethics. Those writers sometimes suggest that beneficence is realized largely by honoring patient preferences; being beneficent actually places the rehabilitation team members squarely back into the lap of being guided by the candidate's wishes, hopes, and desires! But even the most competent person can make poor choices under conditions of disequilibrium and high uncertainty, such as those characteristic of rehabilitation candidates' situations. Philosophers long have argued that fundamental respect for persons may — in carefully prescribed situations — require that the agent not be guided entirely by an individual's desires or wants. The rehabilitation team's judgment of what is optimum for the candidate indicates that team members act as if they hold such a belief. Having decided that it is beneficial to alter the outcomes articulated by the patient, team members act paternalistically.

Paternalism, a complex, much misunderstood, and much debated concept, presumes that beneficence and autonomy can be incompatible, and in some cases beneficence should dominate.[13] Paternalistic behavior is justified by the conviction that an individual's wishes may be overruled in the name of more fully benefitting or preventing harm to the person. This differs from coercion, which is the practice of overruling an individual's wishes without the intent to more fully benefit or prevent harm to the person.

In the context of the rehabilitation team, paternalistic behavior poses a moral challenge by its presumption that the team's judgment should (in some cases) take precedence over the candidate's. Coercion never is justified. The rehabilitation team shifts from a position in which respect for the person is expressed by honoring his wishes to one in which respect is expressed by making an independent judgment regarding his welfare.[11]

Paternalism is thought to encourage candidates into avenues that they would want to pursue. The rehabilitation team has the moral responsibility to deliberate thoughtfully and thoroughly about the person's welfare, regardless of patient desires. Specifically in situations of high uncertainty, limited paternalism (a term employed by some philosophers to express the importance of balancing beneficence with a respect for autonomy) may be useful for fostering a desirable outcome. Limited paternalism assumes that the person acting on the candidate's behalf has made the following assessments:

> . . . the patient has some defect, encumbrance, or limitation in deciding, willing, or acting; there is probability of harm to the patient apart from intervention; [and] the probable good effects of the intervention outweigh the probable bad effects of the intervention and alternative modes of action and non-action . . .[4]

An additional insight into paternalistic interventions by rehabilitation team members is offered by Cross and Churchill.[6] They suggest that "paternalism with permission" is defensible in high uncertainty situations. That is, they argue that when a patient acknowledges that the health professional is in a better position to decide on a course of action, a patient may actually exercise autonomy by appointing the health professional as decision maker. The patient must explicitly acknowledge that he/she chooses to follow the professional's judgment.

Finally, Childress observes that paternalistic behavior is justified only when "the least restrictive, least humiliating, and least insulting alternative has been selected."[4] Paternalistic conduct by a team that failed to hold these rigorous guidelines no longer could be judged as beneficial for the candidate.

Obviously, teams might unintentionally or intentionally limit a candidate's choices for reasons other than consideration of the patient's welfare. Does the rehabilitation team arrangement have checks and balances to prevent coercion of the candidate or punishment of a disliked one? James Groves' study of "the hateful patient" revealed that some types of patients, including those who are not in agreement with the judgment of professionals, are capable of evoking deep-seated feelings of revenge, anger and repugnance among health professionals.[9] The rehabilitation candidate, treated in the health care setting for a long period while intensely interacting with health care providers, is more at risk than most types of patients of feeling indirect or direct repercussions should his conduct be unacceptable to the team. To prevent harmful conduct toward "errant" candidates, team members must be vigilant and bold, calling attention to teammates who are acting in a revengeful manner toward candidates. Failure to try to stop this conduct by team members is a regrettable instance of how neglect can become complicity.

Viewing the situation optimistically, one can point to the character traits of many rehabilitation team members: often they have chosen rehabilitation careers from a genuine commitment to improving the welfare of persons struggling under the weight of severe illness or injury. A team including several such persons can be "leavened" by their influence, increasing the candidate's likelihood of benefitting, compared to treatment conducted by one person or a less caring group. Public documents and policies in rehabilitation medicine (e.g., the Commission on the Accreditation of Rehabilitation Facilities[5]), moreover, emphasize the necessity of the team expending considerable energies to ascertain rehabilitation goals appropriate for an individual candidate.

In summary, where, then, does this discussion of autonomy, beneficence, paternalism, and the challenges of each take us in our search to determine the degree of team success in fostering good rehabilitation outcomes? At the very least, it highlights that although autonomy is a valid moral standard for good rehabilitation outcomes, it is not a sufficient one. Constraints on autonomy must be guided by thoughtful concern for the candidate's welfare, rather than distorted by conflicting interests. The morally responsible approach is for the team to synthesize several moral principles.

An expression of respect for persons by the rehabilitation team involves both respect for their welfare as reflected in their choices and, in rare instances, for their welfare instead of their choices.[3] In the challenge of seeking the best interest of the patient, the team approach can either hinder or enhance a morally good rehabilitation outcome. Part of the team's moral responsibility is to develop habits and procedures that best enable a morally good outcome for each candidate.

Comprehensive health care requires the collaboration of several health care disciplines and perspectives. Physical medicine and rehabilitation, with its explicit emphasis on the candidates's physical, psychological, and emotional well-being, understandably has depended on a team arrangement from its very beginnings. In spite of its shortcomings, there are ample opportunities for the rehabilitation candidate's best interests to be served by a team that utilizes workable moral policies.

Since team-based rehabilitation is a promising ideal, we must attempt to improve the team model. Mechanic and Aikin[12] systematically assess problem areas as they attempt to work out a cooperative agenda for medicine and nursing. Spitzer and Roberts[18] rigorously analyze areas of discord in physician teams. A helpful set of suggestions for the "moral education" of interdisciplinary teams is offered by Thomasma,[19] who maintains that in order "to bring about a concert of moral interests within a team" several steps are necessary: (1) the team must develop a common moral language for discussion of moral issues, (2) team members must have cognitive and practical training in how to rationally articulate their feelings about issues, (3) value-clarification exercises are needed, (4) the team must have common experiences upon which to base workable moral policies, and (5) the team must develop a moral decision-making method for all to use.[19] These authors create optimism about constructive steps that may further refine the rehabilitation team's concept, roles, and functions as a means of fostering positive rehabilitation outcomes.

References

1. Beauchamp TL, Childress JF: Principles of Biomedical Ethics. Oxford, Oxford University Press, 1979, pp 56–59

2. Brown T: An historical view of health care teams. In Agich G (ed): Responsibility in Health Care. Boston, Reidel, 1982, pp 603–778

3. Caplan AL: Informed consent and provider–patient relationships in rehabilitation medicine. Arch Phys Med Rehabil 69: 312–317, 1988

4. Childress JF: Ensuring care, respect, and fairness for elderly. Hastings Center Report 14:27–31, 1984

5. Commission on the Accreditation of Rehabilitation Facilities: Standards Manual. Tucson, CARF, 1986

6. Cross AW, Churchill LR: Ethical and cultural dimensions of informed consent: case study and analyses. Ann Intern Med 96: 110–113, 1982

7. DeJong G: The historical and current realities of independent living: implications for administrative planning. In Workshop Proceedings: Policy Planning and Development in Independent Living, University Center for International Rehabilitation. Ann Arbor, Michigan State University Press, 1980, pp. 2–6

8. Erde E: Logical confusions and moral dilemmas in health care teams and team talk. In Agich G. (ed): Responsibility in Health Care. Boston, Reidel, 1982, pp 193–214

9. Groves JE: Taking care of the hateful patient. N Engl J Med 298:883–887, 1978

10. Haas JF: Admission to rehabilitation centers: selection of patients. Arch Phys Med Rehabil 69:329–332, 1988

11. Jameton A: Nursing Practice: Ethical Issues. Englewood Cliffs, NJ, Prentice-Hall, Inc, 1984, p 126

12. Mechanic D, Aiken LH: Cooperative agenda for medicine and nursing. N Engl J Med 307:747–750, 1982

13. Mill JS: On Liberty (1859). Reprinted in Essential Works of JS Mill. New York, Bantam Books, 1961, p 263

14. Naji S: Teamwork in health care in United States: sociological perspective. Milbank Mem Fund Quar 54:75–91, 1975

15. President's Commission for Study of Ethical Problems in Medicine and Biomedical and Behavioral Research: Introduction and summary. In Deciding to Forego Life-Sustaining Treatment: Report on Ethical, Medical and Legal Issues in Treatment Decisions. Washington, DC, United States Government Printing Office, 1983, pp 1–12

16. Purtilo R: Loneliness, the need for solitude and compliance. In Withersty D (ed): Communication and Compliance in the Hospital Setting. Springfield, IL, Charles C Thomas Publishers, 1981, pp 91–115

17. Rothberg JS: Rehabilitation team practice. In Lecca PJ, McNeil JS (eds): Interdisciplinary Team Practice, Issues and Trends. New York, Praeger Publishers, 1985, pp 23–24

18. Spitzer WO, Roberts RF: Twelve questions about teams in health services. J Community Health 6:1–5, Fall 1980

19. Thomasma D: Moral education in interdisciplinary teams. Surg Technologist 2:17, 1982

Chapter 5
Questions to Consider

1. Do you agree with Emanuel and Emanuel that the ideal physician–patient relationship should be understood in terms of the deliberative model? If so, why? If not, why not?
2. To whom does a competent, caring nurse owe her or his primary allegiance — the patient, the physician, the health care facility, the nursing profession, herself or himself? Is it possible to assign priorities to these allegiances? How should conflicts between the conflicting allegiances of a nurse be resolved?
3. On what basis might limited paternalism be justified in the context of rehabilitation? Does this justification differ from how limited paternalism might be justified in acute care, or emergency medicine, or family medicine?

Further Readings

Bayles, Michael D. 1987. Interprofessional ethics in health care. *International Journal of Applied Philosophy* 3(3):21–28.

Baylis, Françoise, and Jocelyn Downie. 1992. *Codes of ethics: Ethical codes, standards and guidelines for professionals working in a health care setting in Canada.* Toronto: Department of Bioethics, Hospital for Sick Children.

Buchanan, Allen. 1978. Medical paternalism. *Philosophy and Public Affairs* 7:370–90.

Caplan, Arthur L. 1988. Informed consent and provider–patient relationships in rehabilitation medicine. *Archives of Physical Medicine and Rehabilitation* 69:312–17.

Gert, Bernard, and Charles M. Culver. 1976. Paternalistic behaviour. *Philosophy and Public Affairs* 6:45–57.

Levine, Robert J. 1987. Medical ethics and personal doctors: Conflicts between what we teach and what we want. *American Journal of Law and Medicine* 13:351–64.

May, William F. 1977. Code and covenant or philanthropy and contract? In *Ethics in Medicine,* Stanley J. Reiser, Arthur J. Dyck, and William J. Curran, eds. 65–76. Cambridge, Mass.: M.I.T. Press.

Mechanic, David, and Linda H. Aiken. 1982. A cooperative agenda for medicine and nursing. *New England Journal of Medicine* 307:747–50.

Miller, Bruce L. 1981. Autonomy and the refusal of lifesaving treatment. *Hastings Center Report* 11(4):22–28.

Thomasma, David. 1983. Beyond medical paternalism and patient autonomy: A model of the physician–patient relationship. *Annals of Internal Medicine* 98:243–48.

Thorne, Sally E., and Carole A. Robinson. 1989. Guarded alliance: Health care relationships in chronic illness. *IMAGE* 21 (3):153–57.

Yeo, Michael. 1991. *Concepts and cases in nursing ethics.* Peterborough, Ont.: Broadview Press.

Chapter 6

Consent

Chapter 6

Introduction

Forasmuch as the lawe of God . . . allowes no man to touch the life or limme of any person except in a judicyall way, bee it hereby ordered and decreed, that no . . . physitians, chirurgians, midwives, or others, shall presume to exercise or putt forth any act . . . without . . . consent of the patient or patients (if they be mentis compotes) . . . (Laws of the Massachusetts Bay Colony 1649).

You are driving to work, and you notice that your car starts to shake when you apply the brakes. You drop it off at the garage, explain the problem, and leave a phone number where you can be reached when the mechanic has figured out what is going wrong.

It is often easier to understand what is involved in a bioethical dispute by referring to a nonmedical example. In essence, informed consent to medical treatment raises many of the same issues as informed consent to automobile treatment. The question of consent presumes that there is a perceived problem, that a choice needs to be made about how to deal with that problem, that to a degree the consequences of these choices are known and distinct, and that there exists relevant expertise to help you to make and effectuate that choice.

Whether we are speaking of your car's shaking or your hand's trembling, many of the same assumptions are present: you perceive a problem (with your car, or with your health); you need expert help (a mechanic's, or a doctor's) to identify the cause of the problem and what can be done about it. The decision of what to do about the problem is in your hands, but you will likely rely upon that expert to identify the costs (or risks) as well as the benefits of the various approaches possible, and make your decision on that basis.

The automobile example helps us to demystify the basis of informed consent. A knowledgeable and interested consumer might want very precise and detailed information from the mechanic before authorizing a repair; another might want only the sketchiest details, relying upon a trusted mechanic's recommendation. (In the same way, some patients will want to interrogate their doctors closely about testing and treatment choices, while others will want to be spared the grim details.) Just as consent to a garage mechanic is ordinarily specific to person and procedure ("I'm paying you to do it, not somebody else; I agreed to your balancing the tires, not to replacing the brake drum"), so must consent to medical care, ordinarily, be specific to be valid.

Most fundamentally, perhaps, the auto example may make clear something often obscured in the medical context. Although we speak of the basis and limits of a patient's right to accept or refuse medical care, we might more properly speak of the basis and limits of a health care professional's authority to perform a medical or nursing act. The fact that you have asked a mechanic to tell you what is wrong with your car does not obligate you to permit him to do whatever he thinks is best — still less to pay for it! That mechanic has no right to touch your car until you have given him permission. In the same way, a physician has no right to treat you without your consent.

In the end, though, cars are not bodies, nor are physicians body mechanics — the view of Bayles (1978) notwithstanding. Underlying any notion of consent will be a view about the physician–patient relationship, based upon the patient's need. A body is far more complicated than a car; the ways in which it can go wrong, more numerous; the potential therapeutic approaches, more diverse. Above all, perhaps, in dealing with our bodies, medicine deals with some of the deepest, most intimate, and most consequential choices that any of us will ever face.

For these reasons, the doctrine of consent to care is one of the cornerstones of current health care ethics. For a consent to a particular intervention to be valid, legally and — in the view of most authors — morally, the permission that it expresses must be provided by a competent person on his or her own behalf; must be given voluntarily, that is, without undue coercion or pressure; and must be informed, that is, provided following the provision of sufficient relevant information in a form which the patient may understand.

Listing the elements of valid consent, though, is only the beginning of wisdom. The very concept of an "intervention" which must be preceded by consent itself raises complications. Some clinical interventions are distinct, simple: for example, an appendectomy. Some interventions are more complex: cancer treatment might involve surgery, followed by chemotherapy and radiation. Some conditions require a variety of interventions at irregular intervals (like asthma); some, regular lifelong treatment (for example, hemodialysis for persons who have lost kidney function). While the surgical model — one intervention, one practitioner, one consent — has dominated theoretical discussions of consent, it may not fit all cases. (What *is* a medical or nursing intervention, anyway? Is consent needed for feeding, dressing, and other forms of custodial care? Each time? Does it make a difference if the feeding is done with a spoon or with a tube into the stomach?)

The other elements of consent also beg some crucial questions:

- How much information is enough? Does every risk of every procedure — and every alternative procedure — need equally to be disclosed? Can patients be as disadvantaged by receiving too much information, of the wrong kind, as by being told insufficient information? The Supreme Court of Canada has held that known and probable risks of a procedure need to be disclosed, as well as special or unusual possibilities (see *Hopp v. Lepp* 1980). This is easy to say, but hard to do. Would you want to be told that, in clinical testing and surveillance, a new and effective antibiotic carried with it a one-in-a-million chance of death due to allergic reaction? Would you also want to be told that your chances of being killed in a traffic accident on the way to filling that prescription are also one in a million?

- What is meant by "voluntary" consent, given without "undue pressure or coercion"? Medical choices are not often happy ones, but rather a choice between the horrible and the worse. A patient has a narrowing of an artery, and is told that without surgery she is likely to have a stroke. Informed consent requires that the patient be given this information — but the patient may feel that the information leaves her no more choice than she would have had when faced by a mugger demanding, "Your money or your life."

The Selections

This chapter's selections, a mixture of philosophical and ethical reflections and court decisions, are chosen to reflect the range of issues that consent raises as a theoretical construction and as a practical requirement for medical treatment.

Reibl v. Hughes together with *Hopp v. Lepp* (1980) represented a revolution in the Canadian legal approach to informed consent. Two distinct but related questions had been the subject of controversy. The first was one of procedure: Has a physician who failed to properly obtain consent to a procedure (e.g., surgery) committed a battery upon the patient, or simply been negligent in performing the duties of a physician? In *Reibl v. Hughes* the Supreme Court of Canada held that a claimed breach of duty, based upon the doctor's having provided the patient with insufficient information, is ordinarily one of negligence. The physician commits a battery only in those cases in which no consent (informed or otherwise) was given to the procedure which was performed; for example, when an operation was performed in spite of a patient's refusal, or when a patient consented to one procedure and the doctor performed quite a different one.

The readings include an edited version of the *Reibl* case, designed to highlight the second, substantive question which it settled as a matter of Canadian law: How much information must a doctor provide to a patient? Many previous courts had held doctors to what is known as a professional standard: a physician must provide that amount of information that the average, reasonable, prudent doctor would have explained to any patient in a similar situation, facing a similar choice. This professional standard considers the task of informing patients to be a medical act, like surgery itself: surgery was not done negligently, in spite of its results, if the doctor in question had acted as any reasonable surgeon would have done; so, too, information is sufficient if it meets the standard that would have been expected of a reasonable doctor explaining a procedure to a patient. Writing in *Reibl*, Chief Justice Bora Laskin rejected that professional standard in favour of a patient-centred one: A consent is sufficiently informed if and only if the explanation provided to the patient included that amount of information that the average, reasonable patient in that patient's situation — as the doctor knew it, or should have known it — would require. As you will see in examining the case, this question of "the patient's situation" may be crucial, and may encompass social and economic factors as well as medical ones.

The second selection is an Ontario case dealing with a related issue at the vague boundaries of consent. The question at issue in *Zamparo v. Brisson*: Has a physician discharged the professional obligation to inform a patient once all relevant information has been explained? Does a physician have an obligation to advise a patient, as well as inform him or her?

Much of the literature about patient consent deals with "input" — for example, the information conveyed to patients — rather than either "processing" (of the information in the course of patient decision making) or "output," the form in which a patient's decision is conveyed. The articles by Nancy Jecker and Erich Loewy address some of these neglected areas. Jecker's paper explores the ethics of consent and refusal in a new sense: Is it ethical for patients to consider the interests of others in accepting or refusing appropriate medical care, and what should be the reaction of health care providers to such patient decisions? Loewy discusses another aspect of consent, the force of a so-called Ulysses contract: patients who provide non-revocable instructions, now, concerning future treatment choices.

References

Bayles, Michael D. 1978. Physicians as body mechanics. In *Contemporary issues in biomedical ethics*, John W. Davis, Barry Hoffmaster, and Sarah Shorten eds., 167–77. Clifton, N.J.: Humana Press.

Ciarlariello v. Schachter, [1993] 2 S.C.R. 119.
Hopp v. Lepp, [1980] 2 S.C.R. 192.
Laws of the Massachusetts Bay Colony. 1649.

21 Reibl v. Hughes

Supreme Court of Canada

. . . LASKIN C.J.C.: — The plaintiff appellant, then 44 years of age, underwent serious surgery on March 18, 1970, for the removal of an occlusion in the left internal carotid artery, which had prevented more than a 15% flow of blood through the vessel. The operation was competently performed by the defendant respondent, a qualified neurosurgeon. However, during or immediately following the surgery the plaintiff suffered a massive stroke which left him paralyzed on the right side of his body and also impotent. The plaintiff had, of course, formally consented to the operation. Alleging, however, that his was not an "informed consent," he sued for damages and recovered on this ground in both battery and negligence. The trial Judge, Haines J., awarded a global sum of $225,000. . . . [On appeal this case went to the Ontario Court of Appeal and then to the Supreme Court of Canada.]

It is now undoubted that the relationship between surgeon and patient gives rise to a duty of the surgeon to make disclosure to the patient of what I would call all material risks attending the surgery which is recommended. The scope of the duty of disclosure was considered in *Hopp v. Lepp*, a judgment of this Court, delivered on May 20, 1980, and as yet unreported [since reported 112 D.L.R. (3d) 67, 22 A.R. 361, [1980] 4 W.W.R. 645], where it was generalized as follows [at p. 81]:

> In summary, the decided cases appear to indicate that, in obtaining the consent of a patient for the performance upon him of a surgical operation, a surgeon, generally, should answer any specific questions posed by the patient as to the risks involved and should, without being questioned, disclose to him the nature of the proposed operation, its gravity, any material risks and any special or unusual risks attendant upon the performance of the operation. However, having said that, it should be added

that the scope of the duty of disclosure and whether or not it has been breached are matters which must be decided in relation to the circumstances of each particular case.

The Court in *Hopp v. Lepp* also pointed out that even if a certain risk is a mere possibility which ordinarily need not be disclosed, yet if its occurrence carries serious consequences, as for example, paralysis or even death, it should be regarded as a material risk requiring disclosure.

In the present case, the risk attending the surgery or its immediate aftermath was the risk of a stroke, of paralysis and, indeed, of death. This was, without question, a material risk. At the same time, the evidence made it clear that there was also a risk of a stroke and of resulting death if surgery for the removal of the occlusion was refused by the patient. The delicacy of the surgery is beyond question, and its execution is no longer in any way faulted. . . . How specific, therefore, must the information to the patient be, in a case such as this, to enable him to make an "informed" choice between surgery and no surgery? One of the considerations weighing upon the plaintiff was the fact that he was about a year and a half away from earning a lifetime retirement pension as a Ford Motor Company employee. The trial Judge noted . . . that "Due to this tragedy befalling him at the time it did, he was not eligible for certain extended disability benefits available under the collective agreement between the Ford Motor Company of Canada Limited and its hourly employees of 10 years' standing." At the time of the operation, the plaintiff had 8.4 years' service with his employer. He stated in his evidence that if he had been properly informed of the magnitude of the risk involved in the surgery he would have elected to forego it, at least until his pension had vested and, further, he would have opted for a shorter normal life than a longer one as a cripple because of the surgery. Although elective surgery was indicated for the condition from which the plaintiff suffered, there was (as the trial Judge found) no emergency in the sense that immediate surgical treatment was imperative. . . .

I think the Ontario Court of Appeal went too far, when dealing with the standard of disclosure of risks, in saying . . . that "the manner in which the nature and degree of risk is explained to a particular patient is better left to the judgment of the doctor in dealing with the man before him". Of course, it can be tested by expert medical evidence but that too is not determinative. The patient may have expressed certain concerns to the doctor and the latter is obliged to meet them in a reasonable way. What the doctor knows or should know that the particular patient deems relevant to a decision whether to undergo prescribed treatment goes equally to his duty of disclosure as do the material risks recognized as a matter of required medical knowledge.

. . . The Ontario Court of Appeal appears to have adopted a professional medical standard, not only for determining what are the material risks that should be disclosed but also, and concurrently, for determining whether there has been a breach of the duty of disclosure. . . . To allow expert medical evidence to determine what risks are material and, hence, should be disclosed and, correlatively, what risks are not material is to hand over to the medical profession the entire question of the scope of the duty of disclosure, including the question whether there has been a breach of that duty. Expert medical evidence is, of course, relevant to findings as to the risks that reside in or are a result of recommended surgery or other treatment. It will also have a bearing on their materiality but this is not a question that is to be concluded on the basis of the expert medical evidence alone. The issue under consideration is a different issue from that involved where the question is whether the doctor carried out his professional activities by applicable professional standards. What is under consideration here is the patient's right to know what risks are involved in undergoing or foregoing certain surgery or other treatment.

The materiality of non-disclosure of certain risks to an informed decision is a matter for the trier of fact, a matter on which there would, in all likelihood, be medical evidence but also other evidence, including evidence from the patient or from members of his family. It is, of course, possible that a particular patient may waive aside any question of risks and be quite prepared to submit to the surgery or treatment, whatever they be. Such a situation presents no difficulty. Again, it may be the case that a particular patient may, because of emotional factors, be unable to cope with facts relevant to recommended surgery or treatment and the doctor may, in such a case, be justified in withholding or generalizing information as to which he would otherwise be required to be more specific. . . .

. . . Can it be said that a reasonable person in the patient's position, to whom proper disclosure of attendant risks has been made, would decide against the surgery, that is, against the surgeon's recommendation that it be undergone? The objective standard of what a reasonable person in the patient's position would do would seem to put a premium on the surgeon's assessment of the relative need for the surgery and on supporting medical evidence of that need. Could it be reasonably refused? . . .

. . . It could hardly be expected that the patient who is suing would admit that he would have agreed to have the surgery, even knowing all the accompanying risks. His suit would indicate that, having suffered serious disablement because of the surgery, he is convinced that he would not have permitted it if there had been proper disclosure of the risks, balanced by the risks of refusing the surgery. Yet, to apply a subjective test to causation would, correlatively, put a premium on hindsight, even more of a premium than would be put on medical evidence in assessing causation by an objective standard.

I think it is the safer course on the issue of causation to consider objectively how far the balance in the risks of surgery or not surgery is in favour of undergoing surgery. The failure of proper disclosure pro and con becomes therefore very material. And so too are any special considerations affecting the particular patient. For example, the patient may have asked specific questions which were either brushed aside or were not fully answered or were answered wrongly. In the present case, the anticipation of a full pension would be a special consideration, and, while it would have to be viewed objectively, it emerges from the patient's particular circumstances. So too, other aspects of the objective standard would have to be geared to what the average prudent person, the reasonable person in the patient's particular position, would agree to or not agree to, if all material and special risks of going ahead with the surgery or foregoing it were made known to him. Far from making the patient's own testimony irrelevant, it is essential to his case that he put his own position forward.

The adoption of an objective standard does not mean that the issue of causation is completely in the hands of the surgeon. Merely because medical evidence establishes the reasonableness of a recommended operation does not mean that a reasonable person in the patient's position would necessarily agree to it, if proper disclosure had been made of the risks attendant upon it, balanced by those against it. The patient's particular situation and the degree to which the risks of surgery or not surgery are balanced would reduce the force, on an objective appraisal, of the surgeon's recommendation. . . .

In saying that the test is based on the decision that a reasonable person in the patient's position would have made, I should make it clear that the patient's particular concerns must also be reasonably based: otherwise, there would be more subjectivity than would be warranted under an objective test. Thus, for example, fears which are not related to the material risks which should have been but were not disclosed would not be causative factors. However, economic considerations could reasonably go to causation where, for example, the loss of an eye as a result of nondisclosure of a material risk brings about the loss of a job for which good eyesight is required. In short, although account must be taken of a patient's particular position, a position which will vary with the patient, it must be objectively assessed in terms of reasonableness. . . .

Relevant in this case to the issue whether a reasonable person in the plaintiff's position would have declined surgery at the particular time is the fact that he was within about one and one-half years of earning pension benefits if he continued at his job; that there was no neurological deficit then apparent; that there was no immediate emergency making the surgery imperative; that there was a grave risk of a stroke or worse during or as a result of the operation, while the risk of a stroke without it was in the future, with no precise time fixed or which could be fixed except as a guess of three or more years ahead. Since, on the trial Judge's finding, the plaintiff was under the mistaken impression, as a result of the defendant's breach of the duty of disclosure, that the surgery would relieve his continuing headaches, this would in the opinion of a reasonable person in the plaintiff's position, also weigh against submitting to the surgery at the particular time.

In my opinion, a reasonable person in the plaintiff's position would, on a balance of probabilities, have opted against the surgery rather than undergoing it at the particular time. . . .

---

22   Zamparo v. Brisson

Ontario Court of Appeal

. . . ZUBER J.A. (dissenting in part): — This is an appeal by the defendant from a judgment of His Honour Judge Huneault of the County Court of the County of Essex awarding the plaintiff judgment in the sum of $21,182.16 plus costs. The defendant, Dennis A.T. Brisson (Dr. Brisson), is a surgeon trained in otolaryngology; the plaintiff, Margaret Zamparo, was his patient. From this relationship flowed this action for malpractice and the judgment which is the subject of this appeal.

In 1971, Margaret Zamparo, a resident of Windsor, was 55 years old. She was a victim of a partial hearing loss in her left ear. This condition had existed for as long as she could remember. When she had colds her hearing problems were aggravated but at other times, save for the necessity of using the telephone against her right ear, she functioned without any serious problems.

Following her husband's death in 1969, Mrs. Zamparo undertook a retraining course in the hopes of securing secretarial work but she was unsuccessful. In 1971, she consulted her family physician Dr. Stojanovic respecting headaches. Dr. Stojanovic detected her hearing loss and referred her to Dr. Brisson no doubt on the premise that the headaches might be connected in some way to the hearing loss.

Dr. Brisson saw her on December 3, 1971, took a history, examined her and performed various clinical tests. . . .

As a result of his clinical findings, Dr. Brisson arranged for audiometric studies to be performed in his office by a technician. Mrs. Zamparo saw Dr. Brisson again on January 19th and January 31st of 1972. Further audiometric and speech tests were performed on March 29, 1972. Shortly thereafter, surgery was scheduled for April 11, 1972. Prior to the surgery, Mrs. Zamparo saw Dr. Brisson in his office on April 10th and on the same day signed a standard form authority for surgical treatment at Grace Hospital.

The surgery to be performed on Mrs. Zamparo is described as a stapedectomy which is a surgical procedure whereby the stapes, one of the three bones of the middle ear is disarticulated from the ossicular chain and removed and replaced with a wire prosthesis. . . .

As a result of the injury to the facial nerve [during the surgery], Mrs. Zamparo suffered a paralysis to the left side of her face. It is that paralysis which is the basis of the damages awarded in this case.

The trial Judge found that Dr. Brisson was negligent in . . . failing to adequately advise Mrs. Zamparo. . . .

. . . [T]he trial Judge made the following significant findings:

1. Dr. Brisson had explained the nature of the surgery to Mrs. Zamparo;
2. He explained the risks involved;
3. Dr. Stojanovic advised Mrs. Zamparo to undergo the surgery;
4. Dr. Brisson did not recommend the surgery nor did he recommend against it. He left it up to the patient;
5. Mrs. Zamparo did not seek medical help because of her hearing difficulty. . . .

. . . [T]he trial Judge said:

In my view, . . . it is part of a surgeon's professional responsibility to give the patient his opinion as to whether or not surgical intervention, although maybe useful, should be performed in an individual case. The surgeon's opinion weighs heavily in a patient's mind when deciding upon elective surgery. The patient has placed his confidence in the surgeon and he is most certainly entitled to his professional opinion. This is an extremely important part of information for the patient to have in order to base his decision. Since Mrs. Zamparo had lived with this condition all or most of her life, had never previously consulted a doctor with a view of correcting her hearing loss, a condition that was so minor as not to preclude her from serving in the Armed Forces for several years, I am convinced that if Dr. Brisson had told the plaintiff that there was no particular need for surgery in her case, as it appears Drs. Barber and Briant would have told her, she would have decided against it. . . .

The surgery involved in this case was elective, i.e., not immediately required, and dependent upon the decision of the patient. The fundamental question posed . . . is whether there is a duty on a surgeon in such a case to give the patient his assessment of the real benefit of surgery and whether such benefit outweighs the risks involved and his recommendation based on such assessment. . . .

The . . . authorities [including *Hopp v. Lepp* and *Reibl v. Hughes*] leave no room to doubt that there rests upon the surgeon a duty to sufficiently inform his patient to enable him to make a choice whether or not to submit to surgery. . . .

In my view, it is self-evident that such a duty demands advice as to whether or not the surgery should be undergone, i.e. — whether it will produce a benefit to the patient which will outweigh the risks inherent in such surgery.

It is not suggested that the surgeon's duty can be discharged by returning the patient to a general practitioner and leaving the problem to him, unless of course, the specialist has transmitted his advice and recommendation to the general practitioner to be relayed to the patient. The fact that a surgeon or specialist is retained demonstrates the need for his advice and recommendation. The fact that a patient may be advised by the referring general practitioner does not as a general rule insulate the specialist against liability to the patient.

In this case the trial Judge obviously accepted the evidence that the proper advice to Mrs. Zamparo would have been a recommendation against surgery. Dr. Brisson, however, failed in his duty to Mrs. Zamparo not by making the wrong recommendation but by making none at all. I agree with the trial Judge that the failure to advise against surgery was negligence. . . .

WILSON J.A.: . . . I think the learned trial Judge imposed too high a duty on Dr. Brisson when he required him to advise Mrs. Zamparo against the surgery. He appears to have proceeded on the basis that:

(1) there is a duty on a surgeon to advise his patient for or against the contemplated surgery; and
(2) in this case the advice should have been against the surgery.

The surgery in this case was elective, almost in the cosmetic category. As I understand it, the election in the case of elective surgery is the patient's election. True, it must be the election of a fully-informed patient, one who has been apprised of the benefits of the surgery and warned of all the risks. The learned trial Judge found, however, that Dr. Brisson had done this, that he had told Mrs. Zamparo all the things the expert witnesses called by the respondent testified that they would have told her. He also gave her the statistics as to the success and failure rate for this type of surgery and the trial Judge found no fault with those. The only thing Dr. Brisson did not do was advise her whether she should have the surgery or not. He left her to make that decision in consultation with her family physician who had referred her to him in the first instance and to whom his full report was directed. Her family physician advised her to have the surgery. The learned trial Judge found that Dr. Brisson failed in his duty to Mrs. Zamparo in that he did not advise her not to have it.

While it may be that a surgeon is under a duty to give his patient his assessment of how the benefits of surgery measure up against the risks of having it, it seems to me that in the case of elective surgery only the patient can truly evaluate the benefits for him or her. There is a substantial subjective element to the evaluation of those benefits which are more than merely physical. There are sociological and psychological aspects, the importance of which will vary from patient to patient. Should the surgeon step outside his area of medical and surgical expertise and tell the patient what is "best" for him or her? . . .

---

23   Being a Burden on Others

Nancy S. Jecker

Individuals facing death are sometimes reluctant to exhaust the income and assets they have accumulated over a lifetime in order to pay for end-of-life care. They also may fear and wish to avoid becoming dependent and reliant on family members for assistance with activities of daily living. In principle, the ethical standard of respecting patients' autonomous choices should support honoring a decision to forgo treatment, irrespective of the reasons for the decision. Nonetheless, our tendency is to discredit decisions to forgo treatment that are made on the basis of the financial or emotional burden treatment places on family members. In this article I ask the following questions: How ought we to think about the various burdens medical treatment imposes on other people? Should patients themselves consider such burdens when making life and death health-care decisions? When they do, should health-care providers and others abide by patients' decisions? I will argue that reasons of justice can support patients' choices to incorporate such considerations into their personal health-care decisions. I will show that respect for patients' well-being and moral integrity can require others to honor patient's preferences made on this basis. Although my defense of these positions is general in spirit and applies to a wide range of health-care decisions, I pay particular attention to the competent patient's refusal of life-extending medical treatment.

The Argument from Justice

At both macro and micro levels, justice is routinely accepted as a legitimate basis for allowing people to forgo lifesaving medical treatment. Thus, most accept the claim that, under conditions of scarcity, society is permitted to allow people to die in order to use its health-care resources in other ways. For example, if there is not enough of a lifesaving resource to provide it to all in need, we may then choose to withhold it from one patient to provide it to another who is more likely to benefit. Even when there is no natural scarcity of health-care resources, the dollars to pay for health care are themselves scarce. Thus, we regard society as justified in choosing to allocate its limited wealth to various goods, including not only lifesaving treatments but also other kinds of health care and other social goods. These decisions are made not only at a societal level, but also within organizations. For instance, insurance companies formulate policies governing how much money will be devoted to lifesaving treatments — such as coronary by-pass surgery — versus other forms of treatment — such as preventive screening for various forms of cancer. Likewise, hospitals make trade-offs between patients by developing policies about how many Medicaid patients to admit. These decisions have life or death consequences, even though the losers in such decisions are often "faceless victims" (such as the Medicaid patient who is turned away from a hospital and whose medical condition subsequently worsens). Finally, smaller groups and individuals also participate in distributive decisions with potential life and death ramifications. For instance, an individual or family may subscribe to an insurance plan that does not cover life-prolonging treatments, such as organ transplantation for certain categories of patients, but provides excellent long-term care benefits.

A common feature these choices share is that they require weighing *competing* values against one another. At stake is not simply how to contain costs, but whether to invest limited resources in one way or another. In each of the above examples, distributive choices entail determining which individuals exert a stronger claim, or which of several priorities should be ranked higher. If the job of justice is to weigh competing claims for scarce goods, then justice naturally directs attention to the *opportunity costs* of using health-care treatments. The opportunities forgone by accepting a certain treatment may include not giving resources to other persons, not investing in other forms of health care, or not investing in other social goods. In short, justice situates isolated acts of treating patients in a broader social context, and fastens the individual to a larger network of persons. In this regard, justice exposes the fallacy of viewing ethical dilemmas in medicine apart from the background choices that structure available options.[1]

In the case of life-extending or lifesaving medical care, justice can give ethical warrant to patients' decisions to forgo treatment and be allowed to die. Patients may decline lifesaving care on grounds of justice, when others have overriding claims to lifesaving resources. Justice also may furnish a basis for forgoing lifesaving medical treatment, where accepting such treatment would also entail accepting finite palliative and caregiving resources to which others have a stronger claim. To explore more fully the role of justice in decisions to decline life-extending treatment, consider the following example.

> Joe is a seventy-one-year-old gentleman who has been diagnosed with oat cell carcinoma of the lung. The tumor is fairly widespread. The physicians treating Joe recommend a combination of radiation and chemotherapy. They point out that this usually increases survival by many months and also provides some palliative care. The patient refuses the recommended course of treatment because he is concerned about the cost that would be borne by his family members, including the cost of his wife staying with him near the hospital. At home, Joe would be cared for on a full-time basis by his daughter, who is a nurse. She has agreed to move in with him and take an indefinite leave of absence from her current job.
>
> In considering his options, Joe reflects along the following lines. First, he observes that the family financial and human resources that would be required to pursue additional months of life are scarce. Second, he judges there are other priorities that have a stronger pull on these resources. For example, his daughter has a young child of her own to care for, and she badly needs to make more time for personal projects that impart meaning and significance to her life. Joe's wife would be financially better able to fend for herself when Joe is gone if the money being spent on medical care were available for her to use. This money was intended to provide financial security in old age, not to be depleted in a short period of time to pay for medical care. Although Joe imagines that, in an ideal world, his resources would be more abundant and his options more robust, the actual choice he faces is how to distribute limited family resources fairly between all.[2]

One consideration at work in Joe's line of reasoning is an ethical ideal that I shall call *just caring*. Just caring requires that persons who care direct their limited resources toward persons or priorities whose claim to be cared for is strongest. When persons who care are blind to justice, they may be tempted to lavish attention on a single object and thereby neglect others who need care more, or as much. In the example described above, the daughter who extends an offer to care for her father responds to her parent's needs in a loving way, but arguably omits considerations of fairness to herself and others to whom she is already devoted. Just caring would require her to restrain her immediate impulse to help her father in order that she might consider the needs of herself and others whom she is called upon to support. Generally speaking, "caring, like loving, needs criteria for it to be helpful caring, just caring, truthful caring, not destructive caring."[3] Thus, it is misleading to think only about caring or loving without concern for justice. Although family members may be disposed to operate "under the canon of mercy, not as an officer of justice,"[4] they should cultivate the ability to step back and consider how to care justly and wisely.[5] Also at work in Joe's reflections is an ethical idea of justice in the family. In situations where life-extending medical treatment is made available by drawing from family wealth or services, the family functions as a commons.[6] A tragedy of the commons occurs when members seek to take more common goods than they are entitled to, or when they refuse to make appropriate sacrifices and contributions. A commons flourishes only when each party is willing to acknowledge resources as shared commodities and respect others' stake in preserving them. To prevent a tragedy from occurring, Joe rightly considers the effect that his individual health-care decisions have for the commons upon which his wife depends. Viewing health-care choices in this light attenuates an exclusive focus on self and prevents persons from becoming morally deaf and dissociated from others. It introduces a role for justice by supporting family members who wish to give up goods in order to secure a fair share for others.

These points make evident that choosing to pursue life-extending medical treatment can place heavy demands on a family's financial and caregiving resources. Family burden is often overlooked in justice debates, but it will increasingly emerge as salient because the demand for family caregiving is expected to grow as the population ages.

Objections

One objection that these remarks may elicit is that dying patients who place other people's monetary or caregiving needs before their own are simply mistaken in their moral assessment. According to this objection, the dying patient's needs always enjoy pride of place, because life itself is of inestimable value. Thus, when others compete for financial resources or caregiving attention, their needs should be overridden when they are for less weighty purposes. The problem that such reasoning encounters is that it runs deeply counter to our implicit choices and values in many other areas. For example, we implicitly accept that life holds finite value whenever we endanger our lives in ordinary activities, such as crossing the street at a busy intersection, flying in airplanes, and driving automobiles. Likewise, when making health-care decisions, we frequently place the goal of extending life alongside the good of improving life's quality. For example, we prefer medications from which death has resulted, such as oral contraceptives, over safer medications that are less convenient. As noted previously, individuals sometimes opt for health insurance plans that offer coverage for certain forms of lifesaving treatment but provide other kinds of benefits. It is simply not true, then, that we can dismiss as misguided a patient's wish to forgo lifesaving treatment in order to avoid becoming a burden to others. Instead, it is consistent with our larger body of beliefs and choices to regard the value of life-sustaining treatment as limited and to allow patients to weigh the emotional and financial costs to others against the cost of giving up additional months of life.

A second objection calls into question the claim that a commons represents a true depiction of family relations. One irritant in this image may be that those who think in accordance with it will be inclined to trammel benevolence and goodwill by introducing a vocabulary of rights and duties into family life. In response, it can be said that love and benevolence need not function as adversaries to rights and duties. Instead, it is possible for these goods to coexist harmoniously: rights and justice improve caring by distinguishing what is wise and helpful caring.

A related concern that the image of a family commons may prompt is that justice is intrusive and out of place in loving relationships; justice entails calculating what people are due and making explicit trade-offs, whereas genuine love must be spontaneous and unconditional. To address this concern, it is important to illuminate the assumptions upon which it is based. First, caring requires separation from justice only if it is imagined that caring is exempt from justice's claims. But the relationships people forge do not make a moral island.[7] Figuring out what one ought, morally, to do is never solely a matter of getting clear about what caring calls for. Instead, caring relationships are circumscribed and undergirded by ethical considerations outside themselves. Second, the idea that the introduction of justice into personal relationships inevitably spoils caring, because it is cold and unfeeling, is based upon the erroneous assumption that justice is a virtue only between strangers. But justice can also be constructed as applying to relationships of goodwill between persons who face competing loyalties.[8] On the latter reading, loving relationships occur in the context of multiple commitments, and justice aims to balance fairly the multiple loyalties people have.[9] If my reasoning is sound, then it is possible to view justice as a family virtue and to picture family resources as a commons in which each member holds a stake. This framework gives moral support to taking burdens on other family members into account when making health-care decisions.

The Argument from Happiness and Integrity

Thus far, I have argued that justice supports patients' choices to take burdens on others into account when making health-care decisions. I now provide reasons why health-care providers and others should honor patients' choices that are made on this basis. My argument will be that permitting patients to act in accordance with their own moral convictions is a prerequisite to patients' happiness and moral integrity.

Aristotle apparently held that performing noble and good deeds is "a thing desirable for its own sake,"[10] and that those who regularly perform such deeds experience a sense of happiness and well-being. One reason that happiness may be an outgrowth of virtuous activity is that persons who practice virtue develop integrity and self-respect. Integrity describes those who abide by moral standards and dispositions that are their own, and who hold strong and deeply felt convictions.[11] Self-respect refers to having a sure sense of one's own worth.[12] Forgoing health-care resources in order to benefit others is an act of integrity when it indicates that one is living up to one's own sense of justice under conditions where this ideal is tested. By contrast, consuming health-care resources generates shame and guilt and undermines integrity when these actions betray one's moral convictions and dispositions.

These remarks suggest a reason why patients should be permitted to regard the burdens their decisions impose on others as important. Permitting such considerations may be a necessary part of honoring patients' moral autonomy and ability to be self-respecting moral agents. When individuals do what they believe is right, this strengthens their sense of moral self-worth and dignity. By contrast, when persons are compelled to disappoint themselves, this lowers their self-estimation. When patients' moral decisions are overridden, they rightfully perceive this as an insult because it conveys that they are not fully capable moral agents. To the extent that the capacity to reflect on choices and form moral opinions is bound up with individuals's sense of their own identity, those who are made to transgress their own moral beliefs will have a less sure sense of who they are and what they hope to be in the world.

Conclusion

I have argued that there is little ethical basis for the unease health providers sometimes feel when patients decline treatment to avoid imposing burdens on others. This leaves us, still, with the lurking question: What is it about taking such burdens into account that troubles so many? I have suggested already that taking burdens to others into account plays havoc with the belief that life is of inestimable value and that we, therefore, must do everything possible to keep patients alive. If there is a price that patients themselves are not willing to pay for additional weeks or months of life, this undermines the belief that life possesses infinite value. Particular lives hold finite, even measurable, value to those who live them. Identifying burdens to others as an ethically valid basis for withdrawing treatment also may prompt unease, because it appears to make a mockery of the cherished idea that human beings are essentially free and unencumbered beings. Patients who consider the burdens they impose on others reveal themselves to be deeply embedded in relationships and social structures to which they owe duties and from which they are entitled to benefits. In point of fact, this perspective hardly makes a mockery of individual autonomy. To the contrary, the idea of autonomy allied with moral responsibility more truly captures original Kantian and Enlightenment views about the function of autonomy in moral life. Kant himself held that individuals become autonomous and self-determined, not by setting themselves free of social and ethical mooring, but by being guided by reason and imposing moral rules and principles upon themselves.[13] On this understanding, a patient who evades her ethical and social responsibilities in reaching treatment decisions is not genuinely autonomous. She is not mastered by her rational and moral self, but succumbs instead to fear of death or weakness of moral will. If this is correct, then the tensions that ethical duties to family members and others introduce into health-care decisions should help to move debates about patient autonomy to a higher ground.

Although I have sketched a partial answer to the question of how we should think about the consideration of burdening others when making health-care decisions, there is a darker side that I have not addressed. Namely, how should we as a society respond to patients who insist that everything possible be done and who simply refuse to take burdens to others into account? How should society answer patients who believe they are owed the best and most expensive care that medicine can offer, regardless of the burdens this imposes?

This darker side of considering the costs of medical treatment has received some attention in recent debates about rationing medicine and reforming the health-care system. Yet most attention has focused on macro policy choices, rather than face-to-face encounters among patients, family members, and health professionals. Ultimately, when explicit policies are in place, the darker side of rationing debates will rear its ugly head. A first step to facing squarely the challenges that lie ahead is to accept and support those who humbly and courageously choose to forgo medical treatment on behalf of valued others.

Notes

1. A.C. Baier, "Alternative Offerings to Asclepius," *Medical Humanities Review* 6, no. 1 (1992): 9–19.
2. Adapted from B.A. Brody and H.T. Engelhardt, eds., *Bioethics: Readings and Cases* (Englewood Cliffs, NJ: Prentice-Hall, 1987), 341, case D.
3. M.A. Farley, "Love, Justice and Discernment: An Interview with Margaret A. Farley," *Second Opinion* 17, no. 2 (1991): 80–91.
4. M. Battin, "Choosing the Time to Die: The Ethics and Economics of Suicide in Old Age," in *Ethical Dimensions of Geriatric Care*, ed. S.F. Spicker, S.R. Ingman, and I.R. Lawson, (Dordrecht, The Netherlands: D. Reidel, 1987), 161–90.
5. C. Gilligan, "Remapping the Moral Domain," in *Reconstructing Individualism*, ed. T.C. Heller, M. Sosna, and D.E. Wellerby (Stanford, CA: Stanford University Press, 1986). 237–52; N.P. Lyons, "Two Perspectives: On Self, Relationships, and Morality," *Harvard Educational Review* 53 (1983): 125–45.
6. G. Hardin, "Living on a Lifeboat," in *Moral Issues*, ed. J. Narveson (New York: Oxford University Press, 1983). 167–78; N.S. Jecker, "The Role of Intimate Others in Medical Decisions," *Gerontologist* 30 (1990): 65–71.
7. N.S. Jecker, "Impartiality and Special Relationships," in *Kindred Matters: Rethinking the Philosophy of the Family*, ed. K. Kipnis, D. Meyers, and C. Murphy (Ithaca, NY: Cornell University Press, at press).
8. J. Kilner, "Who Shall Live?: An African Answer," *Hastings Center Report* 14 (June 1984): 18–22; G. Sher, "Other Voices, Other Rooms," in *Women and Moral Theory*, ed. E.F. Kittay and D.T. Meyers (Totowa, NJ: Rowman and Littlefield, 1987), 178–89.
9. N.S. Jecker and A.O. Berg, "Allocating Medical Resources in Rural America: Alternative Perceptions of Justice," *Social Science and Medicine* 34 (1992): 467–74.
10. Aristotle, *Nicomachean Ethics, in The Basic Works of Aristotle*, ed. R. McKeon (New York: Random House, 1941), 935–1126, at 1102.
11. B. Williams, "Utilitarianism and Moral Self-Indulgence" in B. Williams, *Moral Luck* (Cambridge, England: Cambridge University Press, 1981), 40–53.
12. T.E. Hill, *Autonomy and Self-Respect* (Cambridge, England: Cambridge University Press, 1991).
13. I. Kant, *Groundwork of the Metaphysics of Morals*, trans. H.J. Paton (New York: Harper and Row, 1956). For further discussion of this point, see M.J. Meyer, "Patients' Duties," *Journal of Medicine and Philosophy* 17 (1992): 541–56; E.H. Morreim, *Balancing Act* (Dordrecht, The Netherlands: Kluwer, 1991), chap 7.

---

24   Changing One's Mind:
When Is Odysseus to Be Believed?

Erich H. Loewy

In clinical medicine, physicians often encounter patients who, for a variety of reasons, "change their minds" in circumstances in which critical decisions must be made. Under many conditions, such a change of mind can be accepted as the genuine product of proper reflection; in other situations, such a change of mind may appear to be less than authentic. This article deals with some of the problems involved in evaluating such a change of mind and in then having to act either upon the original or upon the later decision.

A colleague of mine tells the story of his grandmother, who steadfastly had asked to be allowed to die at home rather than to have her life prolonged for only a short time by institutionalization. Her expressed wish was generally followed by the admonition: "and even if I change my mind, don't believe me." We will have later occasion to explore the interesting language (that of "belief") used in this context.

When Odysseus (Ulysses) was coming home, and when he knew that he might be tempted by the sirens, he asked that he be tied to the mast and, no matter how he might plead to be released, not be released until well beyond temptation. He asked, should he be tempted to change his mind, not to be believed. To insure that this would happen, furthermore, he had his men close their ears with wax.[1] Physicians, when handling critical cases, can neither remain below deck nor close their ears. They must deal with these troubling cases as best and as compassionately as they can.

Report of a Case

The patient who forms the background of this discussion was a 58-year-old woman who had chronic obstructive pulmonary disease. She was knowledgeable about her disease, had seen other family members live and die with it, and had seen some of them ventilator-bound. For some years she had steadfastly expressed the desire not to be started on a ventilator unless such an intervention were to be purely temporary, and she had repeatedly expressed her revulsion at the thought of being permanently tied to life-sustaining equipment. She had spoken with her family, who agreed, as well as with her physician, who thought her request reasonable and agreed to it.

When the patient arrived at the hospital in terminal respiratory failure, it was evident that if she were to be placed on a ventilator there would be almost no chance of her ever being weaned. A consultation with a specialist in pulmonary diseases confirmed this. The patient was critically ill, slightly "fuzzy" — albeit grossly oriented — and very anxious. When her physician spoke with her about her decision, she expressed the wish to be placed on a ventilator "even if she would never again be able to be weaned from it."

Shortly thereafter, the patient became more obtunded, so that reasonable conversation with her was impossible.

In this case, as in most such cases, two contradictory wishes confront each other. They are separated from each other by time and circumstance. When patients present us with this problem, we are bound to make a choice that not only reflects our assessment of the case, but also is revealing of us as persons and as moral agents.[2] This article deals with: 1) the problem of changing one's opinion; 2) the criteria for accepting or rejecting a choice as autonomous; 3) the roles of the family and the context in arriving at a decision; 4) a way of resolving such problems; and 5) the resolution of the present case.

Changing One's Opinion

An opinion or a judgment, if it is to be regarded with respect, requires a factual base and the opportunity for reflection and deliberation upon these (understood) facts. An opinion that did not meet these criteria would be discounted. This is not an all-or-nothing proposition: people are more or less informed, are more or less able to understand that information, and have more or less skill for forming a judgment through careful deliberation. When we accept or reject another's judgment or opinion, we generally do so because of such factors. We would discount an uninformed opinion just as we would tend to discount a snap judgment based on undigested facts; we would accept a clearly well-informed and deliberated-upon judgment and we would have cause to question, more or less seriously, an opinion that only marginally met these requirements.

Changing one's opinion is often regarded as being fickle. Yet, persisting in one's opinion despite evidence to the contrary is, at the very least, inflexible and unthinking. The problem seems to reside not in the change itself but in the reason for that change: changing one's opinion without good reason may justly be judged to be capricious; changing it because of new evidence, or because carefully reflecting on old evidence causes one to change, may properly be seen as a sign of thoughtfulness, wisdom, and maturity.

When we say that we have good reason for changing our opinion, then, we imply either new facts or new thoughts about old facts or, at times, both. In either case, we would require both factual or cognitive material and sufficient deliberation to enable us to come to terms with it. When either or both are missing, we tend to discount any opinion, be it the original one or a change.

Unless we have good reason to the contrary, we tend to accept a more recent judgment over an older one. Generally my decision to go to London rather than to Vienna on my next trip will be accepted without much question and my more recent diagnosis will be respected over my initial one. This is so, however, only because the personal circumstances surrounding the making of that judgment are not greatly changed. I am held to be no less competent to make judgments in the latter than I was in the former instance.

Expressing a change in opinion, furthermore, is no guarantee that there has truly been a change. When my colleague's grandmother asked "not to be believed" if she changed her mind, she gave expression to this. In so many words she intimated that when she changed her mind she was not to be believed, would not be authentic,[3,4] and, therefore, would not be telling the truth. It would not be her speaking, it would be another, whom she, like Odysseus, rejected and denied in advance. It would be another, furthermore, whom she (an Odysseus) expected and feared. Both knew themselves well enough to be aware of that "other" lurking underneath their skins. Compelling internal and external circumstances may force us to adopt an unauthentic stance: like Galileo we may recant and may not mean it. We may fear being believed.

Criteria for Autonomous Choice

When patients agree with our decisions, we tend not to examine their ability to make an autonomous choice. Such an attitude, while understandable, is not wholly defensible. Patients who agree with us may do so for a variety of reasons. They may, for example, not wish to choose for themselves; their choice not to choose depends upon their personalities, on prior conditioning or, in this instance, they may simply trust our judgment and prefer not to judge for themselves. When genuine, such decisions not to choose deserve as much respect as do other choices. On the other hand, patients may feel coerced by the physician or by the family, or may fear to "obtrude their wishes against the full power of the medical establishment."[5] Such choices, even when they are consistent with our own recommendations or wishes, are hardly free. Still, when they correspond to our own judgments, we tend to accept them unthinkingly rather than to probe and question.

When our patients choose to do other than what we advise, or when they express wishes with which we may not agree because we do not believe these wishes to be in the patients' best interests, we feel the need to determine the validity of their choices. We consider our choices to be eminently reasonable, sane, and rational, and have trouble conceding such attributes to a choice in conflict with our own. And, in the medical setting, there may often be good reason for this. Most technical decisions (and few, if any, are purely that) made by physicians (whether to treat, operate, or test, for example) stand a better chance of being "right" within the medical framework than do the choices of laymen. However, decisions that deal predominantly with values, and "technical" decisions that are really hidden value judgments (whether, for example, to vigorously treat an infection in a demented person) are another matter. Here the values are the patient's, and doing what is "best" for the patient must be defined, where possible, on the patient's terms. Most, if not all, decisions are composite: they are made on the basis of "technical facts" (themselves not value-free and underpinned by a set of formulating values) as well as on the basis of value judgments. When patients choose to do other than what physicians advise, they may do so because of a dispute over technical facts or they may do so because value judgments are at issue.[6] When patients make choices with which physicians disagree, and when physicians then try to judge the meaning of such dissent, such considerations must be born in mind.

When we accept others' choices, we do so, among other reasons, because we suppose their choices to have been autonomously made. Autonomy here is defined as the capacity for independent thought, decisions, or action. This, of course, is an unachievable ideal.[7] In being dependent upon genetic disposition, on the conditioning of past experience, on the influence of the community, and on one's own precepts, no person is truly independent in thought or decision.[8] The will, in that sense, is certainly not entirely free.[9] Nevertheless, a reasonable or conventional autonomy is vouchsafed to all mature, sentient and rational beings by custom as well as by law.

Autonomy, even conventional autonomy, has its limits.[10,11] It is not an "all-or-nothing" matter but has shades and gradations. It is diminished in the acutely frightened, emotionally harassed, or severely pain-ridden patient, and is difficult to concede to the demented or intoxicated. The determination of autonomy for the purpose of valid consideration in ethical decision making is a recurrent problem whose resolution depends, in part, upon the texture of the specific case.[8] Safeguarding and restoring autonomy is one of the noblest functions of medicine.[12]

To be an autonomous, authentic decision, a decision must meet certain criteria. At the least, it must be: 1) amply informed; 2) the product of sufficient deliberation; 3) free of coercion; and 4) consistent with an enduring world view.[4,8]

Information, of course, must be given in a way that is comprehensible to patients. Persons who truly understand have more than cognitive acquaintance with a subject. Understanding, never complete, has experiential and emotive components: a familiarity, at least, with similar problems and with their implications.

Deliberation appropriate to the topic is a necessary condition of autonomous decisions. Without it, information cannot be processed into understanding and understanding cannot eventuate in choice. Without it, choice remains reflex or random.

Coercion either results in an unauthentic choice, one that is forced against the agent's "better judgment," or distorts understanding, and deforms deliberation. It can, of course, be external (as when patients are coerced by families, physicians, or the medical milieu) or internal (as when patients are coerced by fear, terror, or pain). In either case, significant coercion mitigates against independent and free choice.

Consistency of choices with prior world views stamps choices as authentic; those made in contravention to world views are suspect. Patients who chose in certain ways for their entire lives and who suddenly choose differently may be making an autonomous choice but, more likely, are not. When choices conflict seriously with prior world views, the other criteria of autonomy need to be carefully examined. Such choices may be misinformed, coerced, or made in haste. Further, consistency among various manifestations of a world view, while not a requirement in all circumstances (none of us are entirely consistent in our thoughts or actions), is a desirable subsidiary criterion. World views, of course, change; people may learn better (or worse) and, in effect, may change their philosophies. But such changes occur over time. Only rarely do abrupt changes occur.

Roles of Family and Context

Choosing to heed an earlier or later decision cannot be done out of touch with others concerned with the patient or outside of the context in which such problems occur. A physician's primary duty to his/her patient cannot be discharged by blindly following all the patient's wishes. Patients' wishes may conflict with the physician's own vision of ethical conduct (and necessitate a change of care givers, for neither party can force the other to do that which they hold to be immoral),[6] or the patient's expressed wish may be of doubtful validity. In such instances the patient's family and the patient's context are of great help in arriving at a decision: the patient's understanding, deliberation, and consistency of prior world view can often be helped by understanding the family and the context.

Ideally, physicians can inform their patients, guide their deliberations and become familiar with their world views in an ongoing and enduring relationship. It is a situation of mutuality in which physicians and patients share and in which they become familiar with each other. In such cases, sympathy and understanding for each other's world views slowly evolve. The tendency to distort another's world view and to make it conform to one's own is minimized by such enduring relationships. In today's world such relationships are rare. Often physicians and patients meet in crisis situations as virtual strangers. It is in such situations that an understanding of the patient's autonomous wishes is difficult to obtain. A sense of the patient's wishes can be obtained from the family and others close to the patient, but that sense is inevitably filtered through the hopes, fears, world views and, at times, conflicting interest of those purporting to speak for the patient. An understanding of the context that helped shape the patient's world view is most helpful. (The family members of a Jehovah's Witness who themselves are not Witnesses may judge quite differently than would the patient.) "What the patient would wish" is a judgment difficult to make and, at best, filled with uncertainty. An appreciation by the physician of the patient's prior context as well as a sensitive understanding of the family's interpretation of the patient's wishes (and of their own) will prove most helpful in arriving at discrete judgments in particular cases.

But there is more. Patients and physicians do not operate in a vacuum. In the hospital setting, the caring team as well as the institution have visions of ethical behavior that must be considered. The sensibilities of the moral actors who ultimately must act (and those of the institution in which such actions take place — say, the question of abortion in a Catholic institution) must be taken into account. Certain decisions, felt, perhaps, to be morally acceptable to patient and physician, may be precluded by an institution's dedication to a different vision. A decision, when made, must be implemented within the context of the caring team and of the institution. Since one cannot expect agents to violate their own moral sense, the ultimate choice must, at the least, be acceptable to those involved.

An Attempted Resolution

In deciding what to do in such cases, one can essentially make one of two choices. One may apply a predetermined principle (one, for example, that says that the more recent choice by reason of proximity has greater force and, therefore, must be carried out) or one can adjudicate each case using principles as guidelines but attending to the myriad vagaries that make each case unique. We can, in other words, apply principles in a Newtonian fashion to cases falling into certain categories regardless of the texture of the individual case and its context; or we can use principles as "tools of moral discernment"[13] which help guide, but do not determine, our moral judgments in individual cases.

When patients change their minds under circumstances that raise doubt as to the validity of the change, a careful examination of the criteria for making autonomous choice is often helpful. Such examinations, no matter how mindful of the context and sensitive to the moral actors involved, is unlikely to yield demonstrably and immutably correct results. Patients capable of changing their minds are, obviously, neither totally disoriented nor unconscious. At best, they are fully sentient beings whose autonomy is beyond question; at worst, they are disoriented and incapable of sustained thought. In neither of these extreme cases can there be much question. The vexing questions occupy a middle ground.

When decisions conflict and when both can be considered to be approximately equal autonomous choices the more recent decision will generally rule. All things being equal, we have a prima facie obligation to heed these more recent choices: the person may have had further time for deliberation or may have acquired new facts or a better understanding of old facts, or the context in which the original choice was made may have changed. In dealing with troubling cases such as this one, we cannot so easily apply this rule. We are compelled to ask not only "which judgment is the more recent" but "which judgment truly represents the patient's autonomous will." If one considers autonomy to be, so far as possible, the capacity for independent thought, decision or action,[8] one will have to try to be guided in one's decision by an assessment of the validity of the prior vis-à-vis the present choice. One will, in other words, not only consider which decision was the most recent but also balance the autonomy of one decision against the autonomy of the other. To do this, one will have to consider the four criteria for autonomy and arrive at a judgment as to which decision appears to be the more valid. One must try — but, since one is human, will not succeed altogether — to keep one's own prejudices as to which is the better course from contaminating the judgment. Eventually physicians must act on one or the other decision knowing full well that the judgment made is neither immutably right or wrong.

The Present Case

In essence, three choices were possible in the present case: 1) one could follow the patient's most recent wish and place her on a ventilator knowing that there was virtually no chance that it would ever be discontinued; 2) one could accede to her original desire, refrain from ventilating her and allow her to die; or 3) one could ventilate her sufficiently to allow further deliberation and choice to be made by her.

None of these choices, in and of itself, is "good" in the sense of producing an acceptable outcome. None of them, on the other hand, in and of itself is precluded by ethical considerations. If one were to ventilate the patient, conforming to her most recent wishes, one could readily appeal to the weight of proximity; if one were to ventilate until a further expression of will could be obtained, one could appeal to uncertainty and to the necessity of making sure that the patient's will was indeed genuine; if one were to abide by her original desire, one could appeal to the greater force of the original vis-à-vis the later autonomy. In deciding on which course to follow, physicians must be mindful not to substitute their own sense of the proper course for that of the patient. To the extent that this is possible (and one's own sense of the proper course inescapably will enter into the determination) the decision should be congruent with the patient's own authentic and autonomous choice.[14]

Ventilating this patient, at least long enough to ascertain her "real" will, at first blush seems the better way. It allows time for further deliberation and opts in favor of life. Once, however, patients are placed on ventilators or other life-sustaining devices, removing such devices becomes, in practical terms, a difficult matter. Those who argue that there is a great difference between killing and letting die will argue that removing a ventilator is quite a different matter from not initiating such treatment. The validity of this point (which, to me, seems to depend upon the situation and its context), is a question outside the scope of this paper. The fact remains that in today's hospital setting, removing a ventilator is a quite different matter from failing to initiate such treatment. A situation in which this patient, conscious and pleading to have her initial contract adhered to, is forced to remain on a ventilator is not hard to imagine. The possibility, furthermore, that once removed from a ventilator she would again plead to be placed on it, is not remote. Humanity and compassion would caution one not to initiate the possibility of such a cat-and-mouse game.

Our patient's initial choice is clear and the autonomous nature of her initial decision is not in doubt. It was amply informed, and that information was understood in ways that included the experiential (she had seen others in a similar condition) and, so far as that is possible, the emotive (she was not only familiar with others in this condition but these others had been family members). Her decision had been made over time, had been amply discussed with her physician as well as with family and friends and was, therefore, the product of considerable deliberation. So far as that is possible (and so far as it is possible to judge from the outside), her initial decision had been uncoerced. And it was consistent with a long enduring and often expressed world view (expressed not only in terms of her own case but also in her attitude towards stories with which she had come in contact).

The autonomy of her later decision is certainly in doubt. Judgment here is not right or wrong: as so often when humans confront severe problems, they are forced to make the best judgments and do the best they can. Certainty, in technical or moral matters, is not vouchsafed to us.[15] The patient's knowledge may not have been diminished by her critical situation (albeit certainly not enhanced), but her ability to acquire and digest the particular knowledge of her particular situation at that particular time was severely limited. Understanding, furthermore, was curtailed by her clinical state, and deliberation could not take place. The internal coercion of panic, fear, anoxia, hypercarbia, and the release of stress hormones such as adrenalin was evident. Finally, her decision was entirely inconsistent with an often and emphatically expressed world view. It seemed that rather than pleading for the use of the ventilator she was pleading for comfort or, at least, for surcease from terror.

No right answer is available. The available choices (each blameworthy in itself) had to be sorted out with care and with compassion and humanity. This, inevitably, involves subjective elements. Persons who deal with such problems cannot fail to see themselves in such a situation. And their choices for the patient inevitably reflect such choices for themselves. The converse — making such choices coldly, purely analytically and without empathy — separates the choice from the moral actors and reduces ethics to a cookie-cutting exercise.

Ultimately one has to act. Rightly or wrongly a choice has to be made and a problem has to be resolved. The choice here (with full agreement by family, residents, and nursing staff) was to use a ventilator only if its use would promote comfort and then for as briefly as possible (ultimately this proved not to be necessary), to sedate the patient as required, and to allow her to die with comfort and dignity. Like my colleague's grandmother and like Odysseus, this patient too may well have feared that a decision made under the duress of emotions might not be her authentic self and, in that sense, would be a lie. Odysseus' original plea, we decided, was to be believed.

References

1. Homer: The Odyssey (Transl: Cook A). New York: W.W. Norton & Company, Inc, 1967

2. Churchill LR: Bioethical reductionism and our sense of the human. Man & Med 1980;5:229–249

3. Dworkin G: Autonomy and behavior control. Hastings Center, 1976;6(1):23–28

4. Miller BL: Autonomy and the refusal of life-saving treatment. Hastings Center 1981; 11(4):22–28

5. Ramsey P: The Patient as Person. New Haven: Yale University Press, 1970

6. Loewy EH: Physicians and patients: moral agency in a pluralist world. J Med Humanities Bioethics 1986;7(1):57–68

7. Morison RS: The biological limits on autonomy. Hastings Center 1984;14(5):43–49

8. Loewy EH: Patient, family, physician: agreement, disagreement and resolution. Fam Med 1986;18:375–378

9. Dennett DC: Elbow Room. Cambridge, MA: MIT Press, 1984

10. Siegler M: Critical illness: the limits of autonomy. Hastings Center 1977;7:17–25

11. Jonsen AR, Siegler M, Wisnlade WJ: Clinical Ethics. New York: Macmillan Publishing Co., Inc., 1982

12. Cassel EJ: The function of medicine, Hastings Center 1977; 7(6):16–19

13. Churchill LR, Simarton JJ: Principles and the search for moral certainty. Soc Sci Med 1986;23:461–468

14. Appelbaum PS: Commentary on Can a subject consent to a "Ulysses contract"? Hastings Center 1982;12(4):27–28

15. Loewy EH: The uncertainty of certainty in clinical ethics. J Med Humanities Bioethics 1987;8(1):26–33

Chapter 6

Questions to Consider

1. Mrs. Giovanna Ciarlariello, suspected of having a cerebral aneurysm (weakening of an artery in the brain) that can rupture, resulting in stroke and death, has consented to a cerebral angiogram. This test should locate the site of the aneurysm so that surgical correction could be attempted. During the angiogram Mrs. Ciarlariello begins to

spasm; after calming herself from that reaction, she says, "Enough, no more, stop the test." Her neurologist then assesses her and assures her that five more minutes are required; the patient responds, "Please go ahead." Has she given a valid consent to proceed? (*Ciarlariello v. Schacter*, [1993] 2 S.C.R. 119).

2. John, who has had an extra-marital affair, is concerned that he has acquired a sexually transmitted disease (STD). He goes to his family physician, Dr. Wilson, for an examination. Suppose the province legally requires physicians to report STDs. As part of informed consent, must Dr. Wilson disclose this potential consequence to John prior to the examination?

3. A patient in kidney failure has begun hemodialysis, a treatment that will continue for the rest of the patient's life (barring the possibility of a transplant). For how long is the patient's consent to dialysis valid? Can you describe rules or guidelines for when consent must be renegotiated?

4. Diane has just agreed to emergency surgery. In pain and despondent, she refuses the surgeon's offer to describe to her the nature and consequences of the procedure. She trusts the physician's judgement and is not interested in second-guessing him, she says. Has she provided a valid consent?

5. "Therapeutic privilege" is the name given to the doctrine that a physician may withhold information that would be harmful to a patient. Often, the doctrine is understood broadly, to refer to information that would be physically or emotionally harmful. Some give it a more narrow reading, restricting this privilege to those cases in which providing the information in question would result in the patient's psychological inability

to render an informed decision. When, if ever, would an "average, reasonable patient" agree that this doctrine should apply?

Further Readings

Brody, Howard. 1989. Transparency: Informed consent in primary care. *Hastings Center Report* 19(5):5–9.

Capron, Alexander M. 1993. Duty, truth, and whole human beings. *Hastings Center Report* 23(4):13–14.

Cassell, Eric J. 1985. *Talking with patients*. 2 vols. Cambridge, Mass.: MIT Press.

Cassileth, Barrie R., et al. 1980. Informed consent: Why are its goals imperfectly realized? *New England Journal of Medicine* 302:896–900.

Coy, Janet A. 1989. Autonomy-based informed consent: Ethical implications for patient noncompliance. *Physical Therapy* 69:826–33.

Faden, Ruth R., and Tom L. Beauchamp. 1986. *A history and theory of informed consent*. New York: Oxford University Press.

Feinberg, Joel. 1986. *Harm to self*. Vol. 3 of *The moral limits of the criminal law*. New York: Oxford University Press.

Freedman, Benjamin. 1975. A moral theory of informed consent. *Hastings Center Report* 5(4):32–39.

Lidz, Charles W., et al. 1984. *Informed consent: A study of decisionmaking in psychiatry*, chap. 1–3. New York: Guilford Press.

Meisel, Alan. 1979. The "Exceptions" to the informed consent doctrine: Striking a balance between competing values in medical decisionmaking. *Wisconsin Law Review* 413–88.

———, and Loren H. Roth. 1981. What we do and do not know about informed consent. *Journal of the American Medical Association* 246: 2473–77.

Chapter 7

Competence and Mental Illness

Introduction

The first time I came down to speak with Tim, he was easy to recognize. Sitting on the edge of a high hospital bed, slowly kicking his legs back and forth, with a bright baseball cap pushed back on his balding head, he looked for all the world like a 68-year-old schoolboy waiting for the bell to ring. Tim was well known to the staff, and especially to the psychiatrist who had requested this ethical consultation. A successful businessman and manager until his retirement about five years ago, he has nevertheless required periodic hospital treatment for his bipolar disorder for more than twenty years.

Persons with bipolar disorder (often called by the older diagnostic term, "manic-depressive disorder") may alternate, as the name suggests, between periods during which they are "high" (energetic, outgoing, optimistic) and others in which they are "down" (lethargic, withdrawn, pessimistic, depressed). In between these poles, for periods whose length varies between patients, they are "euthymic," that is, their emotional control and judgement fall within the normal range of behaviour.

A number of facts about bipolar disorder appear to imply that it is a disease, rather than simply a "problem in living." The condition clearly runs in families, suggesting a major genetic component. Everybody suffers from mood swings, but those resulting from bipolar disorder are different: the dips and rises are far more pronounced; the cycles may be fairly regular, appearing to reflect events inside the patient (a changing brain chemistry, for example) more than events in the patient's environment; and apart from the euthymic interval, a patient's judgement often seems very deviant. Finally, bipolar disorder is usually effectively treated medically by lithium.

Tim's cycles have been successfully controlled with lithium. Periodically, however, he would get drunk — Tim is a lifelong binge drinker — and then "forget" to take his medication. He would cycle higher and lower for a period, until he would get so out of control that his daughter would bring him to the hospital for treatment. Since retirement, though, his drinking has gotten out of control. Immediately prior to his current admission, Tim was "high". He had spent $15 000 in the last month, largely by way of gifts to a new friend he had made (a barmaid). His daughter called the police when she became frightened at his conduct. When they arrived, he was throwing sculptures and phonograph records he had been collecting for many years off his second-floor balcony.

The police brought him to the hospital for a psychiatric evaluation of competency, and for treatment. But now the psychiatrist, who has known Tim for years, is uncertain about his own moral obligation to Tim (and, perhaps, to Tim's daughter). Tim's kidney function, under many years' siege from alcohol and lithium, is now functioning at the borderline. If Tim wants to drink himself to death, isn't that his choice? Should Tim be protected from his own choices? The point was brought home to the psychiatrist when Tim told him, pointing to the cast on the psychiatrist's leg (a souvenir of a skiing vacation), "Maybe you should be in the hospital, doc! Maybe somebody should keep you here; next time you might break your neck instead of your leg!"

The questions asked by Tim's psychiatrist are the questions with which this chapter deals: In what sense, if any, can we describe Tim as ill, or his behaviour as symptomatic of illness? Is Tim competent to consent to, or to refuse, treatment for his bipolar disorder? Can we justify treating Tim against his will?

While these questions are commonly framed in the language of mental illness, they are certainly not restricted to persons formally designated as psychiatric patients, still less to patients exhibiting florid and unmistakable delusions and behaviour. When a diabetic patient refuses an amputation, or a kidney patient refuses hemodialysis; when a patient with AIDS has lost twenty percent of his body weight, and been admitted four times with bacterial and fungal infection, yet continues to deny that he is ill; when a chronically ill and frequently hospitalized patient, suffering "hospital fatigue syndrome," asks to be sent home and just to be let alone — in all of these cases and more, suspicion about the person's competency is likely to be raised before any treatment decision is reached.

These kinds of events are not uncommon. Appelbaum and Roth (1983), studying medical and surgical wards of a general (not psychiatric) hospital, found that in some settings these kinds of refusals are encountered more than once every ten days that a patient is in the hospital. In addition, the same sorts of problems frequently occur outside the medical context. The bioethics literature concentrates upon patient competency to consent to medical (and especially psychiatric) treatment. However, competency is also necessary for a person to validly contract for goods or services, to get married, to prepare a will, or to stand trial.

In each of these arenas of competency, Anglo-American courts have favoured a particular conception of competency: in general terms, a person is competent to x (to contract, to marry, to consent to treatment, etc.) if that person understands and appreciates the nature and consequences of *x*, as well as any alternatives to *x* which the person might choose instead. Consider as an example a will whose validity is challenged on the grounds that the testator (the person making the will) was incompetent at the time it was prepared. The law would inquire into whether the testator knew that he was making a will, that is, bequeathing his property to be distributed after his death; was aware of the extent of the estate which he would be leaving; and knew of the "alternatives" he could have chosen — knew, for example, of the existence of the persons who would ordinarily expect to be included within the will (spouse, children, siblings, etc.).

This common legal approach is well illustrated by *Ford v. Wainwright*, a celebrated case decided by the United States Supreme Court in which a new form of competency was described and required. Convicts sentenced to death, it was held, must be competent to be executed: they must understand the nature of the punishment they are to receive and the reason why they have been condemned to death. (It is in the nature of the case that the competency of such persons does not require them to be aware of any alternatives.) (For discussion, see Bonnie 1990.)

Precisely because the medical approach to competency is so distinct from that which the law has chosen, competency to consent to medical treatment poses interesting and intricate dilemmas. From a legal point of view, the focus of a ruling of competency is limited to the decision the person makes in the case at hand. The best evidence available will be the patient's testimony, and its demonstration that the patient understands the nature and consequences of the pending choice. The presumption is always against a finding of incompetency — legally, a person is competent unless proven otherwise — in order to avoid any unjustified infringement upon a person's liberties. By contrast, medical practitioners are more likely to understand patient competency globally, in terms of the whole person, rather than any one particular choice. This global conception of competency is tested by attending to the person's emotional and cognitive capacity to function. For a physician charged with the care of a patient, the most feared kind of error is the opposite of the law's: erroneously finding that a patient is competent, and respecting on that basis a patient decision that will bring harm to the patient.

Thus, while the law, given its values, might want a patient's competency judged in the context of a court hearing (or a quasi-judicial tribunal), medical values indicate that the same question would be resolved better by clinical determination, possibly through a multi-disciplinary case conference. Underlying these differences, in turn, are two radically different views of what kind of decision is involved in a competency determination. For medicine, whether a patient is competent or incompetent is primarily a question of fact, a descriptive issue. For the law, it is in the first instance a normative rather than descriptive question, asking whether that person is a full bearer of the same rights and duties granted to anyone else — especially, the right to determine his or her own fate. By examining the selections in this chapter, dealing with issues associated with definitions of mental illness and their relationship to patients' rights to seek or be free of treatment, you may come to feel that both perspectives need to be respected in the end.

The Selections

A basic issue underlying the relationship between psychiatry and health care ethics is the definition and meaning of mental illness. Critics have often adopted a stance of social relativism, claiming that persons who deviate from accepted social norms are prone to be labelled as mentally ill — which in turn will sometimes imply incompetence, and which may in turn lead to coerced residence in a psychiatric facility and to forced treatment. The point is easy to prove when we consider the psychiatric diagnoses other societies have adopted. In the pre-Civil War United States South, the psychiatric illness "drapetomania" referred to an uncontrollable urge on the part of a slave to run away; similarly, psychiatrists in the former Soviet Union diagnosed and treated persons suffering from "morbus democritus," a pathological attachment to bourgeois values of democracy (see Engelhardt 1974). In a spirited, behind-the-scenes account from a feminist point of view, Karen Ritchie argues that similarly value laden, political judgements were made in the construction of the "Bible" of North American psychiatrists, the Diagnostic and Statistical Manual (DSM). Mobilizing powerful arguments against the view that psychiatric diagnoses describe "real" entities, independent of any particular psychiatric theory, she nonetheless holds out hope that within a theory reliable and valid diagnoses could be established.

Benjamin Freedman's article begins our exploration of the fundamental legal and ethical concept of competency. Many ethicists and most legal systems — buttressed by the information provided by reason of the doctrine of informed consent — hold that whereas competent persons can look after themselves, those who are incompetent are for that reason in need of protection. In the medical and psychiatric contexts, this will imply that others must, on some basis, determine the form of treatment just and appropriate to an incompetent person. But when is a person incompetent? Surveying the major approaches to defining competency, Freedman argues for a "recognizable reasons" theory, by which a person would need to understand the nature and consequences of the medical options available, and in addition be able to choose a course for which recognizable reasons may be offered.

Historically, a court judgement was often needed when a person's competency was doubted. More recently, various jurisdictions have attempted preliminary alternatives to full judicial determination, for example, formal assessment by a psychiatrist. In the province of Ontario, a quasi-judicial process, boards of review, has been tried: assessment by multi-disciplinary panels, incorporating the perspectives of the lay public, as well as of the law and of psychiatry. "In the Matter of The Mental Health Act, R.S.O. 1980, c. 262 as amended, and in the Matter of KV, a Patient at a Hospital in Ontario" provides a glimpse of the kinds of questions these consent tribunals face, and the manner in which they reach their decisions. This tribunal judgement deals with the subtle but fundamental question, Did a schizophrenic person who seems to understand and appreciate all the psychiatrists tell him about treatment, *but who believes them to be mistaken in attributing his aberrant behaviour to mental illness*, satisfy Ontario's standard of competency?

Charles Culver and his colleagues delve further into the concept of competency and its relationship to rationality in the specific context of electro-convulsive therapy (ECT), "shock treatment," used often as a treatment of severe depression (and, less commonly, for other mental disorders). Through a series of case vignettes, the authors ask whether depression itself makes a patient incompetent to consent and whether an irrational decision can nonetheless be judged competent. The authors separate the various elements that underlie a decision regarding forced treatments, and conclude that even when a patient's refusal of treatment like ECT is both irrational and incompetent, the refusal should nonetheless be respected in most cases.

References

Appelbaum, Paul H., and Loren H. Roth. 1983. Patients who refuse treatment in medical hospitals. *JAMA* 250:1296–1301.

Bonnie, Richard J. 1990. Medical ethics and the death penalty *Hastings Center Report* 20(3):12–18.

Engelhardt, H. Tristram, Jr. 1974. The disease of masturbation: Values and the concept of disease. *Bulletin of the History of Medicine* 48(2):234–248.

Ford v. Wainwright, 477 U.S. 399 (1986).

Goldner, Fred. 1982. Pronoia. *Social Problems* 30:82–91.

25   The Little Woman Meets Son of DSM-III

Karen Ritchie

An unusual meeting took place on November 18, 1985. Seven feminist psychologists and psychiatrists were invited, all expenses paid, to meet with a committee of the American Psychiatric Association which was revising the third edition of the Diagnostic and Statistical Manual (DSM-III, 1980), the bible of psychiatric diagnosis. The proposal for the revision (DSM-III-R, 1987) included three diagnoses that some mental health professionals had found objectionable, and because of the vocal opposition to these three, a special committee was named to mediate the dispute.

One disputed diagnosis was premenstrual syndrome. Some of the negative feedback the committee had received was that, although the data are inconclusive, 40% to 60% of women may have symptoms of PMS. The question was raised whether anything experienced by half of a group can be called a disease. In addition, some were concerned that this diagnosis, especially when based on little hard evidence, would only perpetuate stereotypes about the emotional instability of women. Even if it is accepted, it might be more appropriately a gynecologic disorder than a psychiatric one, given the presumed hormonal cause.

A second disorder, paraphilic rapism, would have designated a group of compulsive rapists as having a mental disorder. It was argued that this would allow a rapist to plead insanity and thereby avoid a prison term. The committee found this argument persuasive enough that the diagnostic category was dropped.

The meeting on November 18 dealt with another proposed category, masochistic personality disorder, whose symptoms included remaining in exploitative relationships, sacrificing one's own interests for others, rejecting help so as not to be a burden on others, and turning down opportunities for pleasure.

The discussion evolved into a lively interchange. It centered on three arguments. First, and most pointed, was the problem of women as victims of violence. Several of the women invited to the meeting were experts in this relatively new field. They pointed out that victims of domestic violence, like victims of rape, have traditionally been blamed for causing the attacks, and that to diagnose them as sick, rather than the abusers, would be one more event of victimization. In fact, many abused women believe that staying in the relationship is the best alternative, given their economic dependence and fears of safety for themselves and their children if they leave. The testimony stressed that staying in the relationship may not be self-defeating but may be the least bad of the unpleasant alternatives. This argument was heard by the committee, and eventually an additional stipulation was added that the diagnosis should not be made if the self-defeating behavior is a response to abuse.

A second argument was that the term masochism had undesirable theoretical implications. This term goes back to Freud, who held that femininity involved the trio of passivity, masochism, and narcissism, and that femininity gave preference to "passive aims" (see, for example, Notman, 1982, p. 5, and Caplan, 1985, pp. 18–23). Standard psychoanalytic theory maintains that women obtain pleasure from pain. However, many analysts, and particularly feminist theorists, maintain that the concept is invalid. Because of the association of the term masochism with a theory whose accuracy is in doubt and which many women find offensive, it was argued that a diagnosis by this name should not be included.

This point, too, got a response. The name of the disorder was eventually changed from 'masochistic personality disorder' to 'self-defeating personality disorder'. The reason seems to be not just its association with discredited theories, but its association with *any* theory — the DSM task force, headed by Dr. Robert Spitzer, has made a concerted effort to be "atheoretical with regard to etiology", describing syndromes without attributing causes to them. (DSM-III, 1980, p. 7)

A third argument, like the PMS argument, questioned the validity of labeling abnormal a pattern that is found in many, perhaps the majority, of women. (Although the chief proponent of the diagnosis, Dr. Richard Simons, holds that it is as common among men as among women, he acknowledges that the diagnosis is likely to be made more frequently in women [*New York Times*, 1985]). However, not only are self-effacing characteristics prevalent among women, they are the accepted norm historically, culturally, and often religiously.

This is true particularly, but not exclusively, of Christianity. To use one dramatic example from 1988, Pope John Paul II addressed the proper roles of women in 'On the Dignity and Vocation of Women'. This document stresses that women should not imitate men, but should maintain distinctively feminine traits. For women, there are two options — marriage and motherhood, or virginity. Both choices are characterized by sacrifice — in fact, the words used are the *same* language of self-effacement used to characterize this proposed disorder. The woman, it states, makes a special "gift of self" in marriage, which is inextricable from motherhood (p. 273). And although there are two parents, the mother has the most demanding part — the gestation "literally absorbs the energies of her body and soul" (p. 274). Virginity, the only alternative to marriage and motherhood, also involves sacrifice — it substitutes a "readiness to be poured out for the sake of those who come within one's range of activity" (1988, p. 276). Women are expected to "make a 'sincere gift of self' to others, thereby finding themselves" (p. 281).[1]

The Catholic church is by no means the only denomination that encourages women to be self-sacrificing. Other Christian groups and non-Christians, for example, Muslims, expect similar behavior styles from women. And aside from religion, cultural roles supported by tradition reinforce women's dependence on men. For many women, there are "lifelong restrictions against expressing aggression and against being self-assertive in achieving one's own goals, in circumstances where self-assertion is considered appropriate for males" (Notman, 1982, p. 5). Women may fear that success will "cost them the loss of their relationship with males and of the esteem of the people around them" (ibid., p. 20).

Women are put in a double bind — expected to act in a self-effacing way and then being labeled as sick for doing so. This argument seems to have been presented less clearly than the other two, and the committee apparently did not hear it, or at least did not seem to take it very seriously.[2]

After the women presented their arguments against including masochistic personality disorder, and in their presence, the committee began its deliberation. The feminists were appalled that, so they claimed, criteria, and even whole diagnoses, were created or dispensed with in a session that involved a small group seated around a computer terminal. (It did not help that most of the committee were male and these diagnoses involved primarily women.) One of the invited participants reports that "Each shouted out ideas for criteria coming from their (sic) own experience . . . If the behavior was observable in patients, then a nosology category could be created." However, "one criterion was dropped because a workgroup member piped up with 'I do that sometimes.'" (Walker, 1986, p. 1)

The women asked whether jogging, playing football, or wearing high heels and girdles constituted masochism. The answer they received was that sports activities are not masochistic. Nor is wearing high heels, but wearing a girdle is, unless a woman is over 70. This answer must have contributed to the feminists' dismay over the process (Walker, 1986, p. 1).

One of the feminists reported that the committee offered a compromise — "if we backed off on masochism, they would create a sadistic disorder to cover wife beaters" (*Time*, 1985).[3] The committee, whether it was attempting to placate a vocal group or seriously trying not to be discriminatory, simply missed the points that most concerned the consultants. The offer of adding a new diagnosis disorder, apparently created on the spot, only reinforced the opinion that diagnoses were being made without adequate scientific backing.

The meeting ended abruptly, after mention of a potential lawsuit for violating women's civil rights. Later, in a closed session, the committee formulated its report to the APA's Board of Trustees. The diagnosis was to be retained, with a change of the name to 'self-defeating personality disorder', some modifications in the criteria necessary for the diagnosis, and the stipulation that the diagnosis is not applicable if the behavior is a response to violence. The committee recommended that sadistic personality disorder be added.

After a great deal of controversy involving the Board and the entire membership of the APA, self-defeating personality disorder and PMS, now called late luteal phase disorder, as well as the new sadistic personality disorder, were listed in DSM-III-R in a special appendix entitled 'Proposed Diagnostic Categories Needing Further Study' (1987, pp. 367–374). The disorders, however, were given coding numbers which are required on insurance forms to obtain reimbursement. This is contrary to a precedent set in DSM-III, which included a special research section on sleep disorders (1980, pp. 461–464). Those proposed disorders did not have coding numbers.

Hasty Conclusions

This episode involves so many issues relevant to the philosophy of psychiatry that a book could be written about them. There are, however, some simplistic explanations that could be drawn, but that would be incorrect, or at least incomplete.

One explanation would be that this is fundamentally a political battle, a power struggle of some sort (or that it is politics on the part of one group, the group with which one disagrees). And in fact, both groups accused each other of being more interested in politics than science (Spitzer, 1985; Walker, 1986).

But both groups used political tactics. The feminists used the political tactics of outsiders — first using persuasion, bringing in experts in the field: authors, psychologists and psychiatrists, the chair of the American Psychiatric Association's Committee on Women, and the counterpart for the American Psychological Association. The persuasion was partially successful, but when they did not succeed in eliminating the diagnosis, they threatened to pursue a lawsuit. They called the media, and got wide coverage. At the American Psychiatric Association's next general meeting, there was a demonstration protesting the DSM-III revision process and, specifically, the labeling of women.

For their part, the committee used the political tactics of insiders. They invited the group and paid their way. They tried reasoning and negotiation, and, from their point of view, it did not work. They then resorted to closing ranks. At the meeting in which the Board of Trustees was to decide on the proposal, the American Psychiatric Association's own Committee on Women first saw the proposal 30 minutes before the vote was to be taken, in an apparent attempt to insure that there was not enough time to formulate a considered response. Although the Board's decision was that the manual would make very clear that the diagnoses were provisional and merely needed further study, assigning numbers and listing them in the table in such a way as not to indicate the diagnoses' provisional status appears to have been a political move.

But the fact that political tactics were used does not mean that the entire enterprise is unscientific; it simply means that human beings are doing science. Certainly, science is no stranger to politics. In fact, political factors affect many facets of science, e.g., which investigations are done, which phenomena are observed and recorded and which ignored, which studies are published, and how quickly new theories are accepted, or even whether they are ever accepted at all. In this case, however, the fact that political factors were involved does not explain the disagreement.

A second possible conclusion would be the antipsychiatrists' claim that psychiatry is a failed or immoral endeavour and should be abandoned. Proponents of this view, from Thomas Szasz (see, for example, Szasz, 1974) to the more recent efforts of Masson (1988), have been vocal in denying the validity of psychiatry itself.

The basis of Szasz's argument is that psychiatric disease is a fictional concept, because it is ungrounded in demonstrable biological mechanisms. He would claim that there is no such thing as a psychiatric illness; so a scheme of such illnesses is itself invalid. However, recent advances in biological psychiatry undermine his argument. For example, genetic studies are showing evidence of inheritability of many psychiatric disorders, independent of family environment. Other data correlate mental symptoms with physical or chemical data such as hormone production, brain structures, blood chemistry, etc. Even without evidence, the assertion that disease refers only to biological disorders is not a provable, 'scientific' matter; it is a matter of definition. Instead of coming to agreement with Szasz's position, the profession is expanding the list of behavioral disorders; alcoholism, for instance, has become generally recognized as a disease.

Masson's approach is different. He documents cases of gross abuse of power by certain therapists, both in this century and the last, and concludes that one human should not have that much power over another. He points out that individual therapists sometimes use that power in unethical ways. To be sure, sexual abuse and emotional manipulation do occur. But this is a good argument for better regulation, not proof that regulation is impossible.

He also maintains that this supposedly value-free scientific endeavour is full of assumptions, and that the values of the therapist are often projected onto the patient. For the most part, I agree with this point, and will return to it in a later section.

Another conclusion that might be drawn from the masochism debate is that patients should not be labeled. People are so complex, the argument goes, that they can never be described in shorthand. Furthermore, it is an injustice to the patient, a denial of the individual's humanity and distinctiveness. This argument is often advanced by psychoanalysts, and in fact, setting up the DSM-III task force, Spitzer had problems finding psychoanalysts to serve; many told him they "did not think the task important enough for them to want to do the work" (and some now regret their decision). (See Spitzer, in Klerman et al., 1984, p. 551. This article is an excellent review of the problems with DSM-III.)

However, if a disorder is to be studied, it must have a name and a description. The original purpose of the Research Diagnostic Criteria, a predecessor of DSM-III, was to standardize terminology in order to have better data collection. Diagnoses offer a way to share information among professionals so that treatment can be advanced. The problem arises when the categories are considered to be not just working hypotheses, but descriptions of actual entities. The solution is not to abolish diagnoses, but to regard them with appropriate skepticism.

Conclusions

There are several mistakes that are creating the problems in this case. The first is the failure to recognize that diagnoses can only be made in the context both of a theory of disease and of value judgments concerning health and appropriate human behavior. The DSM committee has made a specific attempt to be purely descriptive, to be 'atheoretical'. But their effort is doomed. If we do not understand the role that theory and values play in diagnosis, we will never understand the confusion that arises when we try to distinguish normal from abnormal behavior.

Let us consider the usual ways of distinguishing disease (or illness) from normal conditions. One would be to reduce normalcy to statistical frequency. Boorse (1982, p. 68) holds that this criterion is appropriate for defining physical disease, although he finds it inadequate for purposes of mental illness. If infrequency is the basis for disease, how can we include PMS (now given the jargonish title late luteal phase disorder)? More relevant here, how many women will fit the criteria for self-defeating personality disorder? Depending on how the therapist applies the criteria, probably the majority.

A condition could be present in the majority of a group and still be considered a disease — for instance, Boorse mentions tooth decay (ibid.) But any entity that is so common should meet more stringent criteria to be considered a disease — there must be general agreement that the condition is undesirable. Tooth decay would meet this criterion, but self-defeating behavior would not.

Let us try another criterion for disease — that of correspondence to some biological design for the organism, i.e., that the behavior is consistent with 'natural' functioning. Is it 'natural' for women to be self-defeating? Now, this is certainly a political question. It has been said that we do not know whether patriarchy is the only possible system because for at least 6000 years we have not tried anything else.

The fact is, women have been under intense pressure for centuries to be self-effacing. Either interpretation is possible. One might conclude that women throughout history have been self-effacing; therefore it must be 'natural'. However, it is more likely that if the church finds it necessary continually to instruct women to be self-sacrificing, it is not 'normal' at all, but requires great effort to overcome the 'natural' impulse. At any rate, the biological design model does not solve the problem here.

A third model for disease would require that the condition cause distress for the individual. According to this model, we could simply ask the woman whether she was bothered by her behavior. While this would work in the case of the individual patient, it is hard to expand the concept to a group — the relevant question is whether being self-defeating causes distress to people in general. The concept of distress depends, among other things, on whether a woman's goals for herself are more or less important than those of her family. We can only determine whether subsuming one's own goals to others constitutes success or failure by reference to some system of values.

There is another model for psychiatric disorders. Behavior foreign to the therapist is likely to be categorized as a maladaption, or as illness. Because most therapists have been men, women's behavior has often been seen as abnormal or unhealthy. Despite the fact that some 60% of psychiatric patients are women, in traditional psychoanalytic theory

[the] male's development and psychic structure were considered central to the theoretical formulations, which described human development from the point of view of the male. The female's developmental path was then examined as a 'variant' of the male's. (Notman, 1982, p. 3)

Men were 'normal' and women were 'other'. This conceptual framework is the basis for a theoretical system that stipulates that 'normal' women are characterized by traits that are unhealthy for men. In a widely read 1972 work, *Women and Madness*, Chessler (pp. 67–68) pointed out that criteria for psychological health — independence, assertiveness, and being self-determining — are typically masculine characteristics, while the feminine — passivity, dependence, and the like, are also characteristics of emotional immaturity. The apparent conclusion is that it is 'normal' for women to be emotionally unhealthy.

If this point seems too extreme, recall that, during the debate over masochism, one committee member's acknowledgment of a particular behavior was enough to remove it from the list of symptoms. *All* diseases occur in a cultural context, and diagnosis cannot be made outside that context. Psychiatry has been making a serious attempt to understand cultural difference and to prepare psychiatrists to deal appropriately with patients from different backgrounds. It can be argued that women do not grow up in the same culture as men of the same race and economic status. It should be no surprise, then, that the concepts of normal and abnormal may not be applied to both in the same way.

There is also a misunderstanding about what diagnoses represent. Kleinman, in *Rethinking Psychiatry*, defines this problem with a story about three baseball umpires discussing how to tell a ball from a strike. The first asserts, "Some are balls and some are strikes, I calls them as they are". The second disagrees, "No, some are balls and some are strikes, I calls them as I see them". But the third answers, "Some are balls and some are strikes, but they ain't nothing until I call them!" (1988, p. 72).

Similarly, psychiatric diagnoses are not real entities. A disease is "a construct that conceptualizes a constellation of signs and symptoms as due to an underlying biological pathology, mechanism, and cause" (McHugh and Slavney, 1983, p. 9). Diseases are only useful tools, language which enables mental health workers to communicate with each other and to pool information which will ultimately benefit the patient. The rapid dissemination of information about newly described problems such as post-traumatic stress disorder and about women as the victims of violence was only possible because words were used to convey a picture of the 'typical' patient — a picture which perhaps never matched any one individual exactly, but was helpful in allowing the mental health worker to deal with individual patients. The job of the therapist is to make the jump from the general, the diagnosis, to the particular, the patient.

However, this is not a morally neutral endeavor. These labels have consequences, some of which are outlined in Talcott Parsons' discussion of the sick role (1951, pp. 436–437). He points out that the sick person is exempt from normal social role responsibilities and from responsibility for the disease. Physicians legitimize this exemption, both individually for the particular patient, and collectively in a diagnostic process such as the DSM.

One of the arguments against masochistic personality disorder was that it could be used against a victim of domestic violence in a custody dispute, i.e., if she has a psychiatric illness, perhaps she is an unfit mother. The DSM-III-R committee deleted paraphilic rape disorder from its list of potential diagnoses because of concern that rapists would use it to avoid prison and not from any conclusion that it 'did not exist' as a separate disorder. They acknowledge, then, that consequences are a valid reason to modify diagnostic categories.

Another of Parson's sick role characteristics is that it carries an *obligation* to get well. While that obligation may be weaker in this age of autonomy and patient's choice, there is still a great deal of power in naming, in designating normal and abnormal. And most people will feel some pressure to correct any behavior that is designated abnormal. The profession has a *moral obligation* carefully to consider the consequences of every diagnosis that appears in the DSM. One wonders, for example, how a Japanese or Iranian psychiatrist would deal with a woman patient whose behavior was consistently self-defeating. Or for that matter, a devout Catholic psychiatrist, faced with such contradictory statements about women's roles. There is simply not enough evidence about the consequences of such a diagnosis to publish it in the diagnostic manual. The feminists are correct in their claim that the committee was not giving enough consideration to consequences.

Another error is the assumption that the essence of science is measurement, and that science should rely only on those things that can be measured. This may be an understandable attempt to get value judgments out of the business of diagnosis, but it is doomed to fail. For example, Vaillant comments that using only numerically measurable criteria for psychiatric diagnosis is

> like trying to make the criterion for drafting professional basketball players that they be at least 7 feet tall. Obviously, measuring the height of a basketball player is a far more reliable procedure than judging his ball handling. But preoccupation with height rather than with ball handling is unlikely to lead to a championship team (Klerman et al., 1984, p. 545).

It is as much a mistake to assume that 'pure science' is value-free as it is to assume that it is theory-free. No amount of measurement will tell us whether self-defeating behavior is normal. For this, we must have a theory of mental health and illness and an idea of whether self-sacrifice is desirable.

The attempt to avoid theory, as Vaillant notes, leads to mistaking reliability for validity. Reliability represents diagnostic consistency. That is, a cluster of symptoms that tend to occur together may be considered to represent a reliable category. But that category means nothing unless it is part of a theory. While data collection is valuable, theory formation is the essence of science.[4]

The task of the DSM group would be difficult enough if psychiatrists agreed on a single theory. The seeming incompatibility of the biologic and psychodynamic schools, to name only two of the groups currently ascendant, makes it even more difficult. The committee has attempted to avoid the conflict by claiming not to ascribe to any theory, but there can be no observation or description without a theory. Psychiatry cannot wait to standardize terminology until there is agreement on theory; good data collection depends on data from several centers, and multicenter studies must establish a common language. But misunderstandings of the type I have outlined will continue to occur until we understand the nature of diagnoses.

Diagnoses come and go, as theories come and go. The foundation of psychiatry cannot be theory, and certainly not 'atheoretical, scientific' observations, but must be the needs of patients. Human suffering (ranging from mild irritation, through anxiety, to the most intense psychic pain) provides the *only* warrant for the existence of psychiatry at all. Theories are valuable only insofar as they provide, immediately or eventually, respite for the individual patient.

The DSM committee members have lost sight of this fact, and have gotten so absorbed in the task that they have forgotten the patient. The feminists were generally correct in their arguments. However, I disagree with their claim that labeling is in itself a disservice. It is only when we begin to invest those labels with an independent truth that we run into trouble.

It is clear that the DSM is trying to serve too many needs. The profession should have at least two lists of disorders. One, the heir to the Research Diagnostic Criteria, would establish common criteria as a foundation for research. It could include anything which anyone found promising as an area for study. But the list that purports to distinguish normal from abnormal, that claims to be a valid map of human behavior, needs to be more carefully considered. Those diagnoses should already have demonstrable reliability and validity; they should fit into some conceptual framework of human behavior that gives them meaning.

Modern psychiatry is in the midst of a major transition regarding its purpose, its underlying theories, its relationship to other professions, and its role in establishing norms for human behavior. The debate over DSM-III is just an example of the ways in which the profession is struggling. It is not my intent to accuse psychiatry of moral or intellectual bankruptcy, as others have done. Rather, I believe it is important to remember that psychiatry rests on a theoretical foundation, or, often, on several sets of conflicting theoretical foundations. In addition, values regarding health and normal behavior are inherent in medicine, and are reflected in psychiatry in a unique way. If the profession can remember this, we may be able to avoid becoming so engrossed with diagnostic methods that we forget the patient.[5]

Notes

1. This document also hints that the servant image is the proper role for males, briefly mentioning Jesus' statement that 'the Son of Man came not to be served but to serve' (p. 265). However, there is great stress on the differences between men's roles and women's roles, with the emphasis on sac-

rifice given as particular to the task of the woman, created at man's side as "a helper fit for him" (p. 280). The point being made is that women's role should not be like men's, and that women should be self-effacing. It does not define the corresponding role of the man.

2. It is missing in a subsequent discussion by Spitzer and his colleagues of objections to the diagnosis. (Widiger et al., 1988.) In a statement that summarizes the problem, Dr. Spitzer said to a reporter that, "even if the culture encourages [self-defeating behavior] among women, it still doesn't make that behavior normal" (*Kansas City Star*, 1986).

3. Dr. Spitzer adamantly objected to the claim that the committee offered any "deals" stating, "We are scientists and not horse traders" (see Spitzer, 1985).

4. The problem of reliability vs. validity in psychiatry is analyzed in McHugh and Slavney (1983, pp. 8–10). Also see Klerman et al., 1984, and Faust et al., 1986.

5. Most of this work was completed while I was a visiting scholar at the Hastings Center. I am grateful for the support of the Center and its staff. I would also like to thank Dr. Alexandra Symonds for her help.

References

Boorse, C.: 1982, "On the distinction between disease and illness," in T.L. Beauchamp and L. Walters (eds.), *Contemporary Issues in Bioethics*, 2nd. edition. Wadsworth Publishing Company, Belmont, California, pp. 64–73.

Caplan, P.: 1985, *The Myth of Women's Masochism*, Methuen, London.

Chessler, P.: 1972, *Women and Madness*, Avon Books, New York.

Diagnostic and Statistical Manual of Mental Disorders (Third Edition) 1980, American Psychiatric Association, Washington, D.C.

Diagnostic and Statistical Manual of Mental Disorders (Third Edition — Revised) 1987, American Psychiatric Association, Washington, D.C.

Faust, D. and Miner, R.A.: 1986, "The empiricist and his new clothes: DSM-III in perspective", *American Journal of Psychiatry* 143, 962–967.

John Paul II: 1988, "Mulieris dignitatem", *Origins* 18, 261–283.

Kleinman, A.: 1988, *Rethinking Psychiatry: From Cultural Category to Personal Experience*, Free Press, New York.

Klerman, G.L. et al.: 1984, 'A debate on DSM-III', *American Journal of Psychiatry* 141, 539–553.

Masson, J.M.: 1988, *Against Therapy*, Atheneum, New York.

McHugh, P.R. and Slavney, P.R.: 1983, *The Perspectives of Psychiatry*, Johns Hopkins University Press, Baltimore.

New York Times: 1985 (November 19), "New Psychiatric Syndromes Spur Protest".

Notman, M.: 1982, "Feminine development: Changes in psychoanalytic theory", in C. Nadelson and M.T. Notman (eds.), *The Woman Patient*. Vol. 2: *Concepts of Femininity and the Life Cycle*, Plenum Press, New York, pp. 3–29.

Parsons, T.: 1951, *The Social System*, Free Press, Toronto.

Spitzer, R.: 1985 (December 30), "Defining masochism" (letter), *Time*, p. 13.

Szasz, T.S.: 1974, *The Myth of Mental Illness*, revised ed., Harper & Row, New York.

Time: 1985 (December 2), "Battling over masochism", p. 76.

Walker, L.: 1986, "Masochistic personality disorder, take two: A report from the front lines", *FTI Interchange*, Feminist Therapy Institute, 4, 1–2.

Widiger, T.A. et al.: 1988, "The DSM-III-R personality disorders: An overview", *American Journal of Psychiatry* 145, 786–795.

26   Competence, Marginal and Otherwise: Concepts and Ethics

Benjamin Freedman

I. Rights and Degrees of Competence

A society that is sensitive to rights is, for that reason, sensitive to persons. On one level, rights functions as a meta-possession: a grounding for the possibility of an individual's possessing anything, a claim that the individual counts, that his wants and interests must be allowed for in our handling of him. Thus, rights serve the function of protecting interests of the personality. Under the regime of rights, desires, inclinations and so on are given protection.

This model rests upon a notion of the personality as a construct pre-dating the "existence" or "conference" of rights. One cannot guard the valuable before one possesses it. Rights, however, do more than this. Legally or morally, they define the limits of the protected personality. When we determine, through rights, the kinds of interests and desires that we shall protect, we also determine to some degree the manner in which persons shall be protected. Those whose desires remain unexpressed cannot have their desires protected under a regime of rights. Those with bizarre or profoundly deviant desires are unprotected in their pursuits: for example, the man with disturbed ideation, who wishes protection from feared disintegration, or spontaneous combustion.

In response to these circumstances, it is common to appeal to a two-fold nature in rights.[1] With respect to those who are competent, the expression of their rights typically takes the form of heeding their wishes. The competent tell us what content to give to their rights. A competent person's right to seek medical care will express itself in *his* decisions as to whether he will seek care, for what condition, and in what form. For the incompetent — the voiceless — we are forced to look elsewhere than at their desires, in giving an expression to their rights. One approach to this has us making decisions in terms of the incompetent's "best interests," as determined by his biological and psychological being, on the one hand, and, on the other, by a community consensus concerning the good for man.

On most accounts, though, this dichotomy — the competent and the incompetent — is not exhaustive. Between them lies a middle ground. Epistemologically, we may term this third group those of dubious competence. This application, however, tells us nothing about *them*. It merely points up the limits of our knowledge, limits which may be attributed more to laziness than to vagueness of the phenomenon. On the borderline between competency and incompetency we face a choice of temperament in choosing a term by which to describe this group. For reasons of brevity and optimism, I will term them the marginally competent.

Practically speaking, as there are three main forms of incompetence, so are there three main groupings of the marginally competent. The first form of incompetence relates to age, infants and small children being a paradigm case of legal and moral incapacity. Between the extremes of infancy and adulthood, the individual's competence is developing. Although in some legal matters the distinction between an "infant" and an adult is firm, this bright line exists only in the legal codes, and is no reflection of reality. As Wilson writes, having described age-based limitations upon capacity, "There is a growing belief among many social observers, however, that many older children have the physical and psychological capacities to act with some autonomy in many areas in which they are now denied independence, that they have a moral right to such autonomy, and that they should be granted corresponding legal rights."[2] For our purposes, the operative words in Wilson's remarks are the qualifiers: "*some* autonomy," not full; "*many*" areas, not all. Though vague and culturally parochial, the period including and surrounding adolescence may serve as the focus for this grouping of the marginally competent.

The second form of incompetence is the presumably stable deficit in intellect and adaptation which is known as mental retardation. The incompetent group would include those with no verbal skills and a very low ceiling on presumed ability to learn. The marginally competent would be those, institutionalized or not, who posses some understanding and some ability to use language to express their wants and desires. The marginally competent are numerically by far the most significant class of the retarded. One estimate has it that for every 1,000 births in the United States, 26 children will be mildly retarded, expressed in their marginal adjustment to adult life; three will be moderately retarded, that is, will never surpass the intellectual attainment of the average seven-year-old; and one will be severely retarded.[3] Given a latitudinous reading of incompetency, then, although between two and three percent of the population are mentally impaired, less than one-half of a percent are totally incompetent.

The third source of incompetency is, loosely, mental illness, whatever its etiology. Those who are prepared to admit the propriety of the concept of mental illness at all will admit that the vast majority of the mentally ill are not wholly incompetent. Even at the fairly extreme end of the pathology, very bizarre behavior might overshadow a core of the personality which is in touch with the world and can respond to it. After noting that the ideal model for a "proxy" or substituted consent to medical treatment is that of a mother on behalf of her infant, one psychiatrist notes:

> If it is a severely crippled, emotionally incompetent adult, it may well be that we can approximate the mother–infant relationship, but most severely ill mental patients are not at all like infants, and while the intellectual insufficiencies may seem as great, the emotional components of the "self" are often vastly different. Mental illness is a fragmented, irrational combination of intact and destroyed faculties.[4]

It seems clear, then, that collectively the marginally competent constitute a very substantial group, deserving of a moral analysis as searching and rigorous as has been provided to their neighbors, the competent and the incompetent. Topically, too, the problems of the moral status of the marginally competent have been increasingly urgent in recent years. Can a mental patient, or a mentally-disturbed prisoner, consent to psychosurgery? Can an institutionalized retarded person consent to sterilization? How should we relate to the adolescent cancer patient? These difficult problems all arise from the twilight status of the marginally competent. It may be that some of the difficulty could be alleviated by the simple recognition that there is a middle classification between the competent and the incompetent. In some discussions, we may have crippled ourselves with our paucity of ethical frameworks. Countless arguments could be mounted over whether a mule is a horse or a donkey, but the path of wisdom might be to simply call it a mule.

The quandaries of the marginally retarded have great theoretical significance, for it is by testing and deepening our understanding of competence that we can clarify the status of the marginally competent. In what follows, then, my *method* will be the clarification of the concept of competence. My *goal* is to achieve an understanding of this concept detailed enough to deal with the vagaries of the human condition.

Before beginning that task, let us face squarely the question of whether competency is an empirical or a moral term. Does it describe a fact in the world, or how we evaluate that fact? A little reflection reveals that in some ways it must do both: a psychiatrist may give expert testimony, in his capacity as a trained observer, about a person's competence seen as a factual matter, and the judge may or may not give this testimony practical effect in deciding how we *ought* to treat that person. Competence is not pure description, then, nor pure evaluation; but, perhaps, an evaluation that stems from certain described facts coupled with a moral theory that tells what those facts mean, how we ought to respond to those facts. A middle step between description and action is always needed, i.e., a moral theory that interprets experience and guides action.

This point — that the ascription of competence has practical implications, and so presupposes a *moral* theory — is surprisingly easy to forget. One of the better writers on questions of competence proposed as his test for competency "the ability to understand and knowingly act upon the information provided." He goes on to say that, "Meaningful decisions concerning this or any other standard, however, can be made only through a careful empirical study of operational results."[5] Yet he never tells us what we should be looking for in these subsequent studies. Should it be the extent to which this standard enhanced the autonomy of the subjects? Or the rational pursuit of their best interests? Should we be looking to see if judgments of competency using this standard accord well with the "intuitive" judgments of psychiatrists, or lawyers, or laymen? We cannot know where to look unless we know what we are looking for. A theory of the values embedded in the ascription of competency, and of its significance, needs to be provided. Insofar as this theory will be one which is intended to guide conscientious action, it will be of necessity an ethical theory.

II. Criteria of Competence: The Background Understandings of Competence

A number of tests for competence have been proposed. "Test" or "criterion" in this context signifies a verbal formula, put in terms of a question, the answer to which will determine whether the person in question is competent or not. As my purpose is moral exploration, rather than legal exposition, I will discuss on their merits and without differentiation proposals put forth by scholars as well as tests actually employed by courts in adjudication in this area.

There are several levels at which tests for competency can be discussed. The first I would term the "general" level. It answers the question: What is the *background* understanding of competency, against which we may judge proposals designed to apply to specific problems?

One sort of general background understanding of competency has been adopted by some members of the medical profession. It has been reported[6] that to test competency, psychiatrists and other physicians often use a functional test. That is to say, if the patient functions well within society, as evinced by an examination of his work history, personal relationships, and so on, he is to be judged competent. Failing these characteristics, he is judged incompetent.

Among lawyers, one can discern a fair amount of agreement on a different background principle of competency. Roth, Meisel and Lidz put the legal understanding as follows:[7] "The test of competency varies from one context to another. In general, to be considered competent an individual must be able to comprehend the nature of the particular conduct in question and to understand its quality and its consequences."

A specific application of this principle may be found in the law of contracts. When is an individual competent to contract? When he can understand the effect of the transaction that the contract effectuates.[8] Given this principle, the question of competence can only be addressed to the situation in question. Someone may be competent, in the sense of understanding what is going on, to engage a house painter at an agreed-upon sum. That same person might be incompetent to contract for futures on the commodities exchange, because he is unable to understand the contingencies involved in that transaction.

It is important to note that the legal background understanding of competency is generally considered to comprise two elements.[9] The first is a bare *knowledge* of what you are doing: the fact that you *are* making a contract; an example is the fact that you have agreed to the doctor's removal of your appendix. The second element requires that you *appreciate* the consequences of the act, including its typical attendant pitfalls or dangers: the fact that, after certain services have been provided, you will be legally required to pay a certain sum; the fact that you will have a scar, etc.

It is not immediately apparent what significance is to be attached to the term, "appreciate." This might simply be another term for knowing, used specifically to apply to dangers. It might, on the other hand, mean that you not merely know of these dangers, but that you also take them into account in making your decision, that you appraise them in a rational way.

What is at stake in choosing between the "functioning" standard (that background understanding of competency imputed to medicine) and the legal background understanding (that one is competent with regard to a particular transaction if he understands information surrounding that situation and appreciates the consequences of his actions)?

The first point of divergence is that whereas the legal standard is rather narrowly focused upon the possession and appreciation of information as a mark of competence, the medical standard looks more broadly at action and behavior and, in particular, interaction. Very broadly speaking, the law has had a traditional inclination to look at people as though they were ambulatory neocortexes. This is an unfortunate perspective even for those who agree that rationality is definitive of humanity, and that obedience to the law can only result from rationality. For surely rationality can express itself actively, rather than by bare ratiocination. Further, even given a mentalist perspective on rationality and thinking, the medical standard is forthright in emphasizing that we can only judge rationality through observable behavior; and in drawing the implication that all behavior, not just speech, should be considered evidential.

The second issue between them might be said to concern the proper scope of competency judgments. In looking at "functioning," medicine might be saying that competency is all of a piece, and so needs to be understood in a global fashion. The law, on the contrary, insists upon an individualized standard. One may be competent to consent to treatment but not to experimentation; one may be competent to prepare this will but not to agree to that contract. Rights of self-determination can be conferred in some areas and arenas, but not in others.

The medical view must surely be rejected, particularly in light of the fact of marginal competence. One's functioning itself is not, after all, of a piece: a person can be relatively successful in his work yet fail dismally at forming personal relationships — a deeply neurotic executive. The institutionalized retarded individual might be unable to work but form close and meaningful personal attachments. When attached to the broad scope of behavior at which medicine might look, a global view — one is competent in all things, or in none — can place an unbearable weight of history upon an individual, and lead to the "labeling" of people in an unjust way.

One issue at hand between these two background views, then, is that of individualization. Is a person's competency to be determined by sole reference to the matter at hand, as the law would have it, or with reference to an entire pattern of behavior, as medicine would have us think? Simply put, since situations of choice differ, competence cannot be an across-the-board affair; and, since situations of choice are similar, competence cannot be entirely determined in an ad hoc fashion.

In exploring the question of individualization, we will first need to distinguish between two approaches to competency, those of policy and of concept; a distinction of major importance for analysis.

What is meant by the policy level? A standard of competency is to *achieve* certain practical things, chief among these being the preservation of a balance between freedom and protection. The policy view judges criteria of competence by the results they yield. Good results, results with which society is pleased, are determinative of good criteria for competence.

Yet behind the policy view, and to some degree presupposed by it, is the *conceptual* level. For it, the basic desideratum of a standard is that it mark off the competent from the incompetent. It does no good to be informed that some need to be protected, others need to have their choices respected, and that a good rule will strike a balance. We need to know who *belongs* in each of these categories. The conceptual view supplies a theory of competency, a theory about why some people — whom we term the competent — are granted the privilege of making decisions, even silly decisions, while this privilege is denied to another class of people. The theory will enable us to distinguish between warranted and unwarranted paternalism, on the basis of qualities which differ across populations. It tells us who is entitled to autonomy, and who is entitled to protection.

Once we understand the concepts and policies underlying a given situation, we can assess the type and level of competence desirable. Some situations obviously require different competencies. A justified imputation of criminal liability, for example, must enquire into aspects of the person different from those needed to be able to fix civil liability. To that extent, we must individualize the question of competence.

On the other hand, some situations are sufficiently analogous that a single test of competence might serve all within the set. The analogies must rest upon similarities between the concepts and/or the policies underlying the situations. A simple example of such a set of situations (or "situation-types"), would be noncapital criminal liability. Consistency demands that at some point the similarity between two situations must be so great that they must both use the same test of competence.

Here is another candidate for a situation-type. It could be argued that the age for consent of medical treatment should not be greater than the age at which one may voluntarily join, or be conscripted into, the armed forces.[10] The age which we fix for service represents society's judgment about when a person is sufficiently mature to be uprooted from his family and to act autonomously, the age at which a person can take responsibility for choices that will govern his entire future course of life. On a conceptual level, it seems that these are the same qualities that are involved in deciding whether to undergo medical treatment.

With regard to policy questions, though, there is clearly a difference between medical consent and armed service. On the one hand, the army might demand physical development of a sort that does not enter into competence for consent; and so it is quite reasonable that a *later* age for army service might be required than is needed for medical consent. On the other hand, policy considerations might constrain us to limit or qualify the age for consent for reasons that stem from the question of financial obligation. An argument for requiring the consent of a parent to a procedure upon a minor who is living at home is that the parent is obligated to pay for the minor's treatment. (This policy consideration might instead be addressed by placing financial liability for the course of treatment upon the minor in the case in which the parent has not consented; in that way we would not have compromised the true question of the minor's competence, as we would do in the event we set a higher age of competence for this conceptually irrelevant circumstance. Policies, unlike concepts, may be achieved in many different ways.)

With regards to the question of individualization, then, neither the legal nor the medical background understandings of competence are fully satisfactory. From the theory of a situation — its policy and conceptual components — emerges a single test of situation-appropriate competence; yet several situations may be served by the same theory. Let me develop this notion of theory a bit further in discussing the tests for competency proposed for consent to medical treatment.

III. Criteria of Competence: Consent to Medical Treatment

In some situations, it is not clear how the background understandings of competence may be applied; and in others, the background understandings seem unacceptably simple-minded. As a result, variant tests of competency are developed. The situation with which I will deal concerns competence to consent to medical treatment. I take this case partly because of its intrinsic interest and importance, and partly because of its symbolic significance. Consent to treatment seems an ideal testing-ground for theories concerning the scope and nature of human autonomy. Also, the concept and policies underlying consent have been explored extensively by courts and scholars.

There are five main tests for competence to consent to, or to refuse, treatment, delineated clearly by Roth, Meisel and Lidz[11] but mentioned by others as well.[12] They are as follows:

1. One is competent to consent to treatment if, in consenting, one achieves a *reasonable result* or is seeking a reasonable outcome.
2. One is competent to consent to treatment if one has followed a rational process in making up one's mind, if one can give or has given *rational reasons* for the choice made.
3. One is competent to consent to treatment if one is *able to express consent* to, or refusal of, that treatment, for whatever reasons and despite the seeming unreasonableness of the outcome.
4. One is competent to consent to treatment if one has the *ability to understand* and knowingly act upon the information which the doctor supplies in the course of "obtaining a consent."
5. One is competent to consent to treatment if one *actually understands* and acts upon the information which is provided by the physician. (This test differs from the previous one in that our judgment is now made on the basis of the assimilation by

the patient of the information provided about this specific procedure. By contrast, the "ability to understand" test could examine the patient's ability to understand, not *this* information, but information of an *equivalent complexity*.)

To make matters a bit more concrete, consider this example: Jones is being seen by Dr. Smith, a psychiatrist. Dr. Smith judges that Jones would benefit from taking Thorazine, a major tranquilizer or anti-psychotic agent. Jones presumably refuses; had he agreed to this "treatment of choice," although in theory he might be competent, incompetent, or somewhere in between, nobody is likely to raise the question in any practical forum. Is Jones competent (in which case presumably his refusal will be effectuated), or incompetent (in which case steps may be taken to initiate proceedings culminating in the legally-sanctioned, forcible administration of the drug)?

This question should be a practical one for psychiatrists. It might be objected that the question of competence is properly one for the courts. While this is of course true, nevertheless someone must initiate the inquiry leading to the proceeding, and psychiatrists are well-placed to do this.

Even with the minimal information given above about Jones, two of the above standards could decide the question of his competence. One would be the reasonable outcome test. Presumably, Dr. Smith would feel that Jones had failed this test, that, in refusing, Jones is *per se* irrational. The test need not lead us to *this* result, however, for although Dr. Smith may be a reasonable man himself, his responses are neither exhaustive or definitive of the repertoire of the reasonable man. A third party, lawyer, psychiatrist, or plumber, might feel that the reasonable man would *always* refuse administration of Thorazine, or, in *Jones's circumstances* would refuse Thorazine. Yet another observer might believe that a reasonable man could swing either way in this choice, that the factors pro and con the administration of the drug are fairly evenly balanced. But the interesting thing about all of these positions is that none of them require more knowledge about Jones. If anything further needs to be learned, it is how the reasonable man would respond.

Nor need we know anything further about this case in order to decide the question of Jones's competence under the third test, that of the "ability to make a choice." *Ex hypothesi*, Jones has chosen to refuse the treatment. Any further knowledge concerning itself with Jones's maturity, intellect, emotional state, and so on, is, for this test, superfluous.

In the case of test 2, we would need to ask Jones why he has refused the treatment, and if those reasons are judged to be rational, his refusal is competent. Suppose Jones indicates that he fears delayed side-effects of the drug, or feels that he is "getting better" and his condition will clear up without the drug, or believes his psychiatrist to be incompetent. These all sound like rational reasons. In contrast, he might say that taking the drug will motivate those who are electrically controlling his behavior to turn him off. This, presumably, will be judged an irrational reason, and a conclusive indication that his decision was incompetent.

The fourth test is not interested in why Jones has refused, but in whether he can understand the information which we feel should be relevant to consent or refusal. Is Jones so mentally defective, or so out of touch with reality, that we cannot get this *kind* of material through? The fifth test, that of actual understanding, asks the same questions, but this time the object of inquiry is whether Jones understands the information provided about the drug. Operationally these tests would proceed as follows: Jones would be informed either about the therapeutic intervention (the reasons for its recommendation, its risk and alternative methods of treatment if any), or else he would be informed of other matters of an equivalent complexity. Smith would query Jones to elicit whether this information has been assimilated; if it has, Jones's refusal or consent would be binding in the sense that it would have been conclusively demonstrated that Jones is competent. . . .

V. A "Recognizable Reasons" Criterion of Competency

. . . Consent is valuable in its protection of freedom. Hence, it is process-centred and must concern itself with what goes into the decision, and not merely with the result. Since it is a result of our rights to freedom, it is person-centered, and depends upon characteristics of the individual himself.

The [criterion] of rational reasons comes closest to satisfying these requirements. Under it, an individual is competent if he can supply rational reasons for his decision. This criterion serves well in that it is process-centered, and in its dependence upon characteristics of the person himself. It can be criticized on the grounds that it is an overly-paternalistic criterion, since it distinguishes between acceptable (rational) and unacceptable reasons for action. This criticism loses its force, however, if latitude is given to the notion of rational reasons, if we are willing to accept as rational reasons arguments which we would not find decisive, but agree are relevant.

Perhaps this point would seem more plausible if instead of speaking of "rational reasons," a phrase which is, anyway, abominably redundant, we spoke of "recognizable reasons." Reasons consist of premises that argue towards a practical conclusion. For a reason to be recognizable, then, it must contain both acceptable premises and a conclusion related to those premises. Since we wish to give latitude to an individual's own value system, one which we do not necessarily share, it is not required that the conclusion "follow" from the premises, in that we believe the premises are *strong* enough to justify the conclusion.

There are two ways in which a person might fail to produce recognizable reasons. The first is by founding his argument upon premises known to be false. . . . The second is by producing reasons which, even if true and weighted heavily, fail to support the conclusion drawn, e.g., by refusing surgery because it's Tuesday. A *non-sequitur* is not an argument.

That which allows us to grant freedom of action in our society is the warranted belief that, by and large, one person's choices will be recognizable by others. It is only given this condition that we can empathize with a person's behavior, and it is only given this condition that behavior becomes sufficiently predictable to enable us to live together in society.

Freedom within society is a reciprocal affair, which requires of me that I order my affairs in the light of what others may be expected to do. It therefore presumes a degree of commonality and predicability of motivation. From this concept of freedom there follows some version of the "rational reasons" criterion of competence; for freedom is only possible in the light of the characteristics possessed by recognizable reasons.

It needs to be noticed, however, that a considerable potential for abuse lurks in such a criterion. People, however competent, are not always prepared to give reasons for their choices. We should also recall that rationality can be demonstrated in the way in which a person orders his life, not merely in the verbal justification he gives for his behavior.

In the light of these considerations, perhaps competence should generally be judged in a dispositional way. If a person has been disposed to be competent — if he has ordered his life within our society, made and carried out long-range plans and so on — then extraordinary strong evidence would need to be produced in attempting to provide that he had failed to achieve a competent decision. The reverse would be true for one with dispositional incompetence. The relevant companion would be with decisions other than medical treatment, but involving equivalent seriousness and complexity, which he has faced; which could, depending on the nature of the proposed medical intervention, require examination of such traditional aspects of adjustment as work-experience, family life, and ability to run an independent household. Perhaps a strong, but defeasible, burden of proof should need satisfaction to treat a "dispositional competent's" decision as incompetent, and vice versa.

With regard to information and its relationship to competence, I am suggesting a reversal of the traditional roles. Traditionally, it was thought that the ascertainment of competence was an issue which needed to be decided prior to the transmittal of information. To the contrary, I believe that information is prior to competence, in that a competent decision includes, but extends beyond, the requirement that the person involved be able to allow the informing process to enter into his decision-making in a substantial way. He must be capable of utilizing the information provided in formulating his reasons.

This burden of informing the person is recognized as a heavy one. If understanding cannot be achieved by the ordinary process, then further methods must be sought. The method of informing chosen must be one designed to enlighten the individual in question. Only when it is clear that no manner of informing the patient will serve does the issue of competence become moot. Since competence is primarily concerned with the manner in which the individual uses the information, the prerequisite to competence is information.

Our discussion also inclines us to an intriguing perspective upon the institutionalized marginally competent. Institutionalization has been said to limit an individual's competence by denying him the opportunity to develop his decision-making capacities and by insulating him from the world of responsibility. Institutionalization does something else as well. It limits the *evidence* of competency. It deprives an individual of a history of successful decision-making, which would have given outside observers confidence in his competency. There is not much which the individual could reasonably do to combat this implication, and so we must act on his behalf: first, by sympathetically examining his attempts at decision-making; second, and more fundamentally, by providing opportunities within the institution for the individual to develop and reveal his capacity to take responsibility for his own actions.

There is no use to assuming competence into existence. Making a decision does not mean a mumbled "yes" or "no"; it assumes an underlying process into which relevant facts about the world enter in a recognizable way. If those relevant facts can by no fashion be communicated, if they cannot be ordered into an argument supporting a conclusion, then competence is not present. Yet a very great wrong is perpetuated in not making the attempt to recognize competence when it is present, albeit veiled. The most serious harm we can visit upon a human being is to tell him that his viewpoint, his innermost self, is of no worth. Whatever the outcome, the very attempt to elicit a competent opinion, if conscientiously carried out, can serve to allay this harm. Whatever the outcome, by entering into his world he is reassured that his is indeed a being of significance to others. . . .

Notes

1. See Freedman, *On the Rights of the Voiceless*, 3 J. Med. & Phil. (1978), and works discussed there.
2. J. Wilson. The Rights of Adolescents in the Mental Health Care System 11 (1978).
3. R. Allen, E. Fersher & H. Weihofen. Mental Impairment and Legal Incompetency 1 (1968 Citing Report of the President's Panel on Mental Retardation (1962).
4. Gaylin, *The Problem of Psychosurgery* in W. Gaylin, R. Neville & J. Meisher, eds., Operating on the Mind 13 (1975).
5. Friedman, *Legal Regulation of Behavior Modification in Institutional Settings*, 17 Ariz L. Rev. 80, 95 (1975).
6. Neuwirth, Heister & Goldrich, *Capacity, Competence, Consent: Voluntary Sterilization of the Mentally Retarded.* Col Human Rights L. Rev. 452 (1975).
7. Roth, Meisel & Lidz, *Tests of Competency to Consent to Treatment*, 134 Am. J. Psych. 279 (1979).
8. Allen et al., *supra note* 3. Appendix A. Part 1.
9. *Id.*, 264.
10. Freedman, *A Moral Theory of Informed Consent*, 5 Hastings Center Rep. (1975).
11. Roth et al., *supra note* 7.
12. See, eg., Friedman, *supra note* 5; G. Annas, L. Glantz & B. Katz, Informed Consent to Human Experimentation: The Subjects Dilemma 153 (1977).

27   In the Matter of The Mental Health Act, R.S.O. 1980, c. 262 as Amended, and in the Matter of K V, a Patient at a Hospital in Ontario

Reasons for Decision

Mr. K V is a patient at a hospital in Ontario. His attending physician has made a determination that he is incompetent to consent to psychiatric treatment and other related medical treatment. Mr. V has applied to the review board for an inquiry into this matter. . . .

The Majority Opinion of Dr. Atcheson and Ms. Hepburn

Mr. V is a gentleman of years of age [*sic*]. Dr. B told the board that Mr. V has a history of paranoid schizophrenia dating back to 1980. He was hospitalized at that time.

After discharge from hospital, Mr. V was maintained on a low dose of anti-psychotic medication until 1990 when he discontinued use of medication. It would appear that his psycho-social and occupational functioning have deteriorated since he ceased taking medication. He broke into and took up residence in an unheated construction trailer without any utilities.

While living in the trailer, Mr. V conceived that he was aware of criminal activities in the community which he believed consisted of counterfeiting. As a result of what he believed to be this awareness of criminal activity, he became frightened that his life was threatened. He believed that he could detect that his life was threatened and that he was being followed. He stated that this belief was confirmed by his "intuition" which permitted him to determine accurately those who proposed to harm him. He approached the police with this information but he was not satisfied that they were taking appropriate actions to protect him.

Mr. V was arrested for breaking a store window. He told the board that he did it in order to draw the attention of the police to himself since he felt that he was being threatened at the time.

Mr. V continued to believe that he was being followed and he believed that he was in danger. He began to carry a container of gasoline in a backpack in the belief that this provided protection for him. He appeared before his probation officer with the gasoline can and this resulted in his apprehension.

Mr. V was admitted to hospital on the 14th of November. Mr. V has been most guarded in his discussions with medical staff. However, after their examination of him, they concluded that he was suffering from paranoid schizophrenia. In reaching this conclusion, staff relied quite heavily on the patient's interpretation of recent events as outlined above. On November 22nd, medical staff concluded that Mr. V was not competent to consent to psychiatric treatment and related medical treatment.

Dr. Bloom, an expert qualified as both a lawyer and a psychiatrist, examined the patient on the evening of December 11th for a period of approximately two hours at the request of counsel for the patient. It was Dr. Bloom's opinion that Mr. V was demonstrating a delusional state, paranoid type (a diagnostic category taken from DSM III), and not paranoid schizophrenia.

Dr. Bloom agreed that, given the symptoms that Mr. V was presenting, it is appropriate that he receive neuroleptic medication and this type of regime should be complemented by supportive psychotherapy.

Dr. Bloom is of the opinion that Mr. V is quite capable of giving consent for treatment. He based his opinion on the fact that the patient was capable of giving a very clear and indeed quite appropriate description at a lay level of the illness of paranoid schizophrenia. The patient further appeared to appreciate that medication is given in the case of paranoid schizophrenia in an attempt to deal with delusional, hallucinatory and behavioural problems in an attempt to modify the course of the illness. Dr. Bloom also noted that the patient had an appreciation of the nature of the side effects that might be experienced from such medication.

In spite of this quite accurate objective description of schizophrenia and the consequences of accepting or refusing medication, Mr. V was of the opinion that he is not suffering from such an illness. Dr. Bloom told the board that he was not able to convince the patient of his diagnosis. In his evidence before the board, Mr. V was quite evasive on the topic and it is our view that he does not accept that he suffers from a serious mental disorder.

Mr. V is diagnosed as suffering from a major mental disorder of a type which is demonstrated by delusional thinking. Although he is able to provide an accurate and intellectual description of schizophrenia and the use of medication, he has no appreciation that he is suffering from a major mental disorder.

Mr. V agrees that he has taken medication in the past and that it has been of some assistance to him. When questioned by his counsel as to why he discontinued medication, he said it was because it slowed down his thinking processes. The patient told the board that one of his reasons for refusing medication at the present time was that he believed that it would slow down his thought process and leave him at some risk because of the danger that he conceived from others. This was obviously a rather inappropriate rationale and his reason for not accepting medication as recommended is clearly related to his delusional thinking.

It is clear from the evidence that Mr. V suffers from a major psychiatric disorder that may be described as a psychotic illness of a paranoid type. This fact is not disputed notwithstanding the somewhat academic debate as to whether the patient is suffering from paranoid schizophrenia or a delusional state of a paranoid type. We note that the evidence indicates that in either of these diagnostic categories the use of neuroleptic medication is indicated as part of the treatment programme.

In our view, it is not sufficient for Mr. V to be capable of providing a description of paranoid schizophrenia which includes a reasonable understanding of the theory of the bio-chemical relationships and an acknowledgement that neuroleptic medication is directed towards stabilizing these bio-medical pathological conditions. The fact is that, although Mr. V can give a theoretical explanation, he does not appreciate that his own delusional thinking is a product of an illness or, for that matter, that he suffers from delusional thinking at all. He believes that his life is threatened and that the abnormal behaviour that he has demonstrated by breaking the window and carrying a container of gasoline in his knapsack was appropriate and was taken as an appropriate step to protect himself from those who might attack him.

We would disagree with Mr. Swadron's position that the patient's rather brilliant description of the theoretical nature of paranoid schizophrenia and the theory with regards to the therapy, consequences of medication and consequences of not receiving medication satisfy the tests for competency set out in the Act.

We do not accept Mr. Swadron's position that it is not necessary for the patient to appreciate that he is suffering from an illness. In our view, it is possible for a patient to be incompetent to consent to treatment for the purposes of the Mental Health Act notwithstanding the fact that he has a knowledge of this disorder.

One of the prerequisites for treatment competency contained in the Mental Health Act is that the patient must have the ability to understand the nature of the illness for which treatment is proposed. In his argument, Mr. Swadron assumes that the word, "for which treatment is proposed" can only have one meaning, namely that the patient must have the ability to understand the illness on a theoretical or academic basis. It is our view that these words refer in fact not to some academic diagnostic category but rather the constellation of symptoms defining the condition from which the patient himself suffers. It follows from this that a patient who is unable to acknowledge the presence of a clearly existent mental disorder is, by definition, not competent to consent to psychiatric treatment. It is simply not possible for a patient whose psychiatric condition denies them the ability to understand or even acknowledge the existence of their condition to make informed, competent decision [sic] with regards to their treatment.

We believe that Mr. V lacks the ability to understand the illness for which treatment is proposed. We therefore conclude that, having failed one of the necessary prerequisites for competency, he is not competent to consent to psychiatric treatment and related medical treatment.

We do not believe that the patient has a meaningful understanding of the relationship between his receipt of medications in the past and his psychiatric condition. He stated that in the past medications had assisted him in dealing with the stress created by the usual problems of living but he does not believe that he was suffering from mental illness during these periods. . . .

Decision

The board confirms that Mr. K V is not competent to consent to psychiatric treatment and related medical treatment.

Dated at North York this 19th day of December, 1991.

---

28   ECT and Special Problems of Informed Consent

Charles M. Culver, Richard B. Ferrell & Ronald M. Green

Can a severely depressed patient validly consent to a course of ECT? Can this patient validly refuse consent? Although the requirement of informed consent is a firm part of the ethical practice of medicine, two separate problems make these questions appropriate and urgent where ECT is concerned. One problem is that ECT is usually prescribed for patients who are seriously depressed and whose ability to consent might therefore be open to question. A second problem concerns the therapy itself: ECT has been held by some to be an intrusive physical technique with inherently unacceptable risks and hence beyond the range of rational choice. While these two problems challenge the validity of informed consent to ECT from different directions, both throw open to question the current practice of employing ECT on the basis of patient consent.

Depression and Competence to Consent

The first of these two problems is not unique to ECT. It is encountered frequently in the field of psychiatry and neurology where the brain, the organ that plays a decisive role in the giving of consent, is often involved in the disease process and may, as with ECT, itself be the direct object of treatment. One might therefore suppose that psychiatry and neurology must be inherently paternalistic when serious mental illness is involved, that is, that they must involve minimal reliance on the patient's expressed wishes regarding treatment and primary reliance on the treatment team's (or family's) judgment concerning what is in the patient's best interests.[1]

In fact, clinical practice does not appear to bear out this supposition. Not only is the patient's consent actively sought in such cases by responsible physicians, but a patient's refusal to consent is usually respected. How can we account for this? Part of the answer seems to be that in the view of most psychiatrists serious mental illness does not usually render a patient incapable of making informed decisions about treatment. Patient A is a case in point.

Case I

Ms. A, a 71-year-old woman, was admitted to our unit with a moderately severe depression. She had had three other depressive episodes over the past 40 years. The third episode, which occurred 6 years earlier, was the most severe. She was initially given antidepressant medication; when this proved ineffective ECT was recommended. Ms. A consented and received a course of eight sessions of ECT, which resulted in a prompt alleviation of her depression and a return to her usual active life.

Ms. A remained symptom-free for 6 years, but then once again, without any clear precipitant, she became depressed, with a significant sleep disturbance, loss of appetite and weight, and occasional thoughts of suicide. She was hospitalized and given antidepressant medication, which, as before, proved ineffective. She readily agreed to a course of ECT. Despite her depression Ms. A appeared to her psychiatrists to be capable of understanding her situation and making an informed decision about her treatment. She understood that ECT would almost certainly alleviate her depression as it had before, and she clearly preferred ECT to the options of no further treatment or some combination of continued antidepressant medication with psychotherapeutic support. After only four treatments, her mood improved substantially, her appetite and sleep pattern returned to normal, and her suicidal thoughts ceased. She was discharged and 6 months later remained in normal mood.

Ms. A seems to us to illustrate a quite unproblematic use of ECT. Most, but not all, depressed patients appear to be as capable of making an informed decision as she was. However, some patients seem to be unable to give or not give consent at all. Occasionally patients withhold consent when their physicians and relatives believe that it would be most reasonable for them to agree. And, although rarely, a severely depressed patient refuses ECT at a time when it appears that he or she will die without it.

The response of psychiatrists to these cases differs widely. In some instances, treatment is initiated independently of the patient's wishes, while in other cases those wishes are respected. The reasons why one course or another is taken are not always clearly articulated, and this lack of clarity is partly due to the inadequacy of terms used to describe patients whose consent is more problematic than Ms. A's was. When psychiatrists and others discuss these cases, terms such as "competence," "rationality," and "capability" are often used. The terms are often used interchangeably, imprecisely, and in a confusing manner. For example, a patient who considers and then refuses what his or her physicians believe to be a very necessary treatment may be labeled "incompetent." On further inquiry it is often the case that there is no independent measure of the patient's competence; rather, the label has come from the treatment-refusal decision. Those doing the labeling have moved from their disagreement with the patient's decision to a label that characterizes the patient as globally incompetent. This kind of linguistic move is confusing at best. Patients who make what appear to be unwise treatment decisions often carry out most of their other activities quite competently. But there is a further danger in this too-quick and too-global labeling: it may reassure the physician that a particular paternalistic insistence on treatment is justified when it may not be. This is because it is easier for most of us to think we are treating an incompetent patient (despite his or her protestations) than to think we are forcing our own treatment decision on a competent patient who disagrees with it.

Because of these difficulties we want to suggest a particular use of terminology in dealing with these matters, which we hope will be clarifying, and a certain associated moral reasoning. We suggest first of all that "competent" and "incompetent" not be used as global attributes of a person but rather be applied more narrowly with respect to particular abilities, for example, that a person be described as "competent to do X" only when certain criteria are met. We will say then that a patient is *competent to decide* about having a particular treatment (such as ECT) when the following are satisfied: 1) the patient knows that the physician believes the patient is ill and in need of treatment (although the patient may not agree), 2) the patient knows that the physician believes this particular treatment may help the patient's illness, and 3) the patient knows he or she is being called upon to make a decision regarding this treatment.[2]

These are deliberately "minimal" criteria because the intent, for reasons explained below, is to consider a patient competent to make a treatment decision unless he or she is *clearly* incompetent to do so.

We suggest further that "rational" and "irrational" be used as attributes of the decisions made by patients. Thus while some patients will be deemed incompetent to make treatment decisions, the rest will be considered competent to make decisions that may be judged rational or irrational. An irrational decision is one based on an irrational belief (e.g., a patient does not believe he or she has cancer despite overwhelming evidence that he or she has) or on an irrational desire (e.g., a patient prefers to die rather than have a gangrenous foot amputated but can give no reason for this choice).[3] This use of "irrational," which will be illustrated in some of the examples below, is meant to accord with the way the term is usually employed, not only by psychiatrists but by people in general.

Thus we would view Ms. A as having been competent to make a treatment decision and would also view her decision as a rational one. We now wish to apply the above terminology to other more troublesome cases to see whether it helps clarify and make explicit the way we (and others) believe it appropriate to respond in such cases.

The Patient Incompetent to Make a Treatment Decision

Case 2

Ms. B, a 69-year-old woman with biopsy-proven unresectable retroperitoneal sarcoma, was admitted to our unit in a profound confusional state that was thought to be a result of delirium, a very severe psychotic depression, or a combination of the two. Approximately I year earlier she had been admitted to the hospital with a similar mental syndrome. At that time a retroperitoneal mass had been identified and biopsied during laparotomy. Treatment with ECT at that time (I year before the present admission) resulted in dramatic clearing of her confusional state and melancholia, enabling Ms. B to resume a satisfying life with her family for a period of about 10 months, when the current confusional state developed.

At this point Ms. B was disoriented to place and time and was severely agitated and restless. She was not able to give understandable answers to most questions, and in general her speech consisted of incoherent babbling. An extensive search for a metabolic, pharmacologic, or structural cause for her mental syndrome yielded no positive results. Her retroperitoneal sarcoma appeared to have increased somewhat in size, but this could not be directly correlated with her change in mental function. Her sarcoma was in no way felt to be immediately life-threatening. Her physicians felt that ECT was again indicated but that she was not competent to give informed consent to any treatment procedure. The hospital attorney was of the opinion that ECT could be used if the unanimous informed consent of her three adult children was obtained. Her children did consent, and a course of ECT was again administered. A similar gratifying improvement resulted.

Ms. B was not competent to decide about having ECT according to our criteria: there seemed no way to make her aware that there was a treatment decision to be made, let alone communicate to her why her doctors believed treatment was necessary.

We believe that under these circumstances it is usually sufficient to allow next-of-kin to make treatment decisions about the patient's care. They are usually in the best position to know the patient's values and to apply those values to the decision at hand. Any position about treatment the patient has *previously* expressed (while competent) should of course be given great weight and should almost always be determinative.

It is because we believe that patients incompetent to make a treatment decision can usually be treated with only next-of-kin's consent, while far more stringent criteria must be met to treat patients who competently decide against treatment, that our criteria for competence are so minimal. We want to allow next-of-kin to represent a patient's interests only in those cases in which it is abudantly clear that the patient is simply unable to represent his or her own interests.

Competently Made Irrational Decisions

As we have indicated, patients can be competent to make a decision, but their decisions can be viewed by their physicians and others as irrational. They may tenaciously hold patently false beliefs about themselves or their conditions, or they may have desires we usually consider to be irrational. Nevertheless, in most instances patients' wishes are and should be respected even when they seem significantly irrational.

Nonetheless, psychiatry (and, to a lesser extent, neurology) seems to be distinguished by a somewhat lesser reluctance than other branches of medicine to override the wishes of patients who make seriously irrational decisions. This probably reflects the judgment that such patients not infrequently make irrational decisions that seem part of the disease from which they suffer and that they can very frequently be expected to reverse their wishes after treatment. However, competence should be accorded considerable respect in the treatment of even severe mental illness, and psychiatrists should require a compelling reason to overrule the wishes of a patient displaying minimal competence to make treatment decisions. Where ECT is concerned this means that if a patient understands the reasons for his or her physician's recommendation of ECT and also knows that consent is being elicited for treatment, this is prima facie a strong reason for respecting the patient's wishes, even when the treatment team disagrees. Ms. C illustrates this situation.

Case 3

Ms. C, a rather frail 55-year-old married woman, was admitted to our unit with a 6-month history of a moderately severe depression. She was transferred to us from a community hospital where her local psychiatrist had tried two different antidepressant medications but had stopped both because of her marked hypotensive response to even the usual low starting dosages.

When she came to us Ms. C was markedly depressed. She had lost a moderate amount of weight and was sleeping poorly but maintained a fairly adequate intake of food and water. We recommended ECT to her. However, she firmly and consistently refused. She had had a close friend who had received ECT; while her friend's depression had improved at the time, she had killed herself a year later. Ms. C acknowledged that ECT "may not have been responsible" for her friend's suicide but said she was terrified of it.

We therefore devised a drug regimen in which we gave her a very small nighttime dosage (10 mg) of desipramine, a tricyclic antidepressant, which we later increased slowly in small (10 mg) increments. We also gave her small morning and noontime doses of methylphenidate, a stimulant. She suffered from significant orthostasis, but with close nursing care this problem proved manageable. After 2 to 3 weeks her depression began to respond. In an additional 2 weeks she was feeling quite well again, and her hypotension had ceased to be a significant problem.

In this case Ms. C's physicians and her husband all felt that ECT should be tried. The probability of significant and rapid benefit was very high and the risk was very small (see below). The alternative to ECT seemed to be a high probability of continued suffering for a long period of time with only slim hope that further alternative treatment might help. The patient's not choosing ECT for the reason she gave seemed on balance irrational to us. However, the harm she risked by not choosing ECT did not seem extreme enough to justify our considering any more coercive efforts.[4] We viewed her as having competently made a decision that was irrational but that should be respected.

In actual fact, we encounter very few patients who refuse ECT. Why should this be so? Probably the most important reason is that we generally suggest ECT only when antidepressant medications have been given an adequate (3–5 week) trial and have failed. Thus ECT-eligible patients have typically been suffering from depression for some time and want to relieve their pain. If we suggested ECT much earlier — for example, as an alternative to trying medications — we would probably encounter more refusals.

Does the fact that someone is suffering a great deal make suspect their consent to a procedure that holds out a very high probability of relief? We believe it explains *why* they usually consent but it does not invalidate that consent; if one were to make that claim, one would have to disallow the majority of patient consents in medicine. Gall bladders and appendices are removed at times of pain, and probably fewer patients refuse these procedures than refuse ECT. Our patients who consent to ECT seem to make that decision for reasons analogous to those used by patients generally: they dislike very much the suffering associated with being depressed, and while they may have some misgivings about undergoing ECT they would prefer undergoing the treatment to the alternative of continued depression. Assuming that ECT is an acceptable treatment (see below), there seems no other rational basis on which it *could* be chosen, either by the patient or by someone representing his or her interests.[5]

However, there are rare cases involving competent patients in which coercive paternalistic intervention occurs and seems justifiable. These are essentially all cases in which ECT appears to be necessary to save the patient's life. Ms. D is an example.

Case 4

Ms. D, a 69-year-old married woman, was admitted to our unit with a depressive illness of 6 months' duration. Approximately 1 year before admission she was discovered on a routine examination elsewhere to have an elevated lactic dehydrogenase. A liver-spleen scan was done and showed her spleen to be enlarged. No further studies were carried out.

Approximately 6 months before her hospitalization Ms. D's husband suffered a heart attack and was subsequently confined to a nursing home. She stated in retrospect that her "world went to pieces" at that time. She gradually became depressed and experienced characteristic changes in appetite, weight, and sleep. She refused to seek medical attention. Eventually her husband called his lawyer, who summoned the police to her home, where they found her in a state of neglect and brought her to the emergency room at her local hospital. She was admitted and noted to be depressed, but was alert, oriented and cooperative. Positive physical findings included anemia, leukopenia, hypoproteinemia, and a further increase in spleen size. She was seen by a consulting psychiatrist, who thought she was significantly depressed and recommended treatment with tricyclic antidepressant medication. She agreed to take the medicine, but did not improve. The patient's internist recommended a bone marrow examination and other laboratory studies. Ms. D refused for reasons that she would not clearly discuss, saying only that she "didn't want to bother." She was transferred to our medical center for a further attempt at evaluation and possible treatment.

Our evaluation confirmed the above impressions. She was seen by a neurologist and by a hematologist, who recomended a CT scan, an EEG, a lumbar puncture, and a bone marrow examination. The patient's clinical condition continued to deteriorate, and she began refusing most food and fluids. She refused to allow most of the recommended diagnostic tests to be performed. Repeated efforts by us and by her family to obtain her consent for these studies were unsuccessful and were now met by her saying that "I deserve to die."

We felt she was indeed at risk of death through malnutrition and electrolyte disturbance resulting from inadequate fluids and nutrition. Her husband and son were informed of the seriousness of the situation. Her son obtained an attorney, went to court, and on the basis of the clinical details we provided, obtained temporary legal guardianship of his mother. He then authorized us to proceed with the diagnostic procedures deemed necessary. These were done despite her objections. The hematology consultant concluded that the most likely hematologic diagnosis was myelofibrosis. Her long-term prognosis from this disorder was thought to be questionable, but her prognosis for the next several years was quite good.

Her son authorized us to proceed with ECT for her now severe melancholia. She was treated initially without her consent and over her stated objections.

After the second treatment she gave verbal consent to further treatments; after the fourth treatment she became brighter in mood, began eating well, and was much more verbal. After a total of 10 treatments Ms. D reported that she felt quite well. She exhibited a mild post-ECT delirium, which subsequently cleared. She was able to express appropriate feelings of sadness about her husband's illness. She told us that she was very grateful we had treated her. At her last follow-up visit, several months after discharge, she was doing quite well.

We viewed Ms. D as entirely competent to make a treatment decision according to our criteria: she knew that her doctors believed she had a very serious depressive illness and that they further believed that ECT was necessary to save her life. She clearly knew that she was being asked to consent to ECT. However, she refused to consent, giving no reason other than her belief that she deserved to die. This choice of nontreatment seemed seriously irrational to us and almost certainly a reflection of her profound depressive illness. Thus we believed that paternalistically forcing treatment on her was justified — that one can universally advocate such an intervention when the harm or evil one is probably forestalling is so great, the evil one is perpetrating is probably so much less, and the patient's refusal is significantly irrational (2).

Because we viewed Ms. D as competent to decide, we made every effort to obtain her consent to treatment. When this was not forthcoming it was only after much discussion among members of the treatment team and the patient's family that (legal) measures were instituted to allow coercive treatment. Thus her wishes (not to have treatment) were taken very seriously and forced us into a searching examination of our own reasoning. Of course, physicians should engage in a similarly thoughtful weighing of risks and benefits whenever any treatment is recommended to and discussed with a patient. However, if the patient does not consent, we believe open discussion with other staff and family members is called for (except in genuine emergency situations) before paternalistic intervention is ever justified. This requirement is stringent but seems desirable whenever a patient competently makes a decision with which his or her own doctors disagree, and it shows why the consent process is so important when ECT (or any other treatment) is involved.

Is ECT an Inherently Irrational Treatment?

A quite different challenge to the validity of consent to ECT is posed by those critics who contend that by its very nature this treatment is not rationally choice-worthy. This appears to be the view, for example, of Friedberg, who has characterized ECT as the deliberate infliction of brain damage, which results in serious mental impairment in the form of memory loss and disorientation (6,7). He considers ECT so un-choice-worthy as therapy that he challenges the moral integrity of physicians who offer it.

Friedberg's rather one-sided and simplistic view of ECT is not shared by the majority of psychiatrists who deal with depressed patients, and it is not borne out by objective studies on the efficacy of side effects of this treatment. The preponderance of evidence suggests that ECT usually effects a dramatic amelioration of depression and that it does so in the overwhelming majority of cases with little or no long-term impairment of memory or other injurious sequelae (8–10). In fact, many psychiatrists feel that ECT is so safe, rapid, and efficacious that to refuse to suggest it to seriously depressed patients (who run a significantly high risk of death because of their illness) is itself irresponsible.

Nonetheless, it seems clear that we do not yet know with sufficient precision the frequency of the significant persistent memory loss that does apparently rarely follow ECT, and we do not know anything about patient characteristics (e.g., age, sex, type of lateralization of brain functions) that may increase its likelihood. Many more studies of the kind reported by Squire (11) are needed.

However, it must be emphasized that the issue of the rationality of consenting to ECT does not depend on obtaining any more factual information than we now have. For example, suppose that Friedberg's very negative portrayal of ECT were exactly correct: it would still not follow that it would be irrational for a patient to choose it or immoral for a physician to offer it. This is because it is not usually considered irrational to take major steps (including even killing oneself) to escape persistent and unbearable pain, and severe depressive illness frequently involves psychic pain of this sort. Thus a patient who chose to undergo some mild brain damage, which would result in mild persistent memory deficits, in order to escape from severe psychic pain that could not be relieved in any other way would not be making an inherently irrational decision.

However, no critic who has examined the evidence (even the same evidence cited by Friedberg; see Frankel's report [9]) believes that Friedberg's very negative appraisal of ECT is correct. The overwhelming majority of patients incur no residual memory loss at all. Thus the best description of the choice confronting the patient is the following:

1. Continued depression on the one hand (or whatever condition it is hoped ECT might alleviate) with, usually, a continuation of prior attempts at therapy, or
2. ECT on the other hand, which is characterized by certain probable benefits (excellent chance of alleviation of depression; usually lesser chance of alleviation of other conditions) and certain risks (very good to excellent chance of no residual effects; lesser chance [perhaps 10%–50% but not yet known] of minor memory problems that may persist 6-12 months; rare chance [perhaps less than 1% but not exactly known] of moderate to marked memory problems that may persist for longer than a year and in extremely rare cases be chronic and disabling). The risk of memory impairment should be adjusted upward in the case of bilateral ECT and downward with right unilateral ECT.

We believe it is this information which should be given to the patient in the early stage of the informed consent procedure. We hope the day will soon arrive when we can be more precise in communicating the magnitude of the risks involved, but we believe the above summarizes the research literature coupled with our own experience. We have found little difficulty in informing patients of these risks and benefits. We do not believe that our current lack of precise knowledge makes the patient's decision inordinately difficult; many treatments for which we ask consent in medicine contain a much greater zone of uncertainty about outcome than does ECT.

Conclusions

ECT appears to be an eminently rational treatment for patients to choose in many clinical situations. The vast majority of very depressed (and other) patients do consent to having ECT when it is recommended, and there seems no basis on which to question the validity of their consent.

However, there are a few patients from whom consent is not forthcoming. A few of these are patients who are incompetent to make a treatment decision at all and their next-of-kin must usually be relied upon.

Finally, some patients do refuse ECT. In some cases their refusal seems rational, e.g., when it objectively seems possible but not probable that ECT will help their condition and/or (very rarely) when ECT itself holds a high risk of morbidity. Usually, given the type of clinical situations in which ECT is recommended, a patient's refusal seems irrational to the treatment team. However, except in extreme cases involving a probable risk of death in the near future without ECT, physicians treating depressed patients will not err morally by respecting their patients' informed decisions about treatment.

Notes

1. For a general discussion of paternalistic medical interventions and when they are and are not justified, see Gert and Culver's work (1,2).

2. These criteria are similar to the criteria employed in most jurisdictions to ascertain that a person has competently made a will: the individual must know he or she *is* making a will, know what his or her assets are, and know who his or her natural heirs are. See Roth and associates' discussion (3) for a useful elaboration of various meanings that have been attached to "competence."

3. The following would be regarded as irrational desires: the desire to die, to suffer pain (physical or mental), to be disabled, or to be deprived of freedom, opportunity, or pleasure. It is not always irrational to desire these things, but it is irrational to desire them without some adequate *reason*. It is sometimes difficult to decide on the adequacy of a person's reason for acting on what would otherwise be an irrational desire. For a fuller account of rationality see Gert's discussion (4, pp. 27–37).

4. For a full elaboration of the features of a case that determine when paternalistic in-

tervention is justifiable, see Gert and Culver's work (2).

5. Using the analysis and terminology proposed by Gert and Duggan (5), we would say that while the decision to consent to medical procedures is often made in the presence of coercive incentives (e.g., suffering and risk of death), it is nonetheless voluntary, i.e., the patient has the ability to will to have or not to have the treatment depending on whether such coercive incentives are or are not present.

References

1. Gert B, Culver CM: Paternalistic behavior. Philosophy and Public Affairs 6:45–57, 1976
2. Gert B, Culver CM: The justification of paternalism. Ethics 89:199–210, 1979
3. Roth LH, Meisel A, Lidz CW: Tests of competency to consent to treatment. Am J Psychiatry 134:279–284, 1977
4. Gert B: The Moral Rules. New York, Harper & Row, 1975
5. Gert B, Duggan TJ: Free will as the ability to will. Nous 13: 197–217, 1979
6. Friedberg J: Electroshock therapy: let's stop blasting the brain. Psychology Today 9(8):13–23, 1975
7. Friedberg J: Shock treatment, brain damage, and memory loss: a neurological perspective. Am J Psychiatry 134:1010–1014, 1977
8. Fink M: Myths of "shock therapy." Am J Psychiatry 134:991–996, 1977
9. Frankel FH: Current perspectives on ECT: a discussion. Am J Psychiatry 134:1014–1019, 1977
10. Greenblatt M: Efficacy of ECT in affective and schizophrenic illness. Am J Psychiatry 134:1001–1005, 1977
11. Squire LR: ECT and memory loss. Am J Psychiatry 134:997–1001, 1977

Chapter 7

Questions to Consider

1. John, an elderly man suffering from depression with paranoid features, has agreed to his psychiatrist's suggestion that he be treated with ECT. He has been informed of the treatment's risks and benefits, and seems to understand them. On the way to treatment, he tells his wife that he has consented to ECT because the prime minister has threatened him with 10 000 years in jail. Should the treatment proceed?

2. Should competency to consent to medical treatment mean the same thing at all times and in all places? Consider Rachel, an infertile woman seeking medical assistance: in Moose Inlet, a small community 700 km south of the Arctic Circle; in Toronto today; in Toronto 50 years ago, or 50 years from now. If Rachel had the same intelligence and psychological makeup in each of these settings, does it follow that she is equally competent in each of them?

3. Paranoia is a recognized mental illness, but what should we do about pronoia? Pronoia involves delusions that other people like you and value you, for example, the belief that when they talk of you behind your back, they must be saying good things about you, or the belief that they are plotting to do good things for you (Goldner 1982).

4. If a person is competent to consent to a treatment, does it follow that that person is competent to refuse it? If competent to refuse, does competency to consent follow?

5. Should persons in the early stages of SDAT (senile dementia of the Alzheimer's type) have a right to prepare a prior directive (a Ulysses contract) about research, offering to serve as research subjects on Alzheimer's trials if and when they are no longer competent to consent?

Further Readings

Appelbaum, Paul S., and Thomas G. Gutheil. 1979. "Rotting with their rights on": Constitutional theory and clinical reality in drug refusal by psychiatric patients. *Bulletin of the American Academy of Psychiatry* 7:306.

Bloch, Sidney, and Paul Chodoff, eds. 1984. *Psychiatric ethics*. New York: Oxford University Press.

Brock, Dan W., and Steven A. Wartman. 1990. When competent patients make irrational choices. *New England Journal of Medicine* 322:1595–99.

Brown, R. 1976. Psychosis and irrationality. In *Rationality and the Social Sciences*, Stanley I. Benn and G.W. Mortimore, eds. 332–55. London: Routledge and Kegan Paul.

Culver, Charles M., and Bernard Gert. 1990. The inadequacy of incompetence. *Millbank Quarterly* 68:619–43.

Drane, James F. 1985. The many faces of competency. *Hastings Center Report* 15(2):17–21.

Kline, Stephen A. 1987. The clinical issues of determining competency. *Health Law in Canada* 8(1):4–6,8.

Ministry of Health, Province of Ontario. 1990. *Enquiry on Mental Competency: Final Report*. Toronto: Queen's Printer for Ontario.

Roth, Loren H., Alan Meisel, and Charles W. Lidz. 1977. Tests of competency to consent to treatment. *American Journal of Psychiatry* 134:279–84.

Savage, Harvey S., and Carla A. McKague. 1987. *Mental health law in Canada*. Toronto: Butterworths.

Szasz, Thomas. 1974. *The myth of mental illness*. New York: Harper and Row.

Weisstub, David N. 1980. *Law and psychiatry in the Canadian context*. Toronto: Pergamon Press.

Chapter 8

Children and the Elderly: Who Should Decide?

Chapter 8

Introduction

As we saw in the chapter on consent (Chapter 6), a morally valid consent (an "informed consent") is given by a competent person, on the basis of relevant information, without undue coercion or pressure. Given these criteria, patients who are not competent, either by virtue of age, mental illness, dementia, or absence of consciousness, may not be able to provide an informed consent to treatment on their own. In such instances, another person (a proxy or surrogate decision-maker) must be empowered to act on the patient's behalf. Two critical questions consequently arise when a patient is incompetent and unable to make health care decisions: "Who should decide?" and "On what basis?"

The first question, "Who should decide?," is procedural, and unless the patient has completed an advance directive appointing someone to make treatment decisions in the event of incompetence (Chapter 13), the appropriate decision-maker is usually assumed to be a member of the patient's family. In defence of this position, it has been argued, for example, that

> the family provides the most significant source of intimacy for many adults as well as the context in which children's own capacities for intimacy are developed. The family must have some significant freedom from oversight, control, and intrusion to achieve intimacy, and one aspect of this freedom or privacy can be the right, at least within some limits, to make important decisions about the welfare of its incompetent members (Brock 1989, 197).

When the incompetent patient is a newborn, an infant, or a child, parents or guardians are typically identified as the legitimate surrogate decision-makers. When the incompetent patient is an adult, a spouse usually acts as surrogate. If there is no spouse, or if the spouse is not competent, adult children may serve as surrogate decision-makers, and if there are no adult children, parents and/or siblings may assume this responsibility.

There are at least two reasons for choosing surrogate decision-makers from among family members. First, it is assumed that families care for their incompetent members and are thus well-suited to make health care decisions on their behalf. Second, it is believed that because families often bear the consequences of decisions about the care of their incompetent members, they should have some input into these decisions. To be sure, however, patients clearly bear the most direct consequences of decisions made on their behalf, and for this reason family input into the decision making process can be constrained.

The second question, "On what basis?," is substantive. It concerns the grounds upon which decisions about the treatment of incompetent persons should be made. A number of possible bases are discussed in the literature. One derives from a familiar biblical saying: "Do unto others as you would have done unto you"; according to this approach, a surrogate decision-maker would make a decision for the patient based on his or her own personal values. Another approach relies on what a hypothetical reasonable patient in circumstances similar to those of the incompetent patient would want (the reasonable patient standard). A third approach requires that the surrogate decision be based on what the actual patient (not some reasonable hypothetical patient) would have wanted in the given circumstances (the substitute judgement standard). Finally, there are appeals to the notion of best interests — the patient's best interests, the family's best interests, or the community's best interests. In each instance, the likely benefits and burdens of treatment and non-treatment are weighed with respect to the patient alone, or the family as well, or perhaps even the community.

Only two of these approaches to surrogate decision making are currently recognized as morally legitimate, however. Specifically, it is widely held (and in some jurisdictions legally required) that if the patient, while competent, expressed clear wishes regarding treatment, the standard for surrogate decision making should be substitute judgement, that is, a decision is to be based on what the patient would want if he or she were competent. If the patient did not express such wishes, or if those wishes cannot be ascertained, the appropriate standard should be the patient's best interests.

When a family member serving as surrogate decision-maker is not acting on the basis of one of these "legitimate" standards (for example, when the surrogate weighs family interests against patient interests), any decision made on behalf of the patient may be questioned, and initiatives taken to replace the surrogate decision-maker. Moreover, when the appropriate standard is the patient's best interests, it is not uncommon for a member of the health care team to assert him or herself as a surrogate for the patient. Conflict between the family and the health care provider, each of whom has a different understanding of what is in the patient's best interests, can result, and an institutional ethics committee may get involved, or on occasion a court might have to resolve the conflict.

The ability to override decisions made by family surrogates, when these are deemed substantively incorrect, marks an important difference between "surrogate consent" and informed consent. A competent patient's right to consent to or refuse medical treatment is almost absolute. In fact, even choices deemed "foolish" from the perspective of some will be respected, provided there is no doubt about the patient's competence (Brock and Wartman 1990). This is not so with surrogate decision making. If the choice made is not one that derives from one of the two appropriate standards discussed above, the surrogate's decision could be overridden. Whereas competent patients can, and typically do, make their health care decisions on the basis of a number of different considerations, surrogate decision-makers may apply only one of two standards, and which standard applies depends on whether the patient, while competent, expressed any wishes about how he or she would want to be treated should he or she become incompetent.

The Selections

The selections for this chapter are carefully chosen to expose a range of responses to the questions, "Who should decide?" and "On what basis?" The first selection, by Ruth Macklin, addresses these questions in general terms with reference to patients who are infants or minor children, comatose or otherwise unconscious, mentally ill, or severely demented. For different reasons, these patients cannot make their own health care decisions. Typically, a family member is empowered to act on their behalf as surrogate decision-maker. The underlying assumption is that the surrogate is well-intentioned and competent. When this assumption proves to be false, or when there is no family member available and willing to serve as surrogate, the state is forced to intervene.

An interesting question that Macklin explores is whether state intervention is ever appropriate when there are relatives willing to act as surrogate decision-maker, or whether in all cases final decision making authority rightfully belongs to family surrogates, provided they are competent to make health care decisions. At issue is whether there are standards or criteria for surrogate decision making that *must* be adhered to for a decision to be "right," or whether any decision made by a rightful decision-maker (i.e., a family member), is thereby "right." Macklin argues that surrogate decision-makers can make decisions that are substantively incorrect (i.e., "wrong") and that it is appropriate for such decisions to be overridden.

The next selection focusses narrowly on decision making for handicapped newborns. At the outset, Robert Weir provides a summary of the criteria for competent surrogate decision-makers. These include relevant knowledge and information, impartiality, emotional stability, and consistency. According to Weir, no one individual can meet all of these criteria. In turn, Weir discusses the respective strengths and weaknesses of parents, physicians, ethics committees, and the courts as surrogate decision-makers and then suggests a serial ordering of decision-makers, starting with the parents.

Of particular interest given the recent increase in the number of ethics committees in Canada (Storch 1990), and the debate as to whether these committees should be decision making or consultative bodies, are the purported benefits of ethics committees as surrogates for newborns. The benefits, according to Weir, are that ethics committees are more likely to satisfy the criteria for surrogate decision-makers; they can help to resolve conflicts between parents and health care providers; they can safeguard the interests of children when parents and physicians agree on a course of action that is not in a child's best interests; and, finally, they can better address the relevant underlying ethical issues. As Weir notes, however, these benefits must be weighed against certain limitations.

Weir's discussion of the relative merits of parents, physicians, ethics committees, and the courts functioning as surrogate decision-makers is followed by a case discussion in which all of the above sought to act as surrogate for a two-year-old patient, Baby L, who had been seriously ill for most of her short life. Her physicians believed that continued treatment was "burdensome and without benefit"; her mother rejected this opinion. The hospital ethics committee supported the physicians' interpretation of what was in the child's best interests, but when the case went to court, a judge ordered that treatment be continued.

John Paris, Robert Crone, and Frank Reardon, writing about the plight of Baby L, argue that when treatment is "futile," disputes between parents and physicians as to what is in a child's best interests should not be resolved by acquiescing to inappropriate parental demands for treatment. Rather, health care providers and ethics committees should be empowered to make treatment decisions on the basis of medical expertise.

The last selection is markedly different. The focus is no longer on children and the procedural question, "Who should decide?", but on adults and the substantive question, "On what basis should decisions be made?" Nancy Jecker, in an examination of the role of adult children in decision making on behalf of their elderly parents, insists that a sharp distinction between surrogate decisions based on either substitute judgement or patient best interests is unhelpful. She notes that not all patients fall neatly into one of two categories: those with previously expressed autonomous wishes (where the standard for surrogate decision making is substitute judgement), and those whose wishes are unknown and cannot be ascertained (where the standard is the patient's best interests). Jecker reminds us that competence is not an "all or nothing" concept, and that in many cases elderly patients have "marginal competence." Jecker argues that family members and intimate others are well placed to help construe or elicit patient wishes and treatment preferences — in which case the preferable standard would not be the patient's best interests. She insists that reliance on this subjective awareness of patient values and wishes is preferable to reliance on the (objective) patient's best interests standard.

References

Brock, Dan W. 1989. Children's competence for health care decisionmaking. In *Children and health care: Moral and social issues*, Loretta M. Kopelman and John C. Moskop, eds. 181–212. Boston: Kluwer Academic Publishers.

———, and Steven A. Wartman. 1990. When competent patients make irrational choices. *New England Journal of Medicine* 322:1595–99.

Storch, Janet, et al. 1990. Ethics committees in Canadian hospitals: Report of the 1989 survey. *Healthcare Management Forum*, Winter, 3–8.

---

29   Deciding for Others

Ruth Macklin

Parents possess awesome decision-making power on behalf of their minor children. For the most part, our society supports that power, recognizing that affection and concern for their children usually lead parents to make decisions in their children's best interests. But there are limits to how parents may decide to act. . . .

When parents make a decision regarding medical care that clearly goes against their child's best interest, the state does not usually take custody of the child or seek foster care. This differs from cases of child abuse and neglect, in which parents forfeit their right to keep their own children and the state assumes custody until a suitable home can be found for those unfortunate children. Typically, in medical situations, a guardian *ad litem* is appointed for the specific and limited purpose of making treatment decisions on behalf of the child. The authority of the guardian ceases once the recommended therapy is completed.

The chief examples of deciding for others occur when infants and children become patients. But they are not the only examples. The need often arises to decide for adults who cannot decide for themselves: comatose or unconscious patients, profoundly mentally retarded persons and those whose mental disturbance is so great as to sever their contact with reality, and severely demented elderly patients all fit this description to some degree. As hard as it is to arrive at a clear, agreed-upon standard for assessing a person's mental capacity to decide for himself, once that difficulty is resolved by a determination that the patient is incompetent, a new set of moral problems arises. Someone must be empowered to decide on the patient's behalf. . . .

The familiar procedural question "Who should decide? has several possible answers. One traditional answer lies in the *parens patriae* doctrine, the legal principle that grants the state broad authority to act in the incompetent person's "best interest." That doctrine — literally, "the state as parent" — supports involuntary-commitment statutes that permit persons in need of care, custody, or treatment to be forcibly placed in institutions. . . .

The *parens patriae* doctrine also underlies the authority of the state to override parental decisions alleged to go against the best interests of their children, as well as the right of the state to remove abused or neglected children from the custody of their abusing parents. Yet critics of this doctrine as it pertains to children argue that the state is too crude an instrument to become an adequate substitute for parents.[1]

The traditional, informal answer to the who-should-decide question is "the family." In most cases involving infants and minor children, the child's parents or guardians should be the decision-makers. And typically in the case of married people, it is the spouse who is presumed to be the natural one appointed in the role of decider. For an elderly person whose spouse is no longer alive, or who is mentally impaired, adult children are usually the ones who serve as surrogates for the patient. But just as the decisions of parents are sometimes thought to be against their children's best interests, so, too, can decisions made by other family members on behalf of their relatives be called into question.

When the content of an ethical decision is questioned, it is the substantive moral position that is under attack. True, cultural values of some sort give rise to the procedural mechanisms a society adopts for handling such problems. In our society, family values occupy a high place, so surrogate decision-makers are usually relatives of the incompetent person, unless they disqualify themselves. But it is not hard to imagine a society (anthropologists have described some) in which authority resides in some unrelated individual — a prophet, healer, or panel of elders. . . .

Parents are generally presumed to be the ones who are "best equipped" to make decisions about medical treatment for their children. Yet doubts can often arise. Simply the fact of their being the little boy's parents did not render the Greens "well equipped" to refuse the standard medical treatment for their son Chad.

Chad Green suffered from leukemia, a disease that is often fatal. His parents, believing in the efficacy of nutritional therapy and laetrile, abandoned chemotherapy, which is known to have an 80 percent rate of cure for children in Chad's age range with his type of leukemia. According to reliable medical data, Chad's "chances" were around eight out of ten for complete recovery if chemotherapy had continued and if the leukemia had remained in remission for eighteen months. Although a court ordered the Greens to resume conventional chemotherapy for Chad, they fled to Mexico to seek the treatments they believed would help. The child died some time later, and it will never be known whether he would have profited from the standard treatment.

Whatever the Greens' "equipment" may have been for making that decision, and whether or not there is a right decision in such cases, many people would argue that Chad's parents had the right and the responsibility to decide for their son. A charitable interpretation would view the Greens not as fanatics seeking a quack therapy but instead as loving parents who wanted to abandon conventional therapy, with its unpleasant side effects, in a desperate search for unproven remedies.

In another highly publicized case the parents of Phillip Becker were far from well equipped to decide to refuse lifesaving heart surgery for him at age thirteen, surgery that could easily correct his heart defect but would not, of course, improve his mental retardation — the ground on which his parents chose to refuse the proposed surgery. Among other things, Phillip Becker had been in a home for handicapped children since birth and was visited by his parents only infrequently. The notion that no one can be presumed to be in a better position than parents to make treatment decisions for their children, and therefore that no one is better equipped to make those decisions, is surely flawed. Yet it remains an open question whether the right to decide nevertheless resides with parents, so long as they are not incompetent as judged by criteria independent of the decision they make on behalf of their children.

The solutions to procedural, who-should-decide questions depend more on law and custom than they do on ethical theory. No moral principle drawn from philosophical ethics dictates an answer to the who-should-decide question. The legal doctrine of *parens patriae* is a curious blend of procedure and substance. It states both who should decide and what principle should guide the decision, requiring that the decision itself be based on the incompetent person's "best interest" — a substantive standard.

Granting decision-making authority for a patient to a family member feels comfortable. Who but a close relative should presume to make decisions for those no longer able to decide for themselves? As comfortable as this "feels," the comfort begins to lessen when probing questions are asked. Should whatever a family member chooses on behalf of an incompetent relative be allowed to stand as final? If not, on what grounds may a relative's decision be questioned? Should the same standard be used in deciding for children as for other incompetent relatives? If not, what basis is there for treating such cases differently?

Just as parents are presumed to be decision-makers for their children, but can nonetheless make decisions that are substantively incorrect, so can other family members make "wrong" decisions for a patient. In the case of adults, two different criteria exist — one substantive, the other procedural — for judging the rightness or wrongness of a third-party decision. The substantive standard is the "best interest" of the patient; the procedural criterion rests on the "substituted-judgment" principle — what the patient would decide, or would have wanted, if he or she were capable of participating in the decision.

The substituted-judgment standard has been the most widely accepted by courts in cases over the past ten to fifteen years. It rests on a solid moral foundation, the adult person's right to self-determination, the right to exercise one's autonomy. If competent persons have that right, then when they are no longer competent their right should still be exercised. The moral and legal theory that supports the substituted-judgment procedure is the right of self-determination.

If the patient has made a living will or otherwise given specific instructions about what he or she would want done when incompetent in the future, that written document or statement is probably the best evidence of the patient's wishes. In the absence of any prior statements by the patient, family members are normally the best source of evidence about what the patient would have wanted, since they are likely to have known the person longest and most intimately.

But many people never discuss these topics with their family or anyone else. Also, families may be mistaken about what their relative would have wanted, substituting their own judgment for that of the patient. Their emotions often play a role, and when asked to consent to an aggressive treatment for the incompetent patient, some family members act out of guilt or fear, ignoring or failing to ascertain what the patient would have wanted. The substituted-judgment doctrine is often hard to apply because of these practical difficulties stemming from uncertainty or ignorance about the patient's actual wishes.

There is another problem of a different sort: the existence of groups of patients to whom the substituted-judgment standard cannot apply. Besides infants and children, who have not yet attained autonomy, others, such as mentally retarded persons or those who have been emotionally disturbed from a young age, have never been competent. These individuals will never develop autonomy in any meaningful sense. When autonomy is so severely diminished, there can be no substituted judgment by another. In these situations the leading moral and legal principle is the old standby, the "best interest of the patient."

Some disturbed, demented, or retarded people have preferences they are able to voice. Care should be taken to respect such preferences, when they are expressed, even if the patient hovers at the border of competency. Doctors and family members should try to strike a balance between respecting the wishes of marginally competent persons and making decisions in their best interest.

As if these two principles were not complicated enough to sort out and apply in practice, the law recognizes still another problematic concept, the "reasonable-person" standard. This legal concept is used in other situations, for example, as a standard of disclosure in the process of gaining informed consent. Its value for determining what doctors disclose to patients lies in the fact that it is a patient-oriented criterion, replacing the earlier, physician-based "reasonable-practitioner" standard. But just as it is hard to determine what a hypothetical "reasonable patient" would want to know before giving informed consent to treatment, so must it be difficult to ascertain what the "reasonable person" would actually decide.

One thing is clear, however. In situations involving incompetent patients, "reasonable" cannot be interpreted to mean "what this patient would want if he or she were competent to decide." That describes the substituted-judgment standard for incompetent patients. An actual patient may be "unreasonable," yet if competent, his wishes should be respected. The "reasonable person" is, by definition, "reasonable." So a potential for conflict exists in the use of the substituted-judgment principle and the reasonable-person standard. And either principle could yield a different decision from the best-interest standard.

Since 1976, when the New Jersey Supreme Court issued its ruling in the case of Karen Ann Quinlan, courts have sought a basis for determining what are the rights of incompetent adult patients. The trend that emerged was to base the rights of incompetent patients on the well-established right of self-determination of competent patients. Embodied in the common-law doctrine of informed consent, the right to self-determination in decisions regarding one's own medical care has been respected for the most part. . . . To base the right of incompetent adult patients on the same rights possessed by competent adults seems natural and consistent. . . .

Despite the recent decline in the use of the best-interest standard for incompetent adult patients, that standard has prevailed in medical situations where the patients are children.

But both the concept of "best interest" and its application to those cases have been attacked. It has been argued that not only is the principle vague and hard to apply, but it is also inappropriate to disqualify parents from their traditional role. The once-simple picture of parents as the sole and proper decision-makers for their children has been altered by a number of different developments. One is the rise of the children's-right and children's-liberation movements, leading to a call for increased decision-making autonomy for adolescents and even younger children. A related development is the idea that children need advocates who will speak on their behalf when parents decide or act wrongly.

Judicial decisions and statutes . . . have lowered the age of consent for a number of medical procedures, particularly those that involve sexuality: obtaining contraceptive information and devices, receiving treatment for venereal disease, and procuring abortions. Despite these exceptions, the general rule holds true that minors . . . cannot grant consent for themselves for medical treatment or to participate in research. Unlike adults, who are presumed competent until determined otherwise, children are held to be incompetent by virtue of their age alone. In addition to matters related to sexuality, other exceptions to the age of consent include treatment for drug abuse, and all forms of therapy for minors who are emancipated, or financially independent, and for "mature minors," ones who are married or who have borne a child.

It is obvious why the substituted-judgment standard does not apply to decision-making on behalf of young children, despite the fact that it is ethically appropriate and has been adopted by courts for adult patients whose wishes before becoming incompetent can be known. However, older children and adolescents should be consulted and their wishes taken into account by parents and physicians. Just as absolute incompetence is rare in adults, the clearest cases being patients who are comatose or profoundly retarded, so, too, with children competency is rarely an all-or-nothing affair. A need exists to draw a line somewhere for legal purposes, so the age of majority is chosen as the time at which an individual is permitted to make his or her own medical decisions. That point is not completely arbitrary, yet it fails to reflect the wide differences in maturity, understanding, and experience among persons growing to adulthood. Any attempt to individualize the notion of competency for children as self-deciders would be so difficult and controversial from a practical standpoint that, as inadequate as chronological age is for marking the distinction between the legally competent and incompetent, it is probably the best that can be devised.

Wherever the legal age of competence is set, cases are bound to arise in which parents make decisions for their children that others deem wrong, misguided, or against the best interest of those children. Inevitably, the question arises whether parents have the unqualified right to make those decisions, or whether mechanisms should be in place to allow unwise parental decisions to be overridden.

A cluster of conflicting values lies at the heart of the controversy about whether parental decisions may be justifiably overridden by the state. One source of conflict is the disagreement about whether there exists a single right answer that can be objectively determined. A second major source of conflict stems from the value of preserving family autonomy and privacy against state intrusion, versus the value of protecting children, when they cannot speak for themselves, against potentially harmful decisions made by their own parents. This second source of conflict can easily become the type of rock-bottom clash of values for which no rational resolution is possible. In that case it falls into a realm of disputed values, where reasonable people disagree in their most deeply held moral commitments. As this controversy illustrates, procedural issues concerning the appropriate decision-maker can give rise to as much disagreement and conflict as substantive disputes about whether a decision itself is morally sound.

A final standard for deciding for others is known as "identity of interests." This principle holds that the interests of the third party and those of the incompetent person are so close that in choosing his or her own interests, the decision-maker will protect the interests of the incompetent individual. Many people would take this to be the proper standard when decisions must be made for children. Yet it could support a wholesale endorsement of parental authority to decide for their own children.

According to this view, an independent determination of a child's interest need not occur or even be possible. In its extreme form this position holds that the interests of parents and their minor children are identical; whatever parents decide is in their children's interest is in their interest. This extreme is untenable, yet there is a sensible core to the identity-of-interests position.

The sensible aspect rests on several assumptions, the chief one being that because children gain a great many of their values from their parents, beginning early in life, it is reasonable to expect them to have internalized those values, and therefore for their interests to coincide with those of their parents. But this very assumption presupposes that it is meaningful to grant that children have interests of their own — interests that may or may not be identical with those of their parents or of the family unit as a whole. Whether the interests of parents and children do coincide is a matter to be factually determined in each specific case. If the idea that children have interests independent of those of their parents is meaningful, then it is possible for those interests to diverge.

A second sound assumption underlying the identity-of-interests view is that children's interests are better served when the family remains a harmonious, autonomous unit, free from the strife and turmoil that can ensue when the state intervenes. Parents can probably perform their nurturing and child-rearing tasks better when the family is intact and when its values remain strong. But this assumption, too, presupposes that children have interests that can be identified independently from those of their parents.

The problem with the identity-of-interests view is that it can too easily degenerate into an extreme position, such as that of Jehovah's Witness parents who refuse lifesaving blood transfusions for their child. If those parents, in accordance with their religious beliefs, judge that their child is better off dead as a result of not having a blood transfusion than alive with a soul condemned to eternal damnation, then the identity-of-interests doctrine would have to consider the interests of parent and child identical. If that doctrine were to prevail, it would be hard to rebut the claim that the interest of a child of Jehovah's Witnesses is precisely what the parents say it is. Fortunately for the children whose lives have been saved by court orders, their interests have been viewed as separate and distinct from those of their parents.

All things considered, I think the best-interest standard — in spite of its shortcomings — should prevail. Underlying this choice is my belief that decisions parents make on behalf of their minor children can have content that is substantively right or wrong. Furthermore, it is unlikely that the state's overriding a family's decision will destroy the family unit or make permanent inroads into its autonomy. A single invasion of family privacy must be weighed against a lifetime of health, well-being, or bodily integrity for the child on whose behalf the state has intervened. It remains important to weigh any potential damage of the child. Family autonomy can be respected, and a deep commitment to family integrity maintained, in the recognition that close and loving family units are in no great danger of being destroyed by an occasional outside intervention aimed at serving the best interests of a child. . . .

Notes

1. Joseph Goldstein, "Medical Care For the Child at Risk," in Willard Gaylin and Ruth Macklin, eds., *Who speaks for the Child? The Problems of Proxy Consent* (New York: Plenum Press, 1982), p. 160.

30   Procedure: Criteria, Options, and Recommendations

Robert F. Weir

Criteria for Proxy Decision Makers

Before addressing the central procedural question ("Who Should Decide?"), it is important to discuss the criteria according to which that question should be answered. Given the ethical context of placing priority on the best interests of handicapped newborns, one must attempt to determine which of the possible decision makers is most likely to promote the best interests of such infants in particular cases. The first procedural question to be addressed is thus, what are the characteristics or qualities that decision makers in neonatal cases should have in order to make responsible decisions about treatment? Any effort to move directly to select a proxy decision maker without taking up this prerequisite question is comparable to recruiting someone to fill a job for which there is no job description.

If any consensus is to be reached on the best possible decision makers, agreement is needed on the characteristics or qualities sought in the persons entrusted with the responsibility of choosing handicapped life or death for neonatal patients who have never been competent. For birth-defective neonates who live and later become competent, it is also important that they believe the best qualified proxies were the persons who actually made treatment decisions on their behalf. Such proxies should meet as many of the following criteria as possible.

I. Relevant Knowledge and Information

Persons deciding to provide or to deny life-prolonging treatment in neonatal cases should have three different kinds of knowledge relevant to such cases. First, they should be knowledgeable regarding the medical fact in particular cases, . . . many of the cases in NICUs are medically complex. Accurate diagnosis is often difficult to do, and physicians sometimes disagree about the prognosis in cases where the diagnosis is clear. In order to make life-and-death decisions, proxies therefore either need to be medically trained or to have accurate diagnostic information and consensus prognostic judgements communicated to them in nontechnical language. Second, proxies should be knowledgeable regarding the family setting into which particular anomalous neonates have been born. In very few situations, if any, should family considerations override a birth-defective newborn's interests in life. Nevertheless, a determination of an infant's best interests depends, in part, on a reasonably accurate understanding of the parent's emotional strength and financial capabilities, the physical and emotional well-being of siblings, and the willingness of family members to accept a seriously handicapped child into the family unit. Third, proxies should be knowledgeable regarding possible alternatives to home care by the biological parents. If the decision concerning handicapped life or death hangs on where that handicapped life will be lived, the decision makers need to have current, accurate information on (a) adoptive parents who will take custody of a handicapped child and (b) institutions that are capable of providing long-term care for handicapped children. The availability of such alternatives to the original family unit can mean the difference between life and death for some anomalous neonates.

2. Impartiality

In any proxy decision made on behalf of an incompetent person, one of the fundamental moral requirements is that of impartiality. For proxies of incompetent patients who have previously been competent, the requirement of impartiality means that such decision makers should determine, as objectively as possible, which medical alternative that person would choose if he or she were still able to choose. For proxies of neonatal patients, the requirement of impartiality means that such persons should determine, as objectively as possible, whether life-prolonging treatment would be in the best interests of the individual neonate in question. To maximize the possibility of being objective, the persons making the treatment/nontreatment decision should be disinterested in the particular case at issue and dispassionate in weighing available alternatives. Only in this manner can proxies hope to determine fairly whether life-prolonging treatment will, on balance, be beneficial or harmful to a particular birth-defective newborn.

3. Emotional Stability

Too often, decisions about nontreatment are made by persons under severe emotional stress. Parents of an anomalous neonate, having expected a normal child, typically respond with a combination of shock, denial, guilt, anxiety, and helplessness.[1] Physicians in charge of an anomalous neonate are also sometimes under serious emotional pressure as a result of the combination of an overly large caseload, too many diagnostic dilemmas, too little time in which to make critical decisions, too little cooperation from problematic parents, and too much interpersonal conflict with other members of the medical team over how to handle borderline cases. The unfortunate result is that some life-and-death decisions are made by persons who are emotionally ill-equipped to make such decisions. There are, however, several alternatives to this current state of affairs: bring in consultants who are not emotionally involved in the particular case in question, build some additional time into the decision-making process (when the medical condition allows such) to give parents and/or physicians respite from the immediate emotional pressures, or turn the decision making in tough cases over to other proxies who are emotionally stable.

4. Consistency

A common requirement of moral decision making is that of consistency from case to case. In terms of the principle of justice, normally similar cases should be handled in similar ways. For proxies making decisions in neonatal cases, this requirement means that all anomalous newborns having the same kind of treatable diagnostic condition should be given treatment for the condition; all anomalous newborns having severe diagnostic conditions that cannot be effectively treated should generally have life-prolonging treatment withheld from them. In this manner it is possible, all other things being equal, to be consistent in handling cases with the same diagnostic condition. In addition it is necessary that proxies be consistent in applying the obligatory/optional distinction to cases. Whether dealing with a range of cases within the same diagnostic category or other cases having multiple anomalies, the requirement of consistency means that proxies should determine whether certain treatment options are optional in particular cases by employing the same pattern of reasoning used in other cases having morally relevant, similar features. Having determined, for instance, that life-prolonging treatment was in the best interests of an anomalous newborn in one case, proxies should arrive at the same conclusion in another case having features that are medically and morally similar.

Who Should Decide?

Unfortunately, no individual involved in neonatal cases is likely to meet all of these criteria. In fact, the applicability of the criteria varies not only from one proxy to another, but also in terms of the particular cases and circumstances that necessitate proxy decision making for neonatal patients. For these reasons it is important to discuss the four major options as decision makers, assess their relative strengths and weaknesses, and put forward the most acceptable alternative for making decisions in neonatal cases.

Parents

Several pediatricians and ethicists think that parents are the appropriate decision makers in neonatal cases. Among the physicians, Raymond Duff, Anthony Shaw and R.B.

Zachary clearly believe that selective nontreatment decisions fall within the scope of parental autonomy. For these physicians, parental autonomy is sufficiently important that they usually choose not to override the decisions of parents with whom they disagree. Among the ethicists, John Fletcher, Michael Garland, Terrence Ackerman, and Richard McCormick think that parental discretion is the most important procedural factor in at least some cases involving decisions about life-prolonging treatment. For these ethicists, parents are the best possible proxies in neonatal cases involving the prospect of long-term, emotionally and financially draining treatment of a seriously handicapped child.

Additional support for parents as proxies comes from other sources. According to one national survey, most pediatricians and pediatric surgeons believe that selective non-treatment is appropriately a matter of parental discretion.[2] The Judicial Council of the American Medical Association agrees: "In desperate situations involving newborns, the advice and judgment of the physician should be readily available, but the decision whether to exert maximal efforts to sustain life should be the choice of the parents."[3] The President's Commission for the Study of Ethical Problems in Medicine also recommends parents as the principal decision makers, especially in borderline cases.[4]

Several reasons are usually given for permitting parents to make these life-and-death decisions.[5] First, parental discretion in deciding about treatment in neonatal cases is only an extension of the discretionary decision-making power that society grants parents in other important matters concerning their children. For instance, society gives parents considerable latitude in providing moral education for their children, in deciding whether their children will attend public or private schools, and in most of the decisions that have to be made about their children's medical care. Second, parents, having anticipated the birth of a child and made certain commitments to the child prior to birth, are the most likely persons to be morally committed to the continuing welfare of the child. Even though the particular child in question is not the normal child the parents wanted, they are still likely to have at least a residual commitment to the child and prefer not to have the child die. Third, parents are the persons who will enjoy the greatest benefits if a handicapped child lives, and they are also the ones who will endure the greatest emotional and financial costs whether the child lives or dies. Because of this more intimate involvement with the child — especially if the child lives — parents are the appropriate decision makers regarding life-prolonging treatment.

There are problems, however, with granting parents the right to make selective nontreatment decisions, and some of the problems have to do with the criteria for proxy decision makers discussed above. For one thing, there is no compelling reason to think that all parents of defective newborns are competent to make decisions about life-prolonging treatment. In fact, given the medical and emotional circumstances in which these decisions have to be made, it is sometimes the case that parents are the least qualified persons to make the decisions. They are certainly the most knowledgeable about the family situation into which an anomalous neonate is born, but they are often hampered in their ability to make decisions by several factors: they may be emotionally devastated by the birth of the child, inadequately informed about the medical facts in the case, virtually ignorant of alternatives to their keeping custody and providing long-term care for the child, and/or unable to understand the medical facts in the case even if given that information.

Another problem is that all parents simply do not promote the best interests of the birth-defective children born to them. In fact, it is a false assumption to think that all parents in these circumstances have the capacity to be either altruistic or impartial toward the handicapped newborns in their families. In some instances, it is clear to observers that parents are impartial in making decisions about treatment. In other instances where there is a conflict of interest between the parents and the handicapped child, it is clear to observers that the parental decision about treatment is contrary to the child's best interests. In promoting their own psychological and financial interests, or protecting their chosen life-style and possibly other children at home, some parents simply cannot make impartial judgments about whether a defective newborn should receive treatment or die untreated. As a result, some ethicists who favor parents as the proxy decision makers recognize that parental autonomy must sometimes be checked: "the state should intervene only when the familial judgment so exceeds the limits of reason that the compromise with what is objectively in the incompetent one's interest cannot be tolerated."[6]

In addition, if birth-defective neonates sometimes live or die merely on the basis of parental discretion, the decisions in these cases may adhere to no ethical principles or criteria generally acceptable by other persons. If parents in such situations are believed to have an absolute right — grounded in parental autonomy — to determine whether their anomalous children are given or denied treatment, there exists virtually no possibility for consistency from case to case. Some infants will live or die depending on their parents' determination of whether severely handicapped life or death is in the infant's best interests, however that judgment is made. Other infants will live or die depending on parental inclination, bias, whim, or whatever, with no attempt to determine which course of action is more beneficial or more detrimental to the infants. And still other infants will live or die because their parents, not having any clear ethical criteria on which to base a decision, are easily persuaded simply to go along with the judgments of physicians in charge of various cases.

Physicians

A second possibility as proxy decision makers in neonatal cases are the physicians responsible for the cases. Among the pediatricians, John Lorber, John Freeman, and Everett Koop favor physicians in the role of decision maker. Each of them thinks that a neonatologist should discuss the relevant facts of cases with parents, but believes that the majority of parents will — and should — go along with the recommendations the medical authority makes.

Among ethicists, Carson Strong thinks that physicians are the best proxies in most neonatal cases because they are most likely to promote the best interests of defective newborns. In contrast to many parents, neonatologists function as patient advocates for the incompetent patients under their care. Often making unilateral decisions to treat neonates aggressively, neonatologists should promote the best interests of their patients except when it appears that prolonging a handicapped child's life would cause a great burden for the family.[7]

For these advocates of physicians as proxy decision makers, there are three reasons for having neonatologists make the treatment decisions in most cases. First, physicians possess specialized knowledge regarding congenital diseases and can make informed predictions concerning the long-term effects of these diseases on children and their families. Especially in terms of this medical knowledge, physicians are better qualified than parents to make decisions about treatment. Even if physicians do not make the final decision about treatment in all cases, their specialized knowledge makes them indispensable as consultants for parents, hospital committees, or courts. Second, physicians usually have a level of objectivity about particular cases that parents simply cannot match. Because emotional stress can overwhelm parents, physicians are often more capable than parents in making an objective assessment of a handicapped newborn's best interests and in making rational decisions about treatment. They can thus be patient advocates, even with their own emotional pressures and time constraints, in a way parents often cannot. Third, given their professional involvement with numerous birth-defective newborns, physicians have recurring opportunities to compare children with the same kinds of anomalous conditions, assess the effectiveness of various treatment possibilities, and make comparative judgments about the longterm handicaps associated with certain conditions. In this respect, physicians are capable of being consistent from case to case in a way parents are not because of the more limited contact parents have with other cases.

Nevertheless, physicians present certain problems when they function as the principal decision makers in neonatal cases, and these problems are particularly evident when individual physicians are granted proxy decision-making power in borderline cases. Although neonatologists are clearly the best qualified decision makers in terms of their medical knowledge of congenital anomalies, that knowledge is limited in several important ways. For instance, the possession of specialized knowledge in neonatal medicine does not enable physicians always to make accurate diagnoses, and it certainly does not enable them to make prognoses that are always correct. To observe these limitations of medical knowledge, one has only to compare the kind of prognostic judgments pediatricians make about children with spina bifida. Moreover, even if medical training in a pediatric specialty brought about greater unanimity in making prognoses than it does, this specialized medical knowledge does not translate into moral expertise. And because treatment/nontreatment decisions are finally moral decisions, once accurate diagnoses and careful prognoses have been made, physicians are no better qualified to make sound moral decisions in these cases than parents or other possible proxies.

A second problem with physicians as proxies has to do with potential conflicts of interest between them and the patients they serve. Although physicians often are able to be more objective than many parents, it is simply not true that physicians are completely impartial in determining the best interests of their patients. Rather, some physicians cast into the principal decision-making role may have their judgments skewed by either of two conflicts of interest. Many, and probably most, pediatric specialists have a serious bias in favor of normal, healthy children. Having cared for numerous handicapped infants and observed the severe problems that confront such infants, pediatricians often tend to view anomalous newborns as living tragedies that should have been terminated prior to birth. To consider prolonging these tragic lives into a seriously handicapped future is a depressing thought, which leads some pediatricians to favor nontreatment in cases in which life appears to be in the infants' best interests.[8] Another bias held by some pediatric specialists is toward research and experimentation. Rather than trying to assess treatment options in terms of the best interests of individual neonatal patients, they tend to view patients — especially those with the most serious, possibly exotic conditions — as relatively rare opportunities to advance the cause of neonatal medicine as a science. Consequently, some seriously defective newborns may be given treatment that will not benefit them but will create research and teaching opportunities for the clinicians in charge of their cases. These two potential conflicts of interest are especially problematic in cases where only one physician (as opposed to a medical team) is allowed to make the final decision regarding life-prolonging treatment.

Furthermore, even though physicians are more capable than parents of being consistent from case to case, they sometimes are not consistent because of the external pressures that influence them. Particularly when treatment decisions are made by individual physicians in charge of cases, those decisions may be substantially swayed by considerations other than the best interests of the child in question or the relationship between two similar cases. The two dominant external pressures on physicians in these situations are the law and assertive parents. For instance, whenever physicians perceive a significant change in legal enforcement patterns (as under the Reagan administration), they sometimes opt for life-prolonging treatment in cases that are medically and morally similar to earlier cases in which they judged such treatment to be optional. Or physicians may simply accede to the demands of assertive parents. The result is that a physician may decide against treatment in a particular case because of parental pressure, even though the same physician in a medically and morally similar case opts for treatment in the absence of such parental pressure.

A Hospital Committee

For some persons who have addressed the issue of selective nontreatment, a hospital committee is a preferable alternative to parents or physicians functioning by themselves as proxies. Among physicians, Norman Fost is the leading advocate for the use of such committees. Given the complexity of selective nontreatment decisions, he thinks that any individual decision maker needs advice from an informed group representing different professional fields. Among attorneys, John Robertson points to the need for due process in treatment decisions. In his judgment, the requirement of due process can be met in neonatal cases only if there is a committee (or at least a physician outside the case, or a patient advocate) to ensure an impartial representation of a defective newborn's interests. In their article, Robertson and Fost state that "even if after reflection one decides that there is a class of defective newborn infants from whom treatment can be justifiably withheld, it does not follow that parents and physicians should be the sole judge in each case of who shall survive."[9]

Among ethicists, Paul Ramsey is convinced that neither parents nor physicians are the best possible proxies. Instead, he says that any decision about the possible termination of an individual's life should be made by a disinterested party. . . .

. . . [A]llowing for variation in committee composition and procedures, there are several reasons for using committees in an advisory role and possibly in the role of proxy decision maker. First, an NICU committee has the possibility of meeting all of the criteria for a proxy decision maker. In contrast to individual physicians and parents, the composite nature of a committee goes a long way toward ensuring emotional stability, impartiality, and consistency on the part of the committee members. Moreover, depending on the expertise of the committee members, a committee is likely to possess the relevant knowledge of the medical facts, family setting, and alternatives to home care that is necessary in making borderline decisions regarding treatment.

Second, an NICU committee can adjudicate conflicts over treatment that sometimes arise between parents and physicians. Without a committee, such conflicts can lead to mutual distrust, power plays, and treatment decisions that may or may not be governed by an objective determination of an infant's best interests. With a committee, especially when parental interests are represented, there is a disinterested party that can discuss the infant's best interests in a context of neutrality between the parents and the attending physician.

Third, such a committee can safeguard an anomalous infant in cases where parents and the attending physician agree on a course of action that is contrary to the infant's best interests. If the committee is called into session by someone other than the attending physician (e.g., by the head neonatologist responding to a report from a nurse or social worker), a selective nontreatment decision by parents and physician can be overruled and the child transferred to another neonatologist's care.

Fourth, depending on the composition of the committee, an NICU committee is likely to be more capable of addressing the ethical aspects of cases than are parents and physicians functioning in relative isolation. Especially if there is a trained ethicist as a regular committee member (not a mere token), this group has the possibility of applying ethical criteria to particular cases and engaging in consistent moral reasoning from case to case.

Of course the use of NICU committees is not without problems. Particularly if the committee moves beyond an advisory role, two or three problems arise. One has to do with logistics and timing. Decisions about treatment in neonatal cases are often made rapidly, in response to a crisis situation with a patient. Even decisions about life-prolonging treatment must frequently be made with dispatch, with a delay in deciding about treatment possibly causing deterioration in a patient's medical condition. Consequently, NICU committees necessarily function in a different manner from committees in other institutional settings. Committee meetings are called as cases and circumstances warrant, and committee members must be ready to make life-or-death decisions in a short period of time. In the relatively few hospitals having these committees, such a procedure seems to work rather smoothly because committee members understand the time constraints involved in the process. However, on occasions when key committee members cannot make meetings, the group decision-making process loses needed expertise and some of its advantages as a proxy decision maker.

A second problem has to do with the mechanics of committee work. Committees are cumbersome ways to make decisions, often frustratingly indecisive, and occasionally simply inept. Assertive, outspoken individuals sometimes dominate committee meetings. Other individuals arrive late or leave meetings early, thus causing needless confusion.

Moreover, it is always possible that the compromises brought about by the group process result in a group decision with which no committee member personally and whole-heartedly agrees. For NICU committees, these inherent difficulties of the committee process can mean failure to meet the criteria for a proxy decision maker. Whether an NICU committee succeeds in being well informed, impartial, and consistent largely depends on the committee's chairperson and the belief by committee members that at least in borderline cases the advantages of the group process outweigh its mechanical difficulties.

In addition to these formal problems, another kind of problem is the reason that some physicians and ethicists reject the alternative of an NICU committee. Simply put, no matter how such a committee is composed or how efficiently it works, any committee placed in an advisory or decision-making role necessarily means a reduction of parental autonomy and physician discretion in neonatal cases. Thus, even if an NICU committee is used only in restricted circumstances, it is open to criticism from persons who seriously believe that the only appropriate decision makers are parents and/or physicians involved in the particular cases in question. By its very nature, an NICU committee is relatively remote from the emotional aspects of cases. Consequently, at least some committee members may never have to deal directly with the parents or infant in a case, and most of the committee members are insulated from the consequences of their group decision. A preferable alternative, for critics of hospital committees, is to have the persons most intimately connected with cases make the decisions that affect not only the child but themselves as well.

Courts

The need for a disinterested party as a proxy decision maker has already led to the involvement of the courts in some neonatal cases. . . .

Few parents or physicians favor turning selective nontreatment decisions over to the courts. For parents, the use of the courts as a proxy means the likelihood of courts-mandated treatment contrary to parental desires. For physicians, the prospect of judicial involvement in neonatal cases means unnecessary legal intrusion into medical matters. Of the physicians, only Norman Fost and Everett Koop give any indication of a possibly appropriate role for courts in some neonatal cases. For ethicists also, there is a dis-inclination to turn to courts to make decisions that can and usually should be made in nonlegal settings.

Among attorneys, of course, there is greater acceptance of courts as proxies. Robert Burt, Dennis Horan, and John Robertson all indicate a willingness to allow courts to protect the best interests of birth-defective newborns and to prosecute parents who jeopardize the lives of their anomalous children by withholding treatment. Paul Freund agrees. Writing in response to the Johns Hopkins case, he argues that neither parents nor physicians are the most appropriate decision makers. Rather, he says that the only way of protecting a defective newborn's best interests is through a disinterested tribunal: "Resort to a court is indicated, not because lawyers and judges have expertise in mongoloidism, which indeed they do not have, but because there all interests can be caught up and valued, and there a guardian *ad litem* for the child can be appointed as spokesman for the child's needs and claims."[10]

In several respects courts share the same strengths and weaknesses as hospital committees functioning as proxies. At least in theory, courts provide an opportunity for disinterested, dispassionate, and consistent reasoning from case to case. They also have the means to ensure that relevant knowledge, information, and opposing points of view are presented for consideration in a public forum. However, they obviously reduce parental autonomy and medical discretion in making treatment decisions, and sometimes cause formidable problems in terms of logistics and timing.

In addition, courts have strengths and weaknesses as proxies that distinguish them from hospital committees. When judges function as proxy decision makers, they have an unparalleled ability to marshal all of the pertinent facts in a case by summoning witnesses, questioning knowledgeable experts, and investigating the merits of several alternative courses of action. Judges also are able, as Freund points out, to appoint a guardian *ad litem* for the purpose of being an advocate of an incompetent patient's best interests. In these ways at least, courts represent a distinctive — and occasionally necessary — proxy in arriving at treatment decisions that are in the best interests of birth-defective newborns.

Even when considered as a proxy of last resort, however, courts have two weaknesses. The first weakness has to do with place. By not being on the scene in the NICU, and having no personal contact with the case under consideration, judges are more remote than other possible proxies. Of course remoteness may lead to greater objectivity, but it may also lead to less sensitivity for and empathy with the persons directly involved in an emotionally difficult case. The second weakness has to do with judges as individuals. In theory, all judges in all legal jurisdictions provide the same opportunity for an objective hearing of cases. In fact, however, the functioning of judges as proxies in neonatal cases sometimes depends on the personal views of the judges. For instance, in cases involving neonates with Down's syndrome complicated by esophageal or duodenal atresia, some judges in some jurisdictions are reluctant to override parental autonomy — and other judges in other jurisdictions override parental autonomy in such cases simply on the basis of a telephoned request from the attending pediatrician.

Figure 8.1   Serial Ordering of Decision Makers

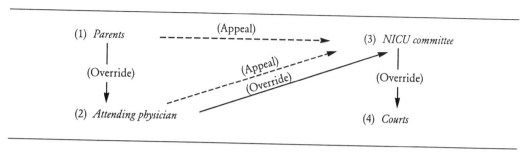

A Serial Ordering of Decision Makers

Because each of these possible proxies is limited in important ways, it is preferable not to regard any of them as the best proxy for all neonatal cases. Instead, as James Childress observes, a serial or sequential ordering of decision makers is preferable for determining the best interests of neonatal patients.[11] By incorporating each of the possible proxies into a sequential decision-making process, and by restricting the circumstances in which these possible proxies can actually function as decision makers for incompetent patients, the best interests of defective newborns are more adequately served and protected than if any of the alternative decision makers is permitted to make unilateral decisions about life-prolonging treatment in all neonatal cases. The use of a sequential arrangement of decision makers also incorporates the possibilities of (a) appeals to a "higher" proxy and (b) overriding the decision of a "lower" proxy when circumstances merit. Represented as a flowchart, this serial ordering of decision makers can and should work in the [manner represented in Figure 8.1].

Parents of defective newborns are the primary decision makers in this serial ordering of proxies. Because of the importance of parental autonomy, decisions about medical treatment for anomalous neonates should not arbitrarily be taken away from parents. When parents are adequately informed by the attending physician regarding the diagnosis and prognosis for their child, they are often capable of making informed decisions that the physician can accept as being medically and morally correct. Moreover, in spite of the emotional stress inherent to these situations, at least parents in less difficult cases are often sufficiently stable emotionally to make decisions that are clearly in the infant's best interests.

However, parents have only a defeasible right to make decisions about treatment or nontreatment. There are at least three circumstances in which parents should not have the final word in such decisions: when they simply cannot understand the relevant medical facts of a case, when they are emotionally unstable, and when they appear to put their own interests before those of the defective newborn. Each of these circumstances happens with some regularity in NICUs. In any such situation, physicians involved in the case — and especially the attending physician — should override parental autonomy to protect the best interests of the child. No birth-defective newborn should be left to die untreated because of the desires or discretion of parents, especially when there appears to be a conflict of interest between the parents and the child.

As previously noted, physicians are sometimes better qualified to be proxies than parents are. Because of their technical knowledge, greater objectivity, and professional involvement with numerous birth-defective newborns, physicians are often capable of determining when parental decisions are contrary to the best interests of anomalous neonates. For instance, when parents refuse to consent to recommended treatment that the neonatologist believes will restore an infant to consciousness, or correct an anomalous condition the infant has, or extend and enhance the infant's life for a significant period of time, there is sufficient reason to think that these particular parents are ill-suited to be proxy decision makers. Given their role as patient advocates, neonatologists in such situations have two appropriate courses of action. They may, in reasonably clear-cut cases, simply override the parents' wishes and provide the necessary treatment. Or in borderline cases, they may choose to override the parents' wishes by referring the cases to the collective wisdom represented by an NICU committee.

There are limits, however, to an attending physician's right to override parental discretion and assume the responsibilities of proxy decision maker. The physician's right to decide, like that of parents, is defeasible. If it appears (to the parents, other physicians, nurses, or social workers) that an attending physician in a case is pursuing interests other than those of the neonatal patient, either the physician should be removed from the case by the head neonatologist, or the major decisions regarding treatment in the case should be turned over to an NICU committee. No birth-defective newborn should be harmed through overtreatment or undertreatment merely because of misplaced respect for medical discretion, especially when there is the possibility of a conflict between the newborn's interests and the physician's research interests.

The NICU committee is the focal point of a serial ordering of decision makers, because it more nearly meets the criteria for proxies in neonatal cases. In hospitals having these specialized committees for neonatal cases (as opposed to hospital ethics committees handling cases from numerous clinical areas), it is possible to arrive at a group consensus regarding the appropriate course of action in at least four different kinds of situations: (1) when there is serious disagreement between parents and the attending physician regarding treatment options; (2) when a newborn has one or more congenital anomalies that place the infant in a treatable diagnostic category, but parents and attending physician have agreed not to provide the necessary treatment; (3) when the major treatment decision in a borderline case hangs on the obligatory/optional distinction, and the attending physician is uncertain on how to make the close call; and (4) in the unlikely event that the attending physician in a particular case thinks that an untreatable, suffering infant should be intentionally killed.

Depending on which of these kinds of situations arises, an NICU committee performs three functions. In situations involving conflict between parents and the attending physician, the committee functions as an in-house appeals board. As such, it may act on an appeal coming from either the parents or the attending physician. In situations in which parents and the physician have agreed on action contrary to an infant's best interests, the committee functions as an institutional check on such abusive practices. Obviously not responding to an appeal from either parents or physician, the committee may carry out this second function on the basis of a report from a concerned nurse or social worker. In the third and fourth kinds of situations, the committee functions primarily as an advisory board for a physician trying to make a tough decision. In addition, however, the committee may represent a procedural safeguard in these situations against the possibly abusive practices of individual physicians.

Courts represent a last-resort proxy that is needed infrequently. In the majority of cases, the responsibilities of proxy decision making are adequately handled by parents or physicians or NICU committees. Even cases requiring adjudication can usually — and preferably — be handled on the hospital scene by NICU committees. However, in rare instances, a judge must override the decision of another proxy when he or she is convinced by the evidence that a particular infant's interests are not being served. Acting on the basis of a report by a concerned nurse or social worker, a judge in such instances may need to have a custody hearing or possibly consider criminal proceedings against parents and/or physicians who are acting contrary to the law. A well-balanced, effectively working NICU committee usually makes such criminal proceedings unnecessary because few physicians (because of peer pressure and administrative pressure) go counter to the recommendations of such committees. . . .

Notes

1. Peter Rothstein, "Psychological Stress in Families of Children in a Pediatric Intensive Care Unit," *Pediatric Clinics of North America* 27 (1980):613–20.

2. Anthony Shaw, Judson G. Randolph, and Barbara Manard, "Ethical Issues in Pediatric Surgery: A National Survey of Pediatricians and Pediatric Surgeons," *Pediatrics* 60 (October 1977): 588.

3. The Judicial Council, *Current Opinions of the Judicial Council of the American Medical Association* (Chicago: American Medical Association, 1982), p. 9.

4. President's Commission for the Study of Ethical Problems in Medicine and Biomed-

ical and Behavioral Research, *Deciding to Forgo Life-Sustaining Treatment* (Washington, D.C.: U.S. Government Printing Office, 1983), pp. 6–8, 197–229.

5. See Richard A. McCormick, S.J., and Robert Veatch, "The Prolongation of Life and Self-Determination," *Theological Studies* 41 (1980): 390–96; and Warren T. Reich and David E. Ost, "Public Policy and Procedural Questions," in Warren T. Reich, editor-in-chief, *Encyclopedia of Bioethics* (New York: The Free Press, 1978), pp. 735–40.

6. McCormick and Veatch, "Prolongation of Life," p. 396.

7. Strong, "Decision Making in the NICU." [Carson Strong, "Decision Making in the NICU: The Neonatologist as Patient Ad-

vocate," *Hasting Centre Report* (forthcoming).]

8. See Rosalyn Benjamin Darling, "Parents, Physicians, and Spina Bifida," *Hastings Center Report* 7 (August 1977): 10–14.

9. John A. Robertson and Norman Fost, "Passive Euthanasia of Defective Newborn Infants: Legal Considerations." *Journal of Pediatrics* 88 (1976): 887.

10. Paul A. Freund, "Mongoloids and 'Mercy Killing,'" in Stanley Joel Reiser, Arthur J. Dyck, and William J. Curran, eds., *Ethics in Medicine* (Cambridge, Mass.: The MIT Press, 1977), p. 538.

11. James F. Childress, *Who Should Decide?* (New York and Oxford: Oxford University Press, 1982), pp. 172–74.

31   Physicians' Refusal of Requested Treatment: The Case of Baby L

John J. Paris, Robert K. Crone & Frank Reardon

. . . The patient, a two-year-old girl, was born at 36 weeks, weighing 1970 g, to a 33-year-old mother who had been pregnant three times before and had given birth to three live infants. The pregnancy was complicated by fetal hydronephrosis and oligohydramnios in the last trimester. Decelerations in the fetal heart rate and thick meconium below the vocal cords were noted at delivery. Apgar scores were 1 at 1 minute, 4 at 5 minutes, and 5 at 10 minutes. The infant was resuscitated, stabilized, and weaned from mechanical ventilation. Over a period of weeks the infant's respiratory function improved, but the neurologic condition remained very depressed, with no responsiveness except to pain.

The infant underwent a gastrostomy at the age of one month, a Nissen fundoplication at four months, and a tracheostomy at seven months. There were intermittent episodes of aspiration and uncontrolled seizures. She was discharged after 14 months with 24-hour nursing care, but was readmitted within two weeks for recurrent pneumonia.

During the next several months she was repeatedly hospitalized for pneumonia and septic shock. At the age of 23 months the child — having been readmitted with worsening pneumonia and sepsis — required mechanical ventilation and cardiovascular support. During those 23 months of recurrent pneumonia and four cardiopulmonary arrests, the mother had continued to demand that everything possible be done to ensure the child's survival.

A meeting of the chiefs of service, primary care physicians, nurses, hospital counsel, and chairpersons of the institutional ethics committee was convened to discuss the advisability of reinstituting mechanical ventilation and cardiovascular support. Given a child with such extensive neurology deficits that she could experience only pain, they agreed unanimously that further medical intervention was not in the best interests of the patient. In their opinion, further intervention would subject the child to additional pain without affecting the underlying condition or ultimate outcome. The child's mother rejected that opinion.

The child was stabilized without mechanical ventilation while the hospital staff sought a facility willing to abide by the mother's decisions on treatment; in the meantime, she contacted an attorney who arranged a hearing in probate court. Before the hearing took place, the institutional ethics committee met to discuss the issue further. One member argued that the slight possibility of recovery to base-line status justified mechanical ventilation. The others were convinced that reinstituting mechanical ventilation would be inhumane.

The issue before the court was what should be done when a parent demands treatment that the physician and other care givers believe to be against the best interests of the child. The judge, indicating a willingness to accede to the mother's request, asked the attorney representing the physicians and the hospital what they would do if the court issued an order for mechanical ventilation. He replied that since the physicians and hospital believed it would violate their ethical obligation to the patient, they would decline to participate in such an action.

The court appointed a guardian ad litem for the child. The guardian asked a pediatric neurologist from another institution to assess the patient's condition and make recommendations about care. It was the consultant's opinion that the patient was severely ill, that she was capable of experiencing pain, and that it was questionable whether she would survive, even with mechanical ventilation. Since the consultant was willing to do everything possible to accommodate the parental wishes, the child was transferred to her care. With that transfer the legal dispute was rendered moot. (Baby L survived the episode. Two years later she remains blind, deaf, and quadriplegic and is fed through the gastrostomy. She averages a seizure a day. Her pulmonary status has improved, but she continues to require intensive home nursing 16 hours a day. Her mental status remains that of a three-month-old infant.)

Discussion

To our knowledge, the medical team's action marks the first time that physicians — even in the face of judicial intervention — have denied a request for potentially life-prolonging medical treatment for a patient in acute crisis. The refusal was based on the team's assessment that unless a reversal or amelioration of the underlying condition could be expected, painful interventions would be futile and inhumane.

The refusal raised the issue of the patient-physician relationship, described by Ingelfinger[1] as one in which patients go to doctors because they think they need help, and physicians with their training and expertise asses the situation and determine whether their skills can be useful. At that point an ethical juncture is met. According to Ingelfinger, "a physician who merely spreads an array of vendibles in front of the patient [or family] and then says, 'Go ahead and choose, it's your life,' is guilty of shirking his duty, if not of malpractice."

It is the physician, not the patient, who must sort out the possibilities, weigh the pros and cons, and recommend a course of action. That responsibility should not be shifted onto the shoulders of the patient in a misguided attempt to respect autonomy. The patient or family can of course accept or reject the physician's recommendation. They are not free, however, to design their own treatment; nor is the physician bound to provide it.

Over the past decade Ingelfinger's perspective has been overshadowed by that of physicians who ask, "What do you want?" Patients and families increasingly reply, "Do everything possible." In an article on medical futility, Lantos and colleagues[2] seem to support that perspective. They insist that even if a physician believes that a therapy will not be beneficial or that the chance of success is low, when the alternative is death, the presumption should favor a request for treatment. For Lantos et al., the goals of the patient and the family, not the physician's assessment of the efficacy of treatment, determine medical futility and thus control decision making.

Moore[3] takes, as we do, a different position. He challenges the validity of instituting "desperate remedies for desperate patients, desperately hopeless from the outset." For him, such patients must be offered more than pain, suffering, and costs: the use of the procedure must be justified by a realistic expectation of prolonged benefit. This demand for appropriate restraint by the physician — even in the face of earnest pleas from the families of desperately ill patients — is echoed in a recent editorial in the

Journal of Pediatrics in which Garfunkel and Denny[4] warn that "the time may be past for beginning to make the hard choices these questions pose."

A balanced approach to such hard choices is found in the report of the President's Commission for the Study of Ethical Problems in Medicine and Biomedical and Behavioral Research.[5] There we read:

> Although competent patients . . . have the legal and ethical authority to forego some or all care, this does not mean that patients may insist on particular treatments. The care available from health care professionals is generally limited to what is consistent with role-related professional standards and conscientiously held beliefs.

The commission also addressed the standard of "best interest" and concluded that the factors to be considered in protecting the welfare of patients who cannot speak for themselves are "the relief of suffering, the preservation or restoration of functioning, and the quality as well as the extent of life sustained." For infants or those with compromised consciousness, the commission added a concern for "the possibility of developing or regaining the capacity for self-determination."

The emphasis is on the physician's reasonable medical judgment. In the case we have described, the medical team believed that Baby L's condition had deteriorated to the point where further treatment would be futile and its imposition inhumane. The mother's wishes did not alter that judgment, nor did they absolve the medical team of its ethical obligations to the patient. Consequently, the team refused the requested treatment.

Here the team was following Thurow's exhortation that physicians must learn to say no.[6] The team did so not — as in Thurow's essay — because of economic consideration (Baby L's medical expenses, although well in excess of a million dollars, were covered by third-party payment), but because in its judgment aggressive interventions in a patient in Baby L's condition would be bad medicine. . . .

A Note of Caution

The issues raised in overriding a family's request for potentially life-saving treatment are complex and difficult. They ought to remain difficult. It is only with the greatest of caution that physicians should consider overturning the presumption for treatment and respect for the family's wishes. The potential for abuse demands that safeguards be designed to ensure that decisions are openly made, principled, and focused on the best interests of the patient. The minimal requirements should include agreement among health care workers, the concurrence of an ethics committee, openness to a second opinion, and a comprehensive note in the patient's chart detailing all the factors considered in the decision.

Conclusion

The case of Baby L was an unprecedented challenge to the medical team and the hospital: a parent's request for aggressive life-prolonging treatment that the staff believed to be futile and inhumane. In refusing the request, the medical team and the hospital declined to violate their professional commitment to their patient. The court acknowledged that no physician or institution can be required to provide an intervention contrary to conscience. The subsequent willingness of another physician to care for the infant as the parent wished does not alter the moral or legal status of the medical team's refusal. The primary obligation of health care providers remains "Do no harm."

Acknowledgements: We are indebted to Dr. David Nathan, physician-in-chief of Children's Hospital, Boston, for his support in the preparation of this paper.

References

1. Ingelfinger FJ. Arrogance. N Engl J Med 1980; 303:1507–11.
2. Lantos JD, Singer PA, Walker RM, et al. The illusion of futility in clinical practice. Am J Med 1989; 87:81–4.
3. Moore FD. The desperate case: CARE (costs, applicability, research, ethics). JAMA 1989; 261:1483–4.
4. Garfunkel JM, Denny FW Jr. Priorities for the use of finite resources: now may be the time to choose. J Pediatr 1989; 115:410–1.
5. President's Commission for the Study of Ethical Problems in Medicine and Biomedical and Behavioral Research. Deciding to forego life-sustaining treatment: a report on the ethical, medical, and legal issues in treatment decisions. Washington, D.C.: Government Printing Office. 1983.
6. Thurow LC. Learning to say "no." N Engl J Med 1984; 311:1569–72.

32   The Role of Intimate Others in Medical Decision Making

Nancy S. Jecker

Individual autonomy has been a fulcrum of bioethical debate since the 1950s and 1960s, and a guiding idea behind a diverse body of bioethics literature. Dominant ideas such as individual autonomy pose the risk of creating conventional categories of thought to which society becomes wedded. Such categories may ignore central aspects of moral experience, thereby fostering illusions that become difficult to dispel. Intimate associations are one domain of moral experience that may elude the world of value delimited by a traditional autonomy model. . . .

. . . The term autonomy entered moral philosophy in the 18th century (Schneewind, 1986), when Kant interpreted it to mean individuals' ability to be governed by moral laws that they themselves author. Inspired in part by feminist thinkers (Gilligan, 1982; Gilligan, Ward, & Taylor, 1989), Blum, Ruddick, and other philosophers (Kittay & Meyers, 1987; Graham & LaFollete, 1989; Pearsall, 1986; Meyers, Murphy, & Kipnis, 1993) now object to what they see as a growing tendency for contemporary theories to be dominated by abstract principles that view autonomous individuals as separate from all of their essential moral relationships. In particular, these critics charge that current theories downplay the significance of special moral relationships, such as friends and family.

Building on this work, this analysis focuses on intimate relations, examining the connection between intimacy and autonomy, with an eye to orchestrating these diverse elements. Specifically, this study shows (1) how the present emphasis on patient autonomy overlooks ways in which intimate relations enable autonomy to function meaningfully; (2) how traditional categories of *competent* and *incompetent* discount intimacy as a tool for accessing patients' subjective experiences; and (3) how intimate associations mark moral boundaries for autonomy because they constitute a setting in which persons give and expend finite human resources. The primary focus is on the role of adult children in decisions affecting elderly parents. Although the implications of this discussion are noteworthy for other forms of intimate associations with patients, they are beyond the scope of this project.

Attending to Context

A distinguishing feature of doctor–geriatric patient relations is that often an adult child or spouse shepherds the geriatric patient to hospital visits. Adelman, Green, & Charon (1987) note that relatives accompany geriatric patients to outpatient visits in 20% of cases at a major urban teaching hospital. Whereas other patient groups such as pediatrics and obstetrics may be joined by third parties, when a third party attends an internal medicine consultation, the patient is generally elderly. Studies also document that adult children frequently are actively involved in home health care and are otherwise assisting and caring for elderly parents (Shanas, 1979; Cicirelli, 1983).

Likewise, family members frequently affect inpatient care for elderly patients in significant ways. For example, I recently observed a patient management conference discussing 14 patients on a geriatric ward of a major university hospital; for 13 patients, family members were mentioned. Their role was most frequently discussed in regard to patient discharge (10 cases) and often had a direct or indirect impact on medical treatment decisions (five cases). Less frequently, the role of the family came up in discussing how to resolve in-hospital patient management problems, such as feeding (two cases), general patient morale problems (one case), and financial difficulties (one case).

The lives of family members themselves are affected profoundly by elderly ill relatives. As Livingston (1987) observes, caring for a sick family member can be a career in itself; illness can mean an added financial strain and may force a change in housing or life style; and, in diseases carrying a stigma, the stigma often attaches to family members as well as patients. Moreover, relatives may react to a patient's illness by developing their own psychopathologies. For example, in stroke, a condition more common among older age groups, 62% of spouses have a high likelihood of significant disturbance in their adjustment to stressful circumstances, ability to cope, general physiological condition, moods, and social functioning (Livingston, 1987). Relatives of patients with myocardial infarction also evidence functional disabilities (Kay, 1982). And, upon learning of a family member's diagnosis of a cancer that threatens survival, one individual reported, "It seemed easier to face death for oneself than to watch someone else . . ." (Anonymous, 1983).

Although a number of studies attest to the fact that adult children perceive themselves to be obligated to meet needs of aging parents (Cicirelli, 1983; Stroller, 1983), this is not always the case. Children may lack the interest or skill to be active players in parents' health care. Overwhelmed by its demands, they may reject filial responsibility altogether (Callahan, 1988); they may form coalitions with health professionals that ignore or discount aging parents (Adelman, Greene, & Charon, 1987; Roscowe, 1981); they may push for overtreatment of relatives out of guilt or insist on undertreatment to escape onerous financial or emotional burdens. In many cases, however, a presumption that family members are good-intentioned and competent is appropriate. In such cases, interpreting their preferences as emotionally maladjusted may be patronizing or cruel (Miles, 1987).

Given the pivotal role family members often play in medical care of geriatric patients, we would do well to review the dynamics of their filial relationships, especially the parent-child relationship. In the past, parents did not live long enough to see offspring enter old age. Today, however, those over the age of 75 are the fastest growing age group in the country, and they have adult children in the 55- to 70-year-old age range. Thus, the dramatic gains in average lifespan in this century have not only brought about an aging society, but also have transformed relationships between parents and children in later life. For the first time, these relationships involve elderly persons at both ends. . . .

. . . An adult son or daughter often will be in a position to bridge communication gaps between parents and health professionals, facilitate exchange of information, convey explanations parents will understand, negotiate treatment decisions, and offer emotional support in dealing with medical problems, treatments, and consequences (Roscowe, 1981). Therefore, incorporating offspring into the decision process often will be justified on the grounds that doing so enhances the patient's own decisional abilities.

Even a well-educated, articulate, and fearless patient stands to benefit from a family facilitator. As Brody (1978) notes, the family is the forum in which the process of "trying on" and "bouncing off" ideas typically occurs: a patient "cannot know what values she holds until she goes through a process of 'trying on' various value stances and 'bouncing them off' others whose opinions and reactions she cares about. . . . Values . . . emerge from the dialogue process . . ." (Brody, 1978).

Rhoden (1988) agrees:

> The family is the context within which a person first develops her powers of autonomous choice, and the values she brings to these choices spring from, and are intertwined with, the family's values. A parent may understand the child's values because she helped to form them, a child may grasp a parent's values because the parent imparted them to her, and a couple may have developed and refined their views in tandem (pp. 438–439).

Gadow (1980) refers to this kind of facilitation and dialogue as "existential advocacy." She describes it as the effort to help persons become clear about what they want to do by helping them discern their values in a situation and, on the basis of self-examination, reach decisions. Such decisions express a reaffirmed, perhaps recreated, complex of values. Only through dialogue, when persons are engaged and their values expressed and responded to, can decisions possibly be *self*-determined.

These thoughts ring true. Surely, shaping moral goals is no easy task. It is not a task many execute confidently or successfully alone.

Intimacy and Access

Let us next consider the role of adult children whose parents are deemed incompetent to make autonomous health care decisions and have provided neither a clear indication of their wishes, such as a living will, nor a clear delegation of decision-making authority, such as a durable power of attorney.

According to the traditional framework concerning surrogate decision making, individuals are judged incompetent if they lack the capacity to give informed consent to medical treatment. In such cases, someone other than the patient chooses the best course of action. Surrogates employ different standards for making this determination. According to a standard of substitute judgment, surrogates strive to speak for the patient by making the choice that the patient would make under the circumstances. Alternatively, where the patient's preferences cannot be ascertained, a choice is based on a best interests standard. Unlike the substitute judgment standard, a best interests model does not depend on what the patient would want, but on an allegedly objective weighing of the burdens and benefits associated with various treatment options.

The framework for considering these issues already casts them in terms of bipolar categories. On the one hand, the patient is either competent or not: either the patient possesses a capacity to form autonomous choices or the patient's authority is transferred to others who do. On the other hand, either others can uncover evidence of the patient's wishes or else efforts to gather evidence are abandoned and judgment is grounded in objective standards.

It is the very clarity of this framework that renders it problematic. By ignoring a significant gray area, which might be termed "marginal competence" (Waymack & Taler, 1988), this bipolar framework discounts the realities of both patients' and families' experiences. In this uncertain space, patients may be formally judged incompetent, yet able to collaborate with intimate others to construct choices consonant with their experience. Likewise, intimate family members may be unable to furnish objective proof of patients' wishes, yet may have access to a rich and detailed knowledge base from which they can build a sense of what constitutes harm or benefit to the patient.

One example of this is a daughter who serves as caregiver for a frail elderly parent. She may be able to look beneath the disoriented conduct and broken phrases to construe or help create some semblance of what the parent values. Evidence is gleaned through partaking in daily rituals with the parent, such as bathing and feeding, and interpreting the parent's responses. Just as a parent comes to know an infant by observing the infant's posture, sounds, eye movements, and facial grimaces, a daughter may gain knowledge about the elderly parent by engaging in sustained, physical nurturing. Through intimate engagement, the caregiver deciphers what the parent holds dear, what counts as pain and comfort, or boredom and interest, to the parent. Her knowledge may be largely "an intuitive, nonverbal sort that is difficult to translate into clear proof" (Rhoden, 1988, p. 392).

These ways of knowing catalyze moral problems for a more traditional model, because they vest those who hold such knowledge with responsibilities that a traditional model denies or even obstructs. The tendency to discount subjective awareness of patients' wishes and defer to a best interests standard is one example of such a problem. According to one group of commentators, few elderly patients have documented or made known their wishes concerning aggressive medical care, for example, by signing living wills or designating a durable power of attorney. "Nor can we easily infer from 'lifestyle' or vaguely expressed 'values' of the patient an acceptable course of action." The upshot is that "in most cases the only appropriate standard will be one that focuses attention on the (objective) best interests of the patient" (Sherlock & Dingus, 1985, pp. 123–124). Thus, the absence of clear proof about patients' preferences, inclines these authors to defer to a more objective measure. Yet this approach effectively dismantles any effort to locate remnants of patients' values through intimate contacts and piece them into meaningful patterns. The result is that, lacking the patient who speaks clearly or leaves trails of objective evidence, the patient as person eludes us.

An alternative approach, that heeds a subjective knowledge base, would grant to families surrogate authority for their incompetent members, or would grant a rebuttle presumption in favor of family authority. As Rhoden (1988) notes, rather than creating a presumption where none exists, this approach simply replaces a present presumption with a more appropriate one:

Courts have adopted medicine's strong presumption for treatment and required that patients overcome it. . . . Judicial acceptance of this presumption silently incorporates the insidious notion that the doctor is rightfully in charge, authorized to treat without consent unless the family can persuade a court otherwise (p. 379).

More explicitly, the ethical considerations that support family authority in decisions for incompetent patients begin with the observation that the familiar categories of competent and incompetent camouflage a realm of patients' subjective experience. If this lived world can be understood, it provides important information for determining what forms of treatment are respectful of or consonant with patients' values. The argument proceeds with the claim that intimacy and patient contact provide a foothold for accessing the subjective experiences of incompetent patients. Moreover, families are a common locus for intimate relations. If so, then family members are prima facie entitled to make surrogate decisions for incompetent members.

This prima facie entitlement might be thought of as following from the family's more general right to privacy. Schoeman (1980), for example, maintains that families possess a right to privacy that holds against society at large and entitles members to exclude others from scrutinizing obtrusions into family occurrences. Thinking of families as possessing a right to privacy or autonomy serves multiple purposes: it safeguards an intimate sphere from third-party intrusions; it enables an intimate group to foster meaningful autonomy for members; and, in the case of vulnerable or compromised persons, it secures protection from decisions by third parties, such as courts, which are inclined to discount the patient's lived world and defer to objective standards.

In response, it might be argued that family members may harbor negative feelings or be emotionally distraught in other ways that color their assessment of treatment options. Such feelings may well hinder thoughtful decision making. Correspondingly, simply being a patient's relative does not guarantee feelings of love and care toward the patient. If not guaranteed, and if these feelings are the grounds for attributing surrogate authority to families, then the grounds for attributing it are undercut.

In reply to these objections it can be said that neither point buttresses the argument for family autonomy. The argument I am defending is not premised on the assumption that family members possess capacities to make disinterested decisions or display purely positive feelings toward patients. To see that this is so, consider the more familiar case of *individual* autonomy. Autonomy entitles individuals to make decisions affecting them, despite the fact that they are immersed in, rather than distanced from, such decisions. Moreover, individuals' autonomy is not legitimately taken away even when their self-love founders. In a similar vein, the family's right to have a hand in health care decisions for incompetent patients is not contingent on objectivity or untainted love toward patients.

Rather, it is the very absence of distance and objectivity that justifies the claim to be surrogate decision makers. Even when family members' love is coupled with feelings of jealousy, envy, and spite, family autonomy does not fall by the wayside. Clearly, this does not mean that families are entitled to use members to vent hostile feelings or that family autonomy should go unchecked. Rather, it implies that filial relations carry moral force even if they are not made in heaven (which they never are).

But what if intimacy is absent in parent–child relationships altogether? Or what if a patient has a close family but finds his or her most intimate contacts outside it? For example, intimacy may be most potent in a friendship or with an unmarried partner. Alternatively, it may be felt most strongly in the daily care a nurse or therapist gives. Rather than challenging intimacy as a basis for surrogate authority, this objection challenges the contention that families are the locus of intimacy.

One important response to this objection is to acknowledge that intimacy, not filial status, is what ultimately provides the moral basis for surrogate authority. This is why the presumption in favor of family authority is presumptive *only*. To justify even a rebuttable presumption, however, we need to recognize how unlikely it is that the state or others will be able to start with no presumptions and go on to make an appropriate determination of where the patient's intimate contacts lie.

Another way of meeting this objection is to broaden the concept of the family to include less traditional associations. For example, New York's highest court recently expanded the definition of *family* as it applies to rent control laws to include "adults who show long-term financial and emotional commitment to each other even if they don't fit the traditional meaning of a family" (Gutis, 1989). The court majority reasoned that a definition of family "should not rest on fictitious legal distinctions or genetic history, but instead should find its foundation in the reality of family life . . . a more realistic and certainly equally valid view of a family includes (persons) whose relationship is long-term and characterized by interdependence." The court's approach thus defies simple formulas and requires considering the "totality of the relationship as evidenced by the dedication, caring and self-sacrifice of the parties" (Gutis, 1989, pp. 1, 12).

Defining *family* in this way avoids the objection noted earlier to granting surrogate authority to families. Admittedly, it may pose other problems, such as the possibility of power struggles between traditional and nontraditional family members. But such conflicts can occur even among members related by blood or marriage. With this emendation, then, a *rebuttable* presumption in favor of family authority emerges as the best means for accomplishing informed surrogate decisions and safeguarding family autonomy. . . .

References

Adelman, R.D., Greene, M.G., & Charon, R. (1987). The physician–elderly patient–companion triad in the medical encounter. *The Gerontologist, 27,* 729–734.

Anonymous. (1983). Cancer care: The relative's view. *Lancet, 3,* 1188.

Areen, J. (1987). The legal status of consent obtained from families of adult patients to withhold or withdraw treatment. *Journal of the American Medical Association, 258,* 229–235.

Blum, L. (1980). *Friendship, altruism, and morality.* London: Routledge and Kegan Paul.

Blum, L. (1987). Particularity and responsiveness. In J. Kagan & S. Lamb (Eds.), *The emergence of morality in young children.* Chicago: University of Chicago.

Brody, H. (1978). The role of the family in medical decisions. *Theoretical Medicine, 8,* 253–257.

Burt, R. (1979). *Taking care of strangers.* New York: Free Press.

Callahan, D. (1988). Families as caregivers: The limits of morality. *Archives of Physical Medical Rehabilitation, 69,* 323–328.

Cicirelli, V.C. (1983). Adult children and their elderly parents. In T.H. Brubaker (Ed.), *Family relationships in later life.* Beverly Hills: Sage.

Evans, R.W. (1983). Health care technology and the inevitability of resource allocation and rationing decisions 1. *Journal of the American Medical Association, 249,* 2047–2053.

Fuchs, V.R. (1984). The "rationing" of medical care. *New England Journal of Medicine, 311,* 1572–1573.

Gadow, S. (1980). Existential advocacy: Philosophical foundation in nursing. In S.F. Spicker & S. Gadow (Eds.), *Nursing images and ideals* (pp. 79–101). New York: Springer.

Gilligan, C. (1982). *In a different voice.* Cambridge: Harvard University.

Gilligan, C. (1986). Remapping the moral domain. In T.C. Heller, M. Sosna, & D.E. Wellbery (Eds.), *Reconstructing individualism* (pp. 237–252). Stanford: Stanford University.

Gilligan, C., Ward, J.V., & Taylor, J.M. (Eds.) (1989). *Mapping the moral domain.* Cambridge: Harvard University.

Graham, G., & LaFollete, H. (Eds.) (1989). *Person to person.* Philadelphia: Temple University.

Gutis, P.S. (1989, July 7). Court widens family definition to gay couples living together. *New York Times,* pp. 1, 12.

Haber, P.A.L. (1986). Rationing is reality. *Journal of the American Geriatric Society, 34,* 761–763.

Hardin, G. (1983). Living on a lifeboat. In J. Narveson (Ed.), *Moral issues* (pp. 167–178). New York: Oxford University.

High, D.M., & Turner, H.B. (1987). Surrogate decision-making: The elderly's familial expectations. *Theoretical Medicine, 8,* 303–320.

Jecker, N.S. (in press). Impartiality and special relations. In D.T. Meyers, C. Murphy, & K. Kipnis (Eds.), *Kindred matters: Rethinking the philosophy of the family.* Lewiston, NY: Edwin Mellen Press.

Jecker, N.S. (1989a). Should we ration health care? *Journal of Medical Humanities and Bioethics, 10,* 77–90.

Jecker, N.S. (1989b). Are filal duties unfounded? *American Philosophical Quarterly, 26,* 73–80.

Jecker, N.S., & Pearlman, R.A. (1989). Ethical constraints on rationing medical care by age. *Journal of the American Geriatric Society, 37.*

Jonsen, A.R., Siegler, M., & Winslade, W.J. (1988). *Clinical ethics* (2nd ed.). New York: Macmillan.

Kay, E. (1982, February), United. *Hospital Update,* 161–170.

Kittay, E.F., & Meyers, D.T. (Eds.) (1987). *Women and moral theory.* Totowa, NJ: Rowman and Littlefield.

Livingston, M. (1987). How illness affects patients' families. *British Journal of Medicine, 38,* 51–53.

Lyons, N.P. (1983). Two perspectives: On self, relationships and morality. *Harvard Educational Review, 53,* 125–145.

Meyers, D., Murphy, C., & Kipnis, K. (Eds.) (1993). *Kindred matters: Rethinking the philosophy of the family.* Ithaca, New York: Cornell Univ. Press.

Miles, S.H. (1987). Futile feeding at the end of life: Family virtues and treatment decisions. *Theoretical Medicine, 8,* 293–302.

Pearsall, M. (Ed.) (1986). *Women and values.* Belmont, CA: Wadsworth.

President's Commission for the Study of Ethical Problems in Medicine and Biomedical and Behavioral Research (1982). *Making health care decisions.* Washington, DC: U.S. Government Printing Office.

Rhoden, N. (1988). Litigating life and death. *Harvard Law Review, 102,* 375–446.

Roscowe, I. (1981). Coalition in geriatric medicine. In M.R. Haug (Ed.), *Elderly patients and their doctors* (pp. 137–146). New York: Springer.

Ruddick, S. (1989). *Maternal thinking*. New York: Beacon Press.

Schneewind, J.B. (1986). The use of autonomy in ethical theory. In T.C. Heller, M. Sosna, & D.E. Wellbery (Eds.) *Reconstructing individualism* (pp. 64–75). Stanford: Stanford University.

Schoeman, F. (1980). Rights of children, rights of parents, and the moral basis of the family. *Ethics, 91*, 6–19.

Shanas, E. (1979). The family as a social support system in old age. *The Gerentologist, 19*, 169–178.

Sherlock, R., & Dingus, M. (1985). Families and the gravely ill: Roles, rules, and rights. *Journal of the American Geriatric Society, 33*, 121–124.

Siegler, M. (1982). Decision-making strategy for clinical ethical problems in medicine. *Archives of Internal Medicine, 142*, 2178–2179.

Stroller, E.P. (1983). Parental care-giving by adult children. *Journal of Marriage and Family, 45*, 851–858.

Thoreau, H.D. (1960). Walden. In S. Paul (Ed.) *Walden and civil disobedience* (pp. 1–227). Boston: Houghton, Miffin.

Waymack, M.H., & Taler, G.A. (1988). *Medical ethics and the elderly*. Chicago: Pluribus.

Yarborough, M. (1988). Continued treatment of the fatally ill for the benefit of others. *Journal of the American Geriatric Society, 36*, 63–67.

Chapter 8

Questions to Consider

1. The mother of a newborn with anencephaly (a serious congenital anomaly that results in absence of the upper brain, and is usually fatal within a few days) insists on aggressive treatment. The neonatologists believe that therapeutic efforts are futile and therefore unwarranted — no amount of treatment will change the outcome. Who decides and on what basis?

2. An elderly male patient has a brain hemorrhage, and surgery is urgently required if he is to have any chance at survival. His only living relative is an estranged son. The father and son have not spoken to each other in the last ten years. The son is contacted by the hospital and is asked whether or not to proceed with the surgery. The son says that he does not care what happens to his father; as far as he is concerned, his father is already dead. Who decides and on what basis?

3. What are the benefits of the reasonable patient standard for surrogate decision making?

4. When, if ever, should family interests outweigh patient interests?

Further Readings

American Academy of Pediatrics, Bioethics Committee. 1994. Guidelines on foregoing life-sustaining medical treatment. *Pediatrics* 93: 532–36.

Baylis, Françoise. 1993. When a child objects to medical treatment: The case of Philip. *Ethics in Medical Practice* 3(1):1–3.

———, and Cate McBurney. eds. 1993. *In the case of children: Paediatric ethics in a Canadian context*. Toronto: Department of Bioethics, Hospital for Sick Children.

Buchanan, Allen E., and Dan W. Brock. 1990. *Deciding for others: The ethics of surrogate decision making*. Cambridge: Cambridge University Press.

Duff, Raymond, and A.G.M. Campbell. 1976. On deciding the care of severely handicapped or dying persons: With particular reference to infants. *Pediatrics* 57(4):487–93.

Hardwig, John. 1990. What about the family? *Hastings Center Report* 20(2):5–10.

High, Dallas. 1990. Old and alone: Surrogate health care decision-making for the elderly without families. *Journal of Aging Studies* 4: 277–88.

Leikin, Sanford. 1989. When parents demand treatment. *Pediatric Annals* 18:266–68.

Moreno, Jonathan. 1991. Foster parents as surrogates for infants and young children. *Mt. Sinai Journal of Medicine* 58(5):2–7.

Nelson, James L. 1992. Taking families seriously. *Hastings Center Report* 22(4):6–12.

New York State Task Force on Life and the Law. 1992. *When Others Must Choose: Deciding for Patients Without Capacity*. Albany, N.Y.: Health Education Services.

Veatch, Robert, and C.M. Spicer. 1992. Medically futile care: The role of the physician in setting limits. *American Journal of Law & Medicine* 18: 15–36.

Chapter 9

Research Involving
Human Subjects

Introduction

It is most important to realize that these Nazi physicians or scientists were not monsters or madmen. The Nazi doctor did not have any physical or immediately recognizable distinction that would set him apart from our family doctor. After my sister and I [in Auschwitz, the Nazi death camp] were selected by [Dr. Josef] Mengele for his experiments on twins and diseases, we had almost daily contact with him. It is from this perspective that I hope to include here a description of the Nazi doctor and his "experiments." In this way, I hope to give the modern scientist/physician a clearer view of the dangers in attitudes involved in scientific research. All we need to do is reverse our priorities, leaving human life as secondary, superceded by science and progress (Susan Seiler Vigorito, "A Profile of Nazi Medicine," in Caplan 1992, 11).

The ethics of research with human subjects is a topic born from the cauldron of horror. During World War II, in Auschwitz and elsewhere, Nazi medical researchers used Jews, Romany (Gypsies), and prisoners of war as human guinea pigs, in macabre experiments in hypothermia (immersing persons in vats of freezing water until the point of death), limb transplantation (chopping off the limbs of two prisoners and attempting to cross-graft), and other grisly studies. Lengthy research programs were designed to find the cheapest and most efficient means of castration and sterilization, as well as techniques of mass murder (see Caplan 1992). The trial of Nazi doctors participating in this research by a judicial tribunal of the Allied nations resulted in their conviction under ethical principles of human experimentation stated by the judges. These principles, which have since become known as the Nuremberg Code, include among their requirements that no subject be enrolled in a medical research study without having given voluntary and informed consent, and that no study be pursued that is expected to result in death or disabling injury to its subjects.

The same pattern appears repeatedly. The revelation of some horribly abusive study of human subjects is followed by a public outcry, a judicial or legislative inquiry, and, ultimately, new guidelines for the ethical conduct of research with human beings. The United States regulations on human research, for example, resulted from Senate hearings into the Tuskegee study. Beginning in 1932, over 400 black males in Alabama were the unwitting subjects of a study of the natural history of syphilis — in other words, What happens to a person infected with syphilis who is never treated? In the 1940s, when penicillin became the standard treatment for syphilis, the subjects were not told of this new treatment; the study continued, with surviving subjects continuing to be untreated, until 1972, when the scandal broke. Similarly, as recently as 1988, the practice of human research in New Zealand was radically altered following a judicial inquiry. The cause of the inquiry: newspaper accounts of a study, begun in 1966 and continued through the mid-1970s, of what happens to women found to have cervical cancer *in situ* who are left untreated. Once again, the subjects were never informed that they were part of a research study, nor that they were eligible for standard surgical treatment of their cancer (see Paul 1988 and McNeill 1993).

These episodes suggest that it is because of, rather than in spite of, abuses of medical research on human beings that reasonably broad agreement on the elements for ethically evaluating such research currently exists. Briefly put, this consensus requires the following:

- First, for a study to be ethical it must be designed properly: It should not be scientifically premature (for example, a new drug should not be tried on humans before any relevant animal models for safety and efficacy have been studied); it should not pose any unnecessary risk to subjects, and those risks that are necessary must be balanced by corresponding benefits; and it must be scientifically valid — that is, its conduct and conclusions should satisfy agreed standards of scientific inference.
- Second, an ethical study must be communicated properly: Competent subjects, and the parents, guardians, or authorized proxies of incompetent subjects, must be allowed to freely choose whether or not to participate, following the provision of as much relevant information as they require.
- Third, for a study to be ethical it must be acceptable by society's standards, as well as those of the scientific community, and by the subjects of the study themselves. For example, in selecting persons to approach for research purposes, society requires that norms of nondiscrimination be respected.

These three principles, identified by the United States' Belmont Commission as the principles of beneficence, autonomy, and justice (respectively), are with adjustments found in other nations' approaches to human research as well. The basic Canadian guidelines, for example, published by the Medical Research Council (MRC) in 1987, state:

> The Standing Committee [on ethics in experimentation] believes that the basic ethical principle in research, as in health care, is respect for life. From this principle flow others: the concept of autonomy, the duty to beneficence, and the duty to justice.

The principles described represent agreement regarding the substantive ethical conduct of research with human subjects — the "what." In addition, there exists broad consensus on procedure, the "how." Prior to beginning research, an investigator must prepare a description of the proposed study (a "protocol"), describing its background (e.g., pharmacology of any new drugs used, previous experience with animals and humans), methodology (who is eligible for the trial, how many subjects are to be enrolled, for how long, what will be done to them), safety precautions (what side effects are expected or possible, what will be done to prevent them, under what circumstances will the study be terminated early because of the occurrence of unanticipated risks), and purpose (e.g., how the study will improve our understanding of or intervention in disease processes). This protocol, accompanied by a consent form (or any other means to be used in explaining the trial to prospective subjects), is submitted to a committee (known in Canada as an REB — Research Ethics Board) independent of the investigator, charged with judging the proposal's acceptability in all aspects, scientific as well as ethical. The REB reviewing a trial — usually established by and lodged within the institution performing the trial — should be composed of members with relevant expertise in science, clinical medicine, and patient safety, and include as well expertise in the normative aspects of human research (ethicists, members of the clergy, and lawyers often serve on REBs), to assure that the trial receives a comprehensive, multidisciplinary review. The REB is also charged with respecting the values of the community; in part for that reason, lay membership is expected as well. While the title of the committee changes from nation to nation — REBs are known in the United States as Institutional Review Boards (IRBs), and in many other nations by other terms (e.g., "research ethics committee"; sometimes, "Helsinki Committee," named after the World Medical Association's guidelines on research with humans, approved in Helsinki in 1964) — its major features are common to most: established by those clinical and academic institutions engaged in research; multidisciplinary expertise in the membership; protective of community values. An REB is given the power to approve, approve with specified modifications, or to disallow research; before reaching a decision, it may require that further information be supplied by the investigator. In many countries — Canada among them — the guidelines expect REBs to play some role in the monitoring of the conduct of research as well.

The Selections

Halushka v. University of Saskatchewan illustrates the way in which guidelines, regulations, and laws concerning research with human subjects have grown out of cases in which the rights of subjects were flagrantly violated. In this case, a student volunteered to participate as a research subject in a seemingly risk-free study that promised to pay well. The research procedure, cardiac catheterization and injection of contrast dye, was in fact at that time highly experimental. In his judgement, Mr. Justice Emmett Hall (later to achieve fame as the "father of Canadian medicare") described what he termed a "full disclosure" standard on behalf of consent to research. At a time when consent to therapy was relatively limited (see the discussion of the professional standard in the introduction to Chapter 6), consent to research would instead require disclosing all facts that any reasonable person might want to consider in deciding to be a subject of research.

Mary Moore and Stephen Berk, in the second selection, provide a retrospective look at a research study of acupuncture as a treatment for chronic pain — an "ethical post-mortem." The study was conducted on patients with common muscle or bone pain of the shoulder. Half of them received acupuncture, while the other half were provided with a "sham" treatment that only imitated acupuncture.

This kind of research design, common in clinical research, is known as an RCT (randomized clinical trial). Subjects are randomly divided into two groups, an "experimental" (acupuncture) and a "control" (sham acupuncture) arm. Many factors, including simple trust in and reassurance by the treating physician, can influence pain, and so the study's control group is selected and treated in ways identical to those of the experimental group except for the intervention. If the acupuncture group does no better than the one being given the placebo, we may conclude that the experimental intervention is not itself effective. The chance distribution of subjects, in which their assignment to group A or B is determined by a random number generator, is needed to eliminate bias. If subject assignment were to be done instead by the investigator, there would be the chance that the healthier patients would be assigned to one group rather than the other.

As Moore and Berk show, an experiment need not involve dramatic, life-and-death choices nor expensive apparatus in order to raise complex ethical issues, including questions of justice in the selection of subjects, the steps that must be taken to safeguard the welfare of persons participating, and of course consent, which is particularly difficult when a subject's knowledge of his or her research assignment (acupuncture or placebo) would invalidate the study's results. With the passage of time, in fact, the authors became convinced that the research they had conducted was unethical in two respects.

Benjamin Freedman's contribution focusses on one aspect of trial design, the choice of the "arms" (different treatment methods) to be tested against one another in controlled clinical research. A controlled trial by definition has at least two arms (for example, drug A versus drug B), but can have more (for example, drug A versus drug B versus surgery). As Canada's *MRC Guidelines* note, "Particular care must be taken . . . to ensure that the subject's best interest is never sacrificed to that of the randomized study" (18). All agree, therefore, that it would be unethical to perform a controlled study in which arm A is in all likelihood less effective or more toxic than B; subjects of research should not be medically disadvantaged by their participation. The ethical concern for an appropriate risk–benefit ratio is sometimes said to require an "honest null hypothesis," that is, genuine uncertainty about which arm is in fact safer, more effective, or both.

This requirement, seemingly so basic to ethical research practice, has led to much confusion. Consider the case when a new asthma drug, drug B, has been discovered, and is to be tested against the current standard asthma treatment, drug A. No clinical investigator would participate in the study, and no drug company or research institution would fund it, unless they were convinced beforehand that B probably has some significant advantage over A. Indeed, even if they had begun the trial in uncertainty, during its conduct they would likely see results that would convince them of one drug's superiority. (Clinical trials of the type we are considering rarely take less than several months to complete, and often last for several years.) How, then, could a doctor invite a patient to join a trial, when there is a 50 percent chance that the patient will receive what the doctor considers the inferior treatment?

Freedman argues for the view that medical care and knowledge are collectively determined by the medical community. As such, a controlled trial is justified provided it begins in a state of "clinical equipoise," uncertainty within the medical community about the comparative merits of the alternative treatments being tested. Clinical equipoise determines the limits of a clinical trial as well; in Freedman's view, a controlled trial must terminate as soon as clinical equipoise has been disturbed (that is, the accumulated evidence has convinced, or if disclosed, would convince, the clinical community of the superiority of one of the tested treatments).

Several ethical aspects of human research, including concepts of consent and of clinical equipoise, have received new attention in the age of AIDS. Activists from the gay community have questioned the view that subjects of research are thereby put at risk, from which they need to be protected. Faced with a diagnosis of AIDS, a dreaded and lethal disease, they have argued that patients with AIDS have a right to experimental treatment at the individual patient's option. It follows from this view that rather than controlled trials in which neither doctor nor patient is told to which treatment arm the patient has been assigned ("double-blind"), researchers should offer patients the opportunity to knowingly opt for a particular nonvalidated treatment (an "open-armed" trial). David Salisbury and Martin Schechter examine the ethical arguments underlying this view, and argue for an alternative: reform of the clinical trial process to permit more access to experimental treatment while at the same time preserving the scientific validity that RCTs offer.

References

Caplan, Arthur L. 1992. *When medicine went mad.* Totawa, N.J.: Humana Press.

McNeill, Paul M. 1993. *The ethics and politics of human experimentation.* New York: Cambridge University Press.

Medical Research Council of Canada. 1987. *Guidelines on research involving human subjects*, 18. Ottawa: Medical Research Council.

Paul, Charlotte. 1988. The New Zealand cervical cancer study: Could it happen again? *British Medical Journal* 297:533–39.

Twenty years after: The legacy of the Tuskegee syphilis study. 1992. *Hastings Center Report* 22(6):29–40.

United States Department of Health and Human Services. 1991. Federal Policy for the Protection of Human Subjects: Notices and Rules. *Federal Register*, Part II, 56(117), 18 June 1991, 28002–280032 (56 FR 28002).

World Medical Association. 1964. *Declaration of Helsinki: Recommendations Guiding Medical Doctors in Biomedical Research Involving Human Subjects.* Revised 1975, Tokyo; 1983, Venice.

33   Halushka v. University of Saskatchewan et al.

Saskatchewan Court of Appeal

. . . The judgment of the Court was delivered by

HALL J.A.: — The appellants Wyant and Merriman were medical practitioners employed by the appellant University of Saskatchewan. The appellant Wyant was professor of anaesthesia and chief of the department of the anaesthetics at the University Hospital. The appellant Merriman was director of the cardio-pulmonary laboratory. As part of their duties in the employ of the appellant University of Saskatchewan, the appellants

Wyant and Merriman conducted and carried out medical research projects, some of which involved the comparative study of anaesthetics. When anaesthetics were administered the subjects were obtained from the employment office.

The respondent, a student at the University of Saskatchewan, had attended summer school in 1961. On August 21, 1961, he went to the employment office to find a job. At the employment office he was advised that there were no jobs available but that he could earn $50 by being the subject of a test at the University Hospital. The respondent said that he was told that the test would last a couple of hours and that it was a "safe test and there was nothing to worry about".

The respondent reported to the anaesthesia department at the University Hospital and there saw the appellant Wyant. The conversation which ensued concerning the proposed test was related by the respondent as follows:

Doctor Wyant explained to me that a new drug was to be tried out on the Wednesday following. He told me that electrodes would be put in my both arms, legs and head and that he assured me that it was a perfectly safe test it had been conducted many times before. He told me that I was not to eat anything on Wednesday morning that I was to report at approximately nine o'clock, then he said it would take about an hour to hook me up and the test itself would last approximately two hours, after the time I would be given fifty dollars, pardon me, I would be allowed to sleep first, fed and then given fifty dollars and driven home on the same day.

The appellant Wyant also told the respondent that an incision would be made in his left arm and that a catheter or tube would be inserted into his vein. . . .

The test contemplated was known as "The Heart and Blood Circulation Response under General Anaesthesia", and was to be conducted jointly by the appellants Wyant and Merriman, using a new anaesthetic agent known commercially as "Fluoromar". This agent had not been previously used or tested by the appellants in any way.

The respondent returned to the University Hospital on August 23, 1961, to undergo the test. The procedure followed was that which had been described to the respondent and expected by him, with the exception that the catheter, after being inserted in the vein in the respondent's arm, was advanced towards his heart. When the catheter reached the vicinity of the heart, the respondent felt some discomfort. The anaesthetic agent was then administered to him. The time was then 11:32 a.m. Eventually the catheter tip was advanced through the various heart chambers out into the pulmonary artery where it was positioned.

The appellants Wyant and Merriman intended to have the respondent reach medium depth of surgical anaesthesia. However, an endotracheal tube which had been inserted to assist the respondent in breathing caused some coughing. In the opinion of the appellant Wyant the coughing indicated that the respondent was in the upper half of light anaesthesia — on the verge of waking up. At 12:16, therefore, the concentration of the mixture of the anaesthetic was increased. The respondent then descended into deeper surgical anaesthesia.

At about 12:20 there were changes in the respondent's cardiac rhythm which suggested to the appellants Wyant and Merriman that the level of the anaesthetic was too deep. The amount of anaesthetic was then decreased, or lightened.

At 12:25 the respondent suffered a complete cardiac arrest.

The appellants Wyant and Merriman and their assistants took immediate steps to resuscitate the respondent's heart by manual massage. To reach the heart an incision was made from the breastbone to the line of the arm-pit and two of the ribs were pulled apart. A vasopressor was administered as well as urea, a drug used to combat swelling of the brain. After one minute and thirty seconds the respondent's heart began to function again.

The respondent was unconscious for a period of four days. He remained in the University Hospital as a patient until discharged 10 days later. On the day before he was discharged the respondent was given fifty ($50) dollars by the appellant Wyant. At that time the respondent asked the appellant Wyant if that was all he was going to get for all he went through. The appellant said that fifty dollars was all that they had bargained for but that he could give a larger sum in return for a complete release executed by the respondent's mother or elder sister.

As a result of the experiment the appellants concluded that as an anaesthetic agent "Fluoromar" had too narrow a margin of safety and it was withdrawn from clinical use in the University Hospital. . . .

If a patient does not die immediately from cardiac arrest, the damage which might ensue can vary in degree from none at all to eventual death with all intermediate degrees possible. Brain damage is the usual cause of death and most of the intermediate damage occurring will be to the brain. The brain cells can be damaged either permanently or temporarily. The portion of the brain most susceptible to damage under these circumstances is that which controls the highest functions, that is, the thinking functions as contrasted to the lowest or automatic functions. . . .

The respondent returned to the University in the fall of 1961. He testified that he became very tired every day and that he had to rest for about three hours before doing his homework. Although this condition did gradually improve, the respondent said that he was never able to complete his homework because of it. The respondent failed in six or seven subjects that year. He said he could not think or concentrate on problems as he had before. He therefore did not try to continue with his University course.

At the time of the trial the respondent was employed as an electrician at Thompson, Manitoba, earning $376 per month. He stated that it was difficult for him to think or concentrate and that he could not understand instructions given to him in the course of the employment unless they were given very slowly. . . .

In my opinion the duty imposed upon those engaged in medical research, as were the appellants Wyant and Merriman, to those who offer themselves as subject for experimentation, as the respondent did here, is at least as great as, if not greater than, the duty owed by the ordinary physician or surgeon to his patient. There can be no exceptions to the ordinary requirements of disclosure in the case of research as there may well be in ordinary medical practice. The researcher does not have to balance the probable effect of lack of treatment against the risk involved in the treatment itself. The example of risks being properly hidden from a patient when it is important that he should not worry can have no application in the field of research. The subject of medical experimentation is entitled to a full and frank disclosure of all the facts, probabilities and opinions which a reasonable man might be expected to consider before giving his consent. . . .

Although the appellant Wyant informed the respondent that a "new drug" was to be tried out, he did not inform him that the new drug was in fact an anaesthetic of which he had no previous knowledge, nor that there was a risk involved with the use of anaesthetic. Inasmuch as no test had been previously conducted using the anaesthetic agent "Fluoromar" to the knowledge of the appellants, the statement made to the respondent that it was a safe test, which had been conducted many times before, when considered in the light of the medical evidence describing the characteristics of anaesthetic agents generally, was incorrect and was in reality a non-disclosure.

The respondent was not informed that the catheter would be advanced to and through his heart but was admittedly given to understand that it would be merely inserted in the vein in his arm. While it may be correct to say that the advancement of the catheter to the heart was not in itself dangerous and did not cause or contribute to the cause of the cardiac arrest, it was a circumstance which, if known, might very well have prompted the respondent to withhold his consent. . . .

34   Ethical Considerations Encountered in a Study of Acupuncture — A Reappraisal

Mary E. Moore & Stephen N. Berk

As the public has become more concerned with human rights, and scientists increasingly have stressed humanistic values, the ethical issues surrounding research with human subjects have come under more and more careful scrutiny. This paper recounts a retrospective ethical analysis of a controlled experiment to study the efficacy of acupuncture to alleviate pain which we completed in 1973.[1] It is hoped that by analyzing in detail the ethical issues involved in this study we will remind others of their importance and stress the need for effective solutions. In the process of reappraisal, we discovered that the traditional doctor/patient relationship has important implications for this type of medical research and we have become critical of our informed consent procedure.

The Study

The purpose of our controlled experiment was to ascertain whether acupuncture was an effective treatment for chronic pain. It was clear from the beginning that this study would have to be conducted using a patient population. An analogue study using experimentally produced pain in healthy volunteer subjects would fall far short of reproducing the "real" pain experience. Common shoulder pain of benign musculoskeletal origin, such as tendonitis/bursitis or osteoarthritis, was chosen for investigation. A second objective was to ascertain whether either susceptibility to hypnosis or a positive treatment setting had an effect on the response to acupuncture.

Subjects were recruited by classified advertisements placed in local newspapers. These advertisements called for people with shoulder pain interested in acupuncture treatment. Forty-two subjects were selected from approximately 200 people who responded. They were randomly divided into two groups. One group was given acupuncture as it was learned from a Chinese-trained physician. The other group was given a "sham" treatment in which the needles did not pierce the skin but merely touched its surface. These groups were subdivided further. Half of each group was assigned to a so-called "positive setting" in which the physician was friendly and talkative. The other half was assigned to a "negative setting" in which the physician interacted as little as possible with the subject. Each subject was independently evaluated by a psychologist to ascertain his degree of hypnotic susceptibility.

Result of the experiment revealed that both the acupuncture and the sham acupuncture relieved shoulder pain in two-thirds of the subjects. This improvement in pain was statistically significant, but acupuncture was not different from the placebo treatment in this respect. Susceptibility to hypnosis appeared to be somewhat related to the success of the treatment but this result did not reach statistical significance. The positive treatment setting was slightly related to successful outcome in the acupuncture group. No such relationship existed for the placebo group. We concluded that acupuncture, as we had been practicing it, was no more effective than a placebo and that its effectiveness might be due to psychological and interpersonal factors rather than to any intrinsic value of the treatment itself.

Cost Benefit Ratio

The overriding consideration involved in planning this or any other human experiment involves an analysis of the cost/benefit ratio. As stated in the World Medical Association's Declaration of Helsinki[2]:

> Clinical research cannot legitimately be carried out unless the importance of the objective is in proportion to the inherent risk to the subject. Any clinical research project should be preceded by careful assessment of inherent risks in comparison to favorable benefits to the subject or to others.

First, we had to evaluate the importance of our objectives. How important was it to ascertain whether acupuncture was a specific treatment rather than simply a placebo? We felt it was overwhelmingly important. As scientists interested in the treatment of pain, we felt a moral imperative to subject acupuncture to a critical test. Not only was acupuncture a novel form of treatment whose efficacy had not yet been scientifically established, but it was one in which the public had an extraordinary interest. Thousands of dollars and the hopes of many suffering people were at stake when we began our investigation in 1973. Patients were being transported by busloads to distant clinics where treatment by means of acupuncture was offered as a magic solution to their problems. Recognizing the great public interest in acupuncture at the time, authorities at the National Institutes of Health (NIH) organized a conference of leading scientists and physicians interested in acupuncture research. This conference concluded that, while acupuncture appeared to hold some promise for the treatment of pain, "Many more well-designed and well-controlled scientific studies are needed before it could be considered for wide use in clinical practice in the United States."[3]

In addition to the generally accepted need for controlled research on acupuncture, we felt a strong personal need for such investigation. We had used acupuncture in a pain clinic for two years in an attempt to help patients with chronic pain. After hearing the questions raised at the NIH conference, we felt it would be *unethical* to continue using this form of treatment without subjecting it to controlled experimentation. Thus the benefits from such experimentation to society at large, as well as to clinical investigators like ourselves, seemed to loom very large.

The individual patient [*sic*] who volunteered for our study also stood to benefit. Those potential subjects who contacted us but did not qualify for our study received professional advice and counsel. Those who were chosen for further evaluation received a free examination by a rheumatologist, followed, in many cases, by an appropriate communication to the patient's physician. Those who did qualify for the acupuncture study were offered the possibility of receiving free acupuncture treatment which we felt, based on our own previous experience, was likely to help their pain. Of the patients with similar complaints treated in our pain clinic, 82% obtained some pain relief.[4] Even those randomly selected for placebo acupuncture had at least one chance in three of obtaining pain relief, since research reveals that in similar experiments, at least one-third of the subjects can be expected to show a powerful placebo response.[5] Finally, if the acupuncture treatment proved more effective than the sham treatment, it was our intention to offer acupuncture to those who had not received it.

On the other side of the coin were the concerns regarding the costs of this experiment. What were the physical and psychological risks to the subject? We knew of no risks involved in the brief standard psychological tests that were used to assess hypnotic susceptibility. The primary risks centered around the acupuncture itself. However, the potential for these hazards seemed to be extremely small. The possibility of infection following skin penetration was considered a minor risk. This concern was further minimized by employing careful sterile techniques and excluding patients with medical histories that would predispose them to infection.

The discomfort caused by the needle stimulation in the acupuncture treatment presented another potential cost (the sham acupuncture involved no discomfort). Having ourselves experienced acupuncture, we felt reasonably sure that the discomfort involved was not likely to be unbearable. Moreover, if a patient found the treatment too uncomfortable, he was given every opportunity to withdraw from the experiment. Still other risks involved the potential of superficial tissue or internal organ injury as a consequence of the "needling" procedure. Because of the peripheral location of the treatment (shoulder and arm), the small calibre of the acupuncture needles, the superficial penetration used, and the experience of the acupuncturist, these potential dangers were also considered to be minimal. Indeed, in two years of previous experience with more than 100 patients, no serious problems had been encountered. Our estimation of these risks proved correct. No deleterious side effects occurred as a result of the study.

Finally, as is the case in the trial of any new therapeutic modality, there was the risk that subjects would enter the experiment and thus be prevented from obtaining a treatment of already proven efficacy. We attempted to eliminate this risk by selecting patients for the study who had benign musculoskeletal problems only. Such problems would not be made worse by a short delay in obtaining more conventional therapy.

Thus, in reappraising the overall pros and cons of our study, we could find no fault with our previous cost/benefit analysis and felt that the overriding benefits clearly justified the small risks encountered.

Experimental Design

Our experimental design employed four experimental groups: true acupuncture in a positive setting; true acupuncture in a negative setting; a sham acupuncture in a positive setting; and sham acupuncture in a negative setting. Subjects were randomly assigned to each group.

Random assignment of subjects to each experimental group is not only advantageous from a scientific point of view, but would appear to be the most ethical way to make such assignments. It eliminates any bias in assigning subjects to treatment groups. The potential for this bias was realized when one of our volunteers was a highly placed person in our own university. Had there been any leeway in the assignment to experiment groups, we probably would have been inclined to give this person *true* acupuncture in a *positive* setting. However, by random selection this individual was assigned to the sham acupuncture in a negative setting. Thus, we found ourselves treating someone we would have liked to impress favorably with a treatment we regarded as less than optimal. The resulting sense of frustration reminded us of our own lack of objectivity and personal bias.

If the experimental design had included a double-blind procedure, such bias and lack of objectivity would have been completely nullified. Under these conditions the experimenter would not have known which treatment he was administering. We could not conceive of a way to double-blind manually performed acupuncture. Consequently, we had to rely on randomization and a strict adherence to a detailed experimental protocol in order to assure an unbiased assignment to treatment groups.

If each person had an equal chance to be assigned to each treatment condition, it was important to justify each of the different experimental manipulations. What about sham acupuncture? Was this use of a placebo justified? We felt that having a condition that approximated acupuncture as closely as possible was *essential* to the test of whether acupuncture's therapeutic efficacy was a function of specific or nonspecific effects. Even Bok, a severe critic of the use of placebos, implicitly recognized the absolute necessity for their use in the evaluation of new forms of therapy: "Consider the cost to the patient. . . . Many temporarily successful new surgical procedures owe their success to the placebo effect alone."[6]

Not only was it important to include a placebo or sham acupuncture condition, it was also important to vary the general setting in which the acupuncture occurred. We believed that much of our previous success with acupuncture might have been because of our enthusiasm for the procedure and to the close, friendly atmosphere that characterized the treatment sessions. Consequently, we deliberately set out to create a negative treatment setting — a relatively neutral, impersonal therapeutic condition to contrast with the positive one. In the negative setting the acupuncturist did not initiate conversation with the patient and made no positive comments concerning the treatment.

Playing out the role of the unenthusiastic therapist proved uncomfortable for our physician acupuncturist. Perhaps this was because she felt (although it had not at all been obvious in advance) that there was a real element of deception involved. The acupuncturist was still a physician. As a physician, she would have normally encouraged the patients and would have comforted those who appeared apprehensive. The negative setting did not allow for this behavior. The physician constrained by such a setting felt somewhat fraudulent.

In retrospect, our experimental design appeared to be ethically justified, but seemed to involve an element of deception that was not fully anticipated beforehand.

Selection of Subjects

Ethical issues arise in the selection of subjects for all human experimentation. It used to be commonplace, and it is still often the practice, for investigators to ask their students, junior colleagues, or their patients to serve as subjects. Such people often "volunteer" in an effort to please the investigator and do not have real freedom of choice. To refuse to serve in the experiment may jeopardize what they regard as a very important relationship. They are, in a sense, a captive population. In recognition of this fact, the Ethical Committee of the World Medical Association in its *Draft Code of Ethics* in human experimentation stated:

No doctor should lightly experiment on a human being when the subject of the experiment is in a dependent relationship to the investigator, such as a medical student to his teacher, a patient to his doctor, a technician in a laboratory to the head of his department.[7]

To avoid any element of coercion, we sought subjects from a population we hoped would be removed from our own sphere of influence. Our advertisements were placed in several newspapers in a large city. As professionals, we had qualms about advertising to attract people to our care. However, since we did not charge for our evaluation or treatment and made no effort to attract such people to stay under our care as patients, we felt that this advertising was ethical. As it turned out, only one of the 42 subjects requested to be followed by us for routine rheumatological care. The majority appeared to have established freely a limited relationship with us.

In retrospect, we were not fully aware that when people in distress volunteer to participate in an experiment involving physicians and treatment, they will to some extent confuse the role of an experimental subject with that of a patient. Despite all explanations to the contrary, most will continue to expect to be treated as patients. Because of their distress, they may fail to "hear" such explanations. Their preoccupation with obtaining symptomatic relief limits their freedom of choice.

Because of our volunteers' expectations and our own unanticipated need to continue to play the role of doctor, we found that we had to assume responsibility for the protection of even would-be subjects. In one such case a prospective subject passed our routine screening questions concerning past difficulties with bleeding. Then, following a ten-minute conversation, he casually mentioned that he was a hemophiliac. After refusing to accept him in the study, we spent some time trying to ascertain why he had assumed acupuncture needles would be harmless and attempted to reeducate him concerning the precautions that should be routine for anyone with hemophilia.

Other examples of our unanticipated obligations concerned patients who called and gave a history of pain that did not sound like musculoskeletal shoulder pain, or who told us of unrelated medical problems for which they were not under a physician's care. By making us aware of these problems they obligated us to intervene with advice. Our typical response was to tell them they were in need of a medical check-up and should call their family physician for an appointment. Occasionally the patient had already consulted his family physician and had been told that the problem was unimportant. In such cases we felt we had to recommend that the patient seek out a specialist for a more sophisticated opinion.

After reappraising the ethical issues involved in our subject selection, we realized that our subjects were being invited to come to a doctor for trial of a new treatment. Because they felt in need of such a treatment they were not completely free to refuse.

Working with these subjects involved many of the same ethical considerations in any patient population.

Informed Consent

The first principle of the Nuremberg Code informs us that three conditions must be met to insure the adequacy of subject consent: explanation, comprehension, and freedom to act.[8] The extent to which the first two conditions were met can be determined by objective assessment procedures. However, the degree of freedom experienced by the subject in his decision-making is more difficult to determine.

In a classic study, Robinson and Merav demonstrated how difficult it sometimes is to provide explanation and achieve comprehension for informed consent.[9] Twenty patients were carefully briefed to their giving consent for major surgery. Even with prompting, only 42% of the consent information was recalled. Moreover, less than 10% of those portions of the briefing related to possible complications of surgery were remembered. Some patients even denied having been informed at all prior to giving consent.

This important study demonstrates how difficult it is to achieve informed consent when patients have serious health problems. The same defense mechanisms that enable them to manage their fears and anxiety apparently interfere with their information processing skills. Threatening information relevant to their health status and the risks of surgery is denied, distorted, or quickly forgotten. The problems of insuring the comprehension necessary for informed consent appear to vary as a function of the threat to safety and health of the individual being informed. As personal threats increase, so does the difficulty of providing valid informed consent. Healthy volunteers for clinical research would be expected to show the best retention and comprehension of procedures and risks.

A study by Woodward tends to support this notion. He recruited healthy volunteers who were asked to swallow a small catheter in order that jejunal secretions could be sampled.[10] All subjects were given a thorough explanation of procedures and risks prior to the signing of an informed consent. At the conclusion of the study Woodward administered a questionnaire to the subjects and found that they retained almost all of the information relevant to the informed consent. He concluded that volunteers who have no special medical education can assimilate and comprehend a great deal of sophisticated information and recognized that this is particularly true when the volunteers are not threatened by health or safety concerns.

Our subjects fell somewhere between the extremes of preoperative patients on the one hand, and normal volunteers on the other. They were people with health problems who volunteered for clinical research aimed at a possible solution to their problems.

These patients were not as ill or as frightened as the preoperative patient, but not as carefree as the healthy volunteers. Consequently, we felt it necessary to provide conditions that would maximize comprehension and retention of information relevant for informed consent. Therefore, we provided subjects with information at two points prior to their signing the consent form. Information regarding the experimental nature of the study, the time demands, and the inconveniences involved was provided during an initial phone contact. Those volunteers who appeared appropriate for the study were then asked to come into the hospital for a thorough medical evaluation and detailed discussion of the purpose, procedures, risks, and demands of the study. Care was taken to use nontechnical language and to provide an atmosphere to encourage questions and discussion. Only after the investigators were satisfied that all the information presented had been understood was a request made to sign the consent form.

In retrospect, we now feel we could have done more to insure the efficacy of our informed consent procedure. Our subjects had chronic pain problems. In all likelihood they listened to our information, heard what they wanted, and volunteered in hopes of finding relief for their discomfort. Our disclosure procedures might have been enhanced by requiring the completion of a questionnaire, as Woodward did, prior to the signing of the informed consent. This short quiz could have been used to help assess the amount of information that the subject had retained and understood.

In addition to the question of whether the subjects understand the information supplied to them, there is the question of how much information concerning the experiment should be supplied. Can any information be deliberately withheld? We deliberately withheld from our subjects the fact that there was to be a placebo group and that there was to be a negative treatment setting. Our consent form simply asked all the subjects to volunteer "for treatment with acupuncture needles." It also specifically stated that acupuncture was "still in an experimental stage." This formulation was true but certainly not the whole truth.

We felt that the decision to withhold information about the placebo and the treatment milieu was crucial. The validity of the experiment seemed to hinge on the degree to which the patients' expectations in the experimental setting duplicated those of the patients who had received acupuncture in a clinical setting. If we had informed the subjects of our experimental manipulation we felt they would have become suspicious and less hopeful of obtaining pain relief. We considered that the element of deception involved in withholding information was justified because the sham acupuncture and negative setting posed no risks for the subjects. Besides, we had built in a debriefing session at the end of the experiment in which our "deception" was revealed. Subjects were told they had received either true acupuncture or an "imitation" of it. This would set the record straight at a time when the subjects' reactions would not affect the experimental data.

There is some research addressed to the effects of informing the subject of experimental manipulation. Park, Covi, and Uhlenhuth reported studying 15 subjects at the Johns Hopkins Hospital.[11] The subjects were told they would be receiving placebo therapy for their anxiety-based complaints. Care was taken to insure they understood the term "placebo." Of the 15 subjects who completed treatment 14 reported symptomatic relief. None of the feared negative effects of disclosure occurred. All subjects complied with procedures, showed no hostility, and gave the expected results. However, it is interesting to note that poststudy interviews revealed that many of the subjects believed all along that they had been receiving real treatment. They did not "buy" the placebo story perhaps because they felt that the doctors at a major hospital would surely be employing genuine treatment.

Resnick and Schwartz[12] reported different findings in their study of disclosure. They attempted to replicate a standard verbal conditioning study in a college student population. Two experimental groups were used. One group received standard briefing procedures which *excluded* information concerning the verbal conditioning. The second group was briefed on the entire procedure. The results from the second group demonstrated that full disclosure prevented the expected conditioning effects. In addition, subjects in the full disclosure group were uncooperative, missed study sessions, felt manipulated, and were defensively suspicious throughout the study. None of these problems were observed in the limited disclosure group. The authors concluded that caution should be exercised in informing subjects because the amount of information supplied could influence the outcome of the study.

The conflicting results obtained by these two studies can be understood if one takes the different subject populations into account. In the first study, the subjects were chronically ill people who went to a hospital for treatment. Regardless of the investigators' statements concerning treatment, they had high expectations of finding relief. Consequently, their motivations and needs distorted their perception of the disclosed information. Resnick and Schwartz used healthy college students who had little or no personal investment in the study. They had no need to arrive at the stated goals of the experiment, and probably resented the manipulation involved. Thus it appears that the impact of full disclosure will differ according to the expectations, needs, and motivations of the subject population.

In looking back on our decision to withhold information from the subjects, we came to feel that we could not in good conscience make the same decision today. We would also not expect our institution's research review committee for the protection of human subjects to approve such a protocol today. The intervening years have raised the level of consciousness concerning the treatment of human subjects. We now agree with Lasagna that major experimental manipulations should be revealed beforehand to the subject, while the details of study procedures may be kept from him.[13]

Today we would inform our volunteers that half would receive placebo acupuncture and that the treatment milieu would be different for different subjects. However, no one would know the experimental group to which they had been assigned until the end of the experiment. We do not now believe that this disclosure would have negatively affected the outcome or have led to unnecessary resistance. All subjects came with the complaint of pain and were hopeful of finding relief. It is unlikely that information concerning treatment would have turned them away or diminished their expectations. In addition, we now agree with Bok[6] who, in her article on the ethics of placebos, emphasized the fact that no encounter between doctor and patient stands alone. The experience of one encounter affects each succeeding one. Once deceived by a doctor, a patient may view future physician contacts with hostility and suspicion.

Debriefing

Debriefing in the context of human research is the process of reviewing the research experience once it has been completed and of disclosing the aims and outcomes of the research to the subject. Perhaps, most importantly, it provides an opportunity to identify and correct any negative responses that a subject may have acquired as a consequence of his participation in the study. Holmes[14] reviewed a number of studies that used debriefing sessions to screen for and eliminate negative responses that occurred following the use of deception methodology. He views the debriefing procedure as entailing two processes: dehoaxing and desensitizing. Dehoaxing strategies focus on relieving any anxiety engendered by the disclosure that the subject has been deceived. Desensitizing procedures are concerned with altering the subjects' feelings regarding the behavior that he demonstrated during the study. Depending on the study, one or both of these methods are required. Holmes' review indicates that these debriefing procedures have been effective in eliminating unpredictable negative responses. In addition, effective debriefing makes the subject a partner in the research endeavor and acknowledges his unique contribution to it.

From the beginning we had built into our study the concept of debriefing. One week following the last treatment each subject met with our psychologist for a 30-minute debriefing session. The first ten minutes of this session were devoted to the completion of a brief questionnaire which attempted to elicit the subject's ratings of

Table 9.1   Ratings of Acupuncturist Enthusiasm and Friendliness (Ratings were on a scale of 0 to 6, 6 being the most positive)

Treatment	Positive Setting		Negative Setting	
	Friendliness		*Friendliness*	
	Mean	5.82	Mean	5.36
	S.D.	.41	S.D.	1.12
ACUPUNCTURE				
	Enthusiasm		*Enthusiasm*	
	Mean	4.73	Mean	4.73
	S.D.	.91	S.D.	1.49
	Friendliness		*Friendliness*	
	Mean	6.00	Mean	6.00
	S.D.	.00	S.D.	.00
PLACEBO				
	Enthusiasm		*Enthusiasm*	
	Mean	5.20	Mean	4.20
	S.D.	1.03	S.D.	1.32

the acupuncturist and the treatment. Regardless of the treatment setting, the subjects tended to rate the acupuncturists as being friendly and enthusiastic (Table 9.1). Apparently, our negative setting was not strong enough to overcome the subjects' powerful pre-dispositions to see physicians in the positive light. In the questionnaire it was revealed to the subject for the first time that there had been a placebo treatment. Each subject was asked to guess whether he had received the "real" acupuncture or the "imitation" of it. There was no difference between the acupuncture group and the placebo group in their estimation of the type of treatment they had received (Table 9.2). Thus it was clear that our subjects had not perceived the two types of acupuncture differently.

The debriefing went on to reveal to each subject whether he had received acupuncture or sham acupuncture and to discuss his reaction to this disclosure. Those who had received the placebo treatment showed surprise but no evidence of anger or the feeling of having been cheated. Subjects were curious about the placebo phenomenon and were eager to talk about their responses and feelings in association with it.

The American Psychological Association's *Ethical Principles in the Conduct of Research with Human Participants* (1973) stresses the importance of effective debriefing.[15] Principle 8 states that following data collection "Ethical practice requires the investigator to provide

Table 9.2   Extent to Which Subjects in the Acupuncture and Placebo Groups Guessed That They Had Received "Classic Acupuncture" versus "Imitation Acupuncture"

Treatment	Total Subjects	Those Guessing "Classic Acupuncture"	Those Guessing "Imitation Acupuncture"	Those Who Didn't Know
Acupuncture	22	7 (32%)	2 (9%)	13 (59%)
Placebo	20	6 (30%)	2 (10%)	12 (60%)

that participant with a full clarification of the nature of the study and remove any misconception that may have arisen." Principle 9 states that "Where research procedures may result in undesirable consequences for the participant, the investigator has the responsibility to detect and remove or correct these consequences, including, where relevant, long-term after-effects."

Unfortunately, there is less stress in the ethical guidelines for physicians on the importance of full debriefing. We feel that debriefing is every bit as important in the context of medical experimentation as it is in psychological experimentation. It may be even more important since experience with medical personnel is more apt to color a subject's future real-life relationships.

Just as informed consent may be difficult to achieve at one sitting, so may adequate debriefing. One can conceive of a situation involving stress or deception in which follow-up debriefing sessions might be scheduled to check on the effectiveness of the initial debriefing. We might have contacted our subjects after some time had elapsed to ascertain how they were doing and to recheck on their perceptions and reactions to what had gone on in the experiment. Some debriefing would seem to be essential to any human experiment. We deplore the tendency for many medical researchers to feel, as is sometimes explicitly so stated in their informed consent that their responsibility for the subject is terminated when the last bits of data have been collected.

Summary

In summary, this reappraisal of our acupuncture study has highlighted a number of ethical concerns. These important issues need to be recognized and effectively dealt with by all who conduct research with human subjects. We believe that we handled most of these ethical issues well. However, other issues were either unanticipated or, upon reflection, appeared to have been ineffectively resolved.

Before any study is begun one must be sure that the risks are minimal and the benefits substantial. Our own analysis of this cost–benefit ratio seems to have been well thought out. An enormous need existed for a controlled evaluation of acupuncture therapy. Our experiment provided an excellent mechanism for such an evaluation and exposed the human subjects to minimal risks. In fact, the volunteers accrued more benefits than had been initially anticipated.

The problems involved in choosing subjects for clinical research are many. Volunteer *patients* by virtue of their illness will always present with some limits on their freedom of choice. In addition, their desire for symptomatic relief will lead to distortion of information relevant to the risks involved in the study. Consequently, in order to insure the most valid informed consent procedure possible, we concluded that one must adhere to several basic rules. First, if possible, the volunteer should be chosen from a group of potential subjects removed from the researchers' sphere of influence. Second, information relevant to the informed consent should be offered several times prior to the signing of any release form. Finally, short tests should probably be employed to assess the amount of information that a subject has understood and retained.

The ethics involved in the use of placebos have been the source of considerable controversy. It is our feeling that their use in controlled experimentation is ethically justifiable. The scientific evaluation of new treatments is mandatory and can only be accomplished by using control group procedures. However, it should be common practice to inform all subjects of the possibility of a placebo treatment. We do not feel that this disclosure will seriously affect subject cooperation or study outcome in clinical research. Our experimental design appropriately employed a placebo control group and two treatment settings. We allowed our subjects as much freedom of choice as possible in volunteering for the experiment. However, we deceived them by not informing them of the placebo conditions and the existence of a negative treatment setting. We now feel that this deception was unethical and unnecessary.

The impact of the traditional doctor/patient relationship on clinical research often goes unrecognized. We did not anticipate the degree to which this relationship would permeate our experimental settings. Much of our experimental design, subject selection, and informed consent procedures made the assumption that such a role relationship could be minimized easily. We now realize that such an assumption was incorrect. It is clear to us now that human research involving doctors and patients must always proceed from the assumption that the subject will expect the researcher to behave like a doctor. Each volunteer will expect to some degree to receive treatment for his ailment and to be dealt with in good faith. Anything that the subject may perceive as a deviation from such expectations must be explained clearly beforehand. These explanations must be reinforced at several points, checked on during the informed consent procedure, and discussed in debriefing sessions following the conclusion of the study.

It is our feeling that medical research must pay more attention to the needs of the subject following completion of the data collection. It is unfortunate that debriefing procedures are often ignored. It is impossible, as we discovered, to anticipate all effects that a study will have on subjects. Consequently, well thought-out debriefing procedures would appear to be mandatory from an ethical point of view.

References

1. Moore ME, Berk SN: Acupuncture for chronic shoulder pain. Ann Intl Med 84: 381–384, 1976.
2. World Medical Association: Declaration of Helsinki: N Engl J Med 271:473, 1964.
3. Proceedings NIH Acupuncture Research Conference, DHEW Publication No. (NIH) 74:165, 1973.
4. Moore ME: Some experiences with acupuncture in the treatment of chronic pain. Del Med J 48:457–465, 1976.
5. Beecher HK: The powerful placebo. JAMA 159:1602–1606, 1955.
6. Bok S: The ethics of giving placebos. Sci Am 231:17–23, 1974.
7. World Medical Association, Ethical Committee: Draft Code of Ethics on Human Experimentation. Brit Med J 2:1119, 1962.
8. Katz J: Experimentation with Human Subjects. New York, Russell Sage Foundation. 1972, p 305.
9. Robinson G, Merav A: Informed consent: recall by patients tested postoperatively. Ann Thor Surg 22:209, 1976.
10. Woodward WE: Informed consent of volunteers: a direct measurement of comprehension and retention of information. Clin Res 27:248–256, 1979.
11. Park LC, Covi L, Uhlenhurt EG: Effects of informed consent on research patients and study results. Nervous and Mental Dis 145: 349–354, 1967.
12. Resnick J, Schwartz T: Ethical standards as an independent variable in psychological research. Amer Psychol 28:134–139, 1973.
13. Lasagna L: Drug evaluation problems in academic and other contexts. Annals of the New York Academy of Sciences 169: 503–508, 1970.
14. Holmes DS: Debriefing after psychological experiments: I. Effectiveness of postdeception dehoaxing. Amer Psychol 31:858–867, 1976.
15. American Psychological Association: Ethical standards for psychologists. Amer Psychol 18:56–60, 1963.

35   Equipoise and the Ethics of Clinical Research

Benjamin Freedman

There is widespread agreement that ethics requires that each clinical trial begin with an honest null hypothesis.[1,2] In the simplest model, testing a new treatment B on a defined patient population P for which the current accepted treatment is A, it is necessary that the clinical investigator be in a state of genuine uncertainty regarding the comparative merits of treatments A and B for population P. If a physician knows that these treatments are not equivalent, ethics requires that the superior treatment be recommended. Following Fried, I call this state of uncertainty about the relative merits of A and B "equipoise."[3]

Equipoise is an ethically necessary condition in all cases of clinical research. In trials with several arms, equipose must exist between all arms of the trial; otherwise the trial design should be modified to exclude the inferior treatment. If equipoise is disturbed during the course of a trial, the trial may need to be terminated and all subjects previously enrolled (as well as other patients within the relevant population) may have to be offered the superior treatment. It has been rigorously argued that a trial with a placebo is ethical only when investigating conditions for which there is no known treatment[2]; this argument reflects a special application of the requirement for equipoise. Although equipoise has commonly been discussed in the special context of the ethics of randomized clinical trials,[4,5] it is important to recognize it as an ethical condition of all controlled clinical trials, whether or not they are randomized, placebo-controlled, or blinded.

The recent increase in attention to the ethics of research with human subjects has highlighted problems associated with equipoise. Yet, as I shall attempt to show, contemporary literature, if anything, minimizes those difficulties. Moreover, there is evidence that concern on the part of investigators about failure to satisfy the requirements for equipoise can doom a trial as a result of the consequent failure to enroll a sufficient number of subjects.

The solutions that have been offered to date fail to resolve these problems in a way that would permit clinical trials to proceed. This paper argues that these problems are predicated on a faulty concept of equipoise itself. An alternative understanding of equipoise as an ethical requirement of clinical trials is proposed, and its implications are explored.

Many of the problems raised by the requirement for equipoise are familiar. Shaw and Chalmers have written that a clinician who "knows, or has good reason to believe," that one arm of the trial is superior may not ethically participate.[6] But the reasoning or preliminary results that prompt the trial (and that may themselves be ethically mandatory)[7] may jolt the investigator (if not his or her colleagues) out of equipoise before the trial begins. Even if the investigator is undecided between A and B in terms of gross measures such as mortality and morbidity, equipoise may be disturbed because evident differences in the quality of life (as in the case of two surgical approaches) tip the balance.[3-5,8] In either case, in saying "we do not know" whether A or B is better, the investigator may create a false impression in prospective subjects, who hear him or her as saying "no evidence leans either way," when the investigator means "no controlled study has yet had results that reach statistical significance."

Late in the study — when P values are between 0.05 and 0.06 — the moral issue of equipoise is most readily apparent,[9,10] but the same problem arises when the earliest comparative results are analyzed.[11] Within the closed statistical universe of the clinical trial, each result that demonstrates a difference between the arms of the trial contributes exactly as much to the statistical conclusion that a difference exists as does any other. The contribution of the last pair of cases in the trial is not greater than that of the first. If, therefore, equipoise is a condition that reflects equivalent evidence for alternative hypotheses, it is jeopardized by the first pair of cases as much as by the last. The investigator who is concerned about the ethics of recruitment after the penultimate pair must logically be concerned after the first pair as well.

Finally, these issues are more than a philosopher's nightmare. Considerable interest has been generated by a paper in which Taylor et al.[12] describe the termination of a trial of alternative treatments for breast cancer. The trial foundered on the problem of patient recruitment, and the investigators trace much of the difficulty in enrolling patients to the fact that the investigators were not in a state of equipoise regarding the arms of the trial. With the increase in concern about the ethics of research and with the increasing presence of this topic in the curricula of medical and graduate schools, instances of the type that Taylor and her colleagues describe are likely to become more common. The requirement for equipoise thus poses a practical threat to clinical research.

Responses to the Problems of Equipoise

The problems described above apply to a broad class of clinical trials, at all stages of their development. Their resolution will need to be similarly comprehensive. However, the solutions that have so far been proposed address a portion of the difficulties, at best, and cannot be considered fully satisfactory.

Chalmers' approach to problems at the onset of a trial is to recommend that randomization begin with the very first subject.[11] If there are no preliminary, uncontrolled data in support of the experimental treatment B, equipoise regarding treatments A and B for the patient population P is not disturbed. There are several difficulties with this approach. Practically speaking, it is often necessary to establish details of administration, dosage, and so on, before a controlled trial begins, by means of uncontrolled trials in human subjects. In addition, as I have argued above, equipoise from the investigator's point of view is likely to be disturbed when the hypothesis is being formulated and a protocol is being prepared. It is then, before any subjects have been enrolled, that the information that the investigator has assembled makes the experimental treatment appear to be a reasonable gamble. Apart from these problems, initial randomization will not, as Chalmers recognizes, address disturbances of equipoise that occur in the course of a trial.

Data-monitoring committees have been proposed as a solution to problems arising in the course of the trial.[13] Such committees, operating independently of the investigators, are the only bodies with information concerning the trial's ongoing results. Since this knowledge is not available to the investigators, their equipoise is not disturbed. Although committees are useful in keeping the conduct of a trial free of bias, they cannot resolve the investigators' ethical difficulties. A clinician is not merely obliged to treat a patient on the basis of the information that he or she currently has, but is also required to discover information that would be relevant to treatment decisions. If interim results would disturb equipoise, the investigators are obliged to gather and use that information. Their agreement to remain in ignorance of preliminary results would, by definition, be an unethical agreement, just as a failure to call up the laboratory to find out a patient's test results is unethical. Moreover, the use of a monitoring committee does not solve problems of equipoise that arise before and at the beginning of a trial.

Recognizing the broad problems with equipoise, three authors have proposed radical solutions. All three think that there is an irresolvable conflict between the requirement that a patient be offered the best treatment known (the principle underlying the requirement for equipoise) and the conduct of clinical trials; they therefore suggest that the "best treatment" requirement be weakened.

Schafer has argued that the concept of equipoise, and the associated notion of the best medical treatment, depends on the judgment of patients rather than of clinical investigators.[14] Although the equipoise of an investigator may be disturbed if he or she favors B over A, the ultimate choice of treatment is the patient's. Because the patient's values may restore equipoise, Schafer argues, it is ethical for the investigator to proceed with a trial when the patient consents. Schafer's strategy is directed toward trials that test treatments with known and divergent side effects and will probably not be useful in trials conducted to test efficacy or unknown side effects. This approach, moreover, confuses the ethics of competent medical practice with those of consent. If we assume that the investigator is a competent clinician, by saying that the investigator is out of equipoise, we have by Schafer's account said that in the investigator's professional judgment one treatment is therapeutically inferior — for that patient, in that condition, given the quality of life that can be achieved. Even if a patient would consent to an inferior treatment, it seems to me a violation of competent medical practice, and hence of ethics, to make the offer. Of course, complex issues may arise when a patient refuses what the physician considers the best treatment and demands instead an inferior treatment. Without settling that problem, however, we can reject Schafer's position. For Schafer claims that in order to continue to conduct clinical trials, it is ethical for the physician to offer (not merely accede to) inferior treatment.

Meier suggests that "most of us would be quite willing to forego a modest expected gain in the general interest of learning something of value."[15] He argues that we accept risks in everyday life to achieve a variety of benefits, including convenience and economy. In the same way, Meier states, it is acceptable to enroll subjects in clinical trials even though they may not receive the best treatment throughout the course of the trial. Schafer suggests an essentially similar approach.[5,14] According to this view, continued progress in medical knowledge through clinical trials requires an explicit abandonment of the doctor's fully patient-centered ethic.

These proposals seem to be frank counsels of desperation. They resolve the ethical problems of equipoise by abandoning the need for equipoise. In any event, would their approach allow clinical trials to be conducted? I think this may fairly be doubted. Although many people are presumably altruistic enough to forgo the best medical treatment in the interest of the progress of science, many are not. The numbers and proportions required to sustain the statistical validity of trial results suggest that in the absence of overwhelming altruism, the enrollment of satisfactory numbers of patients will not be possible. In particular, very ill patients, toward whom many of the most important clinical trials are directed, may be disinclined to be altruistic. Finally, as the study by Taylor et al.[12] reminds us, the problems of equipoise trouble investigators as well as patients. Even if patients are prepared to dispense with the best treatment, their physicians, for reasons of ethics and professionalism, may well not be willing to do so.

Marquis has suggested a third approach. "Perhaps what is needed is an ethics that will justify the conscription of subjects for medical research," he has written. "Nothing less seems to justify present practice."[4] Yet, although conscription might enable us to continue present practice, it would scarcely justify it. Moreover, the conscription of physician investigators, as well as subjects, would be necessary, because, as has been repeatedly argued, the problems of equipoise are as disturbing to clinicians as they are to subjects. Is any less radical and more plausible approach possible?

Theoretical Equipoise versus Clinical Equipoise

The problems of equipoise examined above arise from a particular understanding of the concept, which I will term "theoretical equipoise." It is an understanding that is both conceptually odd and ethically irrelevant. Theoretical equipoise exists when, overall, the evidence on behalf of two alternative treatment regimens is exactly balanced. This evidence may be derived from a variety of sources, including data from the literature, uncontrolled experience, considerations of basic science and fundamental physiologic processes, and perhaps a "gut feeling" or "instinct" resulting from (or superimposed on) other considerations. The problems examined above arise from the principle that if theoretical equipoise is disturbed, the physician has, in Schafer's words, a "treatment preference" — let us say, favoring experimental treatment B. A trial testing A against B requires that some patients be enrolled in violation of this treatment preference.

Theoretical equipoise is overwhelmingly fragile; that is, it is disturbed by a slight accretion of evidence favoring one arm of the trial. In Chalmers' view, equipoise is disturbed when the odds that A will be more successful than B are anything other than 50 percent. It is therefore necessary to randomize treatment assignments beginning with the very first patient, lest equipoise be disturbed. We may say that theoretical equipoise is balanced on a knife's edge.

Theoretical equipoise is not appropriate to one-dimensional hypotheses and causes us to think in those terms. The null hypothesis must be sufficiently simple and "clean" to be finely balanced: Will A or B be superior in reducing morality or shrinking tumors or lowering fevers in population P? Clinical choice is commonly more complex. The choice of A or B depends on some combination of effectiveness, consistency, minimal or relievable side effects, and other factors. On close examination, for example, it some-times appears that even trials that purport to test a single hypothesis in fact involve a more complicated, portmanteau measure — e.g., the "therapeutic index" of A versus B. The formulation of the conditions of theoretical equipoise for such complex, multidimensional clinical hypotheses is tantamount to the formulation of a rigorous calculus of apples and oranges.

Theoretical equipoise is also highly sensitive to the vagaries of the investigator's attention and perception. Because of its fragility, theoretical equipoise is disturbed as soon as the investigator perceives a difference between the alternatives — whether or not any genuine difference exists. Prescott writes, for example, "It will be common at some stage in most trials for the survival curves to show visually different survivals," short of significance but "sufficient to raise ethical difficulties for the participants."[16] A visual difference, however, is purely an artifact of the research methods employed: when and by what means data are assembled and analyzed and what scale is adopted for the graphic presentation of data. Similarly, it is common for researchers to employ interval scales for phenomena that are recognized to be continuous by nature — e.g., five-point scales of pain or stages of tumor progression. These interval scales, which represent an arbitrary distortion of the available evidence to simplify research, may magnify the differences actually found, with a resulting disturbance of theoretical equipoise.

Finally, as described by several authors, theoretical equipoise is personal and idiosyncratic. It is disturbed when the clinician has, in Schafer's words, what "might even be labeled a bias or a hunch," a preference of a "merely intuitive nature."[14] The investigator who ignores such a hunch, by failing to advise the patient that because of it the investigator prefer B to A or by recommending A (or a chance of random assignment to A) to the patient, has violated the requirement for equipoise and its companion requirement to recommend the best medical treatment.

The problems with this concept of equipoise should be evident. To understand the alternative, preferable interpretation of equipoise, we need to recall the basic reason for conducting trials: there is a current or imminent conflict in the clinical community over what treatment is preferred for patients in a defined population P. The standard treatment is A, but some evidence suggests that B will be superior (because of its effectiveness or its reduction of undesirable side effects, or for some other reason). (In the rare case when the first evidence of a novel therapy's superiority would be entirely convincing to the clinical community, equipoise is already disturbed.) Or there is a split in the clinical community, with some clinicians favoring A and others favoring B. Each side recognizes that the opposing side has evidence to support its position, yet each still thinks that overall its own view is correct. There exists (or, in the case of a novel therapy, there may soon exist) an honest, professional disagreement among expert clinicians about the preferred treatment. A clinical trial is instituted with the aim of resolving this dispute.

At this point, a state of "clinical equipoise" exists. There is no consensus within the expert clinical community about the comparative merits of the alternatives to be tested. We may state the formal conditions under which such a trial would be ethical as follows: at the start of the trial, there must be a state of clinical equipoise regarding the merits of the regimens to be tested, and the trial must be designed in such a way as to make it reasonable to expect that, if it is successfully concluded, clinical equipoise will be disturbed. In other words, the results of a successful clinical trial should be convincing enough to resolve the dispute among clinicians.

A state of clinical equipoise is consistent with a decided treatment preference on the part of the investigators. They must simply recognize that their less-favored treatment is preferred by colleagues whom they consider to be responsible and competent. Even if the interim results favor the preference of the investigators, treatment B, clinical equipoise persists as long as those results are too weak to influence the judgment of the community of clinicians, because of limited sample size, unresolved possibilities of side effects, or other factors. (This judgment can necessarily be made only by those who know the interim results — whether a data-monitoring committee or the investigators.)

At the point when the accumulated evidence in favor of B is so strong that the committee or investigators believe no open-minded clinician informed of the results would still favor A, clinical equipoise has been disturbed. This may occur well short of the original schedule for the termination of the trial, for unexpected reasons. (Therapeutic effects or side effects may be much stronger than anticipated, for example, or a definable subgroup within population P may be recognized for which the results demonstrably disturb clinical equipoise.) Because of the arbitrary character of human judgment and persuasion, some ethical problems regarding the termination of a trial will remain. Clinical equipoise will confine these problems to unusual or extreme cases, however, and will allow us to cast persistent problems in the proper terms. For example, in the face of a strong established trend, must we continue the trial because of others' blind fealty to an arbitrary statistical bench mark?

Clearly, clinical equipoise is a far weaker — and more common — condition than theoretical equipoise. Is it ethical to conduct a trial on the basis of clinical equipoise, when theoretical equipoise is disturbed? Or, as Schafer and others have argued, is doing so a violation of the physician's obligation to provide patients with the best medical treatment? [4,5,14] Let us assume that the investigators have a decided preference for B but wish to conduct a trial on the grounds that clinical (not theoretical) equipoise exists. The ethics committee asks the investigators whether, if they or members of their families were within population P, they would not want to be treated with their preference, B? An affirmative answer is often thought to be fatal to the prospects for such a trial, yet the investigators answer in the affirmative. Would a trial satisfying this weaker form of equipoise be ethical?

I believe that it clearly is ethical. As Fried has emphasized, [3] competent (hence, ethical) medicine is social rather than individual in nature. Progress in medicine relies on progressive consensus within the medical and research communities. The ethics of medical practice grants no ethical or normative meaning to a treatment preference, however powerful, that is based on a hunch or on anything less than evidence publicly presented and convincing to the clinical community. Persons are licensed as physicians after they demonstrate the acquisition of this professionally validated knowledge, not after they reveal a superior capacity for guessing. Normative judgments of their be-havior — e.g., malpractice actions — rely on a comparison with what is done by the community of medical practitioners. Failure to follow a "treatment preference" not shared by this community and not based on information that would convince it could not be the basis for an allegation of legal or ethical malpractice. As Fried states: "[T]he conception of what is good medicine is the product of a professional consensus." By definition, in a state of clinical equipoise, "good medicine" finds the choice between A and B indifferent.

In contrast to theoretical equipoise, clinical equipoise is robust. The ethical difficulties at the beginning and end of a trial are therefore largely alleviated. There remain dif-ficulties about consent, but these too may be diminished. Instead of emphasizing the lack of evidence favoring one arm over another that is required by theoretical equipoise, clinical equipoise places the emphasis in informing the patient on the honest disagreement among expert clinicians. The fact that the investigator has a "treatment preference," if he or she does, could be disclosed; indeed, if the preference is a decided one, and based on something more than a hunch, it could be ethically mandatory to disclose it. At the same time, it would be emphasized that this preference is not shared by others. It is likely to be a matter of chance that the patient is being seen by a clinician with a preference for B over A, rather than by an equally competent clinician with the opposite preference.

Clinical equipoise does not depend on concealing relevant information from re-searchers and subjects, as does the use of independent data-monitoring committees. Rather, it allows investigators, in informing subjects, to distinguish appropriately among validated knowledge accepted by the clinical community, data on treatments that are promising but are not (or, for novel therapies, would not be) generally convincing, and mere hunches. Should informed patients decline to participate because they have chosen a specific clinician and trust his or her judgment — over and above the consensus in the professional community — that is no more than the patients' right. We do not conscript patients to serve as subjects in clinical trials.

The Implications of Clinical Equipoise

The theory of clinical equipoise has been formulated as an alternative to some current views on the ethics of human research. At the same time, it corresponds closely to a preanalytic concept held by many in the research and regulatory communities. Clinical equipoise serves, then, as a rational formulation of the approach of many toward research ethics; it does not so much change things as explain why they are the way they are.

Nevertheless, the precision afforded by the theory of clinical equipoise does help to clarify or reformulate some aspects of research ethics; I will mention only two.

First, there is a recurrent debate about the ethical propriety of conducting clinical trials of discredited treatments, such a Laetrile.[17] Often, substantial political pressure to conduct such tests is brought to bear by adherents of quack therapies. The theory of clinical equipoise suggests that when there is no support for a treatment regimen within the expert clinical community, the first ethical requirement of a trial — clinical equipoise — is lacking; it would therefore be unethical to conduct such a trial.

Second, Feinstein has criticized the tendency of clinical investigators to narrow excessively the conditions and hypotheses of a trial in order to ensure the validity of its results.[18] This "fastidious" approach purchases scientific manageability at the expense of an inability to apply the results to the "messy" conditions of clinical practice. The theory of clinical equipoise adds some strength to this criticism. Overly "fastidious" trials, designed to resolve some theoretical question, fail to satisfy the second ethical requirement of clinical research, since the special conditions of the trial will render it useless for influencing clinical decisions, even if it is successfully completed.

The most important result of the concept of clinical equipoise, however, might be to relieve the current crisis of confidence in the ethics of clinical trials. Equipoise, properly understood, remains an ethical condition for clinical trials. It is consistent with much current practice. Clinicians and philosophers alike have been premature in calling for desperate measures to resolve problems of equipoise.

Acknowledgements: I am indebted to Robert J. Levine, M.D., and to Harold Merskey, D.M., for their valuable suggestions.

References

1. Levine RJ. Ethics and regulations of clinical research. 2nd ed. Baltimore: Urban & Schwarzenberg, 1986.
2. *Idem.* The use of placebos in randomized clinical trials. IRB: Rev Hum Subj Res 1985; 7(2):1–4.
3. Fried C. Medical experimentation: personal integrity and social policy. Amsterdam: North-Holland Publishing, 1974.
4. Marquis D. Leaving therapy to chance. Hastings Cent Rep 1983; 13(4):40–7.
5. Schafer A. The ethics of the randomized clinical trial. N Engl J Med 1982; 307: 719–24.
6. Shaw LW, Chalmer TC. Ethics in cooperative clinical trials. Ann NY Acad Sci 1970; 169:487–95.
7. Hollenberg NK, Dzau VJ, Williams GH. Are uncontrolled clinical studies ever justified? N Engl J Med 1980; 303:1067.
8. Levine RJ, Lebacqz K. Some ethical considerations in clinical trials. Clin Pharmacol Ther 1979; 25:728–n41.

9. Klimt CR, Canner PL. Terminating a long-term clinical trial. Clin Pharmacol Ther 1979; 25:641–6.

10. Veatch RM. Longitudinal studies, sequential designs and grant renewals: what to do with preliminary data. IRB: Rev Hum Subj Res 1979; 1(4):1–3.

11. Chalmers T. The ethics of randomization as a decision-making technique and the problem of informed consent. In: Beauchamp TL, Walters L, eds. Contemporary issues in bioethics. Encino, Calif.: Dickenson, 1978:426–9.

12. Taylor KM, Margolese RG, Soskolne CL. Physicians' reasons for not entering eligible patients in a randomized clinical trial of surgery for breast cancer. N Engl J Med 1984; 310:1363–7.

13. Chalmers TC. Invited remarks. Clin Pharmacol Ther 1979; 25:649–50.

14. Schafer A. The randomized clinical trial: for whose benefit? IRB: Rev Hum Subj Res 1985; 7(2):4–6.

15. Meier P. Terminating a trial — the ethical problem. Clin Pharmacol Ther 1979; 25: 633–40.

16. Prescott RJ. Feedback of data to participants during clinical trials. In: Tagnon HJ, Staquet MJ, eds. Controversies in cancer: design of trials and treatment. New York: Masson Publishing, 1979:55–61.

17. Cowan DH. The ethics of clinical trials of ineffective therapy. IRB: Rev Hum Subj Res 1981; 3(5):10–1.

18. Feinstein AR. An additional basic science for clinical medicine. II. The limitations of randomized trials. Ann Intern Med 1983; 99:544–50.

36　AIDS Trials, Civil Liberties and the Social Control of Therapy: Should We Embrace New Drugs with Open Arms?

David A. Salisbury & Martin T. Schechter

The unique challenges posed by AIDS (acquired immune deficiency syndrome) have ramifications far beyond the bounds of the disease itself. Nowhere is this felt more acutely than in the biomedical research and drug regulatory communities. AIDS activists compel researchers and government regulators to re-evaluate the conventional wisdom concerning tests of new therapies.[1] Anyone who thinks this problem is specific to AIDS should consider that changes could affect the way in which all new therapies are evaluated.

The demands have occasionally been extreme. The AIDS epidemic has provided some groups with an opportunity to call for an end to most government regulation of investigational therapies, which they believe should be used solely with the informed consent of the recipient (*New York Times*, Jan. 27, 1987: A21). Other AIDS groups have called for a ban on the use of placebos. The AIDS Coalition to Unleash Power (ACT UP) has called placebo trials "a medically sanctioned form of Russian roulette",[2] and *Le Manifeste de Montréal*, published by a coalition of AIDS groups at the Vth International Conference on AIDS, held June 4 to 9, 1989, in Montreal, stated that "placebo trials must be regarded as inherently unethical when they are the only means of access to particular treatments".[3]

Other, less extreme demands require thoughtful consideration by the medical community. Most AIDS groups recognize the need for valid scientific study of new agents but are frustrated by logistic and bureaucratic delays. Many have questioned the randomized, controlled trial as being paternalistic, coercive and an infringement on fundamental civil rights. Civil liberties experts have presented powerful arguments in favour of enhanced rights to self-determination in the context of AIDS.[4] AIDS groups have suggested alternative trial configurations, such as the open-arm clinical trial, that they believe would provide earlier access to nonvalidated therapies and be more compassionate and ethical than traditional trials.

In this article we review the concept of open-arm clinical trials and present their advantages and disadvantages. We need to find a solution that optimizes individual freedoms at a minimum cost to scientific validity and public protection. As stated by Dixon,[4] whatever the solution it "should be as broad as possible to reflect the respect of Canadians for personal self-determination in that which affects us most personally and intimately, and as narrow as is necessary to leave materially undisturbed the public interests served by the social control of therapy".

A New Reality

Many must wonder why these issues are prominent now, in the AIDS era. "What is special about AIDS", observes Dixon,[4] "is that persons with AIDS possess . . . the political power needed to confront the therapeutic system with a case for the rights of all catastrophically ill patients. . . . They have added their very powerful voice to what has traditionally been an either silent or politically disorganized constituency."

At the extreme some AIDS groups want to end regulation; they openly support the importation and distribution of nonvalidated therapies and have even fostered the sharing of investigational drugs in clinical trials.

Delaney[5] described the situation in which "AIDS study centers throughout the [United States] tell of widespread concurrent use of other treatments; frequent cheating, even bribery, to gain entry to studies; mixing of drugs by patients to share and dilute the risk of being on placebo; and rapid dropping out of patients who learn they are on placebo". Although this is likely the activity of a few, it can have devastating effects on therapeutic progress. We believe that most AIDS groups appreciate the importance of trials in advancing the goals of therapy; however, they want an equal say in the design and conduct of the research intended to help people with AIDS, and they have the organization and resources to raise challenging questions about that research.

Therefore, the AIDS research community faces a new reality. It has always had to contend with the scientific, bureaucratic and logistic barriers that inevitably impede biomedical research, but now there is a highly organized and politically astute patient population, however heterogeneous in its objectives. Unless the legitimate concerns of this community are addressed through dialogue and unless the right of a dying person to self-determination and the right of the state to public protection are reconciled, therapeutic progress could be seriously threatened. As Dr. Jere T. Goyan,[6] dean of pharmacology, University of California at San Francisco, stated, "We need to consider alternative study designs that offer the patient the maximum hope for cure and the opportunity for some control over his or her destiny. . . . What I am suggesting is the need for a reexamination of all the assumptions on which the scientific requirements of the present system are based."

Illustrative Case

Consider an investigational antiviral agent, drug X, intended for use early in HIV (human immunodeficiency virus) infection to prevent or postpone deterioration and AIDS. A phase-III randomized clinical trial is proposed that pits drug X against the standard therapy, which at present would be placebo, although zidovudine (AZT) could soon become the standard therapy as a result of current placebo-controlled trials; the trial would then compare drug X with AZT.

In a conventional randomized controlled trial eligible consenting subjects are randomly allocated to receive either drug, and their outcomes are monitored. In such a trial with an open arm (Figure 9.1) the eligible subject is offered either the open arm or the clinical trial. Subjects who choose the open arm would receive drug X in an unblinded fashion and would be monitored; those who choose the clinical trial would be randomly assigned to either the experimental or the control group. In this design the open arm is offered to the same people who are eligible for the controlled trial.

The open-arm concept is not new; it can be said to exist whenever the experimental intervention is already available outside of the trial. For example, in a randomized

Figure 9.1   Design of Randomized Controlled Trial with Open Arm

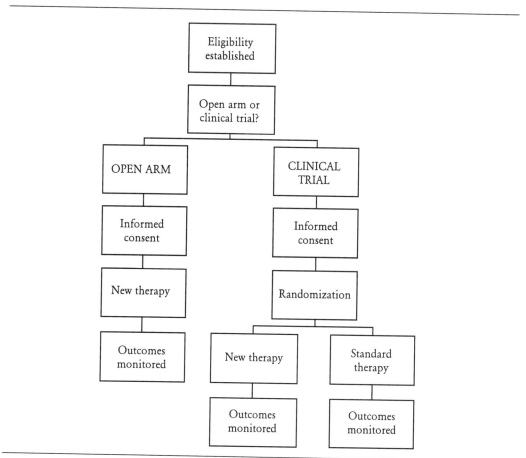

trial that compared mastectomy with lumpectomy for breast cancer, since both therapies were available in the community open arms already existed at the time of the trial.[7] However, in the present context open-arm trials are both novel and controversial; the investigational therapy is neither validated for the clinical condition nor available outside the context of the trial. Under such circumstances, in the conventional trial the only access to the nonvalidated therapy is through participation in the randomized trial; in the open-arm trial direct access is provided for participants who choose the open arm.

Ethical Requirements of a Controlled Clinical Trial

Aside from informed consent a clinical trial has two main ethical requirements. The first is "equipoise" — a term used by Fried[8] and Freedman[9] to indicate a state of genuine uncertainty about the relative merits of the therapies under consideration. In other words, the trial must begin with an "honest null hypothesis".[9] If, for example, there were reasonable consensus that drug X was clearly superior to the standard therapy a state of equipoise would not exist and the trial would be unethical. The second requirement is that the trial must be designed and executed so that equipoise is either disturbed or established. Therefore, the trial must provide conclusive scientific evidence that drug X is superior or inferior to the standard therapy or that the therapies are equally effective. This implies that the trial must have both internal and external validity and that in the case of a negative result the power must be sufficient for the result to be considered conclusive. A trial that is unlikely to resolve the underlying scientific question is a disservice to the study subjects and to potential recipients.

The Case for Open-Arm Trials

The open-arm design has its greatest support among AIDS community groups and their advocates. At the Workshop on HIV Clinical Trials, in London, Ont., Nov. 17 to 18, 1988, a coalition of people with AIDS requested that all trials of experimental treatments include an open arm. They argued that open-arm trials are inherently more ethical and compassionate than randomized controlled trials since they offer patients more control over their medical treatment. The randomized format is thought to be coercive because subjects are forced into the trial as the only way to receive the experimental agent. Delaney[5] asserted, "Many patients and their advocates find it morally repugnant to deny potentially life-saving treatment to the masses to force a few into clinical studies."

A related advantage to the open-arm design is the commitment of the remaining participants, who enter the randomized trial. ACT UP[10] claimed that "if the people who enrol in a trial are truly desperate to get the drug at any cost they will do whatever it takes to enter a protocol. . . . If, however, the drug is available outside the trial to those who absolutely need it, those people who enrol in a trial will more likely be those who can abide by the rigors of the trial." Delaney[5] stated that the volunteers who remained "would be more likely to act as pure research subjects, entering studies not solely out of a desperate effort to save their lives".

Since people who elect to enter the open arm would be followed up, they constitute a case series of subjects taking the new drug and thus provide some scientific information about side effects and toxicity and some circumstantial evidence of benefit. If the open arm contains subjects who were technically ineligible for the trial but for whom the drug might ultimately be prescribed, it can provide actual experience with the drug that would not otherwise be forthcoming from the trial.

Community groups and advocates have often cited the advantage that more people would have access to the new drug and its clinical benefit at an earlier stage in its evaluation. Without open access patient groups have created large "underground" networks to purchase and distribute putative therapies for HIV infection. As Delaney[5] noted, "While most of this is benevolent, there is every reason to expect that it will become less so over time as entrepreneurs learn to exploit it." Proponents argue that open arms would obviate the need for such networks and avoid the possibility of exploitation.

The Case against Open-Arm Trials

In general some useful information about side effects and toxicity would be provided by people who elect to enter the open arm. However, valid scientific evidence of efficacy and effectiveness would be unavailable because of the lack of an adequate control group. Historical or contemporaneous control groups from other populations might be constructed, but there are well-known methodologic problems with such an approach.[11]

The potential for an open arm to introduce bias is great. Subjects who enter and complete the controlled trial will differ from those who enter the open arm by virtue of volunteer and compliance biases.[12] Thus, the controlled trial could be carried out in a biased subset of the total potential recipients. The extent of the bias would depend on the relative proportions of eligible subjects who choose the open arm or the trial. If in the early stages of the trial 90% of all the eligible subjects chose the open arm, the bias could be severe, and the trial might no longer be considered ethical. Conversely, if 90% of the eligible subjects chose the randomized trial the bias would be minimal. The extent of the bias could be assessed through a comparison of outcomes between the open-arm participants and those randomly allocated to receive the new therapy.

An open arm may cause recruitment and sample-size problems. There appears to be little incentive for eligible subjects to enter the randomized controlled trial. Those who want the drug can choose the open arm, whereas those who do not want it need only avoid the trial altogether. Such an option was exercised by women who avoided a randomized trial of lumpectomy versus mastectomy[7,13] and simply sought out their desired therapy. As a result that study had severe recruitment problems and might have failed had the randomization not been modified.[14] If the presence of an open arm in an HIV trial were to create recruitment problems the randomized trial would fail to reach its recruitment target. In addition, subjects would always have the option to switch to the open arm to receive the drug. Thus, the presence of an open arm could increase the likelihood of withdrawal from the clinical trial and thus create analytic complications and exacerbate sample size problems. The trial might end up with insufficient statistical power to detect important differences.

More likely the open arm would lead to recruitment problems that would force the investigators to lengthen the recruitment period and hence the study's duration. This would postpone the resolution of the scientific question. The participants in the ultimately inferior arm of the trial would experience longer exposure to the inferior treatment. Freedman[15] warned that "the failure to complete these trials will serve neither the patients themselves — who serve as guinea pigs for treatments of unproved efficacy, and pay for the privilege — nor future patients who are denied the advantage of prior validation of treatments".

Finally, we turn to the argument that open-arm trials are more compassionate since they allow earlier access to the experimental therapy. Most researchers do not accept that rigorous evaluation through clinical trials is coercive, unethical and lacking in compassion. Richman[16] stated that "on the contrary, properly designed clinical studies of experimental drugs will relieve the most suffering and do the most good, certainly in the long run, and almost certainly in the short run", and "the open distribution of unproved drugs is not compassionate and this approach in fact often delays access of needy patients and health care workers to the critical information that will prolong life and reduce suffering". For these reasons many believe that open-arm trials are unethical. There is a "catch-22" to the argument that open-arm trials allow more people access to the new drug earlier. This will be an advantage only if the drug turns out to be beneficial. For example, an open-arm trial of cyclosporine therapy for AIDS would have exposed many more subjects to a therapy now known to be harmful.[17] Of over 70 agents introduced for possible HIV therapy only 1 has reached the stage of demonstrated clinical effectiveness: many, including cyclosporine,[17] castanospermine[18] and dextran sulfate,[18] have been shown to be possibly harmful.

Rebuttal

Charges of paternalism greet the argument that people with HIV illness must be protected from the potential harmful effects of untested therapies. Advocates of patients with AIDS contend that it is equally possible for new therapies to do more good than harm and that people with serious illnesses should have the opportunity to make informed decisions whether to take the risk. The arguments concerning the possible adverse effects of open arms on recruitment into clinical trials are countered by several points. First, AIDS groups have recognized these concerns and have promised to work to ensure sufficient numbers of subjects. They want to test the viability of open-arm trials rather than argue the hypothetical possibilities of recruitment problems. Proponents indicate several attractions of clinical trials besides access to novel therapy; these include specialized medical care, intensive follow-up, possible beneficial cointerventions that may not otherwise be available and access to health care in countries without universal health insurance.

Alternative Trial Design

We believe there are alternatives to open-arm trials that address the concerns of AIDS groups and meet the scientific demands for rigour. The most compassionate and ethical approach is rapid but valid evaluation of promising new therapies. Several techniques can be applied to improve the rapidity and increase the acceptability of randomized clinical trials of HIV therapies with minimal cost to scientific integrity.

The first alternative involves various techniques known collectively as sequential analysis[19] — analysis of the results of a trial on a continuing or frequent interim basis so that the trial can be ended as soon as a definitive result is available. Although blinded sequential analyses with tight, prespecified stopping rules entail some scientific drawbacks, including the tendency to produce biased estimates of the treatment effect, the advantages in the current climate of HIV clinical evaluation outweigh the drawbacks. These techniques can be advantageous only when the delay between the entry to the trial and the outcome is short relative to the period of recruitment.

There is no absolute reason why a randomized trial must distribute subjects equally to the experimental and control arms. The unbalanced design is an alternative in which two-thirds of the subjects, for example, are allocated to the new therapy and one-third to the standard. This is simple to do, addresses some of the same issues as an open arm and only loses some statistical power relative to a balanced design. There is, however, no compromise to internal validity.

There is also no reason why all trials must use the same classic type I and type II error levels; these levels should be determined on the basis of the societal costs of making false-positive and false-negative errors and not simply convention. It seems ludicrous to maintain the same levels for trials of HIV therapy that one would use for a trial of acne lotion. Thus, we might agree to accept a greater chance than the usual 5% of falsely accepting a new drug for AIDS as being superior to standard therapy. This would reduce the number of subjects required and lead to earlier termination if the drug were clearly beneficial or harmful. A price would have to be paid in the form of an increased false-positive rate, but it is preferable to a state of therapeutic anarchy.

The question of access to nonvalidated therapies unltimately comes down to an assessment of two important rights: the individual right to self-determination and the right of the state to effect some form of control to protect the public and advance science. With regard to chronic illness Dixon[4] explored these rights through two of the avenues open to migraine sufferers: "one in which they have an absolutely unfettered right to scour the earth for novel therapies for their affliction, and in which they will have no practical chance of success; and another in which they relinquish a measure of their therapeutic autonomy to a social and scientific authority that will organize a search for a cure in terms of the scientific method". Under these conditions Dixon argued that the latter was the rational choice and judged "a very limited parternalism acceptable given the very substantial benefits gained through its narrow operation". However, the balance is said to shift in the presence of a life-threatening condition such as AIDS in which life expectancy is often exceeded by the reasonable expectancy of a therapeutic advance. Dixon claimed that under these conditions "a catastrophic illness induces a special set of circumstances which can make the personal freedom to seek therapy of paramount importance".

Another alternative to the open-arm trial is the "catastrophic threshold", which stems from the recognition of the enhanced rights mentioned in the previous paragraph. Under this proposal for the study of a new therapy a point in the natural history of HIV illness should be defined so that patients beyond this threshold would have access, under close supervision, to the new agent while it was being evaluated in clinical trials involving people who are at earlier stages of the disease. The threshold would be shifted as the therapies and our understanding of the natural history of AIDS change. The precise definition of the threshold would be reached through consensus among investigators, sponsors, regulators, community groups and other interested parties. In general the catastrophic threshold at a point in time is meant to identify seriously ill patients for whom clinical science has little to offer, primarily those for whom there is no standard therapy at that point and those who have failed to respond to the standard therapy of the day.

At present the threshold might be defined to include people with AIDS or severe immune dysfunction who have failed to respond or are intolerant to AZT or who have an AIDS manifestation for which there is no worthwhile therapy. Under this definition all people with AIDS would be considered catastrophically ill except those responding well to AZT. The provision of the catastrophic threshold would clearly have cost implications for government and drug sponsors alike.

The catastrophic threshold is similar in spirit to the Emergency Drug Release Programme, in which a physician may request an unapproved drug for a patient on compassionate grounds. However, the threshold would be based on clear criteria derived through consensus and would provide a mechanism for wider release of the drug to all those beyond the threshold; such people would be followed up in an uncontrolled, separate, "catastrophic open arm" of the trial.

In some ways the catastrophic threshold is similar to the "parallel track" proposal in the United States, in which a separate arm runs parallel to the clinical trial for people who would not otherwise enter the trial and who meet certain additional criteria.[10,20] However, the parallel track is proposed for situations other than those we have delineated; for example, it would be available to patients with a disease as severe as that of subjects in the controlled trial but for whom the trial is geographically inaccessible. We prefer the catastrophic threshold because geographic inaccessibility should not be a problem in Canada owing to the impending nation-wide network for HIV clinical trials. If it were to remain a problem the best solution would be not the open distribution of untested drugs in regions with less access but, rather, the expansion of the trials to include all regions.

In the United States the parallel track would also be open to people who are ineligible for the trial but for whom the new drug is absolutely contraindicated. For example, patients who take other medications concomitantly or have certain prespecified conditions are customarily excluded from trials so that the evaluation of drug toxicity and side effects is more pure. An alternative would be to relax the eligibility criteria to include virtually all patients for whom the new therapy is not absolutely contraindicated; if necessary the analysis could be stratified to screen out the statistical "noise" created by their inclusion. Moreover, additional data about actual drug effectiveness would be provided, and considerable resentment and confusion might be avoided. For example, with a parallel track a person in the controlled trial might know of someone at the same stage of HIV infection who has open access to the new drug because of apparent loopholes in the trial's eligibility criteria. The argument that the expanded eligibility criteria would enlarge the trial and increase its costs is not valid, because all of the participants in the parallel track would have received the drug and been followed anyway. We believe that the minimal compromise to scientific purity, if any, would be outweighed by the trial's greater applicability to affected people and the attendant improvement in trial acceptability and recruitment that might arise.

Conclusions

We recommend that HIV clinical trials be rapidly deployed and sequential analysis be used with strict stopping rules, when possible, to provide scientifically valid information in the shortest time. In addition, such techniques as unbalanced randomization and relaxation of conventional confidence levels should be considered. Eligibility criteria should be as relaxed as possible to include all patients for whom the new drug might eventually be used. A catastrophic threshold should be defined so that people whose clinical condition places them beyond the threshold may still receive the agent, in a closely monitored fashion, while it is being evaluated through clinical trials involving people whose HIV infection is at an earlier stage. We believe that this combination of strategies is superior to open-arm trials. The combined strategy will provide the validity required by science as well as the expediency, compassion and human rights demanded by affected people inside and outside of the trial.

Acknowledgements: We are indebted to Mr. Jeff Braff and Drs. Mary Fanning, Gary Garber, Julio S.G. Montaner, Stanley Read, Walter Schlech, Chris Tsoukas, Mark Wainberg, John Dixon and Samuel Sheps for helpful discussions.

This work was supported by National Health Research Scholar award 6610-1496-48 to Dr. Schechter from the National Health Research and Development Program, Department of National Health and Welfare.

References

1. Palca J: AIDS drug trials enter new age. *Science* 1989; 246:19–21
2. *A National AIDS Treatment Research Agenda*, AIDS Coalition to Unleash Power, New York, 1989; 3
3. Le Manifeste de Montréal. *AIDS Action News* 1989; 6: 4–5
4. Dixon J: *Catastrophic Rights*, BC Civil Liberties Association, Vancouver, 1989; 6–11
5. Delaney M: A case for patient access to experimental therapy. *J Infect Dis* 1989; 159: 416–419
6. Goyan JT: Drug regulation: Quo vadis? *JAMA* 1988; 260: 3052–3053
7. Fisher B, Bauer M, Margolese R, et al: Five-year results of a randomized clinical trial comparing total mastectomy and segmental mastectomy with or without radiation in the treatment of breast cancer. *N Engl J Med* 1985; 312: 1665–1673
8. Fried C: *Medical Experimentation: Personal Integrity and Social Policy*, North Holland, Amsterdam, 1974: 50–56
9. Freedman B: Equipoise and the ethics of clinical research *N Engl J Med* 1987; 317: 141–145
10. *Parallel Track Program for AIDS and HIV-related Therapies*. AIDS Coalition to Unleash Power. New York, 1989: 6
11. Sacks H, Chalmers TC, Smith H Jr: Randomized versus historical controls for clinical trials. *Am J Med* 1982; 72: 233–240
12. Sackett DL: Bias in analytic research. *J Chronic Dis* 1979; 32: 51–63
13. Taylor KM, Margolese RG, Soskolne CL: Physicians' reasons for not entering eligible patients in a randomized clinical trial of surgery for breast cancer. *N Engl J Med* 1984; 310: 1363–1367
14. Redmond C, Bauer M: *Pre-randomization: Progress Report of the National Surgical Adjuvant Project for Breast and Bowel Cancer (NSABP)*, NSABP Headquarters, Pittsburgh, 1980: 69–72
15. Freedman B and the McGill/Boston University Cooperative Research Group on Law, Ethics, and Policy on HIV: Nonvalidated therapies and HIV disease: a critique and a proposal. *Hastings Cent Rep* 1989; 19 (3): 14–20
16. Richman DD: Public access to experimental drug therapy: AIDS raises yet another conflict between freedom of the individual and

welfare of the individual and the public. *J Infect Dis* 1989; 159: 412–415

17. Phillips A, Wainberg MA, Coates R et al: Cyclosporine-induced deterioration in patients with AIDS. *Can Med Assoc J* 1989; 140: 1456–1460

18. Izaguirre CA, Drouin J: The anti-HIV drugs castanospermine (CSP) and dextran sulfate (DS) also allow the growth of in vivo infected CD4+ T-cells [abstr]. Presented at the Vth International Conference on AIDS. Montreal, June 4–9, 1989

19. Armitage P: *Sequential Medical Trials*, Blackwell Sci, Oxford, 1975

20. Marshall E: Quick release of AIDS drugs. *Science* 1989; 245: 345–347

Chapter 9

Questions to Consider

1. Many clinical studies are funded by drug companies to test "me-too" drugs: drugs whose chemical composition is so similar to a currently standard medication that the new drug is expected to be as safe and effective as the standard, but distinct enough as not to infringe upon the patent rights of the company manufacturing the standard drug.

    a. What effect should this have upon a research ethics committee's consideration of one such study's risk–benefit ratio?

    b. How should the fact of drug company sponsorship, and the company's motivation, be handled in the informed consent process?

    c. Assume that the drug company is having difficulty in getting subjects to enrol, and therefore wishes to offer them a financial incentive. How, if at all, could this be ethically done?

    d. The same question, but this time the company has failed to attract doctors to participate as clinical investigators: What ethical incentives can be provided? Should these be disclosed to prospective subjects?

2. What are good reasons for requiring that research ethics committees include a layperson (non-physician, non-scientist) among their membership? What qualities should such a person bring to the review process? Should the choice of a layperson be affected by where the research is to be done — for example, in a general hospital; in a children's hospital; in a residence for the developmentally handicapped?

3. Primary pulmonary hypertension is a devastating illness that kills its victims within months. Currently, a patient's only hope is to receive a heart–lung transplant, but most patients die before a suitable donor is found. A newly developed drug that has been used in a small number of patients seems remarkably safe and effective, but it costs $1000 per day per patient. The drug's developer wishes to perform a placebo-controlled trial, to demonstrate that the drug can keep patients alive long enough for heart–lung donors to be found. Should a research ethics committee approve this trial? Would you enrol as a subject if you were diagnosed as suffering from primary pulmonary hypertension?

4. A five-year study of breast cancer therapy, involving thousands of patient/subjects in over 100 North American hospitals, is in its third year. As with most studies of this size and length, this trial has established a data-monitoring committee that confidentially examines its early results to see whether the difference between patient reaction on the two arms of the trial is so great that the trial should be stopped prematurely. You are a biostatistician and a member of the study's data-monitoring committee, as well as of your local hospital's research ethics committee. At the last meeting of the monitoring committee you argued that patients on one trial arm have done so badly that the trial should be stopped now. You were outvoted, five to three. Should you inform the local research committee of the preliminary results, and your view? Let us say that you did: How should that local committee react?

Further Readings

Alexander, Leo. 1949. Medical science under dictatorship. *New England Journal of Medicine* 241: 39–47.

Appelbaum, Paul S., et al. 1987. False hopes and best data: Consent to research and the therapeutic misconception. *Hastings Center Report* 17(2):20–24.

Chalmers, Thomas C. 1990. Ethical implications of rejecting patients for clinical trials. *Journal of the American Medical Association* 263:865.

Freedman, Benjamin, Abraham Fuks and Charles Weijer. 1992. Demarcating research and treatment: A systematic approach to the analysis of the ethics of clinical research. *Clinical Research* 40:653–60.

IRB: Review of Human Subjects Research (six times yearly). [The only journal dealing in its entirety with ethical issues arising in the conduct of human research.]

Levine, Carol, Nancy N. Dubler and Robert J. Levine. 1991. Building a new consensus: Ethical principles and policies for clinical research on HIV/AIDS. *IRB* 13(1–2): 1–17.

Levine, Robert J. 1986. *Ethics and regulation of clinical research*, 2nd ed. Baltimore, Maryland: Urban and Schwarzenberg, Inc.

———. 1988. Uncertainty in clinical research. *Law, Medicine and Health Care* 16:174–82.

Office of Protection from Research Risks, National Institutes of Health. 1993. *Protecting Human Subjects: Institutional Review Board Guidebook*. Washington, D.C.: U.S. Government Printing Office.

Ramsey, Paul. 1970. *The patient as person*. Chapters 1 and 6. New Haven: Yale University Press.

Sieber, Joan E. 1992. *Planning ethically responsible research: A guide for students and internal review boards*. Newbury Park, CA.: Sage Publications.

Part Three

Decisions Near the Beginning and End of Life

Chapter 10

Genetics

Chapter 10

Introduction

Genetic testing involves the diagnosis and classification of genetic disease. A common genetic test is prenatal diagnosis.

> A pregnant woman waits anxiously . . . for laboratory test results. She nursed her older brothers and watched helplessly as they slowly withered away and died of muscular dystrophy. She can't bear the thought of having a baby with muscular dystrophy. But she doesn't know if she can face an abortion should the tests reveal that her unborn baby has the disease (Stockton 1979).

For most women who undergo prenatal genetic testing, the test results are normal — the fetus is not afflicted with a genetic disease. For a small percentage of women, however, prenatal testing reveals a serious genetic disease in the fetus, and the woman is confronted with a difficult choice about whether to continue the pregnancy. Treatment of genetic disease identified *in utero* is rarely an option.

Whereas genetic testing involves the testing of an individual, genetic screening involves genetic testing of a population as a whole, or a subset of the population, to identify unaffected carriers of deleterious genes.

> Tay-Sachs carriers — people who have the Tay-Sachs gene — are ten times more prevalent among the Jewish population who have their ancestral origins in central and eastern Europe. These are the Ashkenazi Jews. Among couples of this background the disease is present in about one in every 3000 births. Among the non-Jewish population, it is much lower, perhaps one in every 300 000 births. So we wanted to attempt mass screening in this Jewish population (Stockton 1979, 64–65).

The objectives of genetic testing and screening are many and varied. They include the prevention of genetic disease through reproductive counselling, the offer of effective treatment, the recruitment of research subjects, the study of the prevalence and natural history of genetic disease, and the determination of eligibility for employment or life insurance (Fost 1992). Below is a brief summary of currently available tests with some indication as to how the knowledge obtained serves the primary objective of preventing (decreasing) genetic disease.

Pre-implantation genetic testing is currently available in a research context to couples who will be using *in vitro* fertilization (IVF) and who are at risk of conceiving a child with an X-linked disorder (such as hemophilia or Duchenne muscular dystrophy), cystic fibrosis, or Tay-Sachs disease. First, the human embryo is created outside of the body using IVF; when the embryo reaches the eight-cell stage, one or two of the blastomeres (cells) are removed for genetic testing to determine if the embryo is afflicted with (or in the case of X-linked disorders has a 50 percent chance of being afflicted with) a genetic disease for which testing is available. On the basis of this genetic testing, a decision is then made about whether to transfer the embryo to the uterus. Effective treatment of the genetic disorder identified in the developing embryo is not possible; even if it were, it would not generally be deemed morally acceptable because treatment would involve germ-line gene therapy.

For those who conceive without the use of assisted reproductive technologies, genetic testing is available during pregnancy to women of late maternal age, to women who have had a previously affected child, and to women with a family history of genetic disease. The two most widely used genetic tests are amniocentesis and chorionic villus sampling (CVS). Amniocentesis is usually done between 16 and 20 weeks gestation. A long, thin needle is inserted through the abdominal wall and into the amniotic sac to remove amniotic fluid, which contains cells from the fetus, for testing. In CVS, usually done between 9 and 12 weeks gestation, a needle is inserted through the abdomen or a catheter is inserted through the vagina and cervix to the placenta to remove a piece of the chorion, the outer tissue surrounding the fetus, for testing. Following prenatal genetic testing, the pregnant woman is provided with information about the genetic health of her fetus(es) and, on this basis, a decision is made concerning the continuation of pregnancy. Effective treatment is rarely possible.

Newborn genetic testing and screening allows for early diagnosis of asymptomatic individuals (i.e., individuals who do not at present have symptoms of the disease). Sometimes this information is useful in promoting well-being; for example, early treatment of newborns with phenylketonuria (PKU) or galactosemia can change the prognosis. More often, however, it is not possible to modify the course of the disease (e.g., Tay-Sachs), and the information obtained is useful mostly in making future reproductive decisions. In Canada, there are approximately 370 000 births per year, and most of these newborns are routinely screened for specific genetic disorders prior to discharge from the nursery and when they are no more than seven days of age (American Academy of Pediatrics 1992).

Asymptomatic testing and screening are also available beyond the newborn period to test for both early-onset genetic diseases such as cystic fibrosis and Duchenne muscular dystrophy, and for late-onset genetic diseases such as Huntington disease (HD). The testing identifies affected individuals before the onset of debilitating symptoms. This allows for timely pre-symptomatic treatment, especially for early-onset diseases, where genetic testing is usually synonymous with diagnosis of disease. Another objective is reproductive counselling — the hope is to influence future reproductive decisions.

Finally, testing and screening are also available to individuals of reproductive age and beyond in order to identify carriers of defective genes. These individuals can be counselled about the risk of having affected children, and the information they receive may influence their decisions about marriage and reproduction. In instances where the person is beyond his or her reproductive years, the information may be of particular importance to their offspring should they intend to start a family.

The Selections

The selections in this chapter focus primarily on prenatal genetic counselling and prenatal diagnosis (PND). The first selection, by Abby Lippman, begins with a critical commentary on that which is typically accepted uncritically, namely, that knowledge in human genetics will fundamentally alter our understanding of the concepts of health and disease. This article is important not only for signalling genetic technology's role in the process of "geneticization," but also for calling into question the touted benefits of prenatal testing and screening. It is widely held that these technologies provide women with reassurance, choice, and control. But according to Lippman, this is only half the story, and we would do well to remember that prenatal testing and screening are public health measures intended to ensure quality control over the product: the "baby." As well, we should understand that prenatal testing responds to "socially constructed needs"; thus, women's needs for testing emerge in tandem with the development of new genetic tests. And, as regards the issue of choice and control, Lippman insists that while prenatal testing and screening do increase control, it is not increased control *for* women, but rather increased control *of* women by geneticists and obstetricians who effectively set the parameters within which women's reproductive choices are made.

The next selection, by Dorothy C. Wertz and John C. Fletcher, can be read as a response to Lippman and similar critics of prenatal genetic testing. Wertz and Fletcher explicitly reject the claim that women are overtly or covertly coerced into availing themselves of prenatal testing either by their physicians (as a result of directive counselling) or by the culture (as a consequence of prevailing attitudes toward those who are cognitively or physically impaired). They further argue that women have not succumbed to the technological imperative — women do not choose to undergo prenatal testing just because it is available. To the contrary, Wertz and Fletcher maintain that most women freely choose to use prenatal testing in order to further their own objective of having a "healthy baby." They also insist that prenatal testing is not a eugenic program that forces women to terminate wanted pregnancies when the fetus is afflicted with a genetic disease. Rather, prenatal testing provides women with an opportunity for informed individual reproductive decision making.

In the last section, Kathleen Nolan highlights the likely impact of the Human Genome Project (an effort to "map" the human chromosomes) on prenatal testing and screening. Specifically, she notes that difficult questions will emerge with the introduction of new genetic probes and markers for genetic diseases that will need to be addressed in a timely and responsible manner. Most important among these questions, according to Nolan, is which diagnostic tests should be included in routine prenatal care and which tests should be considered "optional, unnecessary, or relatively contraindicated"? Moreover, who should make these determinations and on what basis?

Conclusion

The identification and prevention of genetic disease is evidently a public health concern. What is perhaps less obvious, but no less important, is that the availability of genetic testing and screening (which will only increase with the mapping of the human genome) has profound implications not only for those who use these technologies but also for those who are afflicted with, or carriers of, genetic disease. The widespread use of genetic testing and screening profoundly affects the way in which individuals who are cognitively or physically impaired view themselves and are viewed by others. A question this raises for serious consideration is whether sufficient effort has been made to meet the needs of individuals with handicaps, especially in those instances when their handicaps could be overcome by introducing physical changes to the environment and/or by providing needed economic and social support.

In addition to questions concerning our obligations to fetuses, newborns, infants, school children, and adults with genetic disease, there are questions concerning our obligations to family members of affected individuals. For example, what about the young woman in her reproductive years whose 52-year-old mother has just been diagnosed with Huntington disease? The daughter has a 50 percent chance of having the disease.

Does she have a right to information about her mother's diagnosis so that she can make an informed choice about her own reproduction? Aside from problems involving confidentiality, there are also problems of informed choice, access to genetic testing, and discrimination by employers and insurers.

As new laboratory tests for genetic diseases are developed, and as the list of diseases for which genetic testing is available expands, these problems will almost certainly become more complex, casting old philosophical issues in a new light. Brock, for example, has recently explored the potential consequences of the Human Genome Project for our conceptions of equality of opportunity, humans as morally and legally responsible agents, and normality (Brock 1992). He suggests that establishing a relationship between certain genes and specific human characteristics and abilities will lead to demands for therapy to correct genetic disadvantages in the name of equality of opportunity. He further hypothesizes that the mapping of the chromosomes will rekindle the age-old debate about free will and determinism as we better understand the "genetic causal antecedents of human behaviour." And finally, Brock reminds us (as do many others), of the likely impact of the Human Genome Project on our conception of what constitutes good health or normal human development and functioning.

References

American Academy of Pediatrics, Committee on Genetics. 1992. Issues in newborn screening. *Pediatrics* 89:345–49.

Brock, Dan W. 1992. The human genome project and human identity. *Houston Law Review* 29:7–22.

Fost, Norman. 1992. Ethical implications of screening asymptomatic individuals. *FASEB Journal* 6:2813–17.

Stockton, William. 1979. *Altered destinies: Lives changed by genetic flaws*. New York: Doubleday and Co.

37   Prenatal Genetic Testing and Screening: Constructing Needs and Reinforcing Inequities

Abby Lippman

Prenatal Diagnosis: A Technical and a Social Construction

Of all applied genetic activities, prenatal diagnosis is probably most familiar to the general population and is also the most used. Prenatal diagnosis refers to all the technologies currently in use or under development to determine the physi(ologi)cal condition of a fetus before birth. Until recently, prenatal diagnosis usually meant amniocentesis, a second trimester procedure routinely available for women over a certain age (usually thirty-five years in North America),[1] for Down syndrome detection. Amniocentesis is also used in selected circumstances where the identification of specific fetal genetic disorders is possible.[2] Now, in addition to amniocentesis, there are chorionic villus sampling (CVS) tests that screen maternal blood samples to detect a fetus with a neural tube defect or Down syndrome, and ultrasound screening.[3] Despite professional guidelines to the contrary,[4] ultrasound screening is performed routinely in North America on almost every pregnant woman appearing for prenatal care early enough in pregnancy. And although ultrasound is not usually labeled as "prenatal diagnosis," it not only belongs under this rubric but was, I suggest, the first form of prenatal diagnosis for which informed consent is not obtained.[5]

Expansion of prenatal diagnosis techniques, ever widening lists of identifiable conditions and susceptibilities, changes in the timing of testing and the populations in which testing is occurring, and expanding professional definitions of what should be diagnosed *in utero*, attest to this technology's role in the process of geneticization.[6] But these operational characteristics alone circumscribe only some aspects of prenatal diagnosis. Prenatal diagnosis as a social activity is becoming an element in our culture and this aspect, which has had minimal attention, will be examined in depth.

A.   Prenatal Diagnosis and the Discourse of Reassurance

Contemporary stories about prenatal diagnosis contain several themes, but these generally reflect either of two somewhat different models.[7] In the "public health" model, prenatal diagnosis is presented as a way to reduce the frequency of selected birth defects.[8] In the other, which I will call the "reproductive autonomy" model, prenatal diagnosis is presented as a means of giving women information to expand their reproductive choices.[9] Unfortunately, neither model fully captures the essence of prenatal diagnosis. In addition, neither acknowledges the internal tension, revealed in the coexistence of quite contradictory constructions of testing that may be equally valid: 1) as an assembly line approach to the products of conception, separating out those products we wish to develop from those we wish to discontinue;[10] 2) as a way to give women control over their pregnancies, respecting (increasing) their autonomy to choose the kinds of children they will bear,[11] or 3) as a means of reassuring women that enhances their experience of pregnancy.[12]

The dominant theme throughout the biomedical literature, as well as some feminist commentary, emphasizes the last two of these constructions.[13] A major variation on this theme suggests, further, that through the use of prenatal diagnosis woman can avoid the family distress and suffering associated with the unpredicted birth of babies with genetic disorders or congenital malformations, thus preventing disability while enhancing the experience of pregnancy.[14] Not unlike the approach used to justify caesarean sections,[15] prenatal diagnosis is constructed as a way of avoiding "disaster."

The language of control, choice and reassurance certainly makes prenatal diagnosis appear attractive. But while this discourse may be successful as a marketing strategy,[16] it relates a limited and highly selected story about prenatal diagnosis. Notwithstanding that even the most critical would probably agree prenatal diagnosis *can be* selectively reassuring[17] (for the vast majority of women who will learn that the fetus does not have Down syndrome or some other serious diagnosable disorder), this story alone is too simplistic. It does not take account of why reassurance is sought, how risk groups are generated and how eligibility for obtaining this kind of reassurance is determined. Whatever else, prenatal diagnosis *is* a means of separating fetuses we wish to develop from those we wish to discontinue. Prenatal diagnosis does approach children as consumer objects subject to quality control.

This is implicit in the general assumption that induced abortion will follow the diagnosis of fetal abnormality.[18] This assumption is reinforced by the rapid acceptance of CVS, which allows prenatal diagnosis to be carried out earlier and earlier in pregnancy when termination of a fetus found to be "affected" is taken for granted as less problematic.[19] The generally unquestioned assumption that pre-implantation diagnosis is better than prenatal diagnosis also undermines a monotonic reassurance rhetoric.[20] With pre-implantation (embryo) diagnosis, the selection objective is clear: only those embryos thought to be "normal" will be transferred and allowed to continue to develop.[21] Thus, embryo destruction is equated with induced abortion.[22] In perhaps the most blatant example, Brambati and colleagues have proposed the combined use of *in vitro* fertilization, gamete intrafallopian transfer, chorionic villus sampling and fetal reduction to "avoid pregnancy termination among high risk couples" [*sic*], and have stated that the "fetus was reduced" when describing a situation in which this scenario actually occurred.[23]

Thus, while no single storyline is inherently true or false, the reassurance discourse appears to mask essential features of genetic testing and screening that are troubling. Reassurance — for pregnant women or for geneticists[24] — notwithstanding, the story is more complex. Prenatal diagnosis necessarily involves systematic and systemic selection of fetuses, most frequently on genetic grounds.[25] Though the word "eugenics" is scrupulously avoided in most biomedical reports about prenatal diagnosis, except when it is strongly disclaimed as a motive for intervention, this is disingenuous.[26] Prenatal diagnosis presupposes that certain fetal conditions are intrinsically not bearable. Increasing diagnostic capability means that such conditions, as well as a host of variations that can be detected *in utero*, are proliferating, necessarily broadening the range of what is not "bearable" and restricting concepts of what is "normal." It is, perhaps, not unreasonable to ask if the "imperfect" will become anything we can diagnose. . . .[27]

B. Constructing the "Need" for Prenatal Diagnosis

While reassurance has been constructed to justify health professionals' offers of prenatal diagnosis, genetic testing and screening have also been presented in the same biomedical literature as responses to the "needs" of pregnant women. They are seen as something they "choose." What does it mean, however, to "need" prenatal diagnosis, to "choose" to be tested?[28] Once again, a closer look at what appear to be obvious terms may illuminate some otherwise hidden aspects of geneticization and the prenatal diagnosis stories told in its voice.

We must first identify the concept of need as itself a problem and acknowledge that needs do not have intrinsic reality. Rather, needs are socially constructed and culture bound, grounded in current history, dependent on context and, therefore, not universal.

With respect to prenatal diagnosis, "need" seems to have been conceptualized predominantly in terms of changes in cababilities for fetal diagnoses: women only come to "need" prenatal diagnosis after the test for some disorder has been developed. Moreover, the disorders to be sought are chosen exclusively by geneticists.[29] In addition, posing a "need" for testing to reduce the probability a woman will give birth to a child with some detectable characteristic rests on assumptions about the value of information, about which characteristics are or are not of value and about which risks should or should not be taken. These assumptions reflect almost exclusively a white, middle-class perspective.[30]

This conceptualization of need is propelled by several features of contemporary child-bearing.[31] First, given North American culture, where major responsibility for family health care in general, for the fetus she carries and for the child she births, is still allocated to a woman,[32] it is generally assumed that she must do all that is recommended or available to foster her child's health. At its extreme, this represents the pregnant woman as obligated to produce a healthy child. Prenatal diagnosis, as it is usually presented, falls into this category of behaviors recommended to pregnant women who would exercise their responsibilities as caregivers.[33] Consequently, to the extent that she is expected generally to do everything possible for the fetus/child, a woman may come to "need" prenatal diagnosis, and take testing for granted. Moreover, since an expert usually offers testing, and careseekers are habituated to follow through with tests ordered by physicians,[34] it is hardly surprising that they will perceive a need to be tested.[35] With prenatal diagnosis presented as a "way to avoid birth defects," to refuse testing, or perceive no need for it, becomes more difficult than to proceed with it.[36] This technology perversely creates a burden of not doing enough, a burden incurred when the technology is *not* used.[37]

A second feature, related to the first, is that women generally, and pregnant women specifically, are bombarded with behavioral directives[38] that are at least as likely to foster a sense of incompetence as to nourish a feeling of control. . . .[39]

Third, prenatal diagnosis will necessarily be perceived as a "need" in a context, such as ours, that automatically labels pregnant women thirty-five years and over a "high risk" group. . . .[40]

Fourth, as prenatal diagnosis becomes more and more routine for women thirty-five years and older in North America, the risks it seems to avoid (the birth of a child with Down syndrome) appear to be more ominous,[41] although the frequency of Down syndrome has not changed. . . .

Fifth, on the collective level, prenatal diagnosis is generally presented as a response to the public health "need" to reduce unacceptably high levels of perinatal mortality and morbidity associated with perceived increases in "genetic" disorders. This reduction is of a special kind, in that prenatal diagnosis does not *prevent* the disease, as is usually claimed. . . .[42]

"Needs" for prenatal diagnosis are being created simultaneously with refinements and extensions of testing techniques themselves.[43] In popular discourse — and with ge-neticists generally silent witnesses — genetic variations are being increasingly defined not just as problems, but, I suggest, as problems for which there is, or will be, a medical/technical solution. With but slight slipage these "problems" come to be seen as *requiring* a medical solution. This again hides the extent to which even "genetic" disease is a social/psychological experience as much as it is a biomedical one.[44] This process is likely to accelerate as gene mapping enlarges the numbers of individuals declared eligible for genetic testing and screening. Given the extent of human variation, the possibilities of constructing "needs" are enormous.

C. Prenatal Diagnosis and the Social Control of Abortion and Pregnancy

The third element in the prenatal discourse that I will consider here stems from the often told story that testing is an option that increases women's reproductive choices and control. This claim has had much attention in the literature and I will examine it only with respect to how some features of prenatal diagnosis do increase control, but allocate it to someone other than a pregnant woman herself. This is most apparent in the context of abortion.[45]

Without doubt, prenatal diagnosis has (re)defined the grounds for abortion[46] — who is justified in having a pregnancy terminated and why — and is a clear expression of the social control[47] inherent in this most powerful example of geneticization. Geneticists and their obstetrician colleagues are deciding which fetuses are healthy, what healthy means and who should be born, thus gaining power over decisions to continue or terminate pregnancies that pregnant women themselves may not always be permitted to make.

To the extent that specialists' knowledge determines who uses prenatal diagnosis and for what reasons, geneticists determine conditions that will be marginalized, objects of treatment or grounds for abortion.[48] Prenatal diagnosis is thus revealed as a biopolitical as well as a biomedical activity.[49] For example, an abortion may only be "legal" in some countries if the fetus has some recognized disorder,[50] and the justifying disorder only becomes "recognizable" because geneticists first decide to screen for it. Fuhrmann suggests that in Europe, in fact, geneticists significantly influenced legislators establishing limits within which abortion would be at all permissible, by arguing that access to abortion be maintained through a gestational age that reflected when results from amniocentesis might be available.[51] One wonders where limits might have been placed had first trimester chorionic villus sampling been available *before* amniocentesis? Would they have been more restrictive? . . .

V. Conclusion

. . . Prenatal testing and screening are most often presented as ways to decrease disease, to spare families the pain of having a disabled child and to enhance women's choice. The best-selling stories about them speak of reassurance, choice and control. As has also been suggested, this discourse presents a child born with some disorder requiring medical or surgical care as (exhibiting) a "failure."[52] This failed pregnancy theme is reinforced in counseling provided to these families when counselors emphasize how most fetuses with an abnormality abort spontaneously during pregnancy, are "naturally selected," as it were, and how prenatal testing is merely an improvement on nature.

Just as there are several ways to construe reassurance, choice and control, the birth of a child with a structural malformation or other problem, "genetic" or otherwise, can be presented in other than biomedical terms. Is the story claiming that the pregnancy has malfunctioned (by not spontaneously aborting),[53] resulting in a baby with a malformation, any "truer" than the story suggesting that *society* has malfunctioned because it cannot accommodate the disabled in its midst?[54] Social conditions are as enabling or disabling as biological conditions. Why are biological variations that create differences between individuals seen as preventable or avoidable while social conditions that create similar distinctions are likely to be perceived as intractable givens?[55]

While "many people don't believe society has an obligation to adjust to the disabled individual,"[56] there is nothing inherent in malformation that makes this so. Consequently, arguing that social changes are "needed" to enable those with malformations to have rich lives is not an inherently less appropriate approach. Actually, it may be more appropriate, since malformation, a biomedical phenomenon, requires a social translation to become a "problem." Expanding prenatal diagnostic services may circumvent but will not solve the "problem" of birth defects; they focus on disability, not on society's discriminatory practices.[57] They can, at best, make only a limited contribution to help women have offspring free of disabilities, despite recent articles proposing prenatal diagnosis and abortion as ways to "improve" infant mortality and morbidity statistics.[58] Thus, as sociopolitical decisions about the place of genetic testing and screening in the health care system are made, it will be important to consider how problems are named and constructed so that we don't mistakenly assume the story told in the loudest voice is the only — or that the "best seller" is best.

Unarguably, illness and disability are "hard" (difficult) issues,[59] and no one wants to add to the unnecessary suffering of any individual. But being "hard" neither makes illness or disability totally negative experiences,[60] nor does it mean they must all be eliminated or otherwise managed exclusively within the medical system. Women's desire for children without disability warrants complete public and private support. The question is how to provide this support in a way that does no harm. . . .

When amniocentesis was introduced, abortion subsequent to a diagnosis of fetal abnormality was presented as a temporary necessity until treatment for the detected condition could be devised.[61] Advocates assumed that this would soon be forthcoming.

With time, however, the gap between characterization and treatment of disease has widened.[62] New information from efforts at gene mapping will certainly increase the ability to detect, diagnose and screen, but not to treat. A human gene map will identify variations in DNA patterns. Genes that "cause" specific disease, as well as those associated with increased susceptibility to specific disorders, will be found. Simultaneously, prenatal screening and testing are evolving in a context where a "genetic approach" to public health is gaining great favor.[63] All the variations that will be mapped can become targets of prenatal testing. Which targets will be selected in the quest for improved public health? And who will determine that they have been reached? Given the extraordinary degree of genetic variability within groups of people, what does "genetic health" actually mean — and does it matter? . . .

Notes

1. *See infra* note 40 and accompanying text for a discussion of the social, rather than biological bases for categorizing women over 35 as "at risk."

2. Over 150 "single gene" disorders can now be detected, and testing may be carried out for women who have a documented family history of one of these or who are otherwise known to be at increased risk. Testing is not carried out for these disorders without specific indications. *See generally* Antonarakis, *Diagnosis of Genetic Disorders at the DNA Level*, 320 New Eng. J. Med. 153 (1989) (reviewing recent progress in identifying single gene disorders).

3. During an ultrasound examination, high frequency sound waves are projected into the uterus; the sound waves that are reflected back are resolved visually to allow one to "see" the fetus on a television-like display screen. A. Oakley, The Captured Womb: A History of the Medical Care of Pregnant Women 155–68 (1984).

4. *See* E. Nightingale & M. Goodman, Before Birth: Prenatal Testing for Genetic Disease 31–32 (1990). A consensus development conference in the United States recently recommended reserving the use of ultrasound for pregnancies that may require it for specific reasons. Pub. Health Ser., U.S. Dept't of Health & Hum. Serv., Consensus Development Conference: Diagnostic Ultrasound Imaging in Pregnancy 11 (National Inst. of Health Publication No. 667. 1984).

5. See Chervenak, McCullough & Chervenak, *Prenatal Informed Consent for Sonogram*, 161 Am. J. Obstetrics & Gynecology 857, 860 (1989); Lippman. *Access to Prenatal Screening: Who Decides?*, 1 Canadian J. Women L. 434 (1986) [Hereinafter *Who Decides?*]. Chervenak and colleagues have recently called attention to the issue of informed consent for ultrasound, but their conclusions are troublesome. They consider the pregnant woman "the patient's fiduciary," the "patient" to them being the fetus. Chervenak, McCullough & Chervenak, *supra*, at 858. This suggests that the consent process they propose will be coercive.

6. *See generally Who Decides?, supra* note 5, at 434.

7. *Id.*

8. *See, e.g.*, Kolker, *Advances in Prenatal Diagnosis: Social-psychological and Policy Issues*, 5 Int. J. Tech. Assessment Health Care 601 (1989); *see also* Dalgaard & Norby, *Autosomal Dominan. Polycystic Kidney in the 1980s*. 36 Clinical Genetics 320, 324 (1989) (placing importance on "selective reproduction prevention").

9. *See* President's Comm'n for the Study of Ethical Problems in Medical and Biomedical and Behavioral Research, Screening and Counselling for Genetic Conditions. The Ethical, Social, and Legal Implications of Genetic Screening, Counselling, and Education Programs 55 (1983) [hereinafter Pres-

ident's Comm'n] ("In sum, the fundamental value of genetic screening and counselling is their ability to enhance the opportunities for the individual to obtain information about their personal health and childbearing risks and to make autonomous and non-coerced choices based on that information.").

10. *See* B. Rothman, Recreating Motherhood: Ideology and Technology in a Patriarchal Society 21 (1989) (describing the "commodification of life, towards treating people and parts of people . . . as commodities. . . . We work hard, some of us, at making the perfect product, what one of the doctors in the childbirth movement calls a 'blue ribbon baby'"). *See also* Ewing, *Australian Perspectives on Embryo Experimentation: An Update*, 3 Issues Reproductive & Genetic Engineering 119 (1990); Rothman, *The Decision to Have or Not to Have Amniocentesis for Prenatal Diagnosis*, in Childbirth in America: Anthropological Perspectives (K. Michaelson ed. 1988) at 92, 92–98.

11. *See* Hill, *Your Morality or Mine? An Inquiry into the Ethics of Human Reproduction*, 154 Am. J. Obstetrics & Gynecology 1173, 1178–80 (1986).

12. *See generally* Royal College of Physicians of London, Prenatal Diagnosis and Genetic Screening: Community and Service Implications (1989).

13. *See, e.g.*, Women's Rights Litigation Clinic, Reproductive Laws for the 1990s: A Briefing Handbook (1987): *Who Decides?, supra* note 5 at 438.

14. McDonough, *Congenital Disability and Medical Research: The Development of Amniocentesis*, 16 Women & Health 137, 143–44 (1990). McDonough notes that three rationales for amniocentesis emerged from her survey: "The procedure offered those at risk the possibility of 'health'. . . . [it] provided parents with reassurance and avoided abortion. . . . [and it] prevent[ed] disease and disability." *Id.*

15. *See, e.g.*, McClain, *Perceived Risk and Choice of Childbirth Service*, 17 Soc. Sci. & Med. 1857, 1862 (1983).

16. There is no evidence that control, autonomy and reassurance are actually enhanced and not merely assumed to occur. In fact, there have been very few in-depth studies in this area, and the conclusions of these investigations seem to vary with the orientation of the investigator. Studies reported in the social science and feminist literature suggest that prenatal diagnosis removes control; studies reported in the biomedical literature are interpreted to show how reassurance is provided. For an overview of these studies, see Lippman, *Research Studies in Applied Human Genetics: A Quantitative Analysis and Critical Review of Recent (Biomedical) Literature* to be published in Am. J. Med. Genetics (1991). Much more ethnographic work in this area is required.

17. Anon, *WIC Program Shows Major Benefits*, Nation's Health, December 1990; Farrant, *Who's for Amniocentesis? The Politics of Prenatal Screening*, in The Sexual Politics of Reproduction 96, 120 (H. Hofmans ed. 1985); Yankauer, *What Infant Mortality Tells Us*, 80 Am. J. Pub. Health 653 (1990).

18. *See supra* 10–11 and accompanying text.

19. This issue is discussed in A. Lippman, Led Astray by Genetic Maps (speech given, Ottawa, Canada, 1991). Treatment, often said to be a goal of early identification of affected fetuses, becomes even less likely with CVS. Pharmaceutical companies will not be motivated to invest in developing treatments for conditions that "need not occur." Rarely will they base business decisions on their social worth rather than on their financial value.

This situation contains elements of an unusual conflict. Increasingly, geneticists are promising to have treatments available for a wide range of disorders and, for some conditions, therapeutic developments have occurred which make them far more benign than previously. The promises, and the available examples, are likely to be sufficiently persuasive that women "at-risk" may either make use of prenatal diagnosis less frequently or see less reason to abort an affected fetus than today. Yet, at the same time, the very availability of prenatal diagnosis and abortion may be seen as justifications for not investing in the further development of these therapies that parents will have been led to expect. *Cf.* Varekamp,

Suurmeijer, Brōcker-Vriends, Van Dijck, Smit, Rosendaal & Briët, *Carrier Testing and Prenatal Diagnosis for Hemophilia: Experiences and Attitudes of 549 Potential and Obligate Carriers*, 37 Am. J. Med. Genetics 147, 153 (1990) [hereinafter Varekamp] (noticing decrease in hemophilia screening as treatment capabilities increased).

20. *See* Bell, *Prenatal Diagnosis: Current Status and Future Trends*, in Human Genetic Information: Science, Law & Ethics 18–36 (Ciba Foundation Series 1990). *See also* Kolker, *supra* note 8, at 612 (prevention is "clearly cheaper than providing services for those with genetic disorders"); Modell, *Cystic Fibrosis Screening and Community Genetic.* 27 J. Med. Gen. 475, 476 (1990) ("undesirable [diseases] may be all but eradicated"); Dalgaard & Norby, *supra* note 8, at 323–24 ("access to selective reproductive prevention" is important).

21. S. Wymelenberg, Science and Babies: Private Decisions, Public Dilemmas 130 (1990).

22. In fact, some consider the combined procedures of *in vitro* fertilization and embryo diagnosis to be "ethically better" than prenatal diagnosis for detecting problems because it "avoids" abortion. *See* Michael & Buckle, *Screening for Genetic Disorders: Therapeutic Abortion and IVF*, 16 J. Med. Ethics 43 (1990). *But see* J. Testart, Le Monde Diplomatique 24 (1990) (suggesting that it is the very need to consider abortion ("de terribles responsibilités) that is perhaps the best safeguard against ordinary eugenics ("l'eugénisme ordinaire")).

23. Brambati, Formigli, Tului & Simoni, *Selective Reduction of Quadruplet Pregnancy at Risk of B-Thalassemia*, 336 Lancet 1325, 1326 (1990).

24. If nothing else, it is certainly preferable for their public image if geneticists are seen as reassuring women, rather than selecting their offspring.

25. Much of importance has been written about the link between prenatal diagnosis and eugenics: this dialogue, despite its importance, will not be repeated here. *See generally* T. Duster, Backdoor to Eugenics (2) 1990; R. Hubbard, The Politics of Women's Biology 52 (1990); Degener, *Female Self-determination between Feminist Claims and "Voluntary" Eu-*

genics, Between "Rights" and Ethics, 3 Issues Reproductive & Genetic Engineering 87 (1990); Hubbard, *Eugenics: New Tools, Old Ideas*, 13 Women & Health 225 (1987).

26. This point is not merely an argument of critics of prenatal diagnosis. Shaw, a geneticist-lawyer who strongly defends the principle of fetal protection, has written that "any counselor who explains reproductive alternatives and offers a prenatal test to a counselee is a practicing eugenicist and any couple who chooses to avoid having babies with chromosome abnormalities or deleterious mutant genes is also practicing eugenics." Shaw, *Letter to the Editor: Response to Hayden: Presymptomatic and Prenatal Testing*, 28 Am. J. Med. Genetics 765, 765–66 (1987).

27. Rothschild, *Engineering Birth: Toward the Perfectability of Man?*, in 2 Science, Technology and Social Progress 93 (S. Goldman ed. 1989).

28. While those in need are identified explicitly as (certain) pregnant women, it is worth noting that clinical geneticists, themselves, have a need for this technology, too. For instance when a child is born with a malformation, geneticisst likely feel most "helpful" when prenatal diagnosis, a technological palliative for the pains of etiologic ignorance, can be offered. Saving that the malformation is not likely to happen again, given the usually low empiric recurrence risks associated with most of these problems, is not nearly as comforting for genetic counselors as is offering *in utero* detection. Counselors "need" this technique for the satisfactory performance of their jobs no less than they believe a family "needs" prenatal diagnosis to prevent the birth of a second affected child.

29. *See* Lippman, *Prenatal Diagnosis: Reproductive Choice? Reproductive Control?* [Hereinafter *Reproductive Choice?*] in The Future of Human Reproduction 182, 187 (C. Overall ed. 1989) [hereinafter The Future of Human Reproduction] (consideration of prenatal diagnosis as a professional resource).

30. *See* Nsiah-Jefferson, *Reproductive Laws, Women of Color and Low Income Women* in Reproductive Laws for the 1990s 17, 17–58 (S. Cohen & N. Taub eds. 1988) [hereinafter

Reproductive Laws for the 1990s] (discussing potential areas of cultural conflict in genetic counselling).

31. There is an extensive literature on "medicalization" in general and on the medicalization of pregnancy and childbirth *per se* in which this discussion is rooted and from which it derives guidance. *See* e.g., A. Oakley, *supra* note 3, at 275.

32. *See* Oakley, *Smoking in Pregnancy: Smokescreen or Risk Factor? Towards a Maternalist Analysis*, 11 Sociology Health & Illness 311 (1989).

33. *See* Farrant, *Who's for Amniocentesis? The Politics of Prenatal Screening*, in The Sexual Politics of Reproduction 96 (H. Homans ed. 1985); Oakley, *supra* note 32, at 311.

34. *See* R. Hatcher & H. Thompson, Satisfaction with Obstetrical Care among Canadian Women (Health Servs. Res. Unit. Department of Community Health. Queen's Univ. Kingston, Ontario 1987) (result of a survey showing pregnant women's reluctance to question medical authority).

35. *See* Lippman, *supra* note 29, at 182. Physicians may pressure women into being tested even using false information to do so. Marteau, Kidd, Cook, Michie, Johnston, Slack & Shaw, *Perceived Risk not Actual Risk Predicts Uptake of Amniocentesis*, 96 Brit. J. Obstetrics & Gynaecology 739 (1989).

36. *See* Hubbard & Henifin, *Genetic Screening of Prospective Parents and of Workers: Some Scientific and Social Issues*. 15 Int'l J. Health Servs. 231 (1985); Rothman, *The Meaning of Choice in Reproductive Technology*, in Test-Tube Women, *supra* note 31, at 23. I have previously discussed the "burden" of decisionmaking in the context of genetic counseling and a similar "burden" would seem to exist here. *See* Lippman-Hand & Fraser, *Genetic Counseling I: Parents' Perception of Uncertainty*, 4 Am. J. Med. Genetics 51, 58–63 (1979) [hereinafter *Genetic Counseling I*]; Lippman-Hand & Fraser, *Genetic Counseling II: Making Reproductive Choices*, 4 Am. J. Med. Genetics 73 (1978) [hereinafter *Genetic Counseling II*]. This theme is present in contemporary literature as demonstrated by Goldstein's reference to the "momentous decision" that childbearing now involves. R. Goldstein, The Mind–Body Problem 200 (1983).

Hubbard and Henifin, in fact, identify a "new Catch-22" wherein participating in a genetic screening program may lead to a person's being identified as a "genetic deviant," but failure to participate (or to abort a fetus diagnosed with a disorder in *utero*) may lead to her being labeled as a "social deviant." Hubbard & Henifin, *supra*, at 231–48.

37. The degree of this burden is demonstrated by the frequency with which women queried about their reasons for having prenatal diagnosis say that they "had no choice." Sjögre & Uddenberg, *Decision Making During the Prenatal Diagnostic Procedure*, 8 Prenatal Diagnosis: 263 (1988). *See* Kirejczyk, *A Question of Meaning? Controversies About the NRT's in the Netherlands*, 3 Issues Reproductive & Genetic Engineering 23 (1990) (individuals often accept a medical technique because of fear that they might later regret not having done so); *see also* A. Finger, Past Due: A Story of Disability, Pregnancy and Birth (1990): Beck-Gernsheim, *From the Pill to Test-Tube Babies: New Options, New Pressures in Reproductive Behavior*, in Healing Technology: Feminist Perspectives 23 (1988) [hereinafter Healing Technology]; Rapp, *Moral Pioneers: Women, Men and Fetuses in a Frontier of Reproductive Technology*, 13 Women & Health 10 (1987).

38. B. Rothman, *supra* note 30, at 92–97. Women are expected to behave in accordance with norms set up by those in power. *See* Rodgers, *Pregnancy as Justification for Loss of Judicial Autonomy*, in The Future of Human Reproduction, *supra* note 29, at 174.

39. *See*, e.g., Fleischer, *Ready for any Sacrifice? Women in IVF Programmes*, 3 Issues Reproductive & Genetic Engineering I (1990) (Referring to a "code of good conduct" pregnant women ought to follow); *see also* M. De Koninck & F. Saillant, Essai sur la Santé des Femmes (conseil du Statut de la femme 1981); A. Quéniart, Le Corps Paradoxal: Regards de Femmes sur la Maternité (1988); Simkin, *Childbearing in Social Context*, 15 Women & Health 5 (1989) (all discussing the ideology of risk and behavioral expectations in pregnancy).

40. See Fuhrmann, *Impact, Logistics and Prospects of Traditional Diagnosis*, 36 Clinical Genetics 378, 389 (1988). This categorization is more

a cultural than biological creation. *See* Bouret, *Le temps, l'espace en Génétique: Intervention Médicale et Géographique Sociale du gène*, 6 *Science Sociales et Santé* 171 (1988); A. Lippman, The Geneticization of Health and Illness: Implications for Social Practice (manuscript in preparation based on presentation at National Ass'n for Science, Tech. & Soc'y, Washington, D.C., Feb. 2, 1991). It reflects prevailing ideas about the kinds of children women should have and when the probability for them is or is not diminished. *See* Finkelstein, *Biomedicine and Technocratic Power*. Hastings Center Rep. 1990, at 13, 14–16; *see also infra* note 46 for a discussion of the role of genetics in creating these ideas.

41. This may be an example of what Tversky and Kahneman have called the "availability" heuristic. Tversky & Kahneman, *Availability: A Heuristic for Judging Frequency and Probability*, 5 Cognitive Psychology 207 (1973). That is, having become familiar through constant reference to it and to prenatal diagnosis, Down syndrome may be perceived by the general population as "worse" and as more frequent than it is statistically.

42. *See, e.g.*, Modell, *Cystic Fibrosis Screening and Community Genetics* 27 J. Med. Genetics 47, ("Cystic fibrosis . . . is fast becoming preventable. . . . [because] [t]he gene in which mutation can lead to CF . . . has recently been identified . . . [This creates] an imminent need to set up population screening for CF carriers.").

43. These techniques are likely to be driven by financial considerations of the pharmaceutical companies developing them. *See, e.g.*, D. Nelkin & L. Tancredi, Dangerous Diagnostics: The Social Power of Biological Information 33–36 (1989); A. Lippman, *supra* note 19: *cf.* Note, *Patents for Clinical Pharmaceuticals: The AZT Case*, 17 Am. J.L. & Med. 145 (1991) (analyzing the validity of pharmaceutical companies' claims that without a federally-granted monopoly, they would not have the incentive to research and develop orphan drugs).

44. *See* Shiloh, Waisbren & Levy, *A Psychosocial Model of a Medical Problem: Maternal PKU*, 10 J. Primary Prevention 51 (1989).

45. For thorough analyses of the question of women's control, see generally Rapp,

Chromosomes and Communication: The Discourse of Genetic Counseling, 2 Med. Anthropology Q. 143 (1988).

46. In fact, the availability of amniocentesis "influenced legislation so that the upper limit of gestational age for legally tolerated termination of pregnancy was adjusted to the requirements of second trimester prenatal diagnosis in several countries." Fuhrmann, *supra* note 40, at 378. Evidently, geneticists can accomplish what women's groups cannot: a revisioning of abortion.

47. The term "social control" is used in accord with its original use to embrace "the widest range of influence and regulation imposed by society upon the individual." D. Gordon, *Clinical Science and Clinical Expertise: Changing Boundaries Between Art and Science in Medicine*, in Biomedicine Examined 11, M. Lock & D. Gordon eds. (1989), at 257.

48. *Reproductive Choice?, supra* note 29, at 187–192.

49. Finkelstein, *supra* note 40, at 14–16.

50. Fetal abnormality as grounds for abortion is of fairly recent vintage, having first become "legal" in the United States in 1967 in response to a rubella epidemic. The Canadian Medical Association gave its approval the same year. Beck, *Eugenic Abortion: An Ethical Critique*, 143 Canadian Med. Ass'n J. 181, 181–84 (1990). Today, members of the general population as well as physicians regularly and strongly agree that fetal abnormality is a justification for abortion. *See* Annas, *The Supreme Court, Privacy and Abortion*, 321 New Eng. J. Med 1200 (1989); Breslau, *Abortion of Defective Fetuses: Attitudes of Mothers of Congenitally Impaired Children*, 49 J. Marriage Family 839 (1987); Varekamp, *supra* note 19, at 147.

51. *See* Fuhrmann, *supra* note 40, at 383–84. A recent example of the use of genetics to set social policy in this area is the position taken by the American Society of Human Genetics with respect to possible restrictions on abortion under consideration in various parts of the United States. This professional group has proposed as model legislation

> that any pregnant female whose pregnancy has not reached the point of viability and who has been informed by a licensed or certified health care pro-

fessional that her fetus (or fetuses) is/ are likely to have a serious genetic or congenital disorder shall have the right, among other options, to choose to terminate her pregnancy. This right shall extend to situations where the female is at significantly increased risk for bearing a child with a serious disorder for which precise prenatal diagnosis is not available.

Letter from Phillip J. Riley to the author. The merits for/against this position aside, it certainly demonstrates how geneticists seek to influence the resolution of fundamentally political, legal (and ethical) problems.

52.   Dunstan, *Screening for Fetal and Genetic Abnormality: Social and Ethical Issues*, 25 J. Med. Genetics 290 (1988).

53.   Dunstan thus sees genetic screening and "selective abortion" as a "rationalized adjunct to natural processes" in which "defective products" (babies) are "discard[ed] spontaneously." *Id.* at 292.

54.   For a full development of these ideas, see Asch, *Reproductive Technology and Disability*, in Reproductive Laws for the 1990s, *supra* note 30, at 69; Asch & Fine, *Shared Dreams: A Left Perspective on Disability Rights and Reproductive Rights*, in Women with Disabilities 297 (M. Fine & A. Asch eds. 1988).

55.   There would seem to be similar assumptions beneath the transformation of problems with dirty workplaces into problems with women workers who may become pregnant. *See, e.g.*, Bertin, *Women's Health and Women's Rights: Reproductive Health Hazards in the Workplace*, in Healing Technology, *supra* note 37, at 289, 297 (advocating legislation requiring safe workplaces and prohibiting sterility requirements); Woolhandler & Himmelstein, *Ideology in Medical Science: Class in the Clinic*, 28 Soc Sci & Med. 1205, 1206 (1989), at 1205.

56.   Levin, *International Perspectives on Treatment Choice in Neonatal Intensive Care Units*, 30 Soc. Sci. & Med. 901, 903 (1990) (citation omitted).

57.   For a further discussion on this, see McDonough, *supra* note 14, at 149.

58.   Powell-Griner & Woolbright, *Trends in Infant Deaths from Congenital Anomalies: Results from*

England and Wales, Scotland, Sweden and the United States, 19 Int'l J. Epidemiology 391, 397 (1990) (probable that level of infant mortality will be influenced by prenatal screening and selective abortion); Saari-Kemppainen, Karjalainen. Ylostalo & Heinonen, *Ultrasound Screening and Perinatal Mortality: Controlled Trial of Systematic One-Stage Screening in Pregnancy*, 336 Lancet 387, 391 (1990) (Researchers of ultrasound screening in Helsinki, Finland concluded that "[t]he decrease in perinatal mortality of about half in this trial can be explained mainly by the detection of major fetal anomalies by ultrasound screening and the subsequent termination of these pregnancies.").

59.   Lippman, *Genetics and Public Health: Means, Goals and Justices*, to be published in Am. J. Hum. Genetics (1991). *See* A. Finger, *supra* note 37; P. Kaufert, The Production of Medical Knowledge: Genes, Embryos and Public Policy (paper presented at *Gender, Science and Medicine II* conference, Toronto, Ontario, Nov. 2, 1990). Moreover, illness and disability are *hard* (i.e., difficult) issues partly because society defines them as such, in its decisions about how (not) to allocate resources to deal with them. Unfortunately, since resources are always "scarce," the programs or projects that do (not) get supported will merely be those which policymakers choose (not) to fund. No specific choice is inherent in the limited budgets available, although the requirement that choice be made is. In choosing how to deal with health problems, budget limitations may sometimes be secondary to limitations in our visions about what to do. And, in choosing how to approach (even) "hard" issues, genetic prevention is but one possibility.

60.   Asch, *Reproductive Technology and Disability*, *supra* note 30, at 70.

61.   *See* Friedmann, *Opinion: The Human Genome Project — Some Implications of Extensive "Reverse Genetic" Medicine*, 46 Am. J. Hum. Genetics 407, 412 (1990).

62.   *Id.* at 411.

63.   Lippman, Messing & Mayer, *Genome Mapping the Way to Improve Canadians' Health?*, 81 Canadian J. Pub. Health (1990), at 397.

38   A Critique of Some Feminist Challenges to Prenatal Diagnosis

Dorothy C. Wertz & John C. Fletcher

Introduction: The New Critics of Prenatal Diagnosis

In earlier years, most opposition to prenatal diagnosis came from religious groups opposed to abortion.[1] Recently, however, the strongest arguments against widespread use of prenatal diagnostic procedures have come from some feminists[2-4] and some advocates for people with disabilities.[5,6] Although these critics do not represent the entire range of the feminist or disability rights movements, they have provided fuel for political moves that would limit use of prenatal diagnosis and other reproductive technologies, especially in parts of Europe. Since these arguments have important implications for public policy, it is important to examine them carefully. The arguments run as follows: Women are being coerced into having prenatal diagnosis by their doctors and by the culture. There is a "technological imperative" to have prenatal diagnosis simply because it exists. Women feel guilty if they do not use it. Many feel that they "have no choice" about having prenatal diagnosis or aborting a fetus with a genetic condition.[3] Both women and their doctors are pawns of larger economic, class, and patriarchal forces.[2,7,8] Their actions are determined by social interests and by society's rejection of persons with disabilities. Medicine and the biotechnology industry are using prenatal diagnosis to exploit women for professional and monetary gain.

According to the critics, prenatal diagnosis has become a "search and destroy mission"[9] to eliminate fetuses with disabilities. This amounts to discrimination before birth and will lead to reduced benefits for people with disabilities. Society may decide that it is easier and cheaper to prevent their births than it is to care for them. In siding with persons who have been "victimized," many feminists have felt a contradiction between empowerment of people with disabilities and selective abortion of fetuses with disabilities.[2,3,5-8,10-15] Prenatal diagnosis could become a eugenic program comparable with those used in Nazi Germany to eliminate those with "lives not worth living." Individual choices in prenatal diagnosis have social consequences and are therefore eugenic. By aborting fetuses with certain characteristics, women and families are labeling certain kinds of persons as not worthy of life. Assuming that most individuals make similar choices, that these choices will be influenced by prevailing economic and social standards, and that prenatal diagnosis will become routine in most pregnancies, we will sooner or later arrive at a eugenic society. Although all critics defend women's right to abortion, including abortions for genetic disorders or fetal malformations, some regard abortion after prenatal diagnosis as more ethically problematic than abortion of a healthy fetus for even the most "frivolous" reason.[3–6,11,16–18] If a woman does not want to be pregnant at all, so be it. But to not want to continue a pregnancy after unfavorable findings from prenatal diagnosis is to commit a eugenic act.

In sum, according to the critics, the world is *not* better off for having prenatal diagnosis available. Some women may experience genuine relief at avoiding the burden of caring for a child with a disability, but most women experience only increased anxiety and the burden of unwanted decision-making. Some critics claim that most women would not terminate pregnancies after unfavorable prenatal diagnostic findings if they had a real choice, namely the choice of raising the child in a supportive and accepting society. According to this argument, all disability, including mental retardation, is socially constructed and can be overcome.

These arguments should not be regarded as typical of all feminists. There are sound reasons to believe that most feminists, especially those interested in equal rights in employment, support the use of prenatal diagnosis.[19,20] Nor do all activists for disability rights oppose prenatal diagnosis. Patient organizations for people with genetic conditions usually tacitly support prenatal diagnosis or keep an open mind on the issue. They are often reluctant, however, to discuss openly the possibility of aborting fetuses who may be similar to their own living children. Some well-known advocates for people with disabilities also believe in keeping an open mind, although they believe that women should consider carefully and compassionately before terminating for conditions such as blindness or deafness whose effects can be overcome. They also believe that women should be free to make individual decisions about what kinds of children they are able and willing to raise.[5]

It is important to reply to the critics' arguments for two reasons. First, political actions often have unintended consequences. Feminist criticisms of prenatal diagnosis have provided fuel for religious groups and others who wish to ban abortion. Second, the critics' arguments have touched upon areas that give many women a deep unease — social coercion, definitions of normalcy, and class distinctions in access to medical care, to name a few. Many arguments have at least partial validity. In what follows, we examine feminist criticisms of prenatal diagnosis.

Responses to the Critics

The Social Context of Choice

Some feminists have claimed that women say they "have no choice" about having prenatal diagnosis, implying that they have been pressured into it.[3] Yet when asked in surveys or interviews, most women say that they had a free choice, without interference from their partners, family, or doctors.[21-30] Both statements may be true, depending upon the meaning of "choice." If choice is the absence of legal coercion or coercion by partner or family, clearly women have a choice. There is no evidence of direct coercion by doctors, as some have alleged.[31] If choice is interpreted in the broader context of economic and social realities, however, many women may feel that the possible alternative to prenatal diagnosis — raising a child with a disability — is so unattractive that it does not present a real choice. In the liberal tradition or in socialism, freedom of choice means the practical ability to act upon one's decision. . . .[32,33]

. . . In a sense, prenatal diagnosis is an extension of earlier methods to ensure a "better quality" baby. It belongs alongside other methods, such as the cesarean sections that now account for about one fourth of births in the United States and that are performed largely to protect the baby's intellectual potential. Few women have rejected these methods as long as they appeared to produce superior, or at least healthy, babies. Fewer still decided to give birth outside hospitals, where they could avoid use of high technology. Despite the plethora of books on natural birth, independent (lay) midwifery, birthing centers, and homebirth, most women continue to give birth in hospitals. Perhaps 1% of North American women give birth at home.[35] Most women fear that something could go wrong for the baby if they give birth in the absence of high technology, despite considerable evidence that home is as safe as hospital for low-risk women and newborns.[34] Perhaps there is an analogy here with choices about prenatal diagnosis. The choice exists, but the possibility of having a child with a severe birth defect, if the birth could have been prevented, weighs so heavily on women's minds that it is as if they had no choice.

Yet women's stated beliefs that they had a choice are more than "false consciousness." The fact that about 7% in both the United Kingdom[36] and in California[37] have refused maternal serum α-fetoprotein (MSAFP, an indicator of possible spina bifida in the fetus) screening of prenatal diagnosis on moral grounds, even when tests are offered free of charge under national or state health-care systems, suggests that some women are in fact making choices, instead of acting as the puppets of larger social forces.

The history of prenatal diagnosis also points to women's active and personal choices. In contrast to other areas of experimentation in the history of obstetrics, where poor women especially were exploited as research subjects,[34,38,39] the history of prenatal diagnosis suggests that women actively encouraged research in this area. Women who participated in the early experiments with amniocentesis tended to be white, middle-class, well-educated, and vocal, characteristics that encouraged physicians to pursue this line of research with more vigor than they might have otherwise.[40] The actions of individual women, such as Dolores Becker, in suing physicians for not offering prenatal diagnosis have ensured that it became a routine part of obstetrical practice.[40-42] The women (and their husbands) who initiated these suits were not acting as the pawns of social class interests. Many would have sued even if there were optimum social supports for their children, because social support still does not provide them with the child for which they had hoped.

It is extremely difficult, if not impossible, for women to choose to reject technologies approved by the obstetrical profession. Once tests are offered, to reject them is a rejection of modern faith in science and also a rejection of modern beliefs that women should do everything possible for the health of the future child. Women may have more choice about prenatal diagnosis, however, than about most other childbirth technologies, largely because they are not confined to a hospital at the time of testing and because there is strong religious and cultural support in many groups for carrying a child with a disability to term.

Effects of Disability on Women's Lives

If the economic and social cost of a healthy child is greater to women than ever before, on account of women's entry into the workforce, the cost of a child with a disability is enormous. The irony is that women who have invested heavily in their education or careers and who have postponed childbearing until their late thirties or early forties face the highest risks for having children with chromosomal abnormalities. These are the women who have the most to lose, economically and socially. Most of the care for children with disabilities falls on the mother.[43-45] Not only must she give up much of her paid employment, but she must often adopt motherhood as her primary self-identification. In a world where many women now identify themselves as workers, to identify oneself first as a mother places a woman in a position of relative isolation. Furthermore, she may be a mother for the rest of her life. Medicine has greatly extended the lives of people with disabilities, so that most people with retardation now live a nearly normal lifespan. It is not uncommon for parents in their eighties to be caring for children with Down syndrome who are in their fifties.[46,47] When the elderly parents die, care usually falls on the siblings.[48] Some siblings have expressed resentment at the extra attention given to the affected person and their own corresponding neglect in childhood.[48-50]

Most people with mental retardation, perhaps 80%, live at home under the care of parents or relatives.[51,52] This has always been the case. Historically, the majority of people with retardation or developmental disabilities have always lived with their families. Institutions were for those who had no families, or who were violent or profoundly retarded (and almost half of those with profound retardation lived at home). Society has never provided either institutional care or in-home care for most persons with mental disabilities. In 1967, the peak year for institutionalization in the United States, 197,000 persons with mental retardation or developmental disabilities were institutionalized, out of an estimated one to two million. In 1990, 82,000 were institutionalized. Cost-saving is not the only reason for deinstitutionalization. Many child psychologists have argued that children with retardation or developmental disorders are more likely to develop their full potential at home under the care of their parents, than in an institutional setting. It is now virtually impossible for parents in many areas to place a newborn or infant in an institution no matter how severe the retardation. In-home care, even occasional respite care, is difficult to obtain. Under these conditions, the choice of not having prenatal diagnosis appears to be no choice at all, unless a woman is opposed to abortion under most conditions.[53] For pregnant women who will be single parents, as is the case for 22% of white women, 34% of Hispanic women, and 59% of African-American women, the prospect of raising a child with a disability may be even more distressing.[54,55]

Much of the literature on effects of prenatal diagnosis on attitudes toward people with disabilities regards all disabilities as a generic class and treats them as if equal.[2,3,5,6,17,18,56-60] This is not a realistic approach. Most physical and some mental disabilities can be overcome with social support and changes in the physical environment.[61] Some mental and neurologic disabilities, however, require lifetime care and overwhelm the parents' lives. Such disabilities may never be overcome even with massive economic and social support. Although increased support is necessary in the interests of social justice, it may not present an alternative to prenatal diagnosis and selective abortion in all cases. The writings of parents of children with disabilities present a mixed message. Although generally intended to inspire by presenting triumphs over adversity, many of these biographies describe the immense effort and sacrifice on the part of the parents.[62-66] There is no clear outcome that might be labeled "joy."[67] Instead, many parents write as if the grieving process that began at the child's birth continues throughout the child's life, as a never ending sense of loss.[68,69] Parents' accounts represent after-the-fact, largely successful, attempts at coping. Those whose children have mental retardation or behavioral problems have described the immense difficulty of daily life. We do not know what these parents might have done if they had had a choice. Probably many would prefer not to think about the possibility, because to negate the birth of a child like theirs is to devalue both their child and their own coping efforts.

It is impossible to return to a pretechnological state in which women do not have to face the possibility of prenatal diagnosis and abortion. Although some feminists imply that such a return to nature would be desirable,[4] medicine has so transformed nature that we can no longer refer to "what nature intended" as a guide for either prenatal or postnatal decisions. In childbirth, North American lost the sense of nature sometime in the nineteenth century.[34] We must face the fact that we live in a technological age that women themselves helped to bring about.[40,70]

Parents have always made choices — often negative ones — about infants with disabilities: for centuries Europeans exposed or abandoned such newborns, usually placing them where they would not be found by kindly passersby.[71] The Catholic Church made no effort to eradicate this custom. Many of these infants would have died anyway before modern medicine. Although some modern writers have argued in favor of allowing or even helping newborns with severe disabilities to die,[72,73] legal or hospital regulations, together with the urge of perinatologists to save life, effectively prevent this. It is no longer possible for parents to decide whether to have a lifesaving operation on a newborn with mental retardation: in most cases, the hospital will overrule the parents and proceed with the operation.[74,75]

For most parents, choices are now limited to the preconception or prebirth period. Having foreclosed choices that once existed postnatally, medicine now offers new choices prenatally. The increase in use of prenatal diagnosis in Canada,[75-77] Denmark,[78] Germany,[79] the United Kingdom,[36,80,81] and the United States[82-86] suggests rapid uptake of the new technologies. Women who have had amniocentesis and have aborted fetuses with Down syndrome write of their relief at being able to avoid becoming mothers of severely disabled children.[87-92] Even though the decision was often difficult and psychologically stressful, these women believe that prenatal diagnosis freed them to go on with their lives, to continue their careers, and to have healthy children. While sensitive to the need to provide adequate supports for those with disabilities, they believe that prenatal diagnosis will continue to offer the best alternative for many women carrying fetuses with serious mental retardation.[29,30,90-92]

Women could, of course, decide to carry the child to term and place it for adoption, but few do so even though there are waiting lists of people willing to adopt children with Down syndrome. (Adoption is less likely for infants with profound mental retardation or likelihood of death within the first few years.) Most parents apparently consider giving up a child with a disability for adoption as the most socially "deviant" course of action that they could take. Many doctors do not even mention this possibility. If there is a choice that parents feel they really do not have, that choice is probably giving up their baby for adoption, an alternative which receives little social support.

"The Exploitation of Women"

Exploitation is not the same as coercion. As Feinberg has pointed out, exploitation can exist in the absence of coercion, as long as one party benefits disproportionately from an interaction.[93] Critics argue that the new reproductive technologies exploit and aggrandize the medical–scientific establishment or the biotechnology industry. At the extreme, some critics claim that *all* modern technology is a manipulative patriarchal plot against women, or a form of "quality control" that ensures that children meet men's specifications. . . .[94–102]

Another reason why critics label prenatal diagnosis as exploitative is that it is big business for the companies that manufacture the equipment and conduct the tests. Commercialization creates laboratory capacity. It then becomes necessary to increase consumer demand in order to keep the laboratory working at capacity. Labratory capacity in the United States has increased to the point that the original recommendations of government bodies[103] or professional organizations[104,107] about maternal age, which were recognized at the time as arbitrary, have been relaxed. The majority of geneticists would perform prenatal diagnosis for any anxious woman, even without indications of age or family history. In 1985, 78% of United States geneticists would perform prenatal diagnosis for an anxious woman of 25 with no medical or genetic indications for its use, and an additional 11% would offer a referral.[105] More women (76%) than men (61%) geneticists would perform prenatal diagnosis for anxiety alone. Most believed that they were alleviating anxiety. Socially speaking, they were opening the door to making prenatal diagnosis a routine procedure in prenatal care. Most pregnant women are anxious. Not all tests are invasive or risky. The so-called "triple test" (α-fetoprotein, estriol, and human chorionic gonadotropin) is a blood test that poses no risk. It was applied to women in 1992 and may become routine. It serves to determine which women should have amniocentesis. Having proceeded as far as a "positive" blood test that indicates possible bad news, many women will find it difficult to decline further testing.

This is what critics mean by exploitation. The biotechnology industry is making large sums of money, and women are having more tests, which become more difficult to refuse. That most women probably welcome the tests does not change the facts of commercialization. Prenatal diagnosis is already one of the most frequently used procedures in prenatal care[106,107] and could become routine in most pregnancies.

Is Prenatal Diagnosis a Eugenic Program?

The underlying concern of those who criticize prenatal diagnosis is often summarized in the word *eugenics*. Most modern authors associate eugenics with Nazi programs to eradicate Jews, Gypsies, and other "inferior" groups.[108–112] Historians of the eugenics movement in Canada,[113–114] the United States,[115,116] Germany,[117] France,[118] and the United Kingdom[119] remind us that genetics has served corrupt political and social ends.

Eugenics has many meanings, so many, in fact, that the Commission of the European Communities has omitted it from its revised human genome proposal (1989) as lacking precision.[120] According to Paul's excellent review,[33] the various definitions of eugenics include the following dichotomies: (1) intention versus effect, (2) science versus social policy, (3) coercion versus voluntary choice, and (4) individual versus social responsibility. The following paragraphs outlines Paul's argument.

Intention versus Effect   If eugenics means intentions, it does not apply to most abortions following prenatal diagnosis, because women do not abort with the intent of improving the gene pool.[121,122] If eugenics applies to unintended effects of individual decisions, however, prenatal diagnosis and selective abortions could be considered eugenic.[123] Duster believes that individual, private decisions are a "backdoor to eugenics," because their collective results will affect the genetic makeup of the entire population.[125] According to this view, the majority of individuals and families will make similar decisions, because they subscribe to a unified ideal of human health and perfection. The sharp reduction in incidence of certain birth defects, such as Tay-Sachs in the United States and spina bifida or thalassemia in the United Kingdom, suggests that families are making what amount to eugenic decisions in regard to these disorders, which most people regard as serious. For less serious disorders, however, it is less likely that individual decisions will have a eugenic effect in a pluralistic society. Individuals and diverse social groups usually have a wide variety of ideas about what constitutes health, unless they are given biased information.

Science versus Social Policy   Originally, eugenics was defined as a science rather than social policy. Francis Galton, who originally coined the term in 1883, described eugenics as "the science of improvement of the human race germ plasm through better breeding."[125] A few modern definitions follow Galton.[126] Most definitions, however, assume interference with a natural process. The agents of change may be individuals or families rather than (or in addition to) the state or other social institutions. The collective results of individual actions may be unanticipated by or even abhorrent to the individuals who made these decisions. Families will choose the kind of children they want, and the result will be a form of "homemade" eugenics in the absence or direct social policy.[124] It is exactly this kind of eugenics that gives feminists fear.[2–4,7,8,95–99,127–129] They point out that (1) individual decisions are not always truly individual, but occur in a social context that may alter or limit choice,[3] and (2) the collective results of individual decisions may lead to social policies that discriminate against the minority who make different decisions and especially against persons with disabilities.[2] This kind of "eugenic discrimination" could be particularly invidious in a democratic society where it could occur by virtue of majority vote (or at least majority action) rather than by authoritarian decree.

Coercion versus Voluntary Choice   Many people define eugenics as including coercion and/or social goals. For example, Holtzman defines eugenics as "any effort to interfere with an individual's procreative choices in order to attain a societal goal."[130] What people are most likely to find objectionable in eugenics is not the goal, but the coercive means of achieving it. To this way of thinking, policies and practices designed to improve the health of the population cannot be eugenic unless coercive. Yet the history of the eugenics movement, especially in the United Kingdom, points to many noncoercive approaches that were considered as eugenic.[131]

Individual versus Social Responsibility   Individual versus social responsibility is another dichotomy in definitions of eugenics. Actions may be defined as eugenic if their intentions are social (such as preventing the costs to society of raising children with disabilities) and as not eugenic if their intentions are to promote informed choices by individuals. One reason why eugenics has such a negative connotation is that all eugenicists, whether radical, liberal, or conservative, including Francis Galton,[125] Madison Grant,[132] George Bernard Shaw,[133] Bertrand Russell,[134] and Jane Clapperton,[135] believed that individual desires must be sacrificed to the public good. Even John Stuart Mill, who believed in the widest possible scope of individual choice, thought that the state should take responsibility in regard to reproduction. Urging "responsible parenthood," he argued, "to undertake this responsibility — to bestow a life which may be either a curse or a blessing — unless the being on whom it is to be bestowed will have at least the ordinary chances of a desirable existence, is a crime against that being."[133] Echoing Mills's statement, Hungarian obstetrician and geneticist Andrew Czeizel argues that children have a "right to be born healthy" and that the state has the moral and legal responsibility to ensure their healthy birth.[134] Czeizel is the last geneticist to advocate this kind of eugenics openly, but others may tacitly support this view. Feminist critics of new reproductive technologies are uneasy with statements such as Mill's and Czeizel's. They reject interference with women's choices, but are at the same time uncomfortable with both the existence and the social outcomes of these choices.[136]

The Goals of Counseling: Eugenics or Informed Choice?

Most genetic counseling around the world would be considered noneugenic today, because 99 to 100% of counselors strive to be nondirective and to "help the individuals/ couples achieve their parenting goals," and to "help individuals/couples understand their options and the present state of medical knowledge so they can make informed decisions."[137–140] Counselors claim to "tell patients that decisions, especially reproductive ones, are theirs alone and refuse to make any for them" (92%): they also claim to "support any decisions patients make" (94%).[105,138,139] It is not only the nondirectiveness, but the individual and family focus of genetic counseling that places it outside most definitions of eugenics.

As Kevles points out, however, in his concluding chapter "The New Eugenics," during the 1960s, the shift of counseling from concern with improving the welfare of the population to improving the welfare of individuals and families took place partly for political reasons.[115] Many of the early post-World War II geneticists in Canada and the United States sincerely believed in improving the biological quality of the population but rejected any association with the eugenics movement.[33,141] In order to pursue their objectives in politically acceptable ways, they focused on voluntary, individual decision-making. Sheldon Reed coined the term *genetic counseling* in 1947 to replace the earlier terms *genetic advice or genetic hygiene*, which sounded too directive.[142] Kevles believes that this shift in ethos to place the needs and rights of individuals and families above the welfare of the population or gene pool marked a decisive break with the past and that the so-called "new eugenics" is beneficial, because it is devoted to the interests of individuals rather than society.

Ludmerer and others believe that there was no shift in ethos and that the goals of the eugenics movement entered medicine, unpretentiously, through genetic counseling.[116,143] The majority of geneticists in Canada (68%), the United Kingdom (71%), the United States (78%), France (81%), and 15 other nations (74%) still believe that the eugenic goal of "improvement of the general health and vigor of the population" is important.[105,139] A smaller majority in Canada (51%) and substantial percents in the United Kingdom (48%), the United States (47%), France (50%), and 15 other nations (54%) believe that another goal of Kevles' "old" eugenics, namely "reduction in the number of carriers of genetic disorders in the population," is an important goal of counseling.[105] Most (97%) in the United States and 18 other nations (98%) believe that "the prevention of disease or abnormality" is an important goal of counseling.

Labelling a technology "eugenic" does little to clarify the issues. In view of its multitudinous and sometimes contradictory meanings, the word should perhaps be dropped from discussions of prenatal diagnosis altogether. There remains the problem of defining what it is that people fear when they use the word eugenics. The basic fears appear to be (1) coercion into having prenatal diagnosis and abortion; (2) exploitation of women for the benefit of medical or social institutions; (3) excesses or misuses of prenatal diagnosis for "frivolous" purposes such as sex selection; (4) discrimination against people with disabilities, especially if their births could have been prevented. Underlying this final fear is a sense that there may be a deep undercurrent of eugenic thinking in the public, sometimes voiced as a belief that "some people should not have children. . . ."

Effects of Prenatal Diagnosis on Societal Attitudes toward People with Disabilities

Many people fear that increased use of prenatal diagnosis will shift social resources away from people with disabilities.[2–6,36,79,145–149] Most disabilities, however, are not genetic in origin. They result from accidents, aging, viral or bacterial diseases, birth traumas, acts of violence, or environmental exposures. Genetics does not even account for the majority of severe mental retardation. Altogether chromosomal disorders (e.g., Down syndrome), single-gene disorders (e.g., Tay-Sachs, fragile-X syndrome), and developmental malformation syndromes (e.g., neural tube defects) account for about 40% of individuals with an intelligence quotient under 50.[150] Accidents at birth, prematurity, low birthweight, environmental or substance exposures, and unknown factors account for the remaining 60%. Genetic disorders do account for substantial numbers of deaths at early ages, including perhaps 20% of all infant deaths. They are second only to prematurity and birth injuries as causes or perinatal mortality. They are estimated as the second leading cause of death in children between the ages of one and four years and the fourth leading cause in individuals between the ages of 15 and 24 years,[103,150] behind accidents, suicide, and homicide.[144] Nevertheless, genetic disorders are never *the* leading cause of death or disability. Many fetal malformations, including some congenital heart defects, cannot be diagnosed prenatally. Even disorders that can be diagnosed prenatally, such as Tay-Sachs, will not be tested for in low-risk groups and will continue to appear. Other disorders, such as neurofibromatosis, have a high rate of new mutations. This means that disability will always be with us, regardless of what we do with prenatal diagnosis. Society needs to be prepared to offer support to people with disabilities. Even if every pregnancy underwent chromosomal prenatal diagnosis and testing for neural tube defects (an unlikely event, given the negative risk–benefit ratio for younger women) and every woman agreed to abortion (also an unlikely event), society would still have children with birth defects of genetic origin from unsuspected inborn errors of metabolism, new mutations, heart defects, and so on. The majority of birth defects, however, would still originate from prematurity, low birthweight, and environmental exposure, as is the case now.[151] This argues for preventive measures that aim at the social and environmental causes of birth defects. There is no reason why social and economic programs cannot go hand-in-hand with public education about genetics and use of prenatal diagnosis, if desired. There is also no reason why prevention of disabilities — through adequate maternal nutrition, prenatal care, prevention of substance abuse or physical abuse, and prenatal diagnosis — must be at cross-purposes to support for living people with disabilities. It is illogical to argue that support for people with disabilities will be reduced if there are fewer such persons, or that support will be increased if more children with disabilities are born.

It appears unlikely that society will have fewer people with disabilities in the future. As society ages, we can expect more, rather than fewer, people with disabilities of all types, including mental disabilities. It is therefore important to increase, rather than to contemplate decreasing, supports for people with disabilities.

However, those who are concerned about the effects of prenatal diagnosis on attitudes toward disabilities have some legitimate fears. Sooner or later, as health-care budgets are rationed . . . the taxpayers may decide that they do not wish to provide extraordinary support for a child with very limited potential if the birth could have been prevented. This is not to say that the majority of people lack all sympathy for those with disabilities or that this is the beginning of a Nazi extermination program. When treatment is not effective, however, and the state underwrites the cost of care, at some point there must be a limit to the amount expended, so that funds can go to patients whose treatment may be successful. . . . If a woman has prenatal diagnosis and then decides to carry to term a baby with a serious and costly problem that cannot be treated successfully, she may indeed face social opprobrium.[152,153] (She could, of course, have refused prenatal diagnosis, but may still be considered socially irresponsible for doing so.) . . .

Conclusion

Some feminist criticisms of prenatal diagnosis are well taken. Some women do feel social pressure to have prenatal diagnosis: many women find the "choice" of bearing and raising a child with a disability so unattractive under present conditions that it appears tantamount to no choice at all.

Differential use of prenatal diagnosis by different social groups could have a divisive effect on society's views about disability. Increasing fragmentation in American society could lead to reductions in services for those with disabilities. Commercial laboratories do profit from prenatal diagnosis and some have sought to expand its use for social, rather than strictly medical, indications. There are hidden arguments in public health programs, including genetics, that shift attention away from social and cultural causes of ill health or definitions of ill health. Goals of "prevention of disease" or cost–benefit arguments maybe at odds with goals of genetic counseling that stress "helping individuals come to decisions that are best for them." Finally, there are abuses, notably for sex selection.

On the other hand, people always have *some* choice. Sartre characterized the excuse "I have no other choice" as "bad faith." Most women believe they have a choice and some refuse prenatal diagnosis. There is no evidence of coercion by doctors. Women have collaborated actively in encouraging the spread of prenatal diagnosis. Discouraging women from having prenatal diagnosis will not necessarily increase benefits for people with disabilities. The reverse is more likely. An increase in the number of affected children would most likely mean that each individual would receive less, rather than more support. Comparing prenatal diagnosis with coercive eugenic programs or with the death camps does nothing to help either women or people with disabilities. Instead, this line of argument leads only to backlash from anti-abortionists who would like to see women return to traditional — subordinate — roles.

In all, the evidence is that (1) women exercise choice in regard to prenatal diagnosis; (2) there are social pressures to use prenatal diagnosis in a "technological culture," just as there are pressures to give birth in hospitals and to use other birth technologies; (3) women probably have more power over choices about prenatal diagnosis than they do over other technologies used in birth; (4) most women, including most who consider themselves feminists, seem relieved to be able to make the choice implied in prenatal diagnosis; (5) many of the ethical problems in prenatal diagnosis arise from inequalities in our health-care system rather than from the technology itself; and (6) prenatal diagnosis is not a eugenic program.

References

1. Fletcher JC, Wertz DC. Ethics and prenatal diagnosis: Problems, positions, and proposed guidelines. In: Milunsky A ed. Genetic disorders and the fetus. Baltimore: Johns Hopkins University Press, 1992, in press.

2. Hubbard R. The politics of women's biology. New Brunswick, NJ: Rutgers University Press, 1990.

3. Lippman A. Prenatal genetic testing and screening: constructing needs and reinforcing inequities. Am J Law Med 1991a; 17: 15–50.

4. Rothman BK. The tentative pregnancy: prenatal diagnosis and the future of motherhood. New York: Norton, 1986.

5. Asch A. Reproductive technology and disability. In: Cohen S, Taub N, eds. Reproductive laws for the 1990s. Clifton, NJ: Humana Press, 1989:69–127.

6. Saxton M. Prenatal screening and discriminatory attitudes about disability. In: Baruch EH, D'Adamo AF, Seager J, eds. Embryos, ethics, and human rights: Exploring the new reproductive technologies. New York: Harrington Park Press. 1987b:217–224.

7. Hubbard R. Prenatal diagnosis and eugenic ideology. Women's Stud Int Forum 1985; 8: 567–576.

8. Hubbard R. Eugenics: new tools, old ideas. Women & Health 1987;13:225.

9. Schaeffer FA, Koop CE. What ever happened to the human race? Old Tappan, NJ: Revell, 1979.

10. Henifin MS, Hubbard R. Norsigian J. Prenatal screening. In: Cohen S. Taub N, eds. Reproductive laws for the 1990s. Clifton NJ: Humana Press, 1989:155–184.

11. Rothman BK. Recreating motherhood: Ideology and technology in a patriarchal society. New York: Norton, 1989.

12. Wexler NS. The oracle of DNA. In: Rowland LP, Wood DS, Schon EA. Dimauro S. eds. Molecular Genetics and Diseases of the Brain, Nerve, and Muscle. New York: Oxford University Press. 1989:429–442.

13. Zola IK. Medicine as an institution of social control. Sociological Review. 1972; 20: 487–504.

14. Zola IK. In the name of health and illness: On some socio-political consequences of medical influence. Soc Sci & Med 1975; 83: 85–87.

15. Zola IK. Healthism and disabling professions. In: Illich I. Zola IK. McKnight J, Caplan J, Shaiken H, eds. Disabling profession. London: Calder & Boyars, 1977.

16. Hubbard R. Henifin S. Genetic screening of prospective parents and workers: Some scientific and social issues. Int'l J Health Services 1985;15:231.

17. Kaplan D. Prenatal screening and its impact on persons with disabilities. Fetal Diagnosis and Therapy. November 1992, in press.

18. Saxton M. Prenatal screening and discriminatory attitudes about disability. Genewatch. Jan/Feb 1987a:8–11.

19. Luker K. Abortion and the politics of motherhood. Berkeley: University of California Press. 1984.

20. Lasker JN, Borg S. In search of parenthood: Coping with infertility and high-tech conception. Boston: Beacon Press. 1987.

21. Sjögren B, Uddenberg N. Decision making during the prenatal diagnostic procedure: a questionnaire and interview study of 211 women participating in prenatal diagnosis. Prenat Diagn 1988:8(4):263–273.

22. Swert A. Impacts of generic counseling and prenatal diagnosis for neural tube defects. In: Evers-Kiebooms G, Cassiman JJ. Van den Berghe H, D'Ydewelle G, eds. Genetic risk, risk perception, and decision-making. Birth Defects 1987; XXII(2):61–83.

23. Frets PG, Niermeijer M. Reproductive planning after genetic counselling: a perspective from the last decade. Clin Genet 1990; 38: 295–306.

24. Evers-Kiebooms G. Decision making in Huntington's disease and cystic fibrosis. Birth Defects: Original Article Series 1987; 23(2): 115–149.

25. Evers-Kiebooms G, Denayer L. Van den Berghe H. A child with cystic fibrosis: 2. Subsequent family planning decisions, reproduction and use of prenatal diagnosis. Clin Genet 1990;37:207–215.

26. Adler NE, Keyes S, Robertson P. Psychological issues in new reproductive technologies: Pregnancy including technology and diagnostic screening. In: Rodin J. Collins A. eds. Women and new reproductive technologies: Medical, psychosocial, legal and ethical dilemmas. Hillsdale, NJ: Lawrence Erlbaum Associates, Publishers, 1991:111.

27. Rapp R. The power of positive diagnosis: Medical and maternal desicourses on amniocentesis. In: Michaelson KL. ed. Childbirth in America: Anthropological perspectives.

South Hadley, MA: Bergin & Garvey, 1988a:103–116.

28. Rapp R. Constructing amniocentesis: Medical and maternal voices. In: Ginsburg F, Tsing A, eds. Uncertain terms: Negotiating gender in America. Boston: Beacon Press, 1990.

29. Rapp R. Chromosomes and communication: The discourse of genetic counselling. Med Anth Quart 1988b;2(2):143–157.

30. Rapp R. Reproduction and gender hierarchy: Amniocentesis in contemporary America. In: Miller B, ed. Sex and gender hierarchies. Chicago: University of Chicago Press, 1991.

31. Clarke A. Is non-directive genetic counselling possible? Lancet Oct. 19, 1991; 338: 998–1001.

32. Green TH. Liberal legislation and the feedom of contract. In: Nettleship RL ed. Works of Thomas Hill Green. Reprint of 1889 ed. Krauss reprint 1968.

33. Paul DB. Eugenic anxieties and social realities. Social Research October 1992, in press.

34. Wertz RW, Wertz DC. Lying-in: A history of childbirth in America, expanded edition. New Haven, CT: Yale University Press, 1989.

35. Pearse WH. Parturition: Places and priorities. Am J Pub Hlth 1987; 177:923–924.

36. Harris R. Wertz DC. Ethics and medical genetics in the United Kingdom. In: Wertz DC. Fletcher JC. eds. Ethics and human genetics: A cross-cultural perspective. Heidelberg: Springer-Verlag. 1989:388–418.

37. Richwald GA, Clark RD, Crandall B et al. Cost and acceptance of MSAFP screening in public prenatal clinics. Am J Hum Genet 1990:47(suppl):A291.

38. Oakley A. Women confined: Towards a sociology of childbirth. Oxford, UK: Martin Robertson, 1980.

39. Oakley A. The captured womb: A history of the medical care of pregnant women. Oxford, UK: Basil Blackwell, 1984.

40. Cowan RS. A history of prenatal diagnosis. Fetal Diagnosis and Therapy. 1993: 8(Suppl. 1)

41. Andrews LB. Medical genetics: A legal frontier. Chicago: American Bar Foundation, 1987.

42. Elias S, Annas GJ. Reproductive genetics and the law. Chicago: Yearbook Publishers, 1987.

43. Byrne EA, Cunningham CC. The effects of mentally handicapped children on families: A conceptual review. J Child Psychol & Psychiat 1985;26:847–864.

44. Thompson L. Walker AJ. Gender in families: Women and men in marriage, work, and parenthood. J Marr Fam 1989;51:845–871.

45. Marcenko MD, Meyers JC. Mothers of children with developmental disabilities: Who shares the burden? Fam Relat 1991; 40: 186–190.

46. Krauss MW, Seltzer MM. Coping strategies of older mothers of adults with retardation: A life-span developmental perspective. In: Turnbull AP, Patterson J. Behr Sk, Murphy DL, Marquis J. Blue-Banning M., eds. Cognitive coping research in developmental disabilities. Baltimore: Paul H Brookes, 1992, in press.

47. Janicki MP, Wisniewski HM, eds. Aging and developmental disabilities: Issues and approaches. Baltimore: Paul H Brookes, 1985.

48. Seltzer MM, Krauss MW. Sibling relationships of persons with mental retardation in adulthood. In: Stoneman Z. Berman P. eds. Siblings of individuals with mental retardation, physical disabilities, and chronic illness. Baltimore: Paul H Brookes. 1992, in press.

49. Lobato D. Siblings of handicapped children: A review. J Autism & Dev Disord 1983; 13: 347–364.

50. Drotar P. Crawford P. Psychological adaptation of siblings of chronically ill children: Research and practice implications. Dev & Behavioral Pediatrics 1985;6:355–362.

51. Fujura GT, Garza J, Braddock D. National survey of family support in developmental disabilities. Mimeo, IL: University of Illinois at Chicago, 1989.

52. Meyers CE, Borthwick SA, Eyman RK. Place of residence by age, ethnicity, and level of retardation of the mentally retarded/developmentally disabled population of California. Am J Mental Deficiency 1985; 90: 266–20.

53. Petchesky R. Giving women a real choice. Nation 1990;250:732.

54. United States Bureau of the Census. Single parents and their children. Washington: U.S.

Government Printing Office, 1990.

55. United States National Center for Health Statistics. Wanted and unwanted childbearing in the U.S.: 1973–1988. Washington: U.S. Government Printing Office, 1990.

56. Kaplan D. Disability rights perspectives on reproductive technologies and public policy. In: Cohen S, Taub N, eds. Reproductive laws for the 1990s. Clifton, NJ: Humana Press, 1989:241–248.

57. Degener T. Debates across social movements on reproductive technologies, genetic engineering, and eugenics. In: Duncan B. Woods DE, eds. Ethical issues in disability and rehabilitation. World Rehabilitation Fund. New York: Printing Production Services. 1989:73.

58. Degener T. Female self-determination between feminist claims and "voluntary" eugenics, between "rights" and ethics. Issues in Reproductive and Genetic Engineering 1990;(3):87.

59. Finger A. Claiming all of our babies: Reproductive rights and disabilities. In: Arditti R, Klein RD, Minden S, eds. Test-tube women: What future for motherhood? London: Pandora Press, 1984.

60. Finger A. Past due: A story of disability, pregnancy, and birth. Seattle WA: Seal Press, 1990.

61. Carrier JG. Learning disability: Social class and the construction of inequality in American education. Westport, CT: Greenwood Press, 1986.

62. Dorris M. The broken cord. New York: Harper & Row, 1989.

63. DeFord F. Alex: The life of a child. New York: New American Library, 1984.

64. Forecki M. Speak to me. Washington, DC: Gallaudet University Press, 1985.

65. Fraiberg A, Fraiberg L. Insights from the blind: Comparative studies of blind and sighted infants. New York: New American Library, 1979.

66. Spradley TS, Spradley JP. Deaf like me. Washington, DC: Gallaudet University Press, 1985.

67. Retsinas J. The impact of prenatal technology upon attitudes toward disabled infants. In: Wertz DC, ed. Research in the Sociology of Health Care 1991;9:75–104.

68. Wikler L, Waso M, Hatfield E. Chronic sorrow revisited: Parent vs. professional depiction of the adjustment of parents of mentally retarded children. Am J Orthopsychiatry 1981;5:63–70.

69. Simons R. After the tears: Parents talk about raising a child with a disability, New York: Harcourt Brace, 1987.

70. McDonough P. Congenital disability and medical research: The development of amniocentesis. Women and Health 1990; 16(3–4): 137–153.

71. Boswell J. The kindness of strangers: The abandonment of children in western Europe from late antiquity to the Renaissance. New York: Pantheon Books, 1988.

72. Glover J. What sort of people should there be? New York: Penguin Books, 1984.

73. Kuhse H. Singer P. Should the baby live? The problem of handicapped infants. London: Oxford University Press, 1985.

74. Fletcher JC. Coping with genetic disorders: A guide for clergy and parents. San Francisco: Harper & Row, 1982.

75. Guillemin JH, Holmstrom LL. Mixed blessings: Intensive care for newborns. Oxford: Oxford University Press, 1986.

76. Hunter AG, Thompson D, Speevak M. Midtrimester genetic amniocentesis in Eastern Ontario: A review from 1970 to 1985. J Med Genet 1987;24:335–343.

77. Roy DJ, Hall JG. Ethics and medical genetics in Canada. In: Wertz DC, Fletcher JC, eds. Ethics and human genetics: A cross-cultural perspective. Heidelberg: Springer-Verlag, 1989:119–140.

78. Therkelsen AJ, Bolund L, Mortensen V. Ethics and medical genetics in Denmark. In: Wertz DC, Fletcher JC, eds. Ethics and human genetics: A cross-cultural perspective. Heidelberg: Springer-Verlag, 1989: 141–155.

79. Schroeder-Kurth TM, Huebner J. Ethics and medical genetics in the Federal Republic of Germany. In: Wertz DC, Fletcher JC, eds. Ethics and human genetics: A cross-cultural perspective. Heidelberg: Springer-Verlag, 1989:156–175.

80. Farrant W. Who's for amniocentesis? The politics of prenatal screening. In: Homans H. ed. The sexual politics of reproduction.

Aldershot, Hants, UK: Gower Publishing, 1985:96–122.

81. Terzian E, Boreham J, Cuckle HS, Walk NJ. A survey of diagnostic amniocentesis in Oxford from 1974 to 1981. Prenat Diagn 1985;5:401–414.

82. Mulvihill JJ, Walters L, Wertz DC. Ethics and medical genetics in the United States of America. In: Wertz DC, Fletcher JC, eds. Ethics and human genetics: A cross-cultural perspective. Heidelberg: Springer-Verlag, 1989:419–456.

83. Hook EB, Chambers GM. Estimated rates of Down syndrome in live births by one year maternal age intervals for mothers aged 20–49 in a New York State study — implications of the risk figures for genetic counseling and cost benefit analysis of prenatal diagnosis programs. In: Bergsma D, Lowry RB, eds. Numerical taxonomy of birth defects and polygenic disorders. New York: Alan R Liss, 1972.

84. Hook EB, Schreinemachers DM. Trends in utilization of prenatal cytogenetic diagnosis by New York State residents in 1979 and 1980. Am J Pulb Hlth 1983;73(2):198–202.

85. Adams MM, Finley S, Hansen H, et al. Utilization of prenatal diagnosis in women > 35 years, United States. 1977–78. Am J Obstet Gynecol 1981;139:673.

86. Marion JP. Acceptance of amniocentesis by low-income patients in an urban hospital. Am J Obstet Gynecol 1980;130:11–15.

87. Anonymous. When risk factors have little meaning. Br Med J 1989;299:1599–1600.

88. Hodge SE. Waiting for amniocentesis. New Engl J Med 1989;320:63–64.

89. Green R (pseud). Letter to a genetic counselor. J Genetic Counseling 1992;1:55–70.

90. Rapp R. XYLO: A true story. In: Arditti R. Klein RD, Minden S, eds. Test-tube women: What future for motherhood? London Pandora Press, 1984:313–328.

91. Brown J (pseud). The choice. JAMA 1989;262:2735.

92. Eicholz A. Amniocentesis: The experience of invasion and the ambivalence of foreknowledge. In: Offerman-Zuckerberg J, ed. Gender in transition: A new frontier. New York: Plenum, 1989:173–177.

93. Feinberg J. Noncoercive exploitation. In: Sartorius R, ed. Paternalism. Minneapolis: University of Minnesota Press, 1990:201–236.

94. Rothschild J, ed. Machina ex dea: Feminist perspectives on technology. New York: Pergamon Press, 1983.

95. Spallone P. Beyond conception: The new politics of reproduction. Granby, MA: Bergin & Garvey, 1989.

96. Spallone P, Steinberg DL. Made to order: The myth of reproductive and genetic progress. New York: Pergamon Press, 1987.

97. Corea G. The mother machine: Reproductive technologies from artificial insemination to artificial wombs. New York: Harper & Row, 1985.

98. Arditti R, Klein RD, Minden S, eds. Testtube women: What future for motherhood? London: Pandora Press, 1984.

99. Rothman BK. In labor: Women and power in the birthplace. New York: W W Norton, 1982.

100. Whitbeck C. Theories of sex difference. Philosophical Forum 5 (1.2);1973:45–80.

101. Whitbeck C. The moral implications of regarding women as people: New perspectives on pregnancy and personhood. In: Bondeson WB, ed. *Abortion and the status of the fetus*. Boston: D Reidel, 1984: 251–252.

102. Atwood M. The handmaid's tale. Boston: Houghton Mifflin, 1986.

103. United States Department of Health, Education, and Welfare. Antenatal diagnosis. April 1979. NIH Pub. No. 79–1973. Washington, DC. U.S. Government Printing Office. April 1979.

104. Canadian College of Medical Geneticists. Professional and ethical guidelines. Ottawa: CCMG, 1986.

105. Wertz DC. The 19-nation survey: Genetics and ethics around the world. In: Wertz DC, Fletcher JC, eds. Ethics and human genetics: A cross-cultural perspective. Heidelberg: Springer-Verlag, 1989a:1–79.

106. Nightingale EO, Goodman M. Before birth: Prenatal testing for genetic disease. Cambridge, MA: Harvard University Press, 1990.

107. Blatt RJR. Prenatal tests. New York: Vintage Books, 1988.

108. Chorover SL. From genesis to genocide. Cambridge, MA: Massachusetts Institute of Technology Press, 1979.

109. Lifton RJ. The Nazi doctors. New York: Basic Books, 1986.

110. Luria S. Human genome program (letter). Science October 13, 1989;246:873.

111. Mueller-Hill B. Murderous science: Elimination by scientific selection of Jews, gypsies, and others. Germany 1933–1945. Oxford, UK: Oxford University Press, 1988.

112. Proctor RN. Racial hygiene: Medicine under the Nazis. Cambridge, MA: Harvard University Press, 1988.

113. McLaren A. Our own master race: Eugenics in Canada 1885–1945. Toronto, Ontario: McClelland & Stewart, 1990.

114. McLaren A, McLaren AT. The bedroom and the state: The changing practices and politics of contraception and abortion in Canada. 1880–1980. Toronto, Ontario: McClelland and Stewart, 1986.

115. Kevles DJ. In the name of eugenics: Genetics and the uses of human heredity. New York: Knopf, 1985.

116. Ludmerer KM. Genetics and American society. Baltimore: Johns Hopkins University Press, 1972.

117. Adams M, ed. The wellborn science: Eugenics in Germany, France, Brazil and Russia. New York: Oxford University Press, 1990.

118. Schneider WH. Quality and quantity: The quest for biological regeneration in twentieth-century France. Cambridge, UK: Cambridge University Press, 1990.

119. Soloway RA. Demography and degeneration: Eugenics and the declining birthrate in twentieth-century Britain. Chapel Hill: University of North Carolina Press, 1990.

120. Commission of the European Communities. Modified proposal for a Council decision adopting a specific research and technological development in the field of health: Human genome analysis (1990 to 1991). Official Journal of the European Communities, CB–CO–89–485–EN–C. Brussels November, 13, 1989:3.

121. Carlson EA. Human genetics. Lexington, MA: DC, Heath, 1984, glossary V.

122. Carlson EA. Ramifications of genetics. Science April 25, 1986;232:531–532.

123. Wright R. Achilles' helix. The New Republic July 9 & 16, 1990:21–31.

124. Duster T. Backdoor to eugenics. New York: Routledge, 1990.

125. Galton F. Inquiries into the human faculty and its development. London, 1883.

126. Haller MH. Eugenics: Hereditarian attitudes in American thought. New Brunswick, NJ: Rutgers University Press, 1984:ix.

127. Holmes HB, Hoskins BB, Gross M, eds. The custom-made child? Women-centered perspectives. Clifton, NJ: Humana Press, 1980.

128. Holmes HB, Hoskins BB, Gross M, eds. Birth control and controlling birth. Clifton, NJ: Humana Press, 1980.

129. Rodin J, Collins A, eds. Women and new reproductive technologies. Hillsdale, NJ: Lawrence Erlbaum, 1991.

130. Holtzman NA. Proceed with caution: Predicting genetic risks in the recombinant DNA era. Baltimore: Johns Hopkins University Press, 1989.

131. Hogben L. Genetic principles in medicine and social science. London 1931:207.

132. Grant M. The passing of the great race. New York 1916:44–45.

133. Shaw GB. Sociological papers. London 1905:74–75.

134. Russell B. Eugenics. In: Russell B, ed. Marriage and morals. New York: Liveright, 1970: 255–273.

135. Clapperton J. Scientific meliorism. London 1885:10.

136. Fox-Genovese E. Feminism without illusions. Chapel Hill: University of North Carolina Press, 1991.

137. Fraser FC. Genetic counseling. Am J Hum Genet 1974;26:636–659.

138. Sorenson JR, Swazey JP, Scotch NA. Reproductive pasts, reproductive futures: Genetic counselling and its effectiveness. New York: Alan R Liss, 1981.

139. Wertz DC, Fletcher JC. Attitudes of genetic counselors: A multi-national survey. Am J Hum Genet 1988b;42(4):592–600.

140. Wertz DC, Fletcher JC. Ethical decision-making in medical genetics: Women as patients and practitioners in 18 nations. In: Ratcliff KS et al. eds. Healing technology: Feminist perspectives. Ann Arbor: University of Michigan Press, 1989b:221–241.

141. Sorenson JR. Genetic Counselling: Values that have mattered. In: Annas GJ, Elias S,

eds. Gene mapping: Using law and ethics as guides. New York: Oxford University Press, 1992:203–211.

142. Reed SC. A short history of genetic counseling. Soc Bio. 1974;21:332–339.

143. Kessler S. Psychological aspects of genetic counseling. VII. Thoughts on directiveness. J Genetic Counseling 1992;1:9–18.

144. United States Department of Health and Human Services. National Center for Health Statistics. Health USA 1990. Washington, DC: U.S. Government Printing Office, 1991.

145. King's Fund Forum. King's Fund Forum consensus statement: Screening for fetal and genetic abnormality. Br Med J 1987; 295: 1551–1553.

146. Holder AR, Heinifin MS. Selective termination of pregnancy. Hastings Center Rep 1988;18(1):21–22.

147. Hull RT, Nelson JA, Gartner LA. Ethical issues in prenatal therapies. In: Humber JM, Almeder RF, eds. Biomedical Ethics Reviews. Clifton, NJ: Humana Press, 1984: 225–249.

148. Johnson SR, Elkins TE. Ethical issues in prenatal diagnosis. Clin Obstet Gynecol 1988;31:408.

149. Motulsky A, Murray J. Will prenatal diagnosis with selective abortion affect society's attitude toward the handicapped? In: Berg K, Tranoy DE, eds. Research ethics. New York: Alan R Liss, 1983.

150. NICHD. Antenatal diagnosis: Report fo a consensus development conference. Washington, DC: DHEW, 1979, Pub. No. (NIH) 79–173.

151. Yankauer A. What infant mortality tells us. Am J Pub Health 1990;80:653.

152. Billings P, Kohn M, DeCuevas M, Beckwith J, Alper J, Natowicz M. Discrimination as a consequence of genetic screening. Am J Hum Genet 1992;50:476–482.

153. Natowicz MR, Alper JS. Genetic discrimination and the law. Am J Hum Genet 1992;50(3):465–475.

39   First Fruits: Genetic Screening

Kathleen Nolan

And when the woman saw that the tree was good for food, and that it was pleasant to the eyes, and a tree to be desired to make one wise, she took of the fruit thereof, and did eat, and gave also unto her husband with her; and he did eat. (Genesis 3:6)

One of the first fruits of the Human Genome Project will be many new markers for traits and diseases believed to have a genetic base but so far lacking an identified gene (or genes). Most of these markers can be developed into diagnostic tests quite easily, greatly expanding the range of genetic diagnostic options potentially available to individuals for themselves, or as parents and prospective parents.

However, the sheer mass of genetic information that may become available, along with the complex patterns of information offered by many of the new markers, has generated concern about the extent and rapidity with which these new markers should move from the laboratory bench into various clinical uses. In particular, critics of modern obstetric practices have taken note of the ways in which increased diagnostic surveillance can change the character and mood of pregnancy, and they have urged special caution about increased prenatal genetic testing. This paper explores these issues and suggests the need for national standards articulating criteria for introducing and funding new genetic tests as a part of normal prenatal care.

Genetic Testing in Prenatal Care

Having a baby is an exciting and emotionally demanding process for parents. Here is a new life, forged from complex physical and emotional bonds between its parents, and manifesting the powerful and mysterious intertwining of their previously distinct genetic heritages. Whether planned or unanticipated, pregnancy emerges replete with potential: a potential child with an almost infinite range of needs, desires, and attributes.

From a parent's perspective, pregnancy is thus filled with both curiosity and concern. What kind of baby will this be? Who will it look like? Will it be a girl or a boy? Will it be healthy?

This last question — "Will my baby be healthy? — helps propel parents into the obstetrician's or midwife's office, as they seek to fulfill their responsibility to protect and promote the well-being of their developing offspring. Joining with the health professional, they construct a history of the developing fetus via a series of physical examinations and selected diagnostic tests.

Although few parents realize it, none of these tests, singly or in combination, can prove that the pregnancy is proceeding normally. In fact, even directly examining the baby after birth is not fool-proof against unsuspected conditions. Nonetheless, prenatal and even preconceptual screening of various sorts can identify many problems, sometimes at very early stages. Parents and health care professionals have therefore increasingly turned to amniocentesis, ultrasound, alpha-fetoprotein assays, and other tests in an attempt to gain information and to detect and treat conditions for which prenatal interventions are available.

Genetic screening has until recently played a relatively minor role in this process. Because genetic testing was expensive and time-consuming, and because most detectable conditions were quite rare, specialized testing for inherited disorders (other than chromosomal analysis and the diagnosis of disorders of hemoglobin formation, such as sickle cell disease) has not generally been recommended as a part of normal prenatal care, except in those situations where a family history or a previously affected child indicates an increased risk.

However, this aspect of prenatal care may undergo enormous change over the next two decades. The prospect of dozens or even hundreds of relatively inexpensive new genetic diagnostic tests emerging rapidly from the genome project has been held out as likely by both the project's advocates and its opponents. Many of these markers will identify genes related to common illnesses and other traits and conditions that were previously well outside prenatal health professionals' routine range of concerns.

Various professional, political, and policy stances can influence the degree to which the introduction of more genetic markers into normal prenatal care is accepted, or indeed, encouraged. The question is, then, Will such markers actually improve the quality of prenatal care, and at what cost? The need for an answer to this question will only become more pressing if, as some hope, it soon becomes possible to screen maternal blood for fetal lymphocytes, which can be safely and easily subjected to testing with genetic markers.

Diagnostic Options

What prenatal diagnostic tests to pursue has always been something of a judgment question. Risks for Down syndrome and other chromosomal abnormalities increase precipitously at a maternal age of approximately thirty-five years, leading health care professionals to recommend amniocentesis at that point; nonetheless, the majority of infants with Down syndrome in the United States are actually born to younger mothers, where the frequency of chromosomal abnormalities is lower but the number of births is much higher. Alpha-fetoprotein screening is also becoming more common despite concerns about its low predictive value (requiring expensive follow-up testing for many women whose pregnancies will ultimately prove uneventful) and despite the absence of treatment (other than abortion) for many of the problems the screening identifies.

In addition, serious debate has attended consideration of both routine prenatal screening for HIV infection, which some health professionals advocate, and elective screening for identification of fetal sex, which some parents request for personal reasons (including the desire to abort a fetus of an unacceptable sex).

The fruits of the genome project hold the potential to multiply these options exponentially. We can reasonably expect the development of genetic probes for most major, early onset genetic diseases caused by a single gene, but researchers will also likely discover markers that provide some degree of information about the genetics of a wide range of other conditions, of varying severity and of complex etiology. In fact, genome project and other federally sponsored research has already led to the development of markers for late onset diseases such as Huntington chorea and adult onset polycystic kidney disease, as well as for susceptibility or vulnerability to various abnormal blood lipid patterns and certain forms of cancer.

Markers for these "contingent conditions" — conditions that are related to the presence of certain genes but not fully or immediately predicted by them — may turn out to be very plentiful. Moreover, markers will likely be available for behavioral conditions, such as schizophrenia and manic depressive disorder, and conditions of relatively minor severity, such as obesity, freckling, myopia, and some learning disorders. It will also be possible to identify carriers of recessive and sex-linked disorders; they will not themselves manifest the condition, but they will be capable of transmitting its gene(s) to future generations.

Which of these markers to develop into diagnostic tests for widespread use has already proved to be a difficult question for postnatal populations. For example, widespread screening for adult carriers of cystic fibrosis was recently discouraged by two national scientific organizations after substantial study, despite great media excitement about the new developments and the readiness of several biotechnology firms to begin marketing their new diagnostic probes.

Moving the question to prenatal populations introduces several additional layers of complication. First, it is much less clear who is being served by diagnostic testing: is it the parents, who acquire information about their pregnancy and subsequent offspring, or is it the offspring, considered as a second (fetal, embryonic, or pre-embryonic) patient?

Similarly, how are the benefits and burdens of testing to be estimated? Can we say anything intelligent about the importance of diagnosing late onset and other contingent conditions, or conditions of limited severity? What about conditions for which successful postnatal treatment is available? And, again, whose perspective on benefits and burdens should we consider: the parents'? the offspring's? geneticists'? other health professionals'? society's?

We can also responsibly ask, Should any limits be placed on the availability of such probes or the use of such information? Will parents understand what the markers do and do not offer in terms of diagnosis and prognosis? Do we want to have large panels of markers available for prenatal use? Are we willing to have pregnancy decisions, including abortion, turn on the presence or absence of genes for late onset conditions, contingent conditions, or conditions of limited or questionable severity? And, finally, who will pay for whatever testing is available?

Planning for the Introduction of New Markers

One of the main grounds offered in support of efforts to obtain funding for the genome project has been the potential for genetic information to improve medical care. Thus, the very existence of the project serves as an impetus to move newly discovered markers rapidly into the clinical arena. In the absence of prospective planning, new diagnostic tests will likely be introduced rapidly, in response to both market and professional forces.

The market forces are obvious: if biotechnology firms own patents on either the new markers or on techniques for bringing them into the clinical arena, there are clear financial incentives to make testing a more routine part of prenatal care.

The professional forces are also straightforward. First, there is a general tendency in medicine to view new developments, especially those perceived to be of low risk, as beneficial. Despite theoretical support for pilot studies and even randomized clinical trials of new diagnostic or therapeutic interventions, many clinicians assume that care will be improved by offering the new "services," and they are frequently reluctant to wait for formal evaluations of them. . . .

Perhaps more importantly, health care professionals providing prenatal care may feel compelled to use new tests as soon as they become available so they can obtain increased security against possible malpractice suits for failure to diagnose a given condition. The fear of possible wrongful birth suits (and "wrongful life" suits in the few states that allow children as well as parents a cause of action) has been cited as a major factor in the dissemination of alpha-fetoprotein screening, and harried clinicians may attempt to reduce their perceived threat of liability by offering the broadest possible panel of diagnostic tests. This problem is exacerbated by the current absence of any professional or societal guidance about which tests should be considered essential, and which optional, unnecessary, or relatively contraindicated. Even if patients are offered the option of refusing testing, in the absence of mechanisms to provide education about the value of obtaining various types of genetic information, the tendency will likely be for patients to accept everything available, since that is what appears to be "recommended." Moreover, when ignorance is the only alternative, patients may actually prefer a full range of "information," no matter what its relevance and quality.

Providing Guidance

Traditionally, the ethics of prenatal genetic counseling has required that prospective parents be given full information and then be allowed to choose which, if any, genetic diagnostic tests to pursue. Out of respect for reproductive decisionmaking and genetic privacy, and to prevent abuses such as attempts at eugenic control, virtually all genetic counselors espouse the ideals of value-neutral counseling and autonomous decisionmaking. This model is theoretically extremely appealing, and it works well in settings where well-trained counselors are available and affordable, and where counselors and clients share a common cultural background.

Yet the demands of routine prenatal care make it difficult simply to transpose this ethical framework into the obstetric or primary care clinic. The volume of patients is large, there is little enough time as it is to attend to patients' physical and psychological needs, and there are frequently quite prominent gaps between the social and cultural backgrounds of prenatal health care professionals and their patients. Moreover, genetic counselors have in the past generally been able, based on specific clinical indications, to focus their attention on one disease or syndrome at a time, while in the future, decisionmaking will likely encompass a broad spectrum of conditions for which prospective parents may be at no particularly increased risk. In the language of public health specialists, the issue will thus be one of *screening* rather than *testing*.

There are also matters of substance that argue in favor of a new model for providing guidance to prospective parents. Most importantly, the benefits of widespread screening have yet to be documented, and there are potential burdens that also need investigation, including increased anxiety about the pregnancy or about the parent's own health, risks associated with follow-up testing, possible changes in insurance coverage, overall increased costs, and the general effect on families and society of having parents prospectively evaluate their offspring in this fashion. Thus, while *access* to a broad range of genetic screening should remain available to those who specifically request it, new markers should not be offered as part of normal prenatal care.

Who, then should decide which markers to incorporate into routine practice? Individual health professionals are poorly suited, both because of financial and liability pressures and because most lack sufficient information to guide such decisionmaking. Geneticists have a useful role to play, but are likely to be reluctant to issue sweeping recommendations without public input lest they rekindle fears of eugenics. Regulatory agencies are too insulated and also too bureaucratic, lacking the flexibility that will be necessary if recommendations are to be based on information somewhat less rigorous than formal pilot studies and controlled trials.

The default solution would be to let financial matters take precedence, considering as routine only those markers that are covered through state or federal funding or through private insurance. Yet this alternative too is unresponsive to the desire to have public input into decisionmaking, and it is unclear that it would totally alleviate clinicians' concerns about liability.

No doubt a perfect solution is unattainable. A reasonable pragmatic approach, however, might be to seek out the guidance of professional geneticists and genetic counseling organizations, asking them to help develop procedures for gathering information, generating interdisciplinary and public comment, and making nonbinding recommendations about which tests *need* to be offered routinely in order to meet standards of normal prenatal care. . . .

Leaving the Garden

When Adam and Eve ate of the fruit of the tree of knowledge of good and evil, they were expelled from the Garden of Paradise and entered a world of suffering and toil. So too may we be leaving behind what some would consider blissful days of ignorance about our future genetic legacies. We will soon have the power to evaluate ourselves and our prospective offspring, to peer into previously opaque genetic mysteries, to gain an understanding that seems clear. Whether we will reap benefits from seeking this knowledge, collectively and as individuals, is still quite uncertain. Thus, if we truly seek wisdom, we must consider most carefully in what manner and how deeply we will taste the genome project's tempting fruits.

Chapter 10

Questions to Consider

1. Do individuals or couples at increased risk of having a child with a specific genetic disorder have a moral obligation to seek genetic counselling and testing? Is it morally wrong to have a child with a genetic disorder when the conception or birth of that child could have been avoided?

2. Do women who use prenatal diagnosis (PND) freely choose to do so? Discuss with reference to the articles by Lippman and by Wertz and Fletcher.

3. Should PND and elective termination of pregnancy be available for all disorders that can be diagnosed by DNA technology? Or, should society, medical geneticists, and/or prospective parents decide which disorders are serious enough to justify the options of PND and termination?

4. A 34-year-old mother of two boys is pregnant for the third time. She and her husband intend to complete their family at three, and they desperately want a baby girl. The woman tells her doctor that she will only continue the pregnancy if the fetus is female. She asks her physician for prenatal genetic testing to determine fetal sex. Should the physician comply with this request?

5. Should individuals or couples who are at risk for a specific genetic disorder have full, limited, or no access to ARTs (see Chapter 12, Assisted Reproductive Technologies)?

   a) Should access depend upon a willingness to accept donor gametes to eliminate or minimize the chance of having a child with a serious disease or disorder?

   b) Should access depend upon a willingness either to undergo pre-implantation diagnosis and to discard any affected embryos or to undergo prenatal testing and to abort any affected fetuses?

   c) Should access depend upon the nature of the inherited disease? Consider, for example, Tay-Sachs — a genetic disease characterized by mental and physical retardation, blindness, and spasticity that usually results in death prior to age four. Compare this disease to Huntington's disease, also a fatal genetic disease, but one that does not normally develop until middle age at which time progressive odd movements and memory difficulties begin to develop.

6. If a person has a genetic predisposition to aggressive behaviour, should she or he be held morally and/or legally accountable for violent acts committed against members of the community?

Further Readings

Acuff, Katherine, and Ruth Faden. 1991. A history of prenatal and newborn screening programs. In *AIDS, Women and the Next Generation*, Ruth R. Faden, Gail Geller, and Powers Madison, eds. 59–93. New York: Oxford University Press.

Anderson, W. French. 1989. Human gene therapy: Why draw a line? *Journal of Medicine and Philosophy* 14:681–93.

Bartells, Diane, Bonnie LeRoy, and Arthur Caplan, eds. 1993. *Prescribing our future: Ethical challenges in genetic counselling.* New York: Aldine De Gruyter.

Clarke, Angus. 1991. Is non-directive genetic counselling possible? *Lancet* 338:998–1001.

Clayton, Ellen W. 1992. Issues in state newborn screening programs. *Pediatrics* 90:641–46.

Fost, Norman. 1992. Ethical issues in genetics. *Pediatric Clinics of North America, Medical Genetics I* 39(1): 79–90.

Greenspan, P.S. 1993. Free will and the genome project. *Philosophy and Public Affairs* 22:31–43.

Huggins, Marlene, et al. 1990. Ethical and legal dilemmas arising during predictive testing for adult-onset disease: The experience of Huntington disease. *American Journal of Human Genetics* 47:4–12.

Kerem, Eitan, and Abbyann Lynch. 1991. Screening for cystic fibrosis: Ethical and social issues. *American Review of Respiratory Diseases* 143:457–60.

Laberge, Claude M., and Bartha M. Knoppers. 1991. Newborn genetic screening: ethical and social considerations for the nineties. *International Journal of Bioethics* 2(1): 5–12.

Rothman, Barbara K. 1993. *The tentative pregnancy: How amniocentesis changes the experience of motherhood.* New York: W.W. Norton.

Royal Commission on New Reproductive Technologies. 1993. *Proceed with Care: Final Report of the Royal Commission on New Reproductive Technologies* (Chap. 26). Ottawa: Minister of Supply and Services Canada.

Chapter 11

Abortion

Chapter 11

Introduction

Therapeutic abortion (the medically induced destruction and removal of a human embryo or fetus from a woman's womb) is a highly contentious issue in contemporary society. Passionate arguments about abortion rage in the media, the courts, and the legislature, as well as in ethics journals and textbooks. Many people feel strongly about this issue; as a result, the rhetoric with which abortion is discussed is often so charged that it is sometimes difficult for people who are less certain of their positions to admit or explain their own confusion or ambivalence. Making matters more difficult is the fact that there is dispute about even what the proper subject for debate should be: not only are the substantive conclusions of abortion arguments contested, but so, too, is the framing of the questions at issue.

Within the field of health care ethics, discussions of abortion tend to focus on two distinct questions: one has to do with establishing the moral status of abortion, and the other explores the appropriate legal status of the practice. The task of the former is to decide whether abortion is (ever, sometimes, or always) morally permissible, and if so, in what circumstances. The latter has to do with determining whether the state should try to enforce any restrictions on abortion rather than treating it as simply another elective medical procedure. These are separate questions because it is possible for someone to be "conservative" on the moral question (viewing all or most abortions as morally wrong) and "liberal" on the legal one (opposing legal sanctions against abortion), and vice-versa. While law often coincides with morality, law is nevertheless distinct from morality. Law does not and should not attempt to proscribe all morally unacceptable behaviour or prescribe all morally desirable behaviour. For example, gratitude is morally appropriate in certain circumstances, but it would surely be a mistake to try to make it legally mandatory. Nor should law be restricted to matters of moral concern; many laws restrict behaviour that is otherwise morally acceptable (e.g., cautious jaywalking). Because morality and law are related but distinct, it is possible to hold different positions about the moral and legal status of abortion.

Poll after poll reveals that Canadians are quite divided about both the morality and the legality of abortion. Although a majority of Canadians favours moderate moral and legal policies, activist minorities believe that abortion is either always wrong or never wrong, and they work toward a public policy that will either prohibit it altogether or remove all legal barriers (Muldoon 1991). Political action is directed at the law because activists believe it is easier to change public policy than it is to establish a moral consensus about abortion. Consequently, most disagreements about abortion have been played out in the judicial and legislative arenas.

A Brief History of Abortion Laws in Canada

In light of the intense debates, political lobbying, and demonstrations that have become fixtures of current abortion struggles, it seems hard to believe that abortion has not always been an issue of widespread interest in Canadian society. Yet the heavily political character of the abortion controversy is relatively recent. Historically, abortion was first covered by common law, according to which abortion became a matter of legal concern only after the stage of quickening (i.e., the point at which the pregnant woman can feel the fetus move in her womb); beyond that time, abortion would be a misdemeanour. In 1892, the Dominion of Canada passed its first version of the Criminal Code; under its terms, it was a criminal offence to deliberately cause the death of a child not yet a human being unless the action was undertaken to save the mother's life. This remained the law for nearly 80 years.

The provisions for abortion were subject to sweeping amendments in 1969. Under the new rules, it was still a criminal offence to perform or have an abortion, but more exemptions were allowed. Under Section 251 of the revised Criminal Code, abortions were permitted provided that they were performed in an "accredited or approved" hospital, that the hospital had a therapeutic abortion committee consisting of at least three doctors appointed by the hospital board, that the doctor performing the abortion was not a member of the abortion committee, and that a majority of the hospital abortion committee determined that continuing the pregnancy would endanger the life or health of the pregnant woman and issued a certificate to that effect to her doctor.

The attempted legislative compromise left adherents of both poles of the abortion debate unsatisfied. Advocates of a woman's right to choose considered it unduly restrictive because many regions lacked qualifying hospitals with appropriate abortion committees; moreover, there was wide variation in how committees interpreted the idea of a threat to a woman's life or health, and the cumbersome approval process inevitably involved delays which increased the risks associated with abortion. Their opponents focussed on the committees that were especially liberal in their interpretations and argued that this legislation amounted to abortion on demand. Not surprisingly, then, the legislation was challenged by people on both sides of the abortion controversy, although it survived judicial scrutiny for some years.

The Canadian Charter of Rights and Freedoms, proclaimed in 1982, provided new grounds for judicial review of the abortion legislation. The decisive case turned out to be *Morgentaler, Smoling and Scott v. The Queen*, hereafter referred to as *R. v. Morgentaler*. In 1988, a five-to-two majority of the Supreme Court of Canada ruled that section 251 of the Criminal Code infringed on rights guaranteed to women by section 7 of the Charter, and because it was not saved by section 1, it was unconstitutional.[1] The effect of striking down this legislation was to remove abortion and the legal requirements associated with the therapeutic abortion committee process from the Criminal Code.

Subsequent to this decision, the Supreme Court, in 1989, refused to rule on Joseph Borowski's request that they find the fetus a person under the provisions of the Canadian Charter of Rights and Freedoms. The Court held that it would be inappropriate to hear the case because there was no abortion law in effect at that time. Another important Supreme Court decision on abortion was rendered in 1989 in the case of *Tremblay v. Daigle*, in which the biological father of a fetus asked a Quebec court to grant an injunction that would prevent his former girlfriend from getting an abortion. The Supreme Court unanimously ruled that a fetus was not to be considered a person under the terms of the Quebec Charter of Human Rights and Freedoms and denied that a potential father has the right to veto a woman's decision on abortion.

In *R. v. Morgentaler*, the Supreme Court allowed the possibility of the future passage of an abortion law that would be compatible with the Charter. The justices acknowledged that Parliament might have a legitimate interest in the protection of fetuses and suggested that legislators may want to draft new policies to protect fetal life which would not violate women's rights under the Charter. In response, the government tabled Bill C–43 in November 1989 as a means of returning abortion to the Criminal Code. This bill would have made it a criminal act to perform an abortion, but it allowed exceptions if the abortion was performed by a licensed medical practitioner who "is of the opinion that, if abortion is not induced, the health or life of the female person would be likely to be threatened." Although this bill passed the House of Commons, it did not win a majority in the Senate and, as a result, it failed to become law. Hence, abortion is currently free of criminal sanction. Various provincial governments have been eager to fill that gap, however. Some have introduced legislation to restrict the circumstances under which abortions can be performed in accordance with their constitutional authority to provide and regulate health services. Only the federal government can change the Criminal Code, though, and it remains to be seen whether subsequent attempts will be made to recriminalize abortion. In the meantime, advocates on both sides of the abortion debate concentrate on pursuing further court challenges to provincial policies.

The Moral Issues

Most of the debate about the moral status of abortion focusses on the questions of fetal and/or maternal rights. Most authors grant women the right to determine the outcomes of their pregnancies if it can be established that abortion does not violate the rights of the fetus. Hence, in most discussions, the important issue is to determine whether, or at what stage of development, human fetuses (broadly understood to include all stages of embryo development) have a right to life that would outweigh the woman's interest in terminating an unwanted pregnancy. Positions on this matter range from the view that embryos have a right to life from the moment of conception (Noonan 1970), through the view that fetuses acquire a right to life when they develop brain activity (Brody 1973) or some other intermediate stage, to the view that fetuses do not acquire a right to life (or personhood) until birth or even some point in infancy (Tooley 1972; Warren 1973). Other authors argue, however, that the moral acceptability of abortion involves other considerations and cannot be settled by appeal to the question of the moral status of fetuses. For example, in a very famous article, Judith Jarvis Thomson (1971) argues that refraining from aborting amounts to more than not killing; a woman who does not abort her pregnancy must provide her fetus with the necessary conditions of continued life and development, and even if fetuses are persons, it is not clear they have a right to such resources. Other authors ask us to reconceive the debate so that it is not structured as an adversarial contest between women and their fetuses (e.g., McDonnell 1984; Overall 1987).

The Selections

The most significant court decision on abortion in Canada was the 1988 decision in *R. v. Morgentaler*; to provide an idea for the arguments considered decisive, we include a few brief excerpts from the much longer statements of three of the justices who decided this case. Chief Justice Dickson and Madam Justice Wilson write for the majority position that concludes that section 251 is in conflict with the Charter of Rights and Freedoms and therefore cannot stand, although they express different reasons for objecting to it. Both leave the door open for subsequent legislation on abortion, but the differences in their views suggest different directions for such legislation. Mr. Justice McIntyre writes from the dissenting perspective that the Charter does not guarantee women a right to abortion and so legislation restricting abortion should not be viewed as a violation of Charter rights.

Much of the moral debate on abortion focusses on the question of the moral status of the fetus (where this term is used to include all stages of embryo development from fertilization to birth), whether it is the sort of being that should be accorded moral rights. While a few authors (e.g., Thomson 1971 and English 1975) argue that the moral permissibility of abortion can and should be determined independently of the fetus's moral standing, most authors believe that these issues are necessarily related. L.W. Sumner offers a critical review of the leading positions on the question of what status to accord fetuses and presents his own proposal for a developmental view of the fetus, an approach that allows certain sorts of abortions and prohibits others. (Note that Madam Justice Wilson recommends his analysis as the basis for any future abortion law in Canada.)

In contrast, Donald Marquis presents an explicitly conservative view of abortion, in which he argues that killing fetuses (at any stage of development) is morally wrong for the same reason that killing any human being is wrong.

Susan Sherwin strongly disagrees. In her view, adopting a feminist perspective leads to different sorts of reasoning and encourages us to see the moral significance of many dimensions of abortion that are commonly overlooked in traditional approaches to the issue.

Notes

1. Section 7 states: "Everyone has the right to life, liberty and security of the person and the right not to be deprived thereof except in accordance with the principles of fundamental justice." Section 1 states: "The *Canadian Charter of Rights and Freedoms* guarantees the rights and freedoms set out in it subject only to such reasonable limits prescribed by law as can be demonstrably justified in a free and democratic society."

References

Borowski v. Canada (Attorney General), [1989] 1 S.C.R. 342.

Brody, Baruch. 1973. *Abortion and the sanctity of human life. American Philosophical Quarterly* 10:133–40.

Canadian Charter of Rights and Freedoms, Part I of the Constitution Act 1982, being Schedule B of the Canada Act 1982 (U.K.), 1982, c. 11.

Charter of Human Rights and Freedoms, R.S.Q., c. C–12.

Criminal Code, R.S.C., 1970, c. C–34.

English, Jane. 1975. Abortion and the concept of a person. *Canadian Journal of Philosophy* 5:233–43.

McDonnell, Kathleen. 1984. *Not an easy choice: A feminist re-examines abortion.* Toronto: Women's Press.

Muldoon, Maureen. 1991. *The abortion debate in the United States and Canada: A source book.* New York: Garland.

Noonan, John T., ed. 1970. *The morality of abortion: Legal and historical perspectives.* Cambridge: Harvard University Press.

Overall, Christine. 1987. *Ethics and human reproduction: A feminist analysis.* Boston: Allen & Unwin.

Thomson, Judith Jarvis. 1971. A Defense of abortion. *Philosophy and Public Affairs* 1:47–66.

Tooley, Michael. 1972. Abortion and infanticide. *Philosophy and Public Affairs* 2:37–65.

Tremblay v. Daigle, [1989] 2 S.C.R. 530.

Warren, Mary Ann. 1973. On the moral and legal status of abortion, with postscript on infanticide. *The Monist* 57:43–61.

40   Morgentaler, Smoling and Scott v. The Queen

Supreme Court of Canada

DICKSON C.J.C.: — . . . At the most basic, physical and emotional level, every pregnant woman is told by the section that she cannot submit to a generally safe medical procedure that might be a clear benefit to her unless she meets criteria entirely unrelated to her own priorities and aspirations. Not only does the removal of decision making power threaten women in a physical sense; the indecision of knowing whether an abortion will be granted inflicts emotional stress. Section 251 clearly interferes with a woman's bodily integrity in both a physical and emotional sense. Forcing a woman, by threat of criminal sanction, to carry a foetus to term unless she meets certain criteria unrelated to her own priorities and aspirations, is a profound interference with a woman's body and thus a violation of security of the person. Section 251, therefore, is required by the Charter to comport with the principles of fundamental justice.

Although this interference with physical and emotional integrity is sufficient in itself to trigger a review of s. 251 against the principles of fundamental justice, the operation of the decision-making mechanism set out in s. 251 creates additional glaring breaches of security of the person. The evidence indicates that s. 251 causes a certain amount of delay for women who are successful in meeting its criteria. In the context of abortion, any unnecessary delay can have profound consequences on the woman's physical and emotional well-being.

More specifically, in 1977, the Report of the Committee on the Operation of the Abortion Law (the Badgley report) revealed that the average delay between a pregnant woman's first contact with a physician and a subsequent therapeutic abortion was eight weeks (p. 146). Although the situation appears to have improved since 1977, the extent of the improvement is not clear. . . .

The appellants contended that the sole purpose of s. 251 of the *Criminal Code* is to protect the life and health of pregnant women. The respondent Crown submitted that s. 251 seeks to protect not only the life and health of pregnant women, but also the interests of the foetus. On the other hand, the Crown conceded that the court is not called upon in this appeal to evaluate any claim to "foetal rights" or to assess the meaning of "the right to life". I expressly refrain from so doing. In my view, it is unnecessary for the purpose of deciding this appeal to evaluate or assess "foetal rights" as an independent constitutional value. Nor are we required to measure the full extent of the state's interest in establishing criteria unrelated to the pregnant woman's own priorities and aspirations. What we must do is evaluate the particular balance struck by Parliament in s. 251, as it relates to the priorities and aspirations of pregnant women and the government's interests in the protection of the foetus.

Section 251 provides that foetal interests are not to be protected where the "life or health" of the woman is threatened. Thus, Parliament itself has expressly stated in s. 251 that the "life or health" of pregnant women is paramount. The procedures of s. 251(4) are clearly related to the pregnant woman's "life or health" for that is the very phrase used by the subsection. As McIntyre J. states in his reasons, the aim of s. 251(4) is "to restrict abortion to cases where the continuation of the pregnancy would, or would likely, be injurious to the life or health of the woman concerned, not to provide unrestricted access to abortion". I have no difficulty in concluding that the objective of s. 251 as a whole, namely, to balance the competing interests identified by Parliament, is sufficiently important to meet the requirements of the first step in the *Oakes* inquiry under s. 1. I think the protection of the interests of pregnant women is a valid government objective, where life and health can be jeopardized by criminal sanctions. Like Beetz and Wilson JJ., I agree that protection of foetal interests by Parliament is also a valid governmental objective. It follows that balancing these interests, with the lives and health of women a major factor, is clearly an important governmental objective. As the Court of Appeal stated, "the contemporary view [is] that abortion is not always socially undesirable behavior" [at p. 365 C.C.C., p. 654 D.L.R.].

I am equally convinced, however, that the means chosen to advance the legislative objectives of s. 251 do not satisfy any of the three elements of the proportionality component of *R. v. Oakes*. The evidence has led me to conclude that the infringement of the security of the person of pregnant women caused by s. 251 is not accomplished in accordance with the principles of fundamental justice. It has been demonstrated that the procedures and administrative structures created by s. 251 are often arbitrary and unfair. The procedures established to implement the policy of s. 251 impair s. 7 rights far more than is necessary because they hold out an illusory defence to many women who would *prima facie* qualify under the exculpatory provisions of s. 251(4). In other words, many women whom Parliament professes not to wish to subject to criminal liability will nevertheless be forced by the practical unavailability of the supposed defence to risk liability or to suffer other harm such as a traumatic late abortion caused by the delay inherent in the s. 251 system. Finally, the effects of the limitation upon the s. 7 rights of many pregnant women are out of proportion to the objective sought to be achieved. Indeed, to the extent that s. 251(4) is designed to protect the life and health of women, the procedures it establishes may actually defeat that objective. The administrative structures of s. 251(4) are so cumbersome that women whose health is endangered by pregnancy may not be able to gain a therapeutic abortion, at least without great trauma, expense and inconvenience.

I conclude, therefore, that the cumbersome structures of s-s. (4) not only unduly subordinates the s. 7 rights of pregnant women but may also defeat the value Parliament itself has established as paramount, namely, the life and health of the mother. As I have noted, counsel for the Crown did contend that one purpose of the procedures required by s-s. (4) is to protect the interests of the foetus. State protection of foetal interests may well be deserving of constitutional recognition under s. 1. Still, there can be no escape from the fact that Parliament has failed to establish either a standard or a procedure whereby any such interests might prevail over those of the woman in a fair and non-arbitrary fashion.

Section 251 of the *Criminal Code* cannot be saved, therefore, under s. 1 of the Charter.

MCINTYRE J. (dissenting): —

Section 251 of the Criminal Code

. . . I would say at the outset that it may be thought that this case does not raise the Charter issues which were argued and which have been addressed in the reasons of my colleagues. The charge here is one of conspiracy to breach the provisions of s. 251 of the *Criminal Code*. There is no doubt, and it has never been questioned, that the appellants adopted a course which was clearly in defiance of the provisions of the *Code* and it is difficult to see where any infringement of their rights, under s. 7 of the Charter, could have occurred. There is no female person involved in the case who has been denied a therapeutic abortion and, as a result, the argument on the right to security of the person, under s. 7 of the Charter, has been on a hypothetical basis. The case, however, was addressed by all the parties on that basis and the court has accepted that position. . . .

It follows, then, in my view, that the task of the court in this case is not to solve nor seek to solve what might be called the abortion issue, but simply to measure the content of s. 251 against the Charter. While this may appear to be self-evident, the distinction is of vital importance. If a particular interpretation enjoys no support, express or reasonably implied, from the Charter, then the court is without power to clothe such an interpretation with constitutional status. It is not for the court to substitute its own views on the merits of a given question for those of Parliament. The court must consider not what is, in its view, the best solution to the problems posed; its role is confined to deciding whether the solution enacted by Parliament offends the Charter. If it does, the provision must be struck down or declared inoperative, and Parliament may then enact such different provisions as it may decide. . . .

The Right to Abortion and S. 7 of the Charter

The judgment of my colleague, Wilson J., is based upon the proposition that a pregnant woman has a right, under s. 7 of the Charter, to have an abortion. The same concept underlies the judgment of the Chief Justice. He reached the conclusion that a law which forces a woman to carry a foetus to term, unless certain criteria are met which are unrelated to her own priorities and aspirations, impairs the security of her person. That, in his view, is the effect of s. 251 of the *Criminal Code*. He has not said in specific terms that the pregnant woman has the right to an abortion, whether therapeutic or otherwise. In my view, however, his whole position depends for its validity upon that proposition and that interference with the right constitutes an infringement of her right to security of the person. It is said that a law which forces a woman to carry a foetus to term unless she meets certain criteria unrelated to her own priorities and aspirations interferes with security of her person. If compelling a woman to complete her pregnancy interferes with security of her person, it can only be because the concept of security of her person includes a right not to be compelled to carry the child to completion of her pregnancy. This, then, is simply to say that she has a right to have an abortion. It follows, then, that if no such right can be shown, it cannot be said that security of her person has been infringed by state action or otherwise.

All laws, it must be noted, have the potential for interference with individual priorities and aspirations. In fact, the very purpose of most legislation is to cause interference. It is only when such legislation goes beyond interfering with priorities and aspirations and abridges rights, that courts may intervene. If a law prohibited membership in a lawful association it would be unconstitutional, not because it would interfere with priorities and aspirations, but because of its interference with the guaranteed right of freedom of association under s. 2(d) of the Charter. Compliance with the Income Tax Act, 1970–71–72 (Can.), c. 63, has, no doubt, frequently interfered with priorities and aspirations. The taxing provisions are not, however, on that basis unconstitutional, because the ordinary taxpayer enjoys no right to be tax free. Other illustrations may be found. In my view, it is clear that before it could be concluded that any enactment infringed the concept of security of the person, it would have to infringe some underlying right included in or protected by the concept. For the appellants to succeed here, then, they must show more than an interference with priorities and aspirations; they must show the infringement of a right which is included in the concept of security of the person. . . .

. . . I would only add that even if a general right to have an abortion could be found under s. 7 of the Charter, it is by no means clear from the evidence the extent to which such a right could be said to be infringed by the requirements of s. 251 of the *Code*. In the nature of things that is difficult to determine. The mere fact of pregnancy, let alone an unwanted pregnancy, gives rise to stress. The evidence reveals that much of the anguish associated with abortion is inherent and unavoidable and that there is really no psychologically painless way to cope with an unwanted pregnancy.

It is for these reasons I would conclude, that save for the provisions of the *Criminal Code*, which permit abortion where the life or health of the woman is at risk, no right of abortion can be found in Canadian law, custom or tradition, and that the Charter, including s. 7, creates no further right. Accordingly, it is my view that s. 251 of the *Code* does not in its terms violate s. 7 of the Charter. Even accepting the assumption that the concept of security of the person would extend to vitiating a law which would require a woman to carry a child to the completion of her pregnancy at the risk of her life or health, it must be observed that this is not our case. As has been pointed out, s. 251 of the *Code* already provides for abortion in such circumstances.

WILSON J.: — At the heart of this appeal is the question whether a pregnant woman can, as a constitutional matter, be compelled by law to carry the foetus to term. The legislature has proceeded on the basis that she can be so compelled and, indeed, has made it a criminal offence punishable by imprisonment under s. 251 of the *Criminal Code*, R.S.C. 1970, c. C–34, for her or her physician to terminate the pregnancy unless the procedural requirements of the section are complied with.

My colleagues, the Chief Justice and Beetz J., have attacked those requirements in reasons which I have had the privilege of reading. They have found that the requirements do not comport with the principles of fundamental justice in the procedural sense and have concluded that, since they cannot be severed from the provisions creating the substantive offence, the whole of s. 251 must fall.

With all due respect, I think that the court must tackle the primary issue first. A consideration as to whether or not the procedural requirements for obtaining or performing an abortion comport with fundamental justice is purely academic if such requirements cannot as a constitutional matter be imposed at all. If a pregnant woman cannot, as a constitutional matter, be compelled by law to carry the foetus to term against her will, a review of the procedural requirements by which she may be compelled to do so seems pointless. Moreover, it would, in my opinion, be an exercise in futility for the legislature to expend its time and energy in attempting to remedy the defects in the procedural requirements unless it has some assurance that this process will, at the end of the day, result in the creation of a valid criminal offence. I turn, therefore, to what I believe is the central issue that must be addressed.

I. The Right of Access to Abortion

Section 7 of the *Canadian Charter of Rights and Freedoms* provides:

> 7. Everyone has the right to life, liberty and security of the person and the right not to be deprived thereof in accordance with the principles of fundamental justice.

I agree with the Chief Justice that we are not called upon in this case to delineate the full content of the right to life, liberty and security of the person. This would be an impossible task because we cannot envisage all the contexts in which such a right might be asserted. What we are asked to do, I believe, is define the content of the right in the context of the legislation under attack. Does s. 251 of the *Criminal Code* which limits the pregnant woman's access to abortion violate her right to life, liberty and security of the person within the meaning of s. 7?

Leaving aside for the moment the implications of the section for the foetus and addressing only the s. 7 right of the pregnant woman, it seems to me that we can say with a fair degree of confidence that a legislative scheme for the obtaining of an abortion which exposes the pregnant woman to a *threat* to her security of the person would violate her right under s. 7. Indeed, we have already stated in *Re Singh and Minister of Employment and Immigration* (1985), 17 D.L.R. (4th) 422, [1985] 1 S.C.R. 177, 14 C.R.R. 13, that security of the person even on the purely physical level must encompass freedom from the *threat* of physical punishment or suffering as well as freedom from the actual punishment or suffering itself. In other words, the fact of exposure is enough to violate security of the person. I agree with the Chief Justice and Beetz J. who, for differing reasons, find that pregnant women are exposed to a threat to their physical and psychological security under the legislative scheme set up in s. 251 and, since these are aspects of their security of the person, their s. 7 right is accordingly violated. But this, of course, does not answer the question whether even the ideal legislative scheme, assuming that it is one which poses no threat to the physical and psychological security of the person of the pregnant woman, would be valid under s. 7. I say this for two reasons: (1) because s. 7 encompasses more than the right to security of the person; it speaks also of the right to liberty, and (2) because security of the person may encompass more than physical and psychological security; this we have yet to decide.

It seems to me, therefore, that to commence the analysis with the premise that the s. 7 right encompasses only a right to physical and psychological security and to fail to deal with the right to liberty in the context of "life, liberty and security of the person" begs the central issue in the case. If either the right to liberty or the right to security of the person or a combination of both confers on the pregnant woman the right to decide for herself (with the guidance of her physician) whether or not to have an abortion, then we have to examine the legislative scheme not only from the point of view of fundamental justice in the procedural sense but in the substantive sense as well. I think, therefore, that we must answer the question: what is meant by the right to liberty in the context of the abortion issue? Does it, as Mr. Manning suggests, give the pregnant woman control over decisions affecting her own body? If not, does her right to security of the person give her such control? I turn first to the right to liberty. . . .

In my view, the deprivation of the s. 7 right with which we are concerned in this case offends s. 2(a) of the Charter. I say this because I believe that the decision whether or not to terminate a pregnancy is essentially a moral decision, a matter of conscience. I do not think there is or can be any dispute about that. The question is: whose conscience? Is the conscience of the woman to be paramount or the conscience of the state? I believe, for the reasons I gave in discussing the right to liberty, that in a free and democratic society it must be the conscience of the individual. Indeed, s. 2(a) makes it clear that this freedom belongs to "everyone", i.e., to each of us individually. I quote the section for convenience:

2. Everyone has the following fundamental freedoms:

   (a) freedom of conscience and religion; . . .

In my view, the primary objective of the impugned legislation must be seen as the protection of the foetus. It undoubtedly has other ancillary objectives, such as the protection of the life and health of pregnant women, but I believe that the main objective advanced to justify a restriction on the pregnant woman's s. 7 right is the protection of the foetus. I think this is a perfectly valid legislative objective. . . .

. . . It is simply to say that in balancing the state's interest in the protection of the foetus as potential life under s. 1 of the Charter against the right of the pregnant woman under s. 7 greater weight should be given to the state's interest in the later stages of pregnancy than in the earlier. The foetus should accordingly, for purposes of s. 1, be viewed in differential and developmental terms: see Sumner, *Abortion and Moral Theory*, pp. 125–8.

As Professor Sumner points out, both traditional approaches to abortion, the so-called "liberal" and "conservative" approaches, fail to take account of the essentially developmental nature of the gestation process. A developmental view of the foetus, on the other hand, supports a permissive approach to abortion in the early stages of pregnancy and a restrictive approach in the later stages. In the early stages the woman's autonomy would be absolute; her decision, reached in consultation with her physician, not to carry the foetus to term would be conclusive. The state would have no business inquiring into her reasons. Her reasons for having an abortion would, however, be the proper subject of inquiry at the later stages of her pregnancy when the state's compelling interest in the protection of the foetus would justify it in prescribing conditions. The precise point in the development of the foetus at which the state's interest in its protection becomes "compelling" I leave to the informed judgment of the legislature which is in a position to receive guidance on the subject from all the relevant disciplines. It seems to me, however, that it might fall somewhere in the second trimester. Indeed, according to Professor Sumner (p. 159), a differential abortion policy with a time limit in the second trimester is already in operation in the United States, Great Britain, France, Italy, Sweden, the Soviet Union, China, India, Japan and most of the countries of Eastern Europe although the time limits vary in these countries from the beginning to the end of the second trimester (*cf.* Isaacs, Stephen L., "Reproductive Rights 1983: An International Survey" (1982–83), 14 Columbia Human Rights L. Rev. 311, with respect to France and Italy).

Section 251 of the *Criminal Code* takes the decision away from the woman at *all* stages of her pregnancy. It is a complete denial of the woman's constitutionally protected right under s. 7, not merely a limitation on it. It cannot, in my opinion, meet the proportionality test in *Oakes*. It is not sufficiently tailored to the legislative objective and does not impair the woman's right "as little as possible". It cannot be saved under s. 1. Accordingly, even if the section were to be amended to remedy the purely procedural defects in the legislative scheme referred to by the Chief Justice and Beetz J. it would, in my opinion, still not be constitutionally valid. . . .

41   Abortion

L.W. Sumner

Among the assortment of moral problems that have come to be known as biomedical ethics none has received as much attention from philosophers as abortion. Philosophical inquiry into the moral status of abortion is virtually as old as philosophy itself and has a continuous history of more than two millennia in the main religious traditions of the West. The upsurge of interest in the problem among secular philosophers is more recent, coinciding roughly with the public debate of the past fifteen years or so in most of the Western democracies over the shape of an acceptable abortion policy. Despite both the quantity and the quality of this philosophical work, however, abortion remains one of the most intractable moral issues of our time.

Its resistance to a generally agreed settlement stems primarily from its unique combination of two ingredients, each of which is perplexing in its own right. Abortion, in the sense in which it is controversial, is the intentional termination of pregnancy for its own sake — that is, regardless of the consequences for the fetus. Pregnancy, in turn, is a peculiar sort of relationship between a woman and a peculiar sort of being. It is a peculiar sort of relationship because the fetus is temporarily lodged within and physically connected to the body of its mother, on whom it is directly dependent for life support. The closest approximation elsewhere in our experience of this dependency is that of a parasite upon its host. But the host-parasite relationship typically differs in some material respects from pregnancy and is therefore only an imperfect analogue to it.

The fetus is a peculiar sort of being because it is a human individual during the earliest stage in its life history. Although there are some difficult and puzzling questions to be asked about when the life history of such an individual may properly be said to begin, we will assume for convenience that this occurs at conception. It will also be convenient, though somewhat inaccurate, to use the term 'fetus' to refer indiscriminately to all gestational stages from fertilized ovum through blastocyst and embryo to fetus proper. A (human) fetus, then, is a human individual during that period temporally bounded in one direction by conception and in the other (at the latest) by birth. The closest approximations elsewhere in our experience to this sort of being are the gametes (sperm and ovum) that precede it before conception and the infant that succeeds it after birth. But both gametes and infant differ in material respects from a fetus and are also only imperfect analogues to it.

Abortion is morally perplexing because it terminates this peculiar relationship and causes the death of this peculiar being. It thus occupies an ambiguous position between two other practices — contraception and infanticide — of whose moral status we are more certain. Contraception cannot be practiced after conception, while infanticide cannot be practiced before birth. Since an abortion can be performed only between conception and birth, contraception and infanticide are its immediate temporal neighbors. Although both of these practices have occasioned their own controversies, there is a much broader concensus concerning their moral status than there is concerning abortion. Thus, most of us are likely to believe that, barring special circumstances, infanticide is morally serious and requires some special justification while contraception is morally innocuous and requires no such justification. One way of clarifying the moral status of abortion, therefore, is to locate it on this contraception-infanticide continuum, thus telling us whether it is in relevant respects more like the former or the latter.

Of the two ingredients whose combination renders abortion morally perplexing, the peculiar nature of the fetus is the more troublesome. Clarifying the moral status of abortion thus requires above all clarifying the moral status of the fetus. Contraception is less perplexing in virtue of the fact that it operates not on any temporal stage of a human being but only on the materials out of which such a being might be formed. And infanticide is less perplexing in virtue of the fact that it operates on a later temporal stage of a human being, of whose moral status we are more certain. Deciding whether abortion is in relevant respects more like contraception or infanticide therefore requires above all deciding whether a fetus is in relevant respects more like a pair of gametes or an infant. The moral category in which we choose to locate abortion will be largely determined by the moral category in which we choose to locate the fetus. Let us say that a being has *moral standing* if it merits moral consideration in its own right and not just in virtue of its relations with other beings. To have moral standing is to be more than a mere thing or item of property. What, more precisely, moral standing consists in can be given different interpretations; thus, it might be the possession of some set of basic moral rights, or the requirement that one be treated as an end and not merely as a means, or the inclusion of one's interest in a calculus of social welfare. However it is interpreted, whether a being is accorded moral standing must make a great difference in the way in which we take that being into account in our moral thinking. Whether a fetus is accorded moral standing must therefore make a great difference in the way in which we think about abortion. An account of the moral status of abortion must be supported by an account of the moral status of the fetus.

There is also a political question concerning abortion to which we need an answer. Every society must decide how, if at all, it will regulate the practice of abortion. Broadly speaking, three different types of abortion policy are available.¹ permissive policy allows abortion whenever it has been agreed upon between a woman and a qualified practitioner, while a restrictive policy prohibits it altogether. A moderate policy occupies a middle ground between the other two, imposing either (or both) of two constraints on the practice of abortion: a time limit (which stipulates *when* an abortion may be performed) and recognized grounds (which stipulate *why* an abortion may be performed). A view of abortion should tell us which type of abortion policy a society ought to adopt, and if a moderate policy is favored then it should also tell us where to locate the time limit and/or which grounds to recognize. There will clearly be an intimate relation between the determination of the moral status of abortion and the defense of an abortion policy. If abortion is as morally innocuous as contraception, then that seems a good reason for favoring a permissive policy, while if it is as morally serious as infanticide, then that seems a good reason for favoring a restrictive policy.

A complete view of abortion, one that answers the main moral questions posed by the practice of abortion, is an ordered compound of three elements: an account of the moral status of the fetus, which grounds an account of the moral status of abortion, which in turn grounds a defense of an abortion policy. It is not enough, however, that a view of abortion be complete — it must also be well grounded. If we explore what is required to support an account of the moral status of the fetus, we will discover what it means for a view of abortion to be well grounded. The main requirement at this level is a *criterion of moral standing* that will specify the (natural) characteristic(s) whose possession is both necessary and sufficient for the possession of moral standing. A criterion of moral standing will therefore have the following form: all and only beings with characteristic C have moral standing. (Characteristic C may be a single property or a conjunction or disjunction of such properties.) A criterion of moral standing thus determines, both exhaustively and exclusively, the membership of the class of beings with such standing. Such a criterion will define the proper scope of our moral concern, telling us for all moral contexts which beings must be accorded moral consideration in their own right. Thus it will determine, among other things, the moral status of inanimate natural objects, artifacts, nonhuman animals, body parts, superintelligent computers, androids, and extraterrestrials. It will also determine the moral status of (human) fetuses. An account of the moral status of the fetus is well grounded when it is derivable from an independently plausible criterion of moral standing. The independent plausibility of such a criterion is partly established by following out its implications for moral contexts other than abortion. But a criterion of moral standing can also be given a deeper justification by being grounded in a moral theory. The function of a moral theory is to identify those features of the world to which we should be morally sensitive and to guide that sensitivity. By providing us with a picture of the content and structure of morality, a moral theory will tell us, among other things, which beings merit moral consideration in their own right and what form this consideration should take. It will thereby generate and support a criterion of moral standing, thus serving as the last line of defense for a view of abortion.

The Established Views

We are seeking a view of abortion that is both complete and well grounded. These requirements are not easily satisfied. The key elements remain an account of the moral status of the fetus and a supporting criterion of moral standing. Our search will be facilitated if we begin by examining the main contenders. The abortion debate in most of the Western democracies has been dominated by two positions that are so well entrenched that they may be called the established views. The liberal view supports what is popularly known as the "pro-choice" position on abortion.[2] At its heart is the contention that the fetus at every stage of pregnancy has no moral standing. From this premise it follows that although abortion kills the fetus it does not wrong it, since a being with no moral standing cannot be wronged. Abortion at all stages of pregnancy lacks a victim; circumstantial differences aside, it is the moral equivalent of contraception. The decision to seek an abortion, therefore, can properly be left to a woman's discretion. There is as little justification for legal regulation of abortion as there is for such regulation of contraception. The only defensible abortion policy is a permissive policy. The conservative view, however, supports what is popularly known as the "pro-life" position on abortion. At its heart is the contention that the fetus at every stage of pregnancy has full moral standing — the same status as an adult human being. From this premise it follows that because abortion kills the fetus it also wrongs it. Abortion at all stages of pregnancy has a victim; circumstantial differences aside, it is the moral equivalent of infanticide (and of other forms of homicide as well). The decision to seek an abortion, therefore, cannot properly be left to a woman's discretion. There is as much justification for legal regulation of abortion as there is for such regulation of infanticide. The only defensible abortion policy is a restrictive policy.

Before exploring these views separately, we should note an important feature that they share. On the substantive issue that is at the heart of the matter, liberals and conservatives occupy positions that are logical contraries, the latter holding that all fetuses have standing and the former that none do. Although contrary positions cannot both be true, they can both be false. From a logical point of view, it is open to someone to hold that some fetuses have standing while others do not. Thus while the established views occupy the opposite extremes along the spectrum of possible positions on this issue, there is a logical space between them. This logical space reflects the fact that each of the established views offers a *uniform* account of the moral status of the fetus — each, that is, holds that all fetuses have the same status, regardless of any respects in which they might differ. The most obvious respect in which fetuses can differ is in their gestational age and thus their level of development. During the normal course of pregnancy, a fetus gradually evolves from a tiny one-celled organism into a medium-sized and highly complex organism consisting of some six million differentiated cells. Both of the established views are committed to holding that all of the beings at all stages of this transition have precisely the same moral status. The gestational age of the fetus at the time of abortion is thus morally irrelevant on both views. So also is the reason for the abortion. This is irrelevant on the liberal view because no reason is necessary to justify abortion at any stage of pregnancy and equally irrelevant on the conservative view because no reason is sufficient to do so. The established views, therefore, despite their differences, agree on two very important matters: the moral irrelevance of both when and why an abortion is performed. . . .

A Moderate View

We can now catalogue the defects of the established views. The common source of these defects lies in their uniform accounts of the moral status of the fetus. These accounts yield three different sorts of awkward implications. First, they require that all abortions be accorded the same moral status regardless of the stage of pregnancy at which they are performed. Thus, liberals must hold that late abortions are as morally innocuous as early ones, and conservatives must hold that early abortions are as morally serious as late ones. Neither view is able to support the common conviction that late abortions are more serious than early ones. Second, these accounts require that all abortions be accorded the same moral status regardless of the reason for which they are performed. Thus, liberals must hold that all abortions are equally innocuous whatever their grounds, and conservatives must hold that all abortions are equally serious whatever their grounds. Neither view is able to support the common conviction that some grounds justify abortion more readily than others. Third, these accounts require that contraception, abortion, and infanticide all be accorded the same moral status. Thus, liberals must hold that all three practices are equally innocuous, while conservatives must hold that they are all equally serious. Neither view is able to support the common conviction that infanticide is more serious than abortion, which is in turn more serious than contraception.

Awkward results do not constitute a refutation. The constellation of moral issues concerning human reproduction and development is dark and mysterious. It may be that no internally coherent view of abortion will enable us to retain all of our common moral convictions in this landscape. If so, then perhaps the best we can manage is to embrace one of the established views and bring our attitudes (in whatever turns out to be the troublesome area) into line with it. However, results are as awkward as these do provide a strong motive to seek an alternative to the established views and thus to explore the logical space between them.

There are various obstacles in the path of developing a moderate view of abortion. For one thing, any such view will lack the appealing simplicity of the established views. Both liberals and conservatives begin by adopting a simple account of the moral status of the fetus and end by supporting a simple abortion policy. A moderate account of the moral status of the fetus and a moderate abortion policy will inevitably be more complex. Further, a moderate account of the moral status of the fetus, whatever its precise shape, will draw a boundary between those fetuses that have moral standing and those that do not. It will then have to show that the location of this boundary is not arbitrary. Finally, a moderate view may seem nothing more than a compromise between the more extreme positions that lack any independent rationale of its own.

These obstacles may, however, be less formidable than they appear. Although the complexity of a moderate view may render it harder to sell in the marketplace of ideas, it may otherwise be its greatest asset. It should be obvious by now that the moral issues raised by the peculiar nature of the fetus, and its peculiar relationship with its mother, are not simple. It would be surprising therefore if a simple resolution of them were satisfactory. The richer resources of a complex view may enable it to avoid some of the less palatable implications of its simpler rivals. The problem of locating a nonarbitrary threshold is easier to deal with when we recognize that there can be no sharp breakpoint in the course of human development at which moral standing is suddenly acquired. The attempt to define such a breakpoint was the fatal mistake of the naive versions of the liberal and conservative views. If, as seems likely, an acceptable criterion of moral standing is built around some characteristic that is acquired gradually during the normal course of human development, then moral standing will also be acquired gradually during the normal course of human development. In that case, the boundary between those beings that have moral standing and those that do not will be soft and slow rather than hard and fast. The more sophisticated and credible versions of the established views also pick out stages of development rather than precise breakpoints as their thresholds of moral standing; the only innovation of a moderate view is to locate this stage somewhere during pregnancy. The real challenge to a moderate view, therefore, is to show that it can be well grounded, and thus that it is not simply a way of splitting the difference between two equally unattractive options.

Our critique of the established views has equipped us with specifications for the design of a moderate alternative to them. The fundamental flaw of the established views was their adoption of a uniform account of the moral status of the fetus. A moderate view of abortion must therefore be built on a *differential* account of the moral status of the fetus, awarding moral standing to some fetuses and withholding it from others. The further defects of the established views impose three constraints on the shape of such a differential account. It must explain the moral relevance of the gestational age of the fetus at the time of abortion and thus must correlate moral status with level of fetal development. It must also explain the moral relevance, at least at some stages of pregnancy, of the reason for which an abortion is performed. And finally it must preserve the distinction between the moral innocuousness of contraception and the moral seriousness of infanticide. When we combine these specifications, we obtain the rough outline of a moderate view. Such a view will identify the stage of pregnancy during which the fetus gains moral standing. Before that threshold, abortion will be as morally innocuous as contraception and no grounds will be needed to justify it. After the threshold, abortion will be as normally serious as infanticide and some special grounds will be needed to justify it (if it can be justified at this stage at all).

A moderate view is well grounded when it is derivable from an independently plausible criterion of moral standing. It is not difficult to construct a criterion that will yield a threshold somewhere during pregnancy.[3] Let us say that a being is sentient when it has the capacity to experience pleasure and pain and thus the capacity for enjoyment and suffering. Beings that are self-conscious or rational are generally (though perhaps not necessarily) also sentient, but many sentient beings lack both self-consciousness and rationality. A sentience criterion of moral standing thus sets a lower standard than that shared by the established views. Such a criterion will accord moral standing to the mentally handicapped regardless of impairments of their cognitive capacities. It will also accord moral standing to many, perhaps most, nonhuman animals.

The plausibility of a sentience criterion would be partially established by tracing out its implications for moral contexts other than abortion. But it would be considerably enhanced if such a criterion could also be given a deeper grounding. Such a grounding can be supplied by what seems a reasonable conception of the nature of morality. The moral point of view is just one among many evaluative points of view. It appears to be distinguished from the others in two respects: its special concern for the interest, welfare, or well being of creatures and its requirement of impartiality. Adopting the moral point of view requires in one way or another according equal consideration to the interests of all beings. If this is so, then a being's having an interest to be considered is both necessary and sufficient for its having moral standing. While the notion of interest or welfare is far from transparent, its irreducible core appears to be the capacity for employment and suffering: all and only beings with this capacity have an interest or welfare that the moral point of view requires us to respect. But then it follows easily that sentience is both necessary and sufficient for moral standing.

A criterion of moral standing is well grounded when it is derivable from some independently plausible moral theory. A sentience criterion can be grounded in any member of a class of theories that share the foregoing conception of the nature of morality. Because of the centrality of interest or welfare to that conception, let us call such theories welfare based. A sentience criterion of moral standing can be readily grounded in any welfare-based moral theory. The class of such theories is quite extensive, including everything from varieties of rights theory on the one hand to varieties of utilitarianism on the other. Whatever their conceptual and structural differences, a sentience criterion can be derived from any one of them. The diversity of theoretical resources available to support a sentience criterion is one of its greatest strengths. In addition, a weaker version of such a criterion is also derivable from eclectic theories that treat the promotion and protection of welfare as one of the basic concerns of morality. Any such theory will yield the result that sentience is sufficient for moral standing, though it may also be necessary, thus providing partial support for a moderate view of abortion. Such a view is entirely unsupported only by moral theories that find no room whatever for the promotion of welfare among the concerns of morality.

When we apply a sentience criterion to the course of human development, it yields the result that the threshold of moral standing is the stage during which the capacity to experience pleasure and pain is first required. The capacity is clearly possessed by a newborn infant (and a full-term fetus) and is clearly not possessed by a pair of gametes (or a newly fertilized ovum). It is therefore acquired during the normal course of gestation. But when? A definite answer awaits a better understanding than we now possess of the development of the fetal nervous system and thus of fetal consciousness. We can, however, venture a provisional answer. It is standard practice to divide the normal course of gestation into three trimesters of thirteen weeks each. It is likely that a fetus is unable to feel pleasure or pain at the beginning of the second trimester and likely that it is able to do so at the end of that trimester. If this is so, then the threshold of sentience, and thus also the threshold of moral standing, occurs sometime during the second trimester.

We can now fill in our earlier sketch of a moderate view of abortion. A fetus acquires moral standing when it acquires sentience, that is to say at some stage in the second trimester of pregnancy. Before that threshold, when the fetus lacks moral standing, the decision to seek an abortion is morally equivalent to the decision to employ contraception; the effect in both cases is to prevent the existence of a being with moral standing. Such decisions are morally innocuous and should be left to the discretion of the parties involved. Thus, the liberal view of abortion, and a permissive abortion policy, are appropriate for early (prethreshold) abortions. After the threshold, when the fetus has moral standing, the decision to seek an abortion is morally equivalent to the decision to commit infanticide; the effect in both cases is to terminate the existence of a being with moral standing. Such decisions are morally serious and should not be left to the discretion of the parties involved (the fetus is now one of the parties involved).

It should follow that the conservative view of abortion and a restrictive abortion policy are appropriate for late (post-threshold) abortions. But this does not follow. Conservatives hold that abortion, because it is homicide, is unjustified on any grounds. This absolute position is indefensible even for post-threshold fetuses with moral standing. Of the four categories of grounds for abortion, neither humanitarian nor socioeconomic grounds will apply to post-threshold abortions, since a permissive policy for the period before the threshold will afford women the opportunity to decide freely whether they wish to continue their pregnancies. Therapeutic grounds will however apply, since serious risks to maternal life or health may materialize after the threshold. If they do, there is no justification for refusing an abortion. A pregnant woman is providing life support for another being that is housed within her body. If continuing to provide that life support will place her own life or health at serious risk, then she cannot justifiably be compelled to do so, even though the fetus has moral standing and will die if deprived of that life support. Seeking an abortion in such circumstances is a legitimate act of self-preservation.[4]

A moderate abortion policy must therefore include a therapeutic ground for post-threshold abortions. It must also include a eugenic ground. Given current technology, some tests for fetal abnormalities can be carried out only in the second trimester. In many cases, therefore, serious abnormalities will be detected only after the fetus has passed the threshold. Circumstantial differences aside, the status of a severely deformed post-threshold fetus is the same as the status of a severely deformed newborn infant. The moral issues concerning the treatment of such newborns are themselves complex, but there appears to be a good case for selective infanticide in some cases. If so, then there is an even better case for late abortion on eugenic grounds, since here we must also reckon in the terrible burden of carrying to term a child that a woman knows to be deformed.

A moderate abortion policy will therefore contain the following ingredients: a time limit that separates early from late abortions, a permissive policy for early abortions, and a policy for late abortions that incorporates both therapeutic and eugenic grounds. This blueprint leaves many smaller questions of design to be settled. The grounds for late abortions must be specified more carefully by determining what is to count as a serious risk to maternal life or health and what is to count as a serious fetal abnormality. While no general formulation of a policy can settle these matters in detail, guidelines can and should be supplied. A policy should also specify the procedure that is to be followed in deciding when a particular case has met these guidelines.

But most of all, a moderate policy must impose a defensible time limit. As we saw earlier, from the moral point of view there can be no question of a sharp breakpoint. Fetal development unfolds gradually and cumulatively, and sentience like all other capacities is acquired slowly and by degrees. Thus we have clear cases of presentient fetuses in the first trimester and clear cases of sentient fetuses in the third trimester. But we also have unclear cases, encompassing many (perhaps most) second-trimester fetuses. From the moral point of view, we can say only that in these cases the moral status of the fetus, and thus the moral status of abortion, is indeterminate. This sort of moral indeterminacy occurs also at later stages of human development, for instance when we are attempting to fix the age of consent or of competence to drink or drive. We do not pretend in these latter cases that the capacity in question is acquired overnight on one's sixteenth or eighteenth birthday, and yet for legal purposes we must draw a sharp and determinate line. Any such line will be somewhat arbitrary, but it is enough if it is drawn within the appropriate threshold stage. So also in the case of a time limit for abortion, it is sufficient if the line for legal purposes is located within the appropriate threshold stage. A time limit anywhere in the second trimester is therefore defensible, at least until we acquire the kind of information about fetal development that will enable us to narrow the threshold stage and thus to locate the time limit with more accuracy.

Conclusions

We began by noting the special moral problems that the practice of abortion forces us to confront. A healthy respect for the intricacies of these problems and an equally healthy sense of our own fallibility in thinking through them should inhibit us from embracing any view of abortion unreservedly. Nonetheless, of the available options, we have reason to prefer the one that appears, all things considered, to provide the best account of these difficult matters. While both of the established views have obvious and serious defects, many people seem to feel that there is no coherent third alternative available to them. But a moderate view does appear to provide such an alternative.

It does less violence than either of the established views to widely shared convictions about contraception, abortion, and infanticide, and it can be grounded upon a criterion of moral standing that seems to generate acceptable results in other moral contexts and is in turn derivable from a wide range of moral theories sharing a plausible conception of the nature of morality. Those who are dissatisfied with the established views need not therefore fear that in moving to the middle ground they are sacrificing reason for mere expediency.

Notes

1. These categories are adapted from Daniel Callahan, *Abortion: Law, Choice and Morality* (New York: Macmillan, 1970).

2. The terms 'liberal' and 'conservative' as used in the chapter generally, refer respectively to those who think abortion permissible and those who believe it impermissible. Thus, 'liberal' here is not synonymous with 'political liberal' and 'conservative' is not synonymous with 'political conservative.'

3. The sentience criterion is defended in my *Abortion and Moral Theory* (Princeton,

N.J.: Princeton University Press, 1981), 128–46.

4. This position is defended in Judith Jarvis Thomson, "A Defense of Abortion," in *The Rights and Wrongs of Abortion*, ed. Marshall Cohen et al. (Princeton, N.J.: Princeton University Press, 1974); for contrary views, see John Finnis, "The Rights and Wrongs of Abortion," in *The Rights and Wrongs of Abortion*, and Baruch Brody, *Abortion and the Sanctity of Human Life: A Philosophical View* (Cambridge, Mass.: MIT Press, 1975), Chapters 1 and 2.

42   Why Abortion Is Immoral

Donald B. Marquis

. . . All this suggests that a necessary condition of resolving the abortion controversy is a more theoretical account of the wrongness of killing. After all, if we merely believe, but do not understand, why killing adult human beings such as ourselves is wrong, how could we conceivably show that abortion is either immoral or permissible?

II

In order to develop such an account, we can start from the following unproblematic assumption concerning our own case: it is wrong to kill *us*. Why is it wrong? Some answers can be easily eliminated. It might be said that what makes killing us wrong is that a killing brutalizes the one who kills. But the brutalization consists of being inured to the performance of an act that is hideously immoral; hence, the brutalization does not explain the immorality. It might be said that what makes killing us wrong is the great loss others would experience due to our absence. Although such hubris is understandable, such an explanation does not account for the wrongness of killing hermits, or those whose lives are relatively independent and whose friends find it easy to make new friends.

A more obvious answer is better. What primarily makes killing wrong is neither its effect on the murderer nor its effect on the victim's friends and relatives, but its effect on the victim. The loss of one's life is one of the greatest losses one can suffer. The loss of one's life deprives one of all the experiences, activities, projects, and enjoyments that would otherwise have constituted one's future. Therefore, killing someone is wrong, primarily because the killing inflicts (one of) the greatest possible losses on the victim. To describe this as the loss of life can be misleading, however. The change in my biological state does not by itself make killing me wrong. The effect of the loss of my biological life is the loss to me of all those activities, projects, experiences, and enjoyments which would otherwise have constituted my future personal life. These activities, projects, experiences, and enjoyments are either valuable for their own sakes or are means to something else that is valuable for its own sake. Some parts of my future are not valued by me now, but will come to be valued by me as I grow older and as my values and capacities change. When I am killed, I am deprived both of what I now value which would have been part of my future personal life, but also what I would come to value. Therefore, when I die, I am deprived of all of the value of my future. Inflicting this loss on me is ultimately what makes killing me wrong. This being the case, it would seem that what makes killing any adult human being prima facie seriously wrong is the loss of his or her future.[1]

How should this rudimentary theory of the wrongness of killing be evaluated? It cannot be faulted for deriving an 'ought' from an 'is', for it does not. The analysis assumes that killing me (or you, reader) is prima facie seriously wrong. The point of the analysis is to establish which natural property ultimately explains the wrongness of the killing, given that it is wrong. A naturalist property will ultimately explain the wrongness of killing, only if (1) the explanation fits with our intuitions about the matter and (2) there is no other natural property that provides the basis for a better explanation of the wrongness of killing. This analysis rests on the intuition that what makes killing a particular human or animal wrong is what it does to that particular human or animal. What makes killing wrong is some natural effect or other of the killing. Some would deny this. For instance, a divine-command theorist in ethics would deny it. Surely this denial is, however, one of those features of divine-command theory which renders it so implausible.

The claim that what makes killing wrong is the loss of the victim's future is directly supported by two considerations. In the first place, this theory explains why we regard killing as one of the worst of crimes. Killing is especially wrong, because it deprives the victim of more than perhaps any other crime. In the second place, people with AIDS or cancer who know they are dying believe, of course, that dying is a very bad thing for them. They believe that the loss of a future to them that they would otherwise have experienced is what makes their premature death a very bad thing for them. A better theory of the wrongness of killing would require a different natural property associated with killing which better fits with the attitudes of the dying. What could it be?

The view that what makes killing wrong is the loss to the victim of the value of the victim's future gains additional support when some of its implications are examined. In the first place, it is incompatible with the view that it is wrong to kill only beings who are biologically human. It is possible that there exists a different species from another planet whose members have a future like ours. Since having a future like that is what makes killing someone wrong, this theory entails that it would be wrong to kill members of such a species. Hence, this theory is opposed to the claim that only life that is biologically human has great moral worth, a claim which many anti-abortionists have seemed to adopt. This opposition, which this theory has in common with personhood theories, seems to be a merit of the theory.

In the second place, the claim that the loss of one's future is the wrong-making feature of one's being killed entails the possibility that the futures of some actual non-human mammals on our own planet are sufficiently like ours that it is seriously wrong to kill them also. Whether some animals do have the same right to life as human beings depends on adding to the account of the wrongness of killing some additional account of just what it is about my future or the futures of other adult human beings which makes it wrong to kill us. No such additional account will be offered in this essay. Undoubtedly, the provision of such an account would be a very difficult matter. Undoubtedly, any such account would be quite controversial. Hence, it surely should not reflect badly on this sketch of an elementary theory of the wrongness of killing that it is indeterminate with respect to some very difficult issues regarding animal rights.

In the third place, the claim that the loss of one's future is the wrong-making feature of one's being killed does not entail, as sanctity of human life theories do, that active euthanasia is wrong. Persons who are severely and incurably ill, who face a future of pain and despair, and who wish to die will not have suffered a loss if they are killed. It is, strictly speaking, the value of a human's future which makes killing wrong in this theory. This being so, killing does not necessarily wrong some persons who are sick and dying. Of course, there may be other reasons for a prohibition of active euthanasia, but that is another matter. Sanctity-of-human-life theories seem to hold that active euthanasia is seriously wrong even in an individual case where there seems to be good reason for it independently of public policy considerations. This consequence is most implausible, and it is a plus for the claim that the loss of a future of value is what makes killing wrong that it does not share this consequence.

In the fourth place, the account of the wrongness of killing defended in this essay does straightforwardly entail that it is prima facie seriously wrong to kill children and infants, for we do presume that they have futures of value. Since we do believe that it is wrong to kill defenseless little babies, it is important that a theory of the wrongness of killing, easily account for this. Personhood theories of the wrongness of killing on the other hand, cannot straightforwardly account for the wrongness of killing infants and young children.[2] Hence, such theories must add special ad hoc accounts of the wrongness of killing the young. The plausibility of such ad hoc theories seems to be a function of how desperately one wants such theories to work. The claim that the primary wrong-making feature of a killing is the loss to the victim of the value of its future accounts for the wrongness of killing young children and infants directly; it makes the wrongness of such acts as obvious as we actually think it is. This is a further merit of this theory. Accordingly, it seems that this value of a future-like-ours theory of the wrongness of killing shares strengths of both sanctity-of-life and personhood accounts while avoiding weaknesses of both. In addition, it meshes with a central intuition concerning what makes killing wrong.

The claim that the primary wrong-making features of a killing is the loss to the victim of the value of its future has obvious consequences for the ethics of abortion. The future of a standard fetus includes a set of experiences, projects, activities, and such which are identical with the futures of adult human beings and are identical with the futures of young children. Since the reason that is sufficient to explain why it is wrong to kill human beings after the time of birth is a reason that also applies to fetuses, it follows that abortion is prima facie seriously morally wrong.

This argument does not rely on the invalid inference that, since it is wrong to kill persons, it is wrong to kill potential persons also. The category that is morally central to this analysis is the category of having a valuable future like ours; it is not the category of personhood. The argument to the conclusion that abortion is prima facie seriously morally wrong proceeded independently of the notion of person or potential person or any equivalent. Someone may wish to start with this analysis in terms of the value of a human future, conclude that abortion is, except perhaps in rare circumstances, seriously morally wrong, infer that fetuses have the right to life, and then call fetuses "persons" as a result of their having the right to life. Clearly, in this case, the category of person is being used to state the *conclusion* of the analysis rather than to generate the *argument* of the analysis.

The structure of this anti-abortion argument can be both illuminated and defended by comparing it to what appears to be the best argument for the wrongness of the wanton infliction of pain on animals. This latter argument is based on the assumption that it is prima facie wrong to inflict pain on me (or you, reader). What is the natural property associated with the infliction of pain which makes such infliction wrong? The obvious answer seems to be that the infliction of pain causes suffering and that suffering is a misfortune. The suffering caused by the infliction of pain is what makes the wanton infliction of pain on me wrong. The wanton infliction of pain on other adult humans causes suffering. The wanton infliction of pain on animals causes suffering. Since causing suffering is what makes the wanton infliction of pain wrong and since the wanton infliction of pain on animals causes suffering, it follows that the wanton infliction of pain on animals is wrong.

This argument for the wrongness of the wanton infliction of pain on animals shares a number a structural features with the argument for the serious prima facie wrongness of abortion. Both arguments start with an obvious assumption concerning what it is wrong to do to me (or you, reader). Both then look for the characteristic or the consequence of the wrong action which makes the action wrong. Both recognize that the wrong-making feature of these immoral actions is a property of actions sometimes directed at individuals other than postnatal human beings. If the structure of the argument for the wrongness of the wanton infliction of pain on animals is sound, then the structure of the argument for the prima facie serious wrongness of abortion is also sound, for the structure of the two arguments is the same. The structure common to both is the key to the explanation of how the wrongness of abortion can be demonstrated without recourse to the category of person. In neither argument is that category crucial.

This defense of an argument for the wrongness of abortion in terms of a structurally similar argument for the wrongness of the wanton infliction of pain on animals succeeds only if the account regarding animals is the correct account. Is it? In the first place, it seems plausible. In the second place, its major competition is Kant's account. Kant believed that we do not have direct duties to animals at all, because they are not persons. Hence, Kant had to explain and justify the wrongness of inflicting pain on animals on the grounds that "he who is hard in his dealings with animals becomes hard also in his dealing with men."[3] The problem with Kant's account is that there seems to be no reason for accepting this latter claim unless Kant's account is rejected. If the alternative to Kant's account is accepted, then it is easy to understand why someone who is indifferent to inflicting pain on animals is also indifferent to inflicting pain on humans, for one is indifferent to what makes inflicting pain wrong in both cases. But, if Kant's account is accepted, there is no intelligible reason why one who is hard in his dealing with animals (or crabgrass or stones) should also be hard in his dealings with men. After all, men are persons: animals are no more persons than crabgrass or stones. Persons are Kant's crucial moral category. Why, in short, should a Kantian accept the basic claim in Kant's argument?

Hence, Kant's argument for the wrongness of inflicting pain on animals rests on a claim that, in a world of Kantian moral agents, is demonstrably false. Therefore, the alternative analysis, being more plausible anyway, should be accepted. Since this alternative analysis has the same structure as the anti-abortion argument being defended here, we have further support for the argument for the immorality of abortion being defended in this essay.

Of course, this value of a future-like-ours argument, if sound, shows only that abortion is prima facie wrong, not that it is wrong in any and all circumstances. Since the loss of the future to a standard fetus, if killed, is, however, at least as great a loss as the loss of the future to a standard adult human being who is killed, abortion, like ordinary killing, could be justified only by the most compelling reasons. The loss of one's life is almost the greatest misfortune that can happen to one. Presumably abortion could be justified in some circumstances, only if the loss consequent on failing to abort would be at least as great. Accordingly, morally permissible abortions will be rare indeed unless, perhaps, they occur so early in pregnancy that a fetus is not yet definitely an individual. Hence, this argument should be taken as showing that abortion is presumptively very seriously wrong, where the presumption is very strong — as strong as the presumption that killing another adult human being is wrong.

Notes

1. I have been most influenced on this matter by Jonathan Glover, *Causing Death and Saving Lives* (New York: Penguin, 1977), ch. 3; and Robert Young, "What Is So Wrong with Killing People?" *Philosophy*, LIV, 210 (1979): 515–528.

2. Feinberg, Tooley, Warren, and Engelhardt have all dealt with this problem.

3. "Duties to Animals and Spirits," in *Lectures on Ethics*, Louis Infeld, trans. (New York: Harper, 1963), p. 239.

43   Abortion Through a Feminist Ethics Lens

Susan Sherwin

Women and Abortion

The most obvious difference between feminist and non-feminist approaches to abortion can be seen in the relative attention each gives to the interests and experiences of women in its analysis. Feminists consider it self-evident that the pregnant woman is a subject of principal concern in abortion decisions. In most non-feminist accounts, however, not only is she not perceived as central, she is rendered virtually invisible. Non-feminist theorists, whether they support or oppose women's right to choose abortion, focus almost all their attention on the moral status of the developing embryo or the fetus.

In pursuing a distinctively feminist ethics, it is appropriate to begin with a look at the role of abortion in women's lives. Clearly, the need for abortion can be very intense; women have pursued abortions under appalling and dangerous conditions, across widely diverse cultures and historical periods. No one denies that if abortion is not made legal, safe, and accessible, women will seek out illegal and life-threatening abortions to terminate pregnancies they cannot accept. Anti-abortion activists seem willing to accept this price, but feminists judge the inevitable loss of women's lives associated with restrictive abortion policies to be a matter of fundamental concern. . . .

From a feminist perspective, a central moral feature of pregnancy is that it takes place in *women's bodies* and has profound effects on *women's* lives. Gender-neutral accounts of pregnancy are not available; pregnancy is explicitly a condition associated with the female body.[1] Because the need for abortion is experienced only by women, policies about abortion affect women uniquely. Thus, it is important to consider how proposed policies on abortion fit into general patterns of oppression for women. Unlike non-feminist accounts, feminist ethics demands that the effects on the oppression of women be a principal consideration when evaluating abortion policies.

The Fetus

In contrast, most non-feminist analysts believe that the moral acceptability of abortion turns on the question of the moral status of the fetus. Even those who support women's right to chose abortion tend to accept the central premise of the anti-abortion proponents that abortion can only be tolerated if it can be proved that the fetus is lacking some criterion of full personhood.[2] Opponents of abortion have structured the debate so that it is necessary to define the status of the fetus as either valued the same as other humans (and hence entitled not to be killed) or as lacking in all value. Rather than challenging the logic of this formulation, many defenders of abortion have concentrated on showing that the fetus is indeed without significant value (Tooley 1972, Warren 1973); others, such as Wayne Sumner (1981), offer a more subtle account that reflects the gradual development of fetuses whereby there is some specific criterion that determines the degree of protection to be afforded them which is lacking in the early stages of pregnancy but present in the later stages. Thus, the debate often rages between abortion opponents who describe the fetus as an "innocent," vulnerable, morally important, separate being whose life is threatened and who must be protected at all costs, and abortion supporters who try to establish some sort of deficiency inherent to fetuses which removes them from the scope of the moral community. . . .

A Feminist View of the Fetus

. . . On a feminist account, fetal development is examined in the context in which it occurs, within women's bodies rather than in the imagined isolation implicit in many theoretical accounts. Fetuses develop in specific pregnancies which occur in the lives of particular women. They are not individuals housed in generic female wombs, nor are they full persons at risk only because they are small and subject to the whims of women. Their very existence is relational, developing as they do within particular women's bodies, and their principal relationship is to the women who carry them.

On this view, fetuses are morally significant, but their status is relational rather than absolute. Unlike other human beings, fetuses do not have any independent existence; their existence is uniquely tied to the support of a specific other. Most non-feminist commentators have ignored the relational dimension of fetal development and have presumed that the moral status of fetuses be resolved solely in terms of abstract metaphysical criteria of personhood. They imagine that there is some set of properties (such as genetic heritage, moral agency, self-consciousness, language use, or self-determination) which will entitle all who possess them to be granted the moral status of persons (Warren 1973, Tooley 1972). They seek some particular feature by which we can neatly divide the world into the dichotomy of moral persons (who are to be valued and protected) and others (who are not entitled to the same group privileges); it follows that it is a merely empirical question whether or not fetuses possess the relevant properties.

But this vision misinterprets what is involved in personhood and what it is that is especially valued about persons. Personhood is a social category, not an isolated state. Persons are members of a community, they develop as concrete, discrete, and specific individuals. To be a morally significant category, personhood must involve personality as well as biological integrity.[3] It is not sufficient to consider persons simply as Kantian atoms of rationality; persons are all embodied, conscious beings with particular social histories. Annette Baier (1985) has developed a concept of persons as "second persons" which helps explain the sort of social dimension that seems fundamental to any moral notion of personhood:

> A person, perhaps, is best seen as one who was long enough dependent upon other persons to acquire the essential arts of personhood. Persons essentially are *second* persons, who grow up with other persons. . . . The fact that a person has a life *history*, and that a people collectively have a history depends upon the humbler fact that each person has a childhood in which a cultural heritage is transmitted, ready for adolescent rejection and adult discriminating selection and contribution. Persons come after and before other persons. (P. 84–85; her emphasis.)

Persons, in other words, are members of a social community which shapes and values them, and personhood is a relational concept that must be defined in terms of interaction and relationships with others. . . .

No human, and especially no fetus, can exist apart from relationships; feminist views of what is valuable about persons must reflect the social nature of their existence. Fetal lives can neither be sustained nor destroyed without affecting the women who support them. Because of a fetus's unique physical status — *within* and dependent on a particular woman — the responsibility and privilege of determining its specific social status and value must rest with the woman carrying it. Fetuses are not persons because they have not developed sufficiently in social relationships to be persons in any morally significant sense (i.e., they are not yet second persons). Newborns, although just beginning their development into persons, are immediately subject to social relationships, for they are capable of communication and response in interaction with a variety of other persons. Thus, feminist accounts of abortion stress the importance of protecting women's right to continue as well as to terminate pregnancies as each sees fit.

Feminist Politics and Abortion

Feminist ethics directs us to look at abortion in the context of other issues of power and not to limit discussion to the standard questions about its moral and legal acceptability.

Because coerced pregnancy has repercussions for women's oppressed status generally, it is important to ensure that abortion not only be made legal but that adequate services be made accessible to all women who seek them. This means that within Canada, where medically approved abortion is technically recognized as legal (at least for the moment), we must protest the fact that it is not made available to many of the women who have the greatest need for abortion: vast geographical areas offer no abortion services at all, but unless the women of those regions can afford to travel to urban clinics, they have no meaningful right to abortion. Because women depend on access to abortion in their pursuit of social equality, it is a matter of moral as well as political responsibility that provincial health plans should cover the cost of transport and service in the abortion facilities women choose. Ethical study of abortion involves understanding and critiquing the economic, age, and social barriers that currently restrict access to medically acceptable abortion services.[4]

Moreover, it is also important that abortion services be provided in an atmosphere that fosters women's health and well-being; hence, the care offered should be in a context that is supportive of the choices women make. Abortions should be seen as part of women's overall reproductive health and could be included within centres that deal with all matters of reproductive health in an open, patient-centred manner where effective counselling is offered for a wide range of reproductive decisions.[5] Providers need to recognize that abortion is a legitimate option so that services will be delivered with respect and concern for the physical, psychological, and emotional effects on a patient. All too frequently, hospital-based abortions are provided by practitioners who are uneasy about their role and treat the women involved with hostility and resentment. Increasingly, many anti-abortion activists have personalized their attacks and focussed their attention on harassing the women who enter and leave abortion clinics. Surely requiring a woman to pass a gauntlet of hostile protesters on her way to and from an abortion is not conducive to effective health care. Ethical exploration of abortion raises questions about how women are treated when they seek abortions;[6] achieving legal permission for women to dispose of their fetuses if they are determined enough to manage the struggle should not be accepted as the sole moral consideration.

Nonetheless, feminists must formulate their distinctive response to legislative initiatives on abortion. The tendency of Canadian politicians confronted by vocal activists on both sides of the abortion issue has been to seek "compromises" that seem to give something to each (and, thereby, also deprives each of important features sought in policy formation). Thus, the House of Commons recently passed a law (Bill C-43) that allows a woman to have an abortion only if a doctor certifies that her physical, mental, or emotional health will be otherwise threatened. Many non-feminist supporters of women's right to choose consider this a victory and urge feminists to be satisfied with it, but feminists have good reason to object. Besides their obvious objection to having abortion returned to the Criminal Code, feminists also object that this policy considers doctors and not women the best judges of a woman's need for abortion; feminists have little reason to trust doctors to appreciate the political dimension of abortion or to respond adequately to women's needs. Abortion must be a woman's decision, and not one controlled by her doctor. Further, experience shows that doctors are already reluctant to provide abortions to women; the opportunity this law presents for criminal persecution of doctors by anti-abortion campaigners is a sufficient worry to inhibit their participation.[7] Feminists want women's decision-making to be recognized as legitimate, and cannot be satisfied with a law that makes abortion a medical choice.

Feminists support abortion on demand because they know that women must have control over their reproduction. For the same reason, they actively oppose forced abortion and coerced sterilization, practices that are sometimes inflicted on the most powerless women, especially those in the Third World. Feminist ethics demands that access to voluntary, safe, effective birth control be part of any abortion discussion, so that women have access to other means of avoiding pregnancy.[8]

Feminist analysis addresses the context as well as the practice of abortion decisions. Thus, feminists also object to the conditions which lead women to abort wanted fetuses because there are not adequate financial and social supports available to care for a child. Because feminist accounts value fetuses that are wanted by the women who carry them, they oppose practices which force women to abort because of poverty or intimidation. Yet, the sorts of social changes necessary if we are to free women from having abortions out of economic necessity are vast; they include changes not only in legal and health-care policy, but also in housing, child care, employment, etc. (Petchesky 1980, p. 112). Nonetheless, feminist ethics defines reproductive freedom as the condition under which women are able to make truly voluntary choices about their reproductive lives, and these many dimensions are implicit in the ideal.

Clearly, feminists are not "pro-abortion," for they are concerned to ensure the safety of each pregnancy to the greatest degree possible; wanted fetuses should not be harmed or lost. Therefore, adequate pre- and postnatal care and nutrition are also important elements of any feminist position on reproductive freedom. Where anti-abortionists direct their energies to trying to prevent women from obtaining abortions, feminists seek to protect the health of wanted fetuses. They recognize that far more could be done to protect and care for fetuses if the state directed its resources at supporting women who continue their pregnancies, rather than draining away resources in order to police women who find that they must interrupt their pregnancies. Caring for the women who carry fetuses is not only a more legitimate policy than is regulating them; it is probably also more effective at ensuring the health and well-being of more fetuses. . . .

In sum, then, feminist ethics demands that moral discussions of abortion be more broadly defined than they have been in most philosophic discussions. Only by reflecting on the meaning of ethical pronouncements on actual women's lives and the connections between judgments on abortion and the conditions of domination and subordination can we come to an adequate understanding of the moral status of abortion in our society. As Rosalind Petchesky (1980) argues, feminist discussion of abortion "must be moved beyond the framework of a 'woman's right to choose' and connected to a much broader revolutionary movement that addresses all of the conditions of women's liberation" (p. 113).

Notes

1. See Zillah Eisenstein (1988) for a comprehensive theory of the role of the pregnant body as the central element in the cultural subordination of women.
2. Thomson (1971) is a notable exception to this trend.
3. This apt phrasing is taken from Petchesky (1985), p. 342.
4. Some feminists suggest we seek recognition of the legitimacy of non-medical abortion services. This would reduce costs and increase access dramatically, with no apparent increase in risk, provided that services were offered by trained, responsible practitioners concerned with the well-being of their clients. It would also allow the possibility of increasing women's control over abortion. See, for example, McDonnell (1984), chap. 8.
5. For a useful model of such a centre, see Wagner and Lee (1989).
6. See CARAL/Halifax (1990) for women's stories about their experiences with hospitals and free-standing abortion clinics.
7. The Canadian Medical Association has confirmed those fears. In testimony before the House of Commons committee reviewing the bill, the CMA reported that over half the doctors surveyed who now perform abortions expect to stop offering them if the legislation goes through. Since the Commons passed the bill, the threats of withdrawal of service have increased. Many doctors plan to abandon their abortion service once the law is introduced, because they are unwilling to accept the harassment they anticipate from anti-abortion zealots. Even those who believe that they will eventually win any court case that arises, fear the expense and anxiety involved as the case plays itself out.
8. Therefore, the Soviet model, where women have access to multiple abortions but where there is no other birth control available, must also be opposed.

References

Baier, Annette. 1985. *Postures of the Mind: Essays on Mind and Morals*. Minneapolis: University of Minnesota Press.

CARAL/Halifax. 1990. *Telling Our Stories: Abortion Stories from Nova Scotia*. Halifax: CARAL/Halifax (Canadian Abortion Rights Action League).

Eisenstein, Zillah R. 1988. *The Female Body and the Law*. Berkeley: University of California Press.

McDonnell, Kathleen. 1984. *Not an Easy Choice: A Feminist Re-examines Abortion*. Toronto: The Women's Press.

Petchesky, Rosalind Pollack. 1980. "Reproductive Freedom: Beyond 'A Woman's Right to

Choose.'" In *Women: Sex and Sexuality*. Edited by Catharine R. Stimpson and Ethel Spector Person. Chicago: University of Chicago Press.

———. 1985. *Abortion and Woman's Choice: The State, Sexuality, and Reproductive Freedom*. Boston: Northeastern University Press.

Sumner, L.W. 1981. *Abortion and Moral Theory*. Princeton: Princeton University Press.

Thomson, Judith Jarvis. 1971. "A Defense of Abortion." *Philosophy and Public Affairs*, 1:47–66.

Tooley, Michael. 1972. "Abortion and Infanticide." *Philosophy and Public Affairs*, 2, 1 (Fall): 37–65.

Van Wagner, Vicki, and Bob Lee. 1989. "Principles into Practice: An Activist Vision of Feminist Reproductive Health Care." In *The Future of Human Reproduction*. Edited by Christine Overall. Toronto: The Women's Press.

Warren, Mary-Anne. 1973. "On the Moral and Legal Status of Abortion." *The Monist*, 57:43–61.

———. 1989. "The Moral Significance of Birth." *Hypatia*, 4, 2 (Summer): 46–65.

Chapter 11

Questions to Consider

1. Explain the basis for the different conclusions of Chief Justice Dickson and Justices McIntyre and Wilson. What does each consider to be the central matter in *R. v. Morgentaler*? What moral (as opposed to distinctively legal) questions are raised about abortion in the statements of these three judges?

2. What issue does L.W. Sumner consider to be the most morally difficult and important in the abortion debate? Does his own view of abortion avoid the difficulties he finds associated with conservative and liberal views he rejects? Explain.

3. Does Donald Marquis succeed in giving a plausible account of the wrongness of killing adult human beings? Are there any problems in extending this account to fetuses or to embryos in the first stages of development? If correct, is this account sufficient to prove that abortion is almost always wrong?

4. How does the debate on abortion change if we agree to adopt a specifically feminist perspective — that is, what new questions appear and what modifications are encouraged in approaching the traditional questions? How does Susan Sherwin distinguish her view of fetuses from those offered by Sumner and Marquis?

5. What do Sumner, Marquis, and Sherwin agree on, and what do they disagree about? What sort of argument would you imagine each would use if trying to persuade either of the other two of his or her position? (That is, how would Sumner respond to Marquis and Sherwin, Marquis to Sumner and Sherwin, and Sherwin to Sumner and Marquis?)

Further Readings

Baird, Robert, and Stuart Rosenbaum, eds. 1989. *The ethics of abortion, pro-life vs. pro-choice*. Buffalo: Prometheus Books.

Callahan, Sidney, and Daniel Callahan, eds. 1984. *Abortion: Understanding differences*. New York: Plenum.

Engelhardt, H. Tristram, Jr. 1974. The ontology of abortion. *Ethics* 84:217–34.

English, Jane. 1975. Abortion and the concept of a person. *Canadian Journal of Philosophy* 5:233–43.

Feinberg, Joel, ed. 1984. *The problem of abortion* 2nd ed. Belmont, CA: Wadsworth.

Harrison, Beverley Wildung. 1983. *Our right to choose: Toward a new ethic of abortion*. Boston: Beacon.

McInernay, Peter K. 1990. Does a fetus already have a future-like-ours? *Journal of Philosophy* 87:264–68.

Petchesky, Rosalind Pollack. 1984. *Abortion and woman's choice: The state, sexuality, and reproductive freedom*. New York: Longman.

Sumner, L.W. 1981. *Abortion and moral theory*. Princeton: Princeton University Press.

Wertheimer, Roger. 1971. Understanding the abortion argument. *Philosophy and Public Affairs*, 1, 67–95.

Chapter 12

Assisted
Reproductive
Technologies

Chapter 12

Introduction

A number of reproductive technologies are currently available to assist individuals and couples to conceive and have children. These technologies include the following: therapeutic insemination using husband's sperm (TIH), therapeutic donor insemination (TDI), ovulation induction (OI), *in vitro* fertilization (IVF) and embryo transfer (ET) (with or without controlled ovarian hyper-stimulation (COH)), gamete intra-fallopian transfer (GIFT), peritoneal ovum sperm transfer (POST), zygote intra-fallopian transfer (ZIFT), and tubal embryo transfer (TET) (Combined Ethics Committee 1990).

For some, the proliferation and use of these assisted reproductive technologies (ARTs) is morally controversial. The concerns are numerous: 1) the artificiality of the various techniques (procreation and sexual intercourse are disassociated); 2) the moral status of the developing human embryo (whether the embryo has full moral rights, including the right to life, from the moment of conception); 3) the potential physical and psychological harm to the couples (and in particular the women) who avail themselves of these technologies; 4) the potential physical and psychological harm to any offspring; and 5) the research nature of many of the interventions. In addition, there are equally important concerns about issues of control and access, about the language of choice, about the commodification of children, and about the harm to women as a class.

Others are more sanguine. In their view, these technologies are beneficial because they allow infertile individuals and couples to have children who would not otherwise have been born. Research undertaken by the Royal Commission on New Reproductive Technologies (RCNRT) found that 8.5 percent of Canadian couples (approximately 300 000 couples) failed to achieve a pregnancy during one year of unprotected intercourse, while 7 percent of Canadian couples (approximately 250 000 couples) failed to achieve a pregnancy after two years of unprotected intercourse (RCNRT 1993 180). In general terms, ARTs (and especially IVF) are deemed an important treatment option for these infertile couples who desire to have children.

Nonetheless, among the more optimistic, many are troubled by the use of ARTs in combination with adjunct interventions. Embryo cryopreservation (freezing), embryo donation, gamete (ova and sperm) donation, and preconception (surrogacy) agreements can be used in combination with the aforementioned technologies — potentially resulting in controversial reproductive arrangements. For instance:

- A 59-year-old woman gives birth to twins conceived using her 45-year-old husband's sperm and eggs donated by a young woman in her twenties (Schmidt 1993). Some defend the woman's right to have a child; others insist that the child has a right to active, able parents and a suitable family life.
- A five-parent preconception agreement is arranged involving a genetic father (a sperm donor), a genetic mother (an ova donor), a gestational mother (a surrogate), and the social parents (an adoptive mother and an adoptive father). The explanation given for this complex arrangement is that the social parents have an adopted child for whom they want a sibling. They ask the birth parents of their first adopted child to have a second child for them to adopt. The birth parents reject this idea but agree to donate ova and sperm. The social (adoptive) mother, however, cannot carry a child, so her adult daughter from a previous marriage agrees to act as a surrogate (Masciola and Peterson 1993). Some support the social parents' initiative to provide their adopted child with a genetically related sibling. Others are deeply concerned about the confused family relationships.
- A 37-year-old black woman who is married to a white man receives eggs from a white donor. Her hope is to "spare her child any racial discrimination" (Lightfoot 1994). Some are sympathetic. Others are uneasy with the idea of "colour-controlled" babies; they wonder if there are any limits to parents' designing interests in their children.

Consider in this regard the purposeful creation of identical twins or triplets solely to satisfy the whims of prospective parents. At a joint meeting of the American Fertility Society and the Canadian Fertility and Andrology Society in October 1993, researchers at George Washington University announced the successful cloning by blastomere separation of abnormal non-viable human embryos (Kolberg 1993). This was done by dissolving the zona pellucida (the outer membrane) of a two-cell embryo, separating the embryo into two distinct cells, and then placing each cell in an artificial zona pellucida. In relation to ARTs, the supposed benefits of this type of embryo cloning, which are already highly contested, include the ability to increase the number of embryos available for transfer during an IVF cycle for couples who cannot produce the three to five embryos typically transferred, and the ability to create cloned two- or three-cell embryo copies for preimplantation genetic diagnosis (Jones, Edwards, and Seidel 1994).

The cloning of humans, however, also raises the spectre of a future in which the world is populated by superhumans; it is not too difficult to imagine a time when persons of superior intellect, beauty, and physical strength are selectively cloned. Nor is it too far-fetched to think that persons needing an organ transplant would want to create an identical twin to serve as their personal organ donor, or that a vain individual might wish to bestow upon society an exact replica of him- or herself.

Such recent developments in reproductive science, and other proposed revolutionary fertility treatments such as the use of eggs from aborted fetuses for women without functioning ovaries, explain a recurrent theme: our knowledge of reproductive and molecular biology and human genetics is fast outpacing our understanding of the relevant social and ethical issues. And this is happening despite the plethora of proposed guidelines published by government commissions and working groups on the social, ethical, legal, health, and research implications of ARTs.

The Selections

The proponents of ARTs typically emphasize the right to have a baby. Robert Edwards, who, along with Patrick Steptoe, helped create the world's first *in vitro* baby, writes:

> I had no doubts about the morals and ethics of our work. I accepted the right of our patients to found a family, to have their own children. I was blessed, Patrick was blessed, some of our most stringent critics were fortunate to have children of their own. It was a priceless asset. It was a gift, the relationship of parent to a developing human being. . . . The Declaration of Human Rights made by the United Nations includes the right to establish a family (Edwards and Steptoe 1980, 101–102).

The first selection, by Mary Briody Mahowald, concerns the so-called "right" to have a baby. This brief excerpt from Mahowald's book, *Women and Children in Health Care*, succinctly distinguishes different types of rights and gently questions whether the interest (desire) of a person in becoming a parent (i.e., in having a baby) is so fundamental as to constitute a human or a natural right.

The next two selections, in turn, discuss two specific ARTs. Since articles on every method of assisted reproduction could not possibly be included in a single chapter, the focus of this chapter is on IVF (a reproductive technology on which a number of other interventions depend) and preconception agreements (one of the more widely criticized reproductive technologies).

Susan Sherwin, in her article, surveys mainstream bioethics literature on IVF and related technologies. Objections to such technologies, typically raised by theological ethicists, are noted as are the common rebuttals offered by secular non feminist philosophers who focus narrowly on the autonomy of the couple seeking access to IVF. Sherwin then develops a feminist critique of IVF and other methods of assisted reproduction. She encourages the reader to broaden the perspective from which reproductive technologies are evaluated and, in so doing, to acknowledge the "sexist, classist, and often racist assumptions" that determine who controls and who has access to IVF and other reproductive technologies. Sherwin highlights male and class dominance, control by medical specialists, oppression, and discrimination as common features of reproductive programs. She concludes that "IVF threatens to result in a significant decrease in freedom for women as a class."

The next selection, by Christine Overall, begins with a description of two discrete models of preconception agreements (i.e., surrogate motherhood) — the free market model and the prostitution model. The first model views preconception agreements as freely chosen arrangements between consenting parties for mutual benefit. In this view, preconception agreements are morally acceptable. The second model emphasizes the coercion and deliberate exploitation of women who become gestational mothers. In this view, preconception agreements are morally objectionable.

In her paper, Overall critically examines these two models and shows that both are flawed with respect to underlying assumptions concerning reproductive labour and reproductive choice. Overall argues that characterizing gestational motherhood as a job that involves the sale of one's reproductive labour seriously misrepresents the operative power relations. She further insists that arguing about whether a decision to become a gestational mother is an exercise of free choice concerning the use of one's reproductive services ignores a more fundamental issue, namely, whether surrogacy should become a "socially approved 'choice.'"

The chapter concludes with excerpts from press packages released by the Privy Council office to highlight the work of the Royal Commission on New Reproductive Technologies (RCNRT). The first selection outlines the ethical framework and guiding principles used by the RCNRT to generate its final recommendations. As well, there are two summary statements on the RCNRT's recommendations concerning the ARTs dealt with in this chapter — IVF and preconception agreements.

Conclusion

Notably, the most recent national commission to report its findings on the ethical implications of ARTs is the Canadian Royal Commission on New Reproductive Technologies (RCNRT). In October 1989, the federal government of Canada established the RCNRT to examine

in particular:

a) implications of new reproductive technologies for women's reproductive health and well-being;

b) the causes, treatment and prevention of male and female infertility;

c) reversals of sterilization procedures, artificial insemination, *in vitro* fertilization, embryo transfers, prenatal screening and diagnostic techniques, genetic manipulation and therapeutic interventions to correct genetic anomalies, sex selection techniques, embryo experimentation and fetal tissue transplants;

d) social and legal arrangements, such as surrogate childbearing, judicial interventions during gestation and birth, and "ownership" of ova, sperm, embryos and fetal tissue;

e) the status and rights of people using or contributing to reproductive services, such as access to procedures, 'rights' to parenthood, informed consent, status of gamete donors and confidentiality, and the impact of these services on all concerned parties, particularly the children; and,

f) the economic ramifications of these technologies, such as the commercial marketing of ova, sperm and embryos, the application of patent law, and the funding of research and procedures including infertility treatment (RCNRT 1993, 3).

In the fall of 1993, two years behind schedule and after much controversy (Kondro 1992), the RCNRT released its final report entitled, *Proceed with Care: Final Report of the Royal Commission on New Reproductive Technologies*. In this report, the RCNRT concluded that legislation, with criminal sanctions, should be introduced to prohibit the following: 1) embryo research on cloning, ectogenesis, animal/human hybrids, and the transfer of human zygotes to other species; 2) the implantation of fertilized ova obtained from human fetuses; 3) the sale of gametes, zygotes, and fetal tissues; and 4) negotiating, or paying for, preconception agreements. As well, the RCNRT recommended that the federal government establish a National Reproductive Technologies Commission to regulate and license reproductive technologies.

It remains to be seen whether these recommendations are heeded. In the meantime, the debate concerning the moral acceptability of various ARTs continues.

References

Combined Ethics Committee of the Canadian Fertility and Andrology Society and the Society of Obstetricians and Gynaecologists of Canada. 1990. *Ethical consideration of the new reproductive technologies*. Toronto: Ribosome Communication.

Edwards, Robert, and Patrick Steptoe. 1980. *A matter of life: The story of a medical breakthrough*. London: Hutchinson.

Jones, Howard W., Robert G. Edwards, and George E. Seidel. 1994. On attempts at cloning in the human. *Fertility and Sterility* 61:423–26.

Kolberg, Rebecca. 1993. Human embryo cloning reported. *Science* 262:652–53.

Kondro, Wayne. 1992. Canada: Controversy over Royal Commission on reproductive technologies. *Lancet* 340:1214–15.

Lightfoot, Liz. 1994. Infertility Doctors Plan to Use Eggs from Aborted Foetuses. *The Sunday Times* (London, England), Jan. 2, 1–2.

Masciola, Carol, and Susan Peterson. 1993. Five-parent Arrangement a First: Birth, Adoptive Family and Adult Daughter All Join In. *The Gazette* (Montreal), Aug. 2, D8.

Royal Commission on New Reproductive Technologies. 1993. *Proceed with Care: Final Report of the Royal Commission on New Reproductive Technologies*, Vols. 1 and 2. Ottawa: Minister of Supply and Services Canada.

Schmidt, William. 1993. Ethical Storm: Birth by 59-year-old Sparks Debate on Age Limits for Becoming Pregnant. *The Gazette* (Montreal), Dec. 30, F8.

44   Fertility Enhancement and the Right to Have a Baby

Mary Briody Mahowald

. . . Rights may broadly be defined as justified or justifiable claims or entitlements. In applying the concept to concrete circumstances, the immediate questions that arise are: Claims or entitlements to what, for whom, and from whom? In the context of fertility enhancement, the first question is often answered as "the right to have a baby." Generally, the answer to the second question (a right for whom?) is a woman or couple who wish to have a child related to them genetically or gestationally. The answer to the third question (a right from whom?) may be anyone whose involvement is necessary in order to exercise the right to have a baby — for example, a sexual partner, gamete donor, technician or clinician, or possibly an insurance company or government program that funds infertility treatment. At a more basic level, rights may be derived from the "law of nature," "consent of the governed," or from God.[1]

Unfortunately, when rights language is used in common parlance, and often when it is used in formal argument, different types of rights are not distinguished. Among the possible distinctions are human, natural, moral and legal, absolute or prima facie, and positive and negative rights. For each of these, there may be correlative responsibilities or duties.[2]

Human rights involve the basic needs or interests of all human beings.[3] They are thus associated with the principle of justice or concept of equality: all human beings equally deserve to have their fundamental needs or interests fulfilled. In light of their applicability to all humans, human rights may also be construed as natural rights.[4] Within the context of natural law theory, both are identified with moral rights because what is natural to human beings is defined as moral. But moral rights generally include rights based on voluntary action as well as those based on human need or interest.

Moral rights are also broader than legal rights. Jeremy Bentham and John Austin view moral rights as based on public opinion rather than law or statute.[5] In contrast, legal rights assume the existence of a legal system whose rules govern their exercise, often restricting their application to certain groups. Although they often articulate moral or human rights, legal rights are formally stipulated by social conventions enacted through legislative or constitutional processes. Moral rights extend to informal as well as formal agreements or commitments among persons.

Whether or not the right to have a baby is a human or natural right depends on whether having a child is a basic need or interest of those who desire parenthood. Although social stigmas and personal disappointment sometimes accompany childlessness, becoming a parent is not necessary to survival, and therefore not a fundamental human need. Parenthood is in the *interest* of some individuals or couples, but whether this interest is so fundamental that it counts as a human or natural right remains questionable. Other interests, such as professional or economic success, clearly do not count as human or natural rights of individuals. Nonetheless, the right to have a baby is a claim that social convention both informally and formally supports, so long as its exercise does not impugn the rights of others. As a moral right, this right may appeal to obligations of beneficence or charity as its correlate.[6]

The distinction between absolute and prima facie duties has a parallel in discussions of rights. An absolute right is exceptionless in the demand it imposes on others. Although opposite sides of the abortion debate seem to regard their values in this way, it is difficult to see how either the right to life or the right to choose is truly absolute. A right to life does not obligate others to risk their lives in my behalf, and a right to choose is surely limited by the obligation of nonmaleficence. Yet either of these rights seems more compelling than a right to have a baby,[7] and a right to reproduce without another's assistance seems more compelling than a right to fertility enhancement or assisted reproduction. If these rights are not absolute, but may be overridden while recognizing their validity, they are prima facie rights.

The distinction between positive and negative rights, corresponding with a distinction between positive and negative duties, is particularly pertinent to issues of fertility enhancement. A negative right implies another's responsibility not to interfere with the expression of that right. A positive right implies the other's responsibility to support or facilitate its expression. If an individual's or couple's right to have a baby is a positive right, practioners have an obligation to provide infertility treatment to those who require and desire it; if the right to have a baby is a negative right, such assistance is not obligatory. It thus seems clear that the right to have a baby is at most a prima facie negative right of individuals. Health professionals are not obligated to respond affirm-atively to every individual or couple requesting reproductive assistance.

A Right to Have a Baby?

What does it mean, then, to assert one's right to have a baby? Ordinarily, when the claim is made by or on behalf of an infertile person or couple, it means the right to procreate by becoming a biological (genetic or gestational) parent. It may also mean the moral or legal right to become a social parent, through adoption or through one's committed relationship to a biological parent. Using Michael Bayles's terminology, we may therefore distinguish between the right to beget, the right to bear, and the right to rear a child. Presumably, the exercise of these rights is based on a desire on the part of a prospective parent. Bayles argues that the desire "to beget for its own sake" is irrational because fulfillment of the desire "will not contribute to one's life expe-riences."[8] The desire may become rational if begetting is seen as a means to fulfillment of other (rational) desires, such as the desire to rear a child. But the "right to have a baby" deserves analysis on another level, namely, critique of its key terms, *have* and *baby*.

To have has a different meaning when it applies to persons or subjects rather than to objects. To have an object means to own or possess it, and this implies a prima facie right to dispose of the object as one wishes. To own something is to treat it as property, which has no rights of its own. When we use the verb "have" in referring to persons (as in "I have a friend," or "I have a husband"), we refer to the relationship itself rather than to a person. We "have," for example, a relationship of friendship or marriage to a particular person. The "having" of such interpersonal relationships does not imply ownership. Typically, it implies responsibility more than rights. As Antoine de Saint-Exupéry observed in *The Little Prince*, you become "responsible for what you have tamed,"[9] that is, for those with whom you have established ties. If having a baby means having a parental relationship with someone, it fulfills this view of responsibility toward another.

The right to *have* a baby may not be literally equivalent to the right to a son or daughter, but rather a right to "the having" or reproducing of one. In that context the claim to a biological tie with one's progeny is affirmed, and this may be expressed through gamete donation or surrogacy as well as through ordinary means of reproduction. One can then "have" a baby without a commitment to its nurturance. Obviously, this raises problems regarding the baby's rights. But what do we mean by the term *baby* in discussing the right to have one? The simplest and most direct answer is to say we mean a future baby or child, that is, a newborn. Because human gametes, embryos, and fetuses are not yet babies and may never be, the assertion of a right to have any of them is not equivalent to the right to have a baby. Moreover, if embryos and fetuses are not persons, the relationship signified by "having" is probably closer to a property relationship than an interpersonal relationship. Gametes are more like property than embryos or fetuses because they are formed entirely from within the "owner's" body, and are, in fact, a part of that body. . . .

Notes

1. Natural law theory supports the view that rights are based on the nature of human beings. This rationale may reflect the religious belief that nature is defined or ordered by God (Eternal Law). Social contract theorists such as Rousseau and Locke construe rights as derived from consent of the governed.

2. See Benn, *Encylopedia*, 195–99 [Stanley I. Benn, "Rights," in *Encyclopedia of Philosophy*, ed. Paul Edwards (New York: Macmillan Publishing Company, 1967), vol.7.]; H. Tristram Engelhardt, *The Foundations of Bioethics* (New York: Oxford University Press, 1986), 94–97; Tom L. Beauchamp and James F. Childress, *Principles of Biomedical Ethics*, 3d ed. (New York: Oxford University Press, 1989), 56–60; and John Finnis, *Natural Law and Natural Rights* (Oxford: Clarendon Press, 1980). Beauchamp also distinguishes between fundamental and derivative rights. See his *Philosophical Ethics* (New York: McGraw-Hill Book Company, 1982), 194–95. Concerning the correlativity thesis, see Joel Feinberg, "The Nature and Value of Rights," *Journal of Value Inquiry* 4 (1970): 243–57. Feinberg rejects the correlativity thesis for some positive rights.

3. As Alan Gewirth states: "We may assume as true by definition, that human rights are rights that all persons have simply insofar as they are human" (in *Human Rights: Essays on Justification and Application* [Chicago: University of Chicago Press, 1983], 41). But human rights may also be possessed by humans who are not persons, or whose personhood is questionable.

4. See Abraham Irving Melden, *Rights and Persons* (Berkeley: University of California Press, 1977), 1.

5. Jeremy Bentham and John Austin in Benn, *Encyclopedia*, 197.

6. Some philosophers (e.g., libertarians) deny that there are any obligations of charity. Even if beneficence and charity are considered obligatory, however, their obligatoriness is less compelling than the obligation of nonmaleficence. As Hippocrates suggested, not harming is more important than doing good. See "Selections from the Hippocratic Corpus," in *Ethics in Medicine*, ed. Stanley Rieser, Arthur J. Dyck, and William Curran (Cambridge, Massachusetts: MIT Press, 1977), 7.

7. Although the two are often equated, the right to reproduce is not equivalent to the right to have a baby. For a woman, the right to reproduce includes the right to conceive, gestate, and give birth. The right to *have* a baby may be superseded by the child's right not to be harmed, even by a parent.

8. Michael Bayles, *Reproductive Ethics* (Englewood Cliffs, New Jersey: Prentice Hall, Inc., 1984), 13.

9. Antoine de Saint-Exupéry, *The Little Prince*, trans. Katherine Woods (New York: Harcourt, Brace, and World, 1943), 71.

45   New Reproductive Technologies

Susan Sherwin

IVF in Bioethics Literature

IVF is the technology responsible for what the media likes to call "test-tube babies." It attempts to circumvent, rather than cure, a variety of barriers to conception, primarily those of blocked fallopian tubes and low sperm counts. Several stages make up the complex technology of IVF: artificial hormones are administered to stimulate the ovaries to release eggs; the released ova are removed from the woman's body (usually by a surgical procedure known as laparoscopy, although newer, less dangerous techniques of vaginal access are being pursued); semen is collected from the woman's partner (or, more rarely, from an anonymous donor) through masturbation, and the sperm is "washed"; the ova and sperm are than combined to promote fertilization. If all has gone according to plan, then some number of the newly fertilized eggs are transferred directly into the woman's womb, with the hope that one will implant itself in the uterus and pregnancy will continue normally from this point on.[1] This procedure requires that a variety of hormones be administered to the woman (often leading to dramatic emotional and physical changes), that her blood and urine be monitored daily at three-hour intervals, and that the extremely uncomfortable procedure of ultrasound be used to determine when ovulation occurs. In some programs the woman is required to remain immobile for forty-eight hours after the fertilized eggs are introduced to her womb (including up to twenty-four hours in the head-down position). The procedure may fail at any point and, in the majority of cases, it does. Most women undergo multiple attempts and may be dropped from the program at any time. Although many practioners of IVF have tried to obscure the information, IVF is, at best, successful in 10 to 15 percent of the cases selected as suitable.[2]

The issues that bioethicists have judged important in evaluating IVF and other methods of laboratory controlled conception (such as artificial insemination) vary with the philosophic traditions of the authors. Those who adopt a theological perspective tend to object to all forms of reproductive technology, on the grounds that they are not "natural" and undermine God's plan for the family. Paul Ramsey, for instance, is concerned about the artificiality of IVF and other sorts of reproductive technology with which it is potentially associated: "There is as yet no discernable evidence that we are recovering a sense for man [*sic*] as a natural object . . . toward whom a . . . form of "natural piety" is appropriate. . . . Parenthood is certainly one of those "courses of action" natural to man, which cannot without violation be disassembled and put together again" (Ramsey 1972, 220).

Leon Kass argues a similar line in "'Making Babies' Revisited" (Kass 1979). He worries that our conception of humanness will not survive the technological permutations before us and that we will treat these artificially conceived embryos more as objects than as subjects; he also fears that we will be unable to track traditional human categories of parenthood and lineage and that this loss will cause us to lose track of important aspects of our identity.

Philosophers in the secular tradition prefer a more scientific approach; they treat these sorts of concerns as sheer superstition. They carefully explain to their theological colleagues that there is no clear sense of what is "natural," and no sense that demands special moral status. All medical activity, and perhaps all human activity, can be seen in some sense as being "interference with nature," but that is hardly grounds for avoiding such action. "Humanness," too, they point out, is a concept that admits many interpretations; generally, it does not provide satisfactory grounds for moral distinctions of the sorts that Ramsey and Kass propose.

Where some theologians object that "fertilization achieved outside the bodies of the couple remains by this very fact deprived of the meanings of the values which are expressed in the language of the body and in the union of human persons" (Ratzinger and Bovone 1987, 28), secular philosophers quickly dismiss objections against reproduction that occurs without sexuality in a properly sanctified marriage. For instance, Michael Bayles argues that "even if reproduction should occur only within a context of marital love, the point of that requirement is the nurturance of offspring. Such nurturance does not depend on the sexual act itself. The argument confuses the biological act with the familial context" (Bayles 1984, 15).

IVF is a complex technology involving research on superovulation, "harvesting" of ova, fertilization, and embryo implants. It is readily adaptable to technology that requires the transfer of ova and embryos, and hence their donation or sale, as well as to programs for the "rental of womb space"; it also contributes to an increasing ability to foster fetal growth outside of the womb and, potentially, to the development of artificial wombs covering the whole period of gestation. IVF is sometimes combined with artificial insemination and is frequently used to produce "surplus" fertilized eggs, whose moral status is in doubt. Theological ethicists worry that these activities and further reproductive developments that we can now anticipate (for example, human cloning) violate God's plan for human reproduction. They worry about the cultural shift that occurs when we view reproduction as a scientific enterprise, rather than as the "miracle of love" that religious proponents prefer: "[a child] cannot be desired or conceived as the product of an intervention of medical or biological techniques; that would be equivalent to reducing him [*sic*] to an object of scientific technology" (Ratzinger and Bovone 1987, 28). Moreover, they are concerned that we cannot anticipate the ultimate outcome of this rapidly expanding technology; they fear that it leaves us balancing precariously on a slippery slope, in danger of sliding down into yet more troubling practices.

The where-will-it-all-end hand-wringing that comes with this sort of religious futurology is rejected by most secular philosophers; they urge us to realize that few slopes are as slippery as the pessimists would have us believe. In their experience, scientists are moral people and quite capable of evaluating each new form of technology on its own merits. Hence, they argue, IVF must be judged by its own consequences and not the possible result of some future technology with which it may be linked. Samuel Gorovitz is typical of the secular philosophers: "It is not enough to show that disaster awaits if the process is not controlled. A man walking East in Omaha will drown in the Atlantic — if he does not stop. The argument must also rest on the evidence about the likelihood that judgement and control will be exercised responsibility. . . . Collectively we have significant capacity to exercise judgement and control. . . . Our record has been rather good in regard to medical treatment and research" (Gorovitz 1982, 168).

The question of the moral status of the fertilized eggs is another area of controversy for some critics. Superovulation is chemically induced to produce multiple eggs for collection, because the process of collecting eggs is so difficult and the odds against conception on any given attempt are very slim. Therefore, several eggs are usually fertilized at once. A number of these fertilized eggs will be introduced to the womb with the hope that at least one will implant and gestation will begin, but there are frequently some "extras" produced. Moral problems arise as to what should be done with these surplus eggs. They can be frozen for future use; alternatively, they can be donated to other women who cannot produce viable or genetically acceptable eggs, used as research material, or simply discarded. Many clinics are ambivalent about the moral status of these developing embryos, and some choose to deal with the problem by putting them all into the woman's womb or by limiting the numbers of available eggs that are collected. The former option poses the devastating threat of four or more eggs "successfully" implanting and a woman being put into the position of carrying a litter — something her body is not constructed to do.[3] The latter option risks not collecting sufficient eggs to guarantee successful fertilization of some.

Those who take a hard line against abortion and argue that the embryo is a person from the moment of conception object to all these procedures, because each places the fertilized egg at risk and treats it merely as an object; hence, they argue, there is no morally acceptable means of conducting IVF. Nonreligious theorists offer the stand-ard responses to this argument: personhood involves moral, not biological, categories, so a being neither sentient nor conscious is not a person in any meaningful sense. For example, Gorovitz argues: "Surely the concept of person involves in some fundamental way the capacity for sentience, or an awareness of sensations at the very least" (Gorovitz 1982, 173). Bayles says: "For fetuses to have moral status they must be capable of good or bad in their lives. . . . What happens to them must make a difference to them. Consequently some form of awareness is necessary for moral status" (Bayles 1984, 66). Fertilized eggs (which are now called "pre-embryos" by clinicians who are eager to establish their ontological status as distinct from that of embryos and fetuses) do not meet such criteria of consciousness.

Many bioethicists have agreed here, as they have in the abortion debate, that the principal moral question of IVF concerns the moral status and rights of the (pre-)embryo. Once they resolve that question, they can, like H. Tristram Engelhardt, Jr., conclude that because fetuses and their precursors are not persons and because reproductive pro-cesses occurring outside a human body pose no special moral problems, "there will be no sustainable moral arguments in principle . . . against in vitro fertilization" (En-gelhardt 1986, 237). He argues that "in vitro fertilization and techniques that will allow us to study and control human reproduction are morally neutral instruments for the realization of profoundly important human goals, which are bound up with the realization of the good of others: children for infertile parents and greater health for the children that will be born" (Engelhardt 1986, 241).

Nonfeminist moral theorists do express worries about the safety of the process, by which they tend to mean the safety to fetuses with regard to this technique; although there is evidence of a higher incidence of birth complications and defects among IVF-produced fetuses, most bioethicists conclude that the practice is safe enough.[4] There is no mention in their discussion of the dangerous side effects that IVF poses for women. The bioethics literature has not considered the chemical similarities between clomid, an artificial hormone that is commonly used to increase women's rate of ovulation, and DES, a drug that has belatedly been implicated as carcinogenic for the offspring of women who were prescribed it decades before.[5] The uncertainties surrounding su-perovulation and use of ultrasound and the dangers associated with administering a general anesthetic for egg collection and embryo transfer have not been deemed worthy of attention in the nonfeminist bioethics literature. Women who do succeed in achieving and sustaining pregnancies through this method experience a very high rate of surgical births, but those risks also are generally ignored.[6] Furthermore, most ethical discussions do not explore the significant emotional costs for women that are associated with this therapy. To date, only feminists have raised these issues.

Having disposed of the religious objections, most bioethicists in the secular tradition conclude that the focus of discussion should be on the values of patient autonomy and individual rights. Most judge IVF to be simply a private matter, to be decided upon by the couple concerned in consultation with a medical specialist. The desire to have and raise children is a common one; it is generally thought of as a paradigm case of a purely private subject. Because, for most people, conception is automatically a matter of private choice (or accident), bioethicists generally argue that "it would be unfair to make infertile couples pass up the joys of rearing infants or suffer the burdens of rearing handicapped children" (Bayles 1984, 32). Concern for the desires or needs of individuals is the most widely accepted argument in favor of the use of this technology.

What is left, then, in most of the nonfeminist discussions of IVF, is usually some hand-waving about costs. For instance, Gorovitz says: "There is the question of the distribution of costs, a question that has heightened impact if we consider the use of public funds to pay for medical treatment" (Gorovitz 1982, 177). IVF is an extremely expensive (and profitable) procedure, costing several thousand dollars per attempt. Because it is often not covered by public or private health plans, it is financially inaccessible for most infertile couples.[7] Discussion in the nonfeminist forum generally ends here, in the mystery of how to balance soaring medical costs, with the added comment that IVF poses no new ethical problems.

The Feminist Perspective

A widening of perspective to include all the effects of IVF and other reproductive technologies on the women involved is called for in bioethical evaluations. In theory, mainstream approaches to bioethics could accommodate such concerns, should the philosophers involved think to look for them, and it is significant that, for the most part, they do not appear to have perceived them.

Like their nonfeminist counterparts in bioethics, most feminists are concerned to promote personal freedom. Feminists have a long history of supporting the protection of personal reproductive control in the areas of abortion and contraception. Women's ability to avoid unwanted pregnancies is both personally and politically important. There is a distinction to be drawn between voluntary and involuntary childlessness, however, for where the former is desired, involuntary childlessness can be devastating in specific lives. From the point of view of those whose infertility is involuntary, IVF is likely to be positively valued, because it holds the promise of increasing their own reproductive freedom. Any public policy that restricts access to this technology will be experienced by those in search of relief for their childless condition as a serious interference with their personal reproductive freedom.

Indeed, most arguments in support of IVF are based on appeals to the rights of the individual to choose such technology. Feminists urge us to look carefully at these autonomy-based arguments, however, because as IVF is usually practiced, it does not altogether satisfy the motivation of fostering personal freedom. Like many other forms of reproductive technology, IVF is controlled by medical specialists and not by the women who seek it. It is not made available to every woman who is medically suitable but only to those who have been judged worthy by the designated medical practitioners. In almost every clinic a woman is considered eligible for this procedure only if she is involved in a stable (preferably married) relationship with a male partner. A couple must satisfy the specialists in charge that they have appropriate resources to support any children produced by this arrangement (in addition to the funds required to purchase the treatment in the first place), and they must demonstrate that they genuinely "deserve" this support. In other words, IVF is usually unavailable to single women, lesbian women, or women who are not securely placed in the middle class or beyond. Furthermore, women who are themselves affected by genetic handicaps are likely to be turned down by medical authorities who feel responsible for protecting future generations against the passing on of genetic defects (even if the condition at issue is one that the woman herself has come to terms with). IVF is also refused to those who have been judged as deficient according to the professionals' norms of good mothering.

The supposed freedom of choice, then, is provided only to selected women who have been screened according to the personal values of the experts administering the technology. Because most clinics deny service to single women, IVF may be accurately described as a technique that is available to men who are judged worthy, even though it is carried out on the bodies of their wives. Not only is this a far cry from individually controlled reproductive freedom, the selection criteria serve as one more instrument to establish the superior power and privilege of favored groups in society.

Feminist ethics directs us to examine the practice of IVF within the broader context of medical involvement in women's reproductive lives. There is a clear pattern of ever-increasing medical control over the various aspects of women's reproductive lives. . . .

Viewed in this context . . . the issue of professional gatekeeping and monitoring in IVF is a matter of deep concern. IVF and most other new forms of reproductive technology constitute further areas for medical intervention in women's reproductive lives. They allow still greater decision-making power to be concentrated in the hands of medical specialists.

Some formal indication of "informed consent" is generally sought from clients, but many of the forms of reproductive technology have a poor track record in meeting the ethical demands of consent. Some of these technologies are offered to women as if they were established therapies, although they are still in a highly experimental stage; often the techniques are transferred directly from agricultural experience in animal husbandry, without the benefit of careful clinical trials performed on primates.[8] Other technologies, such as the use of ultrasound and electronic fetal monitors, represent new applications of military research, which have also been used extensively on women's bodies without adequate safety studies (Oakley 1987; Petchesky 1987; Kunisch 1989). Women's experiences with thalidomide, DES, the Dalkon Shield, as well as the widespread use of fetal X rays until the mid-1970s and the belated warnings of the hazards of chemical contraceptives, provide ample reason for women to distrust reproductive technologies that have not yet been thoroughly tested for safety, but most bioethicists have been willing to rely on medical assurances about risks. . . .

Putting IVF in Context

Feminist ethics expands the scope of ethical discussions of IVF and the other forms of new reproductive technologies in other respects. Although feminists share with their nonfeminist counterparts in bioethics an interest in matters of personal freedom, safety, fairness, and the overall contributions to human happiness and suffering that such technology may produce, they also identify many other important moral issues, which must be investigated. In evaluating the new reproductive technologies, a principal concern of feminist ethics is to see how each innovation fits into existing patterns of oppression. Technology is not neutral, so it is important to consider who controls it, who benefits from it, and how each activity is likely to affect women's subordinate status in society.

There are infertile couples with a strong desire to produce a child, and IVF does benefit many of them while it holds out hope to the rest. It is worth keeping in mind, however, that patients are not the only ones who benefit from this technology; IVF also serves the interests (commercial, professional, scholarly, and patriarchal) of the medical specialists who create and manipulate it. As the birth rates drop in the West and the traditional market for obstetric services shrinks, new reproductive technologies fill a potential void in the demand for specialist services. There is the prospect of significant prestige and profit at stake in the development of successful technologies. Michelle Stanworth observes: "Reproductive technologies often enhance the status of medical professionals and increase the funds they can command, by underpinning claims to specialized knowledge and by providing the basis for an extension of service. Such technologies may, in addition, help a profession in its attempts to dominate other competitors for control in an area of work. . . . Perhaps, most significantly, new technologies help to establish that gynecologists and obstetricians 'know more' about pregnancy and about women's bodies than women do themselves" (Stanworth 1987, 13). Renate Klein is blunter; she claims that "it is not the concerns of people with fertility problems that matter most. Much higher priority is given to the concerns of those who invent, practise and promote the new technologies" (Klein 1989, 247).

Moreover, it is important to investigate why so many couples feel compelled to seek technological solutions to involuntary childlessness. Why do people place such emphasis on the desire to produce their "own" child? With respect to this question, theorists in the mainstream tradition of bioethics seem to shift to previously rejected ground and suggest that this is a natural or, at least, a proper desire. Engelhardt, for example, says, "The use of technology in the fashioning of children is integral to the goal of rendering the world congenial to persons" (Engelhardt 1986, 239). Bayles more cautiously observes that "a desire to beget for its own sake . . . is probably irrational"; nonetheless, he immediately concludes: "These techniques for fulfilling that desire have been found ethically permissible" (Bayles 1984, 31). Robert Edwards and David Sharpe confidently state "the desire to have children must be among the most basic of human instincts, and denying it can lead to considerable psychological and social difficulties" (Edwards and Sharpe 1971, 87). They do not seem interested in probing the desire to procreate or the expectations placed on people to develop such desires. . . .

These observations are not meant to deny that involuntary childlessness is a cause of great unhappiness for many people. Many individuals and couples suffer from their inability to procreate when they choose to do so; many are indeed eager to pursue whatever techniques might be offered to relieve this condition. Their motivations cannot be dismissed as irrational or misguided or judged unethical. As long as the technology that offers relief from their condition is available, it is appropriate for individuals to seek access to it.

Feminist ethics asks us to look at the social arrangements and cultural values that underlie people's drive to assume the risks that are posed by IVF and its variants. In our culture involuntary childlessness is made all the more painful by the fact that many adults have no opportunity for emotional attachment to children outside their own home. Children are valued as privatized commodities that reflect the virility and heredity of their parents. Because adults are often inhibited from having warm, stable interactions with the children of others, those who wish to know children well may find that they must have their own.

Moreover, many women are persuaded that their most important purpose in life is to bear and raise children; they are told repeatedly that their lives are incomplete, that they are lacking in fufillment if they do not have children. Furthermore, many women do face a hollow existence without children. Far too often children remain their one hope for real intimacy and for the sense of accomplishment that comes from doing work one judges to be valuable. Children are sometimes the only means women have to secure their ties to their husbands, in a culture that makes a husband a financial and social necessity for many women. . . .

From the point of view of feminist ethics, the central question is whether IVF and other forms of reproductive technology threaten to reinforce the lack of autonomy that most women now experience in our culture — even though these technologies appear to increase particular aspects of freedom for some women. Although the new reproductive technologies are advertised as increasing women's autonomy, feminists mistrust them as long as they remain intertwined with key social forces that are oppressive to women in general and, especially, to women who are multiply oppressed. By accepting the presupposition that (particular) women ought to bear children, even if they must risk their lives to do so, IVF implicity reinforces many of the sexist, classist, and often racist assumptions of our culture. It helps to support the existing power structures, because it provides reproductive assistance to the affluent and accepts the view that it is more important for the privileged to produce children of their own genetic type than to adopt a child of a different background. On our revised understanding of freedom, the contribution of this technology to the general autonomy of women collectively seems largely negative.

Therefore, it seems appropriate to resurrect the old slippery-slope arguments against IVF. Women's existing lack of control in reproductive matters begins the debate on a pretty steep incline. Technology with the potential to remove further control of reproduction from women makes the slope very slippery indeed. IVF is a technology that will always include the active involvement of designated specialists; it will never be simply a private matter for the couple or women concerned. Although offered under the guise of increasing some individuals' reproductive freedom, IVF threatens to result in a significant decrease in freedom for women as a class. . . .

Notes

1. A very useful description of the process involved in this technique and its variations can be found in Birke, Himmelweit, and Vines (1990). [Birke, Lynda, Susan Himmelweit, and Gail Vines. 1990. *Tomorrow's Child: Reproductive Technologies in the 90's*. London: Virago.]

2. Therefore, Klein (1989) concludes, "In reality, it is a *failed* technology" (1). [Klein, Renate D. 1989. *Infertility: Women Speak Out*

about Their Experiences of Reproductive Medicine. London: Pandora Press.]

3. Multiple births are a relatively frequent occurrence in IVF and other technological responses to infertility; the preferred technological solution to this iatrogenic problem is the new technique of selective abortion, wherein some fetuses in the womb are given a lethal injection and the other(s) are allowed to continue their development.

4. Having a healthy baby with an uncompli-

cated birth is an extremely rare achievement for IVF technology. A survey conducted by the Australian government reported that fewer than 5 percent of cases resulted in an unproblematic, live birth (cited in Klein 1989).

5. For a discussion of some of the already apparent dangers of clomid use in the treatment of infertility, including deaths attributed to irresponsible prescriptions, see Klein (1989).

6. Beck-Gernsheim (1989) reports that over half of the women who give birth to IVF babies do so by cesarian section (36). [Beck-Gernsheim, Elizabeth. 1989. "From the Pill to Test-Tube Babies: New Options, New Pressures in Reproductive Behaviour." In *Healing Technologies: Feminist Perspectives*, ed. Kathryn Strother Ratcliff. Ann Arbour: University of Michigan Press.]

7. The province of Ontario is remarkable exception; it does include IVF under the rubric of provincially funded medical services. In Britain only one clinic is fully funded under the National Health Service, and waiting lists are extremely long (Doyal 1987; Birke, Himmelweit, and Vines 1990). [Doyal, Lesley. 1987. "Infertility — A Life Sentence? Women and the National Health Service." In *Reproductive Technologies: Gender, Motherhood and Medicine*, ed. Michelle Stanworth. Minneapolis: University of Minnesota Press.]

8. When I raised this point in a panel discussion on the ethics of reproductive technologies at the University of Alberta, the gynecologist on the panel explained the reason for this omission: primates are expensive research animals. Although I do not mean to imply that there are no ethical problems in the experimental use of animals, animal experimentation and careful documentation are usually demanded before any new medical technology can be implemented; but here, where the technology is directed exclusively at women, no such research was performed. Further, the women on whom this technology is practiced are not advised of this omission; many assume that they are undergoing an established treatment, rather than participating in a broad, uncontrolled clinical trial.

References

Bayles, Michael. 1984. *Reproductive Ethics*. Englewood Cliffs, N.J.: Prentice-Hall.

Birke, Lynda, Susan Himmelweit, and Gail Vines. 1990. *Tomorrow's Child: Reproductive Technologies in the 90's*. London: Virago.

Edwards, Robert G., and David J. Sharpe. 1971. "Social Values and Research in Human Embryology." *Nature* 231:87.

Engelhardt, H. Tristram, Jr. 1986. *The Foundations of Bioethics*. Oxford: Oxford University Press.

Gorovitz, Samuel. 1982. *Doctors' Dilemmas: Moral Conflict and Medical Care*. New York: Oxford University Press.

Kass, Leon. 1979. "'Making Babies' revisited." *Public Interest* 54: 32–60.

Klein, Renate D. 1989. *Infertility: Women Speak Out about Their Experiences of Reproductive Medicine*. London: Pandora Press.

Kunisch, Judith R. 1989. "Electronic Fetal Monitors: Marketing Forces and the Resulting Controversy." In *Healing Technology*. See Beck-Gernsheim 1989.

Oakley, Ann. 1987. "From Walking Wombs to Test-Tube Babies." In *Reproductive Technologies*. See Doyal 1987.

Petchesky, Rosalind Pollack. 1987. "Foetal Images: The Power of Visual Culture in the Politics of Reproduction." In *Reproductive Technologies*. See Doyal 1987.

Ramsey, Paul. 1972. "Shall We Reproduce?" *Journal of the American Medical Association* 220: 1484.

Ratzinger, Joseph Card, and Alberto Bovone. 1987. "Instruction on Respect for Human Life in its Origin and on the Dignity of Procreation: Replies to Certain Questions of the Day." Vatican City: Vatican Polyglot Press.

Stanworth, Michelle, ed. 1987. *Reproductive Technologies*. See Doyal 1987.

46   Surrogate Motherhood

Christine Overall

. . . I shall present two different points of view about surrogate motherhood, which I call the free market model and the prostitution model.[1] Of the two, the prostitution model is better. But it shares with the free market model certain assumptions about reproductive labour and reproductive choice, assumptions which, I shall show, turn out to be highly implausible, and only obscure our understanding of what surrogate motherhood really is.

II The Free Market Model

According to the free market model, surrogate motherhood is, at its best, a desirable, useful, and indeed necessary service which uncoerced women may offer for purchase by childless but fertile men and their infertile wives.

This approach is defended by lawyer John A. Robertson, who regards surrogate motherhood as one type of what he calls 'collaborative reproduction,' that is, reproduction in which '[a] third person provides a genetic or gestational factor not present in ordinary paired reproduction.'[2] Other types include adoption and the use of artificial insemination by donor [AID]. For Robertson, there are few, if any, important social or moral differences among the various forms of collaborative reproduction.[3] Indeed, in some respects resort to surrogate motherhood may be preferable to agency adoption, because it is

> an alternative to the nonmarket, agency system of allocating children for adoption, which has contributed to long queues for distributing healthy white babies. This form of independent adoption is controlled by the parties, planned before conception, involves a genetic link with one parent, and enables both the father and the mother of the adopted child to be selected in advance.[4]

Robertson lists other benefits of surrogate motherhood, such as the alleviation of suffering and satisfaction of desires of the infertile.[5] But it is clear that for Robertson, the major benefit of the use of a surrogate is that it involves the uncoerced exercise of economic choice. The commissioning couple obtains the type of child they want[6] and at the time they choose. The couple freely decides to invest their money in their preferred form of consumer good: a child. As one adoptive mother of a baby born to a surrogate said, 'My God, people spend more on a Mercedes than we spent on Alexander. It's an alternative for people who want infants.'[7]

Of course, since the cost of hiring a surrogate mother is now $22,000 to $25,000,[8] and growing, this service is not, in fact, available to all. Robertson calls it 'a consumption item for the middle classes.' Its limited accessibility is not, he claims, unjust to poor couples, because it does not leave them worse off than they were before.[9] Philosopher Michael D. Bayles also uses this defence and mentions some others. He says that the price will drop if many women decide, because of the attractive fees, to become surrogates, and more children will become available for adoption. 'In general,' says Bayles, 'one should not accept limitations on otherwise permissible activities because poor people cannot afford them, but should try to raise the income of the poor or subsidize the activities so that poor people can afford them.'[10]

Furthermore, the surrogate, like the commissioning couple, also exercises free choice, according to Robertson. Equality of opportunity has been extended: like the sperm donor, a woman is now free to sell her reproductive capacities.[11] She chooses, in effect, a particular type of temporary (though by no means part-time!) job. Robertson states that surrogates 'choose the surrogate role primarily because the fee provides a better economic opportunity than alternative occupations. . . .'[12] Thus, Jane Doe chooses to be a surrogate mother rather than a waitress, let's say, because the pay for the former is (or appears to be) better. High school guidance counsellors take note: female students should be alerted to the existence of this new employment opportunity.

It should be remarked at this point that there might be some question as to how rewarding the payment for surrogate mothering really is. Much of the money paid by the couple goes toward lawyers' fees, medical and travel expenses, and insurance; surrogate mothers usually receive about $10,000.[13] This means that a woman who becomes pregnant at the very first attempt at artificial insemination would earn around $1.50 per hour for her full-time 24-hour-per-day 'job' as a pregnant woman.

Nevertheless, says Robertson, the payment of a fee (such as it is) is crucial to the surrogate mothering contract, for 'few surrogates will volunteer for altruistic reasons alone.' A ban on fees is not necessary to protect the surrogate from coercion or exploitation, since the surrogate has made 'a considered, knowing choice, often with the assistance of counsel, before becoming pregnant.'[14] Bayles elaborates this suggestion. Poor women, he says, are not exploited in being offered attractive payments to be surrogates. After all, 'other people are attracted by large fees to become lawyers or physicians.' It is true that poor, uneducated women might not have many alternative forms of employment, but this fact is not a good reason to ban even this form of opportunity. In fact, it would be unjust to deprive them of the opportunity, providing their decision to become a surrogate is an informed one.[15] Philosopher Alan Rassaby expresses this idea more bluntly. 'Given a choice between poverty and exploitation,' he says, 'many people may prefer the latter.'[16]

Robertson does not fail to recognize some potential problems in surrogate motherhood. These problems mainly concern the possibility of psychological suffering of the parties to the contract between the surrogate and the commissioning couple, harms to the child, the artificial manipulation of the natural process of reproduction, and difficulties resulting from noncompliance with the contract. Robertson apparently regards such problems as just a manifestation of the pains of the human condition: they are not unique to surrogate motherhood. Furthermore, they can be significantly diminished by providing good medical and legal services.

Robertson summarizes his discussion of possible problems in surrogate motherhood in a most significant statement. 'The morality of surrogate mothering,' he says, 'depends on how the duties and responsibilities of the role are carried out, rather than on the mere fact that a couple produces a child with the aid of a collaborator.'[17] For Robertson what is important is 'not what we do — but how we do it.'[18] No further analysis of 'what we do' in surrogate mothering is needed. All that is required is reasonable 'public scrutiny, through regulation of the process of drawing up the contract rather than its specific terms,'[19] of how surrogate mothering is carried out.

III The Prostitution Model

At the very least, the free market model for surrogate motherhood seems naive. Among its problems are the assumptions that the commodification of babies is morally acceptable; that the high cost to the commissioning couple, along with the low fee to the mother, is not unjust; that surrogate mothers choose freely to sell their services at a fair price and are therefore not the victims of exploitation; that the practice of surrogate motherhood requires only legal regulation in order to prevent problems; and that *what* surrogate motherhood is is in no need of further analysis.

The second point of view on surrogate motherhood, which I have called the prostitution model, is, at first sight, quite different from the first, for it calls into question at least some of the assumptions made by the free market model. It is usually advanced by feminist writers, but it is nowhere as fully expressed and developed as the free market model. Instead, it is necessary to piece it together from a variety of rather brief commentaries.

According to this second point of view, surrogate motherhood is a type of deliberate exploitation of women's reproductive capacities, and is in that way akin to prostitution.

An outline of this sort of analysis is provided by Mary Kay Blakely, in a short paper whose very title, 'Surrogate Mothers: For Whom Are They Working?' invites us to examine our underlying assumptions about surrogate motherhood. She suggests that the practice is governed by racist and sexist beliefs.[20] Surrogate motherhood, she says, raises issues concerning ownership of children, 'the conceit of patriarchal genetics,'[21] infertility as a failing in women, and finally 'guilt and money, and how women earn both.'[22] But these comments just hint at a feminist analysis, and Blakely herself never answers the provocative question in the title of her paper.

In response to Blakely's paper, another writer[23] states that recognition of a woman's right to control her own body and to make decisions about childbearing do not imply a license to exploit one's body. Surrogate mothers may feel a sense of fulfillment at least partly because childbearing has been, historically, almost the only realm for which women gain recognition.[24] Thus, while women should have a 'right to choose' in regard to surrogate motherhood, 'society's endorsement of this choice as a valid female occupation' would be a mistake, because it would serve as an affirmation of the tradition of fulfillment through childbearing.

A possible answer to the question, for whom are surrogates working, is provided by feminist Susan Ince. In her investigation of the operation of a surrogate motherhood broker, she found that the infertile wife, who is the raison d'être of the surrogate industry, is 'notably absent' from the surrogate motherhood relationship. The company investigated by Ince urged each 'girl' to find ways to include the biological father (the husband of the infertile woman) in her pregnancy and birth, for example, by sending a 'nice note' to the father after conception, and later, a tape of the baby's heartbeat.[25] Furthermore, the contract used by the company makes it clear that it is the father who is the purchaser; it is he to whom the child-product belongs, and to whom it must be delivered.[26] The preeminence of the father over his infertile wife is emphasized by the fact that her consent is not usually required for his participation in the surrogate motherhood arrangement. (This contrasts with the regular procedures governing the use of AID: consent of the husband is usually required before a women is artificially inseminated.) Thus, Susan Ince's analysis suggests that the true employer of the surrogate is not the so-called commissioning couple, but only the male who provides the sperm.

That suggestion renders more plausible the claim that surrogate motherhood is like prostitution. The comparison is used briefly by philosopher Mary B. Mahowald, who also challenges the assumption of the free market model that women freely choose the job of surrogate mother. Expressing concern about women's right to self-determination regarding their own bodies, she writes,

Most prostitutes are driven to their "trade" by economic and emotional pressures largely beyond their control; and surrogacy? What either practice says about society is more telling than what it says about the individual. Accordingly, we might more appropriately critique the social conditions that make these options genuine and unavoidable for individual women, than worry about the legal complaints arising from their practice.[27]

Finally, feminist Andrea Dworkin has also written about surrogate motherhood in the course of a longer discussion of prostitution. She argues that the scientific separation of sex from reproduction, and of reproduction from sex, now 'enable women to sell their wombs within the terms of the brothel model.'[28] Thus, reproduction can become the sort of commodity that sex is now. All reproductive technologies 'make the womb extractable from the woman as a whole person in the same way the vagina (or sex) is now.'[29] A surrogate mother is, Dworkin says, a 'reproductive prostitute.'[30]

IV The Two Models: Similarities and Critique

The free market model and the prostitution model of surrogate motherhood appear to be rather different. The former states that surrogate motherhood is a freely chosen arrangement between two or more human beings operating to the potential benefit of all concerned. The latter sees surrogate motherhood as akin to prostitution, a type of exploitive employment by men into which the women involved enter, not freely, but out of economic necessity or social coercion. The two viewpoints are, consequently, sharply divided as to the moral justification of the practice: the free market model regards it as acceptable, the prostitution model as morally questionable; and also as to social policy, with the free market model seeing surrogacy as in need only of legal regulation, while the prostitution model sees it as necessitating a dramatic restructuring of society so that women will not be forced into being surrogate mothers.

Nevertheless, despite these apparent differences, closer examination of the two viewpoints on surrogate mothers reveals that they share several assumptions in common. I shall discuss two items of agreement between them: the first concerns the idea of reproductive labour, which is expressed in this context by treating surrogate motherhood as a job; the second concerns the concept of reproductive choice.

a) Reproductive Labour: Surrogate Motherhood as a Job

In a very literal sense, the surrogate mother is engaging in reproductive labour: her body is doing the work necessary to produce a human being. Moreover, she is being paid for this work. Hence, surrogate motherhood appears to be, or to be like, a job. This is an assumption shared by both the free market model and the prostitution model, and even by the women themselves.[31] Just as, for example, a music teacher might sell her pedagogical services privately to individual students, or a lawyer might sell her legal services to clients, or a prostitute might sell her sexual services to customers, the surrogate mother sells her reproductive services to the commissioning couple, or, more accurately, to a man, or possibly a series of individual men.

To treat surrogate motherhood as a job appears only too consistent with other traditional uses of women's reproductive labour. For, as feminist writers have pointed out, under usual circumstances, such labour is either a species of volunteer work, which women supposedly undertake for sheer love of it, or, in less congenial circumstances, it is a type of slavery.[32] Thus, the fee paid to the surrogate mother at least appears to put reproductive labour on a more equal footing with other forms of paid labour that it ordinarily possesses.

But *if* surrogate motherhood is to be regarded as a job, then we are forced to accept the peculiar implications which follow from it. For example, consider this: The free market model assumes that the surrogate is employed by the commissioning couple; the prostitution model suggests that she is employed by the man who provides the sperm. But closer investigation makes it at least as plausible to say that the surrogate is self-employed.

Surrogate motherhood is similar in several respects to a small-scale, owner-operated business. The woman, after all, operates out of her own home; she provides the equipment for carrying out the labour; and her earnings are controlled (or limited) by the amount of work she is willing to do (that is, by the number of babies she is willing to produce). I would even venture that if the government found out about her income, it would require her to pay taxes directly to the state.[33] The surrogate motherhood brokers who bring buyers and sellers together are not the employers of the women; they explicitly disavow any responsibility for adverse outcomes,[34] and they do not pay the woman for her services. But then, neither are the couple, or the biological father, the employer of the woman, any more than a lawyer's clients or a music teacher's pupils are their employers.

Thus, *if* surrogate motherhood is a job involving the selling of reproductive labour on a private basis, then an answer, at least as plausible as any other, to Blakely's question, for whom is the surrogate working, is: herself.

Now of course, I do not really want to claim that surrogate mothers are self-employed. I simply want to explore the implications that follow from treating surrogate motherhood as a job. They reveal, I think, that there is an error in seeing surrogate motherhood as being, or being like, a job involving the selling of one's reproductive services. For if the surrogate mother is self-employed, then we are led to see her as an individual whose activities must be regulated in order to protect both those who specifically hire her services, and the general public, from any potential dangers or failure of responsibility in her exercise of her vocation.[35] Indeed, legislation to govern surrogate motherhood has already been proposed which is designed to safeguard lawyers, doctors, the commissioning couple, and the potential baby, by providing legal and financial penalties to be exacted if the mother should abort, engage in negligent behaviour, or fail to surrender the child, in violation of the terms of her contract.[36] The idea that the surrogate mother is self-employed thus leads us to a concern for the licensing of surrogates; for setting appropriate fees;[37] for requisite training, qualifications, screening, advertising, insurance, and contracts. Moreover, if surrogate motherhood is a job, then it appears that our only worry, if there is one at all, for the women involved must be whether it is a good job: Our concern will be directed toward improving their working conditions, raising their income, providing insurance, perhaps even offering a pension plan, and so on.

But all of these concerns entirely lose sight of part of what seems to be implicit in, and correct about, the feminist critique of surrogate motherhood: namely, that the surrogate mother is *herself* in need of protection from the lawyers, doctors, and infertile couples who wish to make use of her services. The assumption that surrogate motherhood is, or is like, a job essentially misrepresents the power relations which are defined by the practice. The immediate locus of power in the surrogate arrangement is in a necessarily rather wealthy man who pays the fee and provides the sperm, and in the person, usually a male lawyer, who represents him, and receives a commission for his services. But the wider network of control is constituted by the authority relations defined in patriarchy, in the context of which reproduction is usually labour done by women for men. It seems highly unlikely that in becoming a surrogate mother, a woman is invested with power and independence which she would otherwise not possess in the exercise of her reproductive capacities. As in the case of prostitution, the mere payment of a small fee in no way changes the possibility that she is a victim of exploitation, and the nature of the exploitation is not such that an increase in fees or improved working conditions will change it.

b) Reproductive Choice

But in order to give more substance to this contention, I shall now introduce some analysis of the second item on which the two models of surrogate motherhood agree. Both of them assume that individuals ought, perhaps within certain limits, to have the freedom to choose what sort of job to take up (whether, let's say, to become a secretary or a waitress, or whether to choose self-employment as a doctor or as a surrogate mother). And becoming a surrogate mother is assumed to be, at least potentially, one possible result of the exercise of that free choice, in particular, free choice concerning the use of one's reproductive capacities.

Of course, the two models disagree as to whether this freedom really exists in the case of surrogate motherhood: the free market model says it does; the prostitution model says it does not. And in this respect, the prostitution model is, I would argue, correct. A question raised by the Canadian Advisory Council on the Status of Women about prostitution applies almost verbatim to surrogate motherhood: 'Can a person of minimal education and financial well-being be said truly to choose a way of life that is stigmatized by much of society, that is physically dangerous at times, that leaves her with little control over her earning power, and that can cause her considerable legal complications?'[38]

In one of the few psychological studies so far undertaken on the characteristics of women who apply to be surrogate mothers, it was discovered that 40% of the sample were unemployed or receiving some form of financial aid, or both. Moreover, 72% of the women had an education level of high school graduation or less.[39] The researcher, Philip J. Parker, also found that a large majority of the group had been pregnant previously; when pregnant these women 'felt more content, complete, special, and adequate and often felt an inner glow; some felt more feminine and attractive and enjoyed the extra attention afforded them.'[40] In this sample, 35% of the women either had had a voluntary abortion or had relinquished a child for adoption, a fact which led Parker to surmise that these women 'felt (often unconsciously) that surrogate motherhood would help them master unresolved feelings they had regarding a previous voluntary loss of fetus or baby.'[41] Considering all of these factors, the candidates for surrogate motherhood seem not only to be motivated by very real financial need, but also to be influenced by quite traditional role expectations about the importance of pregnancy and motherhood in women's lives.[42]

It is most ironic that after uncovering this information about applicants for surrogate motherhood, Parker emphasizes the importance of ensuring that every applicant for surrogate motherhood is 'competent' and is 'voluntarily and freely making an informed choice, free of coercion and undue influence.'[43] In my view, there is a fundamental contradiction between the fact that social conditions such as those delineated in Parker's study create the demand for surrogate motherhood, and permit reproductive services to become a commodity, and the fact that the women involved are perceived as able to make a free choice.[44] Yet the free market proponents to surrogate motherhood are likely to use that alleged free choice to defend the practice, by asking, rhetorically, what right the state has to deny women the exercise of her free will in selling her reproductive capacities.[45]

Perhaps the cause of the disagreement between the two models as to whether surrogate motherhood is the result of free choice is a failure to examine what reproductive choice means. Both models appear to assume that the main moral question about reproductive choice is whether or not it exists — in this context, whether the women who become surrogate mothers freely choose this use of their reproductive capacities. But I contend that the idea of reproductive choice is in need of further analysis: It is more complex than proponents of the two models appear to realize.

Sociologist Barbara Katz Rothman has sounded some warnings about the meanings of reproductive choice. Examining the varieties of choices offered by reproductive technology — options for fetal monitoring, contraceptive use, abortion, prenatal diagnosis, and infertility treatments — Rothman argues that apparent expansions of choice often result in the loss of other choices because they become socially less acceptable, or in the existence of choices which we are, paradoxically, forced to make.[46] Thus reproductive choice sometimes turns out to be more apparent than real.

This sort of insight can be applied to surrogate motherhood. We should be asking what options may be foreclosed for some women by the existence of the apparent choice of selling one's reproductive services. To this question I can offer only a tentative response. For individual women, the existence of surrogate motherhood as an apparent choice may tend to obscure or override other possible interpretations of their lives. Just as the overwhelming presence of the role of housewife presented itself, until recently, as the only 'choice' for women, so also surrogacy may appear to be the only possible escape route for some women with few resources and opportunities. A woman may reason, in effect, that if all else fails, she can still become a surrogate mother. If surrogate motherhood becomes a socially approved 'choice,' it will affect how women see the use of their reproductive capacities, and their relationships to their children, as well as the social construction of women's reproductive roles.

So far, what I have said about reproductive choice does not go much beyond what feminists have said about it in other contexts. However, I want to suggest a second reason to reconsider the notion of reproductive choice in the context of surrogate motherhood: it can lead to an uncritical acceptance of the many ways in which women's reproductive capacities may be used. In endorsing an uncritical freedom of reproductive choice, we may also be implicitly endorsing all conceivable alternatives that an individual might adopt; we thereby abandon the responsibility of evaluating substantive actions in favour of advocating merely formal freedom of choice.[47] We must think very carefully about whether surrogate motherhood is a 'choice' which we want to recognize in this way.

This brings me to a more fundamental reservation about the idea of reproductive choice in the context of surrogate motherhood: Is becoming a surrogate mother really the sort of thing one can freely choose? What I am trying to get at here could perhaps be more clearly expressed by asking whether surrogate motherhood is genuinely a part of what we ought to *mean* by the exercise of reproductive choice.

The problem is not merely that surrogate motherhood may not be freely chosen by those women who take it up. The problem is that there is a real moral danger in the sort of conceptual framework which presents surrogate motherhood as even a *possible* freely chosen alternative for women.

Notes

1. There are others—such as Herbert T. Krimmel's view that surrogate motherhood is immoral primarily because of the motivations of the persons involved and the effects on the children produced—which I shall not discuss here. See 'The Case Against Surrogate Parenting,' *The Hastings Center Report* 13 (October 1983), 35–9. Cf. Mary Warnock, A Question of Life: The Warnock Report on Human Fertilization and Embryology (Oxford: Basil Blackwell 1985), 45.

2. John A. Robertson, 'Surrogate Mothers: Not So Novel After All,' *The Hastings Center Report* 13 (October 1983), 28.

3. Bayles also compares the issues surrounding surrogate motherhood to those in AID (23), Cf. Alan B. Rassaby, 'Surrogate Motherhood: The Position and Problems of Substitutes,' in William Walters and Peter Singer, eds., *Test-Tube Babies* (Melbourne: Oxford University Press 1982), 103, and Suzanne M. Patterson, 'Parenthood by Proxy: Legal Implications of Surrogate Birth,' *Iowa Law Review* 385 (1982), 390–1.

4. Robertson, 28

5. Cf. Rassaby, 104.

6. For example, white, not black: '[A]lmost every adopting white couple wants a healthy white baby, and the great majority of young, pregnant, white American women do not give up their babies for adoption' (Cynthia Gorney, 'For Love and Money,' *California Magazine* [October 1983], 91).

7. Ibid., 155

8. Margaret Munro, '"Rent-a-Womb" Trade Thriving Across Canada–U.S. Border,' *The Montreal Gazette* (21 January 1985) D–11

9. Robertson, 29

10. Bayles, 26; cf. Rassaby, 103.

11. *A Matter of Life* also cites this claim as a possible justification for surrogacy: '[C]arrying mothers . . . have a perfect right to enter into such agreements if they so wish, just as they have a right to use their own bodies in other ways, according to their own decision' (45). Cf. Council for Science and Society, Human Procreation: Ethical Aspects of the New Techniques (Oxford: Oxford University Press 1984) 66.

12. Robertson, 29

13. Munro, D–11

14. Robertson, 32–3

15. Bayles, 25

16. Rassaby, 103. Cf. William A.W. Walters and Peter Singer, 'Conclusions — And Costs,' in *Test-Tube Babies*, 138.

17. Robertson, 32

18. Ibid., 33

19. Ibid., 34

20. Advertisements for prospective surrogates usually make it clear that applicants should be white. And the commissioning couple may 'try again' for a boy if the pregnancy produces a female infant (Mary Kay Blakely, 'Surrogate Mothers: For Whom Are They Working? *Ms.* 11 [March, 1983], 18 and 20). She could also have added class considerations. Cf. Rosalind Pollack Petchesky, 'Re-

productive Freedom: Beyond "A Woman's Right to Choose,"' in Catharine R. Stimpson and Ethel Spector Person, eds., *Women: Sex and Sexuality* (Chicago: University of Chicago Press 1980), 92–116, for a discussion of class distinctions in the availability of other reproductive services, such as abortion and contraception.

21. Susan Ince states: 'The need to continue patriarchal lineage, to make certain the child has the sperm and name of the buyer, is primary" ('Inside the Surrogate Industry,' in Rita Arditti, Renate Duelli Klein, and Shelley Minden, eds., *Test-Tube Women: What Future for Motherhood?* [London: Pandora Press 1984], 112).

22. Blakely, 20

23. Susan E. Nash, letter, *Ms.* 11 (June, 1983), 5

24. Some confirmation for this appears in a recent brief discussion of the motives of surrogate mothers. One woman wrote, 'When I first heard of surrogate motherhood, my immediate thoughts were, "Goodness, I could do that! I can't cook, I can't play tennis or do tapestries, but I am good at being pregnant and giving birth."' Quoted in Carl Wood and Ann Westmore, *Test-Tube Conception* (Englewood Cliffs, NJ: Prentice-Hall 1984), 113.

25. Ince, 102

26. Ibid., 112

27. Letter, *The Hastings Center Report* 14 (June, 1984), 43

28. Andrea Dworkin, *Right-Wing Women* (New York: Perigee Books 1983), 181

29. Ibid., 187

30. Ibid., 188

31. Munro, D–11

32. Elizabeth W. Moen, 'What Does "Control Over Our Bodies" Really Mean?', *International Journal of Women's Studies* 2 (March/April 1979), 133

33. I owe these ideas to Ted Worth.

34. Ince, 107

35. This point of view is taken most noticeably by Bernard D. Hirsch, in 'Parenthood by Proxy' *Journal of the American Medical Association* 249 (April 22/29 1983), 2251–2.

36. This seems to be reflected in surrogate motherhood contracts: the contract signed by the mother is often longer, and specifies more limitations, than that signed by the commissioning couple. ('Nothing Left to Chance in "Rent-A-Womb" Agreements.' *The Toronto Star* [January 13, 1985].) See also Theresa M. Mady, 'Surrogate Mothers: The Legal Issues,' *American Journal of Law and Medicine* 7 (Fall 1981), 351.

37. 'One wonders . . . whether fair compensation for being a surrogate mother should be determined simply by market forces,' William J. Winslade, 'Surrogate Mothers: Private Right or Public Wrong?,' *Journal of Medical Ethics* 7 (1981), 154.

38. Canadian Advisory Council on the Status of Women, *Prostitution in Canada* (March 1984), 84

39. Philip J. Parker, 'Motivation of Surrogate Mothers: Initial Findings,' *American Journal of Psychiatry* 140 (January 1983), 117

40. Ibid., 118

41. Ibid.

42. Cf. the finding of Darrell D. Franks, 'Psychiatric Evaluation of Women in a Surrogate Mother Program,' *American Journal of Psychiatry* 138 (October 1981) 1378–9.

43. Philip J. Parker, 'Surrogate Motherhood: The Interaction of Litigation, Legislation and Psychiatry,' *International Journal of Law and Psychiatry* 5 (1982), 352

44. Dworkin, 182

45. Ibid., 180; cf. *Prostitution in Canada*, 69, and Ince, 99.

46. Barbara Katz Rothman, 'The Meanings of Choice in Reproductive Technology,' in *Test-Tube Women*, 23–33. Cf. Kathleen McDonnell, *Not An Easy Choice: A Feminist Re-Examines Abortion* (Toronto: The Women's Press 1984), 71–2, and Petchesky, 101, on abortion as a 'free' choice.

47. An unlimited advocacy of the further development of reproductive choice would seem to imply, for example, an unlimited 'right' to choose the sex of one's children, through selective abortion, a 'right' which appears to be potentially gynecidal. See McDonnell, 79, and Petchesky, 100.

47   Proceed with Care: Final Report of the Royal Commission on New Reproductive Technologies*

Framework for Decision Making

Given the range and complexity of issues on which the Royal Commission on New Reproductive Technologies was asked to make recommendations, it was vital that we establish a way that Commissioners with varying backgrounds and life experiences could together approach the technologies — we needed an ethical framework for decision making. The shape this took is outlined here, so that those who are interested can see how we approached the real-life moral dilemmas facing individuals and society in this field. We adopted as our ethical framework a modified ethic of care and within that orientation, developed a set of guiding principles which we used as a prism through which to view the technologies. In keeping with our policy of keeping the public apprised of our findings and work, this article gives an overview of our approach. The full details of the framework obviously cannot be covered in a short excerpt. The Commission's Final Report will make clear how we have applied it and how our recommendations flow from our ethical stance.

Many traditional ethical theories are based on an understanding of human nature that sees people as individuals in competition with one another who need to protect their own interests and rights. Recent ethical thinking has questioned this view, and tries to take into account that we are all connected to one another in families, communities, and social bonds of all sorts, and that people who are connected in these ways care about each other's welfare — they know no one can enjoy their rights and interests by themselves. The ethic of care gives priority to this mutual care and con-

---

*The following selections are from press packages released by the Privy Council Office to highlight the work of the Royal Commission on New Reproductive Technologies.

nectedness and tries to foster it rather than starting by viewing individuals as adversaries. A large part of ethical deliberation therefore concerns how to build relationships and prevent things that give rise to conflict. We were committed to finding creative ways to remove or reduce conflict, and our focus was on helping society and human relationships to flourish by seeking to foster the dignity of the individual and the welfare of the community.

Conflicts cannot be avoided entirely: no ethical stance can accomplish that. Therefore, as well as this overall ethical perspective, we developed eight guiding principles. These principles — autonomy, equality, respect for human life, protection of the vulnerable, appropriate use of resources, non-commercialization of reproduction, accountability, and balancing individual and collective interests — act as a prism, casting light on issues where conflicts are likely to arise and helping us to reach ethically based conclusions. No one principle automatically "trumps" any other, there is no hierarchy here. Different principles are considered as they apply to specific issues.

Individual autonomy means that people should be free to choose how to lead their lives, particularly with regard to their bodies and their fundamental commitments, such as work, health, family, and sexuality. Clearly this is not an unqualified right — it does not include the right to harm others, for instance, to use force to coerce them, or to undermine human dignity or social stability. We believe that this principle requires that all of society, and especially people considering using new reproductive technologies, must be able to make an informed decision about their involvement. This requires information — on outcomes, costs, and risks.

The principle of *equality*, at its root, means that every member of the community is entitled to equal concern and respect. Equal access to public services such as health care and education is based on this principle, which also forms the basis for our particular concern with ensuring that the interests and concerns of Canadians in all their diversity are taken into account in decisions about new reproductive technologies. That is why, for instance, we have taken particular pains to examine how the technologies affect women, members of racial and ethnic minorities, people with disabilities, and Aboriginal people.

Our *respect for human life* implies that all human life should be treated with sensitivity and respect, not callousness or indifference. In fact, all human tissue should be treated with respect. Although the law does not treat embryos and fetuses as persons, they are connected to the community by virtue of their origins (having been generated by members of the community) and their possible future (their potential to become members of the community). Hence they, too, are deserving of respect.

Protection of the vulnerable requires that the welfare of those who are liable to exploitation, or those who are less capable of looking after themselves be given special consideration. Children obviously fall into this category, including those children who may be born in the future through the use of new reproductive technologies. Furthermore, individuals and couples seeking to use new reproductive technologies, whether because of infertility or because of the possibility of passing on a genetic disease, are vulnerable. It is not in their interest, for instance, that any technique which has not been shown to be safe and effective be offered as a medical treatment. It is also not in their interest to offer any technique without providing adequate information and counselling to assist them in exercising informed choice.

The Commission believes strongly that it is wrong for fundamental decisions about human reproduction to be determined by a profit motive. Introducing a profit motive into the sphere of reproduction is contrary to respect for human dignity and disregards the importance and significance of reproduction in our lives as human beings. *Non-commercialization of reproduction* is, therefore, a basic moral principle, regardless of whether we are talking about sperm, ova, or embryos, or whether we are talking about the people involved in reproduction. While there may be a legitimate, regulated role for commercial interests in some areas of reproductive health care — for example, in the development of drugs or medical devices — it is important to place strict limits on the nature and extent of commercial involvement in this field. In particular, neither women nor children should ever be treated as commodities.

Appropriate use of resources is an important principle recognizing that since resources are finite and needs are many, we must use our resources wisely and effectively. Appropriate roles for *prevention* and acute care must be assessed in light of this principle. Providing a treatment which is not effective is, obviously, a poor use of resources. This principle, therefore, leads to the need for technology assessment and evaluation of medical practices, and the importance of evidence-based medicine.

The principle of *accountability* is the basic democratic principle that those who hold power are responsible for how they use that power. We believe that Canadian society has a right — and a responsibility — to regulate and monitor whether and how new reproductive technologies are used, to ensure that Canadian values, principles, and priorities are being respected. In the past, this has been done through self-regulation by the medical profession. The implications of new reproductive technologies are so profound, however, that it is clear that calls for more widespread public participation in their regulation are legitimate.

Finally, the Commission believes that both *individual and collective interests* are worthy of protection, and that neither one automatically takes precedence over the other. The individual interests encompass those of children born as a result of the technologies, gamete donors, or women or couples seeking assisted conception or pre-natal diagnosis. Collective interests include not only those of society as a whole, but also those of identifiable groups within society, particularly, in this case, women, but also groups such as people with disabilities and members of racial or ethnic minorities.

Ethical issues were the focus of many of the interventions and submissions we received during our consultation process. There was a widespread public perception that the ethical implications of new reproductive technologies require greater attention than they have received to date. The orientation of the ethic of care, and the prism of guiding principles, enabled us to think through the ethical and social implications of new re-productive technologies and to make principled recommendations. Adopting the ethic of care and using the guiding principles within it does not guarantee an easy resolution of all moral issues. It does, however, provide for the Commission, and for Canadians, a constructive and humane way in which to approach difficult moral dilemmas.

(This is based on a draft of the Final Report prepared by the five Commissioners of the Royal Commission on New Reproductive Technologies. The Report is due to be presented to the federal government by July, 1993.)

Main Topics: "In Vitro Fertilization"

IVF is currently offered in a way that is unacceptable. In about half of cases in Canada it is used for indications for which there is not good evidence it is effective, yet it is offered in these cases as a treatment, not as research. As well, there are marked differences in how services are offered, often without clear and understandable infor-mation for patients. Record keeping is unsatisfactory and insufficient to be able to assess outcomes — even such critical aspects as the number of children born. Voluntary guide-lines developed by practitioners for practice are not routinely adhered to. The situation of voluntary regulation in the treatment community has led to practice ranging from excellent to completely unacceptable.

Medical procedures should move from the realm of research to that of treatment only if they can be demonstrated to be effective and beneficial, and only if information on their risks and effects is available. To date, IVF has been proven effective for only one category of infertility disorders — those involving complete blockage of the fallopian tubes. Only for this category of cases is it a treatment proven to be of benefit and therefore a candidate for provincial health-insurance coverage. For all other uses, there is a pressing need to find out for what indications IVF is effective. Until that information is available, IVF for indications other than tubal blockage should be offered only in the context of well designed clinical trials.

Some uses of IVF technology contravene Canadian values, and are unethical, thus they should be banned. These include IVF in support of preconception arrangements and IVF for post-menopausal women, IVF as a profit-making venture, and experimental uses of IVF offered as treatment.

A nationally administered, regulated, standardized system is needed to ensure adherence to rigorous standards of practice and care, useful and standardized record-keeping, access to adequate information and counselling for patients, analysis of any long-term effects, and ongoing monitoring and policy-making.

There is a good opportunity to put in place a well regulated system to provide assisted conception services in Canada. There is a history of voluntary cooperation in the field, and only a relatively small and clearly identifiable number of such facilities and concerned professional organizations.

Main Topics: Preconception Arrangements

A preconception agreement is where a woman agrees to conceive and carry a pregnancy in order to hand over the child to a commissioning person to raise. Our review of the evidence shows that the potential benefits to a few individuals are far outweighed by the harms to others and to society. Commissioners believe strongly that preconception arrangements are unacceptable and should not be encouraged. Preconception arrangements commodify reproduction and children, they have the potential to exploit women's vulnerability because of race, poverty, or powerlessness and leave women open to coercion. Thus they contravene the Commission's ethical principles.

The most appropriate ways to discourage commercial preconception arrangements are by criminally prosecuting those who act as intermediaries, and by making payments for preconception arrangements illegal.

To be effective, prohibitions against preconception agreements must be national in scope and equally enforced in all areas of the country, so federal regulation is necessary. We also recommend that Canada take a lead in discouraging such practices internationally.

We recommend the interests of children born through non-commercial preconception arrangements should be protected by establishing that a child's legal mother is the woman who gives birth to the child. We recommend that the best interests of the child predominate in any dispute over custody.

Chapter 12

Questions to Consider

1.   Do ARTs increase or decrease reproductive choice for women?

2.   Should there be an age limit for access to fertility treatment? For example, with egg donation it is possible to extend a woman's reproductive potential beyond natural menopause (the time at which the woman no longer produces any eggs of her own). Should the government or the medical profession limit the age at which a woman could become pregnant using donor eggs? Would such a decision be sexist given that there is no age barrier to fertility treatments for men?

3.   Some authors have suggested that women who act as "surrogates" are like prostitutes (selling the use of their body to men), and that children born of preconception agreements who are handed over to their "social parents" are like slaves (persons sold to contracting couples). In your view, do commercial preconception agreements involve the sale of a reproductive service (nine months of gestation), or the sale of a product (the newborn)?

4.   To discourage the use of preconception agreements, the RCNRT recommends that payment for, or acting as an intermediary for, preconception agreements be legally prohibited. What are the moral arguments against this particular reproductive technology? Should practices that are morally objectionable to some (to all) be legislated against?

5.   Discuss the RCNRT's summary recommendations on IVF and preconception agreements with specific reference to the ethical framework and the guiding principles.

Further Readings

Baylis, Françoise. 1990. The ethics of ex utero research on spare "non-viable" IVF human embryos. *Bioethics* 4:311–29.

Congregation for the Doctrine of the Faith. 1987. *Instruction on respect for human life in its origin and on the dignity of procreation: Replies to certain questions of the day.* 40. Vatican City: Vatican Polyglot Press.

Corea, Gena, et al., eds. 1987. *Man-made woman.* Bloomington: Indiana University Press.

Glover, Jonathan. 1989. *Ethics of new reproductive technologies: The glover report to the European commission.* DeKalb: Northern Illinois University Press.

Lauritzen, Paul. 1990. What price parenthood? *Hastings Center Report* 20(2): 38–46.

Macklin, Ruth. 1991. Artificial means of reproduction and our understanding of the family. *Hastings Center Report* 21(1): 5–11.

Ontario Law Reform Commission. 1985. *Report on Human Artificial Reproduction and Related Matters*, Vols. I and II. Toronto: Ministry of the Attorney General.

Overall Christine, ed. 1989. *The future of human reproduction.* Toronto: The Women's Press.

Steinbock, Bonnie. 1988. Surrogate motherhood as prenatal adoption. *Law, Medicine and Health Care* 16:44–50.

Chapter 13

Withholding and Withdrawing Life-Sustaining Treatment

Chapter 13

Introduction

A 25-year-old woman suffers from irreversible paralysis from the neck down caused by a neurological disorder. She is dependent upon a respirator to keep her alive. She has been in the hospital for more than two years and thoroughly understands her medical condition and prognosis. She asks her physician to disconnect the respirator.[1]

What should the physician do? Would the answer to this question change if the patient's paralysis was permanent but the respirator dependence was only temporary? What if the patient was requesting the withdrawal of artificial hydration and nutrition rather than the withdrawal of a respirator?

An 88-year-old man has advanced metastatic cancer that is no longer responding to treatment. The health care team meets to discuss the use of CPR (cardiopulmonary resuscitation) should he go into cardiac arrest. The team leader tells the team that the chance of CPR restoring cardiac output is 10 percent and, even with CPR, the patient is expected to live no more than two days. He argues that CPR is futile and therefore a DNR (do not resuscitate) order should be placed on the man's chart without discussing it with him or his family.

What should the team do? Would the answer to this question change if the chance of CPR restoring cardiac output were 50 percent? What if, with CPR, the patient would be expected to live two weeks?

A 57-year-old woman is brought into the emergency room of a large hospital following a serious car accident. She requires an immediate blood transfusion to save her life. She is unconscious, but a living will is found in her wallet. This living will clearly states that the woman is a Jehovah's Witness and therefore rejects blood transfusions.[2]

What should the health care team do? Would the answer to this question change if the woman were conscious, competent, and fully informed about the need for a blood transfusion? What if the woman were unconscious, had no living will, and her daughter refused to consent to the transfusion on her mother's behalf?

These are the sort of questions that arise in discussions of the ethics of withholding and withdrawing life-sustaining treatment. Many attempts to answer these questions have rested upon drawing distinctions and attaching moral significance to them. Distinctions that have been thought to be important include killing versus letting die, active versus passive euthanasia, ordinary versus extraordinary treatment, futile versus non-futile treatment, and present versus prior expressions of wishes. Often, drawing distinctions has led to the drawing of moral conclusions such as the following: killing is morally unacceptable but letting die is morally acceptable; the withholding of futile treatment is morally acceptable but the withholding of non-futile treatment is morally unacceptable; and respecting present expressions of wishes is morally compulsory but respecting prior expressions of wishes is not.

Many other attempts to answer these questions have rested upon placing fundamental values on a hierarchy. Relevant values include the preservation of life, the alleviation of suffering, and respect for autonomy (self-determination).

So, for example, it might be argued that the woman in the third example should have her wishes respected because a) to do so is to allow her to die rather than to kill her and allowing someone to die is morally permissible; b) respect for autonomy is more valuable than the preservation of life; or c) prior expressions of wishes are as much an expression of autonomy as present expressions of wishes and therefore her autonomy should be respected. Alternatively, it might be argued that the woman should be given a blood transfusion because a) there is no morally significant difference between killing and allowing to die and both are morally unacceptable; b) the preservation of life is more valuable than respect for autonomy; or c) only present expressions of wishes are expressions of autonomy and therefore there is no autonomy to respect.

It might be asked, What, if anything, is the moral significance of the distinction between killing and letting die? When, if ever, can the disvalue of suffering outweigh the value of life? It is essential that the distinctions and hierarchies of value that lie beneath so many arguments be carefully examined. Only then will the answer to the question of when, if ever, it is morally permissible to withhold or withdraw life-sustaining treatment come clear.

It should be noted here that Canadian courts have recently been called upon to consider a number of cases involving the withholding and withdrawing of life-sustaining treatment. Recently, a majority of the judges on the Supreme Court of Canada sum-marized the current legal status as follows:

> Canadian courts have recognized a common law right of patients to refuse consent to medical treatment, or to demand that treatment, once commenced, be withdrawn or discontinued (*Ciarlariello v. Schacter*, [1993] 2 S.C.R. 119). This right has been specifically recognized to exist even if the withdrawal from or refusal of treatment may result in death (*Nancy B. v. Hôtel-Dieu de Québec* (1992), 86 D.L.R. (4th) 385 (Que.S.C.); *Malette v. Shulman* (1990), 72 O.R. (2d) 417 (C.A.).[3]

Therefore, it appears that withholding and withdrawing life-sustaining treatment at the request of the patient is legally permissible (indeed, in certain circumstances, is legally compulsory).

Having said this, however, it is important to note that the ethical debate is not resolved by the legal statement. First, what is legal is not always moral and vice versa. Simply because something is legally permissible or compulsory does not mean that it is morally permissible or compulsory. One classic illustration of this point is apartheid in South Africa; apartheid was legal but was (most people would agree) immoral. Second, the legal conclusions drawn by the Supreme Court of Canada are fairly general and do not always provide clear answers to specific questions. For example, is it ethically acceptable to withhold or withdraw life-sustaining treatment from incompetent individuals with no advance directives? Must treatments deemed to be "futile" by the health care team be offered to patients? Even though Canadian courts have spoken on some aspects of the issue of withholding and withdrawing life-sustaining treatment, the ethical debates continue.

The Selections

The selections in this chapter deal with a variety of issues under the broad heading of withholding and withdrawing life-sustaining treatment. Generally, they deal with the conditions under which it is ethically acceptable to withhold or withdraw life-sustaining treatment. Specifically, they deal with the following topics: a) artificial hydration and nutrition; b) futility and CPR (cardiopulmonary resuscitation); and c) advance directives (living wills and durable powers of attorney). These are three of the most hotly contested topics in this area of health care ethics today.

In the first selection, Dan Brock examines the distinctions between killing and allowing to die, causing or not causing death, and withholding ordinary or extraordinary care in the context of withholding or withdrawing life-sustaining food and water. His article is important for its thorough discussion (and ultimate rejection) of the moral significance of these distinctions and for its analysis (and again ultimate rejection) of the moral significance of the distinction between life-sustaining food and water and other forms of life-sustaining treatment.

In the second selection, Robert Truog, Allan Brett, and Joel Frader examine a specific distinction found in debates about the ethics of withholding or withdrawing life-sustaining treatment — that is, futile versus non-futile treatment. They explore this distinction in various contexts: a) patients in a persistent vegetative state; b) DNR (do not resuscitate) orders and CPR; and c) organ-replacement technology. Must all treatment requests made by the family of a patient in a persistent vegetative state be met? May a health care team declare that some treatment is futile and should therefore be withheld or withdrawn? May a patient (or surrogate) demand that CPR be provided even when the health care team believes that CPR will be futile? May a physician place a DNR order on a patient's chart without the patient's consent if she or he believes that CPR would be futile? May a health care team cite futility and unilaterally deny a terminally ill individual access to organ-replacement therapy? Truog, Brett, and Frader note that the distinction between futile and non-futile treatment is increasingly being used to ground moral conclusions — futile treatment need not be provided even upon direct request but non-futile treatment may need to be provided (or at least offered). They conclude that "the notion of futility hides many deep and serious ambiguities that threaten its legitimacy as a rationale for limiting treatment" and "the notion of futility generally fails to provide an ethically coherent ground for limiting life-sustaining treatment . . . The rapid advance of the language of futility into the jargon of bioethics should be followed by an equally rapid retreat."

In the final selection, Jocelyn Downie explores the ethical and legal status of advance directives. Advance directives are directions given by a competent individual concerning what and/or how health care decisions should be made in the event that the individual becomes incompetent to make such decisions in the future. The most common forms of advance directives are living wills (documents that set out what decisions are to be made) and durable powers of attorney for health care (documents that set out who is to make decisions). She asks whether requests for the withholding or withdrawal of life-sustaining treatment should be respected if they are made through advance directives. She also asks whether respect for such requests should be legislatively required. Downie concludes that advance directives should be respected and that such respect should be required by law.

Notes
1. This situation mirrors the Quebec Superior Court decision in *Nancy B. v. Hôtel-Dieu de Québec* (1992), 86 D.L.R. (4th) 385 (Que.S.C.).
2. This situation mirrors the Ontario Court of Appeal decision in *Malette v. Shulman* (1990), 72 O.R. (2d) 417 (C.A.).

3. *Rodriguez v. British Columbia (Attorney General)*, [1993] 3 S.C.R. 519.

References
Ciarlariello v. Schachter (1993), 2 S.C.R. 119.
Malette v. Shulman (1990), 72 O.R. (2d) 417 (C.A.).
Nancy B. v. Hôtel-Dieu de Québec (1992), 86 D.L.R. (4th) 385 (Que.S.C.).

48   Forgoing Life-Sustaining Food and Water: Is It Killing?

Dan W. Brock

The moral permissibility of patients forgoing life-sustaining medical treatment has come to be widely accepted. The issue of forgoing life-sustaining food and water, however, has only very recently gained attention in public policy discussions. One source of resistance to extending this acceptance of a general right to forgo life-sustaining treatment to the case of food and water has explicitly philosophical origins: for a physician to withhold food and water might seem to be not merely to allow the patient to die, but to kill the patient, and therefore wrong. A closely related moral worry is that for physicians to withhold food and water would be to make them the direct cause of their patients' death, which also would be wrong. And finally, many worry that providing food and water is ordinary care, not extraordinary or "heroic," and so must be obligatory.

In each case, a distinction is drawn — between killing and allowing to die, causing or not causing death, and withholding ordinary or extraordinary care — and in each case it is claimed that the former, though not the latter, is morally forbidden. I consider appeal to the intrinsic moral importance of these distinctions to be confused, both in general and as applied to food and water. In the hope of reducing the impact of these moral confusions in the policy debate about forgoing food and water, I will address here both the general meaning and the putative moral importance of these distinctions, as well as their specific application to the case of food and water. The upshot of my argument will be that forgoing food and water does not fall under any special moral prohibitions that would make it in itself morally different than the forgoing of other life-sustaining medical care. I believe that a competent patient has the moral right to forgo any life-sustaining treatment, including food and water. If the patient is incompetent, as is usually the case when forgoing food and water is seriously at issue, the surrogate's decision should reflect what the patient would have wanted if competent, or, in the absence of knowledge of the patient's preferences, reflect an assessment of the benefits and burdens to the patient.

I. Killing and Allowing to Die

Is it killing to forgo food and water? And why is that thought to be important? Since forgoing food and water is obviously behavior leading to death and is known to be such at the time it is done, why is it thought important to ask whether it is killing?

There is a common view, among physicians and much of the general public, that physicians can allow patients to die by stopping life-sustaining treatment, but they cannot kill patients. In this view, killing is wrong, and it occurs in the medical context only as a result of accident or negligence. This is to use the concept of killing normatively, to capture in the category of killings only wrongful actions leading to death. Physicians do, however, stop life-supporting treatments frequently in medical contexts, and rightly believe that they are generally justified in doing so. If they believe that killing is wrong, and occurs in medical contexts only as a result of accident or negligence, then they have a strong motive for interpreting what they do when they stop life support as allowing the patient to die, but not as killing.

I think this interpretation of all stopping of life support as allowing to die is problematic and leads in turn to worries about whether stopping life support is morally justified. Let me, therefore, address directly what the difference is between killing and allowing to die. I will offer two interpretations of that difference: on the first, most stopping of food and water — and of other life-sustaining treatments — will turn out to be killing; on the second, allowing to die.

In the first interpretation, the distinction between killing and allowing to die is the distinction between acts and omissions leading to or resulting in death. When I kill someone, I act in a way that causes that person to die when they would not otherwise have died in that way and at that time. When I allow someone to die, I omit to act in a way that I could have acted and that would have prevented that person dying then; that is, I have both the ability and the opportunity to act to prevent the death, but fail to do so.

Now suppose that the difference between killing and allowing to die is understood as we have just described it. Consider the case of ceasing respirator support: the respirator is turned off and the patient dies. Suppose this is done by a physician who believes it to be justified and who does it with the patient's consent. The patient may have asked to be allowed to die and may understand what is done as allowing him or her to die. But according to this first interpretation of the difference between killing and allowing to die, what the physician has done is to kill the patient, since in turning off the respirator he or she has acted in a way that causes the patient to die in that way and at that time. Now, is that mistaken? Is it mistaken to say that, by turning off the respirator, the physician killed the patient? Physicians, at least, do not commonly understand what they do when they turn off burdensome respirators with patients' consent as killing the patients.

To help see that this might be correctly construed as killing, consider the case of a nephew who, impatient for his uncle to die so that he can inherit the uncle's money, turns off the uncle's respirator. In this case, I think most would understand the nephew to have killed his uncle. We would take it as a piece of sophistry if the nephew defended himself by replying, "No, I merely allowed my uncle to die," or, "I didn't kill my uncle; it was the underlying disease requiring the use of a respirator that killed him."

The difference in the two cases, in my view, is not in *what* the physician as opposed to the nephew does. It is not a difference between killing and allowing to die. The difference is the presence of other morally important factors, most obviously the difference in motivations of the nephew and the physician, as well as whether the patient consented to the respirator being stopped. The difference is not that one and not the other kills, but that one and not the other kills justifiably.

Thus, if the difference between killing and allowing to die is interpreted in terms of the difference between acts and omissions resulting in death, it would seem that when one stops a life-sustaining treatment like a respirator expecting that a patient will die as a result, one thereby kills the patient. My examples also suggest that in some cases one does so with justification, in others not. But is this difference between killing and allowing to die of moral importance? Does the mere difference that one kills in one case, allows to die in the other, in *itself* make the one any more or less morally justified, or wrong, than the other?

Consider the following case:

A patient is dying from terminal cancer, undergoing great suffering that cannot be relieved without so sedating him that he is unable to relate in any way to others. This patient prepared an advance directive in an early stage of his disease indicating that in circumstances like this he wished to have his life ended either by direct means or by withdrawing life-sustaining treatment. In a recent lucid moment he reaffirmed the directive. The attending physician and the patient's family are in agreement that the patient's desire to die ought now to be granted.

Now consider two alternative conclusions to this case. In the first, while the patient is deeply sedated and not conscious, his wife places a pillow over his face and he dies peacefully from asphyxiation. In the second, while the patient is deeply sedated and not conscious, he develops severe respiratory difficulty requiring emergency professional intervention and use of a respirator if he is to live. His wife knows this, is present, and decides not to call the professional staff and thereby not to employ the respirator. Her goal is to allow him to die. The patient dies peacefully.

Suppose we still understand the difference between *killing* and *allowing to die* in terms of acts and omissions resulting in death. In the first outcome, the patient is killed by his spouse, while in the second outcome, the spouse decides not to treat or not to seek treatment and thereby allows him to die. Is there any reason why what the wife does in the first instance is morally (as opposed to legally) worse or different from what she does in the second instance? If not, then what one does if one kills is *in itself* no worse morally than if one allows to die. Of course a particular act of killing may be worse, when other features of the action are considered, than a particular allowing to die. But so also some allowings to die may be morally worse, all things considered, than some killings. And if the mere fact that in one case a person kills, in another allows to die, is not itself a difference of moral significance, then it is also not morally important whether stopping a respirator is interpreted as killing or as allowing to die. Some instances of killing and of allowing to die will be morally wrong; some of each will be morally justified. That what one does is to kill or to allow to die will usually count as a moral reason against doing it; which it is considered to be, however, will not make what one does more or less justified or wrong. Other factors, such as whether the patient consents, and what sort of life could otherwise be offered, will morally differentiate particular killings and allowings to die.[1]

The act/omission difference is the first interpretation of how killing differs from allowing to die, and on that interpretation, as I have briefly argued, killing is not morally worse in itself than allowing to die. There remains, nevertheless, strong resistance to accepting that physicians kill when they stop life-sustaining treatment, as follows on the act/omission interpretation. I have already noted one reason for this resistance: if killing is understood as a normative category, referring only to wrongful actions leading to death, then physicians quite justifiably do not want to understand what they do as killing and therefore wrongful when they stop life-sustaining treatment. They are quite correct that it need not be morally wrong.

There is a second reason for resistance to understanding stopping life-support treatment as killing, and that is a different interpretation of the difference between killing and allowing to die. Very loosely, the distinction is this. If you kill someone, what you do is to initiate a deadly causal process that leads to the person's death. If you allow someone to die, you allow a deadly causal process which you did not initiate to proceed to its result of a person's death.[2] One way to allow to die is simply to omit to act in a way that would have prevented the death. That is an allowing to die on the act/omission understanding of the killing/allowing to die distinction. But another way to allow to die is to act in a way that allows some deadly causal process, which at present is halted, to follow out its course so as to result in death.

Let me say a little bit more about this second way of allowing to die, since it is essential to the common understanding of stopping life support as allowing to die. Why does a physician who stops a respirator allow a patient to die in this account of allowing to die? There is a life-sustaining process in place — the respirator. There is a deadly disease process present which requires the use of a life-sustaining respirator, and which is, in effect, being held in abeyance by the use of the respirator. By the positive action of turning off the respirator, the physician then stops that life-sustaining process and allows the deadly disease process to proceed; the physician thereby allows the patient, as it is often put, to die of the underlying disease. Now, in this account of the killing/allowing to die distinction, the physician does allow the patient to die when there is an independent underlying disease process which is being held in abeyance and the physician takes positive action to remove the system which is holding that underlying disease process in abeyance.

But what about our earlier greedy nephew? In this account of allowing to die, doesn't he too, like the physician, allow to die? Doesn't he do the same as the physician does, though with different motives? He too merely allows the disease process to proceed to conclusion. Proponents of this second interpretation of the kill/allow to die distinction will be hard pressed to avoid accepting that the nephew allows to die, though they can add that he does so unjustifiably. Some will take this implication for the greedy nephew case to show that this second interpretation of the kill/allow to die difference is not preferable to the first act/omission interpretation after all.

There is not space here to argue that the difference between killing and allowing to die on this second interpretation of the distinction also lacks moral importance. I believe that is so, and that pairs of examples similar to the one cited above for the act/omission interpretation can be constructed to show that.

With these two interpretations of the killing/allowing to die distinction now before us, we are finally in a position to consider whether forgoing food and water is killing. Suppose that a decision has been made not to feed a patient and that the choice has been made according to sound procedures and in circumstances in which all concerned agree this course is morally justified. All further feedings are omitted and the patient dies of dehydration or malnutrition. But then the question is raised whether what was done killed the patient or allowed him to die. Since we have already noted more than one interpretation of that difference, we know the question is more complex than it might seem. On the act/omission interpretation of the difference, since we have said that feedings were omitted, it would seem that the patient was allowed to die. On the other hand, if, for example, IV's were in place and a physician had to take positive action to remove them, it would seem we then have an action leading to death, and so a killing. This shows the difficulty in practice of applying the kill/allow to die distinction in its act/omission interpretation. But it also displays the lack of any moral significance in this difference between killing and allowing to die. Suppose that just before the physician enters the patient's room to remove the IV, it falls out on its own, and upon seeing this the physician then deliberately omits to reinsert it so that the patient may die. Could there really be any moral importance attached to whether the physician removes the IV or fails to reinsert it in this case?

To think of omitting to feed the patient as allowing him to die is in keeping with common understandings of related cases. Suppose you consciously omit to send food to persons whom you know are starving in a famine in some distant land. The famine victims die. No one would say that you killed them by not sending food, but rather that you allowed them to die (whether or not you were morally wrong to have done so). Why do some persons, nevertheless, want to use the more active concept of killing and to say that one kills by denying food and water in the medical context? One reason lies in the confusion of thinking that one more strongly morally condemns what is done by calling it killing. If I am correct that killing is in itself no worse than allowing to die, but instead other factors morally differentiate actual killings and allowings to die, then withholding feeding is no worse morally for being killing instead of allowing to die.

There is a second reason why some persons might understand denying food and water to a patient as killing, and it reveals a further complexity in our moral thinking about this issue. I think the clue here is found in the naturalness of speaking of *denying* food and water to the patient. To speak in terms of denying food and water is implicitly to assume that giving food and water in a medical context of patient care is the expected course of events. It is seen as statistically expected, as what is standardly done, or, perhaps at least as important, as what is morally required. It is assumed that the statistically and morally expected course of events is that patients will be given the basic care of food and water, that this is part of the health care professional's moral obligation to care for the patient. If so, then if some patient is not to receive food and water, someone must actively intervene to stop this normal course of events. The decision to omit to give food and water is seen as an active intervention in the normal caring process, making death occur when it would not otherwise have occurred. And so this positive decision not to feed, even if resulting in an omission to feed, is seen as killing. It is important to understand, however, that this line of reasoning gains its plausibility from standard cases in which the patient is able to eat and drink in normal ways and is clearly benefited by being provided with food and fluids. In those cases, providing food and fluids is both statistically and morally expected. In other cases, however, pro-viding food and fluids requires sophisticated medical procedures, for example, total par-enteral nutrition, and may not be of benefit to the patient; then, the assumption that feeding is either statistically or morally expected may be unwarranted. But without that assumption, omitting to feed should not be understood as an active denial of nutrition and therefore as killing.[3]

Some commentators have cited a further reason why stopping feeding, unlike stopping most other forms of life-sustaining treatment, is not allowing to die on the second interpretation I offered above of the killing/allowing to die difference.[4] In that inter-pretation, we allow to die when, by act or omission, we allow a deadly disease process that is being held in abeyance by a life-sustaining treatment to proceed to death. For example, when a respirator is withdrawn, the patient is allowed to die of the underlying disease requiring use of a respirator. But when food and water are withheld, it is said, we introduce a *new* process — that of dehydration or malnutrition — which will result in death. The patient dies from this new causal process we introduce, not from any already present fatal disease process that was being held in abeyance by a life-sustaining treatment. We thereby kill the patient. However, this line of reasoning appears to be mistaken.

Whenever a disease process attacks a patient's normal ability to eat and drink, and artificial means of providing nutrition are required, then feeding by artificial means can be seen as a form of life-sustaining treatment. Forgoing feeding when IV's, nasogastric tubes, and so forth, are required is then to forgo employment of a life-sustaining treat-ment — artificial provision of nutrition — and to allow the patient to die from a disease that has impaired his normal ability to eat and drink. It would seem to be only when the patient's normal human ability to take in nutrition is unimpaired, and a decision is then made not to sustain life and so to stop feeding, that a new fatal process is introduced as opposed to withdrawing a life-sustaining treatment and letting the disease process proceed to death. The vast majority of cases of forgoing food and fluids in the medical context are of the former sort, and so constitute allowing to die, not killing, on the second interpretation of that distinction.

Let me summarize my discussion up to here, since the analysis has become rather complicated. (In my defense, I believe that this complexity is not merely the result of philosophers making simple matters appear complex, but arises instead from existing complexities and confusions in common, nonphilosophical thinking on these issues.) Does one kill, or does one allow to die, by forgoing food and water? On the act/omission interpretation of the difference between killing and allowing to die, one kills if the forgoing involves a positive action to stop feeding, allows to die if one only omits to feed. In cases in which the expected course of events is feeding, any forgoing of feeding, even if it results in an omission to feed, can be seen as actively intervening to change that course of events, and so as killing; however, in many actual forgoings of food and fluids it cannot be assumed that feeding is either the statistically or the morally expected course of events. I have also argued that the difference between killing and allowing to die on its act/omission interpretation is of no moral importance, and so whether forgoing food and water is in any instance morally justified will turn entirely on other matters than whether it is killing as opposed to allowing to die.

In the second interpretation of the kill/allow to die difference, stopping a life-support system like a respirator is understood as allowing the patient to die from the underlying disease process held in abeyance by the respirator. But to forgo food and water is generally to stop the life-sustaining artificial provision of nutrition and to allow the patient to die of the underlying disease process that has impaired his normal human ability to eat and drink; thus, it too is usually to allow to die. However, I have also suggested, though not argued, that, on this second interpretation as well, whether any instance of forgoing food and water is morally justified turns entirely on other questions than whether it is killing as opposed to allowing to die.

II. Cause of Death

I turn now to a related confusion in much discussion of forgoing life-sustaining treatment that concerns a different aspect of the issue about the cause of death than that discussed above. It is related because many persons hold that to stop a life-support process such as feeding is to kill, because one directly causes the patient's death, whereas, when one allows to die, it is the underlying disease process, not the physician, that causes the patient's death.

Questions of causality are exceedingly difficult and complex, but I will try at least briefly to illuminate two important confusions about causing death prominent in discussions about life-sustaining treatment generally, and relevant to forgoing food and water in particular. Consider what can be called a "but-for" sense of causality: but for this, that wouldn't have occurred; but for Jones poisoning the food Smith later ate, Smith would not have died. Consider our greedy nephew again. But for his turning off the respirator, his uncle wouldn't have died: the nephew, therefore, causes the uncle's death. As I suggested above, it would be absurd for the nephew to assert, "No, not I but the underlying disease caused my uncle's death." Now consider the physician who seemingly does the same thing and stops the patient's respirator: he too satisfies the "but-for" condition for the patient's death. But for the physician's stopping the respirator, the patient would not have died; the physician causes the patient's death. Finally, consider stopping feeding. But for that, the patient would not have died; the physician's withholding food and water causes the patient's death.

What I have called a "but-for" sense of causality is *not* by itself an adequate account of ordinary attributions of causality. There, one who kills another (e.g., by giving poisoned food) is considered the cause of the other's death, whereas one who allows another to die (e.g., by not providing food to a famine victim) is not generally said to have caused the other's death. The point is that the broader "but-for" sense of causality seems to provide the necessary control over the outcomes of what a person does ("does" interpreted broadly to include both acts and omissions) to allow ascription of at least prima facie moral responsibility to the person for the outcomes. And the "but-for" causality condition for the death is satisfied both when one kills and when one allows to die, and equally by the greedy nephew, the physician stopping the respirator, and the physician stopping feeding. Why then should we mark any moral difference in these cases because of supposed causal differences when the "but-for" sense of causality is equally satisfied in all of them?

I will consider two responses to my claim that there is no morally important causal difference in these cases, each of which, I think, brings out something interesting about causing death, and about why causal talk is often confusing in this area. The first response is associated with talk of "merely prolonging the dying process," and goes like this: If a patient is terminally ill, then a physician who stops the patient's life-sustaining treatment neither kills nor allows him to die. The physician doesn't kill him; rather, the fatal disease does (more on this shortly). Nor does the physician allow him to die, because to allow someone to die it has to be possible for you to save the person; if the patient is terminally ill, you couldn't save him. So on this response, there's nothing the physician does that causes death, nothing that but for doing it the patient would live. There is more than one confusion in this response. Surely one *can* either kill or not save a terminally ill person. When one either kills or allows to die, what one does causes death in the "but-for" sense of causality. This can only mean that one causes a patient to die *at a particular time* (and, to avoid certain complications of causal over-determination, in a particular way). No one ever prevents someone's death completely, without any qualifications to its being at a particular time (or in a particular way), because we can't make anyone immortal. What we do is to make or allow death to occur earlier than it otherwise would have done, and in that sense what we do does causally affect the person's death, whether or not the person was terminally ill.

It is worth noting that the claim that a physician is never a "but-for" cause of the patient's death would not help in some important cases of stopping food and water even if it was itself sound. I have in mind, especially, permanently unconscious patients who are usually not terminally ill in any plausible sense of "terminally ill." These patients can, and often do, survive for many years in that state. This ought to give some pause to the many commentators who seem prepared to agree that stopping food and water, or for that matter stopping other life-sustaining treatment, can only be justified if the patient is terminally ill.[5] If one believes, as I do, that stopping life-sustaining treatment, including food and water, can be morally permissible with permanently unconscious patients, then one should not endorse a restriction to stopping that treatment only with terminally ill patients.

Let me turn to a second response to my suggestions that it is a broad "but-for" sense of causality that is relevant to moral responsibility for outcomes, and that on this account physicians *do* cause death when they stop life-sustaining food and water or respirators. Consider the legal inquiry into the patient's cause of death. In the case of stopping a life-sustaining respirator, the cause of death would commonly be identified as the underlying disease which resulted in death once the patient was taken off the respirator. Doesn't this suggest that I am mistaken in identifying the physician and what he does as causing death? I think not, and that is because the inquiry into the cause of death is somewhat more complex than it may look at first. It is not simply an empirical inquiry into what conditions played a causal role in the death. It is in part an empirical or factual inquiry of this sort, but it is shaped as well by normative concerns; these are legal concerns when it is a legal inquiry, moral concerns when it is a moral inquiry.

The inquiry into the cause of death is, roughly, something like this: We take all the factors which are "but-for" causes, but for these factors the patient would not have died in that way and at that time. There will be a great many such factors, and we do not actually assemble them all, but rather restrict our selection of the cause from among them. On what basis do we select *the* cause of death from among all the "but-for" causes? We do not do it solely on empirical or factual grounds, we also consider normative grounds. We ask, for example, in the legal inquiry: Among the "but-for" causes, is there anyone who acted in a legally prohibited role with whom the law then wants to concern itself? And we can ask an analogous question in a moral inquiry: Among the "but-for" causes, is there anyone whose action was morally impermissible? This helps to explain "cause of death talk" in our earlier two cases in which respirators were stopped by a physician and by a greedy nephew. The action of each is a "but-for" cause of the patient's death. The physician's action, however, is within a legally protected role. He acts in accordance with a competent patient's right to refuse even life-sustaining treatment, and so the law does not single him out for further concerns when he stops the respirator. The greedy nephew, on the other hand, acts in a legally prohibited role, since (among other things) he acted without the patient's consent, and so the law is concerned further with him. This difference is reflected in our holding the greedy nephew to be the cause of death, while in the case of the physician who also stopped a life-sustaining respirator, the patient's underlying disease is held to be the cause of death.[6]

If this is correct, then it should be no surprise that there is uncertainty and controversy about whether the physician who withholds food and water is the cause of the patient's death. That is a reflection of the uncertainty and controversy that exists about whether stopping food and water is legally and/or morally permissible. If we reach greater agreement on those questions, then it will become clearer whether the physician who stops food and water should be held to be *the* cause of the patient's death. But then it will be the legal and moral permissibility helping determine what or who is *the* cause of death, not whether the physician is the cause being a determinant of legal and moral permissibility.

III. "Ordinary" and "Extraordinary" Treatment

I turn finally to the distinction between ordinary and extraordinary or heroic treatment. Those who employ this distinction usually understand the provision of extraordinary treatment as optional and the provision of ordinary treatment as obligatory. This distinction is most often employed in the case of incompetent patients unable to decide for themselves about treatment. And it may seem especially important to the stopping of food and water, since if any care is ordinary, food and water would seem to be. But what is the ordinary/extraordinary difference? Some understand it to be the degree to which the treatment is (statistically) usual or unusual; others, the degree of invasiveness of treatment; others, the extent to which sophisticated, high technology or artificial treatment is employed; and so forth.

None of these differences, however, are in themselves morally important differences between treatments which could justify distinguishing some as morally obligatory, others as optional. If we understand extraordinary treatments instead as those excessively burdensome to the patient, then we do have a difference of obvious moral importance (and, I believe, the meaning the distinction had in its origin within Catholic moral theology). But to determine whether any treatment is excessively burdensome, those burdens must be weighed against the benefits of the treatment in order to judge whether the burdens are worth undergoing. In this interpretation, whether a treatment is ordinary or extraordinary is determined by an assessment of its benefits and burdens. And then, contrary to initial appearances, even providing food and water may be extraordinary care in those few cases in which the burdens of doing so exceed the benefits.

The point I want to press is that the classification of treatments as ordinary or extraordinary now is doing no work in the reasoning about whether the treatment may be withheld. What is doing all the work in the reasoning is the assessment of the benefits and burdens of the treatment. Only when that assessment has been made, and the burdens judged excessive given the benefits, do we label the treatment extraordinary. We put the label on after the analysis has been completed, and so the labelling of treatments as ordinary and extraordinary adds nothing to the analysis — except confusion. It adds confusion because the difference is so often understood not in terms of the benefits and burdens of treatment, but in one of the senses I noted earlier such as the usualness or artificiality of treatment. Given these multiple understandings, and the fact that the ordinary/extraordinary difference adds nothing of substance to the reasoning about forgoing life-sustaining treatment, I believe we do best to avoid its use.

Conclusions

I will conclude with two points. The first is that I believe the ordinary/extraordinary distinction in its "excessively burdensome" interpretation does at least point to the correct reasoning in decisions about forgoing food and water. It directs us to assess whether the benefits to a patient from continuing food and water outweigh the burdens, given that patient's particular circumstances. It is my view that there are at least some few cases where it may be that the burdens do outweigh the benefits.

Second, I want to emphasize that I have focused only on a few of the moral complexities and confusions about forgoing life-sustaining treatment in general and about forgoing life-sustaining food and water in particular. There are other difficult moral issues involved, such as the relevance of the economic cost and of the effects on persons other than the patient of feeding or forgoing feeding, which I have not addressed. Moreover, sound public policy should reflect additional considerations, such as slippery slope worries about abuse, the symbolic importance of providing food and water, and how authorization to deny it may affect our care of other potentially vulnerable populations. My concern here has been only with a few of the underlying moral considerations which ought to inform public policy in this area.

Notes

1. I discuss and defend the assumptions in this argument from example further in "Taking Human Life," *Ethics* 95:851–865 (1985), from which my example is drawn. Other arguments to the same effect can be found in James Rachels, "Active and Passive Euthanasia," *N. Engl. J. Med.* 292:75–80 (1975); Michael Tooley, "Defense of Abortion and Infanticide," in *The Problem of Abortion*, Joel Feinberg, ed., Belmont, CA: Wadsworth Publishing Co. (1973), at 84–86; and Jonathan Bennett, "Morality and Consequences," in *The Tanner Lectures on Human Value II*, S.M. McMurrin, ed., Salt Lake City: University of Utah Press (1981), at 45–116.

2. The Appellate Court in *Conroy* tried to rely on such a distinction. *In re* Conroy, 464 A.2d 303, 315 (N.J. Super. A.D. 1983).

3. Whether tube feedings are part of expected care is an unsettled issue. See results of a survey of physicians in chapter 4 *supra*. See also an Australian perspective, W.J. Quilty, "Ethics of Extraordinary Nutritional Support," *J. Am. Geriatr. Soc.* 23:12–13 (1984).

4. See, e.g., *In re* Conroy, 90 N.J. Super. 453, 464 A.2d 303 (1983), *rev'd*, 98 N.J. 321, 486 A.2d 1209 (1985).

5. See, e.g., chapter 26 *supra*.

6. *In re* Bartling, 209 Cal. Rptr. 220 (1984). *In re* Quinlan, 70 N.J. 10, 355 A.2d 647, *cert. denied*, 429 U.S. 922 (1976); and Superintendent of Belchertown State School v. Saikewicz, 373 Mass. 728, 370 N.E.2d 417 (1977).

49   The Problem with Futility

Robert D. Truog, Allan S. Brett & Joel Frader

"Futility" is one of the newest additions to the lexicon of bioethics. Physicians, ethicists, and members of the media are increasingly concerned about patients and families who insist on receiving life-sustaining treatment that others judge to be futile. A clear understanding of futility has proved to be elusive, however. Many clinicians view futility the way one judge viewed pornography: they may not be able to define it, but they know it when they see it.[1]

The notion of futile medical treatment may go back to the time of Hippocrates, who allegedly advised physicians "to refuse to treat those who are overmastered by their disease, realizing that in such cases medicine is powerless."[2] More recently, the concept has appeared frequently in court decisions and policy statements.[3-6] The so-called Baby Doe law exempts physicians from providing treatment that would be "virtually futile."[7] The Council on Ethical and Judicial Affairs of the American Medical Association (AMA) recently concluded that physicians have no obligation to obtain consent for a do-not-resuscitate (DNR) order when cardiopulmonary resuscitation (CPR) is deemed futile.[8] The fact that this concept has appeared in law and policy may seem to indicate that it is clearly understood and widely accepted. In reality, however, the notion of futility hides many deep and serious ambiguities that threaten its legitimacy as a rationale for limiting treatment.

Paradigms of Futility

Contemporary discussions of futility have centered primarily on cases involving patients in a persistent vegetative state and those involving the use of CPR. A third type of case, involving organ-replacement technology, has received little attention but is helpful to our understanding of futility.

Futility and the Persistent Vegetative State

The first type of scenario involving the question of futility is represented by the recent Minnesota case of Helga Wanglie.[9] Mrs. Wanglie was an 86-year-old woman who had been dependent on mechanical ventilation and in a persistent vegetative state for more than a year. Her husband insisted that she believed in maintaining life at all cost, and that "when she was ready to go . . . the good Lord would call her."[10] Her physicians, on the other hand, believed that the continued use of mechanical ventilation and intensive care was futile. When attempts to transfer her elsewhere failed, they sought to have a court appoint an independent conservator with responsibility for making medical decisions on her behalf. The judge denied this petition and reaffirmed the authority of her husband as legal surrogate. Three days later, Mrs. Wanglie died.

Cases like that of Mrs. Wanglie seldom reach the courts, but they are probably not rare. A similar case involving a child with severe brain damage was concluded with a settlement favorable to the family before a judicial decision.[11]

Futility in Cases Involving CPR

The second prototypical scenario involves the use of DNR orders. Although the techniques of CPR were originally intended only for use after acute, reversible cardiac arrests, the current practice is to use CPR in all situations unless there is a direct order to the contrary. Since cardiac arrest is the final event in all terminal illness, everyone is eventually a candidate for this medical procedure. DNR orders were developed to spare patients from aggressive attempts at revival when imminent death is anticipated and inevitable. Nevertheless, patients or families sometimes request CPR even when care givers believe such attempts would be futile. Some have argued that in these circumstances a physician should be able to enact a DNR order without the consent of the patient of family.[12–14]

Futility and Organ-Replacement Technology

Although the bioethical debate over the question of futility has been most concerned with cases involving CPR and the treatment of patients in a persistent vegetative state, a third type of futility-related judgment has gone essentially unchallenged. It involves the increasingly large number of interventions that could possibly prolong the life of virtually any dying patient. For example, extracorporeal membrane oxygenation can replace heart and lung function for up to several weeks. Physicians now use this intervention when they expect organ systems eventually to recover or while they await organs for transplantation. However, it could prolong the life of almost anyone with cardiorespiratory failure, reversible or not. Patients thus kept alive may remain conscious and capable of communicating. Care givers do not now offer this therapy to terminally ill patients, presumably because it would be futile. This judgment has gone largely unchallenged, yet it is not obvious why a clinician's unilateral decision not to use "futile" extracorporeal membrane oxygenation is inherently different from a decision not to use "futile" CPR or "futile" intensive care. If all three treatments can be characterized as objectively futile, then unilateral decisions not to offer them should be equally justified.

As it is used in these three cases, the concept of futility obscures many ambiguities and assumptions. These can be usefully grouped into two categories: problems of value and problems of probability.

Futility and Values

It is meaningless simply to say that an intervention is futile; one must always ask, "Futile in relations to what?" The medical literature provides many examples in which the importance of identifying the goals of treatment has not been fully appreciated. The effectiveness of CPR, for example, is often discussed in terms of whether patients who require the procedure can survive long enough to be discharged from the hospital.[15] This definition of success usually implies that short-term survival is a goal not worth pursuing. Patients or family members may value the additional hours of life differently, however. Indeed, physicians and other care givers have repeatedly been shown to be poor judges of patients' preferences with regard to intensive care.[16–18]

Schneiderman and colleagues have argued that treatments that merely preserve permanent unconsciousness or that cannot end dependence on intensive medical care should be considered futile.[19] Although society may eventually endorse decisions to override the previously expressed wishes of patients or the desires of surrogates who demand such treatments, it does not follow that the treatments are futile. Mr. Wanglie would have rejected this conclusion, and there is no reason to dismiss his view out of hand. The decision that certain goals are not worth pursuing is best seen as involving a conflict of values rather than a question of futility.

Certainly in this context, the plurality of values in our society makes agreement on the concept of futility difficult if not impossible. Several groups have therefore attempted to arrive at a value-free understanding of the concept.[20,21] The most promising thus far is the notion of "physiologic futility." As the guidelines on the termination of life-sustaining treatment prepared by the Hastings Center state, if a treatment is "clearly futile in achieving its physiological objective and so offer[s] no physiological benefit to the patient, the professional has no obligation to provide it."[20] For example, the physiologic objective of mechanical ventilation is to maintain adequate ventilation and oxygenation in the presence of respiratory failure, and the physiologic objective of CPR is to maintain adequate cardiac output and respiration in the presence of cardiorespiratory failure. The New York State Task Force on Life and the Law mistakenly concludes that CPR is physiologically futile when it will "be unsuccessful in restoring cardiac and respiratory function or [when] the patient will experience repeated arrest in a short time period before death occurs."[21] CPR is physiologically futile only when it is impossible to perform effective cardiac massage and ventilation (such as in the presence of cardiac rupture or severe outflow obstruction). Saying that CPR is physiologically futile when it will be unsuccessful in restoring cardiac function is like saying that mechanical ventilation is physiologically futile if it cannot restore respiratory function. The immediate physiologic effect of the intervention differs from the broader and more uncertain question of prognosis.

Physiologic futility, understood in narrow terms, comes close to providing a value-free understanding of futility. Unfortunately, it applies to a very small number of real cases involving CPR. Similarly, since in the case of Mrs. Wanglie mechanical ventilation could maintain adequate oxygenation and ventilation, her treatment could not be considered futile in the physiologic sense. Even the use of extracorporeal membrane oxygenation in terminally ill patients cannot be considered physiologically futile, since it can maintain circulation and ventilation. The concept of physiologic futility therefore falls short of providing guidance in most cases resembling those described above.

Futility and Statistical Uncertainty

In most medical situations, there is no such thing as never. Futility is almost always a matter of probability. But what statistical cutoff point should be chosen as the threshold for determining futility? The statement from the Council on Ethical and Judicial Affairs of the AMA concludes that physicians have no obligation to provide futile CPR, but it fails to specify any level of statistical certainty at which the judgment is warranted.[8] The AMA statement fails to acknowledge that this is even an issue. Should each physician decide independently what probability of success should be considered to indicate futility?

Even if we could agree on a statistical cutoff point for determining futility, physicians are often highly unreliable in estimating the likelihood of success of a therapeutic intervention. Psychological research[22,23] has shown that estimates of probability are susceptible to "severe and systematic errors."[22] Empirical studies have corroborated the limitations of clinical assessment in estimating both prognosis[24] and diagnosis.[25] Even in theory, statistical inferences about what might happen to groups of patients do not permit accurate predictions of what will happen to the next such patient. In addition, the tendency to remember cases that are unusual or bizarre predisposes physicians to make decisions on the basis of their experiences with "miraculous" cures or unexpected tragedies.

Schneiderman and colleagues recently argued that a treatment should be considered futile when 100 consecutive patients do not respond to it.[19] But how similar must the patients be? In assessing the efficacy of mechanical ventilation to treat pneumonia, for example, is it sufficient to recall the 100 most recent patients who received artificial ventilation for pneumonia? Or must this group be stratified according to age, etiologic organism, or coexisting illness? Clearly, many of these factors will make an important difference.

Futility and Resource Allocation

Although medical practice has increasingly emphasized patients' autonomy, there is growing pressure on physicians to slow the increase in health care costs by foreclosing some options. Thus, we have a tension between the value of autonomy, exercised in the form of consent to use or omit various interventions, and the desirability of a more Spartan approach to the consumption of medical resources. We promote patients' freedom to request whatever the medical menu has to offer, but we also require that interventions be guided by considerations of cost and the likelihood of benefit.[26] Unfortunately, there is no consensus about what constitutes a just method of balancing the preferences of individual patients against the diverse needs of society.

To some, the concept of futility provides at least a partial solution to this dilemma: it offers a reason to limit therapy without the need to define a fair procedure for allocating resources. This approach allows treatment to be denied on the grounds that they are simply not indicated, apart from the matter of cost. Despite its attractions, there are good reasons why we should not use this concept to solve problems of allocation.

First, arguments based on the futility concept conceal many statistical and value-laden assumptions, whereas strategies based on resource allocation force these assumptions to be stated explicitly. Societies may choose to limit the use of therapies that may be of value and have a reasonable likelihood of success in some cases. For example, the much discussed Oregon plan for allocating Medicaid funds[27] seeks to reflect community values in ranking various health care goals (placing preventive care ahead of cosmetic surgery, for example). Since rationing policies make explicit the values and probabilities that futility-based arguments leave implicit, it is clearly preferable to develop and adopt them rather than use futility arguments as a cover for limiting the availability of scarce and expensive resources.

Another problem with invoking the idea of futility in the debate over allocation is that we have no reason to believe that it is applicable in enough cases to make a difference in the scarcity of medical resources. Although it may be true that beds in the intensive care unit (especially those used for extracorporeal membrane oxygenation) are relatively scarce, it seems unlikely that patients similar to Helga Wanglie occupy an important fraction of those beds, let alone account for a major proportion of the cost of medical care in the United States. From a macroeconomic perspective at least, we must remain skeptical that an appeal to the idea of futility will get us very far.

Moving beyond Futility

Our rejection of futility as a useful concept does not imply that we endorse patients' unrestricted demands for interventions such as those described in our prototypical scenarios. On the contrary, when providers oppose such demands they are usually acting from a profound sense that further treatment would be fundamentally wrong. Our task is to take account of that sense of wrongness without resorting to unilateral, provider-initiated declarations of futility.

In many of the situations in which questions of futility arise, providers believe that the treatment in question would not be in the patient's interests, even from the patient's perspective, and that any insistence by the patient (or surrogate) on further interventions is based on faulty reasoning, unrealistic expectations, or psychological factors, such as denial or guilt. In these circumstances, providers are obligated to make every effort to clarify precisely what the patient intends to achieve with continued treatment. If the patient's goals appear to reflect unrealistic expectations about the probable course of the underlying illness or the probable effect of medical interventions, providers should attempt to correct those impressions. Because inadequate or insensitive communication by providers probably accounts for a substantial proportion of unrealistic requests, such discussions will successfully resolve many conflicts.[14,28] Empirical studies of ethics consultations have demonstrated precisely this point.[29,30]

Although this appeal to the patient's interests may seem to contain some of the same ambiguities as arguments using the concept of futility, there is a subtle but important distinction between the two. Judgments about what is in the patient's interest are properly grounded in the patient's perspective, whereas judgments cast in the language of futility falsely assume that there is an objective and dispassionate standard for determining benefits and burdens. Nevertheless, even after providers make sustained attempts to clarify patients' preferences, some patients or surrogates will continue to demand life-sustaining interventions when the care givers feel deeply troubled about providing them. In many such cases, unrestrained deference to the wishes of the patient or surrogate conflicts with two other values that do not require a unilateral judgment of the futility of treatment: professional ideals and social consensus.

The ideals of medical professionals include respect for patients' wishes, to be sure, but they also include other values, such as compassionate action and the minimization of suffering. Consider, for example, a bedridden victim of multiple strokes who has contractures and bedsores and who "communicates" only by moaning or grimacing when she is touched. Physicians asked to perform chest compressions, institute mechanical ventilation, or use other life-sustaining interventions in such a patient may regard these actions as cruel and inhumane.[31] Moreover, physicians and other care givers have a legitimate interest in seeing that their knowledge and skills are used wisely and effectively. For example, if surgeons were repeatedly pressured to perform operations that they believed to be inappropriate, they would certainly suffer a loss of dignity and sense of purpose. Although appealing to professional ideals can serve as a convenient means of protecting the interests of physicians at the expense of patients' values, these ideals are legitimate factors to weigh against other values. To dismiss this perspective as irrelevant in decision making is to deny an essential part of what it means to practice medicine.

Although we believe that health care professionals should not be required to take part in care that violates their own morals, the law in this area remains uncertain.

On the one hand, courts have upheld a state interest in protecting the ethical integrity of the medical profession. This may provide some basis for protecting doctors who wish to refrain from cruel or inhumane treatment, despite the wishes of the patient or surrogate.[32] On the other hand, in the two cases that have led to court decisions (those of Helga Wanglie[3] and of Jane Doe in Atlanta[33]) the judges upheld the surrogates' decision-making authority. Clearly, this area of the law remains to be defined.

Finally, social consensus is yet another expression of the values at stake in some medical decisions. In a pluralistic society, differences in personal values and interests occasionally run so deep that they cannot be resolved by the introduction of additional facts or by further private debate. At certain critical junctures, the resolution of these conflicts may require an explicit public process of social decision making.[34] Social consensus has been sought, for example, to address the issue of fair allocation of resources.[27] The involvement of society is also essential when the most highly charged questions of morality are at stake, as in the increasingly heated debate over euthanasia.[35]

In the prototypical scenarios described at the outset of this article, an ongoing attempt to achieve social consensus is perhaps most conspicuous with regard to the prolongation of life for patients in a persistent vegetative state. From a legal perspective, the relevant decisions began with the case of Karen Quinlan[36] and have extended through that of Nancy Cruzan.[37] These cases have increased awareness of the ethical issues raised by the situation of patients in a persistent vegetative state and have helped to consolidate the view that it is acceptable to withdraw life-sustaining treatment from patients in such a state. Controversy does remain about who has the ultimate authority to make these decisions. Some hold that the choice must remain with the patient or surrogate, whereas others believe that under some circumstances this prerogative may be overridden. For example, the Hastings Center[38] and the Society of Critical Care Medicine[39] have concluded that providing intensive care to patients in a persistent vegetative state is generally a misuse of resources, and the President's Commission stated that such patients should be removed from life support if such action is necessary to benefit another patient who is not in a persistent vegetative state.[40] It is unclear how this debate will conclude, but the confluence of medical, legal, and ethical thinking about the persistent vegetative state is an example of how social consensus may evolve.

In summary, the Wanglie case demonstrates how the resolution of these conflicts must proceed on many levels. Most such cases will benefit from sustained attempts to clarify the patient's values and the likelihood of the various relevant outcomes, and to improve communication with patients or their surrogates. When this approach fails, physicians and other care givers should ask themselves whether the care requested is consistent with their professional ethics and ideals. When these ideals appear to be violated, either alternative venues for such care should be found or the conflict should be addressed in a public forum. This broader review could be provided through institutional mechanisms, such as the hospital's ethics committee, or by the courts. The public scrutiny that attends such cases will further the debate over the appropriate use of medical resources and foster the development of consensus through legislation and public policy.

Conclusion

In outlining the perspectives of the principal stakeholders — patients and their surrogates, physicians, and society — we have avoided the construction of a rigid formula for resolving conflicts over interventions frequently regarded as futile. Because of clinical heterogeneity, pluralistic values, and the evolutionary nature of social consensus, most clinical decision making on behalf of critically ill patients defies reduction to universally applicable principles.

The notion of futility generally fails to provide an ethically coherent ground for limiting life-sustaining treatment, except in circumstances in which narrowly defined physiologic futility can be plausibly invoked. Futility has been conceptualized as an objective entity independent of the patient's or surrogate's perspective, but differences in values and the variable probabilities of clinical outcomes undermine its basis. Furthermore, assertions of futility may camouflage judgments of comparative worth that are implicit in debates about the allocation of resources. In short, the problem with futility is that its promise of objectivity can rarely be fulfilled. The rapid advance of the language of futility into the jargon of bioethics should be followed by an equally rapid retreat.

References

1. Jacobellis v. State of Ohio. 84 S Ct 1676 (1964).
2. Hippocrates. The art. In: Reiser SJ, Dyck AJ, Curran WJ, eds. Ethics in medicine: historical perspectives and contemporary concerns. Cambridge, Mass: MIT Press 1977: 6–7.
3. Capon AM. In: re Helga Wanglie. Hastings Cent Rep 1991;21(5):26–8.
4. Lantos JD, Singer PA, Walker RM, et al. The illusion of futility in clinical practice. Am J Med 1989;87:81–4.
5. Standards for cardiopulmonary resuscitation (CPR) and emergency cardiac care (ECC).

V. Medicolegal considerations and recommendations. JAMA 1974;227:Suppl:864–6.
6. Appendix A: the proposed legislation. In: Do not resuscitate orders: the proposed legislation and report of the New York State Task Force on Life and the Law. 2nd ed. New York: The Task Force. 1986: 83.
7. 1984 Amendments to the Child Abuse Prevention and Treatment Act. Pub Law 98–457, 1984.
8. Council on Ethical and Judicial Affairs. American Medical Association. Guidelines for the appropriate use of do-not-resuscitate orders. JAMA 1991;265:1868–71.

9.   Miles SH. Informed demand for "non-beneficial" medical treatment. N Engl J Med 1991;325:512–5.

10. Brain-damaged woman at center of lawsuit over life-support dies. New York Times. July 5, 1991:A8.

11. Paris JJ. Crone RK, Reardon F. Physicians' refusal of requested treatment: the case of Baby L. N Engl J Med 1990;322:1012–5.

12. Blackhall LJ. Must we always use CPR? N Engl J Med 1987;317:1281–5.

13. Hackler JC, Hiller FC. Family consent to orders not to resuscitate: reconsidering hospital policy. JAMA 1990;264:1281–3.

14. Murphy DJ. Do-not-resuscitate orders: time for reappraisal in long-term-care institutions. JAMA 1988;260:2098–101.

15. Bedell SE, Delbanco TL, Cooke EF, Epstein FH. Survival after cardiopulmonary resuscitation in the hospital. N Engl J Med 1983;309:569–76.

16. Danis M, Gerrity MS, Southerland LI, Patrick DL. A comparison of patient, family, and physician assessments of the value of medical intensive care. Crit Care Med 1988;16:594–600.

17. Danis M, Jarr SL, Southerland LI, Nocella RS, Patrick DL. A comparison of patient, family, and nurse evaluations of the usefulness of intensive care. Crit Care Med 1987;15:138–43.

18. Danis M, Patrick DL, Southerland LI, Green ML. Patients' and families' preferences for medical intensive care. JAMA 1988; 260: 797–802.

19. Schneiderman LJ, Jecker NS, Jonsen AR. Medical futility: its meaning and ethical implications. Ann Intern Med 1990;112:949–54.

20. The Hastings Center. Guidelines on the termination of life-sustaining treatment and the care of the dying. Bloomington: Indiana University Press, 1987:32.

21. Appendix C: New York Public Health Law Article 29–B — orders not to resuscitate. In: Do not resuscitate orders: the proposed legislation and report of the New York State Task Force on Life and the Law. 2nd ed. New York: The Task Force, 1986:96.

22. Tversky A, Kahneman D. Judgment under uncertainty: heuristics and biases. Science 1974;185:1124–31.

23. Elstein AS. Clinical judgment: psychological research and medical practice. Science 1976;194:696–700.

24. Poses RM, Bekes C, Copare FJ, Scott WE. The answer to "What are my chances, doctor?" depends on whom is asked: prognostic disagreement and inaccuracy for critically ill patients. Crit Care Med 1989;17:827–33.

25. Poses RM, Cebul RD, Collins M, Fager SS. The accuracy of experienced physicians' probability estimates for patients with sore throats: implications for decision making. JAMA 1985;254:925–9.

26. Aaron H, Schwartz WB. Rationing health care: the choice before us. Science 1990; 247:418–22.

27. Eddy DM. What's going on in Oregon? JAMA 1991;266:417–20.

28. Youngner SJ. Who defines futility? JAMA 1988;260:2094–5.

29. Brennan TA. Ethics committees and decisions to limit care: the experience at the Massachusetts General Hospital. JAMA 1988;260:803–7.

30. La Puma J. Consultations in clinical ethics — issues and questions in 27 cases. West J Med 1987;146:633–7.

31. Braithwaite S, Thomasma DC. New guidelines on foregoing life-sustaining treatment in incompetent patients: an anti-cruelty policy. Ann Intern Med 1986;104:711–5.

32. Meisel A. The right to die. New York: John Wiley & Sons, 1989:104.

33. In re: Doe, Civil Action No. D93064 (Fulton County, GA, October 17, 1991).

34. Callahan D. Medical futility, medical necessity: the-problem-without-a-name. Hastings Cent Rep 1991;21(4):30–5.

35. Misbin RI. Physicians' aid in dying. N Engl J Med 1991;325:1307–11.

36. In the Matter of Karen Ann Quinlan, an alleged incompetent. 355. A.2d 647; or 70 NJ 10. March 31, 1976.

37. Annas GJ. Nancy Cruzan and the right to die. N Engl J Med 1990;323:670–3.

38. The Hastings Center. Guidelines on the termination of life-sustaining treatment and the care of the dying. Bloomington: Indiana University Press. 1987:112.

39. Task Force on Ethics of the Society of Critical Care Medicine. Consensus report on the

ethics of foregoing life-sustaining treatments
in the critically ill. Crit Care Med 1990;
18:1435–9.

40. President's Commission for the Study of
Ethical Problems in Medicine and Biomed-

ical and Behavioral Research. Deciding to
forego life-sustaining treatment: ethical,
medical, and legal issues in treatment decisions. Washinton, D.C.: Government
Printing Office, 1983:188–9.

50 "Where There Is a Will, There May Be a Better Way": Legislating Advance Directives[1]

Jocelyn Downie

Introduction

It is estimated that more than ten million living wills have been executed in the United States and that 365,000 living wills have been distributed in Canada by "Dying with Dignity".[2] A recent poll of over 2,000 Ontario physicians indicated that 64% would respect patient wishes as expressed in a "living will"[3] (note that this means that 36% would *not* respect patient wishes). And yet, in almost all parts of Canada, respect for an individual's advance directives concerning medical intervention does not appear to be required by law. In this paper I will argue, on ethical grounds, that the legal status of advance directives for health care in Canada should be revised.

First, I will define the relevant terms used in the debate. . . . Finally, I will canvass and critically assess the arguments made for and against respecting advance directives and the arguments made for and against legally requiring respect for advance directives.

Definitions of Terms

Advance directives are directions given by a competent individual concerning what and/ or how health care decisions should be made in the event that some time in the future the individual becomes incompetent to make such decisions. Advance directives can be divided into two categories: instruction directives (living wills); and proxy directives (durable powers of attorney).

The first common form of advance directive is called a living will. It is a document in which a competent person sets out, in written form, instructions about what and/or how health care decisions are to be made in the event that he or she becomes incompetent. The scope of living wills is most often, but not necessarily, limited to the withdrawal or withholding of life-sustaining procedures from terminally ill patients.

The second common form of advance directives is called a durable power of attorney for health care. Durable power of attorney for health care decisions build on the established legal mechanism of durable power of attorney and explicitly permit Person A to designate Person B to make health care decisions (according to Person A's values) after Person A has ceased to be competent to make health care decisions. In other words, a durable power of attorney for health care is a mechanism by which a competent person designates someone to make health care decisions on his or her behalf should he or she become incompetent. . . .

What Should the Legal Status of Advance Directives Be?

In a comprehensive analysis of the ethics of respecting advance directives, one might expect to start with the question of what kinds of requests made by competent patients should be respected. For example, should a competent individual's request that she not be given a blood transfusion be respected? What if she requests access to Dr. Jack Kevorkian's "suicide machine"? Or a lethal dose of morphine? Answers to these questions might be found in an analysis of arguments involving reference to the value of autonomy and dignity, the disvalue of suffering, the sanctity of life, the edict *primum non nocere*, the danger of slippery slopes and so on. However, I will not here attempt to adjudicate between competing positions on, for example, the place of autonomy relative to the place of life on a scale of values. Instead, for the purposes of this paper, I will leave open the question of the ethical limits on the kind of requests that should be respected if made by competent individuals. Furthermore, I will also leave open the ethical limits on the kind of requests that should be respected if made in advance directives. My question concerns only the relation between these two limits: "Should requests (of the sort that would be respected if made by competent individuals) be respected if made in advance directives?"

Arguments in Favour of Respecting Advance Directives[4]

The arguments in favour of respecting advance directives can be divided into two groups: arguments by analogy, and the consequentialist approach.

Those who argue by analogy in favour of respecting advance directives point to the following two established practices whereby past autonomy is respected:

1. Last Wills and Testaments — it is generally accepted that a person's advance directives concerning the distribution of her possessions and the disposition of her body (burial, cremation, organ donation, etc.) should be respected. When a regular will is executed, there is no actual (but rather past) autonomy left to respect. However, the person's wishes, expressed when competent, are used to guide action. Similarly, it has been argued, a previously competent individual's advance directives should be used to guide action/inaction concerning his/her body.

2. Substituted Judgment — with an incompetent patient, there are two standards that are applied to decision-making: best interests, and substituted judgment. Best interests decisions are based upon a third party's assessment of which action/inaction is in the patient's best interests. This standard is widely advocated for decision-making on behalf of individuals who have never been competent.

   Substituted judgment decisions are based upon the individual's previously expressed values. This standard is widely advocated for individuals who once were competent (and expressed wishes relevant to the decision) but are now incompetent. Given that advance directives for health care are intended precisely to convey an individual's wishes at a time when the individual is no longer competent, they arguably serve as the best foundation available for substituted judgment decision-making. If we use the substituted judgment standard for decisions concerning previously competent individuals (as we tend to try to do), then surely consistency requires that we respect advance directives.

Those who take a consequentialist approach claim that the benefits of advance directives outweigh the burdens. The benefits cited by advocates of advance directives include the following:

1. Promotion of autonomy — advance directives enable competent individuals to determine the course of their lives (and deaths).
2a. Removal of burdens from family and friends — advance directives can remove the decision-making burden from the shoulders of family members or friends who are now often called upon to take responsibility for decisions about life-sustaining treat-

ment. These decisions are fraught with emotional anguish, particularly if the wishes of the patient are unknown. Advance directives address this problem directly, since they convey the patient's wishes.

Advances directives, if they request the withholding/withdrawal of life-sustaining treatment, can also relieve the family and friends of the emotional burdens associated with a long and drawn-out dying process.

2b. Removal of burdens from physicians — advance directives can remove the burden of treatment/non-treatment decisions from the shoulders of physicians. Advance directives can also relieve the physician's uncertainty about whether the family's statements accurately reflect the wishes of the patient.

2c. Removal of burdens from society — advance directives (when, for example, they request the withholding or withdrawal of treatment) can relieve society of the burden of financial support of the life-sustaining treatments. Some people have pointed out that the amount of money spent on individuals during the last four weeks of life is extremely large. *If the individuals do not wish the treatment*, that money could be better spent on, for example, prenatal nutrition programs in our own inner cities or very basic health care programs in Third World countries.

3. Stimulation of communication — the process of preparing advance directives can stimulate discussions about death and dying between patients and their physicians, patients and other health care professionals, as well as patients and their families and friends. Patients might therefore be better prepared (practically and psychologically) for death, health care professionals might become better able to talk about death and dying, and family and friends might be better prepared for the loss of their loved ones.

4. Facilitation of the evolution of a society in which concern for the preservation of life is tempered with concern for respect for autonomy, the alleviation of suffering, and the promotion of dignity.

Thus, there are considerable benefits and at least two analogous situations that can be used to defend respecting advance directives.

Arguments against Respecting Advance Directives[5]

Opponents of respecting advance directives point to at least five concerns:

1. Personal identity — a person who has become incompetent is not the same person she was when she was competent and signed the advance directive. Therefore, pro-

jecting the wishes of the previously competent person onto the presently incompetent individual might project the wishes of one person onto an entirely different person. This, it is argued, would not respect the autonomy of individuals.

2. Changing minds — the individual might change his or her mind between the time the directive was issued and the time when he or she becomes incompetent.

3. Changing treatment options and prognoses — therapeutic options and prognoses might change between the time the directive was issued and the time at which it is to be implemented. Therefore, since the patient could not be fully informed about the options and prognoses at the time of issue, the directive cannot be taken to represent informed choice at the time of implementation.

4. Lack of clarity and specificity — the language of living wills may be unclear, therefore we may not know exactly what the individual's wishes were (the example often cited is the confusion over the terms "ordinary" and "extraordinary" treatment and the problem of interpreting such terms as "no reasonable expectation of recovery" and "no heroic measures").

   Furthermore, no living will is sufficiently detailed to delineate every contingency or possible reaction to a specific situation. Therefore, since a patient may not have anticipated the exact situation, the advance directive cannot be taken to govern the situation.

5. Excessive continuation of treatment — the individual might request *continuation* of treatment rather than cessation and this might place an unacceptable burden on the health care system (if it feels obliged to provide care it cannot afford to provide).

However, except for 1, each of these concerns is practical rather than inherent in the concept of advance directives and, I believe, admits of practical solutions.[6] Consider the following rebuttals to the above arguments:

2. The advance directive can be made easily revocable (for example, by oral renunciation). Furthermore, it can be made explicit in the relevant documents that those who make advance directives are responsible for revoking directives if they change their minds and that, in signing the document, they accept the fact that they will bear the consequences if they do not or cannot do so.[7]

3. It can be required that advance directives be renewed regularly in light of changes in prognoses, treatment options, and the individual's values.

4. Language can be clarified, confusing terms can be avoided, and individuals can be required and assisted to express their wishes *clearly*. For example, an individual who believes that there is a significant difference between ordinary and extraordinary

measures can be advised to clearly describe what he or she considers to be ordinary (for example, antibiotics, food, and water) and what he or she considers to be extraordinary (for example, intensive care life-support systems).

Furthermore, anticipation of the exact situation (noting, for example, specific diseases) may not be necessary if: (a) the living will contains a statement of the individual's general values that can then be *applied* to particular situations; or (b) the individual appoints a proxy through a durable power of attorney to make decisions in particular situations according to general values discussed at the time of appointment.[8]

5. Just as the requests for refusal are limited to those things which, if the patient were competent, would be withdrawn/withheld, requests for treatment can be limited to those things which, if the patient were competent, would be provided.

On the basis of these responses, I conclude that the benefits of advance directives outweigh the burdens, the arguments *for* are stronger than those *against*, and, therefore, advance directives ought to be respected.

Arguments in Favour of Legislatively Adopting Advance Directives

The final question to address is whether respect for advance directives should be legislatively required. There are considerable benefits, I believe, to requiring such respect. These benefits include the following.[9]

1. Provision of a guarantee to patients that their wishes will be respected. This guarantee can serve to diminish patients' anxiety over the dying process and can prevent undertreatment resulting from patients refusing to start something without assurances that prior directives will be respected.

2. Provision of a guarantee of equal access to treatment (and non-treatment) across the country by preventing the situation wherein one patient is allowed to die while another in a relevantly similar condition (and personal context) is kept alive simply because of differences of ethical positions of particular physicians, institutions, or localities. Treatment and non-treatment will not be dependent upon the hospital or physician's service in which an individual happens to have the fortune or misfortune to be a patient.

3. Provision of a means of reducing anxiety among physicians by protecting them from (and letting them feel protected from) legal liability for outcomes. This can, in turn, prevent overtreatment by physicians who overtreat because they fear litigation.

4. Standardization of instruction and proxy directive forms. This may lead to easier identification of these forms, easier processing, and easier completion by patients.

5. Promotion of awareness of rights and obligations (both on the part of patients and health care professionals) since the passage of this kind of legislation would result in (and require) considerable publicity.

6. Avoidance of the slow and labour-intensive process of establishing law through court cases.

Arguments against Legislatively Adopting Advance Directives

Opponents of legislatively requiring respect for advance directives often point to the following dangers:[10]

1. Violation of established patients' rights and potential for overtreatment of those who did not leave any advance directives.

2. Rejection of treatment by patients who may feel pressured to reject treatment for fear of being seen as a potential future burden.

3. Increase in "inappropriate" compliance with directives when the health care professional believes that the advance directive does not accurately reflect the patient's wishes but feels compelled to comply with the directive because of the law.

4. Increase in anxiety about litigation amongst health care professionals and consequent reduction in offering advance directives to patients. People advancing this concern express the opinion that legislative recognition of advance directives will lead to anxiety amongst health care professionals about being forced to follow the "poorly" considered wishes of patients who have completed advance directives and these health care professionals might cease offering advance directives to patients at all.

5. Erosion of the physician/patient relationship (through the decay of trust and promotion of an adversarial attitude).

6. Violation of physician autonomy and diminishment of physician authority.

7. Increase in legal regulation of medical practice.

Possible rebuttals to this list of concerns include the following:

Problem 1 is the most significant of these concerns. There is some evidence that this problem was not avoided in much of the American living will legislation.[11] However, the problem is not insurmountable and can be avoided in two ways. First, careful drafting and implementation of legislation can make it explicit that other rights are not affected by the legislation. Second, careful establishment of (and attention to) a standard of care for individuals who have not prepared advance directives can prevent overtreatment.

Problem 2 can be avoided through careful counselling by health care professionals involved with patients who are considering making advance directives. Just as health care professionals must take care to ensure that a competent patient is not refusing life-sustaining treatment for fear of being seen as a potential future burden, so too they must ensure that competent patients do not prepare advance directives out of the same fear. Since the risk is not seen, in cases of competent patients, to justify disallowing these patients to refuse treatment, it should not be taken to justify disallowing patients to refuse treatment in advance directives.

Problem 3 can be avoided by including a review process in the legislation whereby anyone who feels that the advance directive does not reflect the wishes of the patient can ask the designated body to review the directive and decide whether to authorize overriding it. If this body decides that compliance would be "inappropriate" (that is, would not serve the purposes of respecting advance directives), then the health care professional will not be compelled to comply. However, if this body decides that the compliance would be "appropriate", then the health care professional would be forced to comply or transfer the patient to someone else willing to comply.

Problem 4 can be avoided, in part, by the same process outlined in the discussion of 3[.] (that is, a review process that can be applied to, among other things, "poorly" considered advance directives). The possible reduction in offering advance directives can also be avoided by establishing a system of offering that is not dependent upon health care professionals' fears of future litigation. Consider, for example, the U.S. *Patient Self-Determination Act*. This Act requires that all health care facilities receiving Medicare or Medicaid funds inform their patients about advance directives and the right to refuse life-sustaining treatment. I am not advocating the introduction of such an Act in Canada. I merely raise the Act as an example of a way in which the reduction of offering advance directives can be avoided. . . .

In response to problem 5, legislating advance directives need not have a deleterious effect on the physician/patient relationship. A patient who knows that a physician will not respect his or her advance directive is likely to already have a fairly adversarial attitude. Finally, it can be pointed out that trust has already been eroded between many patients and physicians; many patients do not believe that their physicians will stop treatment at what the patients would consider a reasonable point. Offering patients advance directives might, in fact, help to restore some of this eroded trust.

Fears of physician autonomy being violated — problem 6 — can also be allayed by careful drafting of legislation. Physicians need not be required to participate in something that goes against their consciences (for example, withdrawing treatment). Rather, they can be required to transfer to another physician any patient whose wishes they are not willing to respect. The diminishment of physician authority is something many people would endorse rather than fear. The question is not so much "ought patients to have authority over their own bodies?" but rather "ought physicians to have authority over their patients' bodies?" If the answer to the latter question is no, then the threat to physician authority posed by advance directives is insignificant.

The concern expressed in problem 7 about the increase in legal regulation of medical practice can also be answered in a fairly simple manner. If advance directives ought to be respected and if physicians will not respect them (as many will not), then legal regulation is necessary. There is nothing ethically wrong *prima facie* with legal regulation of medical practice.

Thus, some of these concerns can be answered through careful drafting and implementation of legislation. Those that cannot be answered might best be viewed as the costs of achieving the benefits of respecting and requiring respect for advance directives.

Conclusion

I believe that there are good reasons to respect and to legislate advance directives for health care in Canada. There are indeed some dangers and costs in doing so, but these usually can be avoided through careful drafting and implementation of legislation. When they cannot be avoided, they must be borne as the cost of realizing the benefits. In order to be consistent with the values expressed in our society (for example, the value of autonomy and the disvalue of suffering), legislatures across the country must legally recognize and require respect for advance directives.

There is an urgent need for provincial and territorial legislatures to pay attention to the issue of the legal status of advance directives. Technology enables us to keep people alive far longer than ever before. Technology, however, does not necessarily guarantee that the life prolonged will be one that patients consider to be worth living. Legally requiring respect for advance directives is arguably the best way available to us to ensure that those individuals who can no longer speak for themselves will nevertheless be able to determine both the course of their lives and the course of their deaths.

As Fenella Rouse of the Society for the Right to Die notes:

> Living wills and appointments of agents are admittedly a second best. Nothing is as effective as open informed discussion when the treatment decision must be made. However, in the huge number of

situations in which this is not possible and in an increasingly impersonal medical environment, it seems that living wills and proxy appointments are the best second best available.[12]

Notes

1. The title of this essay "Where There Is a Will, There May Be a Better Way" is taken from Higgs, R., "Living wills and treatment refusal," *British Medical Journal* 295, no. 6608 (November 14, 1987): 1222.

2. American statistics from Rouse, F., "Living Wills and the Right to Refuse Treatment," *IME Bulletin* Supplement 5 (April 1987); 1. Canadian statistics from personal communication with Marilynne Seguin of "Dying With Dignity."

3. "Dying With Dignity" publicity materials.

4. Benefits of respecting advance directives are noted in, for example: Bok, S., "Personal Directions for Care at the End of Life," *New England Journal of Medicine* 295, no. 7 (August 12, 1976): 367–369; Buchanan, A., "Advance Directives and the Personal Identity Problem," *Philosophy and Public Affairs* 17, no. 4 (Fall 1988): 277–302; Fisher, R.H., and Meslin, E.M., "Should living wills be legalized?" *Canadian Medical Association Journal*, 142, no. 1 (1990): 23–26; and Houston, C.S., "Living wills: A solution to the prolonged act of dying? *Canadian Medical Association Journal* 139, no. 3 (August 1, 1988): 241–243.

5. Risks associated with respecting advance directives are noted in, for example: Buchanan, A., "Advance Directives and the Personal Identity Problem"; Davidson, K.W., Hackler, C., Caradine, D., and McCord, R., "Physicians' Attitudes on Advance Directives," *Journal of the American Medical Association* 262, no. 17 (November 3, 1989): 2415–2419; Fisher, R.H., and Meslin, E.M., "Should living wills be legalized?"; and Johnson, D., "Living wills: Their interpretation depends on the situation" *Canadian Medical Association Journal* 139, no. 3 (August 31, 1988); 244–245.

6. The issue of personal identity is too complex to enter into here. It has been a source of controversy in philosophical circles for centuries and is likely to continue as such. Since convincing arguments are not available to either side of the debate (that is, the debate about personal identity and past/present/future autonomy), it seems advisable to remove the issue from the discussion of advance directives and to focus instead on the practical concerns and responses as well as on the arguments by analogy.

7. As an example of someone who *cannot* revoke a directive, consider a person with locked-in syndrome. It might be argued that it is unethical to permit someone to take on the risk of becoming unable to revoke an advance directive. Therefore, until we can prevent people from changing their minds and being unable to revoke, we should not allow advance directives to be signed. This is a legitimate argument. However, it can be argued in response that the cost of people changing their minds and being unable to revoke is outweighed by the cost of refusing to respect advance directives.

8. It should be acknowledged that there can be difficulties in applying an individual's general values to a particular situation and attempting to *deduce* a response. The move from values to particular decisions is a creative, individual one. However, this difficulty can be largely overcome if the individual makes it clear in the advance directive (either through written instruction in a living will or oral instruction to his/her proxy) how he or she makes decisions.

9. Benefits of legally requiring respect for advance directives are noted in, for example: Buchanan, A., "Advance Directives and the Personal Identity Problem"; and Rouse, F., "Living Wills and the Right to Refuse Treatment," in notes 2 and 4.

10. Risks associated with legally requiring respect for advance directives are noted in, for example: Davidson, K.W., Hackler, C., Caradine, D., and McCord, R., "Physicians' Attitudes on Advance Directives"; Fisher, R.H., and Meslin, E.M., "Should living wills be legalized?"; Higgs, R., "Living wills

and treatment refusal"; Lederer, A.D.H., and Brock, D.W., "Commentaries on Case Study: Surgical Risks and Advance Directives." *Hastings Center Report* 17, no. 4 (August 1987): 18–19; and McCarrick, P.M., "Living Wills and Durable Powers of Attorney: Advance Directive Legislation and

Issues," Scope Note 2 (Washington: National Center for Bioethics Literature, 1990).

11.   See, for example, Heintz, L.L., "Legislative hazard: keeping patients living against their wills," *Journal of Medical Ethics* 14 (1988): 82–86.

12.   Rouse, F., *supra* note 2 at page 6.

Chapter 13

Questions to Consider

1.   A 20-year-old man was brought into a hospital one year ago following a car accident. He had suffered severe injuries to his head and he never regained consciousness. He has been diagnosed as being in a persistent vegetative state. His parents ask that the artificially supplied food and water be stopped and he be allowed to die. There is great dissention on the team caring for this man about whether to grant the parents' request. Consider the ethical arguments for and against withdrawal of the artificial hydration and nutrition.

2.   A 45-year old woman is in the intensive care unit. She has advanced breast cancer that is no longer responding to treatment. The health care team has a meeting to discuss the use of CPR should she go into cardiac arrest. The team leader makes the following points: the patient is likely to go into cardiac arrest within days; the chance of CPR restoring cardiac output is 10 percent and, even with CPR, the patient is expected to live no more than two weeks; and the ICU is overcrowded and the bed is desperately needed. The team leader suggests a unilateral DNR order (that is, putting an order not to resuscitate on the patient's chart without discussing it with her or her family). Discuss the ethical arguments in support of and against this suggestion.

3.   A 40-year-old man is brought to the hospital following a car accident. He is unconscious but a living will is found in his wallet. The will states that he is a Christian Scientist and rejects all forms of medical treatment.

Without medical treatment, this patient will die. What should the health care team do? Under what conditions, if any, is treating this patient ethically acceptable? Defend this position.

4.   A 30-year-old woman suffers from irreversible paralysis from the neck down caused by a diving accident. She is dependent upon a respirator to keep her alive. She has been in the hospital for one year and thoroughly understands her medical condition and prognosis. She asks her physician to disconnect the respirator. What should the physician do and why?

5.   List all the distinctions that might be raised in a discussion of the ethics of withholding or withdrawing life-sustaining treatment (e.g., active versus passive euthanasia and killing versus letting die). Discuss the moral (in)significance of four of these distinctions.

Further Readings

Advance Directives Seminar Group, Centre for Bioethics, University of Toronto. 1992. Advance directives: Are they an advance? *Canadian Medical Association Journal* 146:127–34.

Baylis, Françoise E. 1989. Resuscitation of the terminally ill: A response to Buckman and Senn. *Canadian Medical Association Journal* 141:1043–44.

Buchanan, Allen. 1988. Advance directives and the personal identity problem. *Philosophy and Public Affairs* 17:277–302.

Buckman, Robert, and John Senn. 1989. Eligibility for CPR: Is Every death a cardiac arrest? *Canadian Medical Association Journal* 140:1068–69.

Edwards, Miles J., and Susan W. Tolle. 1992. Disconnecting a ventilator at the request of a patient who knows he will then die: The doctor's anguish. *Annals of Internal Medicine* 117:254–56.

Lynn, Joanne, ed. 1986. *By no extraordinary means: The choice to forgo life-sustaining food and water.* Bloomington, IN: Indiana University Press.

Miles, Steven H., and Allison August. 1990. Courts, gender and "the right to die". *Law, Medicine and Health Care* 18:85–95.

Molloy, William, and Virginia Mepham. 1989. *Let me decide.* Toronto: Penguin Books.

Rachels, James. 1975. Active and passive euthanasia. *New England Journal of Medicine* 292:75–80.

Schneiderman, Lawrence J., Nancy S. Jecker, and Albert R. Jonsen. 1990. Medical futility: Its meaning and ethical implications. *Annals of Internal Medicine* 112:949–54.

Solomon, Mildred Z., et al. 1993. Decisions near the end of life: Professional views on life-sustaining treatments. *American Journal of Public Health* 83:14–23.

Winkler, Earl R. 1987. The morality of withholding food and fluid. *Journal of Palliative Care* 3(2): 26–30.

Chapter 14

Euthanasia and Assisted Suicide

Chapter 14

Introduction

Two Canadians afflicted with amyotrophic lateral sclerosis (ALS), also known as Lou Gehrig's disease, who battled to have assisted suicide legalized in this country died five days apart in February, 1994. One was Sue Rodriguez, from British Columbia, who carried her legal fight to the Supreme Court of Canada. The other was Erwin Krickhahn, of Toronto, who decided to have his suicide videotaped but then changed his mind after being disillusioned by the response of the media. Mr. Krickhahn is reported to have died of natural causes. A physician helped Ms. Rodriguez to die. Their efforts to publicize the issue and change the law have forced us to debate the moral and legal permissibility of assisted suicide.

Whether assisted suicide should be legalized in Canada is now before the public and the politicians because on September 30, 1993 the Supreme Court of Canada rejected Ms. Rodriguez's request that a physician be legally permitted to assist her in committing suicide. Over the course of her two-year public and legal campaign, the debilitating effects of ALS on Ms. Rodriguez were dramatic and sobering. Initially she was articulate and self-possessed. But only months before her death, she was confined to a wheelchair and had to struggle to control her body and to speak in an audible, intelligible voice. She knew that eventually she would lose the ability to swallow and speak, and would be unable to breathe without a respirator and eat without a gastrostomy tube. She also knew that throughout the deterioration of her body, her mind would be unimpaired. She would remain aware of her ineluctable progression to virtually total dependency. Ms. Rodriguez said that she would like to live as long as she could with a quality of life that was acceptable to her, but when her suffering became intolerable, she wanted to end her life. At that stage, however, she would lack the physical ability to commit suicide on her own. She would need the assistance of a physician.

Although attempting suicide is no longer a criminal offence in Canada, aiding or abetting suicide is. Ms. Rodriguez contended that section 241(b) of the Criminal Code, which prohibits assisted suicide, violated her rights under the Canadian Charter of Rights and Freedoms. The Supreme Court of Canada rejected her claim in a five-to-four decision. The closeness of the decision reflects how controversial the issue is. In addition to the strong emotions stirred up by matters of life and death, and pain and suffering, there are compelling arguments on both sides. Judgements have to be made about the merit of the individual arguments as well as their comparative importance. Moreover, the issue requires a careful appraisal of the relationship between ethics and public policy, in this case the law. Even if one agreed that it would be *morally* permissible to allow a physician to help Ms. Rodriguez commit suicide, does it follow that the law should be changed to make such assistance *legally* permissible? No one should have to endure the kind of suffering and death that ALS can impose, and that is a good reason for granting Ms. Rodriguez's request. At the same time, there are compelling reasons for criminally prohibiting assisted suicide, not the least of which is the need to protect some highly vulnerable persons. How should one respond to this discrepancy? Should morality and law always be congruent, or are there situations in which they should diverge?

A number of arguments are offered in favour of and against legalizing assisted suicide. A principal argument in support of legalization is that everyone should be able to have a good death. Shana Alexander, a journalist, has written:

> I want a good death; I think I'm entitled to a good death and that we all are. A good death to me seems to be a human entitlement just as much as a good life is. But a good death may be harder and harder for us to get. So I guess I am talking about euthanasia because that's what euthanasia is, a mixture of *thanatos*, "death," and *eu*, which is "good" (Alexander 1993).

If the only way that Ms. Rodriguez could have a good death — a death that preserved her dignity and self-respect and minimized her suffering — was by means of assisted suicide, then, in this view, she should be permitted that. Moreover, a good death means not dying alone. One of the most disturbing features of Dr. Quill's account of how he helped his patient Diane to commit suicide is that she was forced to die by herself (Quill 1991). Because Diane did not want to expose her family or friends to potential legal liability, she made sure that nobody was present when she took the overdose of drugs she had accumulated with Dr. Quill's complicity. In addition, as long as assisted suicide remains illegal, it will be done in secret, sometimes by persons who lack medical expertise. The possibility that a suicide attempt will be botched consequently cannot be ignored. The harm caused by illegal abortions was an argument in favour of decriminalizing abortion; a parallel argument can be made for decriminalizing assisted suicide.

It is also argued that making a choice about the timing and circumstances of one's death is an exercise of the right to autonomy or self-determination. Respecting autonomy means allowing people to make important decisions about their lives according to their own beliefs and values. Deciding how much pain and suffering are tolerable, when life has lost all meaning, and when one's dignity has been eroded are precisely the kinds of important matters that autonomy should protect.

Another argument is that there is no morally relevant difference between discontinuing life-sustaining treatment and assisted suicide. With assisted suicide, the intention, motive, and outcome are the same as when life-sustaining treatment is stopped. In both situations, the intent is to end the pain and suffering of the patient; the motive is compassion or mercy; and the outcome is the death of the patient. In all morally relevant respects, it is argued, stopping life support and assisted suicide are identical. Thus, given that discontinuing life-sustaining treatment is morally (and legally) permissible, assisted suicide should be as well.

In addition, persons who are prevented from committing suicide solely because of their physical incapacities are, it is contended, being discriminated against. They may not legally end their lives solely because they require assistance; people who are not physically disabled are, in contrast, legally permitted to commit suicide. Justice — treating people equally — requires the elimination of this unequal treatment.

Those opposed to the legalization of assisted suicide worry about possible bad consequences. Protection against abuse would, of course, be instituted, but how effective would it be? No procedural safeguards are perfect, especially in the context of such an emotional and controversial issue. Moreover, if abuses were to occur, a backlash might develop that would threaten the progress that has been made in establishing the right of patients to discontinue life-sustaining treatment (Wolf 1989). That progress has taken place against the background of a firm line that prevents the killing of patients. Were that line to be blurred or eradicated, however, the right to have life support stopped might be jeopardized. This is a particular worry in Canada, where explicit legal recognition of the right to have life-sustaining treatment terminated has emerged only recently.

Legalizing assisted suicide might also undermine efforts to develop more effective methods of pain control and better palliative and comfort care. If there is a quicker, more certain, and cheaper way of ending pain and suffering, why devote substantial time, effort, and resources to alternatives that are less assured of success and more costly?

Another worry concerns the slippery slope — the possibility that voluntary assisted suicide might be extended beyond competent persons to persons who are marginally or questionably competent and ultimately might lead to nonvoluntary active euthanasia for patients who are incompetent. This worry is suggested by the history of the right to refuse life-sustaining treatment in the United States. That right was initially recognized for competent patients but then was extended to incompetent patients, to be exercised by proxy or surrogate decision makers. Once competent patients were allowed to die when life was deemed no longer worth living, it was hard to withhold that option from incompetent patients. Why would the same line of reasoning not apply to assisted suicide? And if it did, what would an extension of assisted suicide to incompetent persons mean for people who are comatose or severely mentally handicapped or who suffer from advanced dementia, particularly in a time of increasing financial constraints in health care?

Moreover, we readily assume that because choice is good, more choice is better; giving patients more choices about their deaths therefore seems to be unquestionably good. But is that assumption always correct? The introduction of *in vitro* fertilization has, for example, created new choices for women who have difficulty conceiving, but at the same time it has imposed new burdens on them. One critic of the technology says:

> It is one thing to say that one really would have loved to have given birth, but one cannot, and move on to adoption or to childless living. It is quite another thing to say one would have loved to have given birth but it was too expensive or too difficult or too painful or too dangerous to keep trying. The latter makes much greater demands on a woman's sense of self and of self-worth in this (and most) societies (Rothman 1992).

Legalizing assisted suicide would likewise create new choices and impose new burdens. The very existence of assisted suicide as a legally permissible option would create subtle pressure to choose that option. Vulnerable persons consequently could be induced by economic reasons or the sense of being an imposition on relatives to end their lives when they otherwise would not have.

Finally, the impact of the law itself cannot be ignored. Criminal law, in particular, has profound symbolic and pedagogic effects. Law stands for and exalts those values deemed so vital to the conduct of individual lives and the order of society that they receive both official legal endorsement and the added protection of legal sanctions. But law not only embodies and endorses values, it inculcates them. Law is a powerful force in creating and shaping people's attitudes and values. To remove the criminal prohibition of assisted suicide might not, therefore, be simply a minor correction to a law that needs to be brought in line with changing times. It could have widespread and momentous effects on our views about the value of life and what makes life worth living.

Another aspect of this issue is procedural — how should the matter be resolved? Should the issue of legalization be decided in the courts, or in Parliament, or perhaps by a national referendum? Public opinion polls invariably suggest widespread support for legalization, but how much credence should be given to these polls? Should law be made on the basis of polls in the first place? And despite the results of polls, when legalizing assisted suicide was put directly to voters in Washington and California, it was rejected. How is the disparity between how people respond to polls and how they vote to be explained? How can the issue of physician-assisted suicide be resolved in a way that recognizes its moral, legal, and public policy dimensions?

The Selections

The first two selections take opposite stands on the moral and legal permissibility of assisted suicide and active euthanasia. Dan Brock provides a comprehensive, critical survey of the main arguments for and against voluntary active euthanasia and physician-assisted suicide and concludes that, with certain reservations, both practices should be permitted. Brock argues that the commonly held position that stopping life support is allowing to die rather than killing is mistaken. In his view, discontinuing life support, assisted suicide, and active euthanasia are all killing. But not all killings are wrongful, he points out; and just as stopping life-sustaining treatment can be justified even though it is killing, so can assisted suicide and active euthanasia, even though they are killing. Brock also examines the consequences of assisted suicide and active euthanasia and assesses their likelihood and relative importance. The balance of all these considerations, he concludes, supports permitting both.

The case against assisted suicide and active euthanasia is argued forcefully by Daniel Callahan in the second selection. Callahan insists that there is a morally relevant distinction between killing and allowing to die. A lethal injection, he emphasizes, would kill a healthy person as well as a sick person; withholding or withdrawing treatment, on the other hand, would not affect a healthy person. He also argues that assisted suicide and euthanasia are not private matters protected by the right to autonomy or self-determination. Because they involve at least two people, they require the complicity of society. The likely effects of permitting assisted suicide and euthanasia are so dire, in his view, that they should not be legalized.

The chapter concludes with brief excerpts from three of the opinions in *Rodriguez v. British Columbia (Attorney General)*. The legal issues in this case are complicated and the judgements are lengthy. These short passages are intended primarily to show how the Supreme Court responded to some of the central moral arguments in this debate.

Conclusion

The pressure to legalize assisted suicide, and perhaps active euthanasia as well, is not likely to abate. Given all that is at stake, the public and political discussion of this issue needs to be informed and comprehensive and needs to assess carefully the arguments and considerations raised in this chapter.

References

Alexander, Shana. 1993. Thirty years ago. *Hastings Center Report* 23(6): S5 (supplement).

Criminal Code, R.S.C., 1985, c. C–46, s. 241(b).

Quill, Timothy. 1991. Death and dignity. *New England Journal of Medicine* 324:691–94.

Rothman, Barbara Katz. 1992. Not all that glitters is gold. *Hastings Center Report* 22(4): S4 (supplement).

Wolf, Susan M. 1989. Holding the line on euthanasia. *Hastings Center Report* 19(1): 13–15 (supplement).

51   Voluntary Active Euthanasia

Dan W. Brock

Since the case of Karen Quinlan first seized public attention fifteen years ago, no issue in biomedical ethics has been more prominent than the debate about forgoing life-sustaining treatment. Controversy continues regarding some aspects of that debate, such as forgoing life-sustaining nutrition and hydration, and relevant law varies some from state to state. Nevertheless, I believe it is possible to identify an emerging consensus that competent patients, or the surrogates of incompetent patients, should be permitted to weigh the benefits and burdens of alternative treatments, including the alternative of no treatment, according to the patient's values, and either to refuse any treatment or to select from among available alternative treatments. This consensus is reflected in bioethics scholarship, in reports of prestigious bodies such as the President's Commission for the Study of Ethical Problems in Medicine, The Hastings Center, and the American Medical Association, in a large body of judicial decisions in courts around the country, and finally in the beliefs and practices of health care professionals who care for dying patients.[1]

More recently, significant public and professional attention has shifted from life-sustaining treatment to euthanasia — more specifically, voluntary active euthanasia — and to physician-assisted suicide. Several factors have contributed to the increased interest in euthanasia. In the Netherlands, it has been openly practiced by physicians for several years with the acceptance of the country's highest court.[2] In 1988 there was an unsuccessful attempt to get the question of whether it should be made legally permissible on the ballot in California. In November 1991 voters in the state of Washington defeated a widely publicized referendum proposal to legalize both voluntary active euthanasia and physician-assisted suicide. Finally, some cases of this kind, such as "It's Over, Debbie," described in the *Journal of the American Medical Association*, the "suicide machine" of Dr. Jack Kevorkian, and the cancer patient "Diane" of Dr. Timothy Quill, have captured wide public and professional attention.[3] Unfortunately, the first two of these cases were sufficiently problematic that even most supporters of euthanasia or assisted suicide did not defend the physicians' actions in them. As a result, the subsequent debate they spawned has often shed more heat than light. My aim is to increase the light, and perhaps as well to reduce the heat, on this important subject by formulating and evaluating the central ethical arguments for and against voluntary active euthanasia and physician-assisted suicide. My evaluation of the arguments leads me, with reservations to be noted, to support permitting both practices. My primary aim, however, is not to argue for euthanasia, but to identify confusions in some common arguments, and problematic assumptions and claims that need more defense or data in others. The issues are considerably more complex than either supporters or opponents often make out; my hope is to advance the debate by focusing attention on what I believe the real issues under discussion should be.

In the recent bioethics literature some have endorsed physician-assisted suicide but not euthanasia.[4] Are they sufficiently different that the moral arguments for one often do not apply to the other? A paradigm case of physician-assisted suicide is a patient's ending his or her life with a lethal dose of a medication requested of and provided by a physician for the purpose. A paradigm case of voluntary active euthanasia is a physician's administering the lethal dose, often because the patient is unable to do so. The only difference that need exist between the two is the person who actually administers the lethal dose — the physician or the patient. In each, the physician plays an active and necessary causal role.

In physician-assisted suicide the patient acts last (for example, Janet Adkins herself pushed the button after Dr. Kevorkian hooked her up to his suicide machine), whereas in euthanasia the physician acts last by performing the physical equivalent of pushing the button. In both cases, however, the choice rests fully with the patient. In both the patient acts last in the sense of retaining the right to change his or her mind until the point at which the lethal process becomes irreversible. How could there be a substantial moral difference between the two based only on this small difference in the part played by the physician in the causal process resulting in death? Of course, it might be held that the moral difference is clear and important — in euthanasia the physician kills the patient whereas in physician-assisted suicide the patient kills him- or herself. But this is misleading at best. In assisted suicide the physician and patient together kill the patient. To see this, suppose a physician supplied a lethal dose to a patient with the knowledge and intent that the patient will wrongfully administer it to another. We would have no difficulty in morality or the law recognizing this as a case of joint action to kill for which both are responsible.

If there is no significant, intrinsic moral difference between the two, it is also difficult to see why public or legal policy should permit one but not the other; worries about abuse or about giving anyone dominion over the lives of others apply equally to either. As a result, I will take the arguments evaluated below to apply to both and will focus on euthanasia.

My concern here will be with *voluntary* euthanasia only — that is, with the case in which a clearly competent patient makes a fully voluntary and persistent request for aid in dying. Involuntary euthanasia, in which a competent patient explicitly refuses or opposes receiving euthanasia, and nonvoluntary euthanasia, in which a patient is incompetent and unable to express his or her wishes about euthanasia, will be considered here only as potential unwanted side-effects of permitting voluntary euthanasia. I emphasize as well that I am concerned with *active* euthanasia, not withholding or withdrawing life-sustaining treatment, which some commentators characterize as "passive euthanasia." Finally, I will be concerned with euthanasia where the motive of those who perform it is to respect the wishes of the patient and to provide the patient with a "good death," though one important issue is whether a change in legal policy could restrict the performance of euthanasia to only those cases.

A last introductory point is that I will be examining only secular arguments about euthanasia, though of course many people's attitudes to it are inextricable from their religious view. The policy issue is only whether euthanasia should be permissible, and no one who has religious objections to it should be required to take any part in it, though of course this would not fully satisfy some opponents.

The Central Ethical Argument for Voluntary Active Euthanasia

The central ethical argument for euthanasia is familiar. It is that the very same two fundamental ethical values supporting the consensus on patient's rights to decide about life-sustaining treatment also support the ethical permissibility of euthanasia. These values are individual self-determination or autonomy and individual well-being. By self-determination as it bears on euthanasia, I mean people's interest in making important decisions about their lives for themselves according to their own values or conceptions of a good life, and in being left free to act on those decisions. Self-determination is valuable because it permits people to form and live in accordance with their own conception of a good life, at least within the bounds of justice and consistent with others doing so as well. In exercising self-determination people take responsibility for their lives and for the kinds of persons they become. A central aspect of human dignity lies in people's capacity to direct their lives in this way. The vale of exercising self-determination presupposes some minimum of decisionmaking capacities or competence, which thus limits the scope of euthanasia supported by self-determination: it cannot justifiably be administered, for example, in cases of serious dementia or treatable clinical depression.

Does the value of individual self-determination extend to the time and manner of one's death? Most people are very concerned about the nature of the last stage of their lives. This reflects not just a fear of experiencing substantial suffering when dying, but also a desire to retain dignity and control during this last period of life. Death is today increasingly preceded by a long period of significant physical and mental decline, due in part to the technological interventions of modern medicine. Many people adjust to these disabilities and find meaning and value in new activities and ways. Others find the impairments and burdens in the last stage of their lives at some point sufficiently great to make life no longer worth living. For many patients near death, maintaining the quality of one's life, avoiding great suffering, maintaining one's dignity, and insuring that others remember us as we wish them to become of paramount importance and outweigh merely extending one's life. But there is no single, objectively correct answer for everyone as to when, if at all, one's life becomes all things considered a burden and unwanted. If self-determination is a fundamental value, then the great variability among people on this question makes it especially important that individuals control the manner, circumstances, and timing of their dying and death.

The other main value that supports euthanasia is individual well-being. It might seem that individual well-being conflicts with a person's self-determination when the person requests euthanasia. Life itself is commonly taken to be a central good for persons, often valued for its own sake, as well as necessary for pursuit of all other goods within a life. But when a competent patient decides to forgo all further life-sustaining treatment then the patient, either explicitly or implicitly, commonly decides that the best life possible for him or her with treatment is of sufficiently poor quality that it is worse than no further life at all. Life is no longer considered a benefit by the patient, but has now become a burden. The same judgment underlies a request for euthanasia: continued life is seen by the patient as no longer a benefit, but now a burden. Especially in the often severely compromised and debilitated states of many critically ill or dying patients, there is no objective standard, but only the competent patient's judgment of whether continued life is no longer a benefit.

Of course, sometimes there are conditions, such as clinical depression, that call into question whether the patient has made a competent choice, either to forgo life-sustaining treatment or to seek euthanasia, and then the patient's choice need not be evidence that continued life is no longer a benefit for him or her. Just as with decisions about treatment, a determination of incompetence can warrant not honoring the patient's choice; in the case of treatment, we then transfer decisional authority to a surrogate, though in the case of voluntary active euthanasia a determination that the patient is incompetent means that choice is not possible.

The value or right of self-determination does not entitle patients to compel physicians to act contrary to their own moral or professional values. Physicians are moral and professional agents whose own self-determination or integrity should be respected as well. If performing euthanasia became legally permissible, but conflicted with a particular physician's reasonable understanding of his or her moral or professional responsibilities, the care of a patient who requested euthanasia should be transferred to another.

Most opponents do not deny that there are some cases in which the values of patient self-determination and well-being support euthanasia. Instead, they commonly offer two kinds of arguments against it that in their view outweigh or override this support. The first kind of argument is that in any individual case where considerations of the patient's self-determination and well-being do support euthanasia, it is nevertheless always ethically wrong or impermissible. The second kind of argument grants that in some individual cases euthanasia may not be ethically wrong, but maintains nonetheless that public and legal policy should never permit it. The first kind of argument focuses on features of any individual case of euthanasia, while the second kind focuses on social or legal policy. In the next section I consider the first kind of argument.

Euthanasia Is the Deliberate Killing of an Innocent Person

The claim that any individual instance of euthanasia is a case of deliberate killing of an innocent person is, with only minor qualifications, correct. Unlike forgoing life-sustaining treatment, commonly understood as allowing to die, euthanasia is clearly killing, defined as depriving of life or causing the death of a living being. While providing morphine for pain relief at doses where the risk of respiratory depression and an earlier death may be a foreseen but unintended side effect of treating the patient's pain, in a case of euthanasia the patient's death is deliberate or intended even if in both the physician's ultimate end may be respecting the patient's wishes. If the deliberate killing of an innocent person is wrong, euthanasia would be nearly always impermissible.

In the context of medicine, the ethical prohibition against deliberately killing the innocent derives some of its plausibility from the belief that nothing in the currently accepted practice of medicine is deliberate killing. Thus, in commenting on the "It's Over, Debbie" case, four prominent physicians and bioethicists could entitle their paper "Doctors Must Not Kill."[5] The belief that doctors do not in fact kill requires the corollary belief that forgoing life-sustaining treatment, whether by not starting or by stopping treatment, is allowing to die, not killing. Common though this view is, I shall argue that it is confused and mistaken.

Why is the common view mistaken? Consider the case of a patient terminally ill with ALS disease. She is completely respirator dependent with no hope of ever being weaned. She is unquestionably competent but finds her condition intolerable and persistently requests to be removed from the respirator and allowed to die. Most people and physicians would agree that the patient's physician should respect the patient's wishes and remove her from the respirator, though this will certainly cause the patient's death. The common understanding is that the physician thereby allows the patient to die. But is that correct?

Suppose the patient has a greedy and hostile son who mistakenly believes that his mother will never decide to stop her life-sustaining treatment and that even if she did her physician would not remove her from the respirator. Afraid that his inheritance will be dissipated by a long and expensive hospitalization, he enters his mother's room while she is sedated, extubates her, and she dies. Shortly thereafter the medical staff discovers what he has done and confronts the son. He replies, "I didn't kill her, I merely allowed her to die. It was her ALS disease that caused her death." I think this would rightly be dismissed as transparent sophistry — the son went into his mother's room and deliberately killed her. But, of course, the son performed just the same physical actions, did just the same thing, that the physician would have done. If that is so, then doesn't the physician also kill the patient when he extubates her?

I underline immediately that there are important ethical differences between what the physician and the greedy son do. First, the physician acts with the patient's consent whereas the son does not. Second, the physician acts with good motive — to respect the patient's wishes and self-determination — whereas the son acts with a bad motive — to protect his own inheritance. Third, the physician acts in a social role through which he is legally authorized to carry out the patient's wishes regarding treatment whereas the son has no such authorization. These and perhaps other ethically important differences show that what the physician did was morally justified whereas what the son did was morally wrong. What they do *not* show, however, is that the son killed while the physician allowed to die. One can either kill or allow to die with or without consent, with a good or bad motive, within or outside of a social role that authorizes one to do so.

The difference between killing and allowing to die that I have been implicitly appealing to here is roughly that between acts and omissions resulting in death.[6] Both the physician and the greedy son act in a manner intended to cause death, do cause death, and so both kill. One reason this conclusion is resisted is that on a different understanding of the distinction between killing and allowing to die, what the physician does is allow to die. In this account, the mother's ALS is a lethal disease whose normal progression is being held back or blocked by the life-sustaining respirator treatment. Removing this artificial intervention is then viewed as standing aside and allowing the patient to die of her underlying disease. I have argued elsewhere that this alternative account is deeply problematic, in part because it commits us to accepting that what the greedy son does is to allow to die, not kill.[7] Here, I want to note two other reasons why the conclusion that stopping life support is killing is resisted.

The first reason is that killing is often understood, especially within medicine, as unjustified causing of death; in medicine it is thought to be done only accidently or negligently. It is also increasingly widely accepted that a physician is ethically justified in stopping life support in a case like that of the ALS patient. But if these two beliefs are correct, then what the physician does cannot be killing, and so must be allowing to die. Killing patients is not, to put it flippantly, understood to be part of physicians' job description. What is mistaken in this line of reasoning is the assumption that all killings are *unjustified* causings of death. Instead, some killings are ethically justified, including many instances of stopping life support.

Another reason for resisting the conclusion that stopping life support is often killing is that it is psychologically uncomfortable. Suppose the physician had stopped the ALS patient's respirator and had made the son's claim, "I didn't kill her. I merely allowed her to die. It was her ALS disease that caused her death." The clue to the psychological role here is how naturally the "merely" modifies "allowed her to die." The characterization as allowing to die is meant to shift felt responsibility away from the agent — the physician — and to the lethal disease process. Other language common in death and dying contexts plays a similar role; "letting nature take its course" or "stopping prolonging the dying process" both seem to shift responsibility from the physician who stops life support to the fatal disease process. However psychologically helpful these conceptualizations may be in making the difficult responsibility of a physician's role in the patient's death bearable, they nevertheless are confusions. Both physicians and family members can instead be helped to understand that it is the patient's decision and consent to stopping treatment that limits their responsibility for the patient's death and that shifts that responsibility to the patient.

Many who accept the difference between killing and allowing to die as the distinction between acts and omissions resulting in death have gone on to argue that killing is not in itself morally different from allowing to die.[8] In this account, very roughly, one kills when one performs an action that causes the death of a person (we are in a boat, you cannot swim, I push you overboard, and you drown), and one allows to die when one has the ability and opportunity to prevent the death of another, knows this, and omits doing so, with the result that the person dies (we are in a boat, you cannot swim, you fall overboard, I don't throw you an available life ring, and you drown). Those who see no moral difference between killing and allowing to die typically employ the strategy of comparing cases that differ in these and no other potentially morally important respects. This will allow people to consider whether the mere difference that one is a case of killing and the other of allowing to die matters morally, or whether instead it is other features that make most cases of killing worse than most instances of allowing to die. Here is such a pair of cases:

Case 1. A very gravely ill patient is brought to a hospital emergency room and sent up to the ICU. The patient begins to develop respiratory failure that is likely to require intubation very soon. At that point the patient's family members and long-standing physician arrive at the ICU and inform the ICU staff that there had been extensive discussion about future care with the patient when he was unquestionably competent. Given his grave and terminal illness, as well as his state of debilitation, the patient had firmly rejected being placed on a respirator under any circumstances, and the family and physician produce the patient's advance directive to that effect. The ICU staff do not intubate the patient, who dies of respiratory failure.

Case 2. The same as Case 1 except that the family and physician are slightly delayed in traffic and arrive shortly after the patient has been intubated and placed on the respirator. The ICU staff extubate the patient, who dies of respiratory failure.

In Case 1 the patient is allowed to die, in Case 2 he is killed, but it is hard to see why what is done in Case 2 is significantly different morally than what is done in Case 1. It must be other factors that make most killings worse than most allowings to die, and if so, euthanasia cannot be wrong simply because it is killing instead of allowing to die.

Suppose both my arguments are mistaken. Suppose that killing is worse than allowing to die and that withdrawing life support is not killing, although euthanasia is. Euthanasia still need not for that reason be morally wrong. To see this, we need to determine the basic principle for the moral evaluation of killing persons. What is it that makes paradigm cases of wrongful killing wrongful? One very plausible answer is that killing denies the victim something that he or she values greatly — continued life or a future. Moreover, since continued life is necessary for pursuing any of a person's plans and purposes, killing brings the frustration of all of these plans and desires as well. In a nutshell, wrongful killing deprives a person of a valued future, and of all the person wanted and planned to do in that future.

A natural expression of this account of the wrongness of killing is that people have a moral right not to be killed.[9] But in this account of the wrongness of killing, the right not to be killed, like other rights, should be waivable when the person makes a competent decision that continued life is no longer wanted or a good, but is instead worse than no further life at all. In this view, euthanasia is properly understood as a case of a person having waived his or her right not to be killed.

This rights view of the wrongness of killing is not, of course, universally shared. Many people's moral views about killing have their origins in religious views that human life comes from God and cannot be justifiably destroyed or taken away, either by the person whose life it is or by another. But in a pluralistic society like our own with a strong commitment to freedom of religion, public policy should not be grounded in religious beliefs which many in that society reject. I turn now to the general evaluation of public policy on euthanasia.

Would the Bad Consequences of Euthanasia Outweigh the Good?

The argument against euthanasia at the policy level is stronger than at the level of individual cases, though even here I believe the case is ultimately unpersuasive, or at best indecisive. The policy level is the place where the main issues lie, however, and where moral considerations that might override arguments in favor of euthanasia will be found, if they are found anywhere. It is important to note two kinds of disagreement about the consequences for public policy of permitting euthanasia. First, there is empirical or factual disagreement about what the consequences would be. This disagreement is greatly exacerbated by the lack of firm data on the issue. Second, since on any reasonable assessment there would be both good and bad consequences, there are moral disagreements about the relative importance of different effects. In addition to these two sources of disagreement, there is also no single, well-specified policy proposal for legalizing euthanasia on which policy assessments can focus. But without such specification, and especially without explicit procedures for protecting against well-intentioned misuse and ill-intentioned abuse, the consequences for policy are largely speculative. Despite these difficulties, a preliminary account of the main likely good and bad consequences is possible. This should help clarify where better data or more moral analysis and argument are needed, as well as where policy safeguards must be developed.

Potential Good Consequences of Permitting Euthanasia

What are the likely good consequences? First, if euthanasia were permitted it would be possible to respect the self-determination of competent patients who want it, but now cannot get it because of its illegality. We simply do not know how many such patients and people there are. In the Netherlands, with a population of about 14.5 million (in 1987), estimates in a recent study were that about 1,900 cases of voluntary active euthanasia or physician-assisted suicide occur annually. No straightforward extrapolation to the United States is possible for many reasons, among them, that we do not know how many people here who want euthanasia now get it, despite its illegality. Even with better data on the number of persons who want euthanasia but cannot get it, significant moral disagreement would remain about how much weight should be given to any instance of failure to respect a person's self-determination in this way.

One important factor substantially affecting the number of persons who would seek euthanasia is the extent to which an alternative is available. The widespread acceptance in the law, social policy, and medical practice of the right of a competent patient to forgo life-sustaining treatment suggests that the number of competent persons in the United States who would want euthanasia if it were permitted is probably relatively small.

A second good consequence of making euthanasia legally permissible benefits a much larger group. Polls have shown that a majority of the American public believes that people should have a right to obtain euthanasia if they want it.[10] No doubt the vast majority of those who support this right to euthanasia will never in fact come to want euthanasia for themselves. Nevertheless, making it legally permissible would reassure many people that if they ever do want euthanasia they would be able to obtain it. This reassurance would supplement the broader control over the process of dying given by the right to decide about life-sustaining treatment. Having fire insurance on one's house benefits all who have it, not just those whose houses actually burn down by reassuring them that in the unlikely event of their house burning down, they will receive the money needed to rebuild it. Likewise, the legalization of euthanasia can be thought of as a kind of insurance policy against being forced to endure a protracted dying process that one has come to find burdensome and unwanted, especially when there is no life-sustaining treatment to forgo. The strong concern about losing control of their care expressed by many people who face serious illness likely to end in death suggests that they give substantial importance to the legalization of euthanasia as a means of maintaining this control.

A third good consequence of the legalization of euthanasia concerns patients whose dying is filled with severe and unrelievable pain or suffering. When there is a life-sustaining treatment that, if forgone, will lead relatively quickly to death, then doing so can bring an end to these patients' suffering without recourse to euthanasia. For patients receiving no such treatment, however, euthanasia may be the only release from their otherwise prolonged suffering and agony. This argument from mercy has always been the strongest argument for euthanasia in those cases to which it applies.[11]

The importance of relieving pain and suffering is less controversial than is the frequency with which patients are forced to undergo untreatable agony that only euthanasia could relieve. If we focus on suffering caused by physical pain, it is crucial to distinguish pain that *could* be adequately relieved with modern methods of pain control, though it in fact is not, from pain that is relievable only by death.[12] For a variety of reasons, including some physicians' fear of hastening the patient's death, as well as the lack of a publicly accessible means for assessing the amount of the patient's pain, many patients suffer pain that could be, but is not, relieved.

Specialists in pain control, as for example the pain of terminally ill cancer patients, argue that there are very few patients whose pain could not be adequately controlled, though sometimes at the cost of so sedating them that they are effectively unable to interact with other people or their environment. Thus, the argument from mercy in cases of physical pain can probably be met in a large majority of cases by providing adequate measures of pain relief. This should be a high priority, whatever our legal policy on euthanasia — the relief of pain and suffering has long been, quite properly, one of the central goals of medicine. Those cases in which pain could be effectively relieved, but in fact is not, should only count significantly in favor of legalizing euthanasia if all reasonable efforts to change pain management techniques have been tried and have failed.

Dying patients often undergo substantial psychological suffering that is not fully or even principally the result of physical pain.[13] The knowledge about how to relieve this suffering is much more limited than in the case of relieving pain, and efforts to do so are probably more often unsuccessful. If the argument from mercy is extended to patients experiencing great and unrelievable psychological suffering, the number of patients to which it applies are much greater.

One last good consequence of legalizing euthanasia is that once death has been accepted, it is often more humane to end life quickly and peacefully, when that is what the patient wants. Such a death will often be seen as better than a more prolonged one. People who suffer a sudden and unexpected death, for example by dying quickly or in their sleep from a heart attack or stroke, are often considered lucky to have died in this way. We care about how we die in part because we care about how others remember us, and we hope they will remember us as we were in "good times" with them and not as we might be when disease has robbed us of our dignity as human beings. As with much in the treatment and care of the dying, people's concerns differ in this respect, but for at least some people, euthanasia will be a more humane death than what they have often experienced with other loved ones and might otherwise expect for themselves.

Some opponents of euthanasia challenge how much importance should be given to any of these good consequences of permitting it, or even whether some would be good consequences at all. But more frequently, opponents cite a number of bad consequences that permitting euthanasia would or could produce, and it is to their assessment that I now turn.

Potential Bad Consequences of Permitting Euthanasia

Some of the arguments against permitting euthanasia are aimed specifically against physicians, while others are aimed against anyone being permitted to perform it. I shall first consider one argument of the former sort. Permitting physicians to perform euthanasia, it is said, would be incompatible with their fundamental moral and professional commitments as healers to care for patients and to protect life. Moreover, if euthanasia by physicians became common, patients would come to fear that a medication was intended not to treat or care, but instead to kill, and would thus lose trust in their physicians. This position was forcefully stated in a paper by Willard Gaylin and his colleagues:

> The very soul of medicine is on trial . . . This issue touches medicine at its moral center; if this moral center collapses, if physicians become killers or are even licensed to kill, the profession — and, therewith, each physician — will never again be worthy of trust and respect as healer and comforter and protector of life in all its frailty.

These authors go on to make clear that, while they oppose permitting any one to perform euthanasia, their special concern is with physicians doing so:

> We call on fellow physicians to say that they will not deliberately kill. We must also say to each of our fellow physicians that we will not tolerate killing of patients and that we shall take disciplinary action against doctors who kill. And we must say to the broader community that if it insists on tolerating or legalizing active euthanasia, it will have to find nonphysicians to do its killing.[14]

If permitting physicians to kill would undermine the very "moral center" of medicine, then almost certainly physicians should not be permitted to perform euthanasia. But how persuasive is this claim? Patients should not fear, as a consequence of permitting *voluntary* active euthanasia, that their physicians will substitute a lethal injection for what patients want and believe is part of their care. If active euthanasia is restricted to cases in which it is truly voluntary, then no patient should fear getting it unless she or he has voluntarily requested it. (The fear that we might in time also come to accept nonvoluntary, or even involuntary, active euthanasia is a slippery slope worry I address below.) Patients' trust of their physicians could be increased, not eroded, by knowledge that physicians will provide aid in dying when patients seek it.

Might Gaylin and his colleagues nevertheless be correct in their claim that the moral center of medicine would collapse if physicians were to become killers? This question raises what at the deepest level should be the guiding aims of medicine, a question that obviously cannot be fully explored here. But I do want to say enough to indicate the direction that I believe an appropriate response to this challenge should take. In spelling out above what I called the positive argument for voluntary active euthanasia, I suggested that two principal values — respecting patients' self-determination and promoting their well-being — underlie the consensus that competent patients, or the surrogates of incompetent patients, are entitled to refuse any life-sustaining treatment and to choose from among available alternative treatments. It is the commitment to these two values in guiding physicians' actions as healers, comforters, and protectors of their patients' lives that should be at the "moral center" of medicine, and these two values support physicians' administering euthanasia when their patients make competent requests for it.

What should not be at that moral center is a commitment to preserving patients' lives as such, without regard to whether those patients want their lives preserved or judge their preservation a benefit to them. Vitalism has been rejected by most physicians, and despite some statements that suggest it, is almost certainly not what Gaylin and colleagues intended. One of them, Leon Kass, has elaborated elsewhere the view that medicine is a moral profession whose proper aim is "the naturally given end of health," understood as the wholeness and well-working of the human being; "for the physician, at least, human life in living bodies commands respect and reverence — *by its very nature*." Kass continues, "the deepest ethical principle restraining the physician's power is not the autonomy or freedom of the patient; neither is it his own compassion or good intention. Rather, it is the dignity and mysterious power of human life itself."[15] I believe Kass is in the end mistaken about the proper account of the aims of medicine and the limits on physicians' power, but this difficult issue will certainly be one of the central themes in the continuing debate about euthanasia.

A second bad consequence that some foresee is that permitting euthanasia would weaken society's commitment to provide optimal care for dying patients. We live at a time in which the control of health care costs has become, and is likely to continue to be, the dominant focus of health care policy. If euthanasia is seen as a cheaper alternative to adequate care and treatment, then we might become less scrupulous about providing sometimes costly support and other services to dying patients. Particularly if our society comes to embrace deeper and more explicit rationing of health care, frail, elderly, and dying patients will need to be strong and effective advocates for their own health care and other needs, although they are hardly in a position to do this. We should do nothing to weaken their ability to obtain adequate care and services.

This second worry is difficult to assess because there is little firm evidence about the likelihood of the feared erosion in the care of dying patients. There are at least two reasons, however, for skepticism about this argument. The first is that the same worry could have been directed at recognizing patients' or surrogates' right to forgo life-sustaining treatment, yet there is no persuasive evidence that recognizing the right to refuse treatment has caused a serious erosion in the quality of care of dying patients. The second reason for skepticism about this worry is that only a very small proportion of deaths would occur from euthanasia if it were permitted. In the Netherlands, where euthanasia under specified circumstances is permitted by the courts, though not authorized by statute, the best estimate of the proportion of overall deaths that result from it is about 2 percent.[16] Thus, the vast majority of critically ill and dying patients will not request it, and so will still have to be cared for by physicians, families, and others. Permitting euthanasia should not diminish people's commitment and concern to maintain and improve the care of these patients.

A third possible bad consequence of permitting euthanasia (or even a public discourse in which strong support for euthanasia is evident) is to threaten the progress made in securing the rights of patients or their surrogates to decide about and to refuse life-sustaining treatment.[17] This progress has been made against the backdrop of a clear and firm legal prohibition of euthanasia, which has provided a relatively bright line limiting the dominion of others over patients' lives. It has therefore been an important reassurance to concerns about how the authority to take steps ending life might be misused, abused, or wrongly extended.

Many supporters of the right of patients or their surrogates to refuse treatment strongly oppose euthanasia, and if forced to choose might well withdraw their support of the right to refuse treatment rather than accept euthanasia. Public policy in the last fifteen years has generally let life-sustaining treatment decisions be made in health care settings between physicians and patients or their surrogates, and without the involvement of the courts. However, if euthanasia is made legally permissible greater involvement of the courts is likely, which could in turn extend to a greater court involvement in life-sustaining treatment decisions. Most agree, however, that increased involvement of the courts in these decisions would be undesirable, as it would make sound decisionmaking more cumbersome and difficult without sufficient compensating benefits.

As with the second potential bad consequence of permitting euthanasia, this third consideration too is speculative and difficult to assess. The feared erosion of patients' or surrogates' rights to decide about life-sustaining treatment, together with greater court involvement in those decisions, are both possible. However, I believe there is reason to discount this general worry. The legal rights of competent patients and, to a lesser degree, surrogates of incompetent patients to decide about treatment are very firmly embedded in a long line of informed consent and life-sustaining treatment cases, and are not likely to be eroded by a debate over, or even acceptance of, euthanasia. It will not be accepted without safeguards that reassure the public about abuse, and if that debate shows the need for similar safeguards for some life-sustaining treatment decisions they should be adopted there as well. In neither case are the only possible safeguards greater court involvement, as the recent growth of institutional ethics committees shows.

The fourth potential bad consequence of permitting euthanasia has been developed by David Velleman and turns on the subtle point that making a new option or choice available to people can sometimes make them worse off, even if once they have the choice they go on to choose what is best for them.[18] Ordinarily, people's continued existence is viewed by them as given, a fixed condition with which they must cope. Making euthanasia available to people as an option denies them the alternative of staying alive by default. If people are offered the option of euthanasia, their continued existence is now a choice for which they can be held responsible and which they can be asked by others to justify. We care, and are right to care, about being able to justify ourselves to others. To the extent that our society is unsympathetic to justifying a severely dependent or impaired existence, a heavy psychological burden of proof may be placed on patients who think their terminal illness or chronic infirmity is not a sufficient reason for dying. Even if they otherwise view their life as worth living, the opinion of others around them that it is not can threaten their reason for living and make euthanasia a rational choice. Thus the existence of the option becomes a subtle pressure to request it.

This argument correctly identifies the reason why offering some patients the option of euthanasia would not benefit them. Velleman takes it not as a reason for opposing all euthanasia, but for restricting it to circumstances where there are "unmistakable and overpowering reasons for persons to want the option of euthanasia," and for denying the option in all other cases. But there are at least three reasons why such restriction may not be warranted. First, polls and other evidence support that most Americans believe euthanasia should be permitted (though the recent defeat of the referendum to permit it in the state of Washington raises some doubt about this support). Thus, many more people seem to want the choice than would be made worse off by getting it. Second, if giving people the option of ending their life really makes them worse off, then we should not only prohibit euthanasia, but also take back from people that right they now have to decide about life-sustaining treatment. The feared harmful effect should already have occurred from securing people's right to refuse life-sustaining treatment, yet there is no evidence of any such widespread harm or any broad public desire to rescind that right. Third, since there is a wide range of conditions in which reasonable people can and do disagree about whether they would want continued life, it is not possible to restrict the permissibility of euthanasia as narrowly as Velleman suggests without thereby denying it to most persons who would want it; to permit it only in cases in which virtually everyone would want it would be to deny it to most who would want it.

A fifth potential bad consequence of making euthanasia legally permissible is that it might weaken the general legal prohibition of homicide. This prohibition is so fundamental to civilized society, it is argued, that we should do nothing that erodes it. If most cases of stopping life support are killing, as I have already argued, then the court cases permitting such killing have already in effect weakened this prohibition. However, neither the courts nor most people have seen these cases as killing and so as challenging the prohibition of homicide. The courts have usually grounded patients' or their surrogates' rights to refuse life-sustaining treatment in rights to privacy, liberty, self-determination, or bodily integrity, not in exceptions to homicide laws.

Legal permission for physicians or others to perform euthanasia could not be grounded in patients' rights to decide about medical treatment. Permitting euthanasia would require qualifying, at least in effect, the legal prohibition against homicide, a prohibition that in general does not allow the consent of the victim to justify or excuse the act. Nevertheless, the very same fundamental basis of the right to decide about life-sustaining treatment — respecting a person's self-determination — does support euthanasia as well. Individual self-determination has long been a well-entrenched and fundamental value in the law, and so extending it to euthanasia would not require appeal to novel legal values or principles. That suicide or attempted suicide is no longer a criminal offense in virtually all states indicates an acceptance of individual self-determination in the taking of one's own life analogous to that required for voluntary active euthanasia. The legal prohibition (in most states) of assisting in suicide and the refusal in the law to accept the consent of the victim as a possible justification of homicide are both arguably a result of difficulties in the legal process of establishing the consent of the victim after the fact. If procedures can be designed that clearly establish the voluntariness of the person's request for euthanasia, it would under those procedures represent a carefully circumscribed qualification on the legal prohibition of homicide. Nevertheless, some remaining worries about this weakening can be captured in the final potential bad consequence, to which I will now turn.

This final potential bad consequence is the central concern of many opponents of euthanasia and, I believe, is the most serious objection to a legal policy permitting it. According to this "slippery slope" worry, although active euthanasia may be morally permissible in cases in which it is unequivocally voluntary and the patient finds his or her condition unbearable, a legal policy permitting euthanasia would inevitably lead to active euthanasia being performed in many other cases in which it would be morally wrong. To prevent those other wrongful cases of euthanasia we should not permit even morally justified performance of it.

Slippery slope arguments of this form are problematic and difficult to evaluate.[19] From one perspective, they are the last refuge of conservative defenders of the status quo. When all the opponent's objections to the wrongness of euthanasia itself have been met, the opponent then shifts ground and acknowledges both that it is not in itself wrong and that a legal policy which resulted only in its being performed would not be bad. Nevertheless, the opponent maintains, it should still not be permitted because doing so would result in its being performed in other cases in which it is not voluntary and would be wrong. In this argument's most extreme form, permitting euthanasia is the first and fateful step down the slippery slope to Nazism. Once on the slope we will be unable to get off.

Now it cannot be denied that it is *possible* that permitting euthanasia could have these fateful consequences, but that cannot be enough to warrant prohibiting it if it is otherwise justified. A similar *possible* slippery slope worry could have been raised to securing competent patients' rights to decide about life support, but recent history shows such a worry would have been unfounded. It must be relevant how likely it is that we will end with horrendous consequences and an unjustified practice of euthanasia. How *likely* and *widespread* would the abuses and unwarranted extensions of permitting it be? By abuses, I mean the performance of euthanasia that fails to satisfy the conditions required for voluntary active euthanasia, for example, if the patient has been subtly pressured to accept it. By unwarranted extensions of policy, I mean later changes in legal policy to permit not just voluntary euthanasia, but also euthanasia in cases in which, for example, it need not be fully voluntary. Opponents of voluntary euthanasia on slippery slope grounds have not provided the data or evidence necessary to turn their speculative concerns into well-grounded likelihoods.

It is at least clear, however, that both the character and likelihood of abuses of a legal policy permitting euthanasia depend in significant part on the procedures put in place to protect against them. I will not try to detail fully what such procedures might be, but will just give some examples of what they might include:

1. The patient should be provided with all relevant information about his or her medical condition, current prognosis, available alternative treatments, and the prognosis of each.
2. Procedures should ensure that the patient's request for euthanasia is stable or enduring (a brief waiting period could be required) and fully voluntary (an advocate for the patient might be appointed to ensure this).
3. All reasonable alternatives must have been explored for improving the patient's quality of life and relieving any pain or suffering.
4. A psychiatric evaluation should ensure that the patient's request is not the result of a treatable psychological impairment such as depression.[20]

These examples of procedural safeguards are all designed to ensure that the patient's choice is fully informed, voluntary, and competent, and so a true exercise of self-determination. Other proposals for euthanasia would restrict its permissibility further — for example, to the terminally ill — a restriction that cannot be supported by self-determination. Such additional restrictions might, however, be justified by concern for limiting potential harms from abuse. At the same time, it is important not to impose procedural or substantive safeguards so restrictive as to make euthanasia impermissible or practically infeasible in a wide range of justified cases.

These examples of procedural safeguards make clear that it is possible to substantially reduce, though not to eliminate, the potential for abuse of a policy permitting voluntary active euthanasia. Any legalization of the practice should be accompanied by a well-considered set of procedural safeguards together with an ongoing evaluation of its use. Introducing euthanasia into only a few states could be a form of carefully limited and controlled social experiment that would give us evidence about the benefits and harms of the practice. Even then firm and uncontroversial data may remain elusive, as the continuing controversy over what has taken place in the Netherlands in recent years indicates.[21]

The Slip into Nonvoluntary Active Euthanasia

While I believe slippery slope worries can largely be limited by making necessary distinctions both in principle and in practice, one slippery slope concern is legitimate. There is reason to expect that legalization of voluntary euthanasia might soon be followed by strong pressure to legalize some nonvoluntary euthanasia of incompetent patients unable to express their own wishes. Respecting a person's self-determination and recognizing that continued life is not always of value to a person can support not only voluntary active euthanasia, but some non voluntary euthanasia as well. These are the same values that ground competent patients' right to refuse life-sustaining treatment. Recent history here is instructive. In the medical ethics literature, in the courts since Quinlan, and in norms of medical practice, that right has been extended to incompetent patients and exercised by a surrogate who is to decide as the patient would have decided in the circumstances if competent.[22] It has been held unreasonable to continue life-sustaining treatment that the patient would not have wanted just because the patient now lacks the capacity to tell us that. Life-sustaining treatment for incompetent patients is today frequently forgone on the basis of a surrogate's decision, or less frequently on the basis of an advance directive executed by the patient while still competent. The very same logic that has extended the right to refuse life-sustaining treatment from a competent patient to the surrogate of an incompetent patient (acting with or without a formal advance directive from the patient) may well extend the scope of active euthanasia. The argument will be, Why continue to force unwanted life on patients just because they have now lost the capacity to request euthanasia from us?

A related phenomenon may reinforce this slippery slope concern. In the Netherlands, what the courts have sanctioned has been clearly restricted to voluntary euthanasia. In itself, this serves some evidence that permitting it need *not* lead to permitting the nonvoluntary variety. There is some indication, however, that for many Dutch physicians euthanasia is no longer viewed as a special action, set apart from their usual practice and restricted only to competent persons.[23] Instead, it is seen as one end of a spectrum of caring for dying patients. When viewed in this way it will be difficult to deny euthanasia to a patient for whom it is seen as the best or most appropriate form of care simply because that patient is now incompetent and cannot request it.

Even if voluntary active euthanasia should slip into nonvoluntary active euthanasia, with surrogates acting for incompetent patients, the ethical evaluation is more complex than many opponents of euthanasia allow. Just as in the case of surrogates' decisions to forgo life-sustaining treatment for incompetent patients, so also surrogates' decisions to request euthanasia for incompetent persons would often accurately reflect what the incompetent person would have wanted and would deny the person nothing that he or she would have considered worth having. Making nonvoluntary active euthanasia legally permissible, however, would greatly enlarge the number of patients on whom it might be performed and substantially enlarge the potential for misuse and abuse. As noted above, frail and debilitated elderly people, often demented or otherwise incompetent and thereby unable to defend and assert their own interests, may be especially vulnerable to unwanted euthanasia.

For some people, this risk is more than sufficient reason to oppose the legalization of voluntary euthanasia. But while we should in general be cautious about inferring much from the experience in the Netherlands to what our own experience in the United States might be, there may be one important lesson that we can learn from them. One commentator has noted that in the Netherlands families of incompetent patients have less authority than do families in the United State to act as surrogates for incompetent patients in making decisions to forgo life-sustaining treatment.[24] From the Dutch perspective, it may be we in the United States who are *already* on the slippery slope in having given surrogates broad authority to forgo life-sustaining treatment for incompetent persons. In this view, the more important moral divide, and the more important with regard to potential for abuse, is not between forgoing life-sustaining treatment and euthanasia, but instead between voluntary and nonvoluntary performance of either. If this is correct, then the more important issue is ensuring the appropriate principles and procedural safeguards for the exercise of decisionmaking authority by surrogates for incompetent persons in *all* decisions at the end of life. This may be the correct response to slippery slope worries about euthanasia.

I have cited both good and bad consequences that have been thought likely from a policy change permitting voluntary active euthanasia, and have tried to evaluate their likelihood and relative importance. Nevertheless, as I noted earlier, reasonable disagreement remains both about the consequences of permitting euthanasia and about which of these consequences are more important. The depth and strength of public and professional debate about whether, all things considered, permitting euthanasia would be desirable or undesirable reflects these disagreements. While my own view is that the balance of considerations supports permitting the practice, my principal purpose here has been to clarify the main issues.

The Role of Physicians

If euthanasia is made legally permissible, should physicians take part in it? Should only physicians be permitted to perform it, as is the case in the Netherlands? In discussing whether euthanasia is incompatible with medicine's commitment to curing, caring for, and comforting patients, I argued that it is not at odds with a proper understanding of the aims of medicine, and so need not undermine patients' trust in their physicians. If that argument is correct, then physicians probably should not be prohibited, either by law or by professional norms, from taking part in a legally permissible practice of euthanasia (nor, of course, should they be compelled to do so if their personal or professional scruples forbid it). Most physicians in the Netherlands appear not to understand euthanasia to be incompatible with their professional commitments.

Sometimes patients who would be able to end their lives on their own nevertheless seek the assistance of physicians. Physicians involvement in such cases may have important benefits to patients and others beyond simply assuring the use of effective means. Historically, in the United States suicide has carried a strong negative stigma that many today believe unwarranted. Seeking a physician's assistance, or what can almost seem a physician's blessing, may be a way of trying to remove that stigma and show others that the decision for suicide was made with due seriousness and was justified under the circumstances. The physician's involvement provides a kind of social approval, or more accurately helps counter what would otherwise be unwarranted social disapproval.

There are also at least two reasons for restricting the practice of euthanasia to physicians only. First, physicians would inevitably be involved in some of the important procedural safeguards necessary to a defensible practice, such as seeing to it that the patient is well-informed about his or her condition, prognosis, and possible treatments, and ensuring that all reasonable means have been taken to improve the quality of the patient's life. Second, and probably more important, one necessary protection against abuse of the practice is to limit the persons given authority to perform it, so that they can be held accountable for their exercise of that authority. Physicians, whose training and professional norms give some assurance that they would perform euthanasia responsibly, are an appropriate group of persons to whom the practice may be restricted.

Acknowledgements: Earlier versions of this paper were presented at the American Philosophical Association Central Division meetings (at which David Velleman provided extremely helpful comments), Massachusetts General Hospital, Yale University School of Medicine, Princeton University, Brown University, and as the Brin Lecture at The Johns Hopkins School of Medicine. I am grateful to the audiences on each of these occasions, to several anonymous reviewers, and to Norman Daniels for helpful comments. The paper was completed while I was a Fellow in the Program in Ethics and the Professions at Harvard University.

References

1. President's Commission for the Study of Ethical Problems in Medicine and Biomedical and Behavioral Research. *Deciding to Forego Life-Sustaining Treatment* (Washington, D.C.: U.S. Government Printing Office, 1983); The Hastings Center. *Guidelines on the Termination of Life-Sustaining Treatment and Care*

of the Dying (Bloomington: Indiana University Press, 1987); *Current Opinions of the Council on Ethical and Judicial Affairs of the American Medical Association — 1989: Withholding or Withdrawing Life-Prolonging Treatment* (Chicago: American Medical Association, 1989); George Annas and Leonard Glantz, "The Right of Elderly Patients to Refuse Life-Sustaining Treatment," *Millbank Memorial Quarterly* 64, suppl. 2 (1986): 95–162; Robert F. Weir, *Abating Treatment with Critically Ill Patients* (New York: Oxford University Press, 1989); Sidney J. Wanzer et al. "The Physician's Responsibility toward Hopelessly Ill Patients," *NEJM* 310 (1984): 955–59.

2. M.A.M. de Wachter, "Active Euthanasia in the Netherlands," *JAMA* 262, no. 23 (1989): 3315–19

3. Anonymous, "It's Over, Debbie," *JAMA* 259 (1988): 272; Timothy E. Quill, "Death and Dignity," *NEJM* 322 (1990): 1881–83.

4. Wanzer et al., "The Physician's Responsibility toward Hopelessly Ill Patients: A Second Look," *NEJM* 320 (1989): 844–49.

5. Willard Gaylin, Leon R. Kass, Edmund D. Pellegrino, and Mark Siegler, "Doctors Must Not Kill," *JAMA* 259 (1988): 2139–40.

6. Bonnie Steinbock, ed., *Killing and Allowing to Die* (Englewood Cliffs, N.J.: Prentice Hall, 1980).

7. Dan W. Brock, "Forgoing Food and Water: Is It Killing?" in *By No Extraordinary Means: The Choice to Forgo Life-Sustaining Food and Water*, ed. Joanne Lynn (Bloomington: Indiana University Press, 1986), pp. 117–31.

8. James Rachels, "Active and Passive Euthanasia," *NEJM* 292 (1975): 78–80; Michael Tooley, *Abortion and Infanticide* (Oxford: Oxford University Press, 1983). In my paper, "Taking Human Life," *Ethics* 95 (1985): 851–65, I argue in more detail that killing in itself is not morally different from allowing to die and defend the strategy of argument employed in this and the succeeding two paragraphs in the text.

9. Dan W. Brock, "Moral Rights and Permissible Killing," in *Ethical Issues Relating to Life and Death*, ed. John Ladd (New York: Oxford University Press, 1979), pp. 94–117.

10. P. Painton and E. Taylor, "Love or Let Die," *Time*, 19 March 1990, pp. 62–71; *Boston*

Globe/Harvard University Poll, *Boston Globe*, 3 November 1991.

11. James Rachels, *The End of Life* (Oxford: Oxford University Press, 1986).

12. Marcia Angell, "The Quality of Mercy," *NEJM* 306 (1982): 98–99; M. Donovan, P. Dillon, and L. Mcguire, "Incidence and Characteristics of Pain in a Sample of Medical-Surgical Inpatients," *Pain* 30 (1987): 69–78.

13. Eric Cassell, *The Nature of Suffering and the Goals of Medicine* (New York: Oxford University Press, 1991).

14. Gaylin et al., "Doctors Must Not Kill."

15. Leon R. Kass, "Neither for Love Nor Money: Why Doctors Must Not Kill," *The Public Interest* 94 (1989): 25–46; cf. also his *Toward a More Natural Science: Biology and Human Affairs* (New York: The Free Press, 1985), chs. 6–9.

16. Paul J. Van der Maas et al., "Euthanasia and Other Medical Decisions Concerning the End of Life," *Lancet* 338 (1991): 669–74.

17. Susan M. Wolf. "Holding the Line on Euthanasia," Special Supplement, *Hastings Center Report* 19, no. 1 (1989): 13–15.

18. My formulation of this argument derives from David Velleman's statement of it in his commentary on an earlier version of this paper delivered at the American Philosophical Association Central Division meetings; a similar point was made to me by Elisha Milgram in discussion on another occasion. For more general development of the point see Thomas Schelling, *The Strategy of Conflict* (Cambridge, Mass.: Harvard University Press, 1960); and Gerald Dworkin, "Is More Choice Better Than Less?" in *The Theory and Practice of Autonomy* (Cambridge: Cambridge University Press, 1988).

19. Frederick Schaeuer, "Slippery Slopes," *Harvard Law Review* 99 (1985): 361–83; Wibren van der Burg, "The Slippery Slope Argument," *Ethics* 102 (October 1991): 42–65.

20. There is evidence that physicians commonly fail to diagnose depression. See Robert I. Misbin, "Physicians Aid in Dying," *NEJM* 325 (1991): 1304–7.

21. Richard Fenigsen, "A Case against Dutch

Euthanasia," Special Supplement, *Hastings Center Report* 19, no. 1 (1989): 22–30.

22.   Allen E. Buchanan and Dan W. Brock, *Deciding for Others: The Ethics of Surrogate Decisionmaking* (Cambridge: Cambridge University Press, 1989).

23.   Van der Maas et al., "Euthanasia and Other Medical Decisions."

24.   Margaret P. Battin, "Seven Caveats Concerning the Discussion of Euthanasia in Holland," *American Philosophical Association Newsletter on Philosophy and Medicine* 89, no. 2 (1990).

52   When Self-Determination Runs Amok

Daniel Callahan

The euthanasia debate is not just another moral debate, one in a long list of arguments in our pluralistic society. It is profoundly emblematic of three important turning points in Western thought. The first is that of the legitimate conditions under which one person can kill another. The acceptance of voluntary active euthanasia would morally sanction what can only be called "consenting adult killing." By that term I mean the killing of one person by another in the name of their mutual right to be killer and killed if they freely agree to play those roles. This turn flies in the face of a long-standing effort to limit the circumstances under which one person can take the life of another, from efforts to control the free flow of guns and arms, to abolish capital punishment, and to more tightly control warfare. Euthanasia would add a whole new category of killing to a society that already has too many excuses to indulge itself in that way.

The second turning point lies in the meaning and limits of self-determination. The acceptance of euthanasia would sanction a view of autonomy holding that individuals may, in the name of their own private, idiosyncratic view of the good life, call upon others, including such institutions as medicine, to help them pursue that life, even at the risk of harm to the common good. This works against the idea that the meaning and scope of our own right to lead our own lives must be conditioned by and be compatible with, the good of the community, which is more than an aggregate of self-directing individuals.

The third turning point is to be found in the claim being made upon medicine: it should be prepared to make its skills available to individuals to help them achieve their private vision of the good life. This puts medicine in the business of promoting the individualistic pursuit of general human happiness and well-being. It would overturn the traditional belief that medicine should limit its domain to promoting and preserving human health, redirecting it instead to the relief of that suffering which stems from life itself, not merely from a sick body.

I believe that, at each of these three turning points, proponents of euthanasia push us in the wrong direction. Arguments in favor of euthanasia fall into four general categories, which I will take up in turn: (1) the moral claim of individual self-determination and well-being; (2) the moral irrelevance of the difference between killing and allowing to die; (3) the supposed paucity of evidence to show likely harmful consequences of legalized euthanasia; and (4) the compatibility of euthanasia and medical practice.

Self-Determination

Central to most arguments for euthanasia is the principle of self-determination. People are presumed to have an interest in deciding for themselves, according to their own beliefs about what makes life good, how they will conduct their lives. That is an important value, but the question in the euthanasia context is, What does it mean and how far should it extend? If it were a question of suicide, where a person takes her own life without assistance from another, that principle might be pertinent, at least for debate. But euthanasia is not that limited a matter. The self-determination in that case can only be effected by the moral and physical assistance of another. Euthanasia is thus no longer a matter only of self-determination, but of a mutual, social decision between two people, the one to be killed and the other to do the killing.

How are we to make the moral move from my right of self-determination to some doctor's right to kill me — from *my* right to *his* right? Where does the doctor's moral warrant to kill come from? Ought doctors to be able to kill anyone they want as long as permission is given by competent persons? Is our right to life just like a piece of property, to be given away or alienated if the price (happiness, relief of suffering) is right? And then to be destroyed with our permission once alienated?

In answer to all those questions, I will say this: I have yet to hear a plausible argument why it should be permissible for us to put this kind of power in the hands of another, whether a doctor or anyone else. The idea that we can waive our right to life, and then give to another the power to take that life, requires a justification yet to be provided by anyone.

Slavery was long ago outlawed on the ground that one person should not have the right to own another, even with the other's permission. Why? Because it is a fundamental moral wrong for one person to give over his life and fate to another, whatever the good consequences, and no less a wrong for another person to have that kind of total, final power. Like slavery, dueling was long ago banned on similar grounds: even free, competent individuals should not have the power to kill each other, whatever their motives, whatever the circumstances. Consenting adult killing, like consenting adult slavery or degradation, is a strange route to human dignity.

There is another problem as well. If doctors, once sanctioned to carry out euthanasia, are to be themselves responsible moral agents — not simply hired hands with lethal injections at the ready — then they must have their own *independent* moral grounds to kill those who request such services. What do I mean? As those who favor euthanasia are quick to point out, some people want it because their life has become so burdensome it no longer seems worth living. The doctor will have a difficulty at this point. The degree and intensity to which people suffer from their diseases and their dying, and whether they find life more of a burden than a benefit, has very little directly to do with the nature or extent of their actual physical condition. Three people can have the same condition, but only one will find the suffering unbearable. People suffer, but suffering is as much a function of the values of individuals as it is of the physical causes of that suffering. Inevitably in that circumstance, the doctor will in effect be treating the patient's values. To be responsible, the doctor would have to share those values. The doctor would have to decide, on her own, whether the patient's life was "no longer worth living."

But how could a doctor possibly know that or make such a judgment? Just because the patient said so? I raise this question because, while in Holland at the euthanasia conference reported by Maurice de Wachter elsewhere in this issue, the doctors present agreed that there is no objective way of measuring or judging the claims of patients that their suffering is unbearable. And if it is difficult to measure suffering, how much more difficult to determine the value of a patient's statement that her life is not worth living?

However one might want to answer such questions, the very need to ask them, to inquire into the physician's responsibility and grounds for medical and moral judgment, points out the social nature of the decision. Euthanasia is not a private matter of self-determination. It is an act that requires two people to make it possible, and a complicit society to make it acceptable.

Killing and Allowing to Die

Against common opinion, the argument is sometimes made that there is no moral difference between stopping life-sustaining treatment and more active forms of killing, such as lethal injection. Instead I would contend that the notion that there is no morally significant difference between omission and commission is just wrong. Consider in its broad implications what the eradication of the distinction implies: that death from disease has been banished, leaving only the actions of physicians in terminating treatment as the cause of death. Biology, which used to bring about death, has apparently been displaced by human agency. Doctors have finally, I suppose, thus genuinely become gods, now doing what nature and the deities once did.

What is the mistake here? It lies in confusing causality and culpability, and in failing to note the way in which human societies have overlaid natural causes with moral rules and interpretations. Causality (by which I mean the direct physical causes of death) and culpability (by which I mean our attribution of moral responsibility to human actions) are confused under three circumstances.

They are confused, first, when the action of a physician in stopping treatment of a patient with an underlying lethal disease is construed as *causing* death. On the contrary, the physician's omission can only bring about death on the condition that the patient's disease will kill him in the absence of treatment. We may hold the physician morally responsible for the death, if we have morally judged such actions wrongful omissions. But it confuses reality and moral judgment to see an omitted action as having the same causal status as one that directly kills. A lethal injection will kill both a healthy person and a sick person. A physician's omitted treatment will have no effect on a healthy person. Turn off the machine on me, a healthy person, and nothing will happen. It will only, in contrast, bring the life of a sick person to an end because of an underlying fatal disease.

Causality and culpability are confused, second, when we fail to note that judgments of moral responsibility and culpability are human constructs. By that I mean that we human beings, after moral reflection, have decided to call some actions right or wrong, and to devise moral rules to deal with them. When physicians could do nothing to stop death, they were not held responsible for it. When, with medical progress, they began to have some power over death — but only its timing and circumstances, not its ultimate inevitability — moral rules were devised to set forth their obligations. Natural causes of death were not thereby banished. They were, instead, overlaid with a medical ethics designed to determine moral culpability in deploying medical power.

To confuse the judgments of this ethics with the physical causes of death — which is the connotation of the word *kill* — is to confuse nature and human action. People will, one way or another, die of some disease; death will have dominion over all of us. To say that a doctor "kills" a patient by allowing this to happen should only be understood as a moral judgment about the licitness of his omission, nothing more. We can, as a fashion of speech only, talk about a doctor *killing* a patient by omitting treatment he should have provided. It is a fashion of speech precisely because it is the underlying disease that brings death when treatment is omitted; that is its cause, not the physician's omission. It is a misuse of the world *killing* to use it when a doctor stops a treatment he believes will no longer benefit the patient — when, that is, he steps aside to allow an eventually inevitable death to occur now rather than later. The only deaths that human beings invented are those that come from direct killing — when, with a lethal injection, we both cause death and are morally responsible for it. In the case of omissions, we do not cause death even if we may be judged morally responsible for it.

This difference between causality and culpability also help us see why a doctor who has omitted a treatment he should have provided has "killed" that patient while another doctor — performing precisely the same act of omission on another patient in different circumstances — does not kill her, but only allows her to die. The difference is that we have come, by moral convention and conviction, to classify unauthorized or illegitimate omissions as acts of "killing." We call them "killing" in the expanded sense of the term: a culpable action that permits the real cause of death, the underlying disease, to proceed to its lethal conclusion. By contrast, the doctor who, at the patient's request, omits or terminates unwanted treatment does not kill at all. Her underlying disease, not his action, is the physical cause of death; and we have agreed to consider actions of that kind to be morally licit. He thus can truly be said to have "allowed" her to die.

If we fail to maintain the distinction between killing and allowing to die, moreover, there are some disturbing possibilities. The first would be to confirm many physicians in their already too-powerful belief that, when patients die or when physicians stop treatment because of the futility of continuing it, they are somehow both morally and physically responsible for the deaths that follow. That notion needs to be abolished, not strengthened. It needlessly and wrongly burdens the physician, to whom should not be attributed the powers of the gods. The second possibility would be that, in every case where a doctor judges medical treatment no longer effective in prolonging life, a quick and direct killing of the patient would be seen as the next, most reasonable step, on grounds of both humaneness and economics. I do not see how that logic could easily be rejected.

Calculating the Consequences

When concerns about the adverse social consequences of permitting euthanasia are raised, its advocates tend to dismiss them as unfounded and overly speculative. On the contrary, recent data about the Dutch experience suggests that such concerns are right on target. From my own discussions in Holland, and from the articles on that subject in this issue and elsewhere, I believe we can now fully see most of the *likely* consequences of legal euthanasia.

Three consequences seem almost certain, in this or any other country: the inevitability of some abuse of the law; the difficulty of precisely writing, and then enforcing, the law; and the inherent slipperiness of the moral reasons for legalizing euthanasia in the first place.

Why is abuse inevitable? One reason is that almost all laws on delicate, controversial matters are to some extent abused. This happens because not everyone will agree with the law as written and will bend it, or ignore it, if they can get away with it. From explicit admissions to me by Dutch proponents of euthanasia, and from the corroborating information provided by the Remmelink Report and the outside studies of Carlos Gomez and John Keown, I am convinced that in the Netherlands there are a substantial number of cases of nonvoluntary euthanasia, that is, euthanasia undertaken without the explicit permission of the person being killed. The other reason abuse is inevitable is that the law is likely to have a low enforcement priority in the criminal justice system. Like other laws of similar status, unless there is an unrelenting and harsh willingness to pursue abuse, violations will ordinarily be tolerated. The worst thing to me about my experience in Holland was the casual, seemingly indifferent attitude toward abuse. I think that would happen everywhere.

Why would it be hard to precisely write, and then enforce, the law? The Dutch speak about the requirement of "unbearable" suffering, but admit that such a term is just about indefinable, a highly subjective matter admitting of no objective standards. A requirement for outside opinion is nice, but it is easy to find complaisant colleagues. A requirement that a medical condition be "terminal" will run aground on the notorious difficulties of knowing when an illness is actually terminal.

Apart from those technical problems there is a more profound worry. I see no way, even in principle, to write or enforce a meaningful law that can guarantee effective procedural safeguards. The reason is obvious yet almost always overlooked. The euthanasia transaction will ordinarily take place within the boundaries of the private and confidential doctor–patient relationship. No one can possibly know what takes place in that context unless the doctor chooses to reveal it. In Holland, less than 10 percent of the physicians report their acts of euthanasia and do so with almost complete legal impunity. There is no reason why the situation should be any better elsewhere. Doctors will have their own reasons for keeping euthanasia secret, and some patients will have no less a motive for wanting it concealed.

I would mention, finally, that the moral logic of the motives for euthanasia contain within them the ingredients of abuse. The two standard motives for euthanasia and assisted suicide are said to be our right of self-determination, and our claim upon the mercy of others, especially doctors, to relieve our suffering. These two motives are typically spliced together and presented as a single justification. Yet if they are considered independently — and there is no inherent reason why they must be linked — they reveal serious problems. It is said that a competent, adult person should have a right to euthanasia for the relief of suffering. But why must the person be suffering? Does not that stipulation already compromise the principle of self-determination? How can self-determination have any limits? Whatever the person's motives may be, why are they not sufficient?

Consider next the person who is suffering but not competent, who is perhaps demented or mentally retarded. The standard argument would deny euthanasia to that person. But why? If a person is suffering but not competent, then it would seem grossly unfair to deny relief solely on the grounds of incompetence. Are the incompetent less entitled to relief from suffering than the competent? Will it only be affluent, middle-class people, mentally fit and savvy about working the medical system, who can qualify? Do the incompetent suffer less because of their incompetence?

Considered from these angles, there are no good moral reasons to limit euthanasia once the principle of taking life for that purpose has been legitimated. If we really believe in self-determination, then any competent person should have a right to be killed by a doctor for any reason that suits him. If we believe in the relief of suffering, then it seems cruel and capricious to deny it to the incompetent. There is, in short, no reasonable or logical stopping point once the turn has been made down the road to euthanasia, which could soon turn into a convenient and commodious expressway.

Euthanasia and Medical Practice

A fourth kind of argument one often hears both in the Netherlands and in this country is that euthanasia and assisted suicide are perfectly compatible with the aims of medicine. I would note at the very outset that a physician who participates in another person's suicide already abuses medicine. Apart from depression (the main statistical cause of suicide), people commit suicide because they find life empty, oppressive, or meaningless. Their judgment is a judgment about the value of continued life, not only about health (even if they are sick). Are doctors now to be given the right to make judgments about the kinds of life worth living and to give their blessing to suicide for those they judge wanting? What conceivable competence, technical or moral, could doctors claim to play such a role? Are we to medicalize suicide, turning judgments about its worth and value into one more clinical issue? Yes, those are rhetorical questions.

Yet they bring us to the core of the problem of euthanasia and medicine. The great temptation of modern medicine, not always resisted, is to move beyond the promotion and preservation of health into the boundless realm of general human happiness and well-being. The root problem of illness and mortality is both medical and philosophical or religious. "Why must I die?" can be asked as a technical, biological question or as a question about the meaning of life. When medicine tries to respond to the latter, which it is always under pressure to do, it moves beyond its proper role.

It is not medicine's place to lift from us the burden of that suffering which turns on the meaning we assign to the decay of the body and its eventual death. It is not medicine's place to determine when lives are not worth living or when the burden of life is too great to be borne. Doctors have no conceivable way of evaluating such claims on the part of patients, and they should have no right to act in response to them. Medicine should try to relieve human suffering, but only that suffering which is brought on by illness and dying as biological phenomena, not that suffering which comes from anguish or despair at the human condition.

Doctors ought to relieve those forms of suffering that medically accompany serious illness and the threat of death. They should relieve pain, do what they can to allay anxiety and uncertainty, and be a comforting presence. As sensitive human beings, doctors should be prepared to respond to patients who ask why they must die, or die in pain. But here the doctor and the patient are at the same level. The doctor may have no better answer to those old questions than anyone else; and certainly no special insight from his training as a physician. It would be terrible for physicians to forget this, and to think that in a swift, lethal injection, medicine has found its own answer to the riddle of life. It would be a false answer, given by the wrong people. It would be no less a false answer for patients. They should neither ask medicine to put its own vocation at risk to serve their private interests, nor think that the answer to suffering is to be killed by another. The problem is precisely that, too often in human history, killing has seemed the quick, efficient way to put aside that which burdens us. It rarely helps, and too often simply adds to one evil still another. That is what I believe euthanasia would accomplish. It is self-determination run amok.

53   Sue Rodriguez v. The Attorney General of Canada and the Attorney General of British Columbia

Supreme Court of Canada

[The constitutional questions answered in this decision of the Supreme Court of Canada are:

1. Does s. 241(b) of the *Criminal Code* of Canada infringe or deny, in whole or in part, the rights and freedoms guaranteed by ss. 7, 12 and 15(1) of the *Canadian Charter of Rights and Freedoms*?
2. If so, is it justified by s. 1 of the *Canadian Charter of Rights and Freedoms* and therefore not inconsistent with the *Constitution Act, 1982*?

The Supreme Court held, in a lengthy five-to-four decision, that section 241(b) of the *Criminal Code* is constitutional. Different answers to the two questions are given in the four opinions for the case. Brief excerpts from three of the opinions are provided; the passages selected show how issues discussed in this chapter are pertinent to the Surpreme Court's decision.

The provisions of the *Criminal Code* and the *Charter* discussed in the excerpts are:

Section 241 of the Criminal Code, R.S.C., 1985, c. C–46:

241.   Every one who

(a) counsels a person to commit suicide, or

(b) aids or abets a person to commit suicide,

whether suicide ensues or not, is guilty of an indictable offence and liable to imprisonment for a term not exceeding fourteen years.

Sections 1, 7, and 15(1) of the *Canadian Charter of Rights and Freedoms*:

1.   The *Canadian Charter of Rights and Freedoms* guarantees the rights and freedoms set out in it subject only to such reasonable limits prescribed by law as can be demonstrably justified in a free and democratic society.

7.   Everyone has the right to life, liberty and security of the person and the right not to be deprived thereof except in accordance with the principles of fundamental justice.

15.(1) Every individual is equal before and under the law and has the right to the equal protection and equal benefit of the law without discrimination and, in particular, without discrimination based on race, national or ethnic origin, colour, religion, sex, age or mental or physical disability.

Justice Sopinka (with four others) held that s. 241 does not limit s. 7 rights and assumed, without deciding, that it limits s. 15(1) rights. He concluded that the limitation of s. 15(1) rights is justifiable under s.1. Chief Justice Lamer held that s. 241 limits s. 15(1) rights and is not justifiable under s.1. Madam Justice McLachlin (with one other) held that s. 241 limits s. 7 rights and is not justifiable under s. 1.]

SOPINKA J.: — . . . The effect of the prohibition in s. 241(b) is to prevent the appellant [Sue Rodriguez] from having assistance to commit suicide when she is no longer able to do so on her own. She fears that she will be required to live until the deterioration from her disease is such that she will die as a result of choking, suffocation or pneumonia caused by aspiration of food or secretions. She will be totally dependent upon machines to perform her bodily functions and completely dependent upon others. Throughout this time, she will remain mentally competent and able to appreciate all that is happening to her. Although palliative care may be available to ease the pain and other physical discomfort which she will experience, the appellant fears the sedating effects of such drugs and argues, in any event, that they will not prevent the psychological and emotional distress which will result from being in a situation of utter dependence and loss of dignity. That there is a right to choose how one's body will be dealt with, even in the context of beneficial medical treatment, has long been recognized by the common law. To impose medical treatment on one who refuses it constitutes battery, and our common law has recognized the right to demand that medical treatment which would extend life be withheld or withdrawn. In my view, these considerations lead to the conclusion that the prohibition in s. 241(b) deprives the appellant of autonomy over her person and causes her physical pain and psychological stress in a manner which impinges on the security of her person. The appellant's security interest [in s.7] (considered in the context of the life and liberty interest) is therefore engaged, and it is necessary to determine whether there has been any deprivation thereof that is not in accordance with the principles of fundamental justice. . . .

Canadian courts have recognized a common law right of patients to refuse consent to medical treatment, or to demand that treatment, once commenced, be withdrawn or discontinued (*Ciarlariello v. Schacter*, [1993] 2 S.C.R. 119). This right has been specifically recognized to exist even if the withdrawal from or refusal of treatment may result in death (*Nancy B. v. Hôtel-Dieu de Québec* (1992), 86 D.L.R. (4th) 385 (Que. S.C.); *Mallette v. Shulman* (1990), 72 O.R. (2d) 417 (C.A.). The United States Supreme Court has also recently recognized that the right to refuse life-sustaining medical treatment is an aspect of the liberty interest protected by the Fourteenth Amendment in *Cruzan v. Director, Missouri Health Department* (1990), 111 L. Ed. 2d 224. However, that Court also enunciated the view that when a patient was unconscious and thus unable to express her own views, the state was justified in requiring compelling evidence that withdrawal of treatment was in fact what the patient would have requested had she been competent. . . .

The distinction between withdrawing treatment upon a patient's request, such as occurred in the *Nancy B* case, on the one hand, and assisted suicide on the other has been criticized as resting on a legal fiction — that is, the distinction between active and passive forms of treatment. The criticism is based on the fact that the withdrawal of life supportive measures is done with the knowledge that death will ensue, just as is assisting suicide, and that death does in fact ensue as a result of the action. . . .

Other commentators, however, uphold the distinction on the basis that in the case of withdrawal of treatment, the death is "natural" — the artificial forces of medical technology which have kept the patient alive are removed and nature takes its course. In the case of assisted suicide or euthanasia, however, the course of nature is interrupted, and death results *directly* from the human action taken. . . .

Whether or not one agrees that the active vs. passive distinction is maintainable, however, the fact remains that under our common law, the physician has no choice but to accept the patient's instructions to discontinue treatment. To continue to treat the patient when the patient has withdrawn consent to that treatment constitutes battery (*Ciarlariello* and *Nancy B., supra*). The doctor is therefore not required to make a choice which will result in the patient's death as he would be if he chose to assist a suicide or to perform active euthanasia.

The fact that doctors may deliver palliative care to terminally ill patients without fear of sanction, it is argued, attenuates to an even greater degree any legitimate distinction which can be drawn between assisted suicide and what are currently acceptable forms of medical treatment. The administration of drugs designed for pain control in dosages which the physician knows will hasten death constitutes active contribution to death by any standard. However, the distinction drawn here is one based upon intention — in the case of palliative care the intention is to ease pain, which has the effect of hastening death, while in the case of assisted suicide, the intention is undeniably to cause death. . . . In my view, distinctions based upon intent are important, and in fact form the basis of our criminal law. While factually the distinction may, at times, be difficult to draw, legally it is clear. The fact that in some cases, the third party will, under the guise of palliative care, commit euthanasia or assist in suicide and go un-sanctioned due to the difficulty of proof cannot be said to render the existence of the prohibition fundamentally unjust.

The principles of fundamental justice cannot be created for the occasion to reflect the court's dislike or distaste of a particular statute. While the principles of fundamental justice are concerned with more than process, reference must be made to principles which are "fundamental" in the sense that they would have general acceptance among reasonable people. From the review [of legislation in other countries] that I have con-ducted above, I am unable to discern anything approaching unanimity with respect to the issue before us. Regardless of one's personal views as to whether the distinctions drawn between withdrawal of treatment and palliative care, on the one hand, and assisted suicide on the other are practically compelling, the fact remains that these distinctions are maintained and can be persuasively defended. To the extent that there is a consensus, it is that human life must be respected and we must be careful not to undermine the institutions that protect it.

This consensus finds legal expression in our legal system which prohibits capital punishment. This prohibition is supported, in part, on the basis that allowing the state to kill will cheapen the value of human life and thus the state will serve in a sense as a role model for individuals in society. The prohibition against assisted suicide serves a similar purpose. In upholding the respect for life, it may discourage those who consider that life is unbearable at a particular moment, or who perceive themselves to be a burden upon others, from committing suicide. To permit a physician to lawfully par-ticipate in taking life would send a signal that there are circumstances in which the state approves of suicide.

. . . Given the concerns about abuse that have been expressed and the great difficulty in creating appropriate safeguards to prevent these, it can not be said that the blanket prohibition on assisted suicide is arbitrary or unfair, or that it is not reflective of fun-damental values at play in our society. I am thus unable to find that any principle of fundamental justice is violated by s. 241(b).

THE CHIEF JUSTICE: — . . . I find that s. 241(b) of the *Criminal Code* infringes s. 15(1) of the *Charter*. In my view, persons with disabilities who are or will become unable to end their lives without assistance are discriminated against by that provision since, unlike persons capable of causing their own deaths, they are deprived of the option of choosing suicide. I further find that s. 1 of the *Charter* does not save s. 241(b) of the *Criminal Code*. The means chosen to carry out the legislative purpose of preventing possible abuses do not in my opinion impair as little as reasonably possible the right to equality enshrined in s. 15(1) of the *Charter*. . . .

It was argued that if assisted suicide were permitted even in limited circumstances, then there would be reason to fear that homicide of the terminally ill and persons with physical disabilities could be readily disguised as assisted suicide and that, as a result, the most vulnerable people would be left most exposed to this grave threat. There may indeed be cause for such concern. Sadly, increasingly less value appears to be placed in our society on the lives of those who, for reason of illness, age or disability, can no longer control the use of their bodies. Such sentiments are often, unfortunately, shared by persons with physical disabilities themselves, who often feel they are merely a burden and expense to their families or on society as a whole. Moreover, as the intervener COPOH (Coalition of Provincial Organizations of the Handicapped) observed in its written submissions, "[t]he negative stereotypes and attitudes which exist about the lack of value and quality inherent in the life of a person with a disability are particularly dangerous in this context because they tend to support the conclusion that a suicide was carried out in response to those factors rather than because of pressure, coercion or duress".

The principal fear is that the decriminalization of assisted suicide will increase the risk of persons with physical disabilities being manipulated by others. This "slippery slope" argument appeared to be the central justification behind the Law Reform Commission of Canada's recommendation not to repeal this provision. The Commission stated the following in its Working Paper 28, *Euthanasia, Aiding Suicide and Cessation of Treatment* (1983), at p. 46:

> The principal consideration in terms of legislative policy, and the deciding one for the Commission, remains that of possible abuses. There is, first of all, a real danger that the procedure developed to allow the death of those who are a burden to themselves may be gradually diverted from its original purpose and eventually used as well to eliminate those who are a burden to others or to society. There is also the constant danger that the subject's consent to euthanasia may not really be a perfectly free and voluntary act.

While I share a deep concern over the subtle and overt pressures that may be brought to bear on such persons if assisted suicide is decriminalized, even in limited circumstances, I do not think legislation that deprives a disadvantaged group of the right to equality can be justified solely on such speculative grounds, no matter how well intentioned. Similar dangers to the ones outlined above have surrounded the de-criminalization of attempted suicide as well. It is impossible to know the degree of pressure or intimidation a physically able person may have been under when deciding to commit suicide. The truth is that we simply do not and cannot know the range of implications that allowing some form of assisted suicide will have for persons with physical disabilities. What we do know and cannot ignore is the anguish of those in the position of Ms. Rodriguez. Respecting the consent of those in her position may necessarily imply running the risk that the consent will have been obtained improperly. The proper role of the legal system in these circumstances is to provide safeguards to ensure that the consent in question is as independent and informed as is reasonably possible.

The fear of a "slippery slope" cannot, in my view, justify the over-inclusive reach of the *Criminal Code* to encompass not only people who may be vulnerable to the pressure of others but also persons with no evidence of vulnerability, and, in the case of the appellant, persons where there is positive evidence of freely determined consent. Sue Rodriguez is and will remain mentally competent. She has testified at trial to the fact that she alone, in consultation with her physicians, wishes to control the decision-making regarding the timing and circumstances of her death. I see no reason to disbelieve her, nor has the Crown suggested that she is being wrongfully influenced by anyone. Ms. Rodrgriguez has also emphasized that she remains and wishes to remain free not to avail herself of the opportunity to end her own life should that be her eventual choice. The issue here is whether Parliament is justified in denying her the ability to make this choice lawfully, as could any physically able person.

While s. 241(b) restricts the equality rights of all those people who are physically unable to commit suicide without assistance, the choice for a mentally competent but physically disabled person who additionally suffers from a terminal illness is, I think, different than the choice of an individual whose disability is not life-threatening; in other words, for Ms. Rodriguez, tragically, the choice is not whether to live as she is or to die, but rather when and how to experience a death that is inexorably impending. I do not, however, by observing this distinction, mean to suggest that the terminally ill are immune from vulnerability, or that they are less likely to be influenced by the intervention of others whatever their motives. Indeed, there is substantial evidence that people in this position may be susceptible to certain types of vulnerability that others are not. Further, it should not be assumed that a person with a physical disability who chooses suicide is doing so only as a result of the incapacity. It must be acknowledged that mentally competent people who commit suicide do so for a wide variety of motives, irrespective of their physical condition or life expectancy. . . .

In my view, there is a range of options from which Parliament may choose in seeking to safeguard the interests of the vulnerable and still ensure the equal right to self-determination of persons with physical disabilities. . . . Regardless of the safeguards Parliament may wish to adopt, however, I find that an absolute prohibition that is indifferent to the individual or the circumstances in question cannot satisfy the constitutional duty on the government to impair the rights of persons with physical disabilities as little as reasonably possible.

MCLACHLIN J.: — . . . This justification [protection of the vulnerable] for s. 241(b) embraces two distinct concerns. The first is the fear that unless assisted suicide is prohibited, it will be used as a cloak, not for suicide, but for murder. Viewed thus, the objective of the prohibition is not to prohibit what it purports to prohibit, namely assistance in suicide, but to prohibit another crime, murder or other forms of culpable homicide.

I entertain considerable doubt whether a law which infringes the principles of fundamental justice can be found to be reasonable and demonstrably justified on the sole ground that crimes other than those which it prohibits may become more frequent if it is not present. In Canada it is not clear that such a provision is necessary; there is a sufficient remedy in the offences of culpable homicide. Nevertheless, the fear cannot be dismissed cavalierly; there is some evidence from foreign jurisdictions indicating that legal codes which permit assisted suicide may be linked to cases of involuntary deaths of the aging and disabled.

The second concern is that even where consent to death is given, the consent may not in fact be voluntary. There is concern that individuals will, for example, consent while in the grips of transitory depression. There is also concern that the decision to end one's life may have been influenced by others. It is argued that to permit assisted suicide will permit people, some well intentioned, some malicious, to bring undue influence to bear on the vulnerable person, thereby provoking a suicide which would otherwise not have occurred.

The obvious response to this concern is that the same dangers are present in any suicide. People are led to commit suicide while in the throes of depression and it is not regarded as criminal conduct. Moreover, this appeal is concerned with s. 241(b) of the *Criminal Code*. Section 241(a), which prohibits counselling in suicide, remains in force even if it is found that s. 241(b) is unconstitutional. But bearing in mind the peculiar vulnerability of the physically disabled, it might be facile to leave the question there. The danger of transitory or improperly induced consent must be squarely faced.

The concern for deaths produced by outside influence or depression centre on the concept of consent. If a person of sound mind, fully aware of all relevant circumstances, comes to the decision to end her life at a certain point, as Sue Rodriguez has, it is difficult to argue that the criminal law should operate to prevent her, given that it does not so operate in the case of others throughout society. The fear is that a person who does not consent may be murdered, or that the consent of a vulnerable person may be improperly procured. . . .

In my view, the existing provisions in the *Criminal Code* go a considerable distance to meeting the concerns of lack of consent and improperly obtained consent. A person who causes the death of an ill or handicapped person without that person's consent can be prosecuted under the provisions for culpable homicide. The cause of death having been established, it will be for the person who administered the cause to establish that the death was really a suicide, to which the deceased consented. The existence of a criminal penalty for those unable to establish this should be sufficient to deter killings without consent or where consent is unclear. As noted above, counselling suicide would also remain a criminal offence under s. 241(a). Thus the bringing of undue influence upon a vulnerable person would remain prohibited.

These provisions may be supplemented, by way of a remedy on this appeal, by a further stipulation requiring court orders to permit the assistance of suicide in a particular case. The judge must be satisfied that the consent is freely given with a full appreciation of all the circumstances. This will ensure that only those who truly desire to bring their lives to an end obtain assistance. While this may be to ask more of Ms. Rodriguez than is asked of the physically able person who seeks to commit suicide, the additional precautions are arguably justified by the peculiar vulnerability of the person who is physically unable to take her own life.

I conclude that the infringement of s. 7 of the *Charter* by s. 241(b) has not been shown to be demonstrably justified under s. 1 of the *Charter*.

Chapter 14

Questions to Consider

1. Is there a morally relevant difference between terminating life support and assisted suicide? Suppose the two events feel very different to the health care professionals who perform them? Would that count as a morally relevant difference?

2. An argument for legalizing assisted suicide is that terminally ill patients too often do

not receive adequate pain relief. The reply to this argument is that the proper response is to develop more effective pain control, not to kill patients. But how long should the health care professions, and society, be given to develop more effective and widespread methods of pain control and to implement them? And what would count as evidence that the need for adequate pain control had been met?

3. An argument for legalizing assisted suicide is that it is necessary to relieve the unbearable suffering of some patients. What is the difference between pain and suffering? How does one determine when suffering is unbearable and unrelievable? Who makes that determination? If unbearable and unrelievable suffering is accepted as a reason for assisted suicide, could safeguards that protected against abuse of this justification be written and enforced? Or would the upshot be assisted suicide on demand?

4. If assisted suicide were legalized, should it be performed by physicians? Or could specialists be trained to assist those who want to commit suicide?

5. Proponents of legalizing assisted suicide claim that adequate safeguards against abuse can be developed. What does "adequate" mean here? How does one determine that safeguards are adequate as well as monitor their ongoing adequacy? In developing a system of safeguards, there is a tension between, on the one hand, making access to assisted suicide timely and not unduly burdensome and, on the other hand, preventing widespread manipulation and exploitation. Can this tension be satisfactorily resolved?

6. One of the main arguments against legalizing assisted suicide is that it will lead to a slippery slope. In his opinion in the *Rodriguez* case, Chief Justice Lamer of the Supreme Court of Canada dismissed this objection as too "speculative." What makes a slippery slope argument persuasive? How persuasive is this one?

Further Readings

Battin, Margaret P. 1991. Euthanasia: The way we do it, the way they do it. *Journal of Pain and Symptom Management* 6:298–305.

Browne, Alister. 1989. Assisted suicide and active voluntary euthanasia. *Canadian Journal of Law and Jurisprudence* 2:35–56.

Feinberg, Joel. 1991. Overlooking the merits of the individual case: An unpromising approach to the right to die. *Ratio Juris* 4:131–51.

Kass, Leon R. 1989. Neither for love nor money: Why doctors must not kill. *Public Interest* 94:25–46.

Lowy, Frederick H., Douglas M. Sawyer, and John R. Williams. 1993. *Canadian physicians and euthanasia.* Ottawa: Canadian Medical Association.

Pellegrino, Edmund D. 1992. Doctors must not kill. *Journal of Clinical Ethics* 3:95–102.

——. (1993). Compassion needs reason too. *Journal of the American Medical Association* 270:874–75.

Quill, Timothy E., Christine K. Cassel, and Diane E. Meier. 1992. Care of the hopelessly ill: Proposed clinical criteria for physician-assisted suicide. *New England Journal of Medicine* 327:1380–84.

——. 1993. Doctor, I want to die. Will you help me? *Journal of the American Medical Association* 270:870–73.

Singer, Peter A., and Mark Siegler. 1990. Euthanasia — A critique. *New England Journal of Medicine* 322:1881–83.

Somerville, Margaret A. 1993. The song of death: The lyrics of euthanasia. *Journal of Contemporary Health Law and Policy* 9:1–76.

Van der Burg, Wilbren. 1991. The Slippery Slope Argument. *Ethics* 102:42–65.

Credits

The editors wish to thank the publishers and copyright holders for permission to reprint the selections in this book, which are listed below in order of their appearance.

Part One   The Nature and Context of Health Care Ethics

Chapter 1   Theory and Method in Health Care Ethics

Excerpt from Paul Ramsey, *The Patient as Person: Explorations in Medical Ethics* (New Haven: Yale University Press, 1974), pp xi–xiii. Copyright © 1970 Yale University Press. Used by permission of the publisher.

Excerpt from Peter Singer, *Practical Ethics*, Second Edition (Cambridge: Cambridge University Press, 1993), pp 8–13. Copyright © 1993 Peter Singer. Reprinted by permission of Cambridge University Press.

Excerpt from H. Tristram Engelhardt, Jr., *The Foundations of Bioethics*, (New York: Oxford University Press, 1986), pp 81–3, 85. Copyright © 1986 Oxford University Press.

Excerpt from Tom L. Beauchamp and James F. Childress, *Principles of Biomedical Ethics*, Fourth Edition, (New York: Oxford University Press, 1989), pp 31–33, 37–38, 43. Copyright © 1979, 1983, 1989, 1994 Oxford University Press, Inc. Reprinted by permission.

Rosemarie Tong, "What's Distinctive about Feminist Bioethics?" A shorter version of this article was presented at the 1994 Bioethics Summer Retreat in Bar Harbor, Maine.

Chapter 2   Pluralism and Multiculturalism

Jill Klessig, "The Effect of Values and Culture on Life-Support Decisions," *The Western Journal of Medicine*, Volume 157, Number 3, September 1992, pp 316–22. Reprinted by permission of *The Western Journal of Medicine*.

Antonella Surbone, "Truth Telling to the Patient," *The Journal of the American Medical Association*, Volume 268, Number 13, October 7, 1992, pp 1661–62. Copyright © 1992 American Medical Association. Reprinted by permission.

Edmund D. Pellegrino, "Is Truth Telling to the Patient a Cultural Artifact?" *The Journal of the American Medical Association*, Volume 268, Number 13, October 7, 1992, pp 1734–35. Copyright © 1992 American Medical Association. Reprinted by permission.

Michele Barry, "Ethical Considerations of Human Investigation in Developing Countries: The AIDS Dilemma," *New England Journal of Medicine*, Volume 319, Number 16, October 20, 1988, pp 1083–86. Reprinted by permission of the Massachusetts Medical Society.

Marcia Angell, "Ethical Imperialism? Ethics in International Collaborative Clinical Research," *New England Journal of Medicine*, Volume 319, Number 16, October 20, 1988, pp 1081–83. Reprinted by permission of the Massachusetts Medical Society.

Lisa H. Newton, "Ethical Imperialism and Informed Consent," IRB: *A Review of Human Subjects Research*, Volume 12, Number 3, May/June 1990, pp 10–11. Copyright © 1990 The Hastings Center. Reprinted by permission.

Chapter 3   Health Care in Canada

Excerpt from Jake Epp, *Achieving Health for All: A Framework for Health Promotion*, Health Canada, 1986, pp 2–5. Reproduced by permission of the Minister of Supply and Services Canada 1994.

Excerpt from *Nurturing Health: A Framework on the Determinants of Health*, Ontario Premier's Council on Health Strategy, 1991, pp 1–17. Reprinted by permission.

Excerpt from Raisa B. Deber, "Canadian Medicare: Can It Work in the United States? Will It Survive in Canada?" *American Journal of Law & Medicine*, Volume 19, pp 75–93. Copyright © 1993 The American Society of Law, Medicine & Ethics, Inc. and the Boston University School of Law. Reprinted by permission.

Chapter 4   Resource Allocation and Rationing

John R. Williams and Eric B. Beresford, "Physicians, Ethics and the Allocation of Health Care Resources," *Annals of the Royal College of Physicians and Surgeons of Canada*, Volume 24, Number 5, August 1991, pp 305–9. Reprinted by permission of the publisher.

Benjamin Freedman and Françoise Baylis, "Purpose and Function in Government-Funded Health Coverage," *Journal of Health Politics, Policy and Law*, Volume 12, Number 1, pp 97–112. Copyright © 1987 Duke University Press. Reprinted by permission.

George J. Annas, "The Prostitute, the Playboy, and the Poet: Rationing Schemes for Organ Transplantation," *American Journal of Public Health*, Volume 75, Number 2, February 1985, pp 187–89. Reprinted by permission of journal.

Part Two   Making Decisions

Chapter 5   Patients and Providers

Ezekiel J. Emanuel and Linda L. Emanuel, "Four Models of the Physician–Patient Relationship," *Journal of the Medical Association*, Volume 267, Number 16, April 22/29, 1992, pp 2221–26. Copyright © 1992 American Medical Association. Reprinted by permission.

Ellen W. Bernal, "The Nurse as Patient Advocate," *Hastings Center Report*, Volume 22, Number 4, July–August 1992, pp 18–23. Copyright © 1992 The Hastings Center. Reprinted by permission.

Ruth B. Purtilo, "Ethical Issues in Teamwork: The Context of Rehabilitation," *Archives of Physical Medicine and Rehabilitation 69* (1988): 318–22. Copyright © 1988 W.B. Saunders Company.

Chapter 6   Consent

Excerpt from *Reibl v. Hughes*, [1980] 1 Supreme Court Reports 880. Reprinted by permission.

Zamparo v. Brisson (1981), 32 Ontario Reports (2nd) 75. Used by permission of the Law Society of Upper Canada.

Nancy S. Jecker, "Being a Burden on Others," *The Journal of Clinical Ethics*, Volume 4, Number 1, Spring 1993, pp 16–20. Reprinted by permission.

Erich H. Loewy, "Changing One's Mind: When Is Odysseus to Be Believed?" *The Journal of General Internal Medicine*, Volume 3, January/February 1988, pp 54–58. Reprinted by permission of Hanley & Belfus, Inc., Philadelphia, PA.

Chapter 7   Competence and Mental Illness

Karen Ritchie, "The Little Woman Meets Son of DSM-III," *The Journal of Medicine and Philosophy*, Volume 14, Number 6, pp 695–708. Copyright © 1989 Kluwer Academic Publishers. Printed in the Netherlands. Reprinted by permission of the publisher.

Benjamin Freedman, "Competence, Marginal and Otherwise: Concepts and Ethics," reprinted from *International Journal of Law and Psychiatry*, Volume 4, Number 1/2, pp 52–73. Copyright © 1981, with permission from Elsevier Science Ltd., Pergamon Imprint, The Boulevard, Langford Lane, Kidlington, OX5 1GB, U.K.

"In the Matter of The Mental Health Act, R.S.O. 1980, c. 262 as Amended, and in the Matter of KV, a Patient at a Hospital in Ontario" is an actual case in which the names have been changed to protect confidentiality. Unpublished. Reprinted with permission.

Charles M. Culver, Richard B. Ferrell, and Ronald M. Green," ECT and Special Problems of Informed Consent," *American Journal of Psychiatry*, Volume 137, Number 5, pp 586–91. Copyright © 1980 the American Psychiatric Association. Reprinted by permission.

Chapter 8   Children and the Elderly: Who Should Decide?

Excerpt from Ruth Macklin, "Deciding for Others," in Ruth Macklin, *Mortal Choices: Ethical Dilemmas in Modern Medicine* (Boston: Houghton Mifflin, 1987), pp 99–112. Copyright © 1987 Ruth Macklin. Reprinted by permission of Pantheon Books, a division of Random House, Inc.

Excerpt from Robert F. Weir, *Selective Nontreatment of Handicapped Newborns: Moral Dilemmas in Neonatal Medicine* (New York: Oxford University Press, 1984), pp 255–66. Copyright © 1984 Oxford University Press, Inc. Reprinted by permission.

John J. Paris, Robert K. Crone, and Frank Reardon, "Physicians' Refusal of Requested Treatment: The Case of Baby L," *The New England Journal of Medicine*, Volume 322, Number 14, April 5, 1990, pp 1012–15. Reprinted by permission of the Massachusetts Medical Society.

Nancy S. Jecker, "The Role of Intimate Others in Medical Decision Making," *The Gerontologist*, Volume 30, 1990, pp 65–71. Copyright © The Gerontological Society of America. Reprinted by permission.

Chapter 9   Research Involving Human Subjects

Excerpt from *Halushka v. University of Saskatchewan et al.* (1966), 53 Dominion Law Reports (2d). Reprinted by permission of Canada Law Book.

Mary E. Moore and Stephen N. Berk, "Ethical Considerations Encountered in a Study of Acupuncture — A Reappraisal," *Clinical Research*, Volume 28, Number 4, October 1980, pp 334–42. Reprinted by permission of The American Federation for Clinical Research.

Benjamin Freedman, "Equipoise and the Ethics of Clinical Research," *New England Journal of Medicine*, Volume 317, Number 3, July 16, 1987, pp 141–5. Reprinted by permission of the Massachusetts Medical Society.

David A. Salisbury and Martin T. Schechter, "AIDS Trials, Civil Liberties and the Social Control of Therapy: Should We Embrace New Drugs with Open Arms?" *Canadian Medical Journal*, Volume 142, Number 10 (1990), pp 1057–62. Reprinted by permission of the publisher.

Part Three   Decisions Near the Beginning and End of Life

Chapter 10   Genetics

Excerpt from Abby Lippman, "Prenatal Genetic Testing and Screening: Constructing Needs and Reinforcing Inequities," *American Journal of Law and Medicine*, Volume 17, Numbers 1–2 (1991), pp 15–50. Reprinted by permission of the American Society of Law & Medicine.

Excerpt from Dorothy C. Wertz and John C. Fletcher, "A Critique of Some Feminist Challenges to Prenatal Diagnosis," *Journal of Women's Health*, Volume 2, Number 2, 1993, pp 173–88. Copyright © 1993 Dorothy C. Wertz and John C. Fletcher. Reprinted by permission of Mary Ann Liebert, Inc., Publishers.

Supplement from Kathleen Nolan, "First Fruits: Genetic Screening," *Hastings Center Report*, Volume 22, Number 4, July–August 1992: pp S2–S4. Copyright © 1992 The Hastings Center. Reprinted by permission.

Chapter 11 Abortion

Excerpt from *Morgentaler, Smoling and Scott v. The Queen*, [1988] 1 Supreme Court Reports, 30. Reprinted by permission.

Excerpt from L.W. Sumner, "Abortion," in Donald VanDeveer and Tom Regan, eds, *Health Care Ethics: An Introduction* (Philadelphia: Temple University Press, 1987), pp. 162–83. Copyright © 1987 Temple University. Reprinted by permission of Temple University Press.

Excerpt from Donald B. Marquis, "Why Abortion Is Immoral," *Journal of Philosophy*, Volume 86, Number 4, April 1989, pp. 183–202. Reprinted by permission.

Excerpt from Susan Sherwin, "Abortion Through a Feminist Ethics Lens," *Dialogue: Canadian Philosophical Review*, Volume 30, Number 3, Summer 1991, pp 327–42. Reprinted by permission of the Canadian Philosophical Association.

Chapter 12 Assisted Reproductive Technologies

From Mary Briody Mahowald, "Fertility Enhancement and the Right to Have a Baby," in Mary Briody Mahowald, *Women and Children in Health Care: An Unequal Majority* (New York: Oxford University Press, 1993), pp 93–113. Copyright © 1993 Oxford University Press, Inc. Reprinted by permission.

From Susan Sherwin, *No Longer Patient: Feminist Ethics and Health Care* (Philadelphia: Temple University, 1992), pp 117–36. Reprinted by permission of the publisher.

Excerpt from Christine Overall, "Surrogate Motherhood," in Marsha Hanen and Kai Nelson, eds., *Science, Morality & Feminist Theory* (Calgary, Alta.: The University of Calgary Press). Copyright © 1987 Canadian Journal of Philosophy. Reprinted by permission.

Proceed with Care: Final Report of the Royal Commission on New Reproductive Technologies, "Framework for Decision Making," *Editorial Page Feature*, and "In Vitro Fertilization" and "Preconception Arrangements" in *Main Topics*, pp 16, 19. From the Privy Council Office. Reproduced with the permission of the Minister of Supply and Services Canada, 1994.

Chapter 13 Withholding and Withdrawing Life-Sustaining Treatment

Dan W. Brock, "Forgoing Life-Sustaining Food and Water: Is It Killing?" in J. Lynn ed, *By No Extraordinary Means: The Choice to Forgo Life-Sustaining Food and Water* (Bloomington: Indiana University Press, 1986), pp 117–31. Copyright © 1986 Indiana University Press. Used by permission.

Robert D. Truog, Allan S. Brett, Joel Frader, "The Problem with Futility," *New England Journal of Medicine*, Volume 326, Number 23, June 4, 1992, pp 1560–64. Reprinted by permission of the Massachusetts Medical Society.

Jocelyn Downie, "Where There is a Will, There May Be a Better Way: Legislating Advance Directives," *Health Law in Canada*, Volume 12, Number 3, 1992, pp 73–80. Reprinted by permission of Gilbert Sharpe.

Chapter 14 Euthanasia and Assisted Suicide

Dan W. Brock, "Voluntary Active Euthanasia," *Hastings Center Report*, Volume 22, Number 2, March–April 1992, pp 10–22. Reprinted by permission of The Hastings Center.

Daniel Callahan, "When Self-Determination Runs Amok," *Hastings Center Report*, Volume 22, Number 2, March–April 1992, pp 52–55. Reprinted by permission of The Hastings Center.

Summary of *Sue Rodriguez v. The Attorney General of Canada and the Attorney General of British Columbia*, [1993] 3 Supreme Court Reports 519. Reprinted by permission.

Reader Reply Card

We are interested in your reaction to *Health Care Ethics in Canada*, by Françoise Baylis, Jocelyn Downie, Benjamin Freedman, Barry Hoffmaster, and Susan Sherwin. You can help us to improve this book in future editions by completing this questionnaire.

1. What was your reason for using this book?
   ☐ university course   ☐ college course   ☐ continuing education course
   ☐ professional   ☐ personal interest   ☐ other (specify) _____
   _____

2. If you are a student, please identify your school and the course in which you used this book.

3. Which chapter or parts of this book did you use? Which did you omit?

4. What did you like best about this book? What did you like least?

5. Please identify any topics you think should be added to future editions.

6. Please add any comments or suggestions.

7. May we contact you for further information?
   Name: _____
   Address: _____
   Phone: _____

(fold here and tape shut)

MAIL ➤ **POSTE**

Canada Post Corporation / Société canadienne des postes

Postage paid   **Port payé**
If mailed in Canada   si posté au Canada

Business   **Réponse**
Reply   **d'affaires**

0116870399   **01**

0116870399-M8Z4X6-BR01

Heather McWhinney
Publisher, College Division
HARCOURT BRACE & COMPANY, CANADA
55 HORNER AVENUE
TORONTO, ONTARIO
M8Z 9Z9